Wrought With Steadfast Will

Wrought With Steadfast Will

A History of Emma Willard School

For Maryll —
With appreciation for
her sustained interest in
her alma mater —
Trudy Hanmer

TRUDY J. HANMER

Book design by Jessika Hazelton
Cover photo by Fantasia Hanmer

Printed in the United States of America

The Troy Book Makers • Troy, New York • thetroybookmakers.com

To order additional copies of this title,
contact your favorite local bookstore
or visit www.tbmbooks.com

ISBN: 978-1-935680-048

Contents

For Alice Dodge Wallace '38

whose abiding interest, extraordinary encouragement,
and magnanimous support contributed immeasurably
to this history of her alma mater

Foreword

Although I embarked on this project seriously in 2008, I have really been working on it since I first arrived at Emma Willard School over thirty years ago. Alumnae will readily recognize that the book's title comes from a line in the "Alma Mater." When that song was only ten years old, the editors of *Triangle* acknowledged the aptness of the phrase in defining their school. "Wrought with steadfast will," they wrote in 1921, "is the keynote to life at Emma Willard." I have found it to be the fitting keynote to the school's history as well.

I undertook this project because the story of Emma Willard and the school that is her legacy needed to be told. Most alumnae know—or at least have been told, whether or not they remember all the facts—the story of Emma Willard's life and vision, but that story has never fully been captured as part of women's history and American history. Emma Hart Willard was born just a few months before the Constitutional Convention met in Philadelphia, and the school began while the nation's existence was threatened once again by superior British military force in the War of 1812. In spite of stiff opposition, the ideals of the nation and the ideals of the founder endured.

Leaving office in 1970, Bill Dietel told his successor that the school had "survived war, economic depression, fire, lawsuits, red ink, and shrinking admissions" but assured him that "the alumnae, the parents, the trustees, the faculty and the students are as a group a nearly boundless source of strength." This group, he assured Dennis Collins, "has a capacity for resolving problems, surmounting differences, and breaking new ground [which] is exceeded only by their devotion to the cause of excellent education." What was true in the

1960s was true in the 1820s, the 1860s, the 1930s—and every decade in between. The story of the school's success is the story of all parts of the enterprise wrestling with different challenges at different times but working with steadfast will to continue the founder's vision for women's education.

Another important theme in the history is the way the same qualities that ensured the school's success were qualities that radiated out from Troy through the lives of the graduates and the people they touched. In the 1990s, a controversial advertising campaign boldly stated about Emma Willard students, "Every day we remind them of the marvelous, limitless possibilities the world presents an educated woman. And vice versa." That *vice versa* is timeless. Elizabeth Cady Stanton confronted slavery, Sarah Seward set up a medical clinic in Allahabad for Indian women and children, Harriet House established a school for girls in Bangkok, Nettie Fowler McCormick took the reins of a major corporation, Margaret Olivia Slocum demonstrated women's capacity for philanthropy, Jane Fonda challenged a war, and Mary Lake Polan joined the National Institutes of Health, ensuring women's place in the highest ranks of scientific policymaking. Through the Renaissance Institute, Linda LeSourd Lader provides a forum for leaders of all walks of life to communicate with each other, and through her "Off the Sidelines" Web site, Kirsten Rutnik Gillibrand encourages other women to join her in politics. These are just a few of the more famous alumnae who have presented the world with new possibilities. Thousands of others have opened up possibilities in their homes, towns, and workplaces. They all share a common goal—to be, as Emma Willard put it—"of the best possible . use to themselves and others."

Among other subjects, this book chronicles changes in school rules and regulations and diploma requirements, and it records the expansion of the "downtown campus" and the move "onto the hill." Much of this is bemusing and humorous. Consider the transformation witnessed by maintenance foreman Joseph Gondella, whose career spanned 1931 to 1973. As he put it at his retirement, "I've seen them go from middies and bloomers to clogs and jeans." What has changed is certainly interesting, but what remains is more important. Generations of students have left Mount Ida with a "great sense of purpose . . . the purpose of being prepared for a good and useful life."[1] In the 1820s, Emma Hart Willard believed that if the nation was to survive, it needed the full talents of women, a full half of the population whose contributions were not valued. Two hundred years later, the school continues to send out educated, purposeful young women. They are the embodiment of her "Prophetic Strains." She predicted

> A day will come, when legislative men,
> Pressed by stupendous dangers to the state,
> Will see how women's power, wealth, influence,
> And mind of quick invention, might be turn'd
> By right machinery to great account.

Another important theme is the role of dedicated faculty and staff at every juncture of the school's history. Adolescent girls are rarely, if ever, imbued with a sense of purpose solely by reading the inspiring words of the founder. Emma Willard left the active management of the school in 1838. Her vision has been fulfilled by the hundreds of women and dozens of men who have taught at the school. Some stayed for only very brief periods. In each chapter of the school's history, however, there has been a corps of teachers, staff, and administrators dedicated to carrying on the ideals of the founder, devoted to teaching young women and deeply aware of the importance of their mission. They, too, have "wrought with steadfast will."

In writing this history, I have consulted all kinds of sources, from secondary accounts of education, curriculum, and history to primary documents located in the Emma Willard Archives and in other archives from Troy to Wisconsin. I have also listened to alumnae accounts of their days and faculty and staff memories of their time on campus. Memory provides both the most colorful anecdotes and the most unreliable accounts. Consequently, I have tried at all points where memory is providing the narrative to bolster the account with material from a published source.

That being said, the last three chapters, covering 1980 to 2012, are inescapably colored by my own memories and experiences living and working at the school. As a result, I believe the final chapters are not quite as authentically historical as the earlier ones. There is great freedom in analyzing eras whose inhabitants are no longer alive, and I anticipate that I will receive letters and e-mails from living alumnae and former faculty explaining how I got something or other all wrong. I have never been a fan of instant history, so I view the last few chapters as social science more than history. They are, I hope, an accurate accounting of the major changes, challenges, and opportunities faced by the school in the past thirty years, but I leave it to a future historian to analyze whether or not the decisions I made were the right ones in the long run.

I hope that you enjoy reading this book as much as I have enjoyed writing it.

~Trudy Hanmer

An Influence Which Will Be Enduring

SPRING IN TROY IN 1870 was unusually warm, and by early April the leaves in Seminary Park were green and displayed a fullness not usually seen before May. The entire winter had been mild; for the first time since records began in 1789, navigation on the Hudson had not been suspended because of ice. The warm weather had not been healthy for Mrs. Emma Willard. After a winter of recurring illness, she was sick again, unable to venture from her rooms. In the fall she had given up her house on Ferry Street and had moved into the seminary building to be closer to her son and his family. On April 5, she wrote her last letter, addressed to her sister, Almira Phelps, in Baltimore. The next day she made an entry in her diary, scrawling in a feeble hand that showed few traces of her trademark copperplate penmanship, "have my prayers alone, read the newspapers."[1]

On April 8, she rallied briefly when Gen. William Tecumseh Sherman paid her a call; he was in Troy for the funeral of his West Point roommate and fellow Union general, Henry Thomas. Thomas's widow, Frances Kellogg, had studied at the seminary while Mrs. Willard was at its helm, and although the general had died in San Francisco, his body was returned to Troy for services at St. Paul's and burial in the Kellogg plot in Oakwood. In addition to Sherman, President Grant, Gen. Philip Sheridan, and James A. Garfield, Republican congressman from Ohio, were all in Troy to honor the "Rock of Chickamaugua," as Thomas was known.

By Wednesday, April 12, it was clear that Mrs. Willard would not leave her bed again. For three days her daughter-in-law, son, and granddaughters sat by her side. Then, on April 15, Good Friday, at two in the afternoon, Emma Hart Willard peacefully drew her last breath. At eighty-four, she had outlived all but the youngest of her sixteen siblings. Emily Wilcox, her grand-niece and future head of the seminary, wrote the next morning to her cousin, Emma Willard Dodd, "[H]er friends were prepared . . . as she had been very feeble for some weeks past."[2]

On Saturday, the weather turned. A cold, rainy day, more typical of April in Troy, greeted the members of the seminary's board of trustees as they hastily met in a special session. While her body lay in state at her beloved seminary, the trustees adopted the following resolutions:

> *Resolved*, That we recognize in the life-long devotion of Mrs. Emma Willard to the best and highest interests of the women of our country and in her persevering and successful efforts for advancing the standard of culture, intelligence and Christian devotion in American homes, as teacher advocate and author, a usefulness which is inestimable and an influence which will be enduring.
>
> *Resolved*, That in her decease the cause of female education has lost one of its most intelligent, laborious and untiring friends, and our own institution a co-worker and adviser of the past fifty years whose only motive has been a love and interest which age and infirmity could not weaken or disturb.
>
> *Resolved*, That as a testimony of our respect for her memory as a cultivated and noble Christian woman, we attend the funeral of Mrs. Willard in a body and wear the usual badge of mourning.[3]

The trustees further resolved that a copy of the resolutions be given to Mrs. Willard's family and the Troy newspapers, and entered into the board minutes. The thirteen men then repaired to their homes to celebrate the Easter weekend with their families. All were successful Troy businessmen. Their backgrounds and economic standing reflected the prominence of the Troy Female Seminary (TFS) and the prosperity of Troy. All Christian, the majority were Episcopalians. Joseph Fuller, James Forsyth, and Uri Gilbert were vestrymen at St. Paul's and were looking forward to Easter mass where the new silver communion service would be used for the first time. Collectively, the trustees' assets, as reported in the 1870 census, totaled over $2 million, with Elias Plum, a leather manufacturer, leading the group with an estate worth

$490,000. With real and personal assets for the entire city assessed at slightly more than $16 million, the seminary's trustees clearly ranked in the top socioeconomic echelon of the city.

For the most part, these men were contemporaries of Mrs. Willard's son, John. Jonas Heartt, thirty-seven, the sole trustee under forty, was the youngest, and George Warren at seventy-two, the oldest. Among them they had fathered more than fifty children; of the twenty-eight girls in the group, twenty-one had attended, were attending, or would attend the seminary. In an era when children routinely died before reaching maturity, they lost only two, evidence of the higher standards of hygiene and nutrition their prosperity afforded them. Five had wives who were seminary graduates, including Plum, whose first wife was the only one of his three wives not to have studied at Troy. (Plum's first daughter by his second wife was named for his first wife, and a daughter by his third wife named for his second, giving true meaning to "strong alumnae ties.")

In addition to serving on the seminary board, the trustees were bank directors and trustees of hospitals, orphanages, and colleges. Fuller, Gilbert, Heartt, Forsyth, William Gurley, and William Kemp all sat on the board of the Rensselaer Polytechnic Institute. Silas Stow, George Warren, and Charles Tillinghast were directors of the Troy Savings Bank; Kemp held the same position at Mutual National and Gurley at National Exchange. Giles Kellogg served with John Willard on the board of the Central National Bank of Troy. One or more of them sat on the boards of the Troy Infirmary and Lunatic Asylum, the Church Home for the Relief of the Aged, Infirm and Destitute, and the Troy Orphanage. Kemp was president of the Troy School Board and would later serve as mayor; Gilbert held that office in 1870.

There was money to be made during the Civil War and in the industrial boom that followed. Troy's businesses supplied arms and clothes and all kinds of iron products for the Union troops, and when the war ended, they continued a manufacturing boom to meet the needs of the expanding middle class. Fuller's wealth, generated from his stove manufacturing, had grown from $12,000 in 1860 to

$450,000 by 1870. Kemp, the manager of a brass foundry, had doubled his wealth during the decade, and Gilbert, a streetcar manufacturer, had tripled his, reporting assets of $325,000 in 1870. Gurley's mathematical instruments business had flourished, as had the law practices of Tracy and Kellogg, with the former reporting to the census that his assets totaled $106,000 and the latter $160,000.[4]

By the time Emma Willard died, Troy was famous for its production of cast-iron stoves, iron rails, collars and cuffs, bells, hosiery, and much more. There had long been an entrepreneurial spirit in the city that gave rise to industrial innovation that matched the educational innovations represented by Rensselaer Polytechnic Institute as well as the seminary. The first Bessemer steel plant in the United States was built in Troy in 1865, thanks to the engineering prowess of Alexander Holley, whose mother was an early seminary student. Detachable collars, invented by Hannah Lord Montague in her Third Street flat, had revolutionized the collar industry. The closely guarded secret formula for the ink used in U.S. currency had been created by Troy druggist Titus Eddy, whose wife and four sisters were seminary graduates. Henry Burden's water wheel, erected in 1851, was the largest in the country. Over sixty feet in diameter, it generated energy equivalent to the power of twelve hundred horses and fueled one of the largest iron foundries in the nation. The income the iron works produced would sustain the Burden family fortune into the next century. Meanwhile, it funded the education of the Burden girls at the seminary.

In the early1870s, two iron companies in Troy employed over three thousand workers who produced more than 150,000 tons of steel and iron annually. Twenty-three stove companies, two malleable iron factories, seven machinery plants, and twenty-five collar firms provided work for nearly eight thousand employees. Troy's industries churned out 67,000 dozen pairs of hose, 3,000-plus tons of paper, and about 100,000 barrels of beer each year. They milled 70,000 barrels of wheat and 10,000 barrels of rye, made bells, car wheels, and railroad ties that were shipped throughout the country. Workers' wages varied, with skilled workers in the stove and machinery trade earning between $600 and $700 annually and iron workers hovering in the $400 range. In the garment business, where the workers were predominantly women and children, wages were lower, with annual incomes rarely exceeding $300.[5]

The industries lined the banks of the Hudson and were located in the hills around the various waterways that flowed from the heights east of the river. The industrial owners, including the trustees, lived within a few blocks of the seminary, inhabiting stately homes on Washington Park and elegant brownstones on Second and Third Streets. All employed live-in domestic help. Of the thirty-three servants recorded in the 1870 census as living with trustee families, all but five were born in Ireland. Even Charles Tillinghast, a hardware merchant who reported only $7,000 in assets, had Ellen Glasheen, Catherine Duffy, and Catherine Golden to care for him, his wife, and their three children. As was true at the Tillinghast home, most of the household help was female; Bridgets, Marys, Noras, Annies, Kates, Kittys, and Elizas filled the census rolls. About a third reported that they were unable to read or write. Only William Kemp employed black servants; Charles and William Brown, presumably brothers, were listed along with one Irish servant, Jane Daly.

These men and their wives knew each other and knew the Willards. Their lives intertwined at work, in their philanthropic activities, at church and at home. Elias Plum's daughter Sarah TFS '63 was married to Uri Gilbert's son, Edward. Plum's second wife, Martha Buell TFS '44, was a niece of Sarah Josepha Buell Hale, editor of the *Ladies' Book*, good friend of Emma Willard, and staunch national champion of female education. If in 1870, many Americans still scoffed at the idea of colleges for women, upper-class Troy embraced education for their daughters. Guided by Emma Willard, they had come to expect wives and daughters to have at least a seminary education. They revered the woman who had taught so many of them, and they supported her institution with both their time and money.

And so it was with heavy hearts that they assembled at the seminary on Tuesday to accompany Emma Willard on her last visit to St. Paul's. The procession moved slowly down Second Street, led by Rev.

Thomas Coit and the associate pastor, Eliphalet Nott Potter, whose family had donated the new communion service to the church. Like the trustees, the two ministers had many ties to the seminary and its founder. Coit, nearing retirement at sixty-eight, had, like the favored parishioner whose life he celebrated that day, grown up in the Hartford area. He had been a professor of church history at Trinity College before assuming the leadership of St. Paul's in 1856. A direct descendant of John Winthrop, he claimed a Puritan heritage similar to Emma Hart Willard's lineage, and they had shared many hours of conversation about theology and the changing nature of Protestant religion. Nott, his youthful associate, was destined to become the president of Union College like his grandfather before him. His grandmother, Urania Sheldon Nott, had graduated from the seminary in 1828; his young wife, Helen Fuller, daughter of trustee Joseph Fuller, had graduated just four years earlier, with the class of 1866.

Accompanying the St. Paul's clergy were John Tucker, rector at Holy Cross, Joseph Mulford from Christ Church, E. Solliday Widdemer, pastor at St Luke's, and Richard Adams, who presided over the chapel at Oakwood Cemetery. The casket followed the ministers, borne by four members of the board and accompanied by the rest. Behind the body walked her family, her son and daughter-in-law, granddaughters, great-grandchildren, and other mourners representing "a very large number of the older class of citizens."⁶ Her sister, Almira, was escorted by two men: her son, Charles Phelps, former congressman from Maryland, and William Whittingham, Bishop of Maryland. Next the 150 seminary students marched in a group. Bringing up the rear, according to the account in Tuesday evening's *Troy Budget*, were "Mrs. Willard's domestics." These perhaps included Mary Nugent and Mary Powers, both Irish born, as well as her cook, Henry Savoy, a native of Maryland, and his wife Ellen, listed in the census as a ladies' maid and mentioned frequently in Mrs. Willard's diary as her primary caregiver during her final months. In 1860 Henry had been a slave in Almira's household in Baltimore.

The coffin was covered in black broadcloth with four wreaths and "a floral crown of rare flowers"⁷ adorning the head and foot. Reverend

Coit began the service with a reading from 1 Corinthians: 15:51–55, a lesson traditionally used in the Episcopal rite of burial. He intoned:

> Behold, I shew you a mystery; We shall not all sleep, but we shall all be changed, in a moment, in the twinkling of an eye, at the last trump: for the trumpet shall sound, and the dead shall be raised incorruptible, and we shall be changed. For this corruptible must put on incorruption, and this mortal must put on immortality. So when this corruptible shall have put on incorruption, and this mortal shall have put on immortality, then shall be brought to pass the saying that is written, Death is swallowed up in victory. O death, where is thy sting? O grave, where is thy victory?

The congregation sang "Lord, Let Me Know My End," and "Jesus, Savior of My Soul," the latter said to be the deceased's favorite hymn. For his eulogy, Reverend Coit took as his text Daniel 12:3 ("And they that be wise shall shine as the brightness of the firmament; and they that turn many to righteousness as the stars for ever and ever"). In a lengthy sermon, later published in Troy, he stated that he was suspending his "disinclination" to deliver "personal eulogies" and pronounced that Emma Willard "was the moulder and enstamper of more good mothers than any woman of her native land." In a fit of civic boosterism, he linked her to Troy and Rensselaer Polytechnic, claiming "[F]or the education of women and the scientist, no place in broad America has a title of more worth."[8] At the conclusion of the service, the mourners traveled by carriage to Oakwood Cemetery, where Emma Willard was laid to rest in the family plot with her husband, Dr. John Willard, and her grandchildren, John Hudson Willard, William Lee Willard, Marcia Willard, and an unnamed infant girl.

Reports of Mrs. Willard's death appeared in the nation's newspapers for the next few weeks. Papers in Charleston, San Francisco, Chicago, Brooklyn, Pittsfield, Boston, and Baltimore all reprinted the account of her death from the *Troy Daily Times*. The Troy paper, in a fit of exaggerated civic pride, had claimed, "The news of her death will touch with sorrow more hearts than would the death of any other woman in America" and added, "She occupies the first place in the gallery of American teachers. . . . She may, with truth, be considered the REPRESENTATIVE WOMAN, at the head of the great modern movement for the education and elevation of woman."[9] Philadelphia's *Evening Telegraph* and the *New York Times* carried their own lengthy obituaries. Almost as laudatory as the Troy papers, the *Times* crowned her "the best known teacher in America . . . the pioneer of female education . . . [the founder] of the first scientific female seminary in the country . . . who had more true personal friends North and South than any other woman."[10] That same day the New York State Assembly passed a resolution in her memory in part because of her "historical reputation." *Harper's Weekly* extolled her work, claiming that "the famous seminary" was an institution "well known throughout the length and breadth of the land."[11] Sarah Josepha Hale, her longtime supporter, only one year her junior but still editing *Godey's Ladies Book*, penned a tribute in the September issue of the magazine. She wrote, "In every state of our Union and probably in every important town, there must be some women to whom the name of Mrs. Willard was dear."[12]

The same papers that carried the news of Emma Willard's death carried stories that indicated the world was changing. Buffalo's black citizens were celebrating the passage of the Fifteenth Amendment, and Oberlin had appointed a black professor as chair of the college's mathematics department. In Wyoming, the army had killed Black Bear, an Arapaho chief, one more step in the forced removal of Native Americans to reservations. In Europe the Prince of Wales and his brother-in-law, the kaiser, were not on speaking terms, the beginnings of a family quarrel that would have historic worldwide consequences early in the next century.

Troy was continuing to expand with immigration fueling most of the growth. Census takers were already compiling the ninth federal census that would show Troy had added over seven thousand citizens since 1860 and was closing in on a total population of fifty thousand. As positive evidence of the changing culture of the city, Troy's Jewish community was about to break ground for a new synagogue, Berith Sholom, on the corner of Third and Division Streets just a few blocks from the seminary. To accommodate the growing Roman Catholic population, St. Jean-Baptiste and St. Lawrence opened in 1869, and St.

Michael's and St. Patrick's would follow before the middle of the decade. There were ten Presbyterian churches, seven Episcopal churches, four Baptist, and eight Methodist, including one for the city's black residents. No longer were St. Paul's, First Presbyterian, the Quaker meetinghouse, and the Congregational Parish the only options for Troy's citizens. St. Joseph's Seminary had ordained more than 250 priests in its first decade, providing educated leaders for the burgeoning Catholic churches in New York and points west.

And, most surely unbeknownst to Mrs. Willard, change was coming to the seminary. Unlike the changes in the city, the transformation at the seminary was not positive. In the antebellum years, the school had routinely enrolled more than four hundred students from all over the country and many places abroad. By 1870 there were fewer than three hundred girls registered at the seminary, and many of these were enrolled at the music school. Only twenty-seven diplomas were awarded in June. Over half were day scholars. Fewer than sixty students came from other states, with Pennsylvania and New Jersey the biggest senders at eleven apiece. The South, once a source of the school's wealthiest pupils, was barely represented; three girls from Texas and a girl from New Orleans comprised the entire southern contingent.

And so, as Emma Willard was laid to rest, her son and daughter-in-law must have wondered whether or not the school would survive. At sixty-one, John Willard appeared to have less energy than his mother had had at eighty. The success of the new women's colleges (Mount Holyoke and Vassar were in full operation, and Smith and Wellesley would open midway through the decade), the proliferation of girls' schools throughout the country (many started by seminary graduates), the growth of high schools in cities and towns all over the Northeast and Midwest, and the aging facilities at the school, particularly in the boarding department, meant that the seminary had reached a crossroads.

Within the eulogies to the founder ran a common theme. She had been the pioneer, the visionary, the architect of equal education for girls. Her school had been the model. However, in her very success lay seeds of doubt about the school's future. Perhaps it was time for the leadership in girls' education to pass beyond Troy. As *Harper's Weekly* noted, "[She] lived to see the complete triumph of her views in regard to education."[13] In her final months, Mrs. Willard gave her blessing to the suffrage movement, writing to a suffragist and former student, "I must soon go to my rest . . . [but] I am more and more convinced that [suffrage] is good work and one that will lead to good."[14] With women in the workforce as never before, with growing agitation for women's participation in the political sphere, with high schools and colleges offering all over the country what had once been attainable in Troy alone, what place was left for the founder's institution?

Patriot Breast

THE TWO FULL-LENGTH BIOGRAPHIES and the numerous sketches of Emma Willard's life are remarkably repetitive and uncritical. The saga of her childhood invariably follows the same heartwarming and inspirational plot. Emma Hart, sixteenth child of colonial parents who descended from the heartiest Puritan stock, absorbed from those parents reverence for learning, self-discipline, thrift, a belief in an all-powerful Protestant God, and an extraordinary capacity for hard work. The real story is a bit more complex, a lot more interesting—and just as inspirational.

Emma Hart was born in Berlin, Connecticut, on February 23, 1787, two days after Congress voted to convene in Philadelphia and revise the Articles of Confederation. Her father, Samuel Hart, had served in the colonial army during the Revolution, reaching the rank of captain, a title he bore for the rest of his life. Her mother, Lydia Hinsdale, was Hart's second wife. When baby Emma joined the family, Samuel Hart had already fathered fifteen children and buried three; at least four were in their twenties and no longer at home. Rebecca Norton Hart, first wife of Samuel, had given birth to seven children in nine years, dying three months after the birth of her last son. Rebecca, born in 1760, was the oldest. James, born in 1769, the year his mother died, only survived a year, doubtless one of the many colonial babies who failed to thrive after their mothers succumbed to the diseases so often in attendance at eighteenth-century childbirth. In between Rebecca and James were Samuel Jr., Charlotte, Asahel, Anna, a teenager with consumption who died two years before Emma was born, and Jesse.

With so many children to rear, Samuel lost no time finding a new wife. In 1770, fourteen months after Rebecca's death, he married Lydia

Hinsdale, ten years his junior. She not only took charge of her stepchildren but began adding to the family almost immediately, eventually producing ten more Hart offspring. In 1771 she gave birth to Mary, followed by John in 1773, James in 1774, Theodore in 1776, Lydia in 1778, Betsey in 1781, Huldah in 1783, and Nancy in 1785. Although Huldah lived only a year and Betsey died at age eleven, the rest all grew to adulthood, with most marrying and having children of their own. For such a large family, the siblings were remarkably close. At least thirty-six Hart relatives studied at the Troy Female Seminary (not counting Emma's six granddaughters, all of whom grew up at the seminary). Among her nieces and great-nieces, at least seven were named for their famous aunt.

There would be one more baby after Emma. Almira, born in 1793, when her mother was forty-six, would become the best friend, fellow educator, and lifelong confidante of her sister Emma. Almira later reminisced that she was very much the pampered youngest. She recalled, "The *baby*, the appellation by which I was for many years known in the family, must by no means be crossed in her wishes or caprices, let them be ever so unreasonable."[1]

In many ways the household was a very traditional one. Both the Harts and the Hinsdales, like many prosperous citizens of colonial Connecticut, traced their lineage to early New England settlers, a fact Emma Willard never ceased to celebrate. In a short autobiography, written when she was fifty-five, she asserted, "[T]he best of the old puritan blood, unmingled with any other flows in my veins."[2]

Stephen Hart, patriarch of the paternal line, emigrated from England around 1625, and Robert Hinsdale, first member of the maternal side to see the New World, emigrated from England in 1637. Stephen settled in Cambridge, where he worshipped at First Church, whose pastor was Thomas Hooker. In 1636 Stephen was one of the one hundred congregants who accompanied Hooker to Connecticut when Hooker broke with John Winthrop. Hooker's more liberal policies concerning voting rights and church membership apparently appealed to Stephen Hart; a streak of liberalism with regard to church orthodoxy would pass through the generations to his great-great-grandson, Samuel Hart, and on to Samuel's daughter, Emma. Almira, in contrast, was far more conventional. As one of her biographers has noted, "The God she worshipped . . . was not the mild Anglican God of the church she chose and apparently loved, but rather the stern patriarch of her Puritan forbears."[3]

Puritan Stephen Hart fathered John Hart, who was killed with almost his whole family during King Philip's War. Only one of John Hart's sons, also named John, survived. To Emma Willard, the triumph of the colonists over the Native Americans in this bloody chapter of colonial history vindicated Christians over "savages." In her history text she wrote, "If Philip's war was to the whites disastrous, to the savage tribes it was ruinous."[4] The younger John's son, Samuel, born in Farmington, Connecticut, in 1692, married Mary Hooker, a descendant of his grandfather's pastor. To Emma Willard, this connection with Thomas Hooker was a point of great pride. "In any state," she wrote, "no one can have a higher ancestry than to be descended from its founder . . . [and] there is no better blood than that of Thomas Hooker."[5] In 1738 Mary Hooker Hart gave birth to Samuel, Emma Hart's father.

Meanwhile, her mother's ancestor, Robert Hinsdale, who settled first in Dedham, Massachusetts, had also pushed westward in New England. By 1652 he was farming in Medfield, and in 1673 he arrived in Deerfield, where his grandson, Mehuman, was reportedly the first white child born in the township. In 1675, however, Robert and his sons, Samuel, Barnabas, and John, met the same fate as Stephen Hart and his family. They were massacred in King Philip's War, killed by Metacom's angry Native American warriors. Barnabas Hinsdale left a young son, Barnabas, who eventually married Martha Smith of Hartford. Their son, John, was born in 1706, worked as a blacksmith, and was described as "a man of rare military and literary ability."[6] John married Elizabeth Cole; the sixth of their seven children was Lydia, Emma Hart's mother.

The tendency toward the unorthodox, so evident in the Hart line, also characterized the Hinsdale lineage. Robert Hinsdale's first marriage to Ann Woodward was, according to family lore, a happy one, and they produced eight children, including Barnabas. When Ann died in 1666, Robert married a widow. This time the marriage was not so congenial, and Robert was punished by the colony when he separated from his wife. Just a year before his violent death, he was charged with having "broken the Perfect rule of divine law Mal 2:6; Matt 19:6; and 1 Peter 3:7 & the law of the Colony in the intent if not in the letter [by] living asunder."[7] Sentenced to both a whipping and a fine, he had broken society's rules, just as his great-great-great granddaughter would do in 1838 when she divorced her second husband.

Most descriptions of Emma's parents, Samuel and Lydia Hart, characterize them as classic New Englanders. According to one of Emma's biographers, Lydia "had in full perfection the New-England [sic] trait of making much out of little, and a little out of nothing." Furthermore, she was "practical, quietly executive, severely but unwaveringly industrious."[8] Samuel was "an influential farmer who represented the town in the General Court, honest, hospitable, kind-hearted, with strong desires for intellectual culture, inquiring and very liberal."[9] He was also "literary and scientific."[10] Prepared for Yale when his father died, he had been forced to give up college, but he was an autodidact all his life.

Emma Hart Willard revered her parents. She credited her father for making her "a voracious reader," recalling "the evenings when he sat in his armed chair before the ample fire-place, reading to his family, often from the profoundest works of philosophy, or theology, sometimes from the best books of poetry, and sometimes from the lighter literature, or the politics of the day, interspersed with grave remark, or with playful wit."

She concluded that "such evenings constituted an education."[11] When her father died, she wrote to a brother regarding the settlement of his estate, "[W]ith regard to the property our father left, we children have not, in justice, any claim. . . . But, with mother, the case is different. . . . She has spent more than forty years of hard labor, care and anxiety, . . . and to her care it is owing that our large family have been brought up."[12]

Emma's respect for her parents was rooted in her admiration for their role in the American Revolution, and her thinking about education invariably reflected her commitment to fulfilling revolutionary ideals. She regarded her father's service in the colonial army as heroic, and she dedicated a poem to her mother that extolled her role as a member of the revolutionary generation. Appearing on the frontispiece of every edition of her highly popular *History of the Republic,* the poem, written in 1828, described her mother as one of the "few [who] are left" who "felt the fire of freedom's holy time/Pervade and purify the patriot breast."[13] In reminiscences about childhood conversations around the Hart hearth, Almira commented, "The War of the American Revolution was a never ending theme."[14]

Berlin, the small village where the Hart homestead stood on Lower Lane, had been part of a colonial tract called Tunxis Plantation, which in 1645 was named Farmington and granted a charter by the Connecticut General Court. Initially, Farmington maintained jurisdiction over the villages of Avon, Bristol, Burlington, Plainville, Southington, most of New Britain, Berlin, Bloomfield, Harwinton, and Wolcott. Berlin was set off and incorporated in 1785 and included Kensington, New Britain, and Worthington. When the first national census was taken in 1790, Emma was three, and Berlin contained 2,465 people, including one slave. The Hart household at the time consisted of her parents along with James, Theodore, Lydia, Nancy, and Emma.

Although Berlin's citizenry admired Samuel Hart enough to elect him to the General Court in 1787, his politics were generally more liberal than those of his neighbors. He was a Jeffersonian Republican in staunchly Federalist Connecticut. Nor did he adhere to community orthodoxy with regard to the church. In fact, he ultimately broke with the church, an act that meant "desirable offices were forthwith resigned or barred."[15] He had been elected church treasurer, a post that carried the responsibility for collecting mandatory taxes for the support of the minister. Two of his neighbors, Gideon Williams and Nathaniel Cole, were nonbelievers and jailed for refusing to pay; to add to his discomfort, the arrest warrants bore his name as church treasurer. After calling a meeting of the congregation and finding no support for his position, he resigned as treasurer, left the church, and paid the taxes and fines for the two men. Almira, herself a very devout Episcopalian all of her adult life, wrote admiringly in 1867, "To force men to pay taxes for the support of the Congregational mode of worship, who urged scruples of conscience against it, was, he thought, unworthy of the descendants of men who had fled from persecution in England."[16]

That Samuel Hart continued to be a free thinker long after this incident is clear from a letter to his brother-in-law, Theodore Hinsdale, founder of Hinsdale, Massachusetts, and the pastor of the Congregational Church in that village. Samuel wrote to this Federalist relative in 1799:

> And I cannot say that, where ecclesiastical societies depend on the coercion of Civil law to maintain their constitution and support their worship, I am sorry to have them disunited; or even disbanded. I wish to see people free from the shackles of bigotry and superstition,—united in promoting free inquiry; and agreed in cherishing a principle of benevolence, friendship and charity, not confined to the limits of any denomination, sect, or party; but extending to the whole family of mankind.

He concluded, "By this time, I fear you will think me a disorganizer—jacobin, or democrat."[17] He was correct in his supposition. Almira, who boarded for a few months with this uncle in 1812, described him as "kind . . . but it was evidently a very mortifying circumstance that his sister's family was not *orthodox* in their adherence to the doctrine of Calvinism and John Adams' political faith." As the War of 1812 approached, Theodore Hinsdale prayed nightly for England—"the only bulwark against the infidelity and immorality of the French people."[18] There is no record of his opinion about his niece Emma's later infatuation with France and the Marquis de Lafayette.

Samuel's unconventional ideas included his belief that women should be educated. In this, as in his religious convictions, he broke with the Puritan tradition of John Winthrop. In 1645 Winthrop had expressed the opinion that Ann Yale Hopkins, the wife of Connecticut governor Edward Hopkins, had gone mad because she spent too much time reading and writing. He opined, "If she had attended her household affairs, and such things as belong to women and not gone out of her way and calling to meddle in such things as are proper for men, whose minds are stronger, she had kept her wits, and might have improved them usefully and honorably in the place God had set her."[19]

Unlike Ann Hopkins, Lydia Hart did not go mad even though, in contrast to many of her contemporaries, she could both read and write. Although most colonists taught their daughters to read, primarily so that they could study the Bible, writing was not considered a necessary skill for women. By 1775 about 90 percent of white men in New England could write; fewer than half the white women in the region could do so. The gap would not close until the second quarter of the nineteenth century, by which time the Troy Female Seminary was flourishing.

By marrying a literate woman, Samuel showed that he agreed with Abigail Adams that men were misguided in allowing "such a disparity [in education] in those whom they one day intend for companions and associates."[20] As a Republican, Samuel did not agree with Adams's fervent Federal politics; that the two saw eye to eye on women's education is noteworthy. It reflects a general change in public opinion about educating girls that blossomed after the Revolution.

Samuel apparently taught his young daughter himself. Emma recalled that "He was fifty years my senior . . . yet would he often call me when at the age of fourteen from household duties by my mother's side, to enjoy with him some passage of an author which pleased him, or to read over to me some essay which he had amused himself in writing."[21] In addition, Samuel also sent her—and her sisters—to school. By law each town in Connecticut had to support a district school, and it was the district school in Berlin that Emma first attended. Although it is not known exactly how long she studied there, it is probable that she attended the school only in the summers, as that was the pattern for girls throughout the region. Boys attended "winter school" but were needed in the fields in the summer. Consequently, the summer teachers were often women, the winter teachers always men. In her recollections of her early education in a schoolhouse that she described as a "rude structure," Emma wrote of boys and girls trudging to school "of a cold winter morning."[22] She might have attended winter school, but she might also have been remembering the winter school where she herself taught some years after she attended the Berlin school. District schools taught only basic reading, writing, and arithmetic. Academies, the public ones open only to boys, provided the next level of education.

Emma Hart's education might have stopped with the village school, but in 1802 a Yale graduate, Thomas Miner, opened a female academy in Berlin. Fortuitously, Emma, as well as her other siblings, had recently received a small inheritance from a maternal uncle. She and her next oldest sister, Nancy, used their money to pay the tuition at Miner's academy, studying with him for two years. In a memoir written years later, she wrote of studying grammar, geography, and composition and claimed "that no better instruction was given to girls in any school, at that time, in our country."[23]

The pride in being an American that was so evident in the revolutionary tales told by Samuel Hart was reinforced in the texts used by Thomas Miner. For grammar, Miner followed the practice of the postrevolutionary nationalists, eschewing the traditional colonial grammar books, published in England, for the volume written by Noah Webster. Webster was the first to establish *American* rules for grammar and spelling that differentiated American English from the version used by the tyrannical British. Jedediah Morse's *Geography*, widely used in academies at the time, also celebrated an American point of view. In the preface, Morse wrote, "Europeans have been the ſole writers of American Geography, and have too often ſuffered fancy to ſupply the place of facts, and thus have led their readers into errors." But, he continued, "ſince the United States have become an independent nation . . . the reſt of the world have a right now to expect authentic information."[24] Morse's text would stand as the leading geography until supplanted in the 1820s by Emma's own volume on the subject, initially co-written with William Woodbridge.

After leaving Miner's school, Emma began teaching in a local school for young children, including her sister Almira. From 1804 until 1807, she alternated terms of teaching in Berlin with terms studying in Hartford, where she enrolled at Mrs. Royce's School and the Misses Pattens' School. Although she undoubtedly paid part of her tuition and board from her teaching salary, her older brothers John and Theodore assisted her financially. They had joined the stream of New England peddlers flowing to the South, carrying the tinware that Connecticut Yankees were famed for making. By 1804 they were successful merchants in Petersburg, Virginia, but neither would live to see their sister's seminary in Troy.

In the fall of 1806, Emma was hired to teach the winter school in the academy building where she had studied with Miner. A town historian has noted, "It was a great innovation then for a woman to be placed in charge of a winter school, but Miss Hart was successful in this, as in her other efforts, and her work gave a new impulse to education in Berlin."[25] At nineteen, she was already making her mark in education. And she was already aware of her uniqueness. She later wrote, "I had the uncommon honor (uncommon at that time for a female) to keep the winter school, in what was then the southwest district of this parish."[26]

The following spring, her fame having spread, Emma was invited to take charge of academies in Westfield, Massachusetts, Middlebury, Vermont, and Hudson, New York. She opted for Westfield, perhaps because it was the closest to her family. It was also a prosperous New England village and the largest town in western Massachusetts in 1807. At the close of the Revolution, it had contained 348 families with slightly over 2,200 white and 15 black inhabitants making up the population, and it had continued to grow.

Plans for an academy had started in 1797; it was to be situated facing the town green near the Congregational Church, the town hall, and Palmer's Tavern. A board of trustees was established in 1799, and the opening day was set for January 1, 1800. Newspapers in Northampton and Springfield promoted the new academy, advertising instruction in reading, writing, and grammar for $2 a quarter session. The trustees set the admissions standards in the bylaws. The academy was open to "youths of both sexes who can read and write in a decent manner."[27] The salary for the head teacher, called a preceptor in the bylaws, was set at 70 pounds. (Although Webster had weaned the fledgling country from British spelling and the Uniform Currency Act of 1792 had established the dollar as the monetary unit for the new nation, the pound sterling remained legal currency throughout New England.)

The trustees also stipulated that the preceptor and his assistant teachers "shall declare to the Trustees . . . their belief of the Christian religion, and their firm persuasion of its truth."[28] In the first twenty-five years of the academy's existence, most of the preceptors were Williams College graduates. After attending a Williams commencement,

Nathaniel Hawthorne described the graduates as "schoolmaster-looking."[29] so Westfield's choice of Williams men was apparently apt.

Emma Hart was not the first woman to teach at Westfield Academy. According to school records, a Miss Parnell Fairchild joined the staff in 1802. The first female preceptress, Lucy Douglas, was appointed in 1819, long after Emma Hart had moved on. At the opening of the academy in 1800, the Rev. Joseph Lathrop of West Springfield crafted his sermon around verse 12 of Psalm 144. "May our sons in their youth be like plants full grown, our daughters like corner pillars cut for the structure of a palace,"[30] intoned the reverend. Clearly, the trustees of the Westfield Academy valued education for their daughters as well as their sons, valued Christianity above all, and at the same time supported gender differences.

Emma Hart accepted the role of assistant teacher at the academy, but she only remained "six or eight weeks." The citizens of Middlebury had yet to fill the position that Emma had turned down. Their school for girls had opened in 1800 under Ida Strong, a fellow citizen of Connecticut and graduate of Sarah Pierce's Litchfield Academy, who had succumbed to the harsh northern Vermont winter in 1805. In the late spring of 1807, the Middlebury Female Academy trustees once more urged Miss Hart to take control of their school. Emma, perhaps chafing at the heavy dose of religion mandated by the Westfield trustees, was apparently unhappy at her Massachusetts post. A letter written to her on May 18, signed by both parents, but most likely composed by Samuel, hints at the cause. Addressing her "present unhappiness," he cautioned that there were "subjects enough of a general nature that are uncontrovertible [sic], to afford matter for ordinary conversation: so that, I trust, you will be under no necessity of disclosing any sentiments or opinions of your own which are not congenial with those of the people among whom you reside."[31] In all likelihood, given her father's example with the Congregational Church in Berlin, the "sentiments and opinions" she yearned to express had to do with religion. However, what was sauce for the Hart gander was not appropriate for "one of your sex, age and station," wrote Samuel.

In spite of a counteroffer from the Westfield trustees, Emma left for Middlebury in the late spring to take the helm of the Middlebury Female Academy in time for the summer session. She made the trip to Middlebury alone, probably traveling by stagecoach, a trip that would have taken at least two days. She later recalled that it was "a dangerous journey . . . tho I arrived in safety."[32] As a point of reference, the Boston stagecoach left Middlebury in good weather at 4 A.M. Passengers arrived in Hanover, New Hampshire, after noon and finally reached their destination two days later. The first turnpike company was organized in 1801, the road following the Middlebury River to Woodstock. The federal post road to Boston ran east of the mountains.

The female academy where Emma took charge was located on the second floor of the boys' academy building. Thirty-seven girls were enrolled for the summer session, a number that swelled to sixty the following spring. No matter the size of the school, she taught the girls alone and in one room. Her later description of the Middlebury Female Academy stressed the rudimentary accommodations provided for girls, as well as the energy and ingenuity of the young teacher:

> They were all in one room, and myself the sole teacher.—The discomforts of that room, which had I think as many as ten windows, and only one small smoking fire-place to warm it in that cold climate, I shall never forget. In some cold days, and when the room was so filled with smoke that we were obliged to open the windows, the only expedient to keep my pupils alive was to call them upon the floor—and set them singing and dancing some lively contradance. . . . I always led the ball myself.[33]

At Middlebury Emma boarded with a local physician, Dr. Tudor, who had studied medicine under Benjamin Rush, signer of the Declaration and patron of the Young Ladies Academy in Philadelphia. It is not known whether or not Tudor shared his mentor's belief in women's education, but it is not impossible to imagine conversations around the Tudor dinner table regarding Rush's "Thoughts Upon Female Education," published the year Emma was born. In it Rush outlined a curriculum for "young ladies," which he thought should include English (reading, writing, speaking, grammar), penmanship, arithmetic, geography, chronology, astronomy, natural philosophy, vocal music, dancing, history, and "regular instruction in the Christian religion."[34] He did not approve of either French or drawing.

There is no record of what Emma Hart taught in Middlebury between 1807 and 1809, but she described her schedule in a letter to her parents. Near the end of the first summer term, she wrote, "I go to school generally before nine, and stay till one; come home, snatch my dinner, go again and stay till almost sundown; come home, and dress in a great hurry to go abroad; get home about ten, fatigued enough to go to bed, and lie till seven the next morning, with hardly time enough to mend my stockings."[35]

Some sort of controversy embroiled the female academy during her second year there. Alma Lutz ascribed the difficulty to "denominational jealousy"[36] but offered little documentation on the exact nature of the problem. As she had done from Westfield, Emma wrote to her parents from Middlebury about her challenge in navigating various religious factions. Maintaining that it would be difficult to "avoid making enemies," she wrote,

> To please the greatest number of people, I must attend all the meetings Sunday, go to conference one or two afternoons in a week, profess to believe, among other articles of the creed, that mankind, generally speaking, will be damned. To please another set of people, I must speak in the most contemptible manner of conferences, and ridicule many of the notions of religionists, and praise many things that are disagreeable, such as dancing, playing cards, etc. In this situation I know of no better way to live than to follow the dictates of my own conscience. This would direct me not to ridicule what others find sacred; to endeavor not to treat any in such a manner that they may have reason to personally be my enemies; to have no idea of pretending to believe what I do not believe.[37]

In spite of her avowed intentions, she apparently fell out of favor with some of the trustees or perhaps some of the influential parents of her students. A leading citizen who rallied to her cause was Dr. John Willard. According to Lutz, Willard's "sense of fair play was aroused, and he at once championed the young schoolmistress."[38] Although Lutz provides no support for this statement, its truth is borne out in a letter Samuel Hart wrote to Willard in 1809. Captain Hart maintained "your friendly exertions, & the interference of some others in her be-half, (which, as I understand, introduced you to her acquaintance) was probably the means of saving her from being crowded out of business, and obliged to quit Middlebury."[39] He alluded to both religion and women's rights as possible areas of contention between Emma and her detractors. Lutz opined that Emma was "very much attracted" to her champion because she was "essentially a hero-worshipper."[40]

John Willard, twenty-eight years her senior, definitely fit her idea of a hero. A Revolutionary War veteran, he was one of the pioneers from Connecticut who had moved to Vermont after the war. Credited with being the first physician in the state, he and his first wife, Es-ther Wilcox, settled in Vermont in 1787. Not yet a state, the territory that would become Vermont was the object of a territorial struggle between New Hampshire and New York, both of which wanted to add Vermont's land to their own. Because Vermont had survived the war debt free, many of its citizens questioned joining a union that would obligate them to help pay other states' war debts. For a time the future state organized as an independent republic, electing Thomas Chitten-den as governor. However, after protracted discussions in Congress and some intervention from President George Washington, Vermont joined the nation as the fourteenth state in 1791.

Even though official statehood had not yet been granted, Vermonters were enumerated in the census of 1790. The 85,000 people living in the territory were composed of migrants from the older New England colo-nies, 98 percent of whom claimed English or Scottish roots. The popula-tion more than doubled by 1800, and by 1810 it topped 200,000. Vermont, in fact, was the fastest growing state in the union before the War of 1812.

In going from Connecticut to Vermont, Emma Hart was com-pletely typical of the Vermont migratory pattern. Even Ethan Allen, head of the Green Mountain Boys and Vermont's leading revolution-ary hero, had been born in Connecticut. So had Gov. Thomas Chit-tenden, and, of course, John Willard. When Willard arrived in Ver-mont in 1787, the year Emma Hart was born, Middlebury "was almost wholly a wilderness."[41] However, the village shortly gained a healthy population, and by the turn of the century it was well on its way to becoming the largest town in the state. Not only did it boast Middlebury College, it was also the site of a law school. The town was characterized as "overrun with lawyers—mostly college men from institutions like Yale, Dartmouth and Williams."[42] Timothy Dwight, an early president of Yale and a prolific journal writer, described Middlebury in 1810 as "one of the most prosperous and virtuous towns in New England."[43] Dwight did complain of the clay that clogged Middlebury's roads for many weeks during the wet end-of-winter and early summer months. On the positive side, Middlebury, with transportation so difficult many months of the year, was a completely self-sufficient society.

When Emma Hart came to Middlebury in 1807, many mills and factories stood along the Otter River: leather tanning, iron production, gunsmithing, glass manufacturing, flour milling, and red flannel production all took place along its banks. There was a goldsmith, a silversmith, a potter, a cooper, a saddler, a whitesmith, a blacksmith, and a baker. Shops were plentiful. There were fourteen merchants, two druggists, three jewelers, seven shoemakers, three tailors, eight dressmakers, four cabinetmakers, one bookseller, one bookbinder, five printers, six masons, and more.

Twenty-year-old Emma Hart found much to admire in the town. The high literacy rate among the former Connecticut citizens and the presence of the college and the law school contributed to what she called "a high state of cultivation—much more than in any place I was ever in." "The beaux here," she wrote to her parents, "are, the greater part of them, men of collegiate education."[44] Although her main beau, John Willard, lacked a college degree, he was, nevertheless, a person of no small importance in Middlebury and in the state as a whole.

John Willard was born in Guilford, Connecticut, in 1759, the second son and third child of John and Mary Horton Willard. He had one older brother, Julius, and one younger sister, Hannah. John was eight when his father, a shipbuilder, died. With limited prospects, John went off to sea as a teenager, and during the Revolution, he served as a quartermaster with the Connecticut Volunteers. Captured by the British, he was imprisoned on one of the infamous Jersey ships, an experience that fueled his lifelong antipathy toward the British.

After the war, he apprenticed with a physician, Jonathan Todd, back home in Guilford. He married Esther Wilcox in 1786 and moved to Vermont the next year. His first son, Gustavus, was born in Vermont in 1787, and John buried his wife there a year later. At some point in the 1790s, he married Mindwell Meigs, third cousin of his first wife, and herself a descendant of Puritan New Englanders much like the Harts and Hinsdales. The Meigs patriarch, yet another John, had been born in Massachusetts in 1641 and had made the migration to Connecticut sometime in the late 1600s, dying in Guilford in 1713. His son, also John Meigs, married Hannah Willard of Guilford, so it is very likely that John Willard and his first two wives were distantly related. Given names in the Meigs's family reflected their Puritan roots; in addition to several generations of Mindwells, there were boys named Return, Zekiel, Josiah, and Recompense, girls named Hester, and, in 1711 a set of male twins named Silence and Submit, one of whom was born dead, never uttering a sound, and the second of whom died shortly after birth, ceding to the will of his Puritan God.

Just as Mindwell was his second wife, John was Mindwell's second husband. She had been married first to a Thaddeus Frisbie; together they, too, had migrated from Connecticut to Vermont. When John married her, she already had two children, Laura and Jerusha. In 1796 she gave birth to William Tell Willard, and in 1798 Benjamin Franklin Willard was born. A few years later, John lost his second wife. On August 29, 1804, the *Middlebury Mercury* reported "Died, in this village, Mrs. Willard, consort of John Willard, Esq."

In 1801 John Willard had been appointed marshal of the state by the new president, Thomas Jefferson. A lifelong Jeffersonian Republican, Willard shared Jefferson's agrarian philosophy and his resistance to renewed economic ties with the British, the position championed by Federalist Party leaders. A Middlebury town historian wrote that between 1800 and 1812, "No man . . . had as much influence in controlling the measures of the [Republican] party as he."[45] A practicing physician, an active politician, and a man of considerable property, John Willard, with two children and two stepchildren still at home, needed a third wife. (Gustavus, his oldest son, had emigrated to Ohio.) It is no wonder that the intelligent, energetic, and liberal Emma Hart caught his eye.

Dr. Willard was sensitive about the difference in their ages; after all, Gustavus and Emma were the same age. He apparently addressed this concern in a letter to Samuel Hart. Samuel, however, agreed to the match, and in a letter written to Willard two months after the wedding, quoted an earlier letter he had received from John. Addressing his son-in-law "Dear Sir," he assured him that

> [I]f ever I had any serious objection against my daughter's giving her hand to you, it is fully removed. . . . The circumstance of the disparity of years I consider as sufficiently overballanced [sic] by other considerations. It is true as you observed, that "at best we hold life and all its enjoyments by an uncertain tenure"—and that "we often see the fairest morning shaded by a gloomy cloud, and the sweetest flower nipet by an untimely frost."[46]

In this letter Emma's father draws clear distinctions between his status in society and the position of John Willard, noting "the great disparity there is between your situation, rank & condition in life, and that of Emma." Anticipating a visit from the couple, he continued, "I hope to convince you that by the alliance, you have confered [sic] an honor upon my family without degrading yourself."[47]

Unlike her father, Emma's best friend from home, Hannah Bull, did not approve of the marriage. By marrying at twenty-two, Emma matched the norm for early nineteenth-century white women in New England, but Hannah still felt she was too young. She wrote to her, "I can't bear that you should be married until you have seen more of the world."[48] At least one of Emma's new stepchildren also opposed the union. Writing to Benjamin Willard in 1821, she brought up "a wound," which was Frank's (Benjamin's family nickname) belief that she had married his father "from motives of interest rather than affection." In a striking departure from her father's letter to her husband, she commented, "My standing in society was as good as his."[49] Compare this indignant defense of her social position with her father's hope in his letter to John that "your allying yourself to a family so obscure will be no mortification to you."[50]

The letter from Samuel Hart to John Willard is notable for two other reasons. In it, he worries about his daughter's liberal attitudes. Given her later accounts of his support for the education of women, it is striking to read, "Her liberal sentiments respecting religion; and high notions of female dignity & the rights of women, I was sensible would render her obnoxious." He is surprised and relieved that she has made any marriage at all, and delighted at the catch she has made. He comments, "That she has been able to recommend herself to the notice, and gain the affections of a Gentleman of your natural & acquired abilities, & elevated rank; is an event that has superseded all my previous calculations."

Samuel concludes his remarks about the Willard marriage with his fervent "hope, Sir, that Emma (notwithstanding her high notions of female importance), will prove your loving, faithfull [sic] & obedient wife." In the original letter, "obedient" is crossed out and asterisked. The corresponding asterisk at the bottom of the page carries the note, "I made that cross—Emma."[51] The youthful Emma Hart and the newly minted Mrs. Willard were forceful personalities. In keeping with the tradition of the day, however, marriage for Emma meant retirement from her teaching. As the spring session in 1809 drew to a close, Emma believed she was leaving her career behind her. Ahead was life as the wife of a prosperous, leading citizen of Middlebury. And, if her life followed the pattern of other young white New England wives, she would have at least four children.

In this, as in so many other ways, she would break from the norm. In 1810 she gave birth to John Hart Willard, her only child. The next year Dr. Willard built his family an impressive stone house on Main Street across from the Middlebury College campus. His nephew and namesake came to live with the Willards while he studied at the college. In addition, Almira, Emma's youngest sister, lived with the family from 1810 to 1811; both John and Emma were her teachers as she prepared to be a schoolmistress. John, since 1806 a director of the Vermont State Bank, in 1812 added sheriff of Addison County to his duties. In spite of isolation, long cold winters, ongoing political battles with the Federalists, growing economic troubles as a result of continuing warfare between Napoleon and the British, the Willard family prospered. Although Dr. Willard was often away from home on business, his young wife proved to be a capable manager. An undated letter to her husband during the early years of her marriage captures the scope of her responsibilities. She wrote,

> The winter-apples are gathered; the cider is made—twenty-three Barrels; the potatoes are nearly all in; the buckwheat is gathered, but lies on the barn-floor unthreshed, which, by-the-way, places us in a predicament about the wheat; the cows and hogs have been fed according to your directions; the carrots and garden vegetables are out yet, but will be gathered immediately; no injury has been done to the farm by unruly cattle; Wilcox has let us have a quarter of beef. . . . I have not been five rods from the house since you left, and . . . I count the days when I may expect you home.[52]

There was nothing in Emma Willard's life in 1813 that hinted at the transformation in girls' education she would launch the following year.

Female Education,
the Subject That Interests Me Most

DURING THE FIRST YEARS of her marriage, Emma Willard had every reason to believe that her husband was prospering. He held public office, he traveled to Boston often on Vermont State Bank business, he built her a large brick house on Main Street, and he owned and managed a number of farm properties. She was the wife of a prominent Republican in a predominantly Federalist town, but that was no different from what she had experienced growing up in the household of the iconoclastic Samuel Hart. She admired men of strong conviction. Furthermore, her attention was focused on her child and her home. As she later wrote, during the first years of her marriage, "I spent my time in the true Olde England style, delving over the kitchen fire."[1] All was not as it seemed, however. Political intrigue, the coming war with Great Britain, and, more troubling, his own fiscal imprudence were converging to destroy John Willard's financial stability.

The launching of the Vermont State Bank coincided with a difficult economic period for the United States. Beginning in 1806, relations with Europe worsened, the Federalists favoring ties to England and the Republicans favoring ties to France. The Non-Importation Act of 1806, the Embargo Act of 1807, the Nonintercourse Act of 1809, and Macon's Bill No. 2 were all attempts by the Republican administrations of Thomas Jefferson and James Madison to bring economic pressure to bear on the warring European empires, neither of which respected American shipping rights. Nothing worked. In fact, the most noticeable result of Jeffersonian foreign policy was to plunge the new nation into its first serious economic crisis.

For northern Vermonters, trade on the high seas was not nearly as important as their skyrocketing business dealings with neighboring Canada. When, in 1808, Jefferson extended the embargo against foreign commerce to trade on the inland waters and on land, there was a strong negative reaction throughout upper New England, including Vermont. In a heated contest for governor, the backlash cost incumbent Republican Israel Smith the election. Federalist Isaac Tichenor won. Political fighting remained intense for years as the office see-sawed back and forth between the two parties. Not until 1815 was the governorship firmly secured by the Republicans when the Federalists died out as a viable national party.

In 1806, at the beginning of this period of political and economic turmoil, John Willard was named a director of the newly incorporated state bank. As was the case with regard to foreign relations, the two main parties held divergent opinions about the role of banks. The Federalists favored banks, which were central to Alexander Hamilton's financial vision. The Republicans, party of Jefferson's "yeoman farmer," distrusted banks and banking interests. Between 1803 and 1806, the Vermont state legislature considered a number of bank bills, all of which failed to pass. Finally, a coalition of Federalists and Republicans united behind a bill for a state bank. Republicans reckoned that a state bank would be a people's bank and would not share the agenda of the private interests they feared. However, by circulating local currency, the bank would meet the Federalist goal of reducing Vermont's dependency on out-of-state bank notes.

Among the rules establishing the new bank were requirements for the amount of specie to be kept on hand, limits on the amount of capital, the establishment of a specie-to-credit ratio, and the provision of a state board of directors with the power to regulate the branches of the bank. Within a very short time there were four of these: Burlington, Westminster, Woodstock, and Middlebury. In addition to John Willard, the directors at the Middlebury branch were Horatio Seymour, a successful attorney who favored the Republicans but also tried to appease the Federalists, and Daniel Chipman, also an attorney but a committed Federalist.

By 1811 the state legislature was aware that the Vermont State Bank was in terrible trouble. The bank had failed to adhere to the specie-to-credit ratio; there were far more bills in circulation than hard money to cover them. In the fall of 1812, an investigating committee appointed by the state legislature to audit the bank concluded that the bank needed to be shut down. The Middlebury branch was particularly problematic. The committee recommended suing the directors of that branch, creating a situation in which "the political and personal reputations of three of Middlebury's most able citizens hung in the balance."[2] Dr. Willard could not have been too surprised. As early as 1807 he had written to a client, Litus Hutchinson, that he was worried about the proliferation of unauthorized paper money and its impact on the specie-to-bill ratio.

The charges were numerous. Middlebury's directors were accused of negligence in their hiring and bonding of cashiers and inaccuracy in their annual reporting of the bank's assets. They were also charged with allowing too much of the bank's business to leave their control, having hired an agent in Boston and one in St. Alban's to make loans that they had not approved and, in some cases, knew nothing about. In addition, the directors were charged with making bad loans to risky customers. They did not routinely require that loans be secured by property, and they took an unorthodox approach to collection. Rather than use writs of extent, as the other branches did, they usually sued, with either Chipman or Seymour earning substantial legal fees in the process. Finally, the investigators found that nearly $14,000 was missing from the bank and accused the directors of swindling it.

The erstwhile bankers cut a deal: no trial. Instead, they agreed to submit to the adjudication of the charges by a legislature-appointed special board. Their confidence in this process was not misplaced. Within a short time, all the charges were dropped except the one concerning the missing money. In refuting this charge, the directors explained that it had been stolen in June 1809. Reminded that no break-in had been reported at the time, they responded that a clerk must have left one of the doors to the bank unlocked, and a disreputable merchant named Joshua Henshaw, who operated a store next door, had absconded with the funds. In the fall of 1813, the legislators refused to believe this story and ordered the three men to pay the money.

Meanwhile, the War of 1812 was well under way. The United States and England had been fighting since the spring of 1812. Both Benjamin Franklin Willard and William Tell Willard were in uniform, taking up arms against the British like their father before them. A significant troop encampment had been set up in Burlington as the federal government prepared to counter a British invasion from Canada and tried to stop northern Vermonters and New Yorkers from illegally supplying British forces by border smuggling. James Madison, in his role as secretary of state, wrote to John Willard, warning that "attempts are to be made in [your] district to frustrate the execution of the Embargo laws" and asking him as marshal of Vermont to aid the customs collector of the district of Vermont by giving "him by means of your posse all the aid which the occasion may require and the laws authorize."[3]

A deadly fever, originating in the army camp, swept through the entire state, killing forty-seven people in Middlebury alone. Emma Willard fell ill. In a letter to an old Connecticut friend, Nancy Whittlesey (who would eventually send three daughters to study in Troy), she reported, "I have been confined to my bed eleven days with the disorder that rages here and for one or two days thought myself more likely to die than live." Her toddler son John apparently had the fever as well. In the first of what would be a lifetime of excuses for his behavior, she expressed her sorrow that his poor conduct on a recent visit to Connecticut was a result of "his ill health and some consequent peevishness."[4]

As Emma recovered, the New England economy suffered. The war hurt trade and spiked inflation. Blaming conditions on Republican foreign policies, the Vermont Federalists captured the state legislature and the governor's mansion in the fall of 1815. Chipman, in spite of the guilty verdict hanging over his head, was not only reelected to the legislature but was elevated to speaker of the house. He quickly proposed a bill establishing a new legislative committee to review the outstanding guilty charge. After a very short deliberation and the introduction of a highly questionable deposition from the son of one of Seymour's colleagues, the final charge was dropped. Fourteen-year-old Udney Penniman recalled that his friend, Joshua Henshaw Jr., had once confided to him that he had found a box containing $13,000 or so in his family's home.

On the strength of Penniman's hearsay testimony, the directors were declared fully innocent. Henshaw Sr., now living in Canada, was guilty without a trial, and this version of events, including the later "discovery" of a false key that he had allegedly used to enter the bank, passed into Vermont history and Emma Willard biographies. In the widely accepted version of this tale, Dr. John Willard, falsely accused of embezzlement and exonerated completely, nevertheless suffered financially from the situation because he was ordered, along with his codirectors, to repay the missing funds. His wife, to help him out, returned to her former occupation and opened a school for girls.

Neither Chipman nor Seymour suffered Willard's fate. Daniel Chipman went on from the Vermont legislature to the U.S. House of Representatives and Horatio Seymour to the Senate. John Willard found himself in a different position because, after all the charges were dropped, he was left with a substantial debt of more than $3,000, money that he had borrowed personally from the bank. No longer marshal of Vermont and removed by the Federalists from his post as sheriff of Addison County, he was not a young man. Nor had he practiced medicine for some time. (Not that medicine was lucrative; doctors in New England as late as the 1830s earned on average less than $1,000 a year, about the same as ministers.) The financial ruin Dr. Willard faced in 1813 was not the result of false accusations but his own improvidence.

Decades later, explaining why she opened a school, Emma wrote, "When I began my school in Middlebury, in 1814, my leading motive was to relieve my husband from financial difficulties."[5] In letters to friends written closer to the event, she showed her awareness of the interplay of economic and political factors. To her friends the Tappans she complained, "[M]y husband's political friends intrigued him out of office and in order to divest him of influence that he need not repay them for their treachery [they tried] to divest him of property."[6] Dr. Willard shared his view of the family's financial reverses with his oldest son, commenting, "I have been swindled out of my property not so much by private individuals as public agents."[7] There is little doubt that the bank business, as well as Willard's removal from office, was intertwined with the acrimonious political fighting in the state. There is also little doubt that without this setback, Emma Hart Willard would never have opened her school. It is also highly probable that she was delighted to leave the kitchen for the schoolroom. In a letter written in the spring of 1815, she wrote, "My fondness for my former favorite occupation has revived."[8]

In the spring of 1814, notices in newspapers in Vermont and in northern New York advertised her plan. According to the *Vermont Mirror*, "A boarding school for young ladies" would commence a summer session on May 8. The curriculum would include arithmetic, English grammar, geography, drawing, painting, and embroidery." In addition, "strict attention [would be] paid to the manners and morals of pupils," and all of this would be provided at "reasonable prices."[9]

In her reminiscences, Emma insisted that "it was not until a year or two after, that I formed the design of effecting an important change in education, by the introduction of a grade of schools for women, higher than any heretofore known."[10] Certainly, the curriculum she proposed in the spring of 1814 was not revolutionary. Nevertheless, in later years she always maintained that the Troy Female Seminary was rooted in the soil of Middlebury. She invariably made two important claims for the Middlebury school, that it was here that the "stream of lady-mathematicians took its rise," and that it was here that the first women teachers were intentionally taught. "Here were now forming my future teachers,"[11] she recalled. The latter claim was somewhat more accurate than the former. Although she later recalled teaching geometry to a few select students in Middlebury, advertisements for the school as late as 1818 do not mention this addition to the curriculum. However, Elizabeth Sherrill, Katharine Batty, Elizabeth Henshaw, and Julia Pierpont, all Middlebury pupils, went on to careers as teachers.

In 1814 schools for girls were no longer the exception they had once been. Enlightenment thinking and the American Revolution had given a boost to arguments in favor of women's education in the late eighteenth century. The Founding Fathers did not, as Abigail Adams begged her husband to do, "remember the ladies" in their new constitution and laws. Nevertheless, the idea of some education for women, particularly reading, writing, and arithmetic, had taken hold. Benjamin Rush, signer of the Declaration, was one of the most articulate spokespeople in this regard. John Adams supported education for his daughters, as well as his sons, and Thomas Jefferson also educated his daughters. As Enlightenment thinkers, many of the young nation's leaders believed that rational thought was a key *human* characteristic, one that set women, as well as men, apart from other creatures. Furthermore, they argued that civilization progresses in proportion to the education of the populace. As educational historian Thomas Woody pointed out, "the gradual advance of the female sex to equality with the male sex"[12] was a sign of an advanced society. This measure of civilization's progress was at the heart of Emma Willard's philosophy of education. It was firmly repeated in her history books and later in her work on behalf of Greece. Under Ottoman rule, education for women had been virtually nonexistent; Emma Willard saw the establishment of a girls' school as critical to the success of the newly independent Greece.

She also was a strong proponent of a second widespread rationale for educating women. If the new nation was to survive, if it was to be able to combat ignorance and faction, feared by all as great threats to the success of the new democracy, women had to be educated. As mothers and as wives, they had a role to play in the new republic. It was not a role that would bring them into the public political sphere as legislators or even voters, but it was a political role just the same. They would be the guides and moral compasses for sons who would become the nation's leaders. This ideology, often called republican motherhood, was based on educational equality without political equality. It appears throughout Emma Willard's writings about education and echoes in the writings of contemporaneous educators like Mary Lyon, Catharine Beecher, and Emma's sister Almira. Literate women writing about women's roles and other social and moral topics gradually introduced women's voices to the public arena. This was perhaps unintended, but it proved to be a long-reaching consequence of educating girls.

In the introduction to her *Plan for Improving Female Education*, Emma Willard very explicitly embraces republican motherhood: "Our sex need but be considered, in the single relation of mothers. In this character, we have the charge of the whole mass of individuals, who are to compose the succeeding generation."[13] In a stirring, patriotic finish, she recalls the Revolution and again ties educated mothers to the future success of the nation:

> History . . . points to a nation, which having thrown off the shackles of authority and precedent, shrinks not from schemes of improvement, because other nations have never attempted them; but which, in its pride of independence, would rather lead than follow, in the march of human improvement. . . . Does not every American exult that this country is his own? And who knows how great and good a race of men, may yet arise from the forming hand of mothers, enlightened by the bounty of that beloved country,—to defend her liberties,—to plan her future improvement,—and to raise her to unparalleled glory?[14]

There was another less lofty and less often articulated reason that schools for girls flourished in the early part of the nineteenth century; education was a mark of social status in a nation that was rapidly developing self-conscious socioeconomic classes. Historian Margaret Nash argues persuasively that the growing middle class, particularly after the War of 1812, saw education as a way of differentiating themselves from the manual wage earners in the lower classes, who were also increasingly foreign born. The "true progeny of the Revolution" were "hardworking, moral, Christian doers . . . the backbone of the republic,"[15] and they swelled the ranks of the newly emerging middle and upper middle classes. To this end, state governments and municipalities provided education for boys at the academy level. Girls' education, although increasingly popular, remained a private enterprise. However, where it flourished, as in Middlebury and later Troy, girls' education, like boys' collegiate education, increasingly delineated social class.

The school Emma Willard opened in Middlebury was no different from many other schools for girls, although most were operated by single women, widows, and men. (John Willard's active support of his wife's work marked him as quite extraordinary for the time.) Called "venture schools," these were for-profit enterprises, as was Emma Willard's school. Many advertised in newspapers, many were boarding schools (although, and this was true of Emma's school as well, the boarders often roomed with neighboring families, as well as in the house of the proprietor). In 1814 a Raleigh, North Carolina, newspaper, *The Star,* advertised a female academy in Warrenton run by Jacob Mordecai and offering instruction in all branches of English, plus "Astronomy, Geography and the use of the Globes, Mythology and Blair's Rhetoric, plain and ornamental Neddle [sic] work—Musick [sic], Drawing and the French language." The *Berkshire Reporter* ran a notice about the Female Academy at Pittsfield where "The manners and morals of the pupils will be carefully formed, and directed to the best uses." In Goshen, New York, the *Orange County Patriot* listed the curriculum at the Female Academy as covering spelling, reading, needlework, writing, English grammar, arithmetic, geography, rhetoric, painting and embroidery, French, and music. In Middleton, Connecticut, Miss Hotchkiss's School taught the same subjects, assured the public that "strict attention is paid to the manners and morals of her students," and promised to provide "board in genteel families at a moderate price."[16] In short, Emma Willard's school in Middlebury, at least in the beginning, resembled girls' schools around the country.

The curriculum that she initially followed was known as the English curriculum and was similar to what was offered to boys at public academies. A very few boys studied a classical curriculum, sometimes provided at a public academy or grammar school but often taught by private tutors. The classical curriculum, which consisted of Greek and Latin in addition to English, prepared boys for college. Because fewer than 2 percent of the male population attended college in the early nineteenth century, there was heavy debate about the justification of public support for a classical curriculum. In the eighteenth century, Benjamin Franklin, among others, had argued strenuously for a more practical curriculum for boys in the public schools, one that would prepare them for careers as mechanics, surveyors, and scientists. Nowhere had science become a regular part of the curriculum, for either boys or girls. That Emma Willard rapidly developed a curriculum that included mathematics and science when the school moved to New York is indisputable. That she was one of many educators, of both boys and girls, moving the curricula of seminaries and academies in this direction is also indisputable.

Among these schools was Litchfield Female Academy. In 1814 most people would have pointed to Litchfield as the most famous school for girls in the country. Catharine Beecher, one of its most well-known alumnae, stated unequivocally in her memoirs that in 1810, the year the Beechers moved to Litchfield, "the reputation of Miss Pierce's School exceeded that of any other in the country."[17] Although Sarah Pierce was twenty years older than Emma Willard, they shared similar backgrounds and ideas about education. Miss Pierce was born in Litchfield, Connecticut, the youngest of the six children of her father and mother; after her mother's death, her father, like Emma's, remarried and had several more children. Her older brother, John Pierce, helped finance her education, paying for Sarah to go to school in New York City. When she finished in New York, she returned to Litchfield, and, to support herself, she opened a school for girls in her home in 1792.

Litchfield at the time was a thriving town with a national reputation. In addition to the Litchfield Female Seminary, like Middlebury, the town boasted a law school. Ten percent of the graduates of Litchfield Law School would eventually end up in Congress. Vice presidents Aaron Burr and John C. Calhoun were alumni. In the late eighteenth and early nineteenth century, the main route from Hartford to the Hudson Valley ran through Litchfield, and the town prospered during the American Revolution. Litchfield's prosperity was greatest from the middle of the eighteenth century until 1834. By then both the law school and Miss Pierce's Academy had closed. Without the water resources to support industry or the students to sustain the town's shops and artisans, Litchfield became a sleepy little village. It declined further when railroad lines passed it by. Historical markers still remind visitors of the two great educational institutions the town once boasted.

Sarah Pierce believed in educating girls, in no small part to make them fit companions of the law school students many of them married. (When Origin Storrs Seymour, Democratic representative from Connecticut, took his seat in Congress in 1851, he noted that he "was met and welcomed by thirty members of the House who were graduated by the Litchfield Law School or had married women who were graduated by Miss Pierce's school.") When she retired from the school in 1832, Sarah Pierce described the reasons she believed in educating women.

Like Emma Willard, the single, childless Miss Pierce was a firm believer in republican motherhood. She wrote,

> Our object has been not to make learned ladies, or skillful, metaphysical reasoners, or deep read scholars in physical science. There is a more useful though less exalted and brilliant station that woman must occupy; there are duties of incalculable importance that she must perform: that station is the home; those duties are the alleviation of the trials of her parents; the soothing of the labors and fatigues of her partner; and the education for time in eternity of the next generation of immortal beings.[18]

The "our" referred to her educational partnership with her nephew, John Brace. She had paid for him to attend Williams College; in return, he joined her in 1814 and introduced mathematics, chemistry, natural philosophy (mechanics, hydrostatics, pneumatics, meteorology, electricity, magnetism, and optics), logic, and Latin to the curriculum. At the same time Sarah worked to make the curriculum more systematic and to proscribe the subjects necessary for attaining a "degree." In her *Plan* and in her work in Troy, Emma Willard also stressed the importance of a more systematic curriculum. It was Sarah Pierce, however, who claimed to be "the very first to introduce a more scientific course in female education."[19]

Education at Litchfield, at least after 1814, had a well-defined set of courses that culminated in a course in moral philosophy. Both Sarah Pierce and John Brace taught this class, using as their text William Paley's *Natural Theology*. In this, they followed the pattern set at men's colleges; generally, the moral philosophy course was taught in the final year by the president. Paley's was the most widely used book on the subject. (Emma Willard definitely used Paley's to teach moral philosophy at Troy and also taught this subject to a few students in Middlebury; in Vermont "a Miss Hemingway" tackled the subject first.) Moral philosophy was the capstone of the collegiate curriculum. The Enlightenment had given a boost to science and rational thinking that some Christian clergy feared would create nonbelievers. After all, if scientists unlocked nature's mysteries, making them understandable, faith could be weakened. In his writings, Paley, an Anglican clergyman, "proved" that all good knowledge was evidence of Christianity's truth.

Rather than juxtapose faith and science as opposites, Paley (and Sarah Pierce, Emma Willard, and Almira Phelps, to name a very few of the educators who taught his work) believed that science proved God's existence. For example, he argued that the human body could only be the work of an all-powerful God possessing "an intelligent designing mind."[20] A gifted scientist (the second woman inducted into the American Academy of Scientists) and a true Paley believer, Almira Phelps wrote in the introduction to *Botany for Beginners*, "The study of Botany . . . leads us to love and reverence God."[21] She repeated this theme in all of her texts. In the 1840 edition of *Natural Philosophy for Beginners,* she stated, "[W]hen we speak of the cause of wind or thunder, we mean the secondary cause, believing that God directs the thunderbolt by his omniscient mind."[22]

The practice of teaching Paley to the most senior girls before they left school is one of the clearest indications that some girls' academies and seminaries provided "higher education." Boys' academies did not teach moral philosophy on the assumption that boys would study it in college; with no colleges awaiting them, moral philosophy became the highest course at the girls' schools. Nor was moral philosophy the only area where the curriculum at girls' schools matched the "higher education" provided by colleges. In 1803 Harvard added arithmetic as an entrance requirement, but no other mathematics was required for the degree. History, central to the curriculum at the girls' schools, was neglected by both the boys' academies and the men's colleges. History as preparation for boys' college admission was uncommon before the middle of the nineteenth century, and Harvard did not appoint its first professor of history until 1839. Willard and Pierce both taught ancient history through the use of Charles Rollins's *Ancient History,* a standard text for Yale sophomores. Geography, which was routine fare at girls' schools after the Revolution, had been a college subject for boys in the eighteenth century. Harvard made it an entrance requirement in 1803, Princeton in 1819, Columbia in 1821, and Yale a year later.

Both women favored dancing as a healthy form of physical exercise. Her first winter in Vermont, Emma Willard danced with her students when the school building became so cold they could not sit still any longer. In her *Plan* she advocated "instruction in dancing."[23] In a letter to her sisters, one of Sarah Pierce's students, Nancy Hale, wrote in 1802, "Miss P. approves of our dancing she says we set [sic] so much that it is very necessary that we should dance sometimes for exercise."[24] Both women also encouraged the creation of mourning art, the nineteenth-century practice of memorializing loved ones with needlework pieces that often incorporated the hair of the deceased. However, the two women differed on the appropriateness of including novels in the curriculum. Emma was opposed, writing in an early letter to Almira, "[R]efrain from pampering your imagination too much with novels."[25] Sarah Pierce, in contrast, often read aloud to her pupils from novels that stressed piety and morals. The popular Oliver Goldsmith novel, *The Vicar of Wakefield,* was one of her favorites.

Although both women taught moral philosophy at their schools, Sarah Pierce practiced a Protestant religion strikingly different from the creed followed by Emma Willard. In 1810 Lyman Beecher became the Congregational minister in Litchfield, and his daughters Harriet and Catharine studied with Sarah Pierce. (Beecher also boarded Litchfield students in his home to augment his pastoral salary.) Sarah was one of his parishioners, and she rented pews at the church for her students. The Second Great Awakening was sweeping New England and other parts of the country, and Sarah Pierce embraced its central tenets of personal salvation and the need to be constantly prepared for death. One of the great revivalist preachers of the time, Lyman Beecher served as a chaplain at the Litchfield Academy, helping many students find their own personal salvation. (The Beecher/Pierce connection grew stronger when Lyman's sister-in-law married John Brace.) Sarah Pierce's evangelicism stood in sharp contrast to the "restrained, intellectual and upwardly-mobile [sic] Anglicanism"[26] favored by Emma Willard.

Everything that Sarah Pierce taught or wrote about came back to Christianity. She shared with Mary Lyon a deep piety that manifested itself in simplicity and charity. The "repast" at tea at Litchfield, recalled alumna Anna Richards in 1902, was "very simple—a plate of shaved smoked beef, some preserves and a basket of cake."[27] (In Troy, the food would be ample.) Nor did Pierce believe in material expressions of faith. In 1842 she wrote disdainfully to her nephew, "Now people are emulating Romanists in building and decorating their churches."[28] A decade later Emma would personally pay for an expensive and elaborate brownstone steeple to be erected on St. John's Episcopal Church in Troy. Sarah Pierce also put a great emphasis on personal charity; Emma Willard urged her students to raise money for good causes (a girls' school in Greece, for example), and Pierce had her students sew blankets for impoverished boys studying for the ministry at Andover Theological Seminary. In 1833 the sometimes acerbic Mrs. Willard quoted Thomas Fuller to her students: "Charity should begin at home, but it should not end there." Like Emma, Sarah Pierce was dissatisfied with the textbooks available to her; like Emma, she wrote her own. Hers, however, were heavily religious. For example, her *Sketches of Universal History Compiled from Several Authors for the Use of Schools,* first published in 1811, "intermixed moral with historical instruction."[29] It is no exaggeration to say that religion "was used to justify each subject in the school's curriculum."[30]

In spite of the simplicity and piety that Sarah Pierce promulgated, her students were most definitely wealthy. They mirrored the students Emma Willard enrolled in Middlebury and later in Troy in that their fathers were prosperous farmers, merchants, and professional men. Few Litchfield students came from the South, but they came from all over New England, New York, Canada, and the West Indies. In the first published list of Litchfield students, dated 1802, thirty-six of fifty-nine students came from outside the village, with twenty-one coming from places outside Connecticut, including Georgia and the West Indies. Students from the West Indies were missionaries' children, a phenomenon Emma experienced at Westfield, an academy that also stressed Christian virtue in its rules and curriculum.

Several students who studied at Litchfield later studied in Troy, and among the students at the seminary in the middle of the nineteenth century were girls whose mothers were Litchfield graduates. Maria Tallmadge studied at Litchfield before marrying John Paine Cushman, an attorney in Troy and a Federalist representative to Congress from 1817 to 1819. In 1823, two years after Emma Willard had moved to that city, Cushman wrote to his father-in-law, a member of the Litchfield board of trustees, asking him to procure three boarding places at Litchfield for the daughters of friends. Whether or not he had political reasons for ignoring the new female seminary in his backyard is unknown. Nevertheless, in the 1830s and 1840s, his own daughters, Harriet, Julia, and Mary, attended the Troy Seminary when they were old enough; Julia, the oldest, studied first at Litchfield, enrolling there in 1832, the last year Sarah Pierce ran the school. However, after her mother's alma mater had closed and was no longer an option, she came home to study with her younger sisters at the seminary.

Of the handful of pupils who attended both and whose lives can be traced, all were from Connecticut, Vermont, and New York. All had fathers who were lawyers, judges, or major landowners. One of her biographers has noted that Sarah Pierce herself was "well aware"[31] that she was educating an elite portion of the population. Later, Emma Willard would also be well aware of the elite status of many of her pupils, but she would intentionally balance wealthy students with girls from families of more modest means, perhaps the first woman in the country to do so.

In one other respect the students at Litchfield matched those at Middlebury, in Troy, and at men's colleges. They spanned a very wide age range. Girls as young as nine studied alongside women in their twenties. Harriet Beecher Stowe, one of Litchfield's most famous graduates, entered the school at the age of nine. In Middlebury, Emma Willard taught girls as young as ten. Men's colleges showed a similarly wide range of ages among their undergraduates. In 1814 Yale graduated a class ranging in age from fifteen to twenty-six, and it was not until 1832 that Amherst set a minimum age for admission: fourteen. When Catharine Beecher opened the Hartford Female Seminary in 1823, she required that entering pupils be at least twelve.

In one other respect the two educators seemed more alike than they were. At her two schools in Middlebury and in Waterford and Troy, Emma Willard stressed public examinations as an important part of her students' education. In fact, she later claimed that her method of examination was one of the more original parts of her scheme. The Litchfield Female Academy also held public examinations, as did many other girls' and coeducational academies. It appears, however, that public examinations at most institutions, and certainly at Litchfield, were demonstrations and recitations of memorized material. At her public examinations, at least after 1814, Emma's pupils were actually examined and not provided with questions in advance. This kind of examination was a key facet of her pedagogy and also served to advertise the school. Public examinations, whether they were recitations or true interrogations, were entertainment attended by local citizens and reported fully in the newspapers. Harriet Beecher Stowe remembered her excitement when one of her compositions was read at the year-end examination. At Atkinson Academy, a renowned coeducational school in New Hampshire, a September 1818 program for the "public exhibition" listed thirty performances including orations, declamations and poems, dialogues, vocal music, and a valedictory address. Both boys and girls presented. Only three of the pieces were designated as "original."[32]

And so, as Emma Willard embarked on her educational venture in Middlebury in 1814, she entered a field that was not crowded but growing. Education for girls, although far from universal or systematized, was acceptable, particularly for the striving, increasingly professional white middle class. The nationalistic fervor of the Revolution and the War of 1812, sometimes dubbed "the second American Revolution," supported educated women as the maternal pillars of the republic, without whom the new nation might crumble.

Keeping a school that was better than those around her was Emma Willard's immediate goal. To Fanny Skinner, the wife of the governor of Vermont and the mother of two of her students, she wrote in 1815 with characteristic self-confidence, "[W]hen I compare my labors with what are generally done in schools of a similar kind, I feel some cause to be satisfied with my own." Alluding to the fact that Skinner shared her concern about girls' education, she railed, "They can expend thousands for the education of male youths, but when was any thing [sic] ever done by the public to promote that of females?"

Echoing the theme of republican motherhood, she reasoned,

> When we consider that the character of the next generation will be formed by the mothers of this, how important does it become that their reason should be strengthened to overcome their insignificant vanities and prejudices, otherwise the minds of their sons, as well as of their daughters, will be tinctured by them! I think the business of education is not to counteract the decision of Nature, but to perfect ourselves in Nature's plan.[33]

"Nature's plan," as she explains it in this letter, includes distinct roles for men and women, roles that are complementary and enhanced by the full development of the intellectual capabilities of both men and women. In a letter running to several pages, she does not once invoke God or religion.

Although her personal correspondence in 1815 displays her passion about "female education, the subject that interests me most,"[34] it was unclear that Emma would continue to be the primary breadwinner. She wrote to her widowed brother-in-law Elisha Treat that she could not take her niece Emily as a student because "If Dr. can get his affairs disposed of to advantage we shall remove from Middlebury and he will probably go into business in some city."[35] Her stepson Franklin, away from home studying medicine, urged his father to leave Vermont. Noting that "they have taken our farm," he wrote his father, "If all is to be taken from us, I hope you will conclude to leave Vermont."[36]

There is no record of any effort that John Willard made to move his family from Middlebury and to take up a new occupation. Instead, by 1816 his wife, motivated by finances or ambition or frustration or, most likely, some combination of the three, had determined to do two things. First, she would improve "female education," and second, she would convince the leadership of the nation and the public that girls' schools, like boys' academies, were the responsibility of the taxpayer.

By 1816 she had drafted *A Plan for Improving Female Education*, although it would not be widely published until 1819. She intended to present it to a state legislature, but for two years left the name of the state blank, sending it instead to friends and influential politicians, often asking "in what part of the Union would it be most likely to succeed?"[37] Meanwhile she continued the school in Middlebury, enrolling numbers of students from New York, among them the daughter of Guert Van Schoonhoven, a wealthy landowning descendant of Hudson Valley patroons. His patronage would prove critical as Emma Willard sought an audience for the document that would come to be known as the "magna charta"[38] of girls' education.

To Endow a Seminary for Females

ALTHOUGH NO CATALOG OF THE Middlebury pupils exists, several of these early students, although advanced in age, responded to the questionnaire sent out by the first alumnae association in the 1890s, and others can be identified, at least by last name, from an undated inventory titled, "List of the Names of the Young Ladies Who Boards [sic] at Mrs. Willard's."[1]

From these sources, it is possible to determine that these young women hailed from prominent New England and New York families. Franklin Willard, studying medicine with a Dr. Morris in Cambridge, New York, apparently helped to recruit students and kept an eye out for wealthy ones. Reporting to his stepmother on his success, he wrote, "You will have along with Maria and Catharine, a Miss Stephenson, a daughter of the richest man in Cambridge."[2]

As would be the case in Troy, many of the Middlebury students were relatives of Mrs. Willard, and many others had parents who knew either Emma or John or both. Huldah Chipman, Miranda Aldis, and Mary Seymour were related to Dr. Willard's erstwhile business partners. Susan Skinner, daughter of the Vermont governor, and Charlotte Storrs, daughter of the prosperous Middlebury attorney Seth Storrs, attended. Laura Hart was her niece, and a Miss Norton and a Miss Wells were also relatives on her Hart side. The Treadwell sisters, Margaret and Anne Marie, lived with their aunt, wife of the president of Middlebury, while they studied with Emma Willard, and the Platt girls and Phebe Mooers came from prominent landowning families in northern New York. From the capital district of New York came Elizabeth Van Schoonhoven, as well as the first of many Lansing girls who studied with Mrs. Willard. Julia Pierpont, Elizabeth Sherrill, Katharine Battey, and Elizabeth Henshaw, students at Middlebury, would all become teachers, beginning their careers in Troy.

Emma Willard was well aware of her pupils' family backgrounds, and she considered their fathers to be keys to her future success. She wanted out of Middlebury, with its bitter memories and harsh weather. In 1815 she wrote to her friends the Tappans, who lived in Ohio, "We neither of us like this country. The climate is cold and dreary, and the inhabitants too much resemble the clime."[3] And in 1818 she complained to the Davises (who had moved from Middlebury to Clinton, New York, where Henry Davis assumed the presidency of Hamilton College), "Mid jogs on as usual . . . many objects here are associated with painful recollections and I should prefer to leave them."[4]

Money stood in her way. In a letter to his father, Franklin alluded to the financial struggles the school was facing: "If it is true that the establishment has never produced any profit, then why keep it up where you are, it is useless to wear yourselves out in business without ever gaining anything."[5] Her school was by all accounts successful in terms of numbers, with up to seventy pupils in the summer session and forty in the winter, "which for this place is a large winter school."[6] Still, she struggled to make ends meet. When the Davises urged her to move her school to Clinton, she refused on financial grounds, arguing that the move would be too costly. She maintained "the profits of my boarding school as I manage it are small at the best. . . . I cannot starve [money] out of my boarders—or draw it out by exorbitant charge."[7]

The times were economically difficult and would become more so after the shaky postwar economy slid into a depression in 1819. Bill collecting was always a challenge. In 1817 Emma wrote to Zebulon Shiperd regarding his daughter's tuition, "Do not give yourself too much uneasiness, sir, with respect to Minerva's school bill. We are perfectly sensible that times are hard. . . . If it should not be convenient to you to pay this spring, I hope it will not make any difference with regard to Minerva's returning to school."[8] And in an undated letter to his father, written from Plattsburgh, William, a lieutenant in the army, reported that "cash is very scarce and provisions more so," and he concluded that "Mr. Treadwell can't pay what he owes."[9] (William often conducted business for his father; perhaps he was trying to collect tuition money for the Treadwell sisters. Their father had lost property he owned in Canada as a result of his American sympathies during the War of 1812.)

Emma believed that tuition alone would never provide enough funds to operate a successful school. Critical to her *Plan for Improving Female Education* was her belief that state governments should support girls' education just as they supported boys' education. In addition, she believed that a reliance on tuition meant that families had more control than they should over curriculum and pedagogy. She dreamed of a well-regulated educational system with a rigorous curriculum that was as well structured as what was offered at a boys' academy and used professional teachers who were well trained in their subject matter. Her ambitions were bold, bolder than she expressed publicly. She later recalled, "I knew that I should be regarded as visionary almost to insanity, if I had uttered the expectations which I entertained in connexion [sic] with [my plan]."[10]

Looking across the street from her school to Middlebury College, where "numbers of my pupils had brothers," she "bitterly felt the disparity between the facilities of the two sexes." She "could not and would not believe that the men, willingly and with reflection did us this injustice; and hence I hoped that if the matter was once fairly set before them as legislators they would be ready to correct their error." She began to write, concealing her work "even from my husband, although he agreed with me in my general views."[11] As she wrote she "had it secretly at my heart"[12] to present it one day to a state legislature.

To get the attention she needed for her plan, she determined to "increase . . . [my] fame as a teacher" because "in this way, I should be sought for to go to other places, where influential men would carry my project before some legislature for the chance of obtaining a good and celebrated school."[13] From 1816 to 1818, she quietly sent the plan to the fathers of her students, to former mentors of hers in Connecticut, and to national figures such as former presidents Thomas Jefferson and John Adams. Cornelius Van Ness, Vermont governor and future parent of two Troy Seminary students, conveyed the plan to President James Madison on Mrs. Willard's behalf. In the beginning the document was handwritten; she painstakingly copied the thirty-page manuscript over and over again. She later claimed to have rewritten the plan "as many as seven times" and had thrown out about "three quarters of what it at first contained."[14] In 1818 the Willards had the plan printed in Middlebury so that it could be more widely distributed; it sold for 4 cents.

The *Plan* was tightly written, well argued, and, although steeped in republican rhetoric, very specific. Cogent and persuasive, Emma Willard anticipated the arguments that would be raised in opposition to her scheme and addressed them directly. On the first page, she wrote of "the absurdity of sending ladies to college" and assured her readers that "the seminary here recommended, will be as different from those appropriated to the other sex, as the female character and duties are from the male."[15] She suggested that the education of women, in and of itself, was a noble goal—and set civilized countries apart from "barbarous and despotic nations."[16] However, she argued, the true impact of the education of women was that "it must inevitably raise [the character] of the other sex . . . and elevate the whole character of the community."[17] Republican motherhood required female education. Mothers, she maintained, "have the charge of the whole mass of individuals, who are to compose the succeeding generation." Yet women's education, "devoted to frivolous acquirements," did not prepare them for this "important . . . power." She concluded her introductory argument with an agricultural metaphor: "Would we rear the human plant to its perfection, we must first fertilize the soil which produces it."[18]

A Plan for Improving Female Education was divided into four parts. In the first section, she laid out the "defects"[19] in women's education. Unlike boys' education, which was funded and consequently regulated by the state, girls' education was at "the mercy of private adventurers."[20] (Of course she, herself, was one of these.) These teachers, dependent on tuition for their income, were "liable to become the victims of their [students'] caprice." Believing that "feminine delicacy" meant that women should teach girls and that boarding schools were the best setting for this, she nevertheless found fault with them. They were "temporary institutions," whose directors' "object is present emolument."[21] (As was hers.) Wanting to cut costs, the "preceptresses"[22] crowded girls in the lodging rooms, provided unsuitable classroom space, failed to provide libraries and "other apparatus,"[23] and did not hire enough assistants. In those cases where they hired "masters"[24] to teach a subject (often male music or French teachers), the preceptress lacked the knowledge to evaluate whether or not the teaching was sound.

Because of their funding, boys' schools and men's colleges, which she interchanged somewhat indiscriminately throughout the *Plan,* had the authority to "regulate their qualifications for entrance, the kind and order of their studies, and the period of their remaining at the seminary."[25] Dependent on "individual patronage," instructors at girls' schools could "neither enforce nor purchase compliance,"[26] with any rules they might try to establish. Furthermore, they often taught "showy accomplishments," so that girls had "toys"[27] to display when they returned home, which served as an inducement to their friends to attend the school.

Just as the curriculum and pedagogy of a girls' school were unregulated, so, too, were the teachers in those schools. "Any woman," she wrote, "has a right to open a school in any place; and no one, either from law or custom, can prevent her."[28] Women of "vicious" character, bad reputation, and those who had "contempt for useful knowledge"[29] often duped the public into allowing them to teach their daughters. Rhetorically, she questioned why a woman of "the best and most cultivated talents"[30] would want to be a teacher, given the sordid state of girls' education. "From necessity" was the answer, and, of course, the reason she, herself, a woman of breeding and talent, had opened a school. Although Emma Willard believed that the vast majority of female teachers were clearly substandard, every once in a while "an extraordinary female has occupied herself in instructing."[31] (There is little doubt that she was thinking of herself, her sister Almira, and probably her cousin Nancy Hinsdale, who operated a girls' school in western Massachusetts.)

There were other problems as well. Without regulation, teachers could do whatever they wanted or neglect to do whatever they did not feel like doing. "They can . . . omit their own duties, and excuse their pupils from theirs . . . can make absurd and ridiculous regulations . . . [and] improper and even wicked exactions of their pupils." In short, she concluded because "legislatures, undervaluing the importance of women in society, neglect to provide for their education," female education becomes "the sport of adventurers for fortune."[32] Her argument was colorful and dramatic. That no one had ever made a fortune running a girls' school in the 1700s or early 1800s appeared to be beside the point. That her goal in seeking public support was in part to stabilize her own school's—and her family's—finances went unspoken.

Having identified the defects, she proceeded to outline "the principles by which education should be regulated."[33] Here she framed her central philosophy:

> Education should seek to bring its subjects to the perfection of their moral, intellectual and physical nature: in order, that they may be of the greatest possible use to themselves and others: or, to use a different expression, that they may be the means of the greatest possible happiness of which they are capable, both as to what they enjoy, and what they communicate.[34]

Using this as her basis for measuring education, she suggested that curriculum be designed either to improve the mind or to be useful in life. Female education needed to be systematized. Boys had a distinct period of time when they were expected to study; girls needed this same discrete period.

She returned briefly to a critique of the current principles of female education. Too much of girls' education was "to fit them for displaying to advantage the charms of youth and beauty." Using another agricultural metaphor, she wrote, "Though well to decorate the blossom, it is far better to prepare for the harvest."[35] It was also a serious and common error to base girls' education on "pleas[ing] the other sex." Echoing Enlightenment thinking, she argued, "reason and religion teach, that we too are primary existencies . . . the companions, not the satellites of men." She hastened to explain, however, that under "particular situations" women must "yield obedience to the other sex," especially "when our sex takes the obligations of marriage."[36] (Recall that this is the same woman who nine years earlier had crossed out the word *obey* in her father's letter to John Willard.) In one of the more radical passages in the *Plan*, she deplored the fact that "the taste of men . . . has been made a standard for the formation of the female character" and scorned "a system of education, which leads one class of human beings to consider the approbation of another, as their highest object."[37] Returning briefly to the republican motherhood theme ("[I]t is through the mothers, that the government can control the characters of its future citizens"[38]), she concluded this section by dismissing the "phantom of a college-learned lady."[39]

Having dispensed with the theory of female education, in Part III she outlined the ideal female seminary. First, there should be a building dedicated to the purpose. The rooms, both for recitation and for lodging, should be "commodious." There should be an apartment for resident teachers and rooms to display teaching "apparatus." Second, the school should have its own library, a collection of musical instruments, some good artwork, maps, globes, and "philosophical apparatus" (scientific models such as levers, balances, and pulleys). Third, a board of trustees, "a judicious board of trust," would be "the cornerstone"[40] of the school's prosperity. These trustees would ensure that "suitable instruction" was provided in four areas: "religious and moral; literary, domestic and ornamental." Without saying so directly, she implied that the trustees would also be responsible for selecting the instructors. She wrote, "The trustees would be careful to appoint no instructors, who would not teach religion and morality."[41]

Although religion and morality headed the list of subjects to be taught, they were to permeate the whole curriculum and life of the students, rather than be taught as separate courses. Unlike the trustees at the Westfield Academy or the Litchfield Academy or many other schools and colleges, Mrs. Willard did not explicitly require that the instructors be Christian. She maintained that "religion and morality . . . constitute the true end of all education," expected that the "laws of the institution" would require that the pupils pay "regular attention to religious duties" and spend a part of the Sabbath "hearing discourses relative to the peculiar duties of their sex." Perhaps it went without saying that the teachers and pupils would be Christians, but her lack of specificity stands in striking contrast to the explicit Christianity required by Sarah Pierce or, later, Mary Lyon. The only specific curricular initiative in this section of the plan was the assertion that "the evidences of Christianity, and moral philosophy, would constitute a part of their studies,"[42] language that mirrored the proscribed course of study for seniors at the men's colleges.

Under "literary instruction," the second topic for "suitable instruction," Mrs. Willard grouped a number of subjects. She was not specific about what literature should be taught, claiming it impossible to determine in advance of knowing what preparation students would have prior to entrance and how long their "continuance at the seminary" might be. She did, however, insist that science be taught. Noting that "Natural philosophy has not often been taught to our sex," and asking, "[W]hy should we be kept in ignorance of the great machinery of nature?" Emma echoed Paley in defense of teaching science: "A knowledge of natural philosophy is calculated to . . . enliven piety, by enabling the mind more clearly to perceive, throughout the manifold works of God, that wisdom, in which he hath made them all."[43] Suggesting that new texts would need to be written to educate young women in science, she linked science to housewifery, claiming that "a systematic treatise"[44] on this subject would be needed. (In 1842 *A Treatise on Domestic Economy*, the first comprehensive and widely read book on housewifery, was published by her contemporary and rival, Catharine Beecher. There is no evidence it was used at the seminary.)

Housewifery was not to be confined solely to texts and study. "Domestic Instruction" was the third department laid out in the plan. Again utilizing the rhetoric of republican motherhood—"it is by promoting or destroying the comfort and prosperity of their own families, that females serve or injure the community"—she insisted that a domestic department be included in any good female seminary and should be supervised by a "respectable lady, experienced in the best methods of housewifery, and acquainted with propriety of dress and manners." This woman should meet the pupils every morning; students who entered with a good grasp of domestic duties would not forget what they had learned, and those who entered with a haphazard knowledge would learn what they needed for "the prosperity of their families."[45]

Finally, she described the curriculum for the "Ornamental branches." She specifically recommended "drawing and painting, elegant penmanship, music, and the grace of motion." She specifically excluded needlework, which she explained should "either be taught in the domestic department, or made a qualification for entrance." In any event, it should be "useful" needlework, defined as that "which may contribute to the decoration of a lady's person, or the convenience and neatness of her family." Other needlework she dismissed as "a waste of time."[46] She had always emphasized exercise, and since her first cold winter in Middlebury had promoted dancing. Not only was "exercise needful to the health," but it also provided "recreation [which leads] to the cheerfulness and contentment of youth." She drew a clear distinction between dancing and "balls." Dancing at a female seminary "should be practiced every day, by youth of the same sex, without change of place, dress, or company, and under the eye of those whom they are accustomed to obey."[47]

Although she conceded that some ornamental subjects, specifically drawing, painting, and music, were not "immediately useful," she argued that they were important in "forming character."[48] She was undoubtedly well aware of two market forces bearing on these subjects. First, instruction in these areas nearly always carried an extra charge and often equaled the tuition for the English course; in short, they were moneymakers. Second, wealthy families wanted this kind of instruction for their daughters. Although increasing numbers of fathers sought an academic education for their daughters, they still wanted them to be schooled in the usual refinements. Nowhere in the *Plan* did she mention mathematics or foreign language as suitable subjects, although she taught both in Middlebury.

In the fifth part of her scheme, Mrs. Willard laid out the regulations that "would be needed . . . so . . . that both the instructors and pupils would know their duty."[49] She proposed a term of study lasting three years and an entrance age of fourteen. The order of the curriculum should be "uniform and publicly known"[50] so that students could be classified according to their prior knowledge of the material. She deftly addressed the issue of "public speaking." Men's colleges rewarded "superior scholarship" with invitations to deliver public addresses at graduation. This would never work at a female seminary, she asserted, "[because] . . . public speaking forms no part of female education."[51] Cleverly, however, speaking in public was all right as long as it was part of an examination. Public examinations, to which she would invite "persons of both sexes," served many purposes; they kept both teachers and scholars focused, and they provided a "public test" of the seminary's success. Preparation for them helped students understand and remember material more clearly, and competition to do well at the examination was a better incentive than competing for prizes determined by faculty "making distinctions among [scholars] . . . which are so apt to be considered as invidious."[52]

Having sketched her ideal school, Mrs. Willard concluded with a discussion of the benefits of such a publicly supported seminary. First, she posited that such schools would provide the nation with badly needed teachers for the common schools. Women, having no other occupations open to them, would stay in the teaching field. Young men, in contrast, left teaching as soon as they had the opportunity to read law, study theology, practice medicine, or go into business. Women were more naturally suited to teaching than men were, and they were willing to work for less. Furthermore, by educating this new raft of women teachers in public state-supported seminaries, the state would, in essence, have more control over what was taught in the common schools.

One final time she sounded the call of republican motherhood, explicitly tying the fate of the United States to the education of its female citizens. No republic had ever lasted, and the reason to her was obvious: no republic had ever educated its female population. Historians suggested that wealth corrupted republics, but she did not find that to be a sound argument. "Wealth will be introduced," she claimed unabashedly, and wealth did not have to mean the "destruction of public virtue." Scorning the wealthy women of European republics who had been corrupted by wealth, she argued that education would "preserve among females of wealthy families, that purity of manners which is allowed, to be so essential to national prosperity, and so necessary, to the existence of a republican government." Furthermore, hard study would "preserve female youth from a contempt of useful labour" and help them base their "natural love of superiority" on "intrinsic merit, rather than in the extrinsic frivolities of dress, furniture and equipage."[53] Daringly, she suggested that among women, as among men, there existed some "master spirits" who could not be satisfied by domestic duties and preferred to be "infamous, rather than obscure." Left to their own devices, such women "are unsafe to [the] community." Often in the past, however, such firebrands had become writers, but now there was a new occupation "worthy of their ambition: to govern, and improve the seminaries for their sex."[54]

A woman of ambition, a woman seeking wealth, a woman who wrote extremely well, a woman who had long chafed at the restrictions on women's education, a woman whose vision blended the values and ideals of her Puritan ancestors, revolutionary parents, and republican husband and contemporaries, Emma Willard was, herself, one of the "master spirits." In 1818 she was ready to take her plan public and put it into action. She was ready to leave Vermont, and she was ready to earn real money with her considerable talents.

At the invitation of Guert Van Schoonhoven, the adoptive parent of one of her pupils and a wealthy citizen of Waterford, New York, she and Dr. Willard headed for Albany, New York, in the winter of 1819. The prior summer, when Van Schoonhoven visited his daughter in Middlebury, he had urged her to move the school to Waterford. Encouraged by his praise she shared her plan with him. He asked for a copy of the manuscript, promising to show it to DeWitt Clinton, governor of New York, and John Cramer, an influential politician from Waterford. At the time of Van Schoonhoven's visit, five pupils from Waterford were studying in Middlebury, all, she later recalled, "of the best families."[55]

In spite of Van Schoonhoven's support, Emma Willard was apprehensive about the reception her plan might receive. In 1817 she had presented it to Dr. Davis while he was president of Middlebury, and he had dismissed it with the advice "as a friend . . . to consider that I had something to lose as well as something to gain." He felt that public awareness of her goals "would [not] do me any credit."[56] Sometime after that she and Dr. Willard traveled to Schenectady "for the express purpose" of seeking the advice of Eliphalet Nott, renowned president of Union College. When Dr. Willard called on Nott, he told him that his wife was "desirous to avail herself of his wisdom and experience having some peculiar views on female education." Emma long remembered Nott's reaction:

'Female education Sir! Why it's all wrong.' 'So thinks my wife,' said Dr. Willard, 'and she has been spending much thought to devise a scheme to improve it.' 'It cannot be done' said Dr. Nott . . . and then excused himself from seeing me. Dr. Willard returned to the Inn where he had left me, very angry.

But far deeper was the feeling which his report excited in my breast. <u>There</u> came a chill, a faintness as of death.[57]

Nott's third wife and his daughter-in-law would end up studying in Troy, but that was still far in the future.

Now she waited "with intense feeling" for Clinton's response. She had already "fixed on the state of New York" as the "best"[58] location for her proposed school. The letter from Clinton arrived in early January 1819. He had read the plan and heartily approved of it. He wrote, "Independently of the conclusive considerations which you urge in favor of the claim and capacity of your sex for high intellectual cultivation, the <u>very fact</u> of such a production from a female pen, must dissipate all doubts on the subject."[59] He urged the Willards to go to Albany when the legislature was in session because he planned to ask for public funding for her scheme. They went. For five weeks they rented rooms in Albany and various state legislators called on Mrs. Willard. She read them her plan and discussed it with them, but always in private.

In late March, the Willards were back in Vermont, making plans for the move to Waterford. Emma wrote to a friend, "When we left Albany a bill to incorporate a female academy had passed." Clinton had attached an amendment to the bill providing that the Waterford Female Academy would receive a share of the academy fund, tax dollars distributed to academies throughout New York. Because this would amount to only a few hundred dollars, which Emma felt was "quite inadequate to the objects proposed in my plan," a separate bill was introduced to the legislature for $5,000 specifically for the new academy at Waterford, which failed to pass. Emma did not expect to get the whole amount because of the "numerous calls upon the treasury this year," but she did hope to get something that would "enable us to commence operations and which will be acknowledging the great principle . . . that the public ought to provide for female education."[60] Again she was disappointed. In fact, her school received no state money until 1836.

Meanwhile, Dr. Willard was negotiating for a suitable building in Waterford and asking that the trustees there guarantee at least $50 per quarter in tuition and board. The Rev. Samuel Blatchford had agreed to serve as president of the board, with John Knickerbacker as secretary. The coming of the school was newsworthy. One citizen of Waterford wrote to his son,

> A Mrs. Willard (& her Husband a Doctor) from Middlebury who taught a school there, she has wrote a Manuscript, which is now printed pointing out a plan, & the necessity of a female academy—or College, . . . and they have got a Company Incorporated, Doctor Blatchford President—the Rev. George Upfold, Vice president—they have rented Demarest House for Six hundred dollars per Ann. . . . Mrs. Willard expects to board 40 Scholars herself but I have been asked to board some—I rather have males—but they are not to be got.[61]

Other than expressing his preference for boarding male students, Mr. Kilby had no objections to the new school. "This Mrs. Willard is a very Capable Woman," he wrote, "She expects to be President of the College for they intend to have it a female College—not exactly like a Male one of course."[62] He recommended that his son buy a copy of her plan.

Advertisements for the new institution were placed in newspapers throughout the Northeast. The academy was scheduled to open June 2, 1819. In addition to Emma Willard, there were four assistants. Her niece, Laura Hart, would supervise the dormitory, and Nancy Lovett, Katharine Battey, and Elizabeth Sherrill would assist in academic instruction. The announcement about the new academy mentioned that it had been incorporated by the legislature, and referred to the "plan . . . already before the public." According to the advertisement, which was signed by the president and secretary of the board, the plan was "calculated to give to the female sex, advantages in point of solid mental requirements, and general improvement, in branches of taste, utility and science, beyond what that sex have ever had the opportunity of possessing."[63] Board per quarter was set at $36, tuition at $12, with music an additional $12. Each pupil was responsible for providing her own mattress, teaspoon, tablespoon, candlestick, goblet or tumbler.

Waterford in 1819 was a prosperous town, favorably situated near the juncture of the Mohawk and Hudson Rivers. Unlike the founders of Connecticut or Vermont, the first white settlers in the area had been Dutch, not English. The leading citizens of Waterford were the descendants of Dutch patroons who had owned huge estates along the banks of the Hudson from Manhattan to Saratoga. Van Schoonhovens had lived in the area since the 1600s, and Gen. Guert Van Schoonhoven owned a "palatial home"[64] on Broad Street. The famous Irish balladeer, Thomas Moore, penned "Lines on Cohoes Falls" while visiting at the Van Schoonhoven estate, and politicians such as Clinton and Martin Van Buren were frequent guests. As Mr. Kilby reported to his son, the Willards, or more specifically Dr. Willard, leased the Demarest House for the school. The building was four stories high and located on Broad Street not far from the Van Schoonhovens. Some townspeople, probably the members of the board, agreed to pay half the lease.

Waterford, like Middlebury, had many thriving businesses and was a self-contained community, particularly when the river was frozen. Vandenburghs, Knickerbocksers, Vandecars, and Ten Broecks, all descended from Dutch settlers, operated mercantile establishments in the town. Horace Hudson, who would posthumously become young John Willard's father-in-law, owned a hardware store. There was a drugstore, a tannery, a flour mill, a shoemaker, a jeweler, a blacksmith, a hatter, several lawyers, two butchers, and two physicians, at least one hotel, and two taverns. An academy located in Classical Hall had opened in 1813 and prepared boys for college. Many attended Union in nearby Schenectady, and there had even been an attempt to get Union to move to Waterford.

William Tell Willard was stationed in Florida when his parents moved from Vermont. Although no comprehensive student catalogs exist prior to 1820, the school apparently flourished right from the start. In July 1819, Lieutenant Willard wrote to his parents, "I am happy you succeed so well in the infancy of your establishment in Waterford. If in so short a time you have twenty-eight pupils, I think the plan must succeed and your institution flourish beyond your most sanguine hopes." William apparently accepted at face value that his stepmother had a good plan because he mentioned that "I have never yet been informed what plan the school is founded on. You have told me it is new, but where it differs, I know not."[65]

In addition to William's assertion that things were going well in Waterford, newspaper accounts of the school's first public examination were very positive. In the January 1820 issue of *The Plough Boy,* an Albany newspaper, "A Spectator" reported on the examination that had been held at the school in December. The day-long examination featured oral examinations of students in grammar (including etymology, syntax, prosody, versification, and punctuation), ancient and modern geography, arithmetic, rhetoric, French, ancient history, botany, the first book of Euclid, and natural and moral philosophy. The spectator had nothing but praise for the pupils and their performance:

> While the knowledge which the young ladies displayed in the several branches of science in which they were examined, excited surprise, that so much valuable information could have been acquired in so short a time; the neatness of their dress and the propriety of their demeanor were also noticed with particular pleasure, as evincing that ladies may cultivate the mind, while they pay strict attention to the person; and that science instead of annihilating, does but give a more interesting character to female modesty . . . [the examination's] result, cannot but silence all cavil on the controversial subject of female genius.

The editors of *The Plough Boy* agreed with the writer, appending to his account their wish "that this first attempt to place female education on its true basis, may not only succeed, but give rise to similar institutions in every part of our Union."[66]

Public examinations took place three times a year at Waterford and were often reported in newspapers. In September 1820, at the end of the summer session, the *Albany Gazette* reprinted an article from the *Waterford Recorder* praising the students' performances. Declared the paper, "It is sufficient to say it exceeded all expectation, and reflected the highest credit on the pupils, and particularly on Mrs. Willard, the principal, and her assistants for their unremitted and successful exertions in the cause of literature."[67] And in January 1821, an "Albanian" wrote to the *Gazette* about the "astonishing proficiency" demonstrated at the public examination in December. He wrote,

> [F]or the first time in my life, I had the pleasure of hearing classes of young ladies, from ten to eighteen years of age, demonstrate with correctness and promptitude the most abstruse propositions of Eu-

clid, explain the complicated principles of perspective, traverse the fields of natural philosophy and astronomy, apprehend the evanescent shadows, and expound the metaphysical subtleties of the philosophy of the mind, and trace the nice discriminations of taste and criticism. . . . It was evident from the examination that Mrs. W. has succeeded in infusing into her assistant instructresses and pupils her own elevated principles and just views. The questions were all put without reference to books.[68]

The public examinations in Waterford, in addition to bringing positive press, also provided Emma Willard with her first struggle with her all-male board of trustees. They all came to the first examination, and she had barely begun to question the students when the president of the board announced that he was satisfied and the class could sit down. She later recalled, "It was a critical moment . . . examinations were an indispensable part of my plan."[69] She explained to Blatchford that she intended to proceed, but the trustees were, of course, free to leave. (The early examinations lasted from 9 A.M. to 9 P.M.) Blatchford stayed. Newspaper accounts reported that he delivered a laudatory ovation at the end of the examination. Emma had established her authority in pedagogical and curricular matters.

In most respects, the Waterford Female Academy appears to have been ordered on the lines of the *Plan*, although the age range of the pupils was wider than Mrs. Willard thought appropriate. Money remained an issue, although she later claimed that "to make money was not the breeze which filled my sails."[70] Bills for more appropriations were put before the legislature in both 1819 and 1820 and failed to pass. DeWitt Clinton and Martin Van Buren both supported it, but "a cry of aristocracy" was raised by legislators who felt the school catered to the children of the rich. In an anonymous petition for "Endowing a Female Seminary," signed "Cornelia," she addressed this objection: "it is asserted that such an institution . . . would benefit the rich and not the poor; but can anyone seriously weigh this assertion against the arguments we have advanced, and say that it either outweighs or confutes them?" Deftly turning a negative objection to a positive rationale, she continued,

> But are the daughters of the rich of no consequence to the state?
> On the contrary, can a class of citizens be found, whose influence

over its prosperity is greater? They are the arbiters of fashion, the leaders of public morals and manners, and as education shall form their characters, will they hereafter infuse health and beauty through the political body, or disease and ruin?[71]

For the summer term in 1820, according to the first printed roster of the school, Waterford Female Academy enrolled seventy-seven girls from New York, Vermont, Connecticut, and Canada. Twenty-seven were residents of Waterford, five came from Troy, four from Albany, and five from New York City. Twenty-six came from other towns in New York, three from Canada, one from Connecticut, and six from Vermont. Among them were Lucretia Hudson and Lucretia Paine, future wives of John Willard and William Willard, and Theodosia Hudson, who would spend her entire life teaching at the Troy Female Seminary. Two letters written by Grace Phillips, a student from Cherry Valley, New York, provide a glimpse of everyday life in Waterford. Grace boarded with a local family, and she described her room as containing "a bed, bedding, a high table, a chest of drawers, two shelves."[72] She wrote that she "would much rather board at the seminary,"[73] although she liked the fact that her landlady did her laundry.

Grace reported to her parents that there was no school on July 13 because "many scholars and Mrs. Willard" traveled to Lansingburgh for Reverend Upfold's ordination. (Upfold was the vice president of the board of trustees.) She did not go because she was a Presbyterian. The trip she wanted to make was to visit Troy, but she had not had the opportunity to do so. She worried about the upcoming examination, scheduled for the first week in September, although she apparently studied only three subjects, French, drawing, and rhetoric, choosing "studies I cannot learn at our own Academy." Her description of the French teacher was detailed; although she felt the woman "teaches very well," she did not like the fact that students had "to ascend 37 steps to her room," which was so stuffy "some days we can hardly stay." According to student lore, the French instructor had once been "a great Belle."[74]

A very real indication of the economic turmoil in which the country found itself was the change in tuition from 1819 to 1820. The basic tuition was cut in half; reading, grammar, geography, and arithmetic cost just $6 per quarter. Rhetoric, history, writing, geometry, logic, natural philosophy, elements of criticism, moral philosophy, and the philosophy of the mind were all available for an additional $2 per course. Dancing cost $5, music $10, French, drawing, and painting, $4. Board was set at $2.25, with students furnishing their own bed and bedding.

Coming out of the War of 1812 in 1815, the country had experienced a real estate boom financed on speculation. Banks, including the Second Bank of the United States, issued far more paper money than they had specie to back it. The New York Stock Exchange opened in 1817. In 1818 and 1819, the government was scheduled to pay off the remaining debt from the Louisiana Purchase. To do this the Bank of the United States began "a series of deflationary moves."[75] An enormous contraction ground the economy nearly to a standstill. Banks began to refuse to accept the notes of other banks, and the national bank's public deposits declined from $9 million in the fall of 1818 to less than $3 million six months later. In response to the National Bank's contraction policy, the total bank notes in circulation fell to $45 million in January 1820, from $68 million in 1816. Prices for everything fell precipitously; tuition at Waterford was no exception. The country had experienced its first modern business cycle of "boom, crisis, depression"[76] and in 1821 would begin the last phase of the process: revival.

In the spring of 1821, friends of the Willards again appealed to the legislature for an appropriation. Again it failed. These repeated Senate defeats destroyed Emma's faith in politicians. She wrote, "Once I was proud of speaking of the Legislature as the 'Fathers of the State.' I knew nothing of the maneuvers of politicians [which have] served to disenchant me." She determined that her "cause is better rested with the people than with their rulers."[77] The lease on the building in Waterford would expire in May, and a group of citizens in Troy urged her to come to their thriving city. Writing to her mother, she was optimistic: "It seems now as if Providence had opened the way for the permanent establishment of the school on the plan which I wish to execute. I believe, if Troy will give the building, the Legislature will grant the endowment."[78] In spite of bitter disappointment, she had not lost sight of her goal—the permanent endowment of a female seminary.

We Have Concluded to Go to Troy

ON JANUARY 5, 1789, a number of settlers living on land once owned by Jacob Vanderheyden, the descendant of Dutch patroons, voted to change the name of their settlement to Troy. For over a hundred years, the area had been called Vanderheyden's in deference to the primary landholder. The newcomers to the area were not Dutch, hailed mostly from the New England states, and viewed the location at the headwaters of the Hudson as a logical place for the development of a mercantile center. In their proclamation renaming the village, they noted its "natural advantages on the Mercantile Line," claiming that "it may not be too sanguine to expect, at no very distant period, to see Troy as famous for her Trade and Navigation as many of our first towns."[1]

Like their counterparts in villages throughout New York State—Ithaca, Utica, Rome, Syracuse—they turned to antiquity for a classical name that might capture their hopes of future glory. They were audacious indeed, for the settlement so named contained "five stores and about a dozen dwellings."[2] Within two years, the state legislature had drawn the lines for the counties of Albany and Rensselaer, and on April 1, the legislature set the boundaries for "a distinct and separate town, by the name of Troy."[3] Village charters were granted to Troy and Waterford on the same day in 1794, the language in the legislation suggesting that Waterford was the more important of the two villages.

Undaunted, Troy prospered and grew. By 1791 a Presbyterian Church had been erected on the edge of what would become Seminary Park. The Baptists organized and built their house of worship in 1795. Before 1800 a gristmill, a sawmill, a flour mill, and a paper mill had all been constructed on the Poestenkill. In 1796 Troy's first post office opened; in 1799 the public library was established. Lansingburgh, Troy's northern neighbor, established long before Troy and considered the leading town north of Albany, began to lose citizens and businesses to Troy. Two newspapers, *The Northern Budget* and *The Farmers' Oracle*, moved to Troy from Lansingburgh, as did numerous young businessmen with names like Cluett and Tibbits, who would become leaders in the nineteenth-century city. In 1797 Troy organized a fire department, buying a secondhand engine from New York that could spray an "inch and a half stream of water over an ordinary two story building."[4]

The turn of the nineteenth century brought more improvements. No longer content to do their banking in Albany (a trip that required a half day's travel), Troy's leading citizens petitioned the legislature for a bank charter. On March 31, 1801, the Farmers' Bank was incorporated with capital stock of $250,000 and thirteen directors, including at least six future fathers of seminary students. One month later, the state legislature divided all the counties into towns, delineating the borders of Troy "Southerly by Greenbush, easterly by Petersburgh, northerly by the north bounds of the manor of Rensselaerwyck, and westerly by the county of Albany, including such of the islands in Hudson's river as are nearest the east side thereof."[5]

Over the next two decades, Troy grew rapidly. Methodists, Episcopalians, and Quakers all organized and built churches. St. Paul's, the Episcopal church where Mrs. Willard's funeral occurred, was completed in 1805, in part with contributions from the venerable Trinity Church in Manhattan. St. Paul's installed the first organ in the city. As the population grew, the infrastructure needs of the town expanded as well. A turnpike to Schenectady was established from a point opposite Troy on the west bank of the Hudson. To meet the need for clean water, a series of aqueducts and pipes, first wooden, and, after 1812, iron, was laid throughout Troy to carry the water from a reservoir on Spring Avenue to the residential and business areas. The town was divided into four wards, numbered from south to north. To protect the growing city, a number of independent military companies were formed. At least one of these, the Troy Invincibles organized by Hazard Kimberly, fought in the War of 1812, the same war in which meatpacker Samuel

Wilson acquired the nickname Uncle Sam, which was transferred by the soldiers who ate his beef to the federal government as a whole.

Troy's position at the point where the Hudson became navigable was a key to its prosperity. Regular boat transportation between Albany and Troy began in 1810, and by 1812 a steamboat, *The Fire Fly*, made the trip twice a day, departing from Troy at 7 A.M. and again at 1 P.M. The quarter-mile Hudson crossing from Troy to West Troy took only four minutes; the ferry was powered by two large draft horses and a wheel. By the middle of the decade, DeWitt Clinton was already laying plans for the construction of the Erie Canal. In 1817 the legislature voted to spend $7 million on the project. A major proponent of the canal, Elkanah Watson, inventor, farmer, and "father of the county fair,"[6] would later acquire a daughter-in-law who was a seminary graduate.

Although much of the country, particularly the northeastern portion, suffered during the War of 1812 and the subsequent economic panic, Troy continued to grow and prosper. In 1815 the population topped four thousand, double what it had been ten years earlier. The larger population spurred Troy's citizens to petition to become a city, and a charter to that effect was enacted on April 12, 1816. Geographically, the city of Troy matched the town of Troy, but there were now six wards instead of four, and the city officers were defined as a mayor, a recorder, a clerk, a marshal, a chamberlain, and an alderman, assessor, and constable for each of the wards. Col. Albert Pawling, longtime civic leader, became the first mayor, and William Marcy, future New York State senator, governor, and federal cabinet member, became the first recorder. Both Marcy and Pawling would have relatives who attended the seminary, as did several of the new aldermen, the new city chamberlain, David Buel, city clerk, William Bliss, and city surveyor, William McManus.

These men and other leading citizens of Troy including merchants, industrialists, and bankers strongly supported education at all levels. In 1816 the Troy Sunday School Association, a nondenominational Christian organization, was formed to provide instruction in reading, writing, and basic Bible instruction for workers' children. In 1818 the Troy Lyceum of Natural History began. The first such society in the United States, the lyceum's main lecturer was Amos Eaton, destined to become the founding president of Rensselaer Polytechnic Institute in 1824. The eminent Yale chemistry professor, Benjamin Silliman, traveling through Troy on a trip to Quebec in 1819, commented, "A number of [Troy's] gentlemen have discovered their attachment to science, by the institution of a Lyceum of Natural History, which fostered by the activity, zeal and intelligence of its members, and its lecturer, Mr. Eaton, promises to be a public benefit and to elevate the character of the place."[7]

Because she advertised in the local papers, Troy's businessmen knew that a Mrs. Willard had opened a school for girls in Waterford. Reprinted in those same papers were Governor Clinton's speeches to the legislature supporting the school and urging the legislature to give it the financial backing she craved. Given Troy's growth, its citizens' concern for education, and the increasing visibility of Emma Hart Willard, it is not surprising that by 1820 Troy's leaders hoped to entice the principal of the Waterford Female Academy to move her enterprise to Troy.

In June 1820, however, a devastating fire broke out in the city. Beginning in a stable belonging to Thomas Davis, at 37 First Street, the fire spread rapidly, consuming homes and businesses. The Troy firefighters were unable to stop the blaze; only when fire engines from Albany, Waterford, and the federal arsenal in Gibbonsville (now Watervliet) arrived was the inferno finally quenched. The headline in the weekly *Troy Northern Budget* trumpeted, "An Awful and Destructive Fire,"[8] and the article claimed that more than ninety buildings had been lost, some of them six stories high. Among the burned buildings, nearly seventy were businesses. Businessmen who lost their establishments included Messrs. Heartt, Hart, Betts, Bliss, McCoun, Gale, Warren, Kellogg, Vail, and Buel, all prominent citizens who would eventually be connected to the seminary as parents, trustees, or both. The loss was estimated between $700,000 and $1 million, with insurance covering barely a tenth of the ruination. On July 12, the city called for a day of prayer, and people thronged to the various Protestant churches. The theme at each service was humility and submission to the will of God. For the next few weeks, much of Troy survived on gifts of money, food, and clothing sent by other communities.

The city was far from defeated, however, and the rebuilding began at once. Grain and other produce from farmers in the western part of the state, Pennsylvania, and Ohio poured through Troy on its way to New England and downstate markets. Optimistically, the editor of the *Troy Post* wrote, "The growing preference which the western farmers, who have grain to dispose of, give to this market is an earnest indication of the future increase of the business of this city."[9] Troy Air Furnace, the city's first foundry, opened, as did the Starbuck Plough Manufacturing Company. In the spring, one Martin Russell rode a velocipede from Congress Street to the Waterford Bridge and back, a distance of eight miles, in under an hour. Troy's industriousness, inventiveness, and willingness to try new things were undaunted.

Among the new things to try was girls' education. In March 1821, the common council voted to tax the residents of the first four wards to raise $4,000 to provide a suitable building for Mrs. Willard's school. In explaining the financial arrangement to her mother, Emma wrote, "The corporation [of Troy] have [*sic*] raised four thousand dollars by tax. Another fund has been raised by subscription." With this offer, "We have concluded to go to Troy."[10] In May the lyceum, which was located in the courthouse, hired rooms "in two adjoining houses for ladies' studies and lodging rooms."[11] It had been agreed that the academy would hold classes in the lyceum until a permanent home was secured. The council appointed Jeremiah Dauchy, Ephraim Morgan, Gurdon Corning, Nathan Warren, Lewis Lyman, John G. Vanderheyden, Thomas Skelding, George Smith, James Vandenburg, Richard P. Hart, and Gilbert Reillay to buy a building and enter into a contract with Mrs. Willard. (Reillay would eventually send five daughters to the seminary, and Hart still holds the record. He sent ten.)

Ads were placed in newspapers announcing the opening of the new school on the second Wednesday in May. Each ad read, "Mrs. Willard, having closed the term of her engagement at Waterford, has been induced to remove her School Establishment to Troy. The liberal patronage of the Corporation and Citizens of Troy, she trusts, will enable her to carry into more complete effect her plan of Female Education."[12] Although Waterford students had studied and been publicly examined in geometry, geometry was not listed as part of the curriculum in the advertisement. The courses offered were identical to those at the Waterford Female Academy in 1820. So was the tuition. In addition, boarding students were required to furnish their own "bedding, pitcher, wash-bowl, towels, large and small spoon, tumbler and candlestick."[13]

On the recommendation of the committee, the city purchased Moulton's Coffee House. Constructed in 1795 as a tavern and inn, the building, originally owned by Howard Moulton, a revolutionary army officer, sat between First and Second Streets, just south of Congress Street. The front faced north. Three stories high, the frame building needed a good deal of work. In accordance with a design dictated by Emma Willard, the frame was filled with brick, and a dining room, kitchen, laundry, lecture spaces, and boarding accommodations were outfitted. In August the common council appointed the first board of trustees: David Buel Jr., Joseph Russell, Nathan Warren, Richard P. Hart, Jeremiah Dauchy, James Mallory, William Bradley, and Amasa Paine. The Troy Female Seminary was ready for occupancy when the term began in September.

Much ink has been wasted in educational history in an attempt to unravel the differences between seminaries and academies. Most recent historians of the academy movement of the nineteenth century have concluded that the two were interchangeable. Emma Willard chose to use the term *seminary* rather casually. As she recalled in 1841, "Being at church one Sunday the clergyman prayed as usual for 'our Seminaries of learning.' This, thought I, shall be the name of my projected institution. It is a general appellation and cannot offend; and we shall in this way, so manage that the men shall give us at least their prayers."[14]

On May 8, 1821, *The Troy Post* announced that "The Troy Female Seminary, under the direction of Mrs. Willard, will be open for the reception of pupils, tomorrow morning at nine o'clock."[15] Troy's newspapers that day were filled with mercantile and shipping news, reports from the legislature, and poetry, jokes, and anecdotes. On the front page of the *Post,* the mayor, Esais Warren, whose three daughters would enroll in the seminary, set the assize for a loaf of bread: a shilling paid for a 64-ounce loaf made of superfine flour or a 70-ounce loaf made of common flour.

Messrs. Vail, McCoun, Hart, and Van Veghten, all merchants and all future seminary parents, advertised goods ranging from buffalo robes, shoes, boots, and books to salt, rum, and molasses. P. Heartt and Sons Hardware sold slates, tin plates, ink, lead pencils, needles, rat- and mouse-traps, and candlesticks. L. Stillwell, a milliner, made "leghorn flatts," straw hats, silk hats, and bonnets. A competitor, Eli Dibble, offered to pay for hatting furs, particularly beaver, and boasted, "All Hats . . . are rendered waterproof by a secret process [because] nothing so soon destroys the beauty of a hat as getting it drenched by rain." Jeremiah Greenman, "hair-dresser and wig manufacturer," catered to both men and women. M. J. Lyman and Sons, druggists, touted their cures for "Flatulence and Farted Breath." There were ads for a "black indentured girl" who had run away, and William Strope assured the public that "whereas my wife Dorcas has eloped from my bed and board without any just cause or provocation," he would not be responsible for her debts.

Much of what was advertised was imported: St. Croix rum, Ma-deira, nutmeg, almonds, coffee, sugar, raisins, rice, tobacco, and gin-ger. The schedules and insurance rates for ships plying the Hudson between Troy and New York were front-page news. Among the ves-sels were the *Atlas*, the *Wasp*, the *Venus*, the *Minerva*, the *Canton*, the *Thames*, the *Industry*, the *Sally Ann,* and the *Maria Ann*. These ships were the only source of international news. The *Martha* had arrived in Troy on May 2, bearing newspapers from London dated the end of March. Trojans learned that the king of Sardinia had abdicated and the Austrians had lost a war with the Neapolitans.

Within the first group of students to enroll at the Troy Female Semi-nary were many from local households made prosperous by the bustling trade along the Hudson. Receiving the first pupils at the new school were three of the teachers from Waterford: Elizabeth Sherrill, Angelica Gilbert, and Mary Heywood. Mary Heywood had not always been a model employee; correspondence between the principal and the young teacher reveal something about early faculty negotiations. Heywood was heartily recommended by prior employers. However, much to Mrs. Willard's consternation, she had indicated in 1820 that she would accept a job at Waterford, and then after Mrs. Willard told other candidates the position was filled, she learned from Mary that the salary was not suit-able. In a compromise, Mrs. Willard offered to pay her $3 a week until

October and $2 thereafter, which was what she had been offered in the first place. Somewhat tartly, the preceptress wrote to her, "and pardon me, Miss Heywood, if I think . . . you are under some little obligation to make (if necessary) some trifling sacrifice."[16]

In part to minimize expenses and in part to train future teachers, Emma Willard adopted the practice of assigning older pupils to be assistant teachers. Mary Aiken, Sarah Ingalls, Mary Field, and Elizabeth Whiting all became assistant teachers during the first year at the seminary. Early catalogs included their names, along with this explanation: "By a rule of the Institution, there are occasionally selected from among the best pupils some who spend a portion of their time in discharging the duties of assistant teachers."[17] This practice was greatly in vogue at publicly supported boys' academies. Officially called the Lancastrian system, this method of educating through peer teachers had been introduced to the United States by Joseph Lancaster, an English Quaker. Its virtues were inexpensive labor and added classroom discipline. In the 1820s, three of the ten girls who served as assistants were Emma's nieces.

Nineteenth-century histories of Troy uniformly report that the school opened with ninety pupils, most from New York, but some from Connecticut, Vermont, Massachusetts, Ohio, South Carolina, and Georgia. Because no catalog for 1821 has been found, it is impossible to verify these statistics. However, the catalogs for the rest of the 1820s do exist, and by 1822 the school was certainly thriving. The so-called catalog (really a listing of pupil names and hometowns) for 1822 records 140 pupils for the "present term" (not defined) and 214 pupils for the year. In addition to New York, they hailed from New England (Vermont, Connecticut, Massachusetts, and New Hampshire), Ohio, Louisiana, North Carolina, and Georgia. (By the end of the decade, students from Michigan, Alabama, Mississippi, South Carolina, Pennsylvania, Maryland, Rhode Island, New Jersey, and Washington, D.C., would all make the trek to Troy.) The future wives of Emma's son and stepson, both named Lucretia, were enrolled in 1822.

In addition to Lucretia Hudson and Lucretia Paine, forty-one girls who studied at the seminary in 1822 wrote in to the first alumnae record book, *Mrs. Emma Willard and Her Pupils*, in the early 1890s and can be traced through the federal census from 1850 to 1880. Of this group, eleven had sisters who attended the seminary, and thirteen would send their daughters to the school in the 1840s, 1850s, and 1860s. All but three married. Two of them married widowers whose first wives were also seminary graduates. Their husbands were merchants, bank presidents, lawyers, farmers, railroad presidents, and clergymen. Only two of these men were doctors. Frances Miller married William Seward, governor of New York, secretary of state, and presidential hopeful. All but one of the married women had children who survived to adulthood. Nearly a third of the households included at one time or another in-laws, unmarried sisters, and sisters-in-law. All but four employed servants. In 1850 the net assets of their families ranged from $3,000 to $40,000. By 1870 this amount ranged from $8,000 to $250,000.

The women who attended the seminary in 1822 were typical of the students enrolled during the first decade in Troy. Throughout the 1820s, the young women who attended the seminary came from prominent wealthy families and married well. Many were politically connected. When the Marquis de Lafayette visited the school in 1825, Mrs. Willard chose Elizabeth Cass and Cornelia Van Ness to present the visiting dignitary with the poem she had written for the occasion. Cass was the daughter of Lewis Cass, governor of the Michigan Territory at the time, and destined to become secretary of war, secretary of state, and a candidate for president. Van Ness's father was the governor of Vermont, having succeeded Richard Skinner, whose daughters studied with Willard in Middlebury and Waterford. Mary Cass and Marcia Van Ness would join their sisters at the seminary, and Cornelia Van Ness would marry James Roosevelt, Theodore's uncle and Eleanor's great-uncle.

Nor were these the only politically connected students of the 1820s. In the middle of the decade, Eleanor and Margaret Worthington, daughters of Thomas Worthington, first senator and later governor of Ohio, attended the seminary. Another midwestern politician was Henry Sibley, first governor of Minnesota, whose sister Catharine attended the seminary from Michigan. Their father was an associate of Lewis Cass. Catharine's husband, Charles Trowbridge, was a mayor of Detroit. When he ran for governor of Michigan in 1837, he was defeated by Stevens Mason, whose three sisters were seminary students.

Mary Meech, whose father Ezra represented Vermont in Congress, and Sarah Craig, whose father served as a congressman from New York, also attended. (Mary's sister Jane would follow her to Troy in the 1830s.) Craig married William Havemyer, a reform mayor of New York City in the post–Civil War years. Belinda Buckingham married Samuel Ryan Curtis, a successful Union general in the first two years of the Civil War, who later represented Iowa in Congress. Elizabeth Clemson's husband, George Washington Barton, practiced law with President James Buchanan. Julia Alvord's brother Thomas, with whom she lived after she was widowed, was the lieutenant-governor of New York immediately following the Civil War. Sarah Hinsdale, niece of Emma Willard, was one of ten Hinsdale relatives who attended the seminary between 1823 and 1848; her third daughter married Levi Morton, vice president of the United States under Benjamin Harrison and subsequently governor of New York. Sarah Shaw, whose father Henry was a congressman from western Massachusetts, was a student in 1829; her brother, Henry Wheeler Shaw, was a nationally renowned humorist of the mid to late nineteenth century.

Shaw was just one of the literati connected to the seminary girls of the 1820s. Henry Wadsworth Longfellow's cousin, Catharine Storer, studied at the seminary and then taught oil painting there in the 1830s and 1840s. James Fenimore Cooper's nieces, Georgiana '24 and Hannah Pomeroy '24, were students; Hannah's daughter, Constance Fenimore Cooper Woolson, was a noted writer in the second half of the nineteenth century and a friend of and major influence on Henry James. Eugene Field, the extremely popular children's poet (author of "Wynken, Blynken and Nod"), was reared by his aunt, Mary Field Jones '22, after his parents died. Two of the most celebrated college presidents of the nineteenth century, Mark Hopkins (Williams College, 1836–72) and Eliphalet Nott (Union College, 1804–66), married women who had studied in Troy. Hopkins's wife, Eliza Hubbell, started at the seminary in 1829 and left in 1830; their son Henry was also president of Williams College in the early twentieth century. Urania Sheldon '28 was Nott's third wife; she was thirty-five when she married Nott, and as his health declined, she was very much in charge of the college.

Not marrying did not preclude success. Catherine Burroughs '27 lived out her life in Bridgeport, Connecticut, her childhood home. The public library there still bears her name in recognition of her philanthropy toward that institution. Helen Phelps, stepdaughter of Emma's sister Almira, taught in many places, eventually founding a school in Texas. More typical was Julia Pierpont Warne '25, who went south to teach, married Elias Marks, and with him ran the South Carolina Female College for many years. Elizabeth Sherrill, who was a pupil in Middlebury and a teacher at both Waterford and Troy, also ran a school in the South with her husband, Thomas Twiss, a close friend of Emma's and a mentor to John Willard during his time at West Point.

The catalogs for the 1820s outline the curriculum, the costs of tuition and board, provide lists of students with their hometowns, and identify the members of the faculty, board of trustees, and Committee of Ladies. They were published in August, and the information covered the prior two terms. The school year began on the third Wednesday in September and ran for a "term" of twenty-two weeks, at which point there was a two-week vacation. Each term was divided into two quarters. The second term commenced in March and ended in August, followed by a six-week break. For 1822–23, the fall term began on September 25 and ran until February 26. Classes met on Christmas Day, which was marked by church services and a special dinner. The spring term began on March 19 and ended August 13. From student letters, it is clear that Mrs. Willard occasionally called a holiday, always doing so around the Fourth of July.

The curriculum in Troy was divided initially into two "classes." The first class studied reading, English grammar, geography (ancient and modern), and arithmetic. Tuition was $6 per quarter or $11 a term. The more advanced second class studied "History, Hedges' Logic, Blair's Rhetoric (not abridged), Kaimes' Elements of Criticism, Euclid's Elements of Geometry, and other branches of mathematics introductory to a course of natural philosophy—Natural Philosophy, Stewart's Philosophy of the Mind, Paley's Theology, Evidences of Christianity, Moral

Philosophy either with or without any of the studies contained in the first class."[18] Tuition for this curriculum was $8 per quarter or $14.67 per term. Instruction in drawing and painting, French, music, piano, and dancing were all available, either as single subjects or in combination with the first- or second-class academic program. Prices for these subjects ranged from $5 (dancing) to $12 (French). In addition "a course of lectures" in natural philosophy (now called physics), chemistry, botany, and "other branches of natural history" was provided for $3 per course.

The pricing structure was complicated. For example, those who took drawing and painting were charged "with any of the studies in either the first or second class, in addition to the charge for said class, at the rate of $4 per quarter amounting to $18.34 if the studies are of the first class; and if the studies are of the second class, to $22 for the term, or without any other study, at the rate of $8 per quarter, amounting to $14.67 for the term." In addition to tuition, boarders paid $2.50 per week for board, which included bed, bedding, furniture, and light; the charge was $2 for those boarders who provided their own room furnishings. All boarders paid an additional $1 per quarter "room rent." Fuel was "furnished to the boarders at prime cost," and washing was available for 50 cents per dozen pieces or at a flat fee of $5 per quarter. If parents wanted to do so, they could pay $200 per year—which got their daughters board, bed, bedding, furniture, fuel, light, room rent, washing, and tuition for either the first- or second-class curriculum. Even at that price, however, French, dancing, music, art, and science lectures were extra.

Although most student letters reveal that the pupils opted for the full academic program, it is clear from the circulars that during the first decade in Troy, a girl could study only "ornamental" subjects. It is also clear that these subjects were moneymakers. Beginning with the catalog of 1825, parents were asked to be "particular in directing what, if any of the ornamental branches they wish [their daughters] to pursue."[19] Mrs. Willard obviously wanted to avoid a situation in which a girl signed up for costly music or art lessons without parental permission.

Given the curricular offerings and structure, it is not accurate to say that all of Mrs. Willard's early students studied higher mathematics and science. However, if they wanted these courses, they were certainly available to them at the seminary. Litchfield had a similar curriculum, but Troy's was more extensive. In a letter home in 1823, a student wrote, "Mr. Eaton lectures on Minerology [sic], Zoology, Geology and some other ology, Phrenology, I believe, about the head and the brains coming from a knot in the back of the neck."[20]

As the decade went on, the pricing stayed mostly the same. In 1829 the total cost was still $200 per year, and it included "such a quantity of stationary [sic] as is necessary in pursuing [the course of English studies]."[21] "English studies" was increasingly used throughout the country to describe a liberal arts education; such a curriculum included mathematics and science and was different from the classical education boys studied in preparation for Harvard and Yale and careers in the ministry and law. U.S. history, painting on velvet, Spanish, and guitar were added. The term *day scholars*[22] was used for the first time in 1828. The size of the school nearly doubled, reaching 245 by 1830.

To accommodate the larger student body, Mrs. Willard had enlarged the original building in the summer of 1825, doubling the space. The size of the faculty also increased. Emma Willard believed that one of the distinctive qualities of her school was having "more teachers in proportion to the pupils"[23] than her competitors. In 1825, in addition to Emma Willard, there were 9 teachers and 4 assistants for a school population of 146. Two years later, for a school of 191, there were 14 teachers and 2 assistants.

The catalog for 1825 was the first to include rules, including directions regarding dress. During school hours girls were to wear dresses of "calico, gingham or crape, made in a plain style." There was an admonition to "Parents and Guardians." They were "earnestly requested not to furnish their daughters or wards with expensive laces and jewelry, or any other needless articles of apparel; or leave with them the controul [sic] of any considerable sums of money."[24] In addition, parents were to tell the school which church their daughters would attend. Beginning in 1826, students were allowed to stay at school and "be instructed"[25] during vacations. If the student paid by the year, there was no additional charge for this; day students were also allowed to take classes during the vacation. There is no record of how teachers felt about this, but it is evident from her letters that Mrs. Willard traveled extensively when school was not formally in session.

For any educational institution, catalogs indicate the schedule, rules, and curriculum that school administrators hope to follow. Letters from students to their friends and families give insight into actual student life. Grace Phillips, who began her studies with Emma Willard in Waterford, made the transition to Troy in 1821, and she wrote to a friend at home, "I now find myself in a small room at Troy, with . . . one of the assistant instructresses,"[26] an indication that in spite of their elevation to assistant instructor, these young women were still treated as boarders in their out-of-classroom life. Grace's curriculum included "Logic, Algebra, Natural Philosophy, Botany . . . the lectures delivered by Mr. Eaton on Natural Philosophy and Botany . . . nine in a week, an hour each." Grace also provided a detailed description of her day:

> We rise at a quarter before five, from ten minutes after 5 until 15 before six walk, from this time untill [*sic*] six attend prayers in the court-room, from 6 to 7 recite N. Philosophy, at 7 breakfast, from half past seven untill nine we devote to the duties of our rooms, and exercise, from nine to twelve study, untill one attend a lecture on Botany, at one dine, at two recite Logick, from three to five attend to painting, at five attend prayers, from five untill six recitation in Botany, at six take tea, from seven to eight either to writing or reading, from eight untill nine attend lecture on Natural Philosophy, at ten minutes after ten retire.[27]

In 1822, in a letter to her brother, poet Jonathan Dorr Bradley, Merab confirmed this schedule. She was looking forward to a week's vacation that was to start on July 3 and encompass what was then the largest annual holiday on the American calendar, the celebration of the Fourth of July. She told Jonathan, "We are woke up every morning at half past four and obliged to get up immediately and walk around the town, then we have prayers and then school goes on."[28]

Roommates and rooming conditions were often topics of letters. In June 1821, Julia Bacon wrote to her mother in western Massachusetts complaining about her accommodations. She was in a room with seven other girls and was anxious for the new seminary building to be completed. The tension between additional income for the school and student comfort resonates even in this first decade. In 1823 Emma Clark wrote her mother, "I hope there will not be many more [new scholars] come, for if there does, we shall have to take another one with us as our room was meant for three."[29]

Merab Bradley reported in 1822 to her brother that she was rooming with Frances Skinner, daughter of the Vermont governor. (Merab's father, who had already served in the House of Representatives, would return to Congress as the Vermont representative in 1823.) The rooming together of the daughters of two Vermont politicians seems calculated. Other girls also roomed with students whose backgrounds were similar to their own. Louisa Baker, who was from New Orleans, wrote to her sister Susan that she was rooming with Juliet Magill and Mary Ann Mansfield. Magill, the grandmother of Girl Scout founder Juliette Magill Gordon Low, also had southern roots. Mansfield was the daughter of a professor at West Point where Baker's brother studied. Parents also weighed in on room assignments. Daniel Parker wrote to vice principal Almira Lincoln that he preferred a single room for Sarah, adding, "more especially I do not wish her to have a Catholic roommate."[30]

Emma Cordelia Clark wrote to her mother that the Pomeroy sisters were housed in the room next to her; Emma and the Pomeroys were all from Cooperstown. Far from alienating other students by their togetherness, the Cooperstown clique was popular. Grace Phillips wrote to her mother, "The Cooperstown girls are much beloved here."[31] Emma, in contrast, took exception to the behavior of Julia Campbell, another Cooperstown girl, whom she described as "stiff" and "unsociable." This was unfortunate, she wrote her brother Grosvenor, because "to be sociable and agreeable is the main thing here."[32]

Pairing like-minded roommates was not always done, perhaps because it was not always possible. In the letter Grace Phillips wrote about the schedule, she also mentioned that her roommate, "a Miss Huntington . . . is a very strong Unitarian, we have had several discussions on this point, she brings many as she supposes very weighty arguments, such as the absurdity of the idea that God himself should die or suffer on the Cross."[33] As different as the principles guiding roommate assignments were from today's ruling concepts of diversity and democracy, the results were perhaps quite similar. Late-night sessions in the dormitory did not always involve religion. In an addendum to one of her letters home, Grace wrote, "We have frequently after the bed bell rings, a discussion in Philosophy, or in Logic, demonstrations in Mathematics, lectures in Natural History etc." These were not serious, she assured her parents. In fact, "they are quite as farcical as they are original. . . . It is mostly the only part of the day in which we feel at liberty."[34]

As Grace's letter implies, the seminary was strictly run. In an earlier letter, she complained about the "close restriction" of the students. She explained with some acerbity, "[F]or the violation or neglect of any of the recitations, absence from prayers, walking, absence from rules during study hours, our rooms, or things being in disorder, and many other such mighty crimes, we receive a mark from the monitress, which marks are to be publicly exposed on the day of examination."[35] Student social life outside the seminary was carefully monitored. In 1827 Emma Willard wrote to Samuel Southard, then secretary of the navy, that his daughter Virginia was "a fine scholar," but that she received more invitations to visit with families in Troy "than she can consistently with the rules of the school accept."[36]

Strict as the rules of the school were, then, as now, some parents wanted them to be even tighter. Cornelia Van Ness apparently complained to her father about his limiting her social life to tea with Emma Willard. In response, he wrote to the principal, "[Cornelia] has received many invitations . . . [and tells us] the restrictions of her not visiting except with you leads to many remarks. The truth is we sent her to school, and had no idea that she would be extensively pressed on the score of visiting."[37] Like many a beleaguered father, he relented and added four names to Cornelia's list of approved hostesses.

The big public examination at the end of each term was greeted with much trepidation, and there were smaller quasi-public examinations, both academic and behavioral, each week. On Wednesdays, for an hour prior to dinner, Mrs. Willard read aloud portions of the girls' compositions anonymously and praised or criticized them. On Saturdays, she reviewed their disciplinary demerits, again in a group setting. This system was widely praised, and when Mary Lyon prepared to launch her female seminary in South Hadley, she visited Troy to see the disciplinary system.

Other routines of seminary life, gleaned through student letters from the 1820s, seem incredibly familiar. Food and money, or the lack thereof, are persistent subjects. Emma Clark wrote home, "I write this on purpose to tell you I want something to eat," adding hastily, "We have enough to eat at our meals, but it is so long between them, I get most starved." Leaving nothing to chance, she included the following directions, "I want you should take a box and bake a pie on a square tin and put it in the bottom of the box and fill it up with everything good, some apples, too, for we haven't any." It was October, so apples should have been readily available, but in a curious remark that reveals another school rule, she explained, "We cannot buy them because we are not allowed to go to any store but dry goods and are marked if we go to a grocery shop." The postscript on this letter contained the plaintive addition: "I don't care for petticoats or anything else, if you will only send me something to eat."[38] (We can hypothesize that the food was sent; some time later, she petitioned her mother for "calico or money for calico" as she was "growing out of [her] clothes."[39])

Sarah Ann Parker's widowed father wrote to her that he did not approve of the prunes her uncle had given her after a visit to the seminary. Sternly, he maintained that "I would not have sent them, for I believe the regulations of the Seminary will furnish you with everything that is necessary and proper for your health and comfort." Had he chosen a gift of food for his daughter, he added, it would have been "a bushel of dryed [sic] peaches that every young lady in school might turn pastry cook, and then show her improvement in the science, by reducing her chemistry to practice in a Christmas tart." Perhaps his real objection, however, was that "I remember well that I never liked those boys at school who were always getting cakes and eating them alone."[40]

Money, like food, was a source of back-and-forth communication between parents and daughters. For Lucy Huntington, the issue in 1825 was that her father had sent a "draft," which Emma Willard had taken to a Troy bank, only to be told that she could not have the money because it "was due to the state bank at Albany." The very confident Miss

Huntington sent word to the banker that the money "was for one of Mr. Huntington's daughters . . . and asked if he wished her to let Mr. Huntington know that he refused to pay it."[41] Other letters more commonly chronicle student requests and parental exasperation. Elizabeth Mansfield wrote to Mary Ann, "Your application for money was quite unexpected. . . . I shall send you 5 dollars which is all I can spare at present."[42] Eleanor Worthington mentioned money in letters to her father. In October 1825, she thanked him for allowing her and her sister to continue with music lessons, which cost extra. By December, however, she wrote, "I am rather unhappy that you should think we have too many wants."[43] She then provided an accounting of how she had spent seven of the eight dollars he had sent them. Her purchases included shoes, calico, gloves, bonnet lining, a piece of sheet music, some pins, a stick of sealing wax, a comb, a pencil, and some muslin. She made sure to mention that some of these items were for her sister Margaret. Her father may have cautioned thrift, but he paid for his girls' laundry so that, as he explained in a letter to Emma Willard, "they can concentrate on their studies."[44]

Thriving though it was, the seminary was not without controversy. In 1822, in an apparent response to something Mary Ann had written, her mother, Elizabeth Mansfield, wrote to her, "I regret exceedingly to hear that your Seminary has enemies, but I cannot say that I am much surprised at it. An institution which in some measure places women on a level with men in point of education must be an object of jealousy and terror to the weak and malignant of both sexes."[45] Mrs. Mansfield was clearly a woman of some probity. The wife of Col. Jared Mansfield, a mathematics professor at West Point, she was disappointed when Mary Ann "dropped Euclid"[46] in favor of studying moral philosophy. She also demonstrated keen insight into her husband's views about women. Extending an invitation through Mary Ann for Dr. and Mrs. Willard to stay with the Mansfields on a trip to the military academy, she commented, "Your father is excellent society for learned ladies, though one would think by his conversation sometimes that they were his particular aversion."[47]

Criticism of seminary girls may have been fairly common. In 1824 a group of students hiked up Mount Ida to see the waterfall. Complained one student to her mother, employing both sarcasm and the casual racism of her day and class, "The people as we passed . . . compared us to Zerxes [*sic*] and his army and to a negro [*sic*] funeral and several other respectable comparisons were made." Later in the same letter, she commented that during students' evening walks in Seminary Park, "the men holler at us and call us cattle going to market."[48] Emma Willard was well aware of her critics. In 1826, in a letter to Gideon Granger, father of Mary Ann, she called the men who opposed educating women "tyrants," ranting that they were "stubborn old 'habitants' who think that everything must be, precisely as it has been, and that because their wives are ignorant that it is better that all women should be so."[49]

The experiment was still young, and much as Emma Willard wanted to follow her plan, it is clear that she made compromises to fill her school with paying customers. She stretched the age limit for students well beyond what she had laid out as appropriate in the plan. Sarah Parker, for example, came to the seminary at the age of nine. (Her "roommate" was a teacher, Almira Lee, most likely a Hart relative and probably more of a nanny for Sarah than a friend.) In a letter to her father, Sarah wrote forlornly, "I am 10 years old; this is the first birthday I have been seperated [*sic*] from you." She was studying "dictation, reading, drawing maps, Arithmetic, writing, and sewing"[50] and hoped that her father would agree to pay for lessons in music and French. Daniel Parker was perhaps unusual, but having lost his wife to consumption, he wanted to make sure that Sarah got lots of exercise. He wrote Almira Lincoln, then serving as Emma's second-in-command, that he was very happy "with Sarah's mentioning her gymnastics exercises." He concluded, "I would rather my daughter should have the frame and muscle of a prize fighter than a cramped chest and nerveless frame."[51]

Mrs. Willard compromised in other ways as well. Although she believed in a set period of study, she was forced to enroll girls at irregular times. From 1823 on, the catalog stated, "Pupils cannot be admitted for any period short of one term."[52] Nevertheless, Grace Phillips mentioned in a letter that she had "entered four weeks after the term commenced,"[53] and in a letter to Mills Olcott, a professor at Dartmouth who had inquired about sending his daughters Sarah and Mary to Troy, she responded, "As the term has commenced, the sooner the young ladies are in school, the better."[54] Students enrolled and left at irregular intervals. In March 1823, Merab Bradley mentioned to her father, "Many of Mrs. Willard's best students do not return this quarter. I should think it would make her feel bad."[55] She went on to note that a Miss Whiting would be going home in May, not to return, because her mother was ill.

Perhaps the full plan was not yet in motion, but there is no doubt that the school thrived in Troy. In 1824, in an article widely reprinted in other magazines, including *Harper's*, *The Ladies' Garland* praised the school:

> There is no female institution in the United States superior to the Seminary, in the number of pupils, the distance from which they are collected, and the respectability of the families to which they belong. It has an open and airy situation, in a place which is healthy, easy of access, and which travelers all concur in considering one of the pleasantest in the Union. The inhabitants of Troy are noted for the correctness of their moral habits.[56]

At the end of the decade, Emma's niece Mary Treat, by now a full-fledged teacher at the school, wrote to her father, "This institution under Aunt Willard's superintendence has flourished astonishingly and now seems to be considered the best in the country."[57] The first decade in Troy had been a rousing success. The school and the city had prospered together. In one of his many letters to Emma Willard about his daughter, Daniel Parker remarked on Troy's prosperity. Sarah Anne, he wrote, "had not walked a square in Troy before she remarked to me that the stores contained as many pretty things as the shops of Philadelphia." She was delighted to find that "pineapples and oranges"[58] were available.

Most amazingly, the school's success was accomplished during a decade in which Emma Willard lost her husband, tried desperately to launch her son on a collegiate course, and proved herself to be a highly prolific and commercially successful textbook author. Not only was the founder visionary, she was practical, energetic, and resourceful.

The Mothers of the Next Generation

As the seminary prospered and grew during its first decade, the nation also experienced unprecedented growth and prosperity. The country industrialized and cities mushroomed. Henry Clay's "American Plan," with its emphasis on internal improvements, was adopted by men of all political viewpoints and set both the federal economic agenda and that of many northern states, including New York. Agriculture also thrived. Southern cotton production boomed after the War of 1812 and then suffered a setback during the Panic of 1819. Dropping from 35 cents a pound in January 1818 to 13 cents a pound eighteen months later, this antebellum economic bellwether boomed again in the 1820s.

While some young women found new opportunities by studying at Troy, others left farms to work in the innovative mills of New England, organized according to the Lowell system. Many, including foreign visitors Charles Dickens and Harriet Martineau, heralded the Lowell mills as model factories, but they did not please Emma Willard. Relentless in her pursuit of state funding for girls' education, she wrote to New York's governor William L. Marcy for aid, using as one of her arguments the need to educate the "hundreds of young women who are laboring like mill-horse drudges in factories." In a characteristic appeal to patriotism, she bemoaned the fact that "many of them are the daughters of those who achieved our revolution," further noting, "these are to be the mothers of the next generation."[1] As always, she stressed the theme of republican motherhood.

It might well be that Emma Willard's antipathy toward mills was based on her observation of the Troy mills rather than the model ones in Lowell. According to the city directory, women and children comprised three quarters of the employees in the cotton and woolen mills along the Poestenkill, producing thousands of yards of ribbon, yarn, flannel, and shirting. There is no indication that any of these mill workers attended the seminary, but at least one young woman from Lowell, Welthea Glines, saved enough money to study in Troy. After a year as a student in 1852–53, she continued on as an instructor until 1857 when she left to teach elsewhere, including a stint on the Texas frontier during the Civil War.

Controversial or not, the New England mills were part of the nation's burgeoning industrialism. With Monroe's election to the presidency in 1820, the Jeffersonian Democrats almost completely overpowered the Federalists. Once the party of agrarianism, with the pro-bank Federalists in the minority and the country's first depression behind them, the Democrats were ready to champion industrial growth. Against little opposition, Democrats embraced internal improvements designed to improve transportation systems to carry the goods that accounted for the nation's increased gross domestic product. Like other historians, Emma Willard adopted the phrase the "era of good feelings" to describe this period. In her U.S. history text, she reflected about the 1820s, "The voice of party spirit had died away, and the period is still spoken of as the 'era of good feelings.'"[2]

From an historical perspective, the period may appear monolithic, but one-party rule did not describe New York politics during this era. Martin Van Buren, destined for the presidency, led the "Bucktails," a group of Democrats who challenged the more conservative wing of the party represented by DeWitt Clinton. A state constitutional convention in 1821 presaged Jacksonian democracy by increasing the rights of common people, provided those common people were white men. The new constitution drastically reduced the property qualifications for white male voters but made it almost impossible for free black male New Yorkers to qualify to vote by requiring that they own property worth $250.

Although the new constitution said little about education, the state's Board of Regents, in existence since 1784, shared the reform spirit, greatly liberalizing its view of academy schooling during the 1820s and 1830s.

Since 1792, the state legislature, at the request of the Regents, had supplied classical boys' academies with tax dollars from a supply of money called the literary fund. (This, after all, was the public support Emma Willard had hoped to receive for her Waterford school and continued to seek for the seminary.) Before 1827, money from the literary fund was doled out to boys' academies around the state according to the percentage of students studying a classical—or precollegiate—curriculum.

The literary fund was earmarked for academies that had been incorporated by the Regents, according to a set of requirements first stipulated in legislation passed in 1787. The money was to be spent on scientific apparatus, library books, salaries, and scholarships, the first two items specifically noted by Emma Willard in her blueprint for girls' schools as particularly needing public funding. In annual appeals to the legislature, she routinely stressed the need for taxpayers to provide these things for girls as well as boys. Typically, the *Connecticut Mirror* reported in 1826 that the New York Assembly had passed a bill appropriating for the Troy Female Seminary "$1000 . . . to be applied to the purchase of a library, a philosophical apparatus and other objects."[3] Just as typically, the bill died in the New York Senate.

In spite of the legislature's reference to scholarships, which suggests a democratic approach to education—at least for young men—the literary fund was controversial. In a democracy, asked some, why should tax dollars raised from the general public be spent on academies that educated the very tiny percentage of college-bound youth? Reflecting the democratization of state politics, at least with regard to white males, after 1827 schools enrolling boys who studied the "English course" were also eligible for grants from the literary fund. Early public high schools, for example the first high school in New York City, which opened in 1825, were nearly indistinguishable from academies; they charged tuition, provided both classical and English curricula, and received money from the literary fund. In the 1830s, additional money was made available to academies and high schools that trained teachers for the state's common schools. Again, the money went only to male institutions.

Limited though these reforms may seem from the vantage point of the twenty-first century, they, in fact, put New York in the forefront of progressive democracy. Although the state's stiff property qualification effectively disenfranchised its African American population, the constitution at least allowed for the possibility of black voting. In contrast, the new states that entered the Union between 1820 and 1840 expressly denied black voting rights. In addition, in its support of academies, its regulation of education through a Board of Regents and in its commitment to teacher training, the state led the nation. Emma Willard's dismay at not having her school included in the literary fund must have been doubly frustrating in light of New York's attitude toward public support of male education, regulated curricula, and teacher training for boys' education. All these principles were central to her plan for female education.

New York also led the nation in invention and bold projects. In 1807 Robert Fulton had successfully plied the Hudson with a steamboat, and repeated improvements each year had sliced time off the trip from New York to Albany. Fulton's initial trip from Manhattan to the state capital took thirty-six hours; by 1840 the trip was easily made overnight. New York politician Philip Hone, who, as mayor, represented New York City at the opening of the canal, commented in his diary, "[T]he rapidity of travelling astonish[es] us who remember how it worked before the use of steam . . . , when a week was consumed in a voyage to Albany [from New York City]. Now we dine at Saratoga and arrive in New York before the people are stirring."[4]

During the 1820s, the number of steamboats and the amount of steamboat tonnage doubled. Meanwhile, turnpikes greatly improved land travel; again, New York led the way, with miles of state road construction paralleling the development of the National Road. Funded by the federal government, this artery ran from Washington, D.C., to Wheeling, West Virginia, and was extended to Ohio by 1830. With improved roads, the new states not only sent farm products to the East, they also sent young women to the seminary. During the 1820s, a few girls from Ohio and Michigan made the arduous trek to Troy; in the 1830s, even more girls from these two states enrolled at the seminary. Other new states—including Louisiana, Alabama, and Mississippi—sent more girls to study in Troy as transportation improved.

However, the boldest of the era's transportation projects, by far, belonged exclusively to New York and directly affected the fortunes of Troy. On this topic, the Clintonians led and the "Bucktails" followed. DeWitt Clinton had long believed that the new nation's survival depended on the establishment of an east-west transportation network. As was true of so many things in the first half of the nineteenth century, including the rationale for educating girls, the preservation of the new republic was a major rallying cry for building the canal. Construction on the Erie Canal, in the planning stages for years, began on July 4, 1817, while the Willards were still in Vermont. When it was finished in 1825, the canal stretched nearly four hundred miles from the Hudson River to the Great Lakes. Thomas Jefferson had believed that "Clinton's Folly" was an impossible engineering feat "little short of madness,"[5] but the determined governor and the canal's engineers proved him wrong. "Clinton's ditch," as it was often called, was only 28 feet wide at the bottom and 40 feet wide at the top. After eight years of back-breaking labor, primarily by immigrants who averaged $12 a month for their efforts, a water route from New York City to the Great Lakes was completed. It would ensure New York City's primacy as the nation's leading port and New York State's commercial leadership.

On October 26, 1825, the canal opened. Water from Lake Erie poured into the canal for the first time. At 10 A.M. a cannon roared in Buffalo; cannons strategically placed along the canal and down the banks of the Hudson boomed in turn until the last gun on the Atlantic shore south of Manhattan sounded, and the volley returned up the river and west along the canal, finishing the salute in Buffalo at 1:30 P.M. The *Seneca Chief*, a canal packet, sailed east from Buffalo, carrying DeWitt Clinton and other dignitaries. When the boat reached the Atlantic Ocean on November 4, Clinton poured water from Lake Erie into the ocean; the *Seneca Chief* carried water from the Atlantic Ocean on its return trip to western New York. Eventually, this keg of salt water was poured into Lake Erie, completing the chain.

Students at the seminary may or may not have joined in the grand celebration of the opening of the canal in 1825. Most of the festivities took place in Albany, where a delegation from Manhattan met the packet boat that entered the Hudson from the West. Anna Riker '24, who had studied in Troy for a year, was present because her father, Richard, was the recorder of the City of New York. Other students were aware of the event, and for many, the canal would mean a quicker, easier journey to school. Anne McDowell '26, a student from Ohio, remembered taking a "carriage from Columbus to Sandusky . . . a boat to Buffalo . . . [and] from there we went by canal and stage to Troy."[6] Going to school was not the only memory of the canal cherished by seminary graduates. Lucena Sheldon '27, whose uncle and guardian was involved in canal shipping, remembered traveling on the canal with her family from her home in Rochester for summer visits to relatives in Vermont:

> The half of the ladies cabin was reserved for me. I took my three children, the youngest of whom was a baby, with a nurse. I had my own bed and bedding, baby's cradle, my low rocking-chair and workbasket. I enjoyed every moment. These days of hurry had not dawned. I could read as well as at home. There was no grinding of wheels. We moved continuously and steadily. The children had their books and playthings, and thus the week of our journey passed pleasantly and without fatigue.[7]

There is no record of Emma Willard's attendance at the canal festivities in 1825, which is not surprising because she was still in formal mourning for her husband, who had died the previous May. Earlier, however, she had been invited by DeWitt Clinton to celebrate the opening of the leg of the canal connecting Schenectady and Troy. Martha Lasell '27, who began studying in Troy in 1822, reminisced in the 1890s, "When the Erie Canal was opened, Mrs. Willard was invited by Governor Clinton to attend the celebration and take a sail up to the nine locks. The school accompanied her, and we had a joyous time."[8]

The impact of the canal on Troy was immediate. When the section of the canal around Troy had opened in 1823, the *Trojan Trader* had set out for the west, jumping the gun on Albany. By December 1825, at the close of the first season of shipping, Troy's role in western shipping was well established. Newspapers reported,

> The amount of produce, &c. brought into Troy in 1825 by the Erie and Northern canals is 107,203 tons. Among the articles are 39,433 barrels of flour, 10,922 barrels of salt, 6,889 barrels of provisions,

287,113 bushels of wheat, 53,558 bushels of other grain, 2,403 tons of gypsum, 67,142 gallons and 165 tons of spirits, 20 tons of hops, 48 tons of wool, 134 tons of butter and lard, 154 tons of cheese, 1803 bushels of timothy seed, 5,082 cords of wood, 27 millions of feet of lumber, 1,147,494 feet of timber, 181,814 M of staves, 263 tons of nails, 750 tons of pig-iron, 149 tons of bar iron, 185 tons of marble, 498 tons of lime.[9]

The "amount of merchandize" traveling west from Troy in the same period totaled 13,436 tons. Between 1825 and the end of the decade, Troy's population grew to nearly 11,000, "an increase [that] exceeds by more than half any of equal time preceding." For this growth, the city was "indebted to the opening of the Grand Canal."[10] In addition Troy benefited from the shipping from the north facilitated by the Northern Canal linking Lake Champlain to the Hudson.

Nor was Troy the only beneficiary of the new waterway. Within a year, the tolls on the canal equaled five times the interest on the bonds issued by the state to fund the project. Costing $7 million, the expense of the canal equaled "one-third of all the banking and insurance capital in the state,"[11] an extraordinary commitment. Thus the miracle of transportation proved to be an outstanding financial success for the state as well, and at least one historian has credited the project with insulating New York from the worst of the Panic of 1819. The low wages and low interest rates associated with that economic crisis allowed the canal commissioners to complete the earliest phases of the construction under the projected budget. Perhaps it was no coincidence that the New York Stock Exchange opened the same year as the Erie Canal because the canal had shown how profitable investment finance could be.

The trip from Buffalo to Albany that had taken nearly a month prior to the opening of the canal took just five days on a passenger packet in 1826. (The first student from Buffalo entered the school in 1825.) Tickets cost about 4.4 cents a mile, including meals. For more affluent travelers, elegant packet boats containing bars, libraries, and drawing rooms were available. In spite of this, passenger travel was the lesser portion of the canal's success. For many people the portion of the trip from Schenectady to Troy was too tedious; more than twenty-five locks were necessary to traverse the steep grade to Cohoes Falls. As an alternative, passengers could take a stagecoach from Albany to Schenectady and board a canal packet there; tickets cost 62 cents. By 1831 the Mohawk and Albany, the first steam railroad in the United States, began to provide passenger travel, eventually replacing the uncomfortable stages.

In terms of freight, the canal proved revolutionary and reigned supreme for many decades. In 1823, when all but the final thirty miles from Lockport to Buffalo, had been completed, the *New Hampshire Gazette* reported, "The transportation of a ton of flour from Buffalo will not cost more than ten dollars, freight and toll included—by land it costs 100 dollars or thereabouts."[12] As late as 1851, "one canal boat, drawn by two sorry mules, carried as large a load [of grain] . . . as one locomotive [drawing] twenty cars."[13] Up until the Civil War, the Erie Canal carried more than ten times the freight of all the state's railroads combined, and improvements to the canal ensured its importance as a freight hauler well into the twentieth century.

One of the most amazing things about the planning for and construction of the Erie Canal was its execution by men who were not professionally trained engineers. Elkanah Watson, James Geddes, Benjamin Wright, Canvass White, and Nathan Roberts all worked on the canal, succeeding by trial, error, and mathematical calculation. There was no university in the English-speaking world that trained engineers; just months before the grand opening of the canal, Troy became the home of the first educational institution specifically geared toward technical education. Rensselaer School (today's Rensselaer Polytechnic Institute) was established in December 1824 and granted the first civil engineering degrees in the United States.

From the beginning, Rensselaer was intertwined with the Troy Female Seminary. Its first board president, Samuel Blatchford, had served as president of the board of the Waterford Female Academy. John Dickinson, Guert Van Schoonhoven, and John Cramer, early trustees of Rensselaer, also served as trustees in Waterford and Troy. Most important, however, was the connection forged by Emma Willard and her sister Almira Lincoln with Amos Eaton. Eaton was appointed "Senior Professor." An accomplished lecturer who pioneered laboratory experiments as an effective means of demonstrating scientific theory, Eaton lectured for the Troy Female Seminary students and worked with Almira as she studied science and wrote science texts for students in Troy and elsewhere.

The Troy Lyceum featured Eaton's lectures, and the local papers advertised Eaton's lectures at the lyceum that included "a course of Lectures on Experimental Philosophy and Chemistry . . . apparatus . . . air pump, solar microscope, etc. . . . this course is given at this time, with a particular view to accommodate the Troy Female Academy."[14] When Rensselaer opened, students at the seminary attended scientific lectures there. Wrote Lucretia Davidson to her mother, "I have been to the Rensselaer School to attend the philosophical lectures. They are delivered by the celebrated Mr. Eaton."[15]

In addition to the opening of the canal and the establishment of the engineering institute, another memorable national event touched Troy in the middle of the seminary's first decade. The Marquis de Lafayette (although he had renounced his title, Americans, citizens of the most democratic of nations, obsequiously clung to its use) had been invited to visit the United States. "The Nation's Visitor," as newspapers across the country called him, planned a tour of the entire country, wanting to see in action the republic he had helped to free from England. Nearly fifty years after he had joined the American revolutionary forces under George Washington, Lafayette embarked on a triumphal trip that would last thirteen months and would take him twice to Troy.

Lafayette's visit was officially sanctioned by Congress. In a joint resolution in the winter of 1823, Congress had requested the president "to communicate to him the assurances of grateful and affectionate attachment still cherished towards him by the government and the people of the United States."[16] No American cherished Lafayette more than Emma Willard. In a letter she wrote to him a few years after this visit, she called him "the man who before I knew him I respected more than any other man living."[17] He embodied all that she revered in the revolutionary generation. (When he died in 1834, he was, in fact, "the last surviving general of the Continental line";[18] the anniversary of his death is celebrated annually even in the twenty-first century by American expatriates in Paris, where he is buried.) Emma Willard was eager to make the Troy Female Seminary one of the ports of call for the visiting dignitary, and she was not disappointed.

Newspapers covered every mile of Lafayette's jubilant tour. At sixty-seven, the famous general was in poor health; he had been wounded during the American Revolution and imprisoned with his wife as a result of his activities during the French Revolution. Leaving France on July 12, 1824, he arrived in New York on August 15. His travels until his return voyage to France began September 7, 1825, took him through all twenty-four states; he met with former presidents Jefferson and Adams, current president Monroe, and future presidents Jackson and the younger Adams. He was present for the dedication of the monument on Bunker Hill, and judging from newspaper accounts, he represented the triumph of national unity for the American people. (This in spite of his repeated criticism of slavery.)

By September Lafayette had left New England and was headed to New York. He crossed the Hudson at Greenbush and entered Albany, festooned with arches, one of which read "The Hero Is Welcome," and the other, "We remember thy deeds—We revere thy worth—We love thy virtues."[19] The mayor of Albany, Ambrose Spencer, was a brother-in-law of DeWitt Clinton and would live to see his son serve in Tyler's cabinet and his grandson married to a seminary graduate. He greeted Lafayette with a lengthy speech, reprinted in its entirety in several newspapers. Spencer extolled the visitor's place in American history, saying, "The few surviving statesmen and soldiers of the revolution have gathered around you as a friend and a brother—the generation that has risen up since your departure, cherish the same feelings, and those that will appear in the successive future ages, will hail you as the benefactor of America and the hero of liberty."[20]

At eight the next morning, Lafayette headed for Troy, probably by sloop. Troy's celebration matched the festivities in Albany. A carpeted platform had been specially erected at the landing, a rifle salute was fired, and a committee of dignitaries (all of whom were or would be Troy Female Seminary trustees) met the boat. More ringing patriotic speeches followed, and then the general traveled by open carriage to the Troy House, the leading hotel in the city, where the "piazza was handsomely adorned with festoons of evergreens and roses [in the center of which] was perched a live eagle, with a miniature of Lafayette upon its neck." As the "Nation's Guest" dined "on a cold collation," with his admiring male hosts, a note was handed to him. It read, "The ladies of Troy, having assembled at the female seminary . . . request of general La Fayette that he would grant them an opportunity of beholding in his person, their own, and their country's, generous and beloved benefactor."[21]

When he arrived at the school, Lafayette was escorted from the park to the building under an "arbor of evergreen." Inscribed above the entrance to the arbor were the words, "America commands her daughters to welcome their deliverer La Fayette." Eunice Pawling, wife of the mayor, addressed the general, thanking him for his part in bringing about American independence and presenting the seminary students as "living testimony of the blessings conferred by that independence." She then introduced him to Emma Willard, citing the seminary as "an institution which we consider an honor to our city and country."[22] According to newspaper accounts, two hundred students lined up to greet the general. Mrs. Willard had written a poem for the occasion that was sung by one of the teachers, with the students joining in on the chorus:

> Then deep and dear thy welcome be;
> Nor think thy daughters far from thee:
> Columbia's daughters, lo! we bend,
> And claim to call thee father, friend![23]

Newspapers reported that the general was moved to tears by the tribute, copies of which were presented to him by Cornelia Van Ness and Margaret Worthington, daughters of the governors of Vermont and Ohio. Six-year-old Jane Lincoln, Almira's daughter, presented him with an "elegantly bound"[24] copy of *The Plan for Improving Female Education.* In all, the stop at the seminary consumed so much time that a trip to Lansingburgh was canceled, further fueling the animosity between the two cities that had festered ever since Troy had beaten its northern rival for the title of county seat.

In intervening years, Emma Willard would indeed call Lafayette her friend. Her correspondence with him began as soon as he returned home, and it was definitely two sided. He helped her find a French teacher for the seminary, and he reviewed "those parts of [her history text] . . . in which yourself have [*sic*] been an actor."[25] Before he left the United States for the last time, she saw him briefly when he stopped in Troy once more. Newspapers reported that the visit was conducted with great propriety, a reference to the fact that she received Lafayette privately while she was in mourning for her husband.

Indeed, the months immediately following the general's first visit were unhappy ones for Mrs. Willard. Dr. Willard, who had been in failing health for some time, was dying, most likely from stomach cancer. An active presence at the seminary, he had championed his wife's efforts on behalf of girls' education, and in Troy he served as the school physician and business manager, perhaps more successfully in the latter position. Wrote Emma Clark to her brother one cold winter day, "It is quite sickly here at present . . . the girls are most all sick with sore throats. I hope I shall not be sick here, for the first thing that is seen here when we are sick is the old Dr. Willard with some medicine he obliges us to take."[26] If the students did not appreciate his labors, his wife did. She relied on him to handle the accounts and negotiate leases with the city, his signature required on legal documents in an era before married women gained property rights.

In a sketch for the Addison County Medical Society that she wrote twenty years after his death, Emma Willard expressed no reservations about her husband's professional acumen, intelligence, and political opinions. Describing him as an "excellent practitioner," she commented that he "had on the whole rather a poor opinion of the state of medical science as it existed in his day." He had no time for the bleeding and harsh medicines prescribed by his fellow doctors; devoted to healing children, he favored warm baths, diet, and bed rest. Using this regimen, she proudly reported, "All his measles patients lived."[27]

Twenty years after losing him, she fondly recalled his "large expressive eyes" and great heart, which she dubbed his "lion-mood."[28] She noted his devotion to the cause of female education, writing, "[H]e was, of all men whom I have ever known, the most truly liberal; the most entirely devoid of the pride of sex."[29] She claimed her husband had been a man of prodigious memory and that at one dinner party in Albany, Chancellor

Kent had leaned over to him and asked, "'How come you to know everything?'"[30] Her only concern as she reminisced about her husband was a worry that he had never truly been saved, even though he had joined the Episcopal Church, probably at her urging, late in life.

Dr. Willard's death was a formidable blow at a time when things were going very well for the seminary. From various references to his health in family letters, it would appear that he had been ill off and on for a few years before his death. As early as 1822, Merab Bradley wrote to her brother that he should tell their father that "Doctor Willard is much out of health."[31] Throughout 1824, William, in the South in an attempt to cure his own consumption, worried about his father's health. On September 15, he wrote to his father hoping "your health is better."[32] However, Dr. Willard was failing. Almira wrote to their mother on April 4 that Dr. Willard's death was imminent. Gustavus and William were in Troy (Franklin had died of yellow fever in Cuba two years earlier), and John had been called home from his boarding school in Vermont. The doctor lingered for several more weeks, drawing his last breath on May 29.

In a letter to a former pupil, Emma Willard detailed her husband's last days:

> His sufferings were indescribable. His stomach was the seat of his disease. For weeks before his death he took no food or drink, or medicine (so irritable were the nerves of his stomach), but simple bread water, cooled with ice. . . . He was sensible of his situation and conversed about the disposal of his affairs, told me what he wished should be done and avoided . . . & where he wanted to be buried.[33]

During much of this time, Almira, who had joined her sister at the seminary in 1823 when her own husband died, ran the day-to-day operations of the school. Weary with nursing, Emma earned the sympathies of a niece and presumably other pupils. Three weeks after Dr. Willard's death, Mary Treat wrote to her father Elisha, widower of Emma's sister Lydia, "our dear uncle breathed his last at half past five in the morning." For eight weeks, she noted, "Aunt Willard . . . was by his bedside night and day, taking only the little rest that was absolutely necessary." Mary predicted that her aunt would use work to sustain herself, in spite of a "loss which might have been considered by some as a stroke too weighty for mortals to bear." After all, reasoned Mary, "She has been the means of doing good to the world, and feels it a duty to renew her exertions, which may in time prove to her country, by the enlightenment of the 'fair sex' that her life has been gloriously devoted to their usefulness."[34]

As she recovered from the loss of her husband, Emma found herself facing another personal trial: the education of her son John. Presumably he attended local schools as a young boy, but he was now a teenager. He had studied at Hadley, Massachusetts, with the Rev. Daniel Huntington and was boarding at a school in Bennington, Vermont, run by a Mr. Adams when his father's final illness began. Now, his mother arranged for him to go to Hartford for the summer term to a school managed by Nathan Starr; in exchange, Starr's daughter, Mary, would study in Troy. However, Mrs. Willard was already focused on her son's collegiate education. She had visited West Point many times, and she had friends on the faculty there who had sent their daughters to the seminary.

One of these was Col. Jared Mansfield, a mathematics professor at West Point whose daughter Mary Anne studied in Troy in 1823. John was just fifteen the fall after his father died, and she told Mansfield she wanted him to "enter at sixteen," which was a normal age for West Point cadets in that era. She wrote to the colonel that she had "concluded after deep and anxious thought to send him to your academy if an appointment should be accorded him."[35] Meanwhile, on December 15, 1825, she contacted Capt. Alden Partridge asking that he accept her "only and darling child"[36] into his school in Connecticut and prepare him for West Point.

In the meantime, she wrote to anyone she thought might help her get John his appointment. Jane Meech had studied in Troy in 1824, and her father Ezra was currently serving as the Democratic congressman from Vermont. He couldn't help her and advised that new regulations about appointments to the academy meant that she was better off contacting her own representative in the Troy area. Fortunately for Mrs. Willard, the congressman who represented Troy, William McManus, was also a former seminary parent; however, his political party did not match her husband's, which may account for her turning to Ezra Meech first. She also wrote to John W. Taylor, the Speaker of the

House of Representatives, urging an appointment for her son. Unlike McManus, Taylor supported the Democratic Party; he was also a New Yorker and a graduate of Union College, so there is great likelihood that Mrs. Willard and the Speaker had mutual friends.

Sometime in 1826 the appointment came through, and John was scheduled to begin classes in the summer. In June, Emma Willard and her son visited West Point, taking Eleanor Worthington along with them. She wrote to Eleanor's father, Thomas Worthington, governor of Ohio, "I hope you will not be displeased that I took Eleanor along with me without consulting you." She reported to the governor that the trio had gone on to Manhattan where she had "rented a hack"[37] to show the young people around New York. It appears that she was treating John to a last pleasurable weekend before handing him over to the military.

John Willard, destined to become the principal of the Troy Female Seminary after his mother's retirement in 1838, was clearly a young man with limited scholarly aptitude—or at least, appetite. His older half brother, William, often referred to him in letters to his parents. William's queries inevitably mixed care and concern. Writing from New Orleans, where he was stationed in the winter of 1824, he complained about his latest letters from home, "I cannot find a syllable of Master John! Whether he is at play in Troy or at school elsewhere?"[38] Ten months later William wrote to his father, "I hope John H. is by this time well settled at his school,"[39] and he suggested that John might be sent to him and that he might "if possible . . . reclaim him and that a removal from the scene of his troubles might facilitate my object."[40] In a letter to John, written that same month, William urged him to "reflect before you act."[41]

Although this was advice any older brother might give a younger sibling, it seems clear that John needed special guidance. A month later William wrote to his father that he was in touch with "Brother John" who was then studying in Castleton, Vermont. He urged his father to keep John in school, implying that John wanted to come home: "I do beg and entreat you that your parental kindness and tenderness for the boy may not yield to his inclination to return . . . for although Troy is of all places most dear to him as the residence of his parents & his home, still it is the last place for his acquiring the intellectual attainments he should now be obtaining."[42]

Prepared or not, John entered West Point. He stayed for two years in spite of very bad grades, multiple demerits for failing to follow regulations, and his general unhappiness at being there. In his biography of Emma Willard, John Lord referred to over two hundred letters passing between mother and son while he was at the military academy. Few of these still exist, but an interesting correspondence between the anxious mother and a young instructor at the Point illuminate the parental relationship and the son's issues. Thomas Twiss, who would marry Emma Willard's Middlebury pupil and Troy teacher, Elizabeth Sherrill, graduated from West Point in 1826 and stayed on as an instructor. Emma Willard had made his acquaintance at some point and turned to him for help in keeping John at the Point.

First-year cadets at West Point in the 1820s took only three subjects: mathematics, French, and drawing. From his first term John performed miserably, invariably scoring near the bottom of his class in all three subjects. In addition, he earned multiple demerits for his tardiness, his casual attention to regulations, and his general potential—or lack thereof—to become an army officer. He wrote frequently to two of his cousins, Mary Treat and Betsy Hart, who were studying in Troy. He complained of the homework load—"6 pp geometry and 6 pp Voltaire"[43] every day—and the marching—"We, to be sure, sometimes march on guard (woolens, woolens) just by way of amusement and stand post one or two hours in the evening so cold that it freezes a person's ideas just in the spot where they happen to be at the time he goes on." He also criticized the food: "We have just as much variety as the man had for his eating who had pork and beans one day and beans and pork the next."[44]

Meanwhile, Lieutenant Twiss kept up an optimistic front in his letters to Emma Willard. During his first fall at West Point, Emma complained that John's roommates were having an "unpleasant effect" on him and asked if Twiss would "take [him] for a roommate."[45] In response, Twiss wrote that he had talked to John and "he will not write to you again for permission to resign."[46] Later that year he reported on positive conversations he had had with John's mathematics tutor, future general Robert E. Lee, and in January, he wrote to John's mother that he "has improved beyond my utmost expectations." He also assured the anxious mother that John's demerits came because he was "thoughtless" and comforted her that he "does not neglect his duty willfully."[47] In May, Twiss reported that Lee expected John to pass his mathematics examination. Emma's response was, literally, to praise God. She wrote to Twiss, "Your communications respecting John call forth in the first place my thanks to Him whom it is delightful to consider the author of all our mercies."[48]

John probably passed the examination because he was allowed to return for a second year, but he remained at or near the bottom of the class. In June 1827, Twiss left the Point, planning to join Elizabeth Sherrill in Georgia, where she was teaching; they would be married when they reunited and would run a girls' seminary in Sparta together. Writing in January, Twiss, who apparently had borrowed money from Mrs. Willard, was still excusing John's behavior. He commented, "The change from the tender care of a mother to this place of stern rule and military discipline is so new, so totally different from what is expected, I am not astonished they are homesick . . . [and] neglect their studies."[49]

In 1828 John Willard left West Point, probably at the request of the academy. A year later, he had a new collegiate plan. His cousin Mary Treat wrote to her father in the summer of 1829, "John is to enter Washington College [now Trinity College] at Hartford."[50] A few months later, she expressed some apprehension about his chances for success, writing, "I hope he will distinguish himself <u>there</u> as a scholar."[51] However, it was not to be. According to college records, he took a special course. In 1829 he was enrolled in the "partial course," an "unusual two-year program of studies that led to a diploma certifying 'good conduct and proficiency in learning.'"[52] More practical than the classical course, this curriculum could lead to a baccalaureate degree if students were successful. John Willard, however, never pursued anything higher.

In spite of his academic tribulations, John was by all accounts an amiable young man and devoted son. His mother believed that he was "peculiarly manly" and "serious and contemplative,"[53] but his letters to his cousins clearly indicate his sense of humor and fun. Wrote his mother, "[Y]ou have the appearance of affecting wit, but the affectation of gayety and frolicking does not become you."[54] He, in contrast, wrote to his cousin that he wanted news of "cupids, darts and flames,"[55] certainly not serious subjects, and he complained that "mother never pretends to write any news."[56] In spite of the different viewpoints that mother and son had of his character, he remained a loyal son. As Mary Treat wrote her father, "John is a great comfort to his Mother. . . . We all think much of him, and he is very affectionate to us."[57] When John left Washington College, his mother resolved to provide him with the capstone experience afforded educated young men: a tour of the European continent. Of course, she would accompany him.

A Peculiar Kind of Woman

IN AUGUST 1830, Emma Willard prepared to turn her seminary over to her sister, Almira Lincoln, so that she and her son John could travel to Europe. A thriving institution, the school had a national reputation and a student body numbering 230. Slightly over a hundred were from Troy, and the others hailed from as far away as the West Indies and St. Petersburg, Russia.[1] Schools for girls were flourishing. Catharine Beecher enrolled more than a hundred students at her Hartford Female Seminary, and the Litchfield Female Academy, still headed by the aging Miss Pierce, also had a strong enrollment.

Because she was a widow and the head of a household, Emma Willard was listed in the census of 1830 by name; her residence, according to that record, consisted of five white males, one between the ages of 10 and 15 and four between the ages of 20 and 40, all of whom, with the exception of John, were presumably servants. In addition, there were a hundred white females, including the principal. Seventy-eight of them were 15 to 20 years old, two were under 15, and twenty were over 30.

Although the school was clearly successful, Emma Willard yearned for greater public support for her venture. Five days before she embarked on her trip, she convened a meeting at the school. Almira, the vice principal, reporting on the meeting to Mary Treat, wrote, "The schoolroom was filled with citizens and citizenesses from Mrs. Dickinson, Miss Warren &tc to those who move in a more humble sphere and from the mayor to mechanics." Her older sister's goal was to impress on the crowd the importance of the Troy Female Seminary (TFS) and "the measures necessary on the part of Troy for its permanence." For the first time Emma Willard delivered her own speech and did not require a man to read it for her. Initially, Almira, always the more conservative of the two, doubted the wisdom of this approach but found that "the moment she rose to speak, my fears all dissipated . . . the effect of her address was very powerful." (Another relative, Emma Hart, also in the audience, was less convinced. "Cousin Emma," wrote Almira, "cried bitterly that Aunt Willard was speaking in public."[2])

Having said her piece, Emma packed her trunks and prepared to leave Troy for a year. She had great faith in Almira, a widow with two young daughters who had lived at the seminary since the death of her husband in 1823. Emma had come to rely on Almira. As one of their many nieces studying in Troy wrote to her father, "Aunt Lincoln is of great service to her."[3] Almira was an educator, scientist, and author of two highly successful textbooks, one on botany and one on chemistry. A particularly accomplished botanist who worked closely with professors Amos Eaton at Rensselaer and Benjamin Silliman at Yale, she would eventually be the second woman inducted into the American Academy of Science.

Emma was heading to Europe, a trip she claimed was necessitated by her "ill health."[4] She wrote to Samuel Southard, a TFS parent and a former secretary of the navy (soon to be elected governor of New Jersey and, subsequently, senator), asking for a letter of introduction to the American minister in Great Britain. She explained that she was, "taking a sea voyage [because] my health has of late threatened wholly to desert me."[5] The five years between her husband's death and this journey had been professionally fulfilling and busy—the school had grown, both in terms of pupils and buildings, and her geography and American history textbooks were commercially and critically successful.

In all likelihood, Emma Willard was tired, and she often mentioned problems with her eyesight in letters to family. In addition, she had had an accident some months before, causing at least one niece to be "so anxious about Aunt Willard after her fall."[6] At forty-three, at a time when an American woman's life expectancy was somewhere in the mid-forties, she was, by nineteenth-century standards, an older woman. Although the health benefits of sea air were widely touted, any trip under sail, particularly across the ocean, was fraught with danger. In her first Saturday morning address to the seminary students, Almira cautioned that they might not see the founder again. Always serious and deeply religious, her reverence for both God and her older sister colored her first message to the assembled girls:

> Every receding wave is carrying her from her native country and her loved and cherished institution. . . . like the Ephesians when St. Paul tore himself from them, sorrow most of all, lest we may see her face no more. But let us hope that a life on which so much depends may be preserved, and that a mind whose efforts have been so greatly blessed for the improvement of her sex, may be restored to us . . . enriched by observations of the state of female education in foreign countries.[7]

The average voyage to Europe took well over a month; the Willards left Troy for New York City on September 27 and boarded the *Charlemagne* on October 1. They glimpsed the Eddystone light on the coast of England on October 21 and continued sailing along the coast until they reached Le Havre, France, on October 24. Nor was the journey finished. After waiting for the tide to turn, they were finally transported to land on October 26.

The travel, rough as it was, fueled Emma's sense of adventure, and her account of the voyage illuminates her fortitude. In a letter to her sister, she wrote that she had not been "sea-sick," but that she had not "exercised as much on deck, owing to the roughness of the weather, as I could have wished: but the perpetual motion in which I am kept by the winds and waters; rocking, and rolling, and tossing; holding with might and main, by some fixed object during the day to keep from being shot across the cabin, and grasping the side of my berth at night for fear of being rolled over the side,—all this, though not particularly diverting at the time, is yet very conducive to my health."[8]

Emma undoubtedly had motivations other than health for undertaking her journey. In 1830 the principal of TFS was independent, wealthy, and famous. For Americans of her social position, ardent patriots though they might be, traveling to Europe, especially France, was increasingly popular, in spite of the risks. The travelers were "mostly young, mostly single, mostly well-educated and well-off,"[9] but some were older and well established, for example, James Fenimore Cooper and Samuel F. B. Morse, both of whom had relatives attend the seminary. Nearly all were men; in choosing to travel abroad as the head of her party, Emma Willard again moved beyond conventional norms for women's behavior.

The eagerness to visit Europe on the part of educated Americans ironically grew simultaneously with the establishment of a truly American cultural tradition that had taken root by 1830. In the 1820s, Washington Irving, Cooper, and William Cullen Bryant all created literature with American themes. Irving's short stories, Cooper's novels, and Bryant's poems were uniquely American, but they won international acclaim. Within a few years, American literature would be enriched and enhanced by the publications of Ralph Waldo Emerson, Edgar Allen Poe, and Walt Whitman. Nor was the new American culture limited to letters. Thomas Cole had begun painting American landscapes; his depictions of natural scenes were the first of many pieces that would form the body of work known as the Hudson School.

At the same time that novelists and artists were crafting a new American culture, the American public, the most literate citizenry in the world, was showing an incredible appetite for newspapers and magazines. By 1830 *The American Ladies Magazine* and *Godey's Lady's Book* both catered to a female readership. *Ladies Magazine*, edited by Sarah Josepha Hale, consciously disseminated American stories and poems and supported women's education. When Hale, Emma Willard's good friend and the mother of two seminary students, took over *Godey's* editorship in 1837, she decreed that her new magazine would only publish stories and poems by American authors.

Part of Americans' pride in their homegrown culture came from their sense of history; the new nation, a republic, embodied virtues that the European monarchies, home to despots, frequent wars, and great social inequities did not share. A major theme in Emma Willard's extraordinarily popular American history textbook was the innocence of the new republic in contrast with the venality of the older European civilizations. Comparing the United States with England and France, she maintained, "In comparison with these old and wily nations, the character of America is that of youthful simplicity, of maiden purity."[10]

Europe, however, was still the cradle of Western civilization, and she could not wait to visit. When she first beheld the coast of France, she could

barely contain her excitement. Getting from the ship to shore was yet another dangerous part of sea travel because the passengers were carried to
land in small boats. It rained on the tiny vessel transporting the Willards,
but neither inclement weather nor treacherous seas dampened her enthusiasm, which stemmed, she wrote, from "a life's wish consummated in
seeing Europe."[11] And, of course, there was the added anticipation of seeing her friend, the aging Marquis de Lafayette, one more time. They had
corresponded frequently since his visit to Troy, and she was looking forward to spending time with him and his family. Two years before her trip,
she had expressed her devotion to him, "To be known and sometimes
thought of by the man who before I knew him I respected more than any
other man living, is a happiness which seems so surprising that at times I
half regard my recollections of General Lafayette but delightful dreams."[12]

After landing in Le Havre, the Willards traveled by coach to Paris,
where Lafayette awaited. The trip was made even more exciting by rumors
of civil war. The French government was unstable. The previous July, a revolution had toppled Charles X, and Lafayette, a liberal member of the French
House of Deputies, had supported the installation of Charles's cousin, Louis
Philippe, as king. The French had exchanged one constitutional monarchy
for another, more liberal version. Disdain for monarchy aside, a king supported by her favorite liberal Frenchman was a king Emma could admire.
She wrote to her sister and her pupils about seeing the royal couple at the
opera and daily on the street. She recognized the inconsistency in her admiration for a monarchy, demonstrating a somewhat uncharacteristic—or at
least, seldom revealed—ability to laugh at herself. When the French queen
wore a coat that was a duplicate of one Emma had recently purchased, she
commented, "Republican as I am, I was silly enough to be pleased."[13]

In the company of Lafayette's two daughters, she visited the House
of Deputies to see her marquis, a longtime deputy, in action. After
hearing him speak, her enthusiasm for his leadership swelled. She
concluded, "Lafayette, more than any other man of the present day,
is making history for others to write, and for posterity to read."[14] She
attended Lafayette's regular Tuesday evening soirees, where she met
many members of the French government, the James Fenimore Coo-
pers, and a variety of other American tourists.

By December, however, France was again in turmoil, and there were mobs in the streets of Paris. Confined to her rooms by the danger, she admired Lafayette's role in quelling the trouble. Again, she wrote, "Lafayette has saved France."[15] Perhaps, but the House of Deputies voted to strip him of his title, "commander-in-chief," a move the king supported. In disgust, Emma wrote Almira, "I have done with French politics."[16] In a huff, Lafayette's daughter-in-law complained to Emma, "America remembers the services of my father for fifty years. France can scarce remember them five months."[17]

This ill treatment of her hero was not all that the visiting educator found to criticize about the French. Much of what she disliked stemmed from her staunch Protestantism, which was sorely challenged by Roman Catholic France. To her credit, she attended mass, but the priest, whom she did not like, merely reinforced her disdain for the national French religion. To her, his sermon centered too much on the institution of the church and not enough on "the meek and lowly Jesus, who went about doing good."[18] She was, however, intrigued to learn about and clearly supportive of a group of priests who wanted to revolt against the pope and "acknowledge Jesus Christ as prime head of the christian [sic] church."[19]

She felt herself "debased and degraded" by the chapel in the palace at Versailles because of images that revealed "the impious attempt to paint God the Father as a man."[20] Other artwork elicited similar negative comments. She recoiled at the "horror" of the statues in various cathedrals and denounced as "shabby" the "waxen figures of the Virgin"[21] found in cemeteries. As for the Louvre, she wrote Almira, "Had the interests of virtue and decency been at all consulted, many of the pictures here would have been dismissed as fit only for the abodes of pollution."[22] Nor did she enjoy all the opera, in spite of being seated in Lafayette's box. After seeing *The Barber of Seville,* she wrote, "I like to be amused, but not at the expense of virtue."[23]

She concluded that virtue, the hallmark of republican motherhood, was sadly lacking in France, even among women, whom she, of course, regarded as the guardians of virtue in America. She suggested that American women "have much to teach French women about virtue" but recognized that it would be an uphill battle because it was "harder to teach virtue than to learn vice."[24] She found French women "far from the proper standards in customs which concern their chastity" and reported that a third of the children in Paris were "born out of wedlock." Of course, the Lafayette women were not included among the fallen women of France because they, she assured a correspondent, "are as much American as French."[25]

What particularly annoyed her about French women in general was their belief that they were moral and virtuous. She commented that French women confused respectability with "a person's connexions [sic], style of living, &c.," and "right and wrong relate to the right and wrong of caps and hats, dresses and ribbons."[26] Her lack of pierced ears was apparently a cause for concern among the French women she met. She was pressured to get them "bored," and she wrote that not having pierced ears was viewed as "some kind of deformity." She was amused by one woman who advised her "to fasten ear-rings by strings passing over my ears."[27] Although she did not pierce her ears, she did adopt the French style of headwear, a distinctive turban arrangement that she adhered to for the rest of her life.

As fascinating—and often repugnant—as she found customs in France, she had a more important reason for visiting the country than just experiencing French culture. In addition to seeing Lafayette and the sights of Paris, Emma Willard had come to France to see how the French educated girls. She heartily approved of the public funding the French provided for girls' education, and she visited several girls' schools. Among her first stops was a school at St. Denis, established by Napoleon to educate at public expense the daughters of indigent and deceased army officers. (The seminary's new French teacher, Alphise de Courval, whom Emma had recruited in Paris, was an alumna.) Run by nuns, the school enrolled five hundred girls who were housed in two dormitories. She conceded that the French students' "movements [were] more graceful" than those of the seminary pupils but concluded that compared to her girls in Troy "their faces were generally less beautiful."[28]

Everywhere she went, she found that French schools failed to meet the standards she had set in Troy. At Mademoiselle Morin's school, where the students ranged in age from ten to thirteen, the writing classes were inferior. The teachers followed the educational philosophy of Joseph Jacotot (who believed that all people were born with equal intelligence). Emma pronounced the "méthode jacotot" a "fraud"[29] and criticized student essays for relying too much on imagination and not enough on reason. She also found French schoolgirls' penmanship to be inferior to that of her seminary students. At Madame Place's School, she admired "a room fitted up for gymnastics" but did not approve of the "masculine costume . . . for them to wear in performing these feats."[30]

As much as she had enjoyed France, Emma Willard was also eager to see England and Scotland, and on April 22, 1831, she sailed from Calais aboard the steamboat *Lord Melville*. Just as her first view of the coast of France had thrilled her, so, too, did her first glimpse of England. Inspired by the Dover cliffs, she wrote a poem, "Hail Britain." The daughter of Samuel Hart and widow of John Willard, American revolutionary soldiers, penned these lines: "Land of my fathers, hail!/ The vital stream/Within my veins, true to its ancient source,/Warms through my heart, as I approach thy shores."[31]

Once on land, however, her democratic spirit returned. Overhearing an Englishman remark that his country was more civilized than America, she reported tartly to Almira that, "I was tempted to tell him that . . . in our country, the lower classes of women did not call their husbands 'master' as is the case here." Further, she fumed, "We [have] . . . schools for the education of the higher classes of female . . . far superior in their literary and scientific character, to any which exist [in England]."[32]

She had done some research to arrive at the latter conclusion. Maria Edgeworth, perhaps the most famous female Anglo-Irish writer of the period, had given her a list of the six top girls' schools in the country along with a letter of introduction stating that "the bearer is Mrs. Emma Willard, an American who has a celebrated establishment for the education of young people near New York; and who is well known for her literary productions."[33] She visited all six and found fault with each of them. The list has not survived, and she referred to the various school heads anonymously. "Miss A." was "ignorant," completely misunderstood Mrs. Willard's questions about teaching Euclid and made the mistake of telling her American counterpart that she only ran a school because of the money. The fashionable world traveler harrumphed self-righteously, "Though my means are equal to my limited wishes, yet I labor zealously and devotedly from a sense of duty."[34] She found the other schools and their leaders no better and concluded as she had in France that there was no better school for a young woman than the one she had built in Troy. She headed home, going back to Le Havre to board the *Sully*; the return trip took forty-seven days.

Stormy weather on the return trip led her to write the hymn that has lasted longest of all her poetic attempts. "Rocked in the Cradle of the Deep," set to music by Joseph Knight in 1840, became a standard in mid-nineteenth-century America. Echoes of her sister's fatalistic view of life's fragility ring through the stanzas:

> Rock'd in the cradle of the deep,
> I lay me down in peace to sleep.
> Secure, I rest upon the wave,
> For Thou, O Lord, has power to save . . .
> Tho' stormy winds swept o'er the brine;
> Rous'd me from sleep to wreck and death,
> In Ocean cave still safe with Thee,
> The hope of immortality
> > And calm and peaceful is my sleep,
> > Rock'd in the cradle of the deep.

Another inspiration for this hymn may well have come from the news from home. While she was in Europe, Emma learned of the deaths of her mother and favorite niece Mary Treat. As she sailed for home, she knew that at least two cherished members of her family would not be there to greet her.

Although Almira was an accomplished teacher and proved to be an able administrator in her sister's absence, she had not allowed the founder to be forgotten. At the winter examination (February 1831), the students sang a hymn of farewell that included this stanza:

> "*Sisters!* We see a broken band!
> For *she* is in a foreign land,
> Who first, our grateful love might claim,
> Oh, lov'd and honor'd be her name.[35]

In addition, Almira maintained the same curriculum and rules that her sister had established. Student life was strictly regulated. Mary Gordon, a boarder from Chatham, wrote home, "We are not allowed to walk out without a teacher . . . cannot go out shopping but once a fortnight . . . if we wish to call on a friend or go out elsewhere, we must write a request and send it to the teachers."[36] Students were required to dress modestly. Parents who lived far away were limited to a $50 clothing allowance, to be deposited at the school.

As her sister had done, Almira delivered lectures to the students every Saturday, and these lectures, published in 1833 as *Lectures to Young Ladies*, provide a thorough description of the course of study at the seminary and the rationale behind the choices Emma Willard made for the curriculum she offered.

The curriculum was designed to be the end point in a young woman's education, so it was equal in most respects to the curriculum that the brothers and future husbands of seminary girls were receiving at Williams, Amherst, Union, Yale, and Washington College (now Trinity) in Hartford, institutions most often mentioned in letters and biographical entries written by TFS students and alumnae. (They also referred frequently to male relatives at Rensselaer and West Point, but the curricula at these two colleges was uniquely male, both stressing engineering over the liberal arts.) The age of the girls at the seminary corresponded to the ages of boys at these colleges; generally students entered between fourteen and sixteen. West Point set the minimum age limit for cadets at twelve.

The distinct emphasis on Christianity is jarring to modern readers, but the seminary curriculum was no more focused on religion than that of the men's colleges. For example, there was an aversion to mythology because "[it is] absurd to introduce to the young mind the disgusting fables of ancient heathenism."[37]

The predilection for Christian teachings aside, the curriculum was in many respects very modern. Although the *Lectures* focus on academic studies, they also reveal a progressive concern with the benefits of physical education, something Emma had stressed in her original plan. Walks to the summit of Mount Ida, a hill to the east of the city, dancing, calisthenics, and horseback riding were all encouraged. Girls' seminaries were often criticized for creating sickly young women who devoted too much time to their studies. In fact, a conundrum for Troy was created by the death of Lucretia Davidson, a widely published poet who had died in 1825 shortly after studying at the school. On the one hand, she was described as brilliant and talented—a credit to her education. On the other hand, most accounts of her life described her studies as the reason for her untimely death. (That her mother had already buried seven of her nine children and would lose the ninth a few years after Lucretia's death indicates a family weakness, not a schooling issue, but the image of the wan Miss Davidson, done in by the severity of her studies, persisted.) So it is not surprising that the girls were admonished to exercise regularly and that Almira cautioned, "[M]any of you appear to engage in these exercises with reluctance, as if every moment taken from your studies were time lost."[38]

Foreign languages were another topic. French was the language of choice but needed native speakers if it was to be taught properly; consequently French teachers had to be paid more, and students had to pay extra for French lessons. (Spanish and Italian, in contrast, according to Emma, could be taught well by trained English speakers.) The rationale behind teaching French was that it was more widely spoken than any other language in the world and is "a medium of communication common to the polite, as is Latin to the learned."[39] Emma Willard had taught herself French prior to going to Europe, and she took daily lessons in the language while she was in Paris.

One of her goals while abroad was to recruit a new French teacher for the seminary. She hired Alphise de Courval, who would teach in Troy until her marriage in 1836. Having a native speaker on the faculty was a coup. At least one student switched to TFS to study with Mademoiselle Courval. She was unhappy that her current school could not "afford to hire a French lady," and pointed out that "Mrs. Willard's French teacher is a lady from Paris."[40]

Geography had long been a focus of academy studies for boys. Girls' seminaries brought a new emphasis on history as an accompaniment to geography. Emma's *History of the United States* and the geography texts she penned with William Woodbridge both emphasized the connection between history and geography, the use of visual aids to help students learn, and the necessity of starting with local history or geography to capture students' imagination. Perhaps most radical, however, was her insistence that the study of history at the seminary should focus on "women [and] their influence considered among all people and in all ages. Collect the facts, observations, anecdotes, portraits of characters; in short anything which has had an influence and still has a bearing upon the condition of females."[41]

As it had since the Middlebury days, mathematics claimed a central place in the curriculum. As a minimum, "[for] those who desire a thorough education a knowledge of algebra must therefore be deemed important."[42] Far from seeing mathematics as irrelevant for a woman's education, Emma and Almira viewed women as needing mathematics even more than men because women often "neglect the regulation of the judgment." The female tendency toward unregulated thinking and reliance on feelings could be solved by the "study of maths" that would provide a "most direct way of controlling the imagination, perfecting reason and judgment and inducing a habit of method and love of order."[43]

Scientific study was important for many of the same reasons. Almira championed natural philosophy (physics), chemistry, and biology. Imagine two young people on a ship, she told the girls. The girl will be thinking about her friends at home, and the boy will examine "the construction of the ship . . . its size, the velocity with which it moves."[44] Physics teaches the powers of observation, something she believed girls needed to perfect. Chemistry, the science most often taught to girls because its "applications to domestic economy are numerous and important,"[45] has value in its own right. She had studied chemistry privately with both Amos Eaton, the first president of Rensselaer Polytechnic Institute, and Benjamin Silliman, the chair of the first chemistry department at Yale. In her opinion, "There is in chemistry, poetry to satisfy the most extravagant fantasy, and in the sublime truths of the science are mysteries far surpassing the boldest conception of human genius."[46]

Although there is little record of people objecting to girls studying natural philosophy and chemistry, biology was another matter altogether. Here again, the religiously conservative, naturally circumspect Almira shared the more radical views of her sister. Biology must be taught at the seminary. "However startling the idea may be," she told her students, "I cannot but consider some knowledge of the human anatomy as desirable for females."[47]

Unlike other disciplines that focused on young women's usefulness to themselves and their families, English had wider implications. It could be career preparation at a time when writing was increasingly accepted as "offering proper employment for the exertion of female talents."[48] Authors themselves, Emma and Almira heartily approved of women working outside the home as writers; throughout their lives they championed women writers and corresponded with them both in the United States and abroad. *Letters* was, in fact, dedicated to two French writers, Louise Belloc and Adelaide deMontgolfier, whom Almira admired and Emma met in Paris, creating a lifelong friendship among the four.

The study of English was divided into separate classes in rhetoric, grammar, spelling, criticism, and composition. Because novels were allowed sparingly, literature as a separate study was not a great part of the curriculum in the first two decades. Again, however, there was an inherent conflict between what was preached and what was practiced. The publication of Sir Walter Scott's historical novel *Waverley* in 1814 had brought a modicum of respect to novel reading and writing. As more women wrote novels in the 1820s and 1830s, fiction reading became more and more acceptable. Writing, however, was critical all along. Emma was an excellent writer, and she and Almira both valued the "power of writing with ease and elegance."[49] (Reminiscing years after she had left the school, Anna Johnson '44 said of her letters from her principal, "It was . . . like burning a leaf from the Bible to destroy any of them."[50])

A composition a week was de rigueur at TFS, a requirement that was cause for many student complaints and seems to have been more rigorous than that at other girls' schools, where compositions were written every two weeks. By noon each Wednesday each girl had to deposit her composition in a box especially prepared for that purpose. The corrected compositions were returned on Saturday morning. Students met with teachers to review their individual errors and learned whose composition had been chosen to be read before the rest of the student body.

Most girls' schools in the eighteenth and nineteenth centuries taught what they advertised as "ornamental branches," but Emma Willard heartily disapproved of those schools where girls studied nothing but music, drawing, and needlework. She prided herself on a curriculum that taught music and drawing as a means of personal and intellectual growth, not as accomplishments to be shown off in a parlor. Among her faculty, the teachers who taught drawing and music were most often men, and they were highly paid. To offset the expense of hiring music and drawing "professors" (women were referred to as teachers, no matter their discipline), she charged extra for art and music lessons.

Drawing was considered to be one of the most difficult subjects. No rulers or compasses were allowed, and all was drawn free hand. The great masters were copied in detail, and drawing was also taught in conjunction with geography and the construction of maps. Notebooks from the period contain exquisitely detailed maps, charts, and drawings. However, few students did well in this subject because, unlike other material, drawing could not be simply learned but required innate ability. As Almira commented, "In no art or science perhaps is genius more necessary than in drawing."[51] Just as they shared an ability to write well, the two sisters also drew beautifully, Almira illustrating her science textbooks with intricate botanical drawings and Emma augmenting her history and geography texts with charts. Most notable among these was the "Temple of Time," which was awarded a prize at the London World Exhibition in 1851.

Music, like drawing, had much to recommend it as a course of study, but it was not for showing off. As in art, the great masters were the standard. Almira warned against the lyrics in popular songs, and the girls were encouraged to sing and play the songs based on the poetry of Felicia Hemans, which was full of moral platitudes. (Her most famous poem, "Casablanca," evokes the famous image, "The boy stood on the burning deck.") The seminary contained many pianos and at least one harp for students to use. In addition, guitar lessons were offered most terms. Pamelia Archer, a student in the mid-1830s whose father was a congressman from Maryland, wrote to her sister that she was "surrounded" by music—"Harp, Piano and Fiddle on one side. Guitar and Accordion on the other."[52]

Besides offering a visionary curriculum, Emma and Almira shared a very modern view of students and their parents. In comments foreshadowing the supposed genius of the children of Lake Wobegon and the hundreds of gifted and talented programs that sprang up in the late twentieth century, they noted that "parents are often deceived in the character of their children," and they bemoaned the misguided parents who sent them "a child of dull intellect" and claimed she was "a remarkable genius."[53] It was always Emma's chief educational goal to return a student to her parents improved in some way. Her letters to parents often pointed out flaws and, just as often, pointed to the ways in which she had corrected these imperfections.

Perhaps most radical of all their educational thinking, however, was the implication that barriers to women's full participation in American life would and should fall. Seminary girls would be in the vanguard of this movement. It was their responsibility to make a difference. In *Lectures*, Almira directly urged her pupils to "act fearlessly of human censure" if they are "assigned a more public and conspicuous station."[54] In short, she allowed for the distinct possibility that the seminary girls would be using their station on a wider stage than American women currently occupied. At the same time, however, Almira denounced Mary Wollstonecraft and Frances Wright, leading English feminists, as "monsters."[55] Their unorthodox private lives and unconventional views on marriage prevented most educated women from reading their work, let alone sympathizing with their views on gender and racial equality.

So while Emma traveled in Europe, Almira conducted the school along the plan her sister had outlined, at the same time expanding its scope. Although her letters to her sister have not survived, it is probable that she wrote to her about enrollment and finances. The outlook for 1831 revealed a drop in enrollment, perhaps because of the founder's absence. She had hoped to be back in Troy in time for the summer examination, which always garnered good press for the school. Delays meant that she returned on the final day. She resumed the leadership of her school in the fall of 1831. In 1830–31, 230 girls had registered for one or both terms, 108 from Troy. For 1831–32, only 93 girls enrolled from Troy, and 120 students attended overall.

Almira had personal reasons to wish for her sister's return. She had fallen in love with the father of several seminary students. On

August 17, she wed her second husband, John Phelps, at St. John's. Emma stood by her side. Phelps and his first wife, Lucy Lovell, had at least eight children, six of whom attended TFS: Helen '28, Stella '33, Lucy '33, Elizabeth '35, Eunice '38, and Ann Regina '38—and three of whom subsequently taught there. John and Almira had two more children, a boy, Charles, who grew up to fight for the Union and later serve in the House of Representatives, and a girl, Almira Lincoln, who attended the Patapsco Institute, an Episcopal girls' school in Maryland, that her mother ran for many years after leaving Troy.

With Almira no longer a part of her household, Emma threw herself back into the operations of the school. As vice principal in Almira's place, she hired Sarah Lucretia Hudson, a young woman from Waterford who had studied at the school from 1823 to 1825. In addition to Mademoiselle De Courval, she had brought a young girl from France, Pauline de Fontaine, and was rearing her as her ward. Her first year back sped by, and enrollment picked up. For 1832–33, a total of 214 girls registered, 103 from Troy. Emma's secretary, Frances P. Emerson, wrote to a friend in the spring of 1833, "[T]he greatest danger seems to be that there will be too great a number of scholars."[56] The catalog for 1833–34 listed 252 pupils, and 267 girls registered for at least one term in 1835. According to John Lord, the seminary's income exceeded its expenses throughout the 1830s.

Emma Willard's travel in Europe had heightened her concern and interest in two causes, one old and one new. The older cause, of course, was TFS and its role as the standard-bearer for girls' education. Her new cause was the establishment of a school for girls in Athens.

She feared for democracy, particularly in Greece, where Christianity and democracy were struggling to make a comeback after throwing off the autocratic Muslim rule of the Ottoman Empire nearly a decade earlier. She had been interested in this cause since hearing the social reformer Samuel Gridley Howe speak in Troy about the plight of Greek women and children. As the historian Angelo Repousis has noted, "Both Howe and Willard envisioned a Protestant Greece."[57] When she returned from Europe, she was determined to raise money by publishing the letters she had written and the journal she had kept during her months abroad. Money from this and from private donations would fund the new school, which would be managed by the Rev. John Hill and the Rev. John Robinson whose wife was a TFS graduate. Emma enlisted Almira in the cause and reached out to TFS alumnae, asking them to make donations, and she asked her current students for contributions as well. Writing to her brother, student Harriet Russell asked his advice about the size of gift she should give to the "subscription for Greece."[58]

In 1833 Emma asked the Reverend Peck, pastor of St. John's, to read her paper, "In Behalf of Female Education in Greece," to the public. In arguing for education for Greek girls, Emma went further than she had before in espousing women's rights. She wrote, "Justice will yet be done. Women will have her rights. I see it in the course of events."[59] The women of Troy responded. They organized the Society for the Advancement of Female Education in Greece and within a few weeks had collected close to $1,000 as well as clothing, thread, blankets, and other necessities. Students at the seminary were responsible for making many of the garments sent to Greece. Greek societies were formed in New York, Baltimore, New Haven, and other places in the Northeast, most of them headed by former TFS students.

In August, representatives from the various Greek women's societies held a meeting in Troy; Almira was the keynote speaker. Eventually, the Troy Ladies Greek League raised over $3,000 for the cause, proving to be its strongest supporters. The girls' school founded in Athens was locally known as the "Troy School." Although the Greek school movement was taken over by the Episcopal Church after a few years, it owed its early success to Emma Willard. As Repousis has concluded, the cause of Greek girls' education "was national in scope and applied modern techniques of communication, propaganda, and fundraising . . . a public crusade that defied conventional definitions of 'proper' female behavior."[60]

The plan to fund a school in Greece apparently backfired with the TFS trustees, who seemed unwilling to ask the city for more support for the seminary, particularly if Emma had the money to travel abroad and support a school in Athens. In April 1833, the situation came to a head. She wrote and delivered a memorandum to the board in which she threatened to leave the seminary altogether and return to the farm in Vermont that she still owned. Once there, she would devote herself to writing because "the writing of schoolbooks is that business which has afforded me the most profit with the least care and labor."[61] In considering what to do, she leaned toward leaving: "To retire from my present occupation is therefore the course to which my inclination, my own views of my interest, my health, my personal enjoyment and my fame, would decidedly lead me."[62]

However, she concluded that she could not give up the cause of education just for personal comfort. With a characteristic show of ego, she stated, "I have the satisfaction of believing . . . my labours have had a beneficial effect upon the general frame of society."[63]

More specifically, she claimed, "I have kept a good school, which has brought money into Troy . . . and the whole affair has been to the city, I am happy to say, a profitable concern."[64] Nevertheless, she still believed that Troy owed the seminary more in the way of public support; in a side note on the document, she later added, "To build a permanent institution had been my object from the first."[65] She suggested that "Troy has now the lead . . . in respect to female education [but] other places are seeking to rival us, and we must row onward, or the tide will carry us back."[66]

She urged the trustees to go to the city for an enlargement of the school building and money to hire "a professor of chemistry and natural philosophy who is also a good classics scholar." Contrary to rumor, she had "not been growing rich," and she offered to "lay open the whole state of my affairs"[67] to the board. She wanted $3,000 for the enlargement of the physical plant, and she pledged $500 of her own money toward that end. She needed more dormitory rooms, special-purpose classrooms for drawing, music, and writing, a laundry and a dress department, a more suitable lecture room, an expanded drawing room, a separate office for her, a chapel, and a new examination room. She suggested the construction of separate staircases, on the western end for visitors and on the eastern end for students and teachers.

She also promised to pay $500 of the annual $1,000 salary necessary for the science professor, and she pledged $500 to buy the apparatus he would need to teach properly. She argued that she was able to supply twice the teachers that publicly supported boys' academies provided for their pupils because "of the advantages which my personal reputation gives me and [my] prudent management."[68]

The immediate reason for this confrontation was the necessity to renew the lease that the school had with the city. She did not want to renew the lease for the current building but instead wanted the trustees and the city to make the improvements she wanted in return for an increase in the lease to $1,000. Although she assured the trustees that she believed she worked well with them and they with her, "never a jarring word,"[69] she also wanted a clause that allowed her to give six months' notice, a codicil the trustees struck. (In a note on the document written in 1852, she commented that this showed "a want of confidence in me."[70]) Concluding that women conducted business in a style much different from that used by men, she admitted that "heavy business responsibilities" are "the part of my cares most obnoxious to my tastes and wishes."[71]

She negotiated various minor points of the lease, including, apparently, the prospect of her remarriage. (She thought it unlikely she would do so but refused to take "a vow of celibacy."[72]) In the end, she declared the lease a "peculiar instrument," but then, she noted, "If I had not been somewhat of a peculiar woman, I would not have been here at this time negociating [sic] as I am."[73] Educational visionary, hardheaded businesswoman, world traveler, autodidact, textbook author, and able school administrator, for someone of her era and class, Emma Willard was a "peculiar woman" indeed.

It is Time . . . [to] Enlarge Their Sphere

WHEN IT WAS PUBLISHED, Emma Willard's appeal to the public on behalf of girls' education in Greece carried a subtitle that increasingly applied as much to the existing school in Troy as to the proposed school in Athens. According to the frontispiece, the female seminary in Greece was specifically designed to "instruct female teachers."[1] At home in Troy, Mrs. Willard, who had encouraged her students to teach since her days in Middlebury, moved her school more systematically in the direction of intentional teacher training. Shortly after her return from Europe, she wrote to her friend Thomas Twiss that she was now "sending out teachers." Ever the businesswoman, she declared, "[I]t is an article which I now calculate to keep on hand . . . and I have them to suit various situations."[2] In towns, villages, and plantations throughout the nation, people organizing schools for girls wrote to Troy if they wanted the most well-trained female teachers. In 1873 John Lord spoke of reviewing "hundreds of letters"[3] to Emma Willard asking for recommendations of young women to teach in various academies across the country. By 1837 would-be teachers at the seminary were numerous. In a letter to her brothers, Harriet Russell '39, a student from Connecticut, reported, "There are 60 girls in the school that are preparing to be teachers—40 of them board with Mrs. Willard."[4]

In retrospect, it is easy to see the logic in taking this step toward providing a "normal school" education. Since her earliest days in Middlebury, Emma had expected some of her pupils to be teachers; in fact, the teachers in Middlebury, Waterford, and then Troy were disproportionately drawn from the ranks of her students. An early circular for the school in Waterford named Angelica Gilbert and Elizabeth Sherrill as two of the four assistant teachers; they had both studied in Middlebury. When Sherrill first left Middlebury, she had in fact opened a school in Chester, Vermont, advertising that one of its highlights would be the teaching of geography "on a new improved plan by Mrs. Willard,"[5] indicating that at least to Elizabeth Sherrill, the mention of her teacher and mentor already carried significant educational weight as early as 1818. And, as an early biographer pointed out, Emma Willard's own pedagogy had always centered on teaching students to "understand, remember and communicate."[6] Teaching teachers how to teach was simply an elaboration of the third prong of her academic creed: teaching was a form of communicating what they had learned.

Equipping young women for a career that would give them a measure of independence was, to some, a radical idea. As she did so often, Emma Willard anticipated her critics' charges and deflected them by deft manipulation of the argument. In a letter recapping her belief in the suitability of women to become teachers, she claimed, "I do not wish women to act out of their sphere . . . but it is time [to] enlarge their sphere from the walls of their own houses to the limits of the school district." Anticipating her opponents' reference to biblical injunctions, she commented, "St. Paul has said [women] must not speak in churches, but he has nowhere said they must not speak in schoolhouses."[7]

Her trip to Europe and her tour of leading girls' schools in England and France had convinced her that her school was the best. Consequently, if the burgeoning girls' academies were to have the sort of well-trained teachers that she had written about in her *Plan,* then they should come from the seminary. After all, there were very few places where a young woman could study algebra, geometry, and the other "higher" subjects that Mrs. Willard's seminary offered. And even where some of these subjects were available, the methods used to teach them paled in comparison to the pedagogy at the seminary. There was no reason not to draw her faculty from the ranks of seminary alumnae, and there was every reason to populate new schools with Troy-trained faculty. Her own reputation traveled with her newly minted teachers. As one historian has commented, "Emma Willard's signature on a letter of recommendation was the first form of teacher certification in this country."[8] In addition, sending her pupils to teach elsewhere worked as a form of recruitment. Writing cheerfully to Mary Ann Hadley '37, she commented, "If you have an opportunity to send on any scholars, do not forget the Old Hive."[9]

Mrs. Willard did not limit herself to recommending her pupils as teachers. She also actively advised them on the negotiation of salary. Offered a job in Cortland, New York, Sarah Dutton turned to her principal for advice. Emma replied, "If Mr. Brewster [the head of the Cortland Female Seminary] offers you $200 per annum, I think you had better accept . . . the position."[10] In another letter, written to a Mr. Whittingham asking for a teacher for St. Luke's, an Episcopal school in Manhattan, she recommended her step-niece Helen Phelps and suggested a salary of $1,000 would be appropriate. This relatively high salary was justified because of Helen's experience ("as to the salaries of teachers, they are, and should be as various as their qualifications") and the location of the school in New York City ("the expense of living is also an item to be considered").[11] Helen had been teaching in Hamilton, New York, where the cost of living was half that of the city, by Emma's estimate. Emma Willard actively encouraged her students to teach, often as a way of justifying the expense of their education. In a letter to her great-niece Harriet Hart '34, she urged her to teach in order to "turn to profitable account the expenses you incurred while in Troy."[12]

It is not clear from this letter whether or not Emma wanted Harriet to repay her or simply make good use of her education. Over the years she enrolled hundreds of young women who planned to be teachers, allowing them to come to the seminary for free or at a reduced tuition, with the expectation that they would repay their benefactor out of their teaching salaries. According to John Lord, only about 50 percent of these loans were ever repaid.[13] Existing letters indicate that reminding former students of their obligation was necessary. In 1834 Elizabeth Heartt, serving as Emma's secretary, wrote to Sarah Dutton, then teaching in the South, "[S]he presumes you are prepared at this time to remit to her some money."[14] By 1846 John Willard, in charge of the seminary's business affairs, was so concerned about the outstanding debts of former pupils that he told his mother, "'We must send out an agent.'"[15] Nearly sixty, Emma volunteered, eventually traveling 8,000 miles throughout the United States (visiting every state except Florida and Texas). She left Troy in March and went to the South first as "we had to get round through the south and south-west before the unhealthy season."[16] There is ample evidence that she was wined and dined by former students and proprietors of girls' academies wherever she went, but no record of how much of the debt she retired nor how much the trip cost.

Perhaps because of her own experience when Dr. Willard's finances suffered in Vermont, Emma Willard was particularly sensitive to the needs of middle-class and sometimes upper-middle-class girls and young women to have some way to make money, either to support themselves or their families during hard times. Jane Ruth Bigelow, for example, entered the seminary from Cummington, Massachusetts, in 1827. According to her biographical sketch, her father's "financial reverses"[17] led her to consider teaching. Like dozens of girls before and after her, she studied and then worked as an assistant teacher at the seminary, repaying her tuition with her labor. After a few years under Emma's tutelage, she went south to teach, married Seth Storrs, a lawyer originally from Middlebury, Vermont, whose father had been a neighbor of the Willards. Jane and Seth Storrs had five children who lived to adulthood; Jane died in 1856 in Wetumpka, Alabama. She was fifty and a widow. In 1850, according to the census, her husband had owned twelve slaves; with property (apart from the slaves) valued at $3,500, he was prosperous although not in the planter class. In spite of marrying a slave owner, Jane Bigelow Storrs had apparently remained connected to the literary and educational circles of the North. Lydia Sigourney, a popular poet of the time and a fan of both Emma Willard and the education of women, memorialized Jane's death in "The Parting."[18]

Other early graduates followed Jane Bigelow's example, either by remaining at the seminary to teach for a few years, by returning home to start or teach in a local school, or by striking out to new areas of the country, particularly the West and South, where teachers were in high demand. In her analysis of the feminist values underlying Emma Willard's work as a teacher of teachers, Anne Firor Scott chronicled the lives of some of the more famous of these women. Julia Pierpont, who ran the South Carolina Collegiate Institute at Barhamville with her husband, Elias Marks, studied first at Middlebury and then, when her first husband died, entered the Troy school in 1824, remaining for one year. Urania Sheldon'28 ran the Utica Female Academy before becoming the third wife of the famously successful Union College president (and critic of Emma Willard's *Plan*), Eliphalet Nott. Both Julia Pierpont Warne and Urania Sheldon served as assistant teachers during their time at the seminary. Elizabeth Sherrill, when she left the seminary in 1826, after teaching there for several years, went to Georgia to take over Julia Warne's school in Sparta. There she stayed for many years, running a female academy in Georgia with her husband, Thomas Twiss, former West Point mentor of John Willard.

Although these three women have well-chronicled lives, other early students were also embarking on teaching careers after early seminary training, some until marriage, some with their husbands, and some after widowhood or family financial reversals. Not all taught for the money. Maria Bowers '30 came from a long line of successful New England traders; in fact, she lived in Cuba as a small child with her grandfather, Ebenezer Sage, a Jeffersonian Republican member of Congress from 1809 to 1815. Part of a New England expatriate community in and around Havana, she may have developed her lifelong horror of slavery during her time in Cuba. As a contemporary, Mary Gardner Lowell wrote during a visit to the Sage coffee plantation, "Mr. Sage shuts all the blacks out of the house at night . . . [he] has most noisy dogs and they do not suffer a negro to approach the house without giving alarm . . . on this estate they are all very well clothed. Mr. Sage flogs the little ones if he finds them near the house."[19] Perhaps because of her early exposure to slavery, Maria Bowers did not go south to teach. Instead, she taught in Ogdensburg, New York, and Brooklyn. In the latter place she met her husband, Lucius Bisbee, a successful insurance agent, and retired from teaching.

Another affluent graduate who taught locally before marrying, Abby Dean '29, who came to Troy from Cooperstown, founded a female seminary in Springfield, New York, where she worked until her marriage in 1840. She married twice, and in 1860, she personally listed assets of

$35,000 and was the mother of three adopted children, who, from their names and their birthplace—India—were probably orphaned daughters of missionary friends of Abby and her husband, Daniel Winsor.

Like Abby Dean and Maria Bowers, Ellen Farrand '31 presumably taught for reasons other than money. Born in Burlington, she taught in Canada and Massachusetts before marrying her wealthy industrialist husband, Nathaniel Russell. As a married woman, Ellen no longer taught, but she used her education as a volunteer, serving as the corresponding secretary and a manager (a position similar to that of a trustee) of the New York Colored Home in Manhattan. Elizabeth Riker '24 was another New Yorker who had no financial reasons for pursuing a career. Her father, Richard, was a successful attorney and served as Recorder of the City of New York during his daughters' time in Troy (Elizabeth had a sister, Anne '24). Her mother, Janette Phoenix Riker, was an acclaimed New York hostess. Nevertheless, Elizabeth taught for fourteen years before marrying Edward Spring, whose brother had married her sister and whose father, Gardiner Spring, was the widely known minister of Manhattan's socially prestigious Old Brick Church. Finally, Sarah Hooker '30, whose younger brother, Joseph, pursued the military training at West Point that would culminate in his service to the Union as a general during the Civil War, taught at a girls' seminary in Watertown, New York, before marrying Presbyterian minister M.L.R.P. Thompson. Nicknamed the "Reverend Alphabet," Thompson supported the cause of female education and was credited by his Buffalo parishioners for spearheading the development of a girls' academy there.

Other middle-class and upper-middle-class young women also chose to teach, perhaps for adventure, perhaps for independence, perhaps to widen their marriage prospects and sometimes for something to do when they were widowed early. Eliza Hollister, a Middlebury student, taught in Chittenden County, Vermont, and then in Brome, Quebec, where she met her husband. Anna Treadwell, also a Middlebury student and the niece of the president of Middlebury who had refused to let Emma audit mathematics classes, taught at Onondaga Academy until she married Lewis Redfield, a prosperous Syracuse businessman. Lydia Ely Gardner '24, like Julia Pierpont Warne, came to the school after being widowed. (Poor John Gardner, traveling with his new bride from her parents' home in the Berkshires to their honeymoon in Niagara Falls, made it only as far as Albany, where he died.) Lydia taught for a few years after her time at the school before marrying a second time to prominent Watervliet farmer Martin Van Der Warker.

From the earliest days, there was also another source of teachers at the seminary—relatives of Emma Willard. Given her numerous brothers and sisters and the wide range in their age, the close ties she maintained with her mother's many Hinsdale relatives and the many Willards, it is not surprising that she had a pool of young relatives to tap as students and then teachers. It is a testimony to her extended family's faith in her ability—or possibly, their faith in her ability to make money—that so many of her relatives sent their daughters to Troy. It is also extraordinary how many of them stayed on at the seminary. (The men of the family were also drawn to the place. By 1825 William Lee, a nephew, was teaching there, and he became the business manager in the 1830s. Dr. Willard's namesake and nephew, John D. Willard, settled in Troy and served as the school attorney and a trustee. Her great-nephew, William Hart, also worked at the school in a business capacity in the 1830s before becoming a banker in Troy.)

Although Emma allowed some of her relatives to attend the seminary for free (her niece Mary, for example, whose mother Lydia had died), it is clear from a letter sent to his father by William that not all relatives got a free education. William, in fact, took the job at the seminary temporarily, to help pay his sister's tuition. Sarah '36, had gone south to teach after leaving the seminary, so presumably, she, too, was helping repay the cost of her education. In a letter written three years after Sarah left the seminary, William wrote to his father, "I have an account open with Cousin John."[20] William must have believed in the value of the education he was helping to pay for; his older daughter, Helen, attended the school in the 1860s, and he named a second daughter—who did not survive infancy—Emma.

Her nieces Elizabeth Hart '25, Mary Treat '26, and Jane Lincoln '28 taught in Troy during the first decade, as did Dr. Willard's niece, Mary Willard '23. All of these young women were listed as both students and teachers during part of their time. Early catalogs publicized this arrangement, listing the names of the assistant teachers, whose names could also be found on the student lists for the year. In 1825 two on the list of five assistants were the principal's nieces.

Other family connections included her cousin, Nancy Hinsdale, who served as vice principal for many years and who had run her own female seminary in Pittsfield, Massachusetts. Nancy's niece, Ann Emmons '31, would return to Troy when her first husband, the head of a grammar school in Princeton, died. She served as secretary to Sarah Willard in the 1840s before marrying a local businessman and eventually moving to Oakland, California. And, of course, the early school had two teachers who would become relatives. Sarah Lucretia and Theodosia Hudson had been pupils in Waterford and transferred with the school to Troy. Upon finishing their studies in 1825, both sisters became teachers. Sarah stayed on at the seminary, and Theodosia returned as a teacher in 1834, remaining until 1872. Sarah, of course, married John Willard. Theodosia never married but remained a member of the Willard household until her death in 1887. She is buried in the family plot in Oakwood.

Some of Emma Willard's relatives and many of her other northern pupils had no compunctions about associating with slave owners. Teaching opportunities abounded in the South. Mary Willard taught in Savannah, Georgia, and was joined there by Ophelia Mead '29, a native of Connecticut. Arabella Pearson '29 also taught in Georgia, where she met her husband, slave owner George B. Walker. Unlike most of the schoolteachers who went South, Arabella grew up there, a native of Alabama. Araminta Rice '26, born in Troy, married twice, both times wedding southerners. She taught in South Carolina with Julia Marks and lived until 1893, dying in New Orleans. Girls' education in New Orleans received a boost of another sort when Cynthia McGehee '29 died in 1835, shortly after her marriage to John Walton. McGehee's father and husband took her $30,000 dowry and used it to establish McGehee Seminary. In 1834 a Nashville paper announced the new term at Dr. Weller's Female Seminary, noting he "expects to be assisted by a highly recommended teacher from the celebrated school of Mrs. Willard in Troy."[21]

In the decades leading up to the Civil War, the number of young women going south from Troy remained steady. In 1840 a record number of fifty-four students were reported to the Regents as going from the seminary to teach; thirty-three went south. As late as 1860, the South claimed the majority of the novice teachers, with ten of the seventeen that year heading toward the Confederacy.[22] Some of the students who went south went to teach at established seminaries, but many taught on plantations, where girls lived far from the nearest school. Their brothers, after tutoring, often traveled north or to England for higher education. Some girls made the arduous trip to Troy or later, Farmington, Connecticut, but it was more common for the graduates of the seminary to carry instruction south. Emma Willard encouraged this. Writing to the uncle who was financing her education, Jane Burritt '39, from Vergennes, Vermont, reported, "I requested Mrs. Willard the other day to obtain me a situation as a teacher. She said she thought she would send me to Virginia or further south if I wished."[23] Reflecting in 1833 on a number of her students who were teaching in the South, Emma wrote, "All who go south seem happy."[24] In the middle of the nullification crisis of the early 1830s—the first serious southern threat to the continuation of the republic she held so dear—Emma Willard maintained that sending students to the South was "the way to unite the north and the south and do away [with] nullification and other southern heresies."[25] Never one to minimize her own role in history, she concluded, "I expect to be reckoned a great benefactor to my country for the part I have in thus promoting union."[26]

Emma Willard's increasing focus on educating teachers coincided with a similar movement throughout the Northeast. At least one contemporary admirer described her as "the apostle of the normal school,"[27] and she was certainly among the first to push for teaching as a profession for women. Her allies in this fight included Horace Mann, Thomas Gallaudet, and Catharine Beecher, who were all advocating teacher training for women by the 1830s. Their rationale was two tiered: first, there had rarely been any effort to teach either men or women how to teach, and Mann and Gallaudet, in particular, wanted to professionalize teaching. Too often teachers in local common schools were young men who were earning some money to enable them to go to college to study for the ministry or waiting for the opportunity to read law or apprentice to a doctor. The dominant pedagogical mode was rote memorization, and corporal punishment was the standard inducement to learning.

Reaction against this conventional pedagogy had been sparked by the publication of Johann Heinrich Pestalozzi's books on education. The Swiss educator and idealist, like Emma Willard, did not believe in either rote instruction or physical discipline. The methods he prescribed, in spite of their focus on elementary education, bore a great deal of resemblance to those advocated by Emma Willard and her sister Almira in their textbook instructions to teachers, including hands-on work, particularly in geography and science. Pestalozzi's model teacher was often a woman, as in his famous educational treatise, *Gertrude and Leonard.* Although Emma Willard was undoubtedly familiar with his work, she never called herself a Pestalozzian. In all likelihood, she viewed herself as his equal in teaching mastery. Her use of maps in her geography and history textbooks, which had already earned her great critical acclaim and significant revenue by the 1830s, aligned with Pestalozzi's view that visual displays of information helped children learn. As a recent geographer has written, "Willard believed that information presented *spatially* and *visually* would facilitate memory."[28] Had Pestalozzi been alive in the 1830s, she might have expected him to style himself a Willardian.

By the 1830s, the expansion of the nation meant there were hundreds of thousands of school-aged children who had no access to any teacher. In New York alone, the number of schoolchildren grew from 176,449 in 1816 to 508,848 in 1833.[29] In addition, the removal of the frontier farther and farther from the seat of national government posed a threat to the survival of the republic. Training women teachers was the answer to the shortage and key to continuing the development of an enlightened citizenry. As the reformers, including Beecher, considered the best way to bring more trained teachers into the fold, they looked first to the few strong female seminaries, which were recognized as having sent out many graduates as successful teachers. Troy was on every list. Invited by the American Lyceum to expound on the subject of female teachers, Catherine Beecher responded with "An Essay on the Education of Female Teachers." Miss Beecher asserted that new teacher training schools should be endowed by state legislatures. A reviewer who wished the enterprise of female teachers "Godspeed" praised Beecher's efforts and concluded that any schools to train female teachers should "repeat and extend, and render permanent, those efforts for preparing female teachers, which have been so successfully made at the seminaries in Ipswich, Hartford and Troy."[30]

Some years after leaving Hartford Female Seminary, Catharine Beecher revisited the issue and provided the solution in *True Remedy*, her treatise on women's rights: "But where are we to raise such an army of teachers as are required for this great work? Not from the sex which finds it so much more honorable, easy, and lucrative, to enter the many roads to wealth and honor open in this land. But few will turn from these to the humble, unhonored toils of the schoolroom and its penurious reward. It is WOMAN who is to come at this emergency, and meet the demand."[31] For several years before the publication of *True Remedy*, Beecher traveled throughout the country, recruiting teachers for common schools in the West. Writing to her mother-in-law who was away from Troy, Sarah Willard commented, "Catharine Beecher has recently lectured by proxy (her brother read the lecture) to the ladies of Troy on the subject of locating teachers in the Western States." Sarah had presumably attended the talk as she concluded the letter by saying that Beecher sent her "remembrance" to Emma.[32]

Both Vermont and Massachusetts lay claim to having had the first specific programs for teaching teachers; Samuel Reed Hall had taught male teachers at his Model School in Concord, Vermont, as early as 1822, and Massachusetts is widely credited with the establishment of the first school dedicated exclusively to the training of teachers. Established in Lexington in 1839, this normal school enrolled only women. The state legislature in New York in the 1830s initially chose to support teacher training in a number of ways short of establishing a separate school—and the Troy Female Seminary was finally the recipient of some public money as a result. In 1832, recognizing that a more systematic method of training teachers was needed, the legislature distributed a copy of Samuel Hall's *Lectures on School Keeping* to each of the state's school districts. Addressed to a male audience, the book, first published in 1829, championed the superior methods of Prussian education (strongly influenced by Pestalozzi), but it was not strictly Pestalozzian in its pedagogical suggestions. In the section recommending textbooks, Hall suggested the use of Almira Phelps's recently published botany book but chose to highlight Jedidiah Morse's geography text, not Emma Willard's.

In 1838 New York went further. The legislature voted to subsidize the training of teachers in existing seminaries and academies by requiring those institutions to train teachers in return for state aid. As early as 1828, DeWitt Clinton, champion of female education, had publicly suggested that academies were the place to train teachers. In 1834 New York had "provided a definite system of academic and professional education for teachers in elementary schools,"[33] and now the state was moving into the realm of secondary teacher preparation to meet the needs of the state's burgeoning common school population. The Troy Female Seminary was officially incorporated by the state in 1838, making it eligible for subsidies for pupils preparing to become teachers. Beginning in 1839, in compliance with the state requirement, the school filed annual reports with the Regents.

The report for 1839 listed income from a state appropriation as $395.25. Forty-three young women had been "sent out" as teachers, one each to Pennsylvania, Kentucky, Indiana, and Ohio, two to Maryland, three apiece to North and South Carolina, four to Alabama, eight each to Georgia and Virginia, and eleven to New York. There were 377 girls enrolled at some point during the year, of whom 296 met the Regents requirements for length of attendance.[34] The oldest student, Mary Ketchum, was thirty-three and local. In all likelihood, she was training to be a teacher. A visitor to the school in 1836 had written a very flattering account of his visit to the school when he returned home to Charleston, reserving special praise for "ladies over twenty years of age being educated for teachers."[35]

By 1839 the physical school had grown. The grounds were 50 feet wide and 109 feet deep. Jane Lincoln, a favorite niece and occasional secretary for Emma Willard, wrote to an alumna on her aunt's behalf in 1833, "The Seminary is much altered since you were here. . . . It has been extended as far back as the alley, the roof has been taken off, and a fourth story has been added. There is a balustrade around the roof and a very handsome cornice below which gives the Seminary a very respectable appearance."[36] This expansion had added a fourth floor to the main building, which was now five stories high, including the cellar. This building, the original coffeehouse, continued to be rented from Troy for $1,100 a year. A three-story brick building that had been erected on the seminary grounds in 1828 at a cost of $3,000 contained three laundry rooms, three storage rooms, and "a large oil painting studio" on the first floor, music rooms and bedrooms on the second floor, a studio for drawing and watercolors, a large room for dressmaking and seven rooms used for music, and bedrooms on the third floor. Emma Willard had moved out of the main building to a separate residence on Second Street.

A separate frame building housed the instructor in natural philosophy and chemistry; he had his apartment on the first floor and his classrooms on the second floor. A listing of scientific equipment housed in the chemistry and physics classrooms included a magic lantern with moving slides, a compound microscope, an electricity machine, an iron retort, eight ivory bells and such chemicals as ether, mercury, muriatic acid, red lead, glauber salts, and arsenic.

The youngest pupil in the 1839 report, Mary Cranson, was eight, but she did not sign the official school register, so her hometown is unknown, but given her age, it is likely that she came from Troy. According to Regents reports filed from 1839 to 1872, the youngest students, almost without exception, were Troy girls. There was a practical reason for Troy families to enroll their girls early. Beginning with the 1832–33 school year, the catalogs stated, "Mrs. Willard, entertaining the opinion that the study of language is particularly suitable for children, informs the citizens of Troy who enter their daughters young, and keep them long at the Seminary, that they shall receive a deduction on the price of instruction in French."[37]

In 1839 there were eighteen faculty members, including Sarah Willard, who had assumed the role of principal in 1838. At $2,000 per year,[38] she was the most highly paid employee; Laura Simmons '39, one of the seven Willard relatives on the staff, was paid the least: $300. There were five men on the faculty and ten alumnae. Only one of the men was reported to have received a college degree; Joseph Fellows, Dartmouth graduate, was a veteran teacher of fifteen years who taught Latin, chemistry, and natural philosophy.

The boarding tuition was $240 per year, which had been the tuition since 1835 when Emma Willard raised it for the first time since 1825. She wrote to her patrons in 1835 that "the expenses of living have increased . . . throughout the country, as well as in Troy."[39] She referred to the "late rise in the price of provisions,"[40] probably a harbinger of the inflationary cycle that would lead to the Panic of 1837. She took the opportunity in her announcement of the tuition increase to make yet another plea for public support, writing,

> If with the Principal of the institution, the friends of female education regret that thorough instruction must be too expensive for all to partake who desire it, then let these friends awake to the importance of the measure, for which she petitioned the legislature in 1818, and has repeatedly brought before them since—that the public should show a little munificence to our sex, where they have so much to the other; and found and endow institutions, where public buildings being provided, and a part of the cost of teaching defrayed, the individuals educated need not be taxed with the whole expense.[41]

The 1835 tuition would be reduced in 1841 to $200, where it would remain until 1854, although beginning in 1846, parents were offered a comprehensive fee of $300, which included as many of the special areas of the curriculum as their daughters wished to take. This simplification of pricing must have been a boon to parents as well as to the seminary's business officer who at times was John Willard (a man who had failed arithmetic as a boy at West Point).

In 1839 seven students were "educated for free." These were, according to the report, "mostly daughters of Clergymen of this City, who are always instructed gratuitously in the English branches of education." Another one hundred received partial credit. They were "young ladies who are desirous of preparing themselves for teachers, but are unable to meet the necessary expense of such preparation." That these young women were expected to pay this money back is implied by the statement that "$4,394.78 is due from young ladies who receive their education on credit." The school was debt free and showed total revenues for the year (including donations of $250 and interest of the same amount) at $9,322.31. The lot on which the school stood had been owned by the city of Troy but in 1837 was given "in perpetuity" to the trustees of the seminary. With expenses totaling $7900.00, the profit for the year was $1,422.31. Faculty salaries at $7,000 accounted for the greatest percentage of the expenses, with fuel second. Listed at $500 in the report, this was an estimate carrying the explanation that because of the boarding department, "it is impossible to give a precise amount for this item."[42] (John Willard was no Ian Smith.)

In 1839, as had been the case for over a decade, the curriculum was divided into two departments. Emma Willard—and later, Sarah Willard—took very seriously the "classification"[43] of students and was concerned that they be placed at the appropriate level of study. Students in the first department learned English grammar, reading, arithmetic, the rudiments of geometry, geography for beginners, and geology. In the second department, students could choose among the higher English branches, French, Latin, Italian, drawing, and music. In addition, courses were provided in algebra, astronomy, botany, chemistry, criticism, elocution, history, hydrostatics, logic, orthography, optics, philosophy, rhetoric, painting, trigonometry, Spanish, and scriptures. Some studies—all of the modern languages, Latin, dancing, all visual arts courses, and all music instruction—carried extra fees ranging from $4 per term (Latin) to $20 per term (harp). Weekly compositions, the bane of many students' existence, as mentioned earlier, were due at noon on Wednesday and returned Saturday morning with corrections. One composition each week was read at a Wednesday afternoon meeting of the entire student body and faculty; from these, a few of the best of the best were chosen to be read at the end-of-term examination.

Emma Willard always prided herself on having a greater number of teachers than other schools. In explaining the need for higher tuition, she outlined the courses taught and the number of sections offered in each subject. Each section "recite[d] daily." French had the most sections (nine) with writing a close second (eight). Ten teachers were assigned to correcting the weekly compositions, which were particularly onerous for students. Emma herself believed that "writing compositions . . . is a task much dreaded by all young ladies in any school."[44]

There were five sections of geography and arithmetic, four in history, three in spelling and grammar, two in Latin, geometry, and astronomy, and one each in sixteen other subjects ranging from chemistry, botany, and geology to rhetoric, logic, and the science of music. That not all students took a full load of courses was clear from the reports to the Regents. In these documents, students were listed by name and curricular accomplishment. In 1839, for example, Mary Bigelow, a thirteen-year-old from Troy, learned grammar, translated French history into English, covered sixty pages of Bolmar's *Phrases*, studied Davies's *Arithmetic*, Latin grammar, and finished Jacobs's *Latin Reader*—and that was just her work for the fall term.

The texts she studied were dense and inaccessible, in comparison with today's brightly illustrated books. The full title of the text by Bolmar, for example, was *A Collection of Phrases on Every Topic Necessary to Maintain Conversation: Arranged Under Different Heads; With Numerous Remarks on the Peculiar Pronunciation and Use of Various Words. The Whole So Disposed as Considerably to Facilitate the Acquisition of a Correct Pronunciation of the French.* By working through the first sixty pages during the fall semester, Mary would have learned the uses of *avoir* and *être,* the seasons, the days, common phrases, and vocabulary pertaining to greetings, school, dress, and weather.

Her Latin text was written by a German, Frederic Jacobs, the author of numerous classical texts. By the middle of the eighteenth century, the relevance of the study of Latin was already being questioned. Jacobs, whose livelihood no doubt depended on the continuation of Greek and Latin in the common schools and academies, disdainfully remarked in 1850, "The young are not called upon to learn all that may by possibility be useful at some future period, for if so, as Aristotle facetiously remarks, we should have to descend to learning cookery."[45] In spite of her love for the classics, Emma Willard shrewdly did not dismiss cooking. As Sarah Hale reported, perhaps to ease the minds of skeptical fathers,

"One woman has charge of the bakery, and to her tuition a certain number . . . of the young ladies are consigned, in rotation, every Saturday afternoon. Here they are initiated in the mysteries of pastry and cake-making; and many hints of useful knowledge they doubtless obtain."[46]

Mrs. Hale also praised the seminary for teaching "home-loving sentiments," by which she meant domestic arts. According to her, "Every two pupils have an apartment together, and it is their duty to keep this in order."[47] Writing with Yankee disdain, she went on, "Many of these young ladies are from the rich families of the South, and never, till they entered this school, had their lily hands been laid on the broom and duster; but they soon appear to enjoy these new duties."[48] At least one student from North Carolina corroborated this view, writing to her mother, "I have got to be so much of a housekeeper since I got here that I calculate to make up my own bed & clean my own room when I get home."[49] Room assignments were handled by the principal, and teachers lived among the students. Jane Burritt reported to her uncle that her roommate was "my French teacher from Paris." Rooming with a teacher was not a burden, however, as she "is complete French, full of mischief."[50]

The arithmetic book that Mary and many of her schoolmates used was written by a future seminary father who was a professor of mathematics at West Point. *The Common School Arithmetic*, by Charles Davies, introduced many terms that today's students need not know. Gills, shillings, pounds, 8cwt, and 4cwt peppered the problems along with acres, dollars, tons, and other modern measurements. Take this problem, for example: "A printer uses one sheet of paper for every 16 pages of an octavo book: how much paper will be necessary to print 500 copies of a book containing 336 pages, allowing 2 quires of waste paper in each ream?"[51] If Mary figured the problem correctly, her answer was 24 reams, 5 quires, 12 sheets (and a partridge in a pear tree).

In contrast to Mary's schedule, Abby Coons's curriculum was simple. A thirty-year-old student, also from Troy, she spent the fall semester studying composition, piano, and guitar. Except for her registration for the school years 1839 to 1842, there is no other record of her; she might have been studying to teach music or she might have been an unmarried woman or widow attempting to improve herself. Mary, who stayed at the seminary from 1838 until 1844, was a typical day student, enrolling for "the full English course."[52] It would appear that students had a great deal of latitude in selecting their studies. Abby Champion '39 chose to concentrate solely on oil painting during the fall of 1838 while Charlotte Combs focused on science, electing astronomy, optics, and hydrostatics for the spring semester. As a "senior" that year, she also took moral philosophy. Writing to her mother, Sarah Crocker '37 reported that she had been looking over the course catalog, was interested in taking dancing as a form of weight loss (she described growing fat the previous winter term because she "went months without going out except to church") and asked her mother to tell her "the extra studies you wish me to take."[53]

A slight modification to the dress code was introduced in the catalog for 1837–38. Earlier in the decade, "distant parents" were allowed to provide an amount not "exceeding $50 per term"[54] for clothing. Now parents were instructed to provide their daughters with dresses made of "some inexpensive material . . . in plain style."[55] As for church attendance, parents were requested to select the church they wished their daughters to attend. Of course, Emma was willing to help: "where no church is specified, the pupils will be taken under the special care of the Principal."[56] Dress, manners, and morals were topics of biweekly lectures, delivered on Wednesday and Saturday afternoons. Parents were advised that these lectures were delivered by the principal. From student letters, it appears that these lectures were popular. Mary Elizabeth Williams wrote to her mother in North Carolina that the "book learning" in Troy was adequate, but that she learned "more from [Mrs. Willard's Saturday lectures] than I do all the rest of the week."[57] Among the subjects over the years was the topic of novel reading. Emma, her sister Almira, and then her daughter-in-law, Sarah Lucretia, cautioned the young women in their charge against sensational literature. Although many novels fell in this category, not all fiction was discouraged. Among the nearly two hundred titles held in the seminary library in 1839 were listed *Ivanhoe, Robinson Crusoe,* and the French romance *Paul et Virginie.* In general, the holdings of the library were eclectic, ranging from biographies of Lord Byron, George Washington, Isaac Newton, Oliver Cromwell, and "Mohamet" (Josephine Bonaparte and

Mary, Queen of Scots were the only women whose lives were featured) to books on etiquette, phrenology, and myths.

The public examinations, which had begun in Waterford if not Middlebury, continued to be a major focus of school life. Lasting between six and eight days, they were occasions, reported on in newspapers, attended by parents and local dignitaries, and dreaded by many pupils and some teachers. Mary Huntington '33 wrote her mother that "Mademoiselle deCorval dreads it as much as the scholars, I suspect."[58] Sarah Hale, having attended an examination at which her daughter, Frances '36, probably recited, presented a detailed, although anonymous, account of the exercises in *American Ladies' Magazine*:

> [T]he Examination Hall . . . is spacious and convenient, being about forty feet in length and thirty in width. It is entered by folding-doors from the east, and the young ladies are ranged along the west side, on seats rising above each other . . . In the centre of the room is a long low table . . . behind this, on the lowest seat of the range, sit the class to be examined, the table answering the purpose of a rest for the black boards to be exhibited, of which, in many of the classes, each pupil has one. Immediately in front of the table sits the Principal, with a teacher beside her (each teacher examines the class she has taught), and behind, on each side of the entrance, rows of seats, similar to those for the pupils, are arranged for the spectators. At the left, or south end of the Hall, the music is placed; here on a raised platform is a piano, harp, guitar, &c., arranged in a manner which affords the best facilities to the performers and audience. . . . The examinations are so managed, that every class is heard through the whole studies pursued during the term, different portions being assigned for different days. Between the recitations of each class there is music, on the piano or harp. . . . A composition, from some one of the young ladies, is occasionally read, to vary the proceedings. . . . It has been mentioned, that a long low table is placed before the pupils; here those who are reciting stand, as being more respectful to the visitors. Sometimes the whole class are requested by their teacher, to rise together, and a quick succession of questions is given, requiring short answers; but usually, two stand . . . together, as less embarrassing to the young ladies, the first having recited sits down, and another rises, and so on. In the recitation of Algebra, each young lady comes with a black board (about two feet square); one is directed to exhibit the Algebraic signs, another to give examples in addition, another in

subtraction, &c. Thus, every young lady in the class is busy, as well as the one reciting. They are frequently directed, after making out their own examples to change their boards, that others may explain the operation, thus making one process test the knowledge of two pupils. The table before them is so low, that a young lady of ordinary height can look over her board as she rests it, thus avoiding the awkwardness of posture incident to exhibiting on large black boards, fixed against the wall.[59]

The examinations were a frequent topic in student letters. In 1834 after her examination, Sarah Crocker wrote to a friend that she had made no mistakes ("I did not miss through the whole"), but that "the girls said I was very pale." She contrasted her pallor with the skin tones of a classmate, Miss Clark, who, when examined in algebra and moral philosophy, "did not turn pale like me, but blushed." All in all, she concluded, "It is not such a dreadful thing to be examined, as I thought it was; for they do not ask but a few questions."[60] The review for Sarah Crocker—and presumably for others—was the most difficult part. Every textbook had to be reviewed thoroughly for "we do not know what question will come to us." Virginia Anderson '37 reported in a letter home, "It is so near examination that I have not a minute to breathe, scarcely."[61] Similarly, Mary Elizabeth Williams broke off a letter to her uncle, claiming, "I am to be examined twice this afternoon and cannot write further."[62] Chloe Cole reported triumphantly to her cousin, "Our Examination is finished, and I am still alive."[63] Ann Phelps '38 apparently took exams in stride, but she mentioned in a letter to her father that "Mother visited for the exam."[64] ("Mother" was stepmother Almira Phelps, who may well have served on the examining committee.)

The examinations apparently attracted students from other schools, some of whom decided to switch. Thus Jane Burritt, a student at "Mrs. Richards' school," after watching an examination, to which she had traveled through the Troy streets in "dreadful snow . . . 12 to 20 feet deep,"[65] wrote her uncle in February that she wanted to change schools. By April she was ensconced at the seminary, happy because she was being instructed in French by "a lady from Paris," a luxury she had not experienced before because "Mrs. Richards cannot afford to hire a French lady."[66] Mrs. Richards apparently did not have the literary standards of

Mrs. Willard. Jane regretted having bought a subscription to "the Knick-erbocker." Under Mrs. Willard's tutelage, she now realized it was "too light."[67] (Washington Irving, James Fenimore Cooper, William Cullen Bryant, and a host of other famous writers of the nineteenth century contributed to this literary magazine.) In a timeless student concern, her only worry at her new school was whether or not she would make friends. (In May, however, she reported that she had formed "a fantasti-cal acquaintance"[68] with some of her new classmates.)

Beginning in 1850 the school catalog carried a report of the examin-ing committee from the prior year. It was important to Emma Willard that people of note attend as examiners and observers. In 1837 she wrote to Alonzo Paige, judge from Schenectady and member of the state as-sembly, "Can you not be spared from your high legislative functions to spend a little time observing how the <u>young</u> ideas shoot?"[69] (Paige was married to a seminary graduate and would send three daughters to the school in the 1850s.) Emma wrote often to Lydia Sigourney importun-ing her to be on the committee; although it is not clear whether or not she ever served in this capacity, she did visit the seminary and became a good friend and frequent correspondent of Emma Willard.

The first published report showed a committee composed of three women and five men. Samuel and Sarah Greeley were from Boston, Sarah Peter was from Philadelphia, and Sarah Gould from Rochester. There were four clergymen on the committee, one from Troy, and the others from Boston, Poughkeepsie, and Rochester. The last, Henry Lee, an Episcopalian born in Connecticut, may well have been a relative of Emma Willard's. Sarah Peter was the older sister of the Worthington girls who had attended the school in the 1820s, and by lineage and marriage, she carried significant social cachet. Two of the clergymen, Robbins and Bullions, were probably current parents. According to their report, the examiners rearranged the pupils randomly for the examination, ensuring that all had to be well versed in each of the sub-jects they had studied; this method made it "impossible for any of the pupils to know beforehand on what part they were to be examined."[70]

As the decade drew to a close, then, the school was in good shape and appeared to have a distinctive educational focus. The years between Emma Willard's return from Europe and the filing of the first Regents report were years in which the school attained national recognition. It was a decade in which the United States weathered the first significant constitutional crisis over states' rights, shuddered from the emotional upheaval created by both religious revivalism and reformist impulses, and suffered a significant economic downturn. In the middle of the decade, the school experienced physical change, and at the end of the decade, the seminary lost its founder to marriage, a change that in other female seminaries had often sounded the death knell of the institution. Sheltered as they were, the pupils of the seminary were aware of the prestige of their school and commented on it frequently in letters home. The geographic and religious diversity of their school community set it apart from other schools, and together with their advanced curriculum prepared them better than most young women to face the challenges of the midcentury.

Who Proved the Truth
of Her Mother-in-Law's Creed

AT LEAST ONE VISITOR TO Emma Willard's school worried, "How is the system of the Troy Female Seminary to be perpetuated, when the intelligent head that now presides there is withdrawn?"[1] Given the pattern at other girls' schools, it was logical to think that the seminary might not outlive its founder. Litchfield had closed shortly after Sarah Pierce's death; Hartford would shut its doors within twenty years of Beecher's departure, and its national reputation faded after she left. Most seminaries, as did Emma Willard's, operated as for-profit businesses. When the proprietor left because of marriage, illness, death, dearth of customers, or lack of interest, the school most often closed. There was a boom in female seminaries and academies in the 1830s and 1840s; in fact, advertisements for such institutions filled the columns of newspapers in virtually every state in the Union.[2] By the Civil War, however, their numbers were declining. Except for the Troy Female Seminary, none of these schools still exist. Thomas Woody, in his comprehensive history of women's education, found that "there was developing a new type of secondary institution, the high school, which gradually took over such secondary school functions as had been performed by the academy or seminary."[3]

There is no evidence that by the late 1830s Emma Willard believed she would remain a schoolteacher forever. She had told the trustees at the beginning of the decade that writing was her preferred occupation, and by 1838, she had several bestselling texts on the market and plans for more. The geographies and atlases that she had coauthored with William Channing Woodbridge in 1822 were still in print and selling well. This comprehensive volume included the popular *Geography for*

Beginners. Like this geography, her *History of the United States*, first published in 1828, was rapidly becoming a school standard; she would revise this text many times over the course of the next forty years. It did not go out of print until the end of the century. In 1838 she wrote *Ancient Geography as Connected with Chronology, and Preparatory to the Study of Ancient History: Accompanied with an Atlas.* This was bundled with the eighth edition of Woodbridge's *A System of Universal Geography on the Principles of Comparison and Classification.*

Speculation that the seminary would not outlast its founder was far from illogical. As early as 1833, she had referred to her "successor"[4] in a memorandum to the trustees. What the visitor from South Carolina or any other observer might not have predicted is the circumstance that would draw her from her greatest creation. At the age of fifty-one, the founder would be taken from the school by romance. Apparently, this decision caused quite a stir. As one pupil wrote to her brother, "[Mrs. Willard's] engaging herself made quite a commotion in the city of Troy."[5]

At some point in 1835 or 1836, the widowed Emma Willard had begun a courtship with the widowed Dr. Christopher Yates. Born in 1779, Yates was far closer to her age than Dr. Willard had been. He had local roots; his grandparents, Johannes and Rebecca, had been among the early settlers of Schenectady. Named for his father, he was the youngest of his parents' nine children. His mother, Catharina Lansing, hailed from a prominent Rensselaer County family with deep Dutch roots, and Christopher grew up in Greenbush. He studied medicine under Dr. Samuel Stringer and was licensed to practice in 1802, the same year he married his first wife. The couple had four children, three girls and a boy.

Described by one biographer as "tall, with a slender figure, gentlemanly manners, an intelligent face . . . considerable intellect and culture,"[6] when the courtship began, Yates had been living in Manhattan since 1820. He had published a number of favorably reviewed medical works, particularly his 1832 work on cholera,[7] and was often described as "an eminent"[8] physician. Early in his career, he was appointed a health officer for the city of Albany.

However, Dr. Christopher Yates's reputation was uneven. He had left Albany for New York in 1820, the same year he sued another man for a "criminal conversation"[9] with his wife. It is unclear whether or not his wife accompanied him to Manhattan, but once in Manhattan, he spent a good deal of time homeschooling his only son, Winfield Scott Yates, a young man whose untimely death from consumption in 1833 produced laudatory obituaries touting his genius.[10] A sketch of the younger Yates written after his father's death credited his superior "moral and intellectual foundation" to his father's tutelage.[11]

One of Yates's medical specialties was the treatment of stutterers. Again, the record is mixed. Although some considered him an expert on the matter and credited him with the invention of "Mrs. Leigh's System" for curing stammering, others accused him of having stolen the method from Leigh, who all agreed was a nursemaid hired to help with the Yates children, in particular a daughter who suffered from a stutter.[12] Whether or not the doctor was responsible for inventing the method, it apparently did not work.[13]

The man was certainly controversial. Few obituaries of professional men written in the nineteenth century contain language as derogatory as that used by Dr. Sylvester Willard in his official summary of Yates's life. He concluded, "His judgment seemed to have been often at fault. It might be charity to stop here; but it is truthful to add, that in his character and example, there was nothing to admire, but everything to avoid; and that his influence upon the profession and upon society, was demoralizing."[14] Anna Johnson '44, like many loyal students, certainly shared Willard's opinion, referring to him in a letter written years after the fact as a "villain."[15]

In his biography, John Lord quotes extensively from letters that reveal the contradictory messages Emma Willard received from a variety of people about Yates's character. Nevertheless, she entered into an engagement sometime in late 1836 or early 1837, but then she broke it off. Not surprisingly, news of the whole affair spread through the student body. Mary Elizabeth Williams wrote to her uncle, "Nothing would surprise us at present. In the first place Mrs. Willard's engagement caused quite a commotion and then the suspension of it (as she wishes it expressed) has made quite a romantic soul of it."[16] Elizabeth had heard that the suspension was the result of religious differences, a belief that Willard's early biographers shared. If Lord's account is chronologically accurate, there was yet one more suspension of the engagement in the late spring or early summer of 1838. On the bottom of a letter dated June 7 from Judge Jesse Buel assuring her he held Yates in highest esteem, Emma wrote, "I had suspended my engagement."[17] Lord quotes extensively from Buel's letter and a letter from a Col. William Stone, the husband of one of Emma's friends, who urged her to go ahead with the wedding. At least one student observer regarded the entire affair with skepticism, writing to her uncle, "When I think of her, I can claim that this is no romance."[18]

Eventually persuaded that Yates would be a suitable spouse (and worried that breaking the engagement might lead to a suit for breach of promise), Emma agreed to the wedding, which took place on September 17, 1838, at St. John's Church (Yates was by birth a member of the Dutch Reformed Church). The Troy papers covered the occasion, the *Budget* perfunctorily and the *Troy Whig* more substantially. Newspapers of the era made no attempt at political impartiality, and John Willard, according to his cousin, was a Whig,[19] which perhaps accounts for the more extensive coverage in that journal. In the same issue, the *Whig* endorsed William Seward for governor and mourned the death of Gov. William Clark of Missouri (his more famous legacy was his joint venture across the Louisiana Territory with Meriwether Lewis). Among the social notes was an account of the wedding, including metaphorical reference to the jittery economy that was plaguing the country in the wake of the Panic of 1837:

> A lively business in the matrimonial line commenced in our city yesterday, and that kind of stock is now considerably above par— holders being firm and prices still advancing. Madame Emma Willard, the founder of the Troy Female Seminary—the patron of female education—and the friend and guardian of pretty girls, led the van to Hymen's altar, and set an example, which is being followed in the full tide of successful experiment by almost half the fair ones in our city.[20]

Newspapers throughout the Northeast carried the story, in many cases reprinting verbatim a flowery account from the *Albany Evening Journal*. The Albany story suggested that "Cupid has let fly his arrow in an unexpected quarter." According to the paper the ceremony took place "privately, with the exception of relatives and personal friends, and the pupils of the school." These pupils, noted the paper, were "tastefully dressed for such an occasion, in white, and with bouquets of flowers." The paper concluded with the hope that "these sweet creatures, after being thoroughly educated, may in due season *follow in the footsteps of their illustrious predecessor.*"[21] Follow her to the altar, that is, not the schoolroom!

There is no direct record of how John Willard felt about his mother's marriage, but it was he who delivered his mother's note to Yates when she decided to break off the engagement, and a letter from Almira to her sister implied that John was not happy about the wedding. Writing from her home in Brattleboro, Almira doubted whether or not John would make any "serious opposition" to the marriage, but if he did, then all the more reason to marry—"If you must have a master, better a husband than a child." Married twice herself, she was sensitive to the emotional pain that stepparents could cause just by their existence and reminded Emma that her own two daughters, who viewed their aunt as a "second mother," and John would initially—and understandably—feel as bereft "as if the sun was extinguished in the firmament."[22] If John did harbor doubts, he must have been vastly relieved that two days before her wedding his mother turned over to him most of her property, including the seminary.

It was a most foresighted transaction. In just ten months Emma Willard Yates had returned to the seminary, having left her husband. In October, she was still there. William Hart wrote to his father,

> Aunt Willard is still at the Seminary, but I do not know what she intends to do. Her marriage with Dr. Yates has really been one of the strangest operations I know of. It has ceased however to create much conversation among the Trojans, and I presume the affair will soon be forgotten by them, and could she do the same it would certainly be a happy circumstance but I know she feels it most sensibly . . . her mind is ill at ease concerning it.

To illustrate his aunt's state of mind, he related an incident he had witnessed. He reported overhearing a teacher say, "'Mrs. Yates, it does not seem as though you had been married but had only been absent for a visit.'" The response, "'Would to God it were so.'"[23]

Her stay in Troy was short. By winter she was in Connecticut. Given the number of relatives she still had living in that state, it is logical that she would go there. In addition, she had found work there. An old friend, Henry Barnard, was superintendent of schools for the state of Connecticut, and he engaged her to establish common schools in Kensington, a section of her hometown. Family and work, however, were not the only reasons for choosing this location. Early in the colonial period, Connecticut, a hidebound Puritan colony in many regards, had "adopted a progressive approach to divorce."[24] In New York, adultery was the only legitimate grounds for divorce; in Connecticut, total neglect of duty and fraudulent contract were also grounds. Furthermore, divorces could be obtained either through the courts or the state legislature. Mrs. Yates chose the legislative path, which required a three-year residency, although she made frequent visits to Troy, particularly at holidays.[25] Troy was home. At the beginning of an extended stay in the spring of 1841, she wrote to her niece, "Now I have sat down in the old Seminary with my books around me—my mind to do my work and my assistant to copy it, and I find myself pleasantly situated."[26] In addition, during her self-imposed exile from Troy, John, his wife, and Emma's sister Almira visited her in Connecticut at least once.

Some of her chroniclers have posited that Emma Willard left Troy to avoid embarrassing the school. Certainly, some of her contemporaries were aghast at her unconventional behavior. Sarah Hale, among others, warned her that a woman who had left her husband would be a huge liability in recruiting students for the school. However, there is no hint in extant student letters that her return to the seminary caused any problems for the institution, in spite of Sarah Hale's fears. In her correspondence with Lydia Sigourney in the weeks right after her departure from Yates, Emma wrote that she believed Hale's negative response to her having left Yates was rooted in misinformation. She confided to Sigourney that Sarah Hale had told her brother-in-law John Phelps that "I had done wrong." Supremely confident as always, she assured Sigourney, "Mrs. Hale is too good a woman to condemn a friend unheard,—and she will think differently when she hears both sides."[27]

Regardless of the reason for Hale's disapprobation, her fears proved groundless. The visit to the school by the founder was an occasion for celebration at the school. Writing to a friend at the end of May 1841, Ellen Thompson '43 commented, "Mrs. Emma Willard is here now [and] . . . will remain here a part of the summer. She gave the young ladies and teachers a party . . . There were also some [guests] from the city. Mrs. Emma was very agreeable."[28] The use of her former name was not accidental; she was determined to leave "Mrs. Yates" behind, and petitioning to regain her first husband's surname was part of her divorce proceedings. Outside of newspaper accounts of her marriage and divorce, the name Yates was rarely attached to her. A notable exception is found in the baptismal record of Mary Theodosia Willard, christened at St. John's on July 24, 1842, with her grandmother, Mrs. E. W. Yates, as a witness.[29]

With the help of her brother-in-law John Phelps, an attorney in Vermont, and her nephew Norris Wilcox,[30] marshal of Connecticut, she petitioned for her divorce on the grounds that Yates had tried to take control of her assets, conspired with his daughter Catherine to spend her money, failed to lead a Christian life, and generally ridiculed every value Emma Willard held dear. Newspapers across the country picked up the story as printed in the *Hartford Patriot*, a publication favorable to her cause. As the *Wisconsin Inquirer* explained, they were running the story "not with a view to feed a morbid appetite for scandal, [but] to protect innocence and virtue." The Connecticut paper described Yates as being "in low circumstances as to pecuniary matters" and as a "tyrannical and unprincipled man . . . an open and hardened infidel and debauchee!"[31]

Yates had his supporters in the press as well. In January, a Philadelphia journal wrote a scathing review of a pamphlet Emma had penned shortly before leaving the seminary. Addressed to her former pupils who were engaged in teaching, her "Letter Addressed as a Circular to the Members of the Willard Association for the Mutual Improvement of Female Teachers" was intended to connect them to each other and provide them with resources about teaching methods and materials. (In spite of the increasing presence of women in the teaching force, they were not yet allowed to join professional educational associations.) The anonymous writer wrote a scathing review of the circular, claiming it was a "cunningly devised scheme to aid Mrs. Willard in the collection of her debts." Charging that "her power of analysis is exceedingly feeble; her conceptions are often confused and indistinct; . . . and the ordinary current of her thoughts is very common place," the reviewer belittled Willard's teaching methods and reputation. In summary, the author concluded "her egotism . . . knows no bounds." "Obviously, he opined, "In her mind, Mrs. Emma Willard and the Troy Female Seminary are the two most important entities within the limits of the United States . . . and she looks upon herself as the greatest benefactor of the female sex in this land." Filled with misogyny and written four months after she had left Yates, the article contained the sardonic footnote that since the publication of the circular, "Mrs. W. has availed herself of one of the prerogatives of her sex and has changed her name . . . [and] will hereafter be known as Mrs. Emma Willard Yates."[32]

The *New York Sunday Morning News* reprinted much of this article, introducing it with this statement: "These female boarding schools have long met with our disapprobation, and in future numbers of this paper we hope to expose their character. We have thought the Troy Female Seminary for a long time, worthy of scrutiny."[33] Other papers in Boston and elsewhere challenged "the attempts of a petticoated pedagogue to rule her husband like a schoolboy."[34] Later, when papers erroneously printed the news that she had recovered money from Yates, criticism flared again. Under "Miscellany," *The Brooklyn Eagle* editorialized, "Right! The male creatures ought to pay for such freaks."[35]

In spite of such criticism, Emma's petition was unanimously accepted by the state legislature's divorce commission, although there was some disagreement among the committee members about whether or not she should be suing in Connecticut. The legislature accepted the commission's recommendation, and on May 3, 1843, her marriage to Yates was officially dissolved. She was vastly relieved. A month later, Emma apologized to an old friend for not having written sooner, explaining, "I was in all the agonies of effort and exciting suspense attendant on the affair in which I have been recently engaged, and which has happily terminated."[36] She could return to Troy for good.

It is possible that the apparently seamless transition back to Troy could not have happened without the calm, reassuring presence of Emma Willard's successor, a woman of intelligence, competence, and irreproachable character. As William Hart wrote to his father shortly after Emma had left Yates, "Mrs. John gives great satisfaction as Principal . . . everything seems to be going on prosperously."[37] Emma Willard had handpicked Sarah Lucretia Hudson Willard[38] to lead the school (and it is certainly possible that she chose her to marry John). Born in Waterford, New York, Lucretia Hudson was the oldest of four children (three girls and a boy) born to British immigrants, Sarah and Horace Hudson.

In all likelihood, Horace Hudson Sr. emigrated from England with some resources. He and Sarah Robinson had been married on May 19, 1803, in St. George's Parish, Hanover Square, London, a church that witnessed many upper-class and even royal weddings.[39] Both came from the eastern coast of England, Horace from Wells-Next-to-the-Sea, Norfolk, and Sarah from South Lincolnshire. Horace may have come to the United States first; he entered the country through New Orleans. By 1810, however, he was a successful hardware merchant in Waterford, and Lucretia, the first of their children, had been born. Unfortunately, Horace died early, leaving his widow with four children under ten. When the Waterford Female Academy opened in 1820, Sarah Hudson enrolled Lucretia and her younger sister, Theodosia. Shortly after that, Mrs. Hudson moved to Troy, and in 1822 the two girls were again placed under Mrs. Willard's charge. The youngest of the Hudson sisters, Harriet, studied longest in Troy, joining the school in 1828 and remaining until 1834.

By 1826 Lucretia was a teacher at the seminary. In an unpublished memoir, Emma reminisced about the early promise she saw in her future daughter-in-law:

> Sarah Lucretia Hudson was one of the youngest of my pupils at Waterford during my first year there. She accompanied me to Troy, and went through my whole course of study; and being always the smallest, and at the same time one of the best scholars in every class to which she belonged, she attracted much attention and applause. She more particularly excelled in the different branches of mathematics. . . . Notwithstanding her youth such was her correctness, energy and prudence that I at once made her a teacher.[40]

So talented was the young teacher that when Emma sailed for Europe, she placed twenty-year-old Lucretia in the position of vice principal to assist Almira.

At some point after his return from Europe and his final attempt at education (studying medicine with a local doctor), John Willard proposed to his mother's favorite assistant. Lucretia accepted, and the couple wed on August 5, 1834. She was one year his senior and arguably far better educated than he. Sarah Crocker wrote to a friend, "Miss Sarah Hudson is married to Mr. Willard. They were married in St. John's Church on Tuesday. . . . The carriage was ready at the door for them to start on their journey to Niagara Falls. . . . They appeared to be very happy."[41] Honeymooning in Niagara Falls marked the young couple as wealthy and fashionable, in the vanguard of honeymooning tourists in 1834. Increasingly popular for wedding trips, from the opening of the Erie Canal until the Civil War, "Niagara was the prime touring destination for the affluent."[42]

Within a year of their marriage, Lucretia gave birth to the first of ten children; this firstborn, named for her grandmother, carried the appellation Emma Willard Willard. She would be followed in 1836 by a brother, William Lee, who lived less than a year, in 1838 by a brother, John Hudson, in 1840 by Sarah Hudson, in 1842 by Mary Theodosia, in 1844 by Harriet, in 1846 by Katherine Aldis, and in 1847 by Marcia. Two final babies, Clara, born in 1849, and an unnamed infant girl born in 1853 lived very briefly. In all, Lucretia Willard was pregnant for half of the first eighteen years of her marriage. In this respect she was somewhat different from her fellow seminary graduates. An analysis of her contemporaries found that "Emma Willard's . . . pupils . . . bore fewer children [than their peers]." Only 4.7 percent of the women who studied in Troy between 1821 and 1872 gave birth to more than seven children, whereas 21.7 percent of all American women at the time had families this large.[43]

Student accounts of Lucretia Willard were invariably flattering, as were most of their accounts of the founder. However, there is a difference. Whereas Emma was a subject of student reverence, respect, and awe, they expressed more affection and warmth for Lucretia. Writing to the Willards' oldest daughter in 1892 about her arrival at the seminary with her sister, Eliza Hunt Apthorp'35 reminisced, "Your mother came like a sunbeam into our room." At the same time, she remembered "your imposing grandmother, always so beautifully dressed in black silk, drawing through her fingers a ribbon to which a gold pencil was fastened. . . . Well do I remember my terrors when she stopped me and I had a buttered roll squeezed in my hand surreptitiously; as I felt the melted butter ooze through my fingers." (Eating outside the dining room was forbidden.)

At seventy-five, with the perspective of age, Apthorp concluded,

> I think no school was ever better equipped with teachers who had the capital merit of awakening the minds of their pupils and the atmosphere of the school was very stimulating to hard work which tells in the long run as nothing else does. . . . But it always seemed to me your mother with her radiant face, was more its inspiration than your grandmother was. . . . Your grandmother's great distinction seemed to me to be a supreme confidence in herself, and as a consequence, a stubborn faith in the capacity of her own sex. She took the initiative: that first step which costs so much, but it was your mother practically who proved the truth of her mother-in-law's creed.[44]

Jane Burritt agreed with Eliza Apthorp. Writing to her uncle, she commented, "Mrs. Willard I like better than expected . . . [and] Mrs. John Willard . . . I think is almost equal to her. She is a perfect lady in her manners and so pleasant and amiable in her disposition."[45] And Harriet Randall, who admired the founder immensely, raved, "Mrs. J.W.! The very mention of her name is to arouse all the better feelings of our nature as we reflect on her calm dignity of manner, her wise self-control, her never-wearying kindness."[46]

To her early pupils, Lucretia Willard represented a grown-up elegance that they could hope to obtain in the not too distant future. Mary Mason '45 reminisced in the 1890s about watching a "ball" thrown for "Troy Society" by John and Lucretia: the latter "a vision of a graceful woman in ruby velvet, pale blue ostrich tips in her coiffure, standing upon a slightly elevated dais, receiving her guests with a matchless air of good-breeding."[47] Ellen Thompson '43 wrote to a friend at home in Granville, New York, that she had seen Emma Willard, who was at the seminary working on a revision of her U.S. history text, but that Lucretia "is one of the best persons I think I ever met."[48] Likewise, Margaret Ann Freligh '42 wrote to her mother, "With Mrs. Willard,

I am more and more charmed every day," adding "[she] has 4 pretty children under eight years. The eldest [is] quite advanced in French."[49]

Perhaps it was her role as mother to so many small children that caused her pupils to remark on her "ready sympathy and sweet motherliness."[50] Like so many accomplished nineteenth- and twentieth-century women, Lucretia managed her career while assuming most of the responsibility for tending her children. In a letter to Emma the spring after her seventh child was born, she commented, "I am writing with Katy on my lap."[51] An earlier letter from Lydia Sigourney to Emma Willard mirrored Lucretia's situation. Sigourney was composing a review of Emma's history but was called away "by a moaning from the cradle which I have long been rocking with my foot and whose dear little inmate by her continual claiming upon my care reminds me that I am anything rather than one of the literati."[52]

Nor were her children Lucretia's only private responsibility. For most of her married life, she lived with or next door to her mother-in-law, by all accounts—friendly and critical—a formidable woman. For some period of time until Sarah Hudson's death in 1854, Lucretia's mother also made her home at the seminary. And, of course, Lucretia's unmarried sister, Theodosia, was also part of the household and the school from the 1830s on. Multigenerational families like the Willards were the norm in the mid-nineteenth century. It is estimated that more than 70 percent of all elderly people in the United States lived with relatives in 1850. Emma referred invariably to Lucretia as her "daughter," and there is no hint in any correspondence of any but the warmest, most cordial relations between the two women, whether the topic was the seminary or the children.

In fact, it would appear that Emma's presence helped enormously. Not surprisingly, Lucretia's health suffered in conjunction with some of her confinements. At those times Emma stepped in, conducting examinations, handling school correspondence, and holding things steady until Lucretia could resume her post. After the divorce Emma had toyed with moving to Philadelphia or Hartford, but John wrote to her that they wanted her with them. His mother was in Philadelphia when he wrote to her that she could have the "corner house." He argued, "Our interests are so much united that if there were no other reason it would be almost enough to turn the scale that you could be here to give your advice and counsel and in case of necessity your assistance."[53] And so she did, writing to Harriet Mumford Paige in September 1846, "in my daughter's absence, I am in charge."[54]

Her involvement was often noted in family letters. In 1847 John wrote to Emma that she would have to preside over the opening of the school because they were staying in Hudson for "Lucretia's health."[55] Most likely, his wife was suffering from having given birth to her eighth child, Marcia, only a year after Katherine's birth. At any rate, Emma showed a remarkable willingness to move back and forth and to defer to Lucretia and John. For example, in a letter to a woman who had recommended a pupil, she replied, "Concerning the young woman mentioned by your mother, you had best speak to John and Lucretia."[56] Although she had no formal role after 1838, the founder remained an important presence. School catalogs assured parents that "The Founder of the Institution, Mrs. Emma Willard, has her residence on the Seminary grounds, and is at all times ready to extend to the members the results of her successful experience as an educator."[57]

In contrast, impressions of John Willard at the seminary are few. Students rarely referred to him and then in a matter-of-fact way, referencing his role as bill collector, manager of trunks and travel, or citizen of Troy. Nevertheless, he seems to have been his wife's partner in every way. His step-cousin Helen commented favorably on the relationship between him and Lucretia, writing to her father that "They are amiable, just and generous, efficient and talented, each in their own way."[58] John had lived in a girls' school since he was four. His affection for Troy and the seminary had shone through the homesick boyish letters he wrote during his painful time at West Point, and he seems to have been content to make his mother's enterprise his life's work. At some point in the 1840s, with the help of his mother, he purchased a farm outside of Troy. According to Lucretia, he liked to take the children there for outings.[59]

Other than that reference, it is difficult to form a picture of John Willard as the patriarch of his family until his daughters were much older when he apparently played the role of wealthy indulgent father.[60]

Perhaps he maintained his distance until he was sure they were going to grow up. Almost inevitably in the nineteenth century, particularly in such a large family, some children would not live to maturity. The Willard children who did not survive are invariably referred to as Lucretia's, even by her mother-in-law. When baby William Lee died before his first birthday, the funeral was held at the seminary with the tiny body on display in the parlor. Mary Elizabeth Williams wrote to her mother, "Mrs. Willard's little son left us yesterday afternoon after much suffering. He was a sweet babe."[61] Infant life was fragile, and the death of young children an all too common occurrence. As late as 1900, infant mortality in the United States hovered around 100 deaths per 1,000 live births (compared to 6.89 deaths per 1,000 in 2000).[62]

Parents did not assume that children would routinely reach adulthood. Historian Gail Collins has identified the prevalence of children's death as a theme in nineteenth-century romantic literature. Dying children were almost always imbued with angelic characteristics intended to ease their parents' sorrow with the comforting thought that the innocent baby was in a better place. As Collins points out, the most famous dying child was Harriet Beecher Stowe's legendary creation Little Eva, but she was far from alone either in religion or real life.[63] For those seminary students who married missionary husbands and bore their children in far-off lands, the risk of death was even greater; presumably, so too was their sustaining faith. Mary Hulin '35 married her missionary husband shortly after leaving the seminary and sailed with him to India. By 1847 she was home in the United States, having left her husband and three of her six children in Indian graves.[64]

Among Lucretia Willard's schoolmates and early students, many lost babies and young children. Elizabeth Converse Starkweather '27 bore thirteen children, five of whom died in childhood, including twins, Francis and Fanny, neither of whom reached the age of six months. (She sent four of her remaining sons to the Civil War; miraculously, all returned home.) Mary Morgan '26 had ten children, all of whom predeceased her, although two made it to adulthood. James Fenimore Cooper's niece, Hannah Pomeroy Woolson '24, bore nine children, two of whom died as infants and three of whom, all toddlers, died within a two-week period in March 1840. Maria Patchin Tiffany '31, writing to her brother and sis-ter-in-law (Charlotte Davis Patchin '31), often commented on children's frailty. On her first daughter's second birthday, she had "a burning fever ... and is so delicate that I think it very doubtful if we ever raise her."[65] A year later, this first daughter had died, and she commented about her second child, "I think the twelfth, thirteenth and fourteenth months very trying to children . . . but we must remember that they are but lent to us."[66] (Her second child survived to adulthood, but Maria herself died from compli-cations of childbirth in 1844. The baby did not survive.) Most mothers, at least among those recording their lives for their alma mater in the 1890s, bore their losses stoically, holding fast to an abiding belief that the blame-less infants were in heaven. Occasionally, however, the weight of the loss was too much. Nancy Chapman Slade '38 lost all four of her children over the course of a few days during a scarlet fever epidemic. The griev-ing mother "never recovered from the shock of her great sorrow"[67] and could not bear to remain in her home.

The loss of infants was painful, but nineteenth-century Ameri-cans also regularly experienced the loss of older children to tragic ac-cidents. The death of the Willards' older son was such a tragedy. John Hudson Willard was ten years old, a healthy, active boy, nearly past the age of deadly childhood diseases when he drowned on a July evening while swimming with friends. Given the fact that he, alone, had the potential to carry on the family name, it is notable that his father's feelings are unrecorded and unmentioned. Writing to a niece just days after the heartbreaking event, Emma mourned, "the deeply afflictive providence which has bereaved us of our only boy—drowned Alas in the Mohawk on Friday near sunset." She continued, "Lucretia is calm and is presiding with her usual dignity. But you know a mother's heart, and can feel for her."[68] No mention of the father's heart or sense of loss—but, perhaps, to his credit, John Willard, staunch defender of girls' education—was no more nor no less upset by his son's death than he would have been at the loss of one of his young daughters. Lucretia's demeanor in the face of this tragedy earned the attention of her pupils. The scheduled end-of-term examination was postponed for only one day. Writing about this much later, Mary Drake '48, remembered,

The mother of the lad, reasoning that private griefs should not frustrate the prescribed routine of exercises in which many pupils with their parents and friends who had come from a distance were interested, nerved herself to the trying ordeal of conducting the public examination, and with an heroic self-forgetting presided at the yearly function with a graceful but pathetic dignity that touched every heart.[69]

As it was, John and Lucretia would lose two children in 1848. When John drowned, Lucretia was four months pregnant with Clara, who was born in December and lived only three days. Nor were these the only deaths connected to the seminary that year. Just months before John's drowning, William Lee, Emma's nephew who served as the seminary's business officer, lost his "beautiful child" to croup.[70]

Death by drowning and illness occurred not only in the Willard family but also among the seminary students. A death among the teenage population of a modern boarding school is exceedingly rare, stunningly heartbreaking, and is usually accompanied by significant counseling for surviving students and adult members of the school community trying to bring some sense to seemingly random acts of fate. Survivors are far more likely to rail against any god who could allow such pain rather than to celebrate the victim's early reunion with her divine creator. In the nineteenth century, student deaths were common. What was uncommon—and a point of pride to Emma, her teachers, and her pupils—was that no students had died at the seminary in the first decade and a half after the move to Troy. During a scarlet fever epidemic in the city, a student wrote home, "It is really wonderful, but there has never a death been in this school."[71] A classmate commented in a letter to her relatives, "Troy is generally a very healthy city" but repeated her astonishment that "it is quite remarkable . . . there has never been a death among her pupils."[72] The good health of the student body was often ascribed to the nutritional diet served at the school, touted in catalogs and remarked on in student letters.

Food at the school was plentiful. Susan Storer sent her mother a detailed description of the menu during her first few days at the seminary:

> The first night for tea we had some bread & butter, a cup of tea (first rate tea too) and something that looked like cabbage chopped

up and steamed. . . . The next morning we had mashed potato, ham & eggs, chopped up together as you chop pork and eggs and some of the best coffee I've drank [sic] this good while, for dinner we had oyster soup, and potato, and something that was like your fritters. . . . I didn't like them much and so didn't eat any, for tea we had biscuit & butter & cheese, the next morning we had pancakes, and butter, and sugar or molasses, for dinner we had a boiled dinner, boiled Beef & pork, cabbage, and a boiled Indian pudding, for tea we had bread & butter & gingerbread, this morning hash, and this noon we had something which I will bet you haven't had, and that was green-peas and roasted pig, and tonight we had bread & butter and dried beef, and there is a plenty of all these victuals.[73]

The two deadliest diseases of the nineteenth century were scarlet fever and tuberculosis, and many seminary students and members of their families fell victim to one or the other of these. However, cholera, the scourge of nineteenth-century cities, erupted in Troy periodically and was the most feared of the nineteenth-century medical menaces, even though it claimed fewer victims. With scarlet fever and even more so with consumption, the nineteenth-century term for tuberculosis, patients often lived for weeks or even years, so families could co-exist with the ill and have time to prepare for death. Cholera, however, could strike an able-bodied person down in the course of a few hours with no warning, and the symptoms of the disease (severe vomiting, uncontrollable diarrhea, victims turning blue) were frightening. In 1832, 1849, 1853, and 1866, Troy, along with the rest of the Eastern Seaboard, suffered from epidemics of this dread disease. Cholera centered in cities and was a downside of Troy's urban growth.

Cholera's source, contaminated drinking water, was unknown until 1854, and the actual microscopic bacterium responsible for the contamination was not identified until 1885. Because of its prevalence in crowded areas of cities, most people prior to the Civil War believed that it was a disease of the lower classes, caused by dirty living conditions and intemperate behavior. Emma Willard apparently clung to this upper-class notion. In her U.S. history text, she traced the path of the 1832 wave of "Asiatic cholera" down the Atlantic Seaboard to "some newly arrived Irish emigrants" in Canada.[74] When cholera broke out in Troy in 1832, Emma Willard was away, and Nathan Warren, a member of the board of trustees, ordered classes to stop. One student wrote to relatives in Boston: "It is strange what a revolution the Cholera produces. . . . The Seminary has been in very great agitation. Mrs. Willard being absent, Mr. N. Warren went there and advised the school to be broken up. Think what a fuss!"[75] Her seeming unconcern was echoed at the time of the next big outbreak by another nonchalant student who wrote to her mother complaining that "it is too warm to do anything," and the students were "forbidden on account of the cholera" to drink ice water or eat ice cream. She concluded, "I hope you are not frightened by the cholera. We are not in the least."[76] These students' attitudes toward cholera were more typical than Trustee Warren's seeming panic.

The students' casual dismissal of the disease during both the 1832 and 1849 outbreaks undoubtedly reflected their awareness that as members of the upper—or at least the upper-middle—echelons of society they need not worry about cholera. They were taught this comforting belief by the Willards and by the press of the day. When a rumor of cholera in Troy circulated at the seminary, Mrs. Willard assured the girls that the victims were black women who "died of intemperance."[77] Nathan Beman, the respected zealous abolitionist minister whose Presbyterian church adjoined the seminary grounds, agreed, using cholera as a reason to petition the Troy City Council for temperance laws. Beman insisted that "nine tenths of the destructive power of the cholera is generated by ardent spirits."[78] In cities across the country, the disease was said to afflict "without exception [the] intemperate, dissolute, licentious, filthy [and] imprudent."[79] Young ladies at the Troy Female Seminary had little to fear from the cholera, given their respectable lives.

However, if cholera posed little threat, death was ever present in the form of consumption, fevers, sudden afflictions, and accidents. Consumptive students who became too weak to study left school and died at home, mourned by their classmates. For example, Hannah Lay '41 went home to Mechanicville, New York, just days before her death, and her body was carried back to the seminary for her schoolmates to bid their farewells. The daughter and sister of missionaries, she was apparently both pious and brilliant. The *New-York Evangelist* reported that "The corpse was conveyed to the Seminary where her late earthly shepherds made a solemn address." The paper concluded, "This lesson of Providence . . . has admonished the young that death regards not youth or beauty, and teaches all that loveliness of character, an accomplished mind and surpassing mental capabilities cannot withstand his unerring shafts."[80] Of course, not all who left for health reasons died. Henrietta Collins '42, writing from her home after leaving the seminary, reflected in a letter to a classmate, "Little did I think that '43 would find me an inhabitant upon this sphere and in the fruition of Heaven's richest boon, <u>Health</u>."[81]

The first death to occur at the school took place on May 9, 1841, two decades to the day after the school opened in Troy. Emma Willard reported the death to her niece Harriet Hart: "We lost a pupil by death on Sunday morning with a disease of the heart. She died suddenly. Went to sleep cheerful at night—and waked in eternity."[82] A student reported the loss in greater detail to a friend, but it was only one bit of news in a letter crammed with details about her daily life, her impressions of teachers, fellow students and her roommate, and an account of a party. According to her letter,

> Miss Jane C. Place, one of the pupils, died. She was in usual health Sabbath day, was monitress Sabbath evening. She was very cheerful and appeared in fine spirits and retired to rest as usual. Her roommate awoke about four o'clock in the morning to find her dying and before any assistance could reach her bedside, her spirit had taken its flight. Two physicians were called immediately but it was too late. The vital spark was extinct. . . . Miss Place was a very amiable and pious girl and a very fine scholar. . . . She was engaged to a young man in her native village [Keesville, NY]. . . . She had had an organic affection of the heart and remarked the day before her death that when she died she expected to die suddenly.[83]

For the students and alumnae of the Troy Female Seminary in the nineteenth century, dying suddenly from an accident was as likely, or perhaps even more likely, than dying suddenly from a disease. This is not surprising, given their comparative wealth and its attendant access to good food, clean water, and opportunities for travel. Even the trip to and from school could be harrowing, particularly if it involved water travel. Ocean travel was dangerous, as was travel on the Great Lakes. Isabella Robert '38 was returning to her plantation home in South Carolina after a year of study when she and her cousin, who had been sent north to escort her home, drowned in the wreck of the *Home* off the coast of North Carolina. Charlotte Davis Patchin '31 lost two daughters, including Mary '65, when their packet went down on Lake Erie in June 1868.

Travel on the Hudson could also be perilous. Sarah Slason '47 was a day student when she survived the destruction of the *Swallow*, which crashed in a spring snow squall, April 7, 1845, near Hudson, New York, on a night run from Albany to New York City. A fellow passenger and fellow survivor was Mary Gleason Gardner '35 (whose husband would be murdered during the California gold rush a few years later). Lucy Hurlbut McDaniel '41 drowned when the *Henry Clay* blew up south of West Point after racing another steamboat down the Hudson. The *Henry Clay* won the race, but its overheated boilers exploded.

As Lucretia Willard settled into running her alma mater in the 1840s, Troy and the nation seemed to settle into their maturity as well. The Jacksonian experiment in democracy had widened the suffrage without ripping the republic apart, and the first significant wave of non-Protestant immigrants was being absorbed in the labor force in urban centers that were increasingly industrial and class conscious. Irishmen laid the rails that were fast outpacing canals, and Irish women served as maids, cooks, and nannies in the homes of the growing middle and upper classes. The union had survived in spite of the nullification crisis of the early 1830s and a severe financial panic at the end of the decade. After the addition of seven new states in the wake of the War of 1812, there had been no more growth since the seminary moved to Troy. From 1836 to 1848, the nation again expanded, with the addition of Arkansas, Michigan, Florida, Texas, Iowa, and Wisconsin. Westward expansion and slavery threatened the nation's stability, but the first seemed inexorable and the second still open to compromise. Jane McManus Storm Cazneau '22, the first American woman war correspondent, covered the Mexican War and coined the phrase "manifest destiny,"[84] although her male editor took credit for it. A decade later, William Seward, brother, husband, brother-in-law, and uncle of seminary students, warned that the time for compromise was over, and an "irrepressible conflict" was at hand.

A Band of Sisters

AT THE TROY FEMALE SEMINARY, the two decades leading up to the Civil War were a time of general prosperity, success, and fame. For the most part the state-required annual reports filed by the school reflected a healthy financial picture, steady additions to library holdings and scientific equipment, a strong enrollment, manageable debt, and periodic improvements to the physical plant. The only years during the two prewar decades when the school failed to make a profit were 1843 and 1844, and in 1843 the loss was negligible.[1] In the other nineteen years between 1840 and 1860, the institution made money, peaking at a surplus of $5,405.97 in 1854, a year when enrollment also hit an all-time high. Four hundred and ninety-six students enrolled for part or all of 1854, a still unbroken record. (1854 saw another school record. Fifty women were "sent out as teachers" that year.) In 1854 the number of volumes in the library topped a thousand for the first time. A year later, the debt incurred when the school borrowed $3,000 in 1847 to pay for an additional building constructed in 1846[2] had been paid off, including over $1,100 in interest. By any statistical measure, the seminary was flourishing in the middle of the nineteenth century.

Prosperity was coupled with a new sense of permanency. Although the state never fulfilled Emma Willard's dream of public support, an important change in the relationship between the city and the seminary took place in 1856. After thirty-six years, the school ceased to depend on municipal largesse and no longer paid rent to Troy. Instead, the buildings and property were turned over to the trustees. For the first time, the Troy Female Seminary was truly an independent school. Reporting the change to the Regents, the Willards wrote, "The title to the Academy lot, building, library and apparatus . . . is now actually held by the trustees as a permanent endowment, subject to no other trust than that of promoting education."[3]

Throughout these years, Sarah Willard remained at the helm of the school, although both she and her husband used the term *principal* when signing official documents for the seminary, and they were listed as "principals" in the school catalogs. Sarah's salary in 1840 was $2,000, a significant amount at a time when most teachers earned between $250 and $700 a year. However, in 1860, Sarah's salary remained $2,000. At her retirement twelve years later, it had not changed; for thirty-four years her salary remained the same. Meanwhile, John Willard never reported a salary. Instead, he drew money from the school in good times and covered the deficit with his own funds when the occasion arose. Like his mother, John had an alternative revenue source. In his case, it was property, including at least two working farms in Rensselaer County.

Although John employed an accountant, he was responsible for the overall financial management of the seminary, including the collection of tuition, paying of bills, and maintenance of student funds. It was he who corresponded with parents, typically fathers, about bills. Parents sent money to John Willard to dole out to their daughters for shopping and to use for dressmaking, medical appointments, and transportation home. He apparently had a reputation for being somewhat tightfisted. Anna Shankland Kellogg '59, desperate to get some money from her account for a last-minute trip to New York City over an Easter weekend, mentioned in her diary, "Mr. Willard was searched for, but as usual, when money-matters were around, was 'not to be found.'"[4]

The number of male teachers remained small; including John Willard, who never taught a class, the percentage of men on the faculty never rose above a third of the total. Most of these teachers were specialists in music, French, or dancing. Unlike the women, whose occupation on the census rolls was listed as "teacher," the men were usually styled "professor." Often they were part-time lecturers in science who earned very modest stipends. George Cook, a professor at Rensselaer Polytechnic Institute (RPI), earned $100 annually for his lectures on chemistry. For several years this salary also covered his work maintaining the scientific apparatus used by the students. Like Cook, who was an RPI graduate, most of the men had college educations. Joseph Fellows, a science lecturer in the 1840s, was a Dartmouth alumnus, and when Cook left the school in 1848, he was replaced by another RPI graduate, Benjamin Greene. In 1851 Freeman Sherbrook, who is listed as a teacher in Schenectady in the 1850 federal census, earned $50 in Troy for providing penmanship lessons. Various clergy taught Greek and sacred music from time to time, sometimes for free; quite possibly their daughters attended the school because the daughters of local clergy were "always instructed gratuitously in the English branches."[5] The French teacher was often male and was usually a full-time, well-paid member of the faculty. Auguste Frolich, for example, a native speaker from Strasbourg, earned $600 annually, which was 25 percent greater than the salary earned by Theodosia Hudson, Sarah Willard's sister. As vice principal, she was typically the second most highly paid employee.

The men who taught at the seminary were often criticized by students. In May 1842, Margaret Freleigh '43 wrote to her mother, "I do not like my Latin teacher and am almost disposed to give it up."[6] (Her Latin teacher was most likely Sylvanus Lewis.) Writing to her mother a few years later, Susan Storer '46 commented, "We have the funniest old man for a teacher in French that ever was."[7] On her second day at school in 1856, Anna Kellogg '59 complained to her diary, "I went and took a [music] lesson of the dirtiest looking man I ever saw." She tried to change teachers but was told she had to stick with "Mr. Barnekoy (the dirty man!) for this quarter."[8] And in her copy of the school catalog for 1857, Anna Kellogg jotted one-word descriptions of many of the teachers. Next to the name of the dancing instructor, A. Deuchar, she wrote, "DRUNK!!"[9]

When the alumnae looked back at their schooldays, the male faculty fared no better. In their reminiscences of school life collected in the 1890s, mature women continued to critique the male teachers, often characterizing them as harsh. One recalled "the almost forbidding face of Professor Luce,"[10] referring to John Luce, a language instructor. Sarah Sage '52 and Sarah Numan '49 both had fearful memories of Gustave

Blessner, a piano teacher. Sage remembered "the . . . touch on my shoulder of Mr. Blessner's violin bow, and his quick rebuke, 'No! No! begin again.'"[11] Numan recounted leaving a music lesson in tears when Blessner shouted at her "'Young woman! You play like one blame fool!'"[12]

In contrast, student letters and alumnae recollections of female teachers reveal a community where students and teachers formed strong relationships. According to Sarah Willard, this was an explicit goal of the school. As she reported to the Regents in 1841, it was the principals' intention "to surround [the students] with teachers whom they can respect and love."[13] Anna Bedell '48, studying in Troy with her sisters, Prudence '48 and Martha '48, wrote to their father, "We like it here . . . the teachers are kind and entirely competent to instruct in any branch; the interest they evince in the progress of their pupils is some encouragement to persevere."[14] A few years later, Nettie Fowler wrote much the same thing to her brother, noting, "The teachers are very affectionate and kind, I never knew teachers to take the pupils so much in the bosom of their family."[15]

For some students the affection bordered on romance. Sarah Chapin '55 recalled her fondness for Theodosia Hudson, writing in 1894, "I still like to meet her in my dreaming hours."[16] Adelaide Galusha '55 echoed the sentiment, saying that she was "devotedly attached" to "Miss Hudson" and remembered being "a frequent visitor to her sunny room."[17] Anna Manwaring '35, who taught at the school from 1844 until 1872, was invariably remembered as "dear" and "kind," and Mary Hastings '45, who taught science, mathematics, and English at the school from 1846 to 1859 earned general approbation for her intellect, gift for teaching, and zeal for learning. Many remembered her as their favorite teacher. Helen Van Bergen '57 wrote, "Miss Hastings fascinated us with her enthusiastic experiments in chemistry and brought us into the companionship of the Lake Poets."[18] (When Smith College opened its doors, Mary Hastings was tapped to head its mathematics department, her only certification her Troy Female Seminary diploma.)

Of course not all the female teachers were universally beloved. In 1857 a student complained that she did not want to write a composition on the subject of "The Ministry of Angels" but instead wanted to write on the topic, "Mother—Home and Heaven." She consulted her English teacher, Caroline King '46, but "I came from her room feeling <u>dreadfully</u>, for, instead of <u>encouraging</u> me, as she <u>ought</u> to have done, she <u>completely</u> discouraged me!!!"[19] Such student frustration was unusual—or at least rarely expressed in extant letters. And, perhaps, Miss King was merely following the direction of Sarah Willard who explained in one Regents report that the seminary teachers sought to help students work independently. Using the masculine pronouns common to formal writing, she criticized other schools where "his teacher does so much for him that no effort is left for himself—he has but passively to receive knowledge."[20] For the most part, when female teachers were discussed, students commonly engaged more in the time-honored tradition of criticizing their dress and mannerisms (for example, referring to two faculty siblings as "the nun-like sisters Maverick"[21]). In general, however, the Troy pupils expressed a sense of shared mission with and gratitude for the Willard women and the female teachers who instructed them.

Throughout this prewar period, alumnae and Willard relatives continued to dominate the faculty. Of nineteen faculty members in 1840, there were thirteen alumnae and six women who had blood ties to Emma Willard. Twenty years later, the staff was the same size and included eleven alumnae and four women related to the founder. The only year when the number of alumnae dropped below ten was 1854. Overall, total faculty numbers remained quite stable between 1840 and 1860, ranging from eighteen in 1843 to twenty-eight in 1851. The fluctuation was almost entirely accounted for by part-time teachers who were hired periodically to teach specific subjects such as Italian or hydrostatics or those subjects categorized as "ornamental branches," which included "drawing in pencil and crayon, mapping, water colors, oils, vocal music, piano, harp, organ, guitar and dancing."[22]

The founder remained a presence. For a short period after her divorce was finalized, she had contemplated moving to Philadelphia to be closer to her publisher, A. S. Barnes. She lived there for several months with her niece Emma Willard Lincoln O'Brien and her family but eventually returned to Troy in 1844. From then until her death, she would devote herself mainly to her writing. In addition to text-books, she wrote poetry and essays and contributed to professional journals, and for a while edited a magazine for teachers in New York. She continued to instruct and guide teachers through her writing, both in private correspondence and magazine articles.

One of her most poignant lessons was published in the educational monthly *New York Teacher* in 1855. The prior spring, Harriet Neely, a pupil from South Carolina, had died suddenly in the night, just days before her sixteenth birthday. The next morning Emma had taken on the responsibility of writing to Hatty's mother, Eliza Neely, to give her the news. After introducing herself to Mrs. Neely, Emma explained that Sarah would have written to her, "but something has occurred this morning, among her pupils, which has so shocked and distressed her, that after a short time of intense activity and exertion she has now been obliged to take to her bed." Emma then segued into her purpose for writing: "[T]he cause of my daughter's affliction concerns you, even more than her. It is a beloved pupil that she mourns, but Dear Madam, it is your daughter.[23] Hattie's body was "hermetically sealed in a leaden coffin,"[24] and her sister Elizabeth, also a student at the school, accompanied her sibling's remains to South Carolina. Mrs. Neely wrote back to the Willards on May 10, thanking the Willards and assuring them that she would never "be able to repay you for your kindness, for what you have done for my children."[25] It was Mrs. Neely's letter that Emma published in the journal, along with her explanation of the events, explaining that she was sharing the story as a lesson for "unreasonable parents" who "make the teacher responsible for whatever happens to the child."[26]

Emma's placement of this story in *New York Teacher* is an example of her shrewd marketing. The news of Hatty's death was reported in the *New York Daily Times* under the misleading headline, "Sudden Death of a Young Lady—Suicide." With a dateline from Troy, the article reported that "a Miss Jones, of South Carolina, a pupil in the Troy Female Seminary, was found dead in her bed this morning," adding, "the cause was disease of the heart."[27] Not only was the name wrong, but the "suicide" was reported in the next paragraph and had nothing to do with the seminary or Troy. Such reporting could lead to fears about instability, unhealthy diets, or poor hygiene at the seminary and consequently deter parents from enrolling their daughters. Writing the article in *New York Teacher* gave Emma the opportunity to praise the medical care available at the school. "Physicians," she wrote, "were by her bedside in a quarter of an hour,"[28] and she received immediate attention from the seminary nurse, Lucy Jones.

Student letters corroborate Jones's importance in the lives—and health—of seminary students. They often mentioned her in connection with outbreaks of measles, scarlet fever, and other ailments and generally seemed to feel they were in a healthy place. A contemporary of Hattie Neely's, also from the South, wrote to her brother complaining about the weather, but assured him, "It is impossible for me to be [imprudent about my health] for there are two nurses always running around to see to the girls. The other day I started to go outdoors without my rubbers on and happened to meet one of them and she . . . followed me to my room till she saw me put them on."[29]

Although her writing varied from correspondence to essays to articles about her school and teaching in general, Emma's income derived from her textbooks. In the federal census for 1850, her occupation was listed as "authoress," and her estate was valued at $25,000, making her a very wealthy woman for her time. She revised her history of the United States every few years, and in 1849 published a separate volume on California and the exploits of John C. Fremont. She revised this text in 1853. In it, her account of the "Omnibus Bill" of 1850 was based in part on her attendance in the Senate gallery during Henry Clay's pivotal speech that was so critical to forging the historic compromise. She sent the dying senator the notes she had taken and proudly reported that he felt she had summarized his speech "perfectly."[30] As always a supporter of the Union at any cost, she focused on the necessity for preventing southern secession rather than the shame and horror of continuing slavery.

In 1856 she revised *Last Leaves* again, this time as a promotion for John C. Fremont's bid to become the first Republican president. Her admiration for Fremont was rooted in her belief that he had brought the western part of the nation into the Union. Again her nationalist feelings outweighed her opinions about slavery; she supported Fremont in spite of his abolitionist views.[31] In her preface to the 1856 volume, she even claimed that she had been the first to suggest Fremont as a presidential candidate, pointing to her speculation in earlier editions that his exploits in California might be viewed as good training for the presidency.[32]

Emma also added periodically to her *Universal History*, first printed in 1835. In 1844 she devised a chart, "The Temple of Time," to help students visualize history, claiming that "in history I have invented the map."[33] She matched that bold claim with others. As time went on, she rarely minimized her own importance. In the preface to one edition of her world history text, she asserted, "[T]he success of many schools is due, in no small degree, to [the] adoption and skillful use"[34] of her texts and teaching methods. In truth, whole public schools systems, including New York City, Baltimore, and Hartford, ordered her texts. When the Crystal Palace Exhibition opened in London in 1851, Emma Willard's chronological charts were included among the nearly six hundred entries from the United States. Prince Albert allegedly gave them his favorable attention.

Although retired from active leadership of the seminary, the founder remained committed to the cause of education. Throughout the 1840s, she was an advocate of the common schools movement, and while she was in Connecticut awaiting her divorce, she was first appointed and then elected to oversee the Kensington common schools. She was the first woman elected to a supervisory position in public education, an ironic twist, given her disdain for woman's suffrage. In Kensington, she introduced new textbooks, including her own, initiated public examinations, worked with the teachers, and, in short, "introduced her own methods of discipline and instruction practiced at Troy."[35] Her work in Kensington was novel for public schools, and Henry Barnard, the superintendent of education for Connecticut, encouraged the adoption of her methods throughout the state.

When she returned to New York, common school teachers and administrators sought her as a speaker on education and as an instructor of teachers. In 1845 she spoke to public school teachers and administrators throughout New York, traveling more than seven hundred miles for this purpose. She loved to travel, whether for education or pleasure. In 1850 she lectured at the Smithsonian. She frequently visited relatives in Hartford, Baltimore, and Philadelphia, and in 1854 she returned to England and France and also toured Germany, Austria, and Italy with her sister Almira, who, widowed a second time, was principal of the Patapsco Institute, an Episcopalian girls' school in Maryland.

When Emma Willard was at home, she frequently entertained students, particularly girls whose mothers she had taught in Middlebury and during her first years in Troy. Alumnae daughters seem always to have received her special attention, and the relationships that led to the future alumnae association were nurtured at tea parties in her parlor. When alumnae dropped off their daughters at school, they invariably sought the founder, and her correspondence with former students was extensive. In 1853 Harriet Mumford Paige '23 turned to her former principal when she became worried that her daughters Hatty and Clara were not prepared for their examinations. Emma tutored the girls herself, giving them extra drills, "more than I do for my own granddaughters." Harriet apparently wanted Emma to make sure that the girls were examined only in subjects they could master, but Emma refused, saying, "I cannot interfere to turn aside arrangements made by their principal and teachers for the examination."[36]

Although it seems clear that Emma Willard treated indigent students well (John Lord estimated that she personally provided more than $75,000 in tuition aid to hopeful teachers[37]), it is also clear that the daughters of wealthy patrons were most likely to take tea in her parlor. When Ermina Merick '54 and Nettie Fowler '53 arrived at school, the daughter and niece of successful North Country businessman Eldridge Merick, they, along with Mrs. Merick, were entertained by the founder. Nettie, who as Mrs. Cyrus McCormick would become famous herself, in large part for her philanthropy, wrote in her diary after meeting Madame Willard, "I think [EW] to be a truly noble woman—& pioneer in the cause of female education—by her own exertions she has attained the eminence upon which she stands." Clearly immune to blind hero worship, Nettie concluded, "in some respects I should not wish to imitate her—for 'tis said that she is very <u>egotistical</u>—but if anyone has the right to indulge vanity 'tis her."[38]

Like Nettie Fowler, many other seminary students were aware of their school's founder and her unique legacy as a pathfinder. They often had had experiences with other schools that allowed them to make informed comparisons with Troy. In pre–Civil War America, there was great fluidity in enrollments as students moved from academy to academy depending on family circumstances and finances, and alternating from studying to teaching and back to studying. In 1857 Anna Kellogg confided to her diary, "Dora Waters, Abbie Culver, and I talked more than an hour about teaching. . . . Oh! If I <u>only could teach</u>! I long to teach for just one year! If Mother and Father would only let me go away to teach somewhere, next year, and then the year after, come here and graduate I should be so happy."[39] Anna did not get her wish, but her two friends did. Dora Waters '57 taught at Troy for fourteen years before marrying; she died one year after her marriage, buried with her new baby in her arms. Abigail Culver '58 taught for seven years in Kentucky before marrying a wealthy Chicago merchant and raising a family of three.

Nettie Fowler had attended the Falley Seminary in Fulton, New York, before going to Troy, and she attended Geneseo Wesleyan in Lima, New York, after leaving the seminary. Mary Munson '42, Clara Harrison '50, Mary C. Brainerd '48, and Harriet Holmes '48 all attended Mount Holyoke (originally Mount Holyoke Female Seminary) before going to Troy, and Maria E. Weeks '40 went to Mount Holyoke after Troy. Other prewar students attended Kimball Union, North Pownal Academy, the Convent of the Sacred Heart in St. Louis, and Wheeling Seminary prior to Troy; Hannah Parish enrolled at the Burlington Seminary after leaving Troy. Cross-referencing students from the Cazenovia Seminary with the Troy Seminary yields at least ten girls who studied in both places, including Livia Guernsey '37, who was also an early "female principal" at Cazenovia. In addition, Cazenovia enrolled a number of men who would marry Troy graduates, including J. S. T. Stranahan, "First Citizen of Brooklyn," who, along with his second wife, Clara Harrison '50, dominated Brooklyn's social and philanthropic circles in the second half of the nineteenth century.

Students who had studied elsewhere invariably compared aspects of different schools, and usually the seminary came out on top. Jane Shepard '57 described her room to her mother, cataloguing "a bed-stead and bed, bureau, side board, washstand, book shelves, looking glass, three chairs and two oil lamps," as well as carpeting. Her bed was "furnished with counterpanes—one linen and one cotton sheet, linen pillow cases . . . and a featherbed." All in all she concluded, "It is very nice for a boarding school,"[40] implying that she had attended others.

Food was also a source of comparison, and again the seminary proved superior. Minnie Otis '65 wrote to a friend at home that she longed for "a good apple," but that overall, "we have pretty good vict-uals."[41] After her first week in Troy, Jane Shepard gave her mother an accounting of meals even more detailed than her room inventory. For breakfast they had "potatoes, 'sometimes' pancakes, bread and butter, and tea and coffee." For the noon meal, "dinner," the students were served "mutton, chicken pie, vegetables, potatoes, squash, tomatoes, turnips and corn." They did not always have dessert, but when they did it was "watermelon or baked rice pudding." Supper consisted of "bread and butter, ginger cake and stewed pears." Jane found all of this most satisfactory and was very pleased that "Everything is cooked well, and tastes good and quite home-like."[42]

Students, of course, also compared their work at the seminary with their previous schooling. Academics at other seminaries were ap-parently not as rigorous as those in Troy. Sarah informed the Regents that "we have found it necessary to instruct most of our pupils in the elementary studies; even the most advanced, at their entrance, have been deficient in Spelling, Reading, Grammar and Arithmetic."[43] Net-tie Fowler assured her brother of the seminary's rigor, writing, "I tell you, Eldridge, if any person wants to know anything here they have to study for it. We cannot skip by as I used to at Fulton—not that I did not study there, but it is necessary to study pretty hard here."[44]

A few months later, however, Nettie revised this assessment. She was still determined to work hard for her diploma, as she wrote, "I would earn it <u>or</u> <u>not</u> <u>take</u> <u>it</u>." To her surprise, she had discovered that "even here one may slip through and get a diploma without deserving it."[45] Jane Shepard corroborated Nettie's observations, writing to her mother "they will give diplomas to young ladies even if they cannot learn one [illegible]."[46] Like Nettie, however, she was determined to earn her diploma, although she left herself an escape plan, asking her mother not to mention to anyone that a diploma could be had for less than full effort "for if I should give out the last few weeks and still get my diploma, I don't want anyone to know anything about it." She added darkly, "I have been behind the curtain and found out all these things."[47] Interestingly, when they left the school, neither had earned a diploma.

Diplomas were a relatively new concept for students at the seminary. For years academies had given students some sort of certificate when they left school; at girls' schools, the certificate was sometimes done in needlework, a sampler to be displayed. However, these documents were usually locally conceived and varied widely as to what they represented. For boys going on to college, the mastery of a discrete body of knowledge, particularly in Greek and Latin, was the mark of a successful academy education. The catalog for 1843 is the first to mention diplomas, and the oldest extant diploma for the seminary is dated 1849. The requirement for receiving a diploma was the successful passing of "examinations in the full course of English studies plus Latin or one of the modern languages."[48] Meanwhile, the diploma itself was awarded for "acquaintance with the prescribed course of study and that deportment which entitles her to the Highest Honor of this institution."[49] "Acquaintance with" connotes significantly less rigor than "passing examinations in," and there was no indication on the early diploma that any state curricular requirements had been met.

For girls in earlier, more traditional seminaries, the ability to play the piano, work a piece of embroidery, or converse in French was physical proof of educational attainment. At the Troy Female Seminary, the public examination remained the capstone achievement. In spite of Nettie Fowler's and Jane Shepard's scoffing, most students seem to have approached this exercise with great trepidation and significant study. The results, reported by the examining committee and the newspapers, continued to impress those who observed the proceedings. Nettie studied hard for her own examination, explaining in her journal, "Not that examination is the <u>sole</u> object of all our toil—but we feel that if we are prepared for a thorough examination we will retain the knowledge we possess."[50]

Anna Kellogg, like many other students, agonized over her examination. The night before her first mathematics exercise, she confided to her diary, "<u>Tomorrow</u>! Oh!!! How I dread it—I feel <u>dreadfully sick</u>—was obliged to go to bed, for more than two hours, this morning—took my book with me & studied one moment, the next, the tears would roll down my cheeks—I was in perfect <u>agony</u>." The morning of the exam, she continued in her diary, "Rose early but did not accomplish much—slept but little—am awfully excited—Oh—what—if I <u>should fail</u>!!! Horrible!!!!" And then at noon, she wrote—"12 o'clock—I am through—my fate is decided—I did not <u>fail</u> . . . I <u>did well</u>—I am not ashamed to confess it—though I know, if I had been feeling well, & less frightened, I should have done better."[51]

The examining committees of the 1850s were drawn chiefly from the ranks of education and religion. The committee for 1854 was typical. All male, it included a mathematics professor from West Point, a science instructor from RPI, the superintendent of the New York City public schools, and a teacher from Lansingburgh along with two ministers from Troy, one Episcopalian and one Presbyterian, and an Anglican minister from Maine. There was usually a Ladies' Visiting Committee as well, but their task was primarily to report on discipline and the care of the students in the boarding department, with special attention to discipline, health, and diet.

Beginning in 1845, the examiners' reports were included in the school catalog. The examiners wrote a new report each year, but over the years, the catalogs also contained snippets from earlier reports, some repeated many years in a row. For the most part, the examination's authenticity was one of its signal strengths. From the time she began teaching in Middlebury, Emma Willard had repeatedly argued that a good education taught pupils how to think, not just to memorize facts. She had written all of her textbooks with this principle in mind. To that end, students were examined randomly and never given questions in advance. Nevertheless, in some instances, the answers required memorization of large bodies of material. In 1852 Taylor Lewis, a member of the examining committee, a professor at Union, and the father of Keziah '57,[52] specifically addressed the issue of memorization. After examining a class of girls in Stewart's *Moral Philosophy,* arguably the most complex subject taught at the seminary (and at Union), he wrote, "Some might criticize the degree of rote learning . . . but it is quite a serious question whether, at the present day, we may not be going much too far into the other extreme, and producing looseness of language and consequently, looseness of thought, under the vain pretense of making pupils *express their own ideas in their own words*.[53]

Albert S. Church, one of Lewis's colleagues on the committee and a mathematics professor from West Point, believed that the seminary students utilized a perfect blend of memory and original thought, noting that the "system of instruction . . . pursued at this Seminary [is] calculated to teach the pupil how to think as well as to gain a thorough acquaintance with the various branches of studying." Church did suggest, however, that more attention be paid to elocution because "a defect of utterance" prevented at least one student from doing "full justice to her real attainments."[54] The next year, Amos Hadley, an attorney from Troy, also mentioned the lack of elocution and criticized students for addressing themselves to the blackboard. Mention of these shortcomings contributed to the authenticity of the examiners' reports. However, on balance the reports were always positive. Perhaps most striking was the spirit of camaraderie among the pupils. As the examiners noted, there was "no envy or jealousy," and the students "appeared like a band of sisters, having a common goal in the common success."[55]

The commentary by the ladies' visiting committee provides a picture of the disciplinary system and the regulation of life outside the classroom. Beginning in Middlebury, Emma Willard had relied on older students to help instruct younger ones, and at the seminary this system continued, not only in the classroom but in the dormitory. The main school building during the antebellum years contained both academic spaces and residence halls. Samantha Otis '60 described "a brick building four stories high, on one side . . . surrounded by trees and on the other side there is a yard with a swing and some flowers in it . . . which the girls play in."[56] Boarders roomed on the top three stories, with faculty residences sprinkled throughout. The rooms were arranged on "halls," which one student described this way: "What I mean by the halls is this, the house is a long, narrow building with halls through the centre, with one above another and only one hall upon each floor, and there is [sic] four of these besides the basement. . . . The school-room for day-schollars [sic] is in the fourth hall, which is the highest one.[57]

The Willards lived in the seminary building, presumably on the first or possibly second floor. By 1850 hot and cold running water was carried by pipes into the residential area of the school. These pipes were heated with steam by 1856, a modernization that symbolized the school's prosperity and was newsworthy enough that "the new steam arrangements"[58] were mentioned in a letter to a great-nephew.

The disciplinary system, designed by Emma Willard during her first years in Troy, had changed very little and essentially remained intact until 1872. In each dormitory area, called "halls" by the pupils, there were students appointed as "monitors" under the supervision of a faculty member who was "the officer of the week." Being a monitor was both an honor and a responsibility. Anna Kellogg excitedly noted in her diary after she had been at school two months, "Anna Kellogg Monitress of the House. (first time!) Miss Hopkins officer."[59] Miss Hopkins was Aurelia Hopkins '44, a teacher at the seminary for nearly twenty years. Being monitress carried with it some additional privileges. In 1853 Nettie Fowler wrote to her brother that she had "finished [her] duties as monitress" and so was allowed to stay up later than usual.[60]

A second faculty member assumed the role of "another officer whose duty it is to inspect the interior of each wardrobe and bureau, every third week, and report any disorder in this department." The visiting ladies commended this practice in 1853 as it "hardly leaves it possible for the pupil to form indolent, disorderly or careless habits."[61] The extent to which students were responsible for their own room care varied from boarding school to boarding school. At South Hadley, Mary Lyon's pupils were responsible for room care and a host of other domestic chores. This student labor was designed to defray expenses and teach humility. A contemporary comparison of Mount Holyoke and Troy viewed the Massachusetts pupils as "ready to grapple with the stern realities of life," whereas the Troy girls focused on "scholastic merit."[62] At Miss Porter's School in Farmington, which had begun in 1843, student rooms were maintained by maids who attended to the rooms every day except Sunday. One student reported home, "There are quite a number of servants, some white and some black."[63] In addition, Miss Porter, it was rumored, "visits every room twice a day and opens bureau drawers once a week."[64]

At Troy students appear to have exercised more self-government than was true of students elsewhere. Every week they collected demerits—or "marks"—for a variety of infractions, but they took turns being the monitors who assigned these marks, and behavior was generally very good. Although expulsion existed as the "severest penalty," it was apparently very rarely exercised; the committee noted that it had been "many years"[65] since an expulsion had occurred. Sarah Willard described the governance of the students as "parental," noting "they are treated with confidence, not being continually watched but sufficiently guarded for the detection of errors of conduct."[66] Guarding against "errors of conduct" gave rise to a very elaborate disciplinary system. Monitors gave marks for lapses in room care, study habits, dress, and behavior, but these could be offset by credits, also given out by the monitors. Group disorder of any type resulted in a "general fault mark" for the whole school. From the very beginning, a system of school bells regulated the class day, as well as the hours for dining, rising, and going to bed. Dozens of student letters end abruptly with the writer hurriedly scribbling that a bell has rung.

Life at the school was restrictive by modern standards. In 1853 the Visiting Committee reported approvingly that students "are not allowed to receive visits from gentlemen, unless in special cases at the request of their parents; neither are they allowed to ride or walk with gentlemen."[67] This rule had been in effect since the beginning and was not generally popular. Early on, Virginia Anderson '37 described the restriction on gentlemen callers to her mother:

> Some one of the teachers always find some excuse to come into
> the parlor when gentlemen call on the girls, and if they possibly find
> it out, they generally go in before the young lady comes down, and
> then pretend to be very busily engaged with a book, or paper, but
> their ears are otherwise occupied, and if they hear anything like
> love, it is reported to Mrs. Willard, who takes good care to have that
> young lady always engaged if the gentleman should call again.[68]

The constraints on social mingling were not there to prevent marriage but rather to ensure that seminary girls made good marriages. Both Sarah and Emma celebrated the marriages of their students and often helped with the planning and attended the weddings. When Clara Hulet '57 left abruptly before the end of the term to be married, another student noted in her diary that "Miss Hudson . . . had known she was going for a long time—she is to be <u>married</u>, on <u>Thursday morning</u>, to a President of a college." Clara married the president of Baldwin College. He was a Methodist minister and a widower with four children, which occasioned her classmate's judgment: "Poor girl."[69]

The Willards routinely held "balls" and parties to which suitable young men were invited. Their attitude contrasts sharply with that of Sarah Porter at her seminary. Miss Porter allowed "no waltzing"[70] at social events. An early Farmington pupil wrote home that "there was a great excitement in the school on account of two of the girls being expelled for flirting. They were found in the woods with two of Mr. Hart's boys."[71] (Ironically, those Hart boys were most likely distant cousins of Emma Willard.) Another student wrote that in coming to Miss Porter's, "I have joined the anti-man society,"[72] and yet another commented, "All of the male sex are great bugbears to Miss Porter."[73] A Farmington rule of the 1850s asserted that the "waving of handkerchiefs, making or returning any signals to young men or boys is an offense that will demand dismissal from the school."[74] Apparently, Sarah Porter used literature to reinforce her feelings about boys. Like Sarah Willard, she routinely read to her students (although she did not have the aversion to novels that the Willards had). After hearing Miss Porter read *The Mill on the Floss*, one student reported, "She said it was not at all natural or true to Maggie's character that her infatuation for Stephen should be carried to the pitch it was."[75]

Farmington students often wrote about what they were reading. Novels like *Adam Bede, The Minister's Wooing, The Newcomes,* and *The Marble Faun* were mentioned in letters, along with Shakespeare and current periodicals, especially *The Atlantic.* As one girl told her parents, Miss Porter "buys all the publications which are worth reading."[76] In spite of her broad outlook on literature, Miss Porter did not inspire awe and admiration in her pupils the way that the Willard women did. She was not worldly; she had not traveled; she did not wear fine clothes. She was unmarried, pious, and a devout Congregationalist. Julia Clark, studying at Farmington from Iowa, wrote home, "Miss Porter is about as homely as you can imagine. She is brown as a baked potato, with a big nose and little gray eyes."[77] Sarah Porter's closest confidante was her brother Noah, eventually the president of Yale, but a minister in Springfield, Massachusetts, when his sister opened her school.

Like the Willards, Miss Porter monitored her students' contact with other people. Complained one Farmington girl, "We are always obliged to go everywhere an hour before the performance commences in order to obtain seats together and not be mixed with other people."[78] Another, having run out of postage stamps, explained her tardiness in responding to a letter: "You know we are not allowed to go to the post office."[79] In Troy shopping was strictly regulated, and students were usually accompanied by teachers when they ran errands in the city. On a Saturday in December 1856, Anna Kellogg wanted to have her picture taken as a present for a student who was leaving. She "had permission from Miss Hudson to go the Daguerrian rooms, if we could get a teacher to go with us. We 'procured' Mrs. Smith."[80] Wily schoolgirl that she was, Anna also knew how to skirt the rules. Just the week before she and a friend had used a visit to the dentist as an excuse to go shopping. After the dentist, they went to "Sinsabaugh's for a snack of oyster stew, pickles, crackers, cake, candy, coconut balls, etc. etc. etc." Following that they "went out shopping, which being against the rules, afforded us much pleasure."[81]

Although both the Willards and Sarah Porter had absolute authority to establish social rules for their pupils, Miss Porter, located in Connecticut, also had absolute control over her curriculum in ways that the Troy educators did not. The elaborate reports filed with the New York State Regents outlined in detail the curriculum, the names, ages and salaries of the teachers, and the students' ages and courses of studies. The number of students at the school far exceeded the number who met the requirements for a diploma. Until the 1870s, a seminary education was still the end point for the vast majority of young women, so the "diploma," critical for a boy's entrance to college, did not carry much weight for girls. Even the pioneering seminary students who pursued medicine—Elizabeth Bates '50, Sarah Seward '50, Sarah McNutt '60 and her sister, Frances '60, and Oriana Moon '51—apprenticed to doctors or went on to the Philadelphia Women's Medical College without benefit of an undergraduate college education.

If the number of students reported as meeting Regents requirements fell far short of the total number of students enrolled, the number of students receiving diplomas was even smaller. For example, in 1852 there were 461 students enrolled for any part of the year; of these 287 met the Regents requirements, and 20 received diplomas. The Regents requirements had to do with attendance, age, and curriculum and were designed as a way to dispense state aid per capita. In spite of the school's ineligibility for state aid, each year the seminary reported the number of students who were "not claimed" as Regents students because of "insufficient age or studies" or having been enrolled at the school for fewer than four months. Although the number of public high schools in United States cities grew during this period, doubling from 80 in 1850 to 160 in 1870, attendance was sporadic, particularly before the war. This erratic pattern of school attendance was a focus of the Regents requirements. The attendance issue was partly seasonal; boys worked on farms and attended school only in the winter. Much has been made recently of the fact that girls outnumber boys on college campuses. In fact, researchers have concluded that girls outnumbered boys in New York's high schools and academies before 1850. Given that high school or academy education was the end point for girls, the persistent pattern over time of girls outnumbering boys at the highest end of education is striking.

Troy's citizens continued to have progressive attitudes about education. At some point in the 1840s, a laboratory at RPI was set aside for high school instruction; however, the annual budget for this enterprise plus the eight ward schools totaled only $22,000. In 1849 a formal board of education charged with monitoring the city schools was established with Day O. Kellogg as president and J. T. McCoun as clerk. McCoun's wife and daughter were seminary graduates. That same year Troy abolished fees for public schools, doing so shortly before the legislature abolished such fees for all public schools in the state.

In the 1850s, Troy decided to build a separate free public high school fit for their progressive and economically thriving city. (Troy continued to be a much touted city. In 1851 the new railroad station in the center of the city contained the largest train shed in the United States and the second largest in the world.) By January 1858, a vacant lot on the west side of Fifth Street had been purchased for $3750 and a builder secured. In the fall of 1859, the new high school opened; the building measured 60 feet by 130 feet and cost just under $13,000 to construct. In contrast, that same year the seminary buildings and lot were valued at just over $12,000.

In New York State, the aim of the Regents was centralized control over the curriculum in the new high schools. They did this by establishing strict diploma requirements. Regardless of a diploma's irrelevance for girls with virtually no collegiate prospects, the standards for the state diploma were mirrored by the course of study at the seminary. Adhering to the proscribed state curriculum had two purposes: to ensure that the young women at the seminary were receiving the same education as their male counterparts and to continue to press for state aid for girls' education.

The state requirements reflected a concern that had long been held by seminary principals, including the founder. In her *Plan*, Emma Willard had criticized the irregular attendance patterns of girls and haphazard courses of study at other girls' schools. Twenty years later Sarah Willard wrote, "We are much hindered in our attempts to produce such a plan as will be for the ultimate benefit of the individual . . . by the early age that girls leave the school and the ruinous sentiment that at seventeen they must be <u>finished</u> women."[82] The curriculum as laid out in catalogs in the pre–Civil War decades assumed a girl's entry into the school at seven and graduation at nineteen. Beginning in 1840, there were two "classes" of instruction. The "introductory or first class of English studies" was designed for younger girls and covered "Reading, Grammar, Arithmetic, Woodbridge's Rudiments of Geography; Willard's Geography for Beginners, Mrs. Phelps' Geology."[83] By the early 1850s, the faculty was listed as belonging to departments: there were departments of language, music, drawing and painting, and "English and Scientific,"[84] which was the formal academic program.

In spite of the Willards' desire for "a regular gradation of study,"[85] the reality at the seminary was often quite different. First of all, the age range of the students varied widely; in 1853 the youngest pupil was ten and the oldest forty. Only once in the years between 1839 and 1872 was a seven-year-old girl enrolled, and that was a Willard granddaughter. (In fact, Willard granddaughters were the youngest students on record for nine of the first thirty-four years of Regents reports.) The youngest girls tended to be ten or eleven years old, and, without exception, all of the youngest students were day students. Each year the oldest students enrolled were women whose ages ranged from twenty-three to forty. They were almost invariably boarders, studying in Troy to prepare themselves for teaching.

Just as the pupils failed to follow the optimal age range as prescribed by the seminary principals, they also refused to follow the proscribed curriculum. From letters it would seem that Sarah Willard and Theodosia Hudson met individually and as a group with entering students in order to place them in the right courses; however, it is also clear that the students had a great deal of freedom to elect what they wanted to pursue. Thus Jane Sheppard reported to her mother in 1856 that she had signed up for French, Music, Kames (moral philosophy), Mathematical Astronomy and Chemistry." She had been told by some teachers that "the last three are . . . very difficult studies."[86]

Worried about the work, she nevertheless took comfort in the fact that "Miss [Theodosia] Hudson when she examined me and classified me yesterday told me I could graduate this year without difficulty."[87] Jane, however, suggests to her mother that staying for two years and not studying quite as hard might be preferable, indicating a significant measure of student and family control over the course of study. Likewise, Samantha Otis reported in 1859 that she was "glad" to be studying "Music, French, Grammar, Reading and Writing and Dancing,"[88] a seemingly easy course of study compared to Jane's.

In spite of this carefully crafted academic program, Sarah Willard never forgot her obligation for the moral education of her pupils. Echoing her mother-in-law's philosophy, she assured the Regents that the seminary "aim[s] at the simultaneous and harmonious exercise of the moral, intellectual and social powers." and that "we provide a moral atmosphere in which the best affections of the soul are fostered." The teachers she asserted, "are, almost without exception, religious persons." In addition, "The scriptures are daily read, and the Bible is a textbook for weekly study." In fact, she claimed, "We never lose sight of the moral culture. In all our instruction, the moral motives and end are enforced."[89] She clearly knew her market. Charlotte Baldwin's brother Richard, like many male family members of seminary students, cautioned her, "I trust that you, with all your learning, learn the true grace and modesty that so much adorns the lady that practices them."[90]

By 1860 there were three well-established nondenominational schools where a young woman could receive an academy education: the Troy Female Seminary, Mount Holyoke, and Miss Porter's. Troy was by far the largest, and its students came from the most diverse backgrounds. As Sarah Numan '45 recalled near the end of the nineteenth century, "Many years before the War of the Rebellion, the proud daughters of Southern chivalry gathered within its walls; the distant regions of the Western States and the cities along New England's coast contributed to this pioneer institution, which was, in the hey-day of its fame, the largest of its class in the world." The twenty years in the middle of the century were indeed the seminary's nineteenth-century "hey-day."[91] The diversity that Numan celebrated proved to be the school's most enduring strength in the long run, but in the course of the Civil War, that strength would prove to be a financial challenge.

The House Is Divided

IN MODERN TERMS, the Troy Female Seminary during its first fifty years in Troy was a homogeneous institution. All of the students were white, and close to 100 percent were Protestant. However, compared to other girls' schools and the boys' boarding schools that have survived into the twentieth century, the seminary was an unusually diverse place. Methodists, Unitarians, Episcopalians, Presbyterians, Baptists, Congregationalists, Lutherans, and the odd Quaker or Disciple of Christ mingled freely together. In letters home, a roommate or classmate's religion was a common descriptor, along with her hometown, father's occupation, or family heritage. For example, Jane Shepard '57 described her roommate to her mother as "a Miss Wilkins from Whitehall . . . 21 . . . an Episcopalian."[1] Similarly, Ermina Merrick '54 wrote to her cousin that she was one of three Methodists enrolled for the fall term, the others being "Miss Kennedy and a girl from Texas."[2]

Following a religion with fewer student adherents sometimes forged a bond; when Mary Huntington '33 spied Ann Crosby '32 with a copy of *The Christian Register*, she immediately suspected that Crosby was a Unitarian; in fact, both fathers were widely published Unitarian ministers. Suggesting the importance of religion as a topic among the students, Mary wrote of her conversation with Ann, "I have not told anyone before that Pa is a Unitarian, and I suppose it will spread like wildfire."[3] Being in Troy gave girls the freedom to choose a different religion from their parents as was evident by Ann's response to Mary; she said that her father had sent her the religious paper, and just because he was a Unitarian did not mean she was. Maria Patchin '31, writing to her brother Thaddeus, explained that she was having trouble deciding on a religion.

She had tried the Willards' church and concluded, "I like Episcopacy pretty well, but I tell you, I am afraid of it. I think it is too easy a religion for me. I know it is a fashionable popular church . . . you know they do not require a change of heart of their members and Christ says, 'Except a man be born again, he cannot see the Kingdom of God.'"[4]

In the early 1890s, a group of alumnae arranged for the compilation of *Emma Willard and Her Pupils*, a biographical record of seminary alumnae from the Middlebury years to 1872, arranged by decade. The overwhelming majority of the entries included the woman's religious affiliation, noting in many cases whether or not she had converted to a different sect when she married. The editors made sure to mention fathers and husbands who were ministers, carefully noting their denominations. Many of the women who responded to the questionnaire had married ministers. Of the students from the first decade who responded, twenty-two women married ministers; most had local parishes, but many were presidents of colleges, and some were missionaries, both overseas and in the West and South. Joshua Phelps, for example, husband of Caroline Lee '31, was sent by the Presbyterian Home Mission to preach in Florida, a frontier area populated by Native Americans and American adventurers, all of whom were presumed to need salvation. Caroline accompanied him.

Fifty women who attended the school during the second decade married ministers. Again, their husbands included college presidents and missionaries—the latter group preaching to Native Americans in the West, Indians and "Siamese" overseas, and American sailors at the port of St. Thomas in the Virgin Islands. Perhaps most unusual in the group was William Henry Hoyt, an Episcopalian who was ordained a Roman Catholic priest in 1877 after the death of his wife, Ann Deming '33. She had converted to Catholicism some years before her death. Thirty-six women from the third decade married ministers with responsibilities to congregations from China and Japan to India, and on college campuses and aboard naval ships.

The thirty-three ministers married to graduates from the fourth decade included missionaries to India, Chile, and Liberia, as well as a president of Hobart, the rector of the American Chapel in Geneva, and the chaplain at Randolph-Macon. Alice Van Kleeck married Robert F. Crary, who, in addition to being an Episcopalian minister, was also Robert Fulton's grandson. Among the final group of graduates chronicled in *Emma Willard and Her Pupils*, twenty-nine married ministers, a third of whom were Episcopalian. Fewer students in this last decade married missionaries, but three sailed with their husbands to posts in Syria, West Africa, and Japan, and Mary Lewis, the wife of Rev. Valentine Lewis and a seminary graduate whose maiden name is unknown, accompanied her husband on his ministry to the residents of Chinatown in San Francisco. Among those connected to colleges was Susan Denison '66, who married Edward M. Gallaudet, the first president of Gallaudet University, the innovative college for the deaf founded by his father.

Another student from the fifth decade, Mary Ella Gray '64, was the daughter of E. H. Gray, chaplain of the U.S. Senate and one of four ministers presiding at Lincoln's funeral services in the East Room of the White House. Mary Ella's brother, N. Oscar Gray, married one of her schoolmates, Mary T. Johnson '65. Johnson's brother, Herrick Johnson, was "a foremost theologian" and "a national figure."[5] The Johnson-Gray marriage united two of the most prominent theological families of the day. The Grays were Baptist and the Johnsons, Presbyterian. Not all of the ministers that the seminary women married were nationally renowned, but most were comfortable financially with census records indicating substantial property.

The graduates' religions and church memberships helped to define them and their place in their communities. Connections with prominent clergy, even as parishioners, was worthy of mention in the autobiographical sketches submitted by alumnae. Preachers like Edward Everett Hale, Henry Ward Beecher, and Phillips Brooks were household names and often achieved celebrity status. The women who belonged to their churches wanted their former classmates to know it. Because clergy were among the small percentage of college-educated American men, they were part of the literary elite, often publishing books of their sermons or memoirs of their missionary work. Those with wives who had been educated at Troy found partners who helped with their literary endeavors in addition to handling the typical duties of the pastor's wife. Susan Denison Gallaudet translated a French grammar into English for use at her husband's school, Helen Howe Holcomb '56 wrote about life in India for children and adults, and Harriet Petitt House '42 contributed chapters to a book about life in Siam, in addition to founding a girls' school in Bangkok and adopting a Siamese boy whom she and her husband educated at Williams College. He returned to his native country as a minister.

House's and Holcomb's books definitely show the influence of their seminary training. Both carefully studied the geography of their adopted countries, describing cities, towns, and physical features, using the same style and narrative that Emma Willard had used in her textbooks (which they had studied in Troy). As Emma Willard had done during her trip to France, both women made every effort to learn and communicate in the native languages of the countries where their husbands were posted. Both specifically celebrated the accomplishments of the girls in the regions where they worked, and they highlighted schools for girls and the accomplishments of women as evidence of progress. For example, in *In the Heart of India,* Holcomb wrote that one of her primary motives in writing the book was to show "the kind of stuff of which the women of India are made."[6] In her chapters in a book of missionary reflections on Siam and Laos, Harriet House emphasized the strides the missionaries were making in educating girls and women. She detailed everything she saw, including the colors and patterns of Buddhist temples. However, echoing Emma Willard's dismissal of Catholicism after her tour of French cathedrals, House concluded her travelogue of the temples with reference to "the deluded people [who] spend vast sums on these temples and their idols"[7] and dismissed the Buddhist priests as "self-conceited idlers."[8] Likewise, Holcomb, whose vivid prose brought the rich smells, colors, and customs of India to life, described non-Christian Indians as "poor, bewildered creatures,"[9] and, like the founder, she could think of nowhere on earth better than the United States. In *Bits About India,* she posed the question, "Are you not glad that you live in a country where the life of a human being is considered of more consequence than that of a cow?"[10]

House, living in Siam under King Mongkut, Rama IV, celebrated every move made by the king toward westernization.[11]

Other schools, both boys' academies and girls' seminaries, produced missionaries and writers, but the contrast with Troy with regard to religion was striking. Although Mary Lyon insisted that her students in South Hadley attend two services at the Congregational Church in the village, students in Troy attended services wherever they wanted and sampled different faiths by accompanying friends to their churches. Troy by 1860 had three Baptist, four Episcopalian, two Unitarian, nine Methodist, seven Presbyterian, and five Roman Catholic churches, as well as one Quaker meetinghouse. (Presbyterian and Methodist churches on Liberty Street housed exclusively black congregations.) In addition to requiring attendance at the Congregational Church, Lyon specifically linked her seminary to the preparation of "laborers for Christ's cause," advertised that a South Hadley education would produce "a handmaid to the Gospel,"[12] and actively worked to convert her students to accept Jesus Christ as their savior.

Emma Willard spoke in more general tones of morality and religious principles, invariably reputing sectarianism. She was, of course, unabashedly Christian, but she was far more interested in teaching morality than sectarian theology. When she published *Morals for the Young, or Good Principles Instilling Wisdom* in 1858, the volume was favorably reviewed as an appropriate text for private and public schools because of "its avoidance of all denominationalism."[13] Sarah Willard continued her mother-in-law's practice of reading and interpreting Bible passages at weekly meetings of the entire student body. Like the older Mrs. Willard, she used the Bible as a springboard for homilies about morality and manners.

At Mount Holyoke, by contrast, the four-year curriculum included a specific Bible course each year, with the study of the Gospels forming the foundation in the first year. Rules for observing the Sabbath were outlined in the course catalog, including the admonition that no student could be away from Mount Holyoke on a Sunday during the academic term. The physical description of the school stressed the proximity of the village church. Although the Willards regularly attended church and certainly observed the Sabbath, members of the family were often away for weekends, particularly after 1862 when Sarah and John made frequent visits to their three grown married daughters living upper-class lives in Manhattan.[14]

Seeking to draw paying customers from the ranks of successful Protestant middle- and upper-class America, the Willards were careful not to favor any group,[15] although students frequently accompanied the Willard family to services at St. John's, where church records show that Emma, John, Sarah, and Sarah's sister Theodosia served as witnesses to or sponsors for several student baptisms. In spite of the family's preference for Anglican worship, however, there was no attempt to convert students to the Episcopal faith. Although Emma Willard had an aversion to the more emotional aspects of Protestant faith as practiced by Methodists and "New Light" Presbyterians (a distaste undoubtedly rooted as much in the snobbery alluded to by Maria Patchin as in theological principle), she allowed students to attend revivals and certainly never stood in the way of their conversions. When the famous revivalist Charles G. Finney came to Troy, at least one student attended his preaching and through Finney "found the way of salvation through Jesus our blessed Saviour." She was grateful, she wrote years later, that she had been permitted to go to the revival meetings.[16]

The commitment to inclusion that has been a hallmark of the modern school can trace its beginnings to the religious tolerance practiced by the founder and her immediate successors. In his biography of Emma Willard, John Lord specifically praised her ability to avoid sectarian favoritism (although after leaving the school, he became a lecturer at Mount Holyoke). He wrote, "There is nothing for which I hold Mrs. Willard in more respect than her uniform custom of keeping free from all sectarian influences." He further complimented her ability to secure "the respect of the various clergy of the city, who ever remained her friends."[17] The western edge of the seminary property bordered the grounds of the Presbyterian Church, presided over for forty years by the nationally renowned abolitionist preacher Nathan S. S. Beman. He also served as president of Rensselaer Polytechnic Institute (RPI) during twenty of those years.

Time and again Beman offered to help with religious instruction at the school, and student letters abound with references to his sermons and revivals. Not even this strong presence swayed Emma from her nonsectarian stance. She wrote to Beman that she appreciated his offer and was certainly glad the Presbyterians among her students looked to him for spiritual guidance, but was sure he would agree with her that "it is not proper for a person keeping a school—professedly not for any particular religious sect—to suffer the religious education of that school to become sectarian."[18] To John Lord, the founder's nonsectarianism was "broad and liberal" and provided room for a "seminary of girls from all parts of the country and divers creeds and opinions."[19] An examining committee put it another way, noting in 1861 that in spite of the fact that they found a "truly religious spirit modifying and moulding the whole system of education . . . religion is not ostentatiously thrust forward any where [sic]."[20]

Regardless of Lord's or others' characterization of her broadmindedness, Emma believed that enlightened education was closely tied to Christian teachings. America, as Emma portrayed it in her textbooks, was a great nation because it had evolved from Protestant pioneers. The founding fathers, in spite of their foresight in separating church and state, had, for the most part, been Protestants who routinely quoted the Bible. Even Jefferson, the most progressive theologically of the early presidents, had at one point ordered the teaching of the Bible in the public schools of the District of Columbia. On the eve of the Civil War, America remained an overwhelmingly Protestant nation, and "religion defined the values and assumptions of most . . . Americans."[21] Church attendance was part of nearly everyone's weekly ritual; one historian has calculated that in 1860, four times as many people attended church on Sunday as voted in the presidential election.[22] (The winner, Abraham Lincoln, a Protestant who derived much of his morality from the Bible, was not one of them.)

Like the presidents of men's colleges, the Willards and Mary Lyon and her successors taught moral philosophy to seniors, a course designed to prove that Christianity could be "revealed" by studying science and other subjects. The same examining committee that praised

the lack of ostentation in the seminary's presentation of religious training also complimented the school for "Christian education," writing,
"A wise course of training, therefore, seeks to make every department
of science and art, and every intellectual pursuit a means of moral
cultivation and advancement, and to show step by step, that religion
ought to permeate the occupation and life of every free moral agent.
This principle of christian [sic] education is, we think, the crowning
excellence of the Troy Female Seminary."[23]

The Willards' emphasis on the connection between the study of
the Bible and the moral growth of their pupils was far from unique.
In fact, they were no different from the leaders of most nonsectarian schools at the time. Public schools taught lessons from the Bible,
required daily prayer, and tied morality and character to Christian religious training. McGuffey's *Readers*, first published in 1836 and used
extensively in American public schools until after the Second World
War, used Bible stories to teach children to read. What was different
in Troy was the enrollment of students practicing so many different
branches of Protestantism in a private school.

In private academies for boys and at private colleges, education was
overwhelmingly controlled by Protestant churches, with most institutions adhering strictly to one sect. Colleges that trained young men for
the law and the ministry were invariably headed by Protestant clergymen.
In 1893, when Amherst published its first comprehensive list of graduates, those alumni who were ordained clergymen or foreign missionaries
were specifically highlighted.[24] When RPI, in the business of educating
young men to be engineers, chose Beman as their fourth president, he
was not only the fourth Presbyterian minister to hold the post but also
the last. His successor in 1865, John Winslow, iron manufacturer, was
the first layman. For RPI, Winslow's appointment marked an important
separation of science and religion that would not occur at the liberal arts
colleges and preparatory schools until the end of the century.

What was true for men's colleges was true for the most prominent
boys' schools of the nineteenth century. In 1903 Oscar Fay Adams identified nine boys' preparatory schools as "famous."[25] Seven of them still
exist, although all are now coeducational. All but one—Belmont Hill in

San Francisco, not incorporated until the 1880s—were identified with a single Protestant denomination, some by design and some by custom and location. Andover and Exeter were originally Congregationalist, although Exeter by the 1840s was Unitarian and by the 1850s allowed boys to worship "'at such church as their parents or guardians prefer,'"[26] which was "a non-sectarian choice virtually unheard of in the academies of the nineteenth century."[27] St. Paul's, St. Mark's, Groton, and Shattuck Hall were Episcopalian, and Lawrenceville had strong Presbyterian roots.

The influence of the particular branch of Protestantism practiced at the schools colored everything the boys did. At Andover, classes were held on Christmas and no wine was served, both Christmas celebrations and alcohol regarded by the conservative headmasters as the province of Roman Catholics. Boys at Andover were discouraged from attending Harvard because of its strong Unitarianism. Lawrenceville was Presbyterian, but in spite of the revivalism sweeping through many Presbyterian congregations, it remained traditionalist and nonevangelical. The Episcopal churches took their lead from their respective bishops. St. Paul's was particularly rigid. Its first headmaster, Rev. Henry Augustus Coit, allegedly told a student, "Do not forget, my child, that in the life to come, the Presbyterians will not be upon the same plane as the Episcopalians."[28] Emma and Sarah Willard might have privately agreed with Coit, and Almira, devoting the last decades of her teaching career to an Episcopal school in Baltimore, most certainly did. However, their public practice was far more inclusive.

In her American history texts, widely used in public schools, Emma Willard celebrated the United States as a "Protestant, Christian nation," but beginning in the 1850s, her school enrolled both Roman Catholic and Jewish students. In contrast, Lawrenceville did not admit Catholics until the end of the century, and the enrollment of Jewish students was a twentieth-century phenomenon at most of the boys' schools, as well as at Miss Porter's. Among the Troy students, however, a belief in girls' education trumped any single creed. And for the Willards, the success of the school was the ultimate tenet of faith in the cause of women's education. Families with the resources and the inclination to invest in their daughters' education practiced many creeds.

In 1858 Alice Theresa Grady '62 and her sister, Jane Frances Grady '63, entered the school as day students from Troy; that same year another day student, Miriam Gratz Mordecai '61, enrolled from West Troy. The Grady sisters were Roman Catholic, and Miriam was Jewish. Mordecai's father, Maj. Alfred Mordecai, was the commandant of the arsenal located almost directly across the Hudson from the seminary. He had graduated from West Point in 1823, among the first Jewish boys to do so. After his graduation, he stayed on at the academy to teach, and Emma Willard presumably met him there while John was a student. Mordecai later married Sara Gratz, a member of a prosperous Jewish family from Philadelphia. Although Miriam's religion set her apart from her classmates, her social status did not. Nor did her ambition; after the Civil War, she lived with her sister Laura on fashionable Rittenhouse Square in Philadelphia, and the two of them ran a successful girls' school in the city. At the end of the century, Miriam's nieces, daughters of her brother Alfred Mordecai Jr., enrolled at the seminary. For Miriam and her nieces, being day students made it easier to keep kosher; her father, in contrast, had been forced to attend services in the Christian chapel at West Point. Education for girls had long been a priority for the Mordecai family. Alfred's father Jacob ran a very successful girls' school in Warrenton, North Carolina. Not surprisingly, given the location of his school, many of his pupils were Christian. However, Jewish families from cities like Richmond also sent their daughters to Mordecai's school.

The Grady sisters' presence at the seminary is more difficult to explain. Both parents were born in Ireland. The father was a gardener, the mother a homemaker with three children younger than Jane, and there was an older sister who worked as a dressmaker. In the 1860 census, both Alice and Jane are listed as schoolteachers, age twenty-two and nineteen, respectively, living at home. They had been pupils in 1858 and 1859 and had been joined by their sister, Julia '64, in 1860. It is highly unlikely that either Alice or Jane made enough money prior to entering the seminary to pay for their studies. They most likely received assistance with the understanding that they would pay it back from future wages earned as teachers.

Both women did devote their lives to teaching. However, they did so after becoming Ursuline nuns and spent their entire lives in Ursuline girls' schools. In 1898 Jane wrote in the alumnae record book that she believed she and Alice had been the first Catholic girls at the school. This claim is untrue; earlier students from France and Louisiana were Roman Catholic. Irish Catholic, however, was another thing altogether. Mindful of how unusual this was in the mid-nineteenth century when discrimination toward immigrant Catholics by "native" American Protestants was rampant (and particularly virulent at times in Troy), Jane Grady expressed her gratitude not only for her education but also for "the kindness"[29] shown her and her sister by Emma and Sarah Willard.

It would be misleading to suggest that the Gradys and Miriam Mordecai began a wave of Catholic and Jewish students. Although the numbers were not large, other students of both faiths followed these girls. Some were boarders, another breakthrough at a time when a Presbyterian roommate gave Episcopalian parents cause for concern. In 1860 Florence O'Neill '61 enrolled from Fernandina, Florida, where she lived on a plantation with her parents, of Irish descent like the Gradys, but more like the Mordecais in terms of wealth and social prestige. James T. O'Neill was a judge, planter, and slave owner. Like Florence O'Neill, Sarah "Sallie" Solomons, a Jewish girl who entered the school from Charleston, South Carolina, came from a distinguished family that had been in the United States for generations and was part of the vibrant professional Jewish community with roots in colonial Charleston.

In spite of the unusual diversity—or perhaps because of it—there is no extant evidence in student letters that they experienced any religious discrimination. Parents occasionally expressed concerns about friendship choices, sometimes on religious grounds, but more often because of character or family background. Of course, the two frequently overlapped. In 1857 Anna Kellogg's mother wrote to express her happiness that Anna's interest in revivalism was keeping her from "the worldly temptations" she had feared would present themselves at the seminary. In particular, Mrs. Kellogg had worried that "the influence of gay Southern girls would lead you astray."[30]

The presence of "Southern girls" marked another kind of diversity.

Geographic diversity, particularly domestic geographic diversity, marked the seminary's uniqueness as much as religious diversity did. Beginning in the 1820s, southern girls had journeyed to Troy. In comparison, Mount Holyoke enrolled only sixteen students from the South between 1838 and 1860, ten coming from Virginia, four from Tennessee, and one each from Texas and North Carolina.[31] Before 1860 girls from every one of the eleven Confederate states studied in Troy, in addition to many students from Kentucky, Missouri, Maryland, and other nonsecessionist but slave-owning states. However, girls from many more countries enrolled at Mount Holyoke than enrolled at the seminary. Judging from the list of countries, which included Syria, India, Turkey, Borneo, and Hawaii, these girls were most likely children of missionaries. No one enrolled from France, England, or Scotland, the countries represented on the Troy lists. The differences can be explained by a combination of religious and economic factors. In 1860 tuition and board at South Hadley was $80 year; the $225 charged at Troy was almost three times that.

As the Civil War approached, students and teachers were more acutely aware of the geographic diversity of the seminary. As early as the 1830s, Emma Willard had forbidden attendance at abolitionist gatherings in Troy, even when the speakers were ministers preaching God's love for all humanity. By the late 1850s, with the "irrepressible conflict" increasingly unavoidable, students and teachers began to take sides. Two months after John Brown's historic raid on Harper's Ferry, Dora Waters wrote to her former seminary colleague, Mary Hastings, "the damnable wrong of slavery never seemed so great." She described the mood of the adults: "Mrs. Emma Willard, Mr. Willard, Mr. Arms and Mrs. Smith are the only ones from whom I've heard a decided opinion upon the side of sin and slavery. Miss King, Miss Hopkins and I are the only ones in the right who care enough about it to say what we think. Miss Jones and Miss Wilcox are halting between two opinions."[32]

At Farmington, Miss Porter's students were also aware of John Brown, but the November issue of the school newspaper focused more on Brown's background than his cause. According to the article, Brown's "exploits . . . [have] suddenly raised him from the obscure position he is so eminently fitted to occupy."[33]

Several months after Brown's raid, Troy captured national attention when Charles Nalle, a fugitive slave who had escaped captivity in Virginia, was arrested by federal marshals under the provisions of the Fugitive Slave Act. Nalle was working as a coachman for Uri Gilbert, seminary trustee. His attorney was Martin Townsend whose daughter and wife were seminary graduates. Troy reputedly had many abolitionists who aided in the work of the Underground Railroad, and a crowd of black and white sympathizers managed to assist Nalle in making his escape. Emma Willard, aware of the work of the Underground, used its existence to argue that most northerners did not favor abolition. Shortly after South Carolina's secession, she wrote, "That the great body of the Northern people acknowledges Southern rights in this respect [right to own slaves] is evident from the fact that run-away slaves have had to pass through an underground rail road. If their escape had been generally approved, there would have been no need of the rail road being <u>underground</u>."[34]

In the fall of 1860, girls from Georgia, Mississippi, Florida, Virginia, Louisiana, Alabama, and South Carolina, as well as students from Missouri, Kentucky, and Maryland, enrolled at the school, eighteen in all, a typical southern representation. There had been sixteen the year before. Isabelle McKennan '61 wrote to her sisters in Pittsburgh that the students in the "girls' parlour [sic]" have "regular battles about Lincoln and Douglas and Bell and Everett."[35] Edward Everett was the running mate of John Bell, the Constitutional Union candidate, and as an educator and politician from Massachusetts, Everett was probably more familiar to seminary students than Bell, the Tennessean. At Farmington, the students were more resoundingly supportive of Lincoln. One student wrote her sister a few days after the voting, "On Tuesday quite a good deal of enthusiasm prevailed here on the subject of the election . . . there is general rejoicing because Lincoln is elected."[36] The election results were more muted at Troy. Sarah wrote her grandmother, who was visiting New York City, "The girls had quite a discussion on politics on election day but that seems to have died out, and they are much more engaged in talking of the party they had last night."[37]

Although she could not vote, Emma Willard favored Bell, a candidate whose platform was consistent with her quest for unity at all costs. After the election, she explained, "I was a Unionist before the late Presidential election, and in favor of the Union candidate." As a good citizen, she supported Lincoln, "the constitutionally elected head of the nation," who was, she wrote approvingly, "struggling according to his oath to maintain its existence."[38] Sarah Willard expressed the same sentiments in a letter to a former classmate. She was glad that Lincoln had been elected because she believed his "more vigorous Administration" would "restore the Union."[39]

Meanwhile, Lincoln's election had spurred the secession of South Carolina, and by April, seven southern states had left the Union. The firing on Fort Sumter that month created even greater tension. The Willards were mindful of their southern students. Isabelle McKennan reported to a friend that there were Union flags hanging on all the stores and the courthouse and that "We are very anxious to hang out our flag here, but Mrs. Willard would not permit [it] for she said the Southern girls among us feel very badly [sic] now and if we were to hang flags out it would make them feel worse." In a fit of defiant patriotism, Isabelle concluded, "she can't prevent us from wearing red, white and blue ribbons."[40] At Farmington there was no such compromise with southern feelings. Addie Coe wrote home, "Farmington seems quite aroused on the subject of the war," and "Miss Porter has a beautiful flag on the observatory."[41]

Somewhat frivolously, the students in Troy "played war," setting up two groups as Fort Sumter and Fort Pickens. Isabelle wrote that "Nellie Merrill was the telegraph and we sent messages to each other." In spite of her participation in this game, Isabelle was cognizant of the potential loss that a civil conflict would bring. She watched the troops drilling in front of the courthouse and observed, "Some of them are so young." She reflected, "When I left home last September, how little I thought so many changes would take place before I returned, or that I was bidding many of my friends good-bye for the last time. For surely we cannot expect them all to return from such a bloody war (as everyone predicts this is going to be) alive."[42]

In the meantime, Emma Willard was doing everything in her power to stop the impending conflict. As soon as South Carolina seceded, she devised a plan for a petition for peace signed by women all over the country, including former students from all sections of the nation. By February she had traveled to Washington, D.C., where she was joined by her sister Almira and niece Myra. Almira had long lived in Baltimore and employed black servants. Emma W. Willard, writing to her grandmother, mused about her cousin Myra in 1861, "It did not seem she could be so much of a Southerner."[43] Myra's half sister, Stella Phelps Hatfield '33, had married a slave-owning teacher in Alabama. In spite of her family's southern predilections or perhaps because of them, Almira had helped her sister collect four thousand signatures that were presented to each house of Congress. The "memorial" to which the signatures were attached "was presented by Emma Willard, in the name and by the authority of American women."[44] Nearing seventy-four years old, she adhered to two of her lifelong principles: the supremacy of the Union and the role that educated women could play in its preservation. The congressional petition, authored by Emma, described the United States as "a continent in extent, an island in security—its harbors opening on the great oceans, it exceeds in geographical position and commercial advantages, any nation of the present or the past," and she expressed her hope that peace might be achieved by "that sex whose mission on earth is peace, duty, and righteousness."[45]

Their efforts, of course, failed. Although she advocated compromise with the South, John Lord maintained in his biography that Emma Willard "detested slavery."[46] Perhaps, but she was convinced that black Americans could not care for themselves without white supervision. Her attitude toward black Americans was founded on her exposure to slavery through her southern students and their families. With typical confidence, she explained her suitability to speak with authority on the topic:

> With regard to the great subject of American slavery, . . . I had advantages to understand it, that few possess; for as principal of the Troy Female Seminary for twenty years I had pupils from every state of the South . . . [and] many of my Northern pupils going South to teach married there, and became the mothers of Southern families. I have since visited and spent weeks at their homes, and I have seen with what care and kindness they treat their servants. (I hate the word slaves and I think we should get rid of it.)[47]

She supported the colonization movement, a position she had taken in her U.S. history texts, viewing Liberia as a "safety-valve for drawing off our surplus coloured population" and supporting the emigration of American blacks to that country "as a means of changing the present degradation of Africa into Christian civilization."[48]

In 1862 she returned to Washington to present to members of Congress her proposal for ending the war by reaching a compromise with the South over slavery. She titled her document *The African in America,* but it was generally called by its subtitle, *Via Media,* by which she meant a middle road that would allow the North and South to come together on the question of slavery. The proposal stressed the supremacy of the white race over the black race and an ordering of society where white men took precedence over white women (and everyone else). It called for the abolition of the harsher aspects of slavery, particularly the involuntary separation of families by sale, the removal of northern blacks—especially the few with talent who might stir up trouble if they remained in the United States—to Africa, and the development of a system of "regulated servitude" for southern ex-slaves. To illustrate her points, she used a number of cloying anecdotes from enlightened slave owners and grateful slaves, all representing the happiness that whites and blacks could have when their relative positions were understood.[49]

In light of her great work and vision for girls' education, the narrow bigotry in *Via Media* is difficult to read. Sadly, it was her last major publication. It stands in bleak contrast to Sarah Porter's actions with regard to slavery. At the same time that Emma Willard was distributing her work on slavery, a student in Farmington wrote, "Went to church to hear a contraband by the name of Davis speak. He sat behind the desk between Dr. Porter and Mrs. Paine and seemed to feel quite an equality with them. He has been a slave . . . and he says that he knows of no condition worse except being in hell. He certainly has great talent, for he is entirely without education. . . . I believe that some society has sent him out as proof of the capabilities of the black man."[50]

There is limited consolation in knowing that she had the courage of her convictions. In traveling to Baltimore and Washington during the war, Emma Willard was risking her life. She knew this. In response to

Sarah's worries about her, she replied simply, "I felt that I *must* come."[51] Her last wartime trip, undertaken in 1864, resulted in her capture by Confederate soldiers, an incident widely reported in northern newspapers. She was released unharmed, the soldiers' chivalry undoubtedly reinforcing her view of genteel southerners, even though she was forced to walk some distance in the hot sun, a challenge for the 77-year-old.

By the spring of 1862, only two students were left at the school from the South, and one was from the border state of Maryland. Neither responded to the alumnae questionnaire, so little is known about their reasons for remaining in the North. Most of the southern girls had left the seminary in May 1861 before the close of the term, assured of safe travel by government passes arranged by the Willards. For the remainder of the war—and for the remainder of the Willards' supervision of the school, which ended in 1872—the number of students from the Confederate states never reached ten, and some of the students who signed the roster during Reconstruction from Louisiana, Texas, or Georgia were actually transplanted northerners whose fathers were businessmen or federal officials.

The war featured prominently in the alumnae responses of the 1890s, providing a set of human profiles that demonstrate the deprivation, despair, and devastation behind the statistics of this deadliest of American conflicts. Seminary girls had fathers, husbands, brothers, and sons on both sides of the conflict. Not surprisingly, most of these men were officers, and many on both sides were graduates of West Point. Sarah French '54 married West Pointer John T. Greble. Lieutenant Greble fell at Big Bethel in 1861, earning the distinction of the first regular army officer killed in the war. Another West Pointer, Union general Joseph "Fighting Joe" Hooker, was the brother of Sarah Hooker '30. William R. Terrill, husband of Emily Henry '57, was a West Point graduate who considered resigning from the U.S. army when the war broke out. Deciding he had to honor his oath, he drove a wedge between himself and his Confederate brother. Both died in battle. Col. Robert Chilton, husband of Laura Mason '38, made the opposite decision, resigning his federal commission to join the Confederate army where he served as adjutant on Robert E. Lee's staff. Louisa Van Cleve '30 had married Camillus

Davies, a West Point graduate. Their son, William Davies, was killed in 1862 fighting for the Confederacy. Harriet Axtell '49, who lived much of her childhood in Florida, where her family had moved for her father's health, married Edward R. Platt, a West Pointer stationed in Tampa. When the war broke out, General Platt was assigned to the Army of the Potomac, and Harriet moved to Washington, D.C., with him. Emma Gardner '37 became the second wife of Alexander Mouton. Born in New York, she moved to a plantation in Louisiana with her husband. Alfred, his son from his first marriage, and Emma's brother Franklin were both West Point graduates, the latter a classmate of Ulysses Grant. The elder Mouton, who had served Louisiana as senator and governor, chaired the state secession convention in 1861. Emma Mouton's stepson and brother both became Confederate generals, Alfred dying in battle.

Seminary alumnae who had gone South to teach found themselves with friends and relatives on both sides of the conflict. Writing to the school in 1896 on behalf of her deceased mother, Marion McDonald Moore '50, her daughter recollected that Marion suffered during the war, as did so many seminary graduates "for her loved ones were numbered among the factions on both sides."[52] The Albany-born Marion had taught in Fishing Creek, South Carolina, in the 1850s, where she married Dr. Thomas Moore. She did not survive the war, succumbing to pneumonia contracted while fleeing from Sherman's advance.

Often the young teachers who had gone South found themselves in a perilous situation, cut off from northern families. Caroline Townsend '41, born in Indiana and reared in Massachusetts, rode out the war in Austin, Texas. Pamelia Alden '57, however, managed to return to her home in New Jersey early in the war. In 1864 Isadora Bishop '56 died trying to reach her Vermont home; that same year a fellow alumna from Vermont, Martha Jamieson '60, successfully made the trek from South Carolina to Michigan where her family had relocated.

Alumnae were particularly proud of relatives who fought in significant battles. William, son of Lucretia Root Brewster '23, was a colonel in the New York volunteer regiment, the "Excelsior Brigade," which fought at Gettysburg, the battle where Catharine Cady Wilkerson '37 lost her older son. He was a seventeen-year-old lieutenant at the time of his death. Mary Warren Ingram '50 lost her husband in the Battle of Shiloh. He died fighting for the Confederacy. Herman Canfield, father of Fitie '65, died at the same battle, fighting for the other side. Caroline Woodward Jamieson '37 lost her husband, a Union surgeon, at Murfreesboro. Brig. Gen. William Duffield, husband of Ann Ladue '47, was wounded in the same battle. Virginia Anderson Bullitt '37 lost her son, William, a Confederate officer, at the Battle of Rocky Ridge, and Maj. Alonzo Truman, son of Relief Smith Mason '35, accompanied Sherman on his march through Georgia.

The war also took its toll on alumnae and their family members who were not soldiers. Fleta Puckette Jeffries '56 lost her husband to disease during the siege of Vicksburg. Josephine Pope '57 died when Yankee troops forced her to flee from her home. When Yankees burned the city of Columbia, South Carolina, William B. Johnston, husband of Eliza Britain '40, lost his newspaper business. Sarah Ingersoll Cooper '55 and her husband, newspaper editor Halsey Cooper, were forced to abandon his newspaper in Chattanooga because of their Union sympathies. Similarly, the pro-Union Harriet Randall '37 and her husband fled Tennessee, giving up the lucrative textile mills he had built there. Charlotte Storrs '55, whose parents were Vermont natives, grew up in Alabama and attended the seminary just before the war broke out. Her three brothers fought in the Confederate army, and she and her sister were left in charge of the family plantation. In a long sentimental entry in the alumnae book, she told of managing the plantation without white male help, hiding family possessions so the Yankees could not get them, making do with limited food and receiving support from slaves who did not want to abandon her. Perhaps because of her parents' northern roots, Storrs somehow managed to continue communication with northern friends. She concluded, "Bitter as was this war, it did not . . . sever the bond of friendship that had united the pupils of the Willard Seminary.[53]

The thousands of women who responded to the alumnae survey support her optimistic conclusion. The ties among the former seminary girls were deep and closely woven. Julia Galusha Howlett '42 and her husband, Dr. Richard G. Banks, were forced to flee from their home in Hampton, Virginia, when Yankee troops took over the town.

A Union soldier from Troy raiding the Banks's home happened upon a composition book Julia had used at the seminary. After the war he was speaking of it in Troy, and Julia's sister learned of it; she asked him for it and mailed it back to its owner.

Although few women made it onto the battlefield during the Civil War, seminary women contributed to the Union and Confederate war efforts in many ways. They made bandages, raised money, staffed the Sanitary Fairs organized to raise money for Union troops, made uniforms for Confederate troops, and nursed soldiers. After Abraham Lincoln created the Sanitary Commission, northern women contributed greatly to its success. Catherine Wendell Rice '26 worked for the Sanitary Commission of the Northwest, and Mary Newel Castle '32 for the Sanitary Commission of northern Ohio. Ann Adams Filley '28 worked on the Mississippi Valley Sanitary Fair in St. Louis, an enormous enterprise that raised $600,000 for the Union effort, and Sarah Hoyt Spelman '56 was a key member of the New York City Sanitary Fair committee, which raised an unsurpassed $2 million. Sarah Willard took her mother-in-law to the Troy Sanitary Fair in 1864, writing to John that they had enjoyed "the novelty of it."[54]

With thousands of wounded soldiers in hospitals all over the country, overwhelmed male doctors reluctantly allowed women to serve as nurses. Again, seminary women played their part. Caroline Dusinbury '40, Ann Adams Filley, and Charlotte Henry '42 all nursed wounded soldiers. While Dusinbury and Filley worked at hospitals near their homes, Henry traveled to a federal hospital in Beaufort, South Carolina. Almira Vaughn '52 accompanied her husband Andrew Morrison to the front and ended up nursing soldiers under fire at the Battle of Fredericksburg. Oriana Moon '51, an 1857 graduate of the Philadelphia Medical College for Women, got a temporary appointment at the Confederate hospital connected to the University of Virginia in Charlottesville. While there, she met her husband, also a doctor. Together they provided medical care for thousands of wounded Confederates.

Other seminary alumnae worked for the war in less conventional ways. Ellen Hathaway Brown '40 and her daughter, Ellen Brown Flagg '60, both wrote about the war as "correspondents" for newspapers in their respective cities, the elder Ellen in Providence, Rhode Island, and the younger one in Troy. The adventurous Welthea Glines '53, who had enrolled at the seminary after working as one of the Lowell girls in the mills of Massachusetts, was in Texas teaching school when the war broke out. She volunteered as a mail carrier, traveling by pony from Kimball, Texas, to Fort Graham. The war had just broken out when Sarah Tracy '38, a Troy native, had begun working as secretary to the Mount Vernon Ladies' Association for the preservation of the first president's home. She remained at Mount Vernon, protecting it from soldiers and is credited with saving the historic site.

Emily Virginia Mason '34, loyal southerner, nursed both Confederate and Yankee soldiers at a number of hospitals in Virginia. After one battle, a Union doctor, whose wife had gone to the seminary with her, asked for her assistance, which she did for "sweet charity's sake."[55] She also remained in contact throughout the war with one of her sister Laura's classmates, Elizabeth Chew '38, who was living in Connecticut and taking care of girls orphaned by the war. Emily, herself, took responsibility for dozens of Confederate girls orphaned by the war. Emily's niece, Dorothea Mason '57, was married to a northern soldier, and at one point during the war, Emily obtained a pass to travel to Dorothea's home in New Jersey to help care for an ailing family member. The trip caused some newspapers to speculate that she was a Confederate spy.

The Willards escaped the worst of the war. Their only close relative in the military was Charles Phelps, Almira's only son. A brigadier general, he was awarded the Medal of Honor for his actions at Spotsylvania. He was wounded in that battle, but not severely, and extant family letters make no mention of his service. John was too old to serve, and given his miserable time at West Point, he probably had little military inclination; had the younger John Willard survived childhood, however, he would have been exactly the right age to enlist. At least two of Almira's stepdaughters stayed in Alabama throughout the war, and Almira, although close to her son, clearly had southern sympathies after more than two decades in Maryland. Early in the war, Emma wrote approvingly to Almira, who was somewhat reluctantly supporting the

North. Emma understood Almira's conflict, writing, "I sympathize in your divided feelings and in your love for your Maryland friends."[56]

During the war the school's enrollment fluctuated from 301 in 1861 to 245 in 1862, recovering to 263 in 1863 and jumping to 329 in 1864, where it remained for the next two years. The comprehensive boarding tuition was still $300, and the inflation accompanying the war meant the school ran deficit budgets in 1862 and 1863, deficits covered by John Willard personally, according to the annual reports to the Regents. In 1862 nine graduates left the seminary to teach, all to posts within New York State; they were the last group of teachers reported to the Regents. Although earlier historians have speculated that the war and the loss of southern students destroyed the seminary's viability as a boarding school, that may not be accurate. In 1864 the school's revenues exceeded expenses, and John Willard drew nearly $575 from the surplus. He did so again in 1867. It was not until the late 1860s that the school ran annual deficits, and even then there was a profitable year. In 1870 revenue exceeded expenses by over $1,300.

The Willards' decision to leave the seminary probably evolved over the course of the 1860s and was rooted in personal as well as business reasons. During that decade, three of the girls married, all of them to wealthy men living in Manhattan. Mary wed first, in 1862 becoming the wife of Theodore Gaillard Thomas, a native South Carolinian with a medical practice in Manhattan. Katharine and Emma both married in 1866, Emma becoming the second wife of Henry Joel Scudder, a prominent Manhattan attorney, and Katharine the wife of successful businessman Howard Lapsley. Emma had six children, Katherine and Mary four apiece. Sarah traveled to New York for her grandchildren's births, reporting back to John in Troy details of each confinement. In May 1864, she was at Mary's side when her first son and the Willards' first grandchild was born. She wrote to John in Troy that "the boy is a fine, large fellow," adding warmly, "accept the grandmother's love to the grandfather."[57] The baby's great-grandmother, "Grandma Willard," as the girls called her, also made several trips to Manhattan during this time.

Extant letters among the family reveal a closely knit, supportive group, rejoicing in the births of the next generation, reminiscing about family times and clearly enjoying life in the bigger city. The Civil War had fueled the establishment of New York as the financial capital of the nation. Local businessmen from smaller cities all over the Northeast moved their banking enterprises to New York if they could. Russell Sage, for example, headed for Manhattan in 1869, leaving Troy behind. The Willard women, who once shopped in Troy, now shopped for themselves and their grandmother in New York. The Willard girls also enjoyed the summer resort life of the upper classes. Even during the war, they vacationed in fashionable Newport, Rhode Island. In August 1861, Mary wrote to her grandmother that she and her sisters, Sarah and Katie, had seen a Rhode Island regiment home on furlough after fighting at Bull Run,[58] and in 1865 Emma wrote to a cousin that the girls had spent the summer in Rhode Island where they had a horse and carriage "furnished by their father." Home for the fall, they proved to be "quite accomplished at driving," and their grandmother "trusted them to drive me."[59]

By the 1870s, Mary and her family were routinely mentioned in the society pages when they traveled to the Hamptons. Dr. Thomas was one of the main developers of the seaside towns at the end of Long Island as a resort. A renowned gynecologist, he was responsible for a surgical breakthrough when he performed the first vaginal ovariotomy. Until 1863 he was a respected member of the faculty at the New York University Medical College, and from 1863 on, he held the chair of gynecology at Columbia University College of Physicians and Surgeons. Thomas prescribed for his wealthy clientele the restorative powers of spending time by the ocean, and he and his family practiced what they preached.

So when the school began losing money, John and Sarah perhaps had little interest in the work necessary to keeping it going. With the death of the founder in 1870, John Willard no longer had to worry about disappointing his mother by closing the institution she had built. He and Sarah decided to retire. They were both in their early sixties and comfortably well off, John having inherited property from his mother in Ohio, Vermont, and West Troy, as well as her copyrights. They had two unmarried daughters living with them who could—and would—care for them in their old age. In 1868 they had lost their youngest daughter, Marcia, who succumbed to consumption after a long struggle. They were close to their grandchildren. Writing from New York at the birth of another Scudder baby, Sarah reported to John, who had left her there, "[Eddie] says . . . Granpa come back."[60] (Eddie would later live with his grandparents in Troy, and when he died at the untimely age of twenty-three, he was buried near them in Oakwood Cemetery.)

In May 1872, the Troy newspapers carried news of the Willards' resignation and speculation about the fate of the school. At the examination in June, the last one conducted by Sarah Willard, the examining committee as usual praised the performance of the pupils, citing the high quality of the education they had received. Sarah Willard was the final speaker at the ceremony. She bade farewell to the institution she had "loved so long and so well" and prophetically called on the alumnae in the audience to preserve its future, appealing to their "common heritage"[61] as graduates of Troy. She and John moved out of the seminary to a brownstone on Second Street, less than a block from the school. In August, John placed a notice in *Harper's* announcing, "The Household furniture, musical Instruments, Patterns, Models and good will of this institution will be sold on very moderate terms."[62] Accompanying their parents in their retirement were daughters Harriet and Sarah, and Sarah's sister, Theodosia Hudson, the longtime vice principal. Sarah and John would live for another decade, dying within three months of each other in 1883.

At any rate, the rumors were quelled with the appointment of Emily T. Wilcox '56. A teacher of astronomy, physics, and mathematics at the school since her graduation, this great-niece of the founder would be the final member of the Willard family to head the school. She would also be the last principal without a college degree.

The Task of Reviving
a Dying Institution

FIVE YEARS AFTER THE END of the Civil War, the United States, the city of Troy, and the Troy Female Seminary (TFS) were poised at the beginning of a decade that would bring huge changes to all three entities. The Gilded Age, with its vast excesses, was a time of cultural, scientific, educational, political, artistic, and literary change that foreshadowed the twentieth century. In fact, in the late nineteenth century, writers, artists, and musicians created works in the United States and in Europe that defined standards throughout the 1900s. Electricity was harnessed for household use, and oil was "discovered"; the uses of both transformed the way Americans lived, worked, and communicated. The United States began to wield world power, and great European empires expanded their rule, laying the groundwork for the international conflagrations of the coming century. American economic and political interests in Asia escalated. In spite of two devastating depressions, the first in 1873 and the second in 1893, the American economy expanded dramatically, fueled by unprecedented immigration, rapid urbanization and industrialization, and nearly unchecked capitalism. During the Gilded Age, as one historian has noted, "manufacturers made the U.S. economy the largest and richest on earth."[1]

In the winter of 1870, Congress, for the first time since the secession of South Carolina, included representatives from every state in the Union. The Senate included Hiram Revels from Mississippi, the first African American to serve in that body. The following summer the first railroad train arrived in Manhattan from the Pacific coast. In the early 1870s, Degas, Manet, Renoir, Winslow Homer, and Whistler were all painting, Dostoevsky, Tolstoy, Nietzsche, and Jules Verne were writing, Darwin published his evolutionary theory, Stanley found Livingstone in interior Africa, P. T. Barnum hawked "The Greatest Show on Earth," and Yellowstone was established as a national park. In 1872 Joseph and Lyman Bloomingdale opened a department store in Manhattan, and Aaron Montgomery Ward began a mail-order business. In 1873 Levi Strauss patented his uniquely structured denim pants. In the 1870s, Joseph Bulova opened a jewelry store, and Aaron Spalding began to sell sporting goods. Dmitri Mendeleev's periodic table of elements fascinated the scientific world, and Luther Burbank produced his namesake potato that is still the most widely cultivated in the world. The Prussians, after successfully defeating the French, consolidated the German empire, significantly changing the balance of power in Europe. The defeated French found redemption in Asian conquest, adding Vietnam to the colonial territory that became French Indochina. Meanwhile, the United States attempted—unsuccessfully—to open Korea, the "Hermit Kingdom," to trade.

Before the decade ended, Trollope, Zola, Henry James, Gilbert and Sullivan, Wagner, Eliot, Browning, Twain, Rodin, Dvořák, Brahms, Tchaikovsky, and Henry George would create novels, poems, operas, symphonies, operettas, sculptures, and economic treatises that would be studied and discussed well into the twenty-first century. American literary icons Tom Sawyer, Daisy Miller, and the four March sisters entered the collective cultural consciousness. *Swan Lake* was performed for the first time. In this same decade Bell made his first telephone call, Edison patented the first mimeograph machine, Bissell invented a carpet sweeper, and a practical mechanical typewriter went on the market, all inventions that would revolutionize women's work inside and outside their homes.

In short, a time traveler from the twenty-first century would feel comfortable with much of the landscape of the late nineteenth century. Of course, there were exceptions. Great expanses of the frontier were still largely untamed. This was the "cowboy and Indian" era, later mythologized and immortalized by Hollywood, comic books, and pulp fiction. Cattle towns like Abilene, Wichita, and Dodge City were home to lawmen like Wyatt Earp and Bat Masterson, whose exploits were often only slightly less violent than the outlaws they chased. East Coast newspapers carrying ads for the latest inventions designed to ease the domestic burden also reported on frontier warfare, especially the escapades of men like bank robber Jesse James and his brothers and the notorious Billy the Kid. A few Troy graduates worked and lived in Indian territory; M. Emilia Wells Rockwell '52 wrote a novel about her experiences as a pioneer wife on the Iowa frontier.[2] Others had sons and husbands who fought in "Indian Wars."[3] Two notable women worked on behalf of the beleaguered aboriginal tribes. The fight to preserve Native American rights, even as their rights were more and more diminished by their confinement on reservations, was spearheaded by the National Women's Indian Association founded by Mary L. Bonney Rambault '36.[4] Erminnie Platt Smith '54, one of the first widely respected female anthropologists, learned Iroquois, studied native folklore, and wrote well-received scholarly papers on native ethnology.

If Emma Willard had proved that women could learn geometry in the first half of the century, by the end of the second half of the century, Calamity Jane and Annie Oakley would prove that women could shoot a rifle. These colorful figures aside, it was a time of change and increased opportunity for most women. In spite of an atmosphere in which the postwar Texas constitution barred idiots, lunatics, paupers—*and women*—from voting, the innovations, inventions, and prosperity of the era significantly altered women's lives, particularly those of white women. By 1900 the typewriter and the telephone switchboard would provide many women with new career options and a new working status, midway between the factory and the schoolroom. The use of electricity in homes and refrigeration in warehouses began to change women's relationship with housework. Mass production of brand-name products—Armour Meats and Procter & Gamble are examples of two modern companies that began marketing their goods nationally in the 1870s—also reduced the amount of time middle-class and upper-middle-class women had to spend producing food and everyday commodities for their families. The Colgate Company sold Cashmere Bouquet soap and the first flavored toothpaste. Soap, once the responsibility of housewives who boiled fireplace ashes and animal fat to make barrels of the family's cleanser, could now be bought in cakes. (James Colgate, one of the two sons of the Colgate founder, married Susan F. Colby '38.) Another small but revolutionary breakthrough came with the acceptance of the retail sale of women's underwear. Until 1876 women's "drawers," like soap, had been made at home and by hand.

Women's education was changing as well. The pioneering period had come to an end. Education for girls, at least through high school, was no longer a radical phenomenon. Public high schools, overwhelmingly coeducational, proliferated after the Civil War. From under two hundred in 1870, the number leaped to eight hundred in 1880, triple that in 1890, and triple that again by 1900.[5] Although the percentage of the population of eligible teenagers receiving high school diplomas remained very small (still less than 10 percent in 1900), the number of girls attending high school quickly outpaced the number of boys. By 1890 an impressive 56 percent of high school students were female, a ratio that would remain very stable through the first decades of the twentieth century.[6]

Not surprisingly, the increase in girls' high school attendance paralleled an increasing interest in women's collegiate education. Emma Willard had specifically eschewed the term *college* in her *Plan for Improving Female Education*. She anticipated her critics by acknowledging "the absurdity of sending ladies to college,"[7] she allayed their fears by dismissing "the phantom of a college-learned lady," and she defined college education as "a masculine education."[8] By 1870 many women, including her own graduates, thought that her reluctance to have women attend college was as outmoded as her use of the word *ladies*.

The seminary catalog for 1870–71 revealed some institutional ambivalence. On the one hand, it proclaimed forthrightly, "the day has dawned when a liberal and accurate education is considered possible for young women as well as for young men." On the other hand, the author, presumably Sarah Willard, appeared to disparage the "blue-stockings" of higher education, noting that some institutions "cast out upon society . . . characters . . . who despise the lowly round of cares and duties in which so much of their future will be occupied." For Sarah, the duties of home and hearth still took precedence; as always she adhered to her mother-in-law's faith in the power of republican motherhood. She was not unaware of the ongoing discussion about the best way to educate young women, however, and noted that the year had been one of "great interest in girls' education."[9]

Sarah Willard referred implicitly to the founding of Smith and Wellesley, plans for which had been announced in 1870 and 1871, respectively. The first college for women, Georgia Female College, had been chartered in 1836, but its location in the South and its curriculum distance it from the women's college movement of the second half of the century. The self-proclaimed "mother of women's colleges," Elmira, opened in 1855, and a few western institutions had opened their doors to women: Oberlin in 1833, Lawrence in 1847, and Antioch in 1853. In 1855 Bates, founded by radical abolitionists, was the first liberal arts college in the East to welcome female students. Amos Eaton had welcomed TFS students to his scientific lectures at Rensselaer from the beginning, but no woman matriculated at the institute for the full course until well into the twentieth century.

When Smith and Wellesley opened in the 1870s, they joined Vassar, the institution that lays legitimate claim to being the first significant college for women in terms of curriculum, facilities, and intention. The beneficiary of the wealth and vision of Hudson River Valley brewer Matthew Vassar, the college opened in 1861. (The longtime assistant to Vassar's first "lady principal" was Ann Eliza Morse '50.) Wellesley and Smith, both opened in the 1870s with munificent gifts from single donors, patterned their programs on Vassar. Mount Holyoke made the transition from seminary to college nearly two decades later, joining the other three as a premier institution for women, although Mary Lyon did not have the luxury of a single munificent benefactor and was obliged to raise the money for her institution by personal fund-raising. By the end of the century, Bryn Mawr, Barnard, and Radcliffe would round out the membership of the elite Seven Sisters. Sarah Barnard Porter '26 did not live to see the college named for her brother, Columbia president, F. A. P. Barnard, but Clara Harrison Stranahan '50 served as one of the college's first trustees. Barnard died shortly before the college opened; he was succeeded by Seth Low, whose step-mother, Anne Bedell Low, graduated from Troy in 1838.

As sure as these colleges were about their equality with the men's colleges, and as different as they were in their determination to be colleges rather than seminaries, their literature still echoed the Troy founder at times. For example, as Smith prepared for its first class, the Massachusetts Board of Education reported, "It is the design of the trustees, as it was evidently of the founder, not to add to the number of such schools, seminaries or academies, as now exist for young ladies, but to realize completely and truly the idea of a *woman's college*. They would secure to young women a culture fully equivalent to that afforded young men by our best New England colleges, and yet differing from that as woman differs from man in her physical and mental constitution, and in the sphere of her active life."[10]

In spite of the Smith trustees' adherence to the concept of the separation of men's and women's spheres, education for women was given the ultimate stamp of approval by Henry Ward Beecher at the Amherst commencement in 1871. Already regarded as the most famous clergyman in America, and not yet the subject of scandal, Beecher informed the assembly, "America is for universal education. If a man be black, and is fully prepared, or if a woman is fully qualified, [college] doors will open to them."[11]

By 1870 the seminary compared poorly with the new colleges. In its early decades, the curriculum, ages of the students, and attendance patterns had matched and sometimes exceeded the offerings at some men's colleges. However, the Willards had made few changes since 1850. On the surface, the school had weathered the war years and the loss of its affluent southern families. Southern girls had been replaced in the late 1860s and early 1870s by students from newly wealthy families who emerged from the oilfields of Pennsylvania. A dozen or so students from Tidioute, Titusville, and Franklin enrolled at Troy during these years. Nevertheless, between 1867 and 1872, the year the Willards retired and closed the boarding department, the school budget ran in the red four of five years, sustaining a $2,100 loss on a total budget of $17,000 in 1872. The tuition had been raised in 1862 and again in 1865 and 1867, a reflection of wartime inflation. The final hike to a comprehensive boarding fee of $500 (day tuition remained unchanged at $28 per year) meant that a TFS education cost more than the education at Vassar ($400), Elmira ($300), and Amherst ($345), among others.

In spite of this escalating cost, the value of the seminary property and buildings had not altered since 1846 when the seminary building was extended one last time. In 1870 the value of the seminary lot and buildings, as reported to the Regents, remained $12,100, the same as it had been in 1846. Meanwhile, Vassar's property was valued at more than $400,000, Elmira's at $136,000, and even Troy High occupied a building worth $28,000. Across the Hudson River, the Albany Academy assessed its buildings and grounds for the Regents at $90,000. (The Albany Female Academy made no report.) The scientific apparatus, long a source of pride for the seminary, was valued at less than half that of the Albany Academy, two thirds that of Troy High, and less than 10 percent of Vassar. Vassar had over $8,000 in astronomy equipment alone, which was to be expected, given the presence on the faculty of famed female astronomer Maria Mitchell. Given these statistics, it is not surprising that the visiting committee at the final examination of the Willards' tenure concluded that the "buildings and appliances are entirely inadequate to the demands of a first-class, or even of a second-class institution."[12]

Interestingly, the total number of students enrolled at the seminary did not decline as precipitously as the physical plant in the last few years of the Willards' tenure. There had been a dip in enrollment the first year of the Civil War—301 were registered in 1861 and only 245 in 1862—but by 1864 enrollment topped 300 again, staying there until 1867. From 1868 until 1872, the enrollment hovered around 260, rising to 295 in 1870 before plunging to 238 in 1872. Sheer numbers were not the problem; the school's budgetary troubles rested on the significant decline in students enrolling for the academic course. Since the late 1830s, New York State had mandated that students who wished to pursue a high school course had to pass preliminary examinations in arithmetic, spelling, geography, and grammar. In the first year that the seminary administered the examinations, more than 70

percent of the students were reported as meeting the Regents requirements. Throughout the 1850s, the number hovered in the 60th to 70th
percentile. During the war years the number qualifying declined a bit,
with a high of 58 percent in 1863.

In 1867, however, there was a tremendous change. Sarah reported to the Regents that only 37 percent of the students met Regents
requirements, and by 1872, only a quarter of the pupils reached that
standard. Concurrent with these declining numbers was an increase
in advertising for pupils nationwide. It seems clear that John Willard
was making a last-ditch effort to attract the qualified paying customers the school needed. Advertisements appeared in newspapers
throughout the country and in national magazines. Perhaps hoping
to recapture southern students—or perhaps targeting the children of
wealthy northerners making money in the former Confederacy—he
advertised in the *Atlanta Constitution* and the New Orleans *Daily
Picayune*. In addition to printing the seminary ad, the latter editorialized, "Mothers sending their daughters off to receive an education should examine closely the standing of an institution. . . . Many
schools rise and fall in a year or so; here is one, however that has
been in successful operation for fifty years."[13] Extant bills from John's
business papers include a $15 invoice for a month of daily adver-
tisements in the *New York Evening Express* and one for $12 for six
months of advertisements in the *Christian Herald*, a Presbyterian
weekly published in Cincinnati.[14] A recurring advertisement appeared in *Harper's Weekly* from August 26 until October 14, 1870,
and then again from September 3 to October 22, 1871. Given that
the school year began in late September, the timing of these ads is
puzzling. At any rate, they did not have the desired effect.

If there was a formal announcement of the school's decision to close
the boarding department at the end of the 1871–72 school year, it has
not survived. Esther "Hettie" Gurley '71 kept a scrapbook of the activities surrounding her class's graduation, and there is no hint of impending change in her careful record of class activities. She noted that the
salutatorian mentioned that Emma Willard was "a household word on
both sides of the Atlantic," hardly an indication that the school's reputa-

tion was in danger. The one sign of change was positive. The valedictorian, Jennie Bancroft, was headed to college. After attending Albany Normal School, she would become the first Troy graduate to earn a doctorate; she later became the dean of women at Northwestern University.

In spite of the normality surrounding the graduation ceremonies in June, the trustees concluded sometime in the fall of 1871, presumably in accordance with John and Sarah Willard, that the school could not continue as it was.[15] Mindful that the citizens of Troy had been originally responsible for Emma Willard's moving her school to their city, they decided to appeal to Troy's general population for help. They wanted two things: first, public support for the idea that the city would transfer to the trustees the title to the buildings and lot and second, money to refurbish and rebuild. Their plea on behalf of the seminary was circulated throughout the city and appeared in the papers in early November.[16]

The appeal began with a short history of Emma Willard's beginnings in Middlebury and Waterford and highlighted the "prominent and public-spirited" men who financed her move to Troy. A quick summary of the financial relationship between the city and the seminary followed. The initial capitalization had included $4,000 from the city and an additional $5,000 from individual citizens; this was to be repaid "without interest" by the $500 annual rent paid by the Willards. (At the time, Dr. John Willard was handling the business matters of the school.) In 1826 Troy advanced $3,000 for the addition, simultaneously raising the rent to $700. The "brick building now used for music instruction, laundry, etc., was erected at a cost of $3,500"[17] in 1828. Three years later, a piece of land between the school buildings and the park was purchased by the city for the school for $1,500, and in 1833, Troy paid for an extension of the main building out to the alley running to Ferry Street. The rent was raised again—to $1,100. All told, the city had spent slightly more than $20,000 on buildings and grounds for the female seminary over the course of twelve years.

Other additions and improvements had been made and paid for by the trustees or the Willards themselves. Each year John budgeted $500 for ordinary repairs (an amount that was generous in 1838 but woefully inadequate by 1870 as deferred maintenance issues piled up). In the 1850s, he spent $7,000 installing steam heat, water and gas pipes, and over $1,000 to build a separate kitchen, bakery, and boiler house behind the main building. In 1846 the trustees purchased a lot from the Presbyterian Church and built a final addition to the western end of the main building.

The trustees figured that the city's expenditures had been more than repaid by the fifty years of rent. In fact, they calculated "the Seminary . . . has paid to the city a cash interest of more than seven percent on its cost; and, taking into account the improvements to the property by steam, gas, and water fixtures, etc., an amount very largely in excess of this—a fact which probably can hardly be truly stated with regard to many pieces of property . . . in Troy which cost their owner $20,000 forty years ago, and have been held by him from that time."

The trustees also stressed the "indirect pecuniary advantages" of having the seminary in Troy—specifically, "the large amounts brought from abroad and expended here by pupils and their friends." Finally, they concluded that "pecuniary advantages" aside, the prestige of the school and the attendant publicity it had brought to Troy should be reason enough for the citizenry to support its renovation. The seminary, they claimed, had "done more to give name and fame to the city of Troy than anything else which has ever existed in it."[18]

The trustees were well aware, however, that the school's reputation was threatened by the dire need of new facilities. They cited Vassar's prosperity and warned,

> While schools have come up in every section of the country splendidly endowed with buildings, furniture, library and apparatus of the first order and most attractive character, our Seminary is in a building originally constructed in the cheapest possible manner, and in many parts actually so thoroughly worn out as not to be worth repairing; with furniture such as serves its purpose, but not such as should be; with library and apparatus sufficient for ordinary use, but by no means equal to the fullest requirements of such an institution as this is, and thus far has been, but cannot long continue to be.

In concluding their appeal, they promised that if the city "will convey to [the trustees] in trust for the sole purpose and uses of a Female Seminary, its interest in the property now occupied for this purpose," then the trustees would "use such means as in their belief will secure an amount sufficient to erect buildings, and provide furniture, library, apparatus, etc., such as shall be adapted to the requirements of the institution." They ended with the grim prediction that without the support of the citizens of Troy, the seminary "shall dwindle into an ordinary girls' school, or be blotted out."[19]

The petition was signed by hundreds of Troy's citizens and presented by the trustees to the mayor and the Common Council in May 1872. The petition requested that the property be turned over to the board. Mayor Thomas Carroll and Common Council president Dennis O'Loughlin denied the petition. Political power in Troy had changed hands and was passing from the men and their fathers who had always sat on the seminary board to the sons of the Irish immigrants who had manned their factories and staffed their homes during the 1850s and 1860s. Their Irish-American daughters had not benefited from the school. It had no place of reverence in their family lore. From the first mayor of Troy, Albert Pawling, to Thomas Carroll, the twenty-fifth mayor of Troy, all but two of the men who served as mayor had daughters, nieces, or wives who attended the seminary. Thomas Carroll was one of the two. Carroll and the Irish Americans who followed him in office had no such ties. There was some compromise, however. The Common Council agreed to sell the school to the trustees for $50,000.

The Troy newspapers carried news of the Willards' resignation and speculated about whether or not the trustees would be able to raise the money. The city had given them one year to complete the task. Word of the school's troubles and the closing of the boarding department spread. Almira, now the family matriarch, had learned of the impending change. "Emily Wilcox has written to me," she wrote John, and she was "thinking much of what is about to take place among you."[20] In June, Gustav Schirmer, the music publisher whose company still exists, requested John recommend his services to "the new management."[21] That same month, Dr. William Baker of Des Moines, Iowa, enclosed a note to John with a check for his daughter's account. "I trust," he wrote, "that you will continue the school for a year or more as I regret changing."[22] But 1872 was to be Annie Baker's last year in Troy. It would be twenty-three years before the school could welcome another pupil from Iowa or anywhere else outside the immediate capital region.

Annie Baker was one of seventy boarders in the spring of 1872 and the only one from Iowa. Pennsylvania was represented by seventeen students, Massachusetts by four, Connecticut by two, and Vermont, New Jersey, Nebraska, and Delaware by one apiece. Of the six students who met the requirements for a high school diploma, four were boarders. The only common subjects for these six scholars were composition and the study of moral philosophy. Four students went on to college: Mary Sanford and Marie Antoinette Whitman to Vassar, Sarah Judson and Jessie Babcock to Wellesley (although the latter did not go for another decade and then to take a "special course"). None of the four future collegians earned a diploma from the seminary.

By far the most interesting members of the class of 1872 were the Price sisters, Cora and Lucy, whose mother, Elizabeth Paine Price, was also an alumna. Their older sister, Lily, listed on the seminary rolls in 1866, was soon to marry wealthy New York businessman Louis Hammersley, and when he died, she inherited his millions. As was the practice among impoverished Gilded Age British nobility, the eighth Duke of Marlborough married the wealthy American widow, making her the eighth duchess. He proceeded to spend her inheritance from her first husband on renovations to the ancestral mansion, Blenheim Palace, where his nephew, Winston Churchill, had been born just three years after Lily left the seminary. In contrast, her two sisters remained in Troy.

In the 1870s, as had been the case since the 1820s, Willard relatives attended the school. This was true for at least two of the members of the final boarding class. John and Sarah's granddaughter, Mary Scudder, Emma Willard Scudder's twelve-year-old stepdaughter, studied there only one year. She was the only girl in her generation to do so. By the time her half sister, named Emma Willard for her mother and famous ancestor, was ready for school, the seminary no longer took boarding students. Emma studied at day schools in Manhattan. However, Emma Willard's male great-grandchildren all went to boarding school, most to St. Paul's, and Willard Scudder spent his life teaching there.[23]

The second relative at the school in 1872 was a Hudson relation.

Emma Scudder's classmate and cousin, Katharine D. Hudson, Sarah Willard's niece and one of the few earning a diploma, had been at the school for thirteen years. Just two years earlier, another namesake of the founder, Sarah's great-niece, Emma Willard Peck, had graduated. (She was the granddaughter of Sarah Willard's brother Horace.) Bills for her schooling found in John Willard's business papers indicate that Willard relatives—at least ones as wealthy as the affluent Pecks—paid tuition just like other patrons. The correspondence from her father to John Willard, addressed to "My dear Uncle," indicates that, like other parents, Horace Peck at times took issue with the cost of his daughter's schooling. Paying a bill for $547.03, he complained that "the charges on the extras are too high."[24]

At the examination in June, the last one conducted by Sarah Willard, the examining committee praised the performance of the pupils, citing the high quality of the education they had received. They were blunt, however, in their assessment of the seminary facilities and referred to "the present crisis in the affairs of the institution." They concluded that the buildings were "utterly incompetent to vie with the rising splendors of Vassar."[25] Concerned about the fate of the school, the examining board added an unprecedented "appeal and a remonstrance" to their usual report. They tied the reputation of the seminary to the reputation of Troy and, echoing the trustees, warned against "the extinction of the institution which has done more than all our factories together to give our city an honorable name."[26] They worried that Troy's "renown as the homestead of female education shall be utterly merged in its reputation for stoves and bells and collars and horseshoes."[27] Stoves and bells and collars and horseshoes were filling the city's and its citizens' bank accounts, however, and the fate of the subscription to preserve the seminary hung in the balance.

William Gurley and his brother Lewis, both trustees, spearheaded the fund-raising effort. The drive began at once, with John Willard an early and generous contributor, donating $2,000 to the cause. Other gifts ranged from the $5,000 pledged by J. L. Thompson and Sons to $5 and $10 donations. Trustee gifts ranged from $500 to $2,500. Ultimately, more than $53,000 was raised; the extra was set aside to provide new furnishings and equipment to renovate the part of the building slated to be used as a day school. On May 8, 1873, nearly a year to the day after the city had agreed on the terms of the sale with the seminary trustees, William Gurley, on behalf of the board, handed Mayor William Kemp a certified check for $50,000.[28] Over $10,000 of the subscription consisted of unpaid pledges, but the Gurley brothers had covered the difference between the $41,245 actually raised and the sale price. The timing was fortuitous. Less than six months later, the bottom fell out of the American postwar economy, and the United States entered a depression whose effects lingered for the rest of the decade.

As the city prepared to hand over the property to the trustees, there was apparently some concern about the board's intentions. The week before the sale was finalized, the *Troy Daily Whig* reported, "Citizens are anxious to know what is to be done with the property."[29] Occupying nearly a full city block in a central location, the old buildings had the potential to become a major blot on the municipal landscape. Troy, perhaps more than other cities, had sympathized with the victims of the great fire in Chicago in 1871 because nine years earlier, the city had suffered its own devastating conflagration. Since the Troy fire in 1862, the city had been engaged in the erection of brick and stone buildings to replace wooden ones. Industries using electrical machinery and housing for larger urban populations needed new structures, particularly in downtown areas. The census of 1870 counted Troy's population as close to 50,000; the city ranked twenty-eighth in the nation in size.

The *Troy Northern Budget* proudly reported on the physical changes in the city. Troy, it boasted, "is rapidly passing from the motley look of the antique decayed village to the broader and brighter look of a modern city of the larger size."[30] Among the new structures was the acoustically spectacular music hall being built by the Troy Savings Bank. In 1872 the combination bank and concert venue was rising on a location that had been home to "a huddle of tumble down and unsightly old wooden buildings."[31] Even famous landmarks were being replaced. The Vanderheyden mansion, once the stately home of the city's first family, was slated for demolition and "had been allowed to sink to the level of a tenement house and a very poor one at that."[32]

To allay citizens' fears about the fate of the seminary buildings, the *Whig* reprinted an interview between a reporter for a rival paper and William Gurley. Gurley offered assurances that the seminary would remain a school, claiming, "It is the object of the trustees to make it an institution of learning second to none of its kind." He commented that the trustees hoped eventually to reopen the boarding department, and he spoke of an ongoing appeal "for funds to make all necessary repairs and put the building in a condition to receive boarders." In the meantime, he asserted, "it will be repaired somewhat, and will be kept open as a day school for young ladies in the city." When asked if the trustees would consider mortgaging the property to raise the funds to reestablish the boarding department more quickly, he responded that they would not. "Although we would like to tear the old buildings down and rebuild at once," Gurley stated, "we will be obliged to content ourselves with what we have until someone generously makes us a donation for that purpose."[33] Troy, it seemed, did not have a Matthew Vassar or Sophia Smith. The trustees' goal would not be met for more than twenty years.

During the year in which the trustees were raising the money to buy the property, the school had already begun to operate exclusively as a day school. For the first time since its opening in 1814, there were no boarders. The circular for the 1872–73 academic year announced that "[the school] will be opened as a Day School . . . under the charge of Miss Emily T. Wilcox, for many years one of the leading teachers of the institution." To reassure its future clientele that the transition would be seamless, the circular also noted that Theodosia Hudson "and other ladies who have been connected with the Seminary" would be staying on. Furthermore, the school "will be organized by Mrs. Willard."[34] Sarah was not yet fully retired.

Emily Wilcox is an elusive historical figure. Her pedigree, her schooling, her career, and her tenure are matters of record, but she herself did not leave the written legacy her predecessors did. Unlike Emma Willard, who was clearly a presence in Troy, Emily Wilcox, according to one of her admirers, was so self-effacing "that she was practically unknown in the city whose daughters she was training up!"[35] According to one of her former pupils, writing at the time of Miss Wilcox's retirement in 1895,

Emily was not eager to take on the job of principal. In a letter to the editor of the *Troy Times*, "A Friend of Emma Willard School" wrote, "When called to the task of reviving a dying institution, she shrank from it."[36] There is some corroboration of Wilcox's reluctance. As late as June 1873, a Troy newspaper reported that the trustees were considering fifteen to twenty candidates for the position, even though Wilcox had already run the school for a year. The article suggested that the frontrunners for the job were the Rev. R. G. Williams and his wife.[37] The Williamses, Episcopalians, had been the founding leaders of St. Margaret's School in Waterbury, Connecticut. To put a cleric at the head of the Troy Female Seminary would have been a dramatic departure from the founder's vision and unlikely in light of the fact that the trustees were not all Anglican. The Gurleys, for example, were Baptists.

At any rate, Emily Wilcox, perhaps not willing, but certainly able, got the job. The circular for 1873–74 made it clear that she now had the position and the title. When the school opened in September, it was "under the charge of Miss Emily T. Wilcox, Principal."[38] There was no mention of Sarah Willard, and her sister, Theodosia Hudson, longtime vice principal, had also retired. Hudson was replaced by Mercy Plum Mann '65. Mann had taught at the seminary for several years after her graduation, but when the Willards retired, she had gone to teach at Madame Da Silva's and Mrs. Bradford's English, French and German Boarding and Day School for Young Ladies and Children in Manhattan. (It is a fortunate that uniforms with the school name embroidered on them were not yet the style.) Not a Willard relative in 1873, Mann would become one in 1883 by marrying Sarah's nephew John Hudson Peck, future president of RPI.

When Emily Wilcox took the helm of the seminary, she was thirty-eight years old. Born in Middletown, Connecticut, she was the granddaughter of Emma Willard's older sister Lydia, who died at age thirty-five, the year before her sister opened her school in Middlebury. Lydia and her husband Elisha had four children, the oldest of whom, named Emily, married Asa Wilcox and became the mother of Emily Treat Wilcox in 1834. Family lore had it that when Emily got old enough to go away to school, she chose to study with Mary Lyon at her South

Hadley Seminary. Not happy with this decision, her great-aunt Emma quickly persuaded her family to send her to Troy. Whether or not Emily wanted to study with Lyon is impossible to know, but there is no record of her on the Mount Holyoke student lists for the 1850s. Prior to going to Troy, she had attended the public high school in Meriden, Connecticut, and a normal school in New Britain. At any rate, she was registered at Troy in 1854 and remained a student for two years. Her seminary education was the last formal education she received, but it apparently provided her with a firm foundation in arts and sciences. Over the course of her seminary career, she taught, among other subjects, algebra, arithmetic, grammar, reading, composition, mythology, physiology, Latin, mechanics, hydrostatics, astronomy, geometry, and natural philosophy. It is very likely that she shared her illustrious great-aunt's penchant for auto didactics.

She also shared Emma Willard's reverence for the Hart family and was an early member of the Daughters of the American Revolution because she could trace her lineage to Capt. Samuel Hart. Like Emma she was raised a Congregationalist, but once in Troy she moved away from the family religion, although not as far away as the Willards. She was a regular congregant at the First Presbyterian Church. During her time as principal, she lived in Emma Willard's house on the corner of Second and Ferry Streets, right at the edge of the seminary property, less than a block away from the Willards' last home. She and the Willard granddaughters were contemporaries, and she remained close to her second cousins, the two unmarried sisters who lived near her in Troy. Among her very few surviving letters is one to Sarah Willard signed, "Your cousin, Emily."[39]

In the Regents report for 1872, Emily Wilcox's salary was listed at $680, the same amount as three other teachers, two of whom had been at the school far longer than she, perhaps an indication of John and Sarah's regard for her skills. Caroline King at sixty-two was the eldest, and her thirty-three-year tenure was twice that of Wilcox. Twenty-year veteran Mary Smith also made the same salary. Abby Wadleigh '63, a relatively inexperienced twenty-seven, also made $680, presumably because she held the post of librarian as well as teacher. Other than Sarah Willard, however, the only two teachers more highly paid than Emily Wilcox were Vice Principal Theodosia Hudson and the French teacher, whose salary at more than $1,100 was even higher than Hudson's. Understandably, the transformation from boarding to day school decimated the faculty. By 1873, in addition to the principal, there were five teachers, including Mary A. Green, who had graduated in 1871. Mercy Mann was the only teacher remaining from the Willard years.

The faculty was not the only thing that had changed. The circular for 1873–74 outlined a revised curriculum in some detail. During the 1860s, the curriculum had been divided into three classifications, with the academic department the highest. The "full course" was intended to educate girls from ages seven to eighteen and was very carefully laid out with suggested courses for each year in each of the departments, which included primary and intermediate in addition to the academic. In the late 1860s, the Regents imposed a new examination procedure on all schools in the state offering an academic course (the equivalent of the curriculum at the state's public high schools).

At the seminary, this meant that for the last few years of the Willards' tenure, the classes were arranged according to regulations established by the Board of Regents. The girls in Class III were those who had been at the school prior to the adoption of the newly rigorous Regents examination and "though not having passed the . . . written examination . . . were allowed by the Regents as classified or higher English students." Class II included students who had passed the written examination and were "provisionally admitted to the academic class," and Class I was reserved for those who had passed the "preliminary academic examination" and "who have subsequently pursued classical or higher English studies or both for at least four months of the said academic year."[40] Nothing was specifically outlined as the formal course of study, although students in their final year continued to study moral philosophy with the principal. Few students earned a Regents-approved diploma, although many received the Regents certificate for passing the written examination qualifying them for the academic course. According to state reports in the 1870s, more students earned diplomas at Troy High than at the seminary, but because the report did not identify graduates by gender, it is impossible to know how many of the Troy High graduates were female. Alumnae records at Vassar, Smith, and Wellesley demonstrate that some Troy girls who were not seminary girls attended those colleges.

Emily Wilcox clearly intended to regularize the academic life of the school. The circular for 1873–74 announced that "a class for graduation will be formed at the opening of the school,"[41] signaling for the first time that a high school diploma was the highest goal of a seminary education. The three-class system was discontinued. Now there would be two: a "First Class" for older students and a "Second Class" to prepare for the first. The more advanced group had the option of choosing among physical geography, universal history, natural philosophy, natural history, algebra, geometry, astronomy, physics, chemistry, botany, rhetoric, literature, elements of criticism, Butler's *Analogy,* Hamilton's *Intellectual Philosophy* (which had replaced Butler as the capstone text), and composition. The preparatory students took arithmetic, geography, grammar, reading, spelling, U.S. history, chronology, penmanship, outline drawing, and composition. Piano, French, German, and a variety of visual arts courses, including oil painting and watercolor, were offered for a fee. Tuition for the regular academic courses remained at $28 per year.

The circular also assured the potential seminary parents that "it is intended to maintain in all respects the very high grade of scholarship for which this school has so long been distinguished."[42] There is no reason to dispute the claim that the courses offered exemplified a "very high grade of scholarship," but there was still no discernible ordered pattern to an individual's education. As had always been the case, some girls took art or studied music, others concentrated on learning French, and some took the courses outlined by the Regents as meeting the state diploma requirements. The latter, however, were few. In 1893 the school printed a list of pupils who had attended the seminary under Wilcox. There were more than seven hundred girls on the list. In addition, the school provided a list of students who had earned high school diplomas during that same time period. There were three in 1874, none in 1875, six in 1876, none in 1877, 1878, or 1879, nine in 1880, none in 1881, three each in 1882 and 1883, none in 1884, seven in 1885, five in 1886, two in 1887, four in 1888, seven in 1889, four in 1890, six in 1891, none in 1892, and four in 1893.

Brought up to revere Emma Willard and trained as a teacher by Sarah Willard, Emily Wilcox was nevertheless more modern than either of her relatives, and she strove to bring a more modern curriculum to the school. She was undoubtedly influenced by David Nelson Camp, regarded by his biographers as a modern professional educator. He had headed both the high school and the normal school Wilcox attended in Connecticut, and he later moved onto the national educational arena, serving as an assistant to Henry Barnard when Barnard was the U.S. commissioner on education. Camp has been given credit for providing "the specific bridge by which students of moral philosophy in the antebellum world after the war turn to moral science and experimental psychology."[43] In alignment with this educational philosophy, Emily Wilcox focused on science more than morality. Beginning in the early 1880s, the seminary catalogs no longer listed moral philosophy among the advanced offerings, and by 1893, Emily Wilcox's classes included psychology, a subject "in which she was especially interested."[44]

Her interest in psychology, like Camp's, stemmed from her love of science and her desire to give education a rational, more scientific framework. She instituted the Troy chapter of the Dana Natural History Society, which was an organization for girls and women wishing to study science. Wilcox, herself, was a member of the Association of American Women Scientists and was reported in the school's alumnae compendium as having contributed a paper to that organization.[45] She was, by all accounts, an excellent classroom teacher. In 1866 the examining committee singled out her classes in physiology and natural science for special commendation.[46] The editors of the 1890s biographical record described her as "much beloved,"[47] and at least some of her former students were more than a little miffed at the idea that her reputation was being overshadowed by Emma and Sarah Willard at the reunion celebration in 1895. Wrote one, "She undertook the work as a labor of love and carried it successfully to the future, thus forming the connecting link between the old Troy Female Seminary and the new Emma Willard School."[48] Her cousin Sarah agreed, claiming that the successful continuation of the seminary after her parents' retirement was "chiefly owing to Miss Wilcox's untiring and intelligent devotion."[49]

Given her gift for teaching, her desire to modernize the curriculum, and her apparent reluctance to seek the spotlight (a trait she most surely did not inherit from her great-aunt), it is disheartening to think about her life at the school during the 1870s and 1880s. The trustees' plans for renovation were halted by the depressed economy after the 1873 panic, and for much of her tenure, Emily Wilcox had to compromise her educational principles to balance the budget. Not only were students allowed to pursue their own course of study, by 1880 the school offered "a supplemental course" for students who did not attend the regular session. As the catalog explained it,

> To meet a new social demand, which has of late been evinced in many ways, young ladies are everywhere forming reading-clubs or engaging in private study of art, literature and history. . . . With a view of supplying to young ladies seeking literary culture adequate means of acquiring it, the trustees have introduced a supplementary course of study under the direction of the Principal of the Seminary. This class will be limited to young ladies not attending school, and will meet for reading, criticism and conversation, in the afternoon, at the Reception room of the Seminary. Recitations will not be required, but careful preparation for the class meetings expected.[50]

At $10 a quarter, this supplemental course had the potential to bring in more dollars for the school but also meant additional work for the principal. A new rule provided a further indication that the school—or at least its pupils—had lost the academic focus of earlier days.

By the 1880s, there was no unanimity among the trustees about the future of the school. Plans to reopen the boarding department were rarely mentioned. The annual catalogs implied that the benefits of a day school surpassed those of a boarding school, maintaining, "The school thus affords to citizens of Troy unexcelled facilities for the thorough and economical education of their daughters, *while surrounded by home influence and parental care*" (emphasis added).[51]

A turning point came in 1886. The federal government made a generous offer to buy a significant parcel of seminary land to use for a post office. The Troy papers covered the trustees' debate over whether or not to accept the offer. At a meeting of the board on February 17, James Forsyth moved the sale, which was seconded by Joseph Fuller. Charles Tillinghast and Walter Warren agreed with them. As Forsyth put it, "I think it is in the best interests of the seminary to get funds with which to equip itself for effectual work. . . . The competition of rival institutions is so overwhelming that we can never recover the prestige the seminary had forty years ago." Forsyth saw no future for the school as a residential institution. In his opinion, securing the money to put the day school on firm financial footing was the best that the trustees could hope to accomplish.

The Gurley brothers, John Hudson Peck, Uri Gilbert, and Henry Ludlow opposed the motion. Peck argued that the seminary was "more than a building," and he optimistically suggested they would be able to build new buildings soon. To sell the land, he argued, would be "suicidal." Lewis Gurley added that "to sell would be like strangling an institution we are bound to protect."[52] By the narrow vote of five to four, the seminary grounds were preserved. Forsyth left the board, followed by Fuller two years later. Lewis Gurley immediately pledged $10,000 to build new buildings; surprisingly, Charles Tillinghast, who had voted for the sale, pledged an additional $5,000.

The trustees' recommitment to the seminary's future appeared to energize the school and give Emily Wilcox the latitude she needed to make some academic changes. The curriculum, as outlined in the catalog for 1885–86, was more specific and detailed required work in each year at both the intermediate and advanced levels. Then in 1887 William Gurley, the president of the board of trustees, died. His brother Lewis took over as president, and to honor his brother, he increased his pledge, promising a new building for the seminary in honor of his brother and his sister Clarissa, a member of the class of 1838. His gift launched the rebirth of the seminary, ensuring its continuation into its second century.

The Best Work Women
of Wealth Can Do

IN AN UNDATED NEWSPAPER clipping from *The Troy Press*, an anonymous writer described the diminished seminary. Respectfully, but fatalistically, he wrote, "Bathed in sunshine half the day and clothed in shade the other half, the Troy female seminary building, like some honored old citizen, is passing the remainder of its days in peaceful retirement . . . its energy . . . like the last pulse-beats of a dying man."[1] The newspaper account accurately portrayed the old school building, but the school itself was far from dying. Its pulse beat steadily on, fed solely by local infusions of students. In fact, as the 1880s drew to a close, plans for the seminary's rebirth were well under way. After the critical meeting in 1886 where the trustees decided not to sell any portion of the school property, they were determined to modernize the school plant and reopen the boarding department. The men on the board would be aided in their efforts by the alumnae. The combined work of these two groups at the end of the nineteenth century ensured both the school's modernization and its renewed national reputation as it approached its second century.

At the height of the Gilded Age, Troy became the "Collar City." Still prosperous, the city had seen its major industry shift from iron to collars. When Troy had first begun manufacturing collars, Amos Eaton had famously and erroneously scoffed that "it was apparent folly for anyone to venture time and money in so petty an undertaking."[2] By the 1880s, collars were no longer "a petty . . . undertaking" being made as piecework by women in their homes. Earl and Wilson, Corliss Brothers, Cluett, Coon and Co., and George P. Ide and Co. were only the largest of the dozens of collar companies that occupied huge new factory buildings near the center of the city that were devoted to turn-ing out brand-name collars, cuffs, and shirts. Troy, once the second largest iron-producing municipality in the country, was now synony-mous with collars. At the height of the city's iron industry, 75 percent of the nation's stoves were manufactured in Troy; by 1889, only 25 percent of the nation's iron stoves were Troy products. Estimates of the percentage of the city's working population engaged in the collar and shirt industry ranged from 75 to 90 percent, and Troy's collars and cuffs monopolized the national market.

Just as the school had long provided opportunities for young wom-en, the collar factories provided opportunities for a different segment of the city's female population. *The Troy Press*, always a civic booster, bragged about the economic opportunities these factories represented for young working women, boasting there was "nowhere else in the world [where] a woman can earn as good wages, or find such steady, congenial work as in Troy, and certainly nowhere can be seen such a large number of well-dressed, pretty and intelligent girls engaged in a respectable and lucrative occupation as in the collar shops of this city."[3]

Troy's workers were relatively well paid. "Collar girls" earned anywhere from $8 to $15 a week, depending on their skill and speed. Their wages compared favorably with teachers who typically earned between $350 and $700 per year. Urging Congress to maintain the protective tariff, one manufacturer described "the living of our girls" compared to German workers whose products they hoped to keep out of the American market:

> The American working girls, on collars, never go to work with-out hats, gloves, or jackets, wear veils, eat ice cream, bananas, eggs, chickens, ham sandwiches, buy jewelry, go to theaters and concerts, and spend their earnings freely. And what does the German girl do? Wears no hat to go to work in, no gloves or jackets, but a shawl, a calico dress and apron, no drawers . . . ; they never indulge in ice cream or soda water, chicken or broiled steak, except perhaps on Christmas or at a wedding.[4]

The lives of the collar workers were undoubtedly less rosy than the picture painted for Congress; after all, they had gone on strike in 1886 to protest wages and working conditions. However, with 90 percent of America's male population buying detachable collars made in Troy, the work was plentiful and steady. The new factories were heralded for their light and space. The city's centennial chronicle described the Ide plant as having "spacious, many-windowed workrooms,"[5] and the factory of Earl and Wilson as "admirably planned and sanitarily fitted."[6]

Just as they were for the railroad industry and so many other industrial concerns of the Gilded Age, protective tariffs were a boon to the collar industry; in 1893 Troy collar factory owners testified before Congress that the tariff kept out cheap, poor quality foreign goods. The industry, they protested, was not "enlarged by protection [but] saved."[7] In other words, argued the factory owners, without the tariff, Troy's collar industry would not survive. In reality, congressional protection supported a sort of complacency about the continued prosperity of the collar industry that would prove disastrous in the twentieth century. Buoyed by laws restricting competition, Troy was dangerously dependent on this one industry, to an extent that would not be fully realized for over thirty years.

Other changes accompanied the shift in manufacturing. Although Troy was still wealthy, major urban areas in the Midwest and West rivaled it in terms of population. Pittsburgh, Cincinnati, Cleveland, Detroit, St. Louis—and, of course, Chicago and San Francisco—outpaced it. Troy, which had ranked in the top twenty-five cities in population at the start of the Civil War, barely made it into the top fifty in 1890, ranking forty-sixth. In 1860 no city in the country, including New York, had numbered a million people. In 1890 New York, Chicago, and Philadelphia all topped a million, with Brooklyn close behind. Troy's population, by contrast, stood at 60,956.

In another shift, Troy's political and economic interests were no longer as closely intertwined. The city's politicians and industrialists were no longer one and the same; "boss" politics accompanied the Irish takeover of the city's elections. In addition, in the two decades following the Civil War, many wealthy Trojans had moved to Manhattan, which had rapidly become the world's economic center. Russell Sage was the most famous of New York City's moneyed former Trojans, but he was not alone. Eddys, Mallarys, Vails, and Burdens, the descendants of founding Troy families, as well as the three married Willard granddaughters, joined the migration of the affluent down the Hudson to Manhattan.

In the late 1880s, Troy was preparing to celebrate its first one hundred years. Its citizens raised money to build a monument to the soldiers and sailors who had died in the Civil War, money to construct an ornate stone complex on Spring Avenue to house the Troy Orphan Asylum, money to erect a beautiful building on Second Street, a few blocks from the old seminary, for the Young Women's Christian Association. The city had dozens of "street railways," designed to carry workers from their homes in South Troy and Lansingburgh to the prosperous factories in the center and northern parts of the municipality. There were 11 miles of granite-paved streets and 21 miles of sewers, improvements that marked Troy as a progressive, modern, and healthy place to live. Downtown Troy was home to Frear's, a huge department store (fifty-four departments in all) doing over a million dollars' worth of business by 1890, both in the store and through a mail-order business that rivaled Montgomery Ward and predated Sears, Roebuck. In 1895 Frear would move his "cash bazaar" a few blocks east to a beautiful four-story marble building. As was true of the collar factories, Frear's building was notable for its skylight and magnificent iron staircase.

The prosperity of the Gilded Age also brought social change. The growing disparity between the very wealthy and the middle class was accompanied by a fascination with the wealthy coupled with a desire on their part to be more and more exclusive. In 1887 the *Social Register* began to document the names of the wealthiest, most well-connected Americans. At the same time newspapers expanded their society columns. As one historian has observed, "Society journalism spread outwards to every American city . . . virtually every community in the country contained an inner circle of old, wealthy families, and a large, socially ambitious, discontented penumbra of those with unsatisfied aspirations."[8]

Troy's society pages often focused on two local favorites: the financier Russell Sage and Lily, Duchess of Marlborough, whose parents, Cicero and Elizabeth, still lived on Second Street. When Lily entertained Lady Colin Campbell (whose divorce had been occasioned in part by her alleged affair with Lily's husband, the eighth Duke of

Marlborough), all of Troy's papers (as well as papers in larger cities) reported on the event. "Already a Sensationalist"[9] trumpeted *The Troy Press*, and the *Morning Telegram* featured "How Lillie [sic] Is Entertaining Lady Campbell."[10] Not to be outdone, the *Troy Northern Budget* reported that the "American duchess" was planning to renovate Blenheim Palace, beginning with a roof repair rumored to cost more than £30,000. Blenheim, under the new duchess's regime, was to "be the scene of regal hospitality and gayety [sic]."[11] Not everyone was pleased by the marriage. When the newlyweds returned to the parish of Woodstock, where Blenheim was located, the rector refused to ring the traditional wedding bells, claiming that "'my creed and my church protest against such marriages.'"[12] *The Troy Press* sided with the royal couple, claiming that Lily was "Troy's own," and "not every American city can boast of a live Duchess!"[13]

Meanwhile, Russell Sage, who had begun his career as a clerk in Troy, provoked almost as much press coverage. A "robber baron" of the Gilded Age, Sage had begun to amass his fortune as a young man in the dry goods business in Troy. Eventually moving into railroads and finance, Sage was reputed to be tight with his money. *The Troy Daily Times*, while acknowledging "he often clings to and squeezes a half dollar until . . . he makes the American eagle scream," also pointed out that the millionaire "is reputed to do acts of kindness of which he never speaks" and is "not so mercenary as his general reputation would warrant."[14] Although he built the foundations of his fortune in Troy and represented Troy's district in Congress from 1853 to 1857, Sage had moved to New York in 1863. In 1869 two years after the death of his first wife, Maria Winne '38, Sage married Margaret Olivia Slocum '47. At his second wife's urging, Sage would be critical to the renewal of the seminary's fortunes.

Perhaps Russell Sage, in spite of his reputation for penuriousness, was also influenced by his fellow millionaire industrialist, Andrew Carnegie. In 1889 Carnegie, who disliked the idle rich—and, for that matter, the idle poor—wrote "Wealth," in which he formulated a philosophy of private responsibility called the "social gospel." He argued that the wealthy who filled the columns of the *Social Register* and the social pages ought to use their money for philanthropic purposes. While Carnegie and Sage had millions to give away, others of more modest, yet still substantial, means were inspired to give away thousands for the institutions they supported.

In Troy, these people included the Gurley brothers, William and Lewis. Their father, Ephraim, a native of Londonderry, Ireland, had built an iron foundry in Troy around the time Emma Willard opened her school in Middlebury. He died when his sons were toddlers, but his wife managed to educate her sons at Rensselaer Polytechnic Institute (RPI) and Union and her daughter, Clara, at the seminary. In the 1840s, William, the older son, helped establish a business for the manufacture of surveying instruments. When his brother joined him in 1851, they became the sole owners of the business, and the mathematical instruments firm of W. and L. E. Gurley was launched. In the 1860 census, William listed respectable assets of $40,000, and Lewis a modest $500. By 1870, however, each brother reported assets of $100,000 to the census taker. The Civil War had created a demand for their precision products, which included sights for cannons and "fuses for artillery projectiles."[15] In 1876 their surveying instruments won prizes at the Centennial Exhibition in Philadelphia.

William and Lewis both had daughters who attended the seminary. William's daughters with his wife Maria Kenney '45, were Clara '67, Esther '71, and Mary '80. Lewis's daughters were Grace '86 and Edith and May, both 1895 graduates. In 1866, when his oldest daughter was in her final year at the school, William first joined the board of trustees, remaining there until 1887 and serving as treasurer from 1872 to 1880. His brother Lewis joined the board in 1879, most likely at the request of John Willard, who served as president of the trustees from 1879 to 1882. It is very likely that William's wife played a role in his active trusteeship. Not only was Maria Kenney Gurley a graduate of the school, she was also a close friend from childhood of Mary Hastings, the seminary alumna and teacher whose advocacy of her alma mater never wavered, even after she left Troy to teach at Smith and Wilson Colleges. Furthermore, after William's death, she continued to be a significant donor to the school.

When John Willard's final illness forced his retirement from public life in 1882, William took over the board presidency. It was he who arranged for the printing of the memorial resolutions in the Troy papers when John died in March 1883. Willard's death was covered by the local papers in greater detail than Sarah's, which occurred three months after his. A typical obituary stressed his civic accomplishments and his warm personality. John was "prominently identified with the business interests of Troy," not only in connection with the seminary but also as a director of the Commercial Bank, the Central National Bank, and the Troy and Boston Railroad Company. He was a member of the vestry of first St. John's and then St. Paul's. He was credited with bringing steam heat into the seminary, one of the "earliest [Trojans] to introduce residential steam heat." Giving a glimpse into the private man, this account concluded, "Children have always been fond of Mr. Willard."[16]

As trustees, William Gurley and John Willard worked closely together. Many of William Gurley's papers and ledgers have been preserved, and they reveal just how actively he and John Willard were involved in the day-to-day operations of the school during the 1870s and 1880s. From canceled checks it is clear that as board treasurer and then president, Gurley's duties included paying salaries and overseeing all expenses. He also took an active role in hiring. John Willard also aided in hiring, wrote advertising copy, ordered repairs to the seminary buildings, and approved school invoices.

No detail was too small for their attention. A typical entry for 1883, for example, listed $5.03 to be reimbursed to Emily Wilcox. The items for reimbursement included $1.68 for "ribbons for diplomas," $.35 for a "globe for hall lamp," and $.10 for a "messenger boy." Given that Wilcox was being paid $300 per quarter, it is no wonder that she needed reimbursement; what is less understandable is why the male board members insisted on maintaining control of the seminary's finances, right down to the level of petty cash. At first glance such patent distrust of the principal's ability to manage money seems at odds with their commitment to women's education and, in John's case, at least, firsthand knowledge of the sharp business acumen of his mother.

The budget during these years was extremely tight. There was no

clerk or business manager on the school payroll, so the board's officers handled financial matters just as Dr. John Willard, Robert Battey,
and William Lee had done for the founder and that John Willard had
done during the years that he and Sarah ran the seminary. Emily Wilcox presumably was too busy teaching and overseeing the academic
side of things to oversee the business of the school. On very rare occasions she approved an expense. For example, she signed off on 85
cents worth of laboratory equipment on December 6, 1882, and on
June 26, 1883, she contracted for the rental of five dozen chairs and an
"extension table," probably for that year's commencement ceremony.
On even rarer occasions, Mercy Mann, who served as Emily Wilcox's
second in command, approved a bill, as she did in April 1882, approv-
ing $3.18, the price for cleaning 53 yards of Brussels carpet.

Letters to Gurley indicate that job seekers often wrote directly to
board members. Gurley received appeals from women seeking French
positions and men wanting to be janitors. In 1872 Gurley had convinced Mercy Plum Mann '65 to return to the school to assist Emily
Wilcox. Mann, who had taught at the school for a few years after her
graduation, was teaching at a girls' school in New York and earning
over a thousand dollars a year. She assured Gurley that she wanted to
return. "I well know the work to be done in the school," she wrote, but
she asked for a salary of $1,100.[17]

Gurley replied immediately that the salary was "not unreasonable" and that he was extending an offer to her "unofficially" because
he felt the institution's success as a day school, although not yet assured, would be greatly helped by announcing her return.[18] Given that
Wilcox's salary was only $1,200, it is not surprising that Gurley wrote
Mann that "for obvious reasons I wish the amount to be considered
strictly confidential."[19] Gurley wrote the salary checks for all employees, so it was possible that Emily Wilcox did not know what her teachers made. At any rate, Mann accepted the offer and stayed at the seminary for a decade, retiring from teaching in 1883 when she married
John Hudson Peck. Peck, a nephew of Sarah Willard, was president
of RPI and a seminary trustee, and both Pecks were very involved in
seminary affairs until their deaths well into the twentieth century.

In his initial correspondence with Mercy Mann, William Gurley implied that the fate of the seminary had been uncertain, but he assured her that the monies to buy out the city's interest were available. He confided that "my brother and I . . . have determined to make up what may not be subscribed by the first of May."[20] Although this was the first significant financial contribution that the Gurley family made to the school, it was far from the last. Throughout the 1880s, according to school ledgers,[21] Paul Cook, William's son-in-law, associate at the instruments factory, and the treasurer of the board of trustees while first William and then Lewis held the presidency, routinely transferred cash to the school account to cover expenses. Some, but not all, of this money was repaid. Between 1873 and 1885, the school took in $119,917.52 and spent $120,104.85. There was rarely more than $200 cash on hand, and periodically parts of the old buildings were sold off. In 1878 the sale of a "Boiler, Old Building, Chimney, &tc." realized $356.[22]

It is also clear from the school ledgers of the 1880s that Gurley and John Willard spent a good deal of time and money on the constant repair of the campus. Invoices for masons, plumbers, wallpaper hangers, carpet cleaners, and carpenters abound. John Willard approved much of this work, carefully writing "correct" and his initials next to the number of hours a repair had taken. In 1881 repairs to a fireplace grate, for example, took "3/4 day," and Thomas Howe, a carpenter born in Ireland, received $1.75 for the accompanying day's labor. In 1884 plumber James Maguire earned 40 cents an hour for a three-hour repair, and his unnamed assistant earned $1.75 for a day's labor, which was probably ten hours. In addition, the school was assessed several hundred dollars for paving Ferry Street and was taxed on properties that were not being used for educational purposes. These included lots on the northwest corner of Ferry and Second Streets, 43 Ferry Street, and the "Buell House." The city water bill, which typically ran between $30 and $40 per year, was figured according to the number of "water closets" in use, both at the school and at 85 Second Street, Emma Willard's residence, where Wilcox and many of her teachers lived.

In 1887, before he could realize his plans for the school, William Gurley died. The "insidious disease" that had plagued him for "two or three years before his death"[23] was most likely cancer. *The Troy Daily Times* reported that Gurley was attended in his final illness by Dr. Sands, the Saratoga physician who treated President Grant in his final struggle with throat cancer. It had been just a year since Gurley had pledged $10,000 to erect a new building for the school. His brother Lewis, taking over the presidency of the board of trustees, was determined to give a building to the school that would memorialize not only his brother but also his older sister Clara. Clara had been one of the first "normal" students at the school, studying under Emma Willard from 1835 to 1838, then teaching in Georgia for a few years before returning to Troy for more study in 1840. She died of typhoid fever just a year later. The new building would be the first major step in achieving William Gurney's dream of restoring the seminary to its former glory as the nation's leading girls' boarding school.

At nearly the same time that Lewis Gurley was hatching his plan, three other separate movements with nearly the same aims were forming throughout the country. Elsewhere in Troy, Chicago, and in New York City, alumnae of the seminary plotted ways to revive their "hibernating"[24] alma mater. By 1889 Troy alumnae were determined to raise the money for a statue in honor of Emma Willard. Invoking the spirit of republican motherhood, Jane Foster Bosworth[25] penned an appeal. Referring to the statue of Joan of Arc erected by the French people, she wrote, "Infinitely more fitting would it be if the 10,000 women who at the Troy female seminary have been led to noble aims and high endeavors, should cooperate with the men whose homes these cultivated women have elevated and adorned, and erect at Troy a statue of Mrs. Emma Willard."[26]

A committee was formed to raise money for the statue. Calling for "a lasting memorial to the most eminent educator of her sex,"[27] the committee was chaired by Susan Colegrove '47, the wife of Charles MacArthur, proprietor of *The Troy Northern Budget*, one of the city's daily newspapers. Francis N. Mann Jr., whose wife, mother-in-law, mother, sisters, daughters, and sundry aunts and cousins (including Mercy Mann Peck) had attended the seminary, served as treasurer. Mann was a lawyer and businessman, and his father had served on the board ex officio when he was mayor of Troy. The other members of the committee included George B. Cluett, owner of one of the city's most prominent collar factories; attorney Charles I. Baker; and Fanny Seymour '66, wife of Charles E. Patterson, prominent local lawyer and former speaker of the New York State Assembly; Elizabeth Hart '37, wife of John Griswold, former mayor and iron manufacturer responsible for the construction of the "Monitor"; and Harriet C. King '70, wife of William S. Kennedy, insurance salesman. In short, the committee reflected Troy's prominent businessmen, as well as alumnae or alumnae connections across six decades. What they proposed was nearly unprecedented. When the statue committee was formed, the only statue in the United States commemorating a real woman was the Margaret Haughery memorial in New Orleans, dedicated in 1884.

Just as the Statue Association began its work, another alumnae group was forming. Motivated in part by news of the statue plans in Troy but also by the movement for women's organizations that was beginning to take hold among upper-class women, C. Evelyn Baker Harvier '68[28] invited all former seminary graduates living in New York City to a tea at her home in the fall of 1890. Enough responded to plan the next steps. On April 25, 1891, a group of forty-eight alumnae met again at the Harviers' home. A planning committee was selected and met five days later at the home of Ruby Gould '60, who was married to former Troy physician Dr. Charles E. Simmons, a prominent doctor in Manhattan. In addition to Evelyn Harvier and Ruby Simmons, the committee consisted of Margaret Olivia Slocum Sage '47, Mary Hastings '45, Frances D. Eaton Pierson '55, Sarah A. Hoyt Spelman '49, and Mary L. Seymour Eddy '56 whose sister, Fanny Patterson, was a member of the Troy statue committee. On May 5, this group convened at the Sage home on Fifth Avenue to take up the work of arranging a governance structure for the organization and writing a constitution and bylaws.

Olivia Sage was certainly the wealthiest member of the nascent association, and the others were also well-to-do. However, money and the Troy Female Seminary were not the only things they had in common. All were active in good causes; many of them, including Hastings, Pierson, Spelman, and Sage had taught school after leaving the seminary, and all had an abiding interest in women's education. Pierson was recently widowed; her second husband had been Henry R.

Pierson, the chancellor of the University of New York. Mary Eddy was an alumna daughter; her husband had left his father's successful ink manufacturing business in Troy to found his own successful chemical company in New York. Spelman, the wife of a prosperous Brooklyn dry goods merchant, was an active volunteer who served for many years as the treasurer of the Brooklyn Industrial School and Home for Destitute Children. The group reflected the religious diversity that had characterized the TFS, and they were politically diverse as well. Some had husbands who were active Democrats; others were married to ardent Republicans. In spite of their social prominence, none of them, including Sage, were members of the elite "400" that defined the top of Manhattan society, at least according to the famous Mrs. Astor.

However, they were members of the growing women's club movement that had gained momentum after the Civil War. Most prominent among the women's organizations in Manhattan was the Sorosis Club, founded in 1868 as a group for professional women who were excluded from similar male organizations. Evelyn Harvier was an early member of Sorosis and a supporter of the successful movement to consolidate all women's clubs under the umbrella of the General Federation of Women's Clubs. Both Spelman and Pierson were also members of Sorosis. Although no TFS graduates were directly involved in the formation of either Sorosis or the General Federation, the title "Mother of Clubs"[29] was bestowed on Lucinda Hinsdale Stone, Emma Willard's first cousin once removed on her mother's side. Stone, who along with her husband, helped found Kalamazoo College was, like the women forming the seminary alumnae association, dedicated to the idea that the purpose of women's clubs was the advancement of women. In a classic bit of nineteenth-century pseudo science, Stone's biographer claimed that a phrenologist "had found [Stone's head] to be strikingly similar to the head of the well-known educator, Mrs. Emma Willard," even though he did not know of their familial connection.[30]

The first order of business for the new association was a name. Originally the group favored Alumnae Association of the Troy Female Seminary, but some members felt this was too narrow and would exclude nongraduates (defining alumnae as graduates only). The next proposal,

"Emma Willard Alumnae Association," was determined too exclusive because it technically referred only to those women who had studied with the founder. At a meeting in late May, held at the Eddys' house, on a motion by the founder's granddaughter, Sarah Willard, who had traveled to New York for the occasion, the name "Emma Willard Association of the Troy Female Seminary" was adopted. Next the group decided on its agenda for the coming years. Olivia Sage, elected president, chaired the meeting. Her fellow officers were Sarah Spelman, recording secretary; Fanny Eddy, treasurer; and Evelyn Harvier, corresponding secretary. There were seven vice presidents: Mary Patterson and Elizabeth Griswold from Troy; Harriette Dillaye '37, longtime TFS teacher and colleague of Olivia Sage at the Ogontz School; Emma Willard Scudder '53; Clara Harrison Stranahan '50, wife of Brooklyn's leading citizen; and Manhattan residents Mary Lillie Baxter '62, wife of William W. Baxter, and Jane Warren Townsend '50, wife of Randolph W. Townsend. Mrs. Baxter's father had made a small fortune with an iron safe factory in Troy, and her husband's family had prospered in the Vermont marble business. The Baxters split their time between Philadelphia and New York where she was active in volunteer organizations. Jane Townsend's husband was a prominent New York attorney; in addition to supporting her own alma mater, in 1910 she bequeathed $50,000 to Yale to endow a history professorship in memory of their only son who had died in his freshman year.

These were women of means who, for the most part, had administrative experience in volunteer organizations. They swiftly developed an agenda for the Emma Willard Association (EWA). First, they planned to bring together as many alumnae as they could for an annual banquet, the first one to be held in October at the Waldorf-Astoria. Second, they planned to appeal to all alumnae for money to support the statue project. Third, they wanted to organize a memorial to Emma Willard to be displayed at the upcoming World's Columbian Exposition in Chicago, whose organizers had already announced there would be a special building dedicated to women's accomplishments. All of these goals undergirded the single most important goal: the perpetuation of Emma Willard's fame and the restored prosperity of her greatest achievement, their alma mater.

A contemporary of the alumnae commented, "The 'Emma Willard

Women' are a power in the land; cultured, ambitious, refined and womanly . . . an honor to themselves and to the School of learning in which they were equipped and trained. The wisdom of their famed preceptress has . . . made light their intellectual pathway."[31] True, but in the early years there was some dissension in the ranks. The third goal of the New York group brought them into conflict with alumnae in the Midwest. At the same time that the New York contingent was meeting, Florence Montgomery Taylor '66 of Canton, Illinois, was rallying the midwestern alumnae in anticipation of the fair. She wanted the Troy alumnae to join with the South Hadley alumnae in an exhibit. Harriet Dillaye, among others, was scornful of Florence Taylor's attempts to combine a reunion of Mary Lyon's pupils with Emma Willard's pupils. Mary Hastings apparently concurred because Dillaye wrote to Hastings that she agreed with her that "the E.W.A. can have nothing to do with the reunion of the Lyons [sic] School." Mrs. Taylor's "*real* Alma Mater"[32] suggested Dillaye disapprovingly, was located in South Hadley.

With no alumnae relations office at the school to navigate this controversy, it was left to the alumnae to settle their own differences. Although they had not been at school together, Olivia Sage had developed a close friendship with Nettie Fowler McCormick '53 during the brief period of time in the 1860s when the Russell Sages and the Cyrus McCormicks lived near each other in Manhattan. By the 1890s, Nettie McCormick was a powerful widow, both socially and financially, and any reunion of the Emma Willard alumnae in Chicago would be enhanced by her participation. Nettie McCormick, whose financial resources at least equaled those of Olivia Sage, was an appropriate confidante for Sage; since her husband's death in 1884, she had not only carried on the philanthropic work he had started but also guided her son in the management of the McCormick Harvesting Machine Company.

Nettie Fowler and Olivia Slocum shared similar backgrounds because both had grown up in upstate New York, Nettie in Clayton and Olivia in Syracuse. Nettie was orphaned at an early age but knew no economic hardship because she was taken in by a wealthy uncle. Olivia's parents were part of her life until she was an adult, but her father's wildly fluctuating finances made her home life unstable. When she went to the seminary, she, too, lived with an uncle. For both women, Emma Willard and her school had provided a haven, albeit for different reasons. The McCormicks had worked together on their philanthropic causes, particularly those pertaining to theology and education. It is not surprising that as early as the fall of 1891, Olivia Sage turned to Nettie McCormick to share her hopes for persuading Russell Sage to fund the school's revival.[33]

Meanwhile, the first banquet and reunion of the Emma Willard Association took place at the Plaza Hotel in New York on October 15. The preparations were elaborate. The *New York Times* covered the event in great detail, and their coverage was reprinted in papers around the country. The guests ranged from Mary Landon '24 to Anna Lomax, newly minted graduate of the class of 1891, who were seated side by side. The entire event, from its floral arrangements to its menu choices, from its speakers to their topics, set a standard for classy and classic alumnae gatherings that would become a trademark of the school's events on into its third century. Unlike modern reunions and even off-site alumnae gatherings, however, this one was completely the work of the alumnae association—with the head of school in attendance as an invited guest.

A significant difference from modern reunions was the inclusion of graduates from all classes instead of a five-year rotation. The five-year rotation was already in vogue at colleges, including RPI, so the inclusion of everyone from the seminary was most likely a deliberate decision. Given the fiscal goals of the organization, reaching out to as many alumnae as possible made good sense. Reunions on school campuses were also well established. By 1891 a bit of doggerel in a songbook at Miss Porter's implied that spring reunions had quite a history at the school. Their alumnae were already dubbed "the Ancients," and the Farmington poem satirized their reunions:

> Her aunts, sister, and cousins were all here before,
> They come back each year late in May.
> Oh, 'tis then that she feels a cold shiver of dread,
> For she knows that those 'Ancients' will say,
> Now when we were here...[34]

The first reunion of the Emma Willard Association looked back, as is true at most reunions, but its larger order of business was the future.

Mrs. Sage presided over the meal and subsequent meeting at the Plaza. Accompanying her at the head table, which was festooned with pink flowers (pink was the signature choice of the alumnae), were most of the association's officers plus Nettie McCormick and a number of invited guests, including Martha J. Lamb, a founder of the *Magazine of American History*, which published flattering accounts of the history of the seminary, Helen Gould, daughter of multimillionaire Jay Gould, and opera star Florence Rice Knox. At the start of the luncheon, which began at 2 o'clock, Mrs. Sage presented the association with "a large portrait of Mrs. Willard on an easel decorated with pink ribbons."[35] For the next two hours, more than 160 women dined on a sumptuous seven-course banquet beginning with *huitres* and ending with fruit, cheese, and *café noir*. Between the fifth and sixth courses, they cleaned their palates with "sorbet, Emma Willard," and one of the seven dessert choices was "pudding, Troy Female Seminary."[36]

The meeting began around 4 o'clock. According to the *Times*, two hours passed (perhaps not swiftly) as speaker after speaker "indulged in reminiscences and paid eulogistic tributes to Mrs. Emma Willard."[37] Each of these tributes was lengthy, and all were reprinted in full in the first annual report of the alumnae association. Emma Scudder read reminiscences written by Harriette Dillaye, who was prevented from attending because of illness. Mercy Peck and Frances Nason spoke about their schooldays. Peck reviewed the lives of the teachers she admired, including Anna Manwaring, Theodosia Hudson, Emily Wilcox, and Caroline King, reserving special praise for Sarah and John Willard. Peck, who had had the experience of teaching elsewhere, concluded about Sarah, "Mrs. Willard's system made teachers. . . . Nobody knew so well as [her teachers] how rare a principal she was."[38] Peck viewed John Willard as Sarah's perfect partner in the enterprise: "unwearied in his endeavors to adapt the building to its work, sparing neither time nor means to render it healthful, convenient, cheerful and comfortable."[39] Nason claimed the 1850s as "The Golden Age of the Troy Female Seminary," and referring to the hundreds of students who studied there, declared, "I glorify the rank and file of this school army."[40] Clara Stranahan recalled her pride when she returned home from school with her Troy diploma, "the first document of the kind ever given to a woman in that town."[41] Emily Wilcox delivered a more formal address on "The Higher Education of Women," overtly calling for the seminary to become a college: "There is the Vassar path, the Wellesley and Bryn Mawr avenues, but where the Willard center whence all should radiate? . . . now its loyal daughters see that the way is well open for them to do for this grand old mother of colleges all that is necessary to place it in the first rank of colleges."[42]

The speeches were interspersed with Florence Rice Knox singing Emma Willard's most famous hymn, "Rocked in the Cradle of the Deep." There were reports from Patterson on the statue fund, and Fanny Eddy gave a treasurer's report. Two subscription books were circulated so that the attendees could contribute to the statue or a new Emma Willard Scholarship Fund. Olivia Sage made the first contributions, $100 apiece in each book. No other donation came close to hers; the next largest in either fund was $10. Evelyn Harvier announced that the Sorosis Club had made a contribution to the scholarship fund, and she also mentioned that Mrs. Grover Cleveland had been invited to attend but regretted because she was "engaged in the higher education of women."[43] This announcement was met with applause from the crowd; presumably they were applauding Frances Cleveland's support of women's higher education (she was the second first lady with a college degree), but it is conceivable that the mostly Republican crowd (by marriage) might have been cheering the absence of the Democratic former first lady.

With annual dues set at a dollar, and wealthy women making scholarship and statue donations in the single digits, the association was far from economically successful. In her speech, Emily Wilcox had stressed the importance of an endowment, referring to an unnamed school that "like other private schools wanting endowment . . . [is] extinct."[44] Nevertheless, it was a start, and the crowd voted to make the reunion banquet an annual event. Among other news from Troy, they heard details of the groundbreaking for Gurley Hall. A mostly local event, this occasion had included singing by the seminary pupils, prayers, and a keynote address by Troy clergymen and the laying of a cornerstone by Lewis Gurley. The stone contained a box of Emma

Willard's writings.[45] The dedication, planned for June, would provide an occasion for a full reunion. Instead of waiting a year, many of the alumnae in attendance at the first New York banquet would meet in Troy in the spring for the dedication of Gurley Memorial Hall.

The new building was finished in mid-May. The construction made national newspapers when the tree planted by Lafayette was cut down to make room for the new building.[46] Better press followed when the building was completed. Designed by local but nationally prominent architect Marcus Cummings (whose wife was Clara Sheldon '69), the Romanesque building was constructed of Long Meadow brownstone edged with Barre granite. Facing Second Street, at almost a right angle to the old school building, it had a basement and two upper stories dedicated to school activities. The gymnasium, located in the basement, had a separate entrance, a dressing room, and a bathroom, five rooms to house a resident janitor and his family, a chemistry laboratory, and a classroom. On the first floor there was a reception room, the principal's office, the library, four classrooms, and a room dedicated to "day scholars." Given that there were as yet no boarders, this room was most likely a gathering space where students could store coats, boots, and other possessions they would not want to carry all day. The second floor contained the assembly hall, complete with raised stage, four classrooms, and another bathroom. Maria Gurley and her children paid for the furnishings, which cost more than $5,000.

Troy alumnae were not to be outdone when it came to the dedication ceremony. They were ready to show off the "Collar City." Preparations for the out-of-town guests were elaborate. The local alumnae committee arranged for special tickets on the Citizens' Line, which ran an early morning steamboat from Manhattan. Carriages met the guests at the dock and drove them to the new YWCA building on Second Street,[47] just three blocks from the school. Dubbed "Seminary Day"[48] by the Troy newspapers, June 8 was an occasion for civic pride, and the downtown businesses were decorated in special bunting for the occasion. Flags flew from downtown residences, and two large portraits, one of Emma Willard and one of Lewis Gurley, were prominently displayed in the window at 28 Second Street, home of Ella Crane Wilkinson '71. Souvenirs in the form of small handpainted fans with pink bows celebrated the school's years in Troy, bearing in gilt the message, "T.F.S., 1821–1892." For alumnae who had attended the school before the great fire of 1862, the city's transformation from a place of wooden buildings to a metropolis with modern "fireproof" multistory edifices must have been startling.

Eager to display their city, the Troy alumnae had arranged a carriage ride from the Y past many landmarks familiar to the former pupils and ending at the Willard family plot in Oakwood Cemetery. The return trip deposited the visitors at the old seminary building. Here they gathered in the old examination room for a meeting of the Emma Willard Association, Mrs. Sage presiding. The meeting began with Susan MacArthur reading from the book of John about the miracle of turning water into wine, and then Frances Nason said a prayer. Emily Wilcox delivered an "Address of Welcome," in which she urged them to "linger awhile within [the old building's] walls before they give their greetings . . . to that fairer building, wherein we trust shall be sustained the soul and spirit of this older one."[49] Mrs. Sage responded that she hoped that "all these efforts in building, statue and reunions be but the beginning of a great work which shall make this seminary second to none in the land."[50] Sarah Willard, who was out of town tending to her sick sister Harriet, had sent a letter of greeting, which was read to the assembly by Susan MacArthur. The business portion of the meeting followed with the usual reports on fund-raising; Olivia Sage announced that the first scholarship fund had been completed. A total of $2,000 had been raised to send a young woman to study at Middlebury.[51] Martha Read Mitchell '38[52] had matched Sage's $100 contribution to the statue fund. Mitchell, married to Alexander Mitchell, one of Wisconsin's wealthiest citizens, demonstrated by her participation in the fund that the rift with the midwestern alumnae had been healed.

Florence Taylor's presence at the meeting in Troy was further indication that the two groups were working together. Specific plans for the Columbian Exposition were tabled until the fall meeting. In the meantime, there were two more speakers. Anne Anderson, the head of the Albany Female Academy,[53] a sister institution also founded in 1814, addressed the conflicting claims as to which institution was the oldest with deft humor: "I am told there is a chronological difference between these two institutions which threatens thoroughly amicable relations; *mirabile dictum*, these sisters disagree as to which has the honor of precedence in age."[54] The controversy did not matter, she concluded, because "Both are old; both are historic; both have enriched the communities in which they were planted" and, most importantly, "both have sent out into the world noble types of good historic womanhood."[55]

After Anderson came the star of the day: Elizabeth Cady Stanton. As Sage's most recent biographer has shown convincingly, Stanton had been personally invited by Sage to speak at the meeting.[56] Sixty years after finishing her education in Troy, Stanton was the most famous— or infamous—graduate of the TFS, and it seems from some accounts of the speech that current students may have been present for this part of the meeting. Stanton was embarrassed by neither her politics nor her age. For her, "the hey-day of a woman's life is on the shady side of fifty."[57] She was "old," she admitted, and acknowledged that it was probably a good thing that none of her classmates were there because "probably our ideas would differ on every subject, as I have wandered in latitudes beyond the prescribed spheres of women."[58]

Noted for her significant girth, Stanton centered her reminiscences about her schooldays on food. (This no doubt amused any teenagers in the audience.) As she spoke in the old assembly hall, she remembered "the dining-room . . . with its viands that never suited us, because, for-sooth, we had boxes of delicacies from home, or we had been out to the baker's or confectioner's and bought pies or cocoanut [*sic*] cakes, candy, and chewing-gum—all forbidden, but that added to the relish."[59]

In addition to nostalgia for the scenes (and tastes) of her school-days, Stanton's speech contained a ringing call for scholarships. Fund-ing scholarships, she maintained, was "the best work women of wealth can do."[60] She revealed a sophisticated understanding of fund-raising, explaining that "there are two kinds of scholarships equally desirable: a permanent one, where the interest of a fund, from year to year will sup-port a succession of students; and a temporary one, to help some worthy individual as her necessities may require."[61]

When Stanton concluded, the assembled alumnae sang "Blessed Be the Tie That Binds" and took one last tour of the old seminary building before adjourning to the YWCA, where current seminary students, adorned with the ubiquitous pink ribbons that marked all EWA occasions, served them lunch. No wine was served, perhaps in deference to the many active temperance workers among the crowd, but the recording secretary noted, "there was a sympathy more fragrant than wine, and we pledged each other in the liquid glance of beaming eye to a constancy that shall never fail."[62]

The main event, the dedication of Gurley Hall, took place after lunch. The festivities included the seminary students singing about the new building to the tune of "America," a solo of "Rocked in the Cradle of the Deep," congregational singing of the "Doxology," an invocation and benediction by local ministers, the reading of a very lengthy memorial poem by its author, Benjamin H. Hall,[63] speeches by Lewis Gurley and John Hudson Peck, and a keynote address by the Rev. H. M. King of Providence, Rhode Island. King was a prominent Baptist minister and temperance leader who had recently moved to Rhode Island from a parish in Albany. Given the Gurleys' strong Baptist beliefs, it is likely that Lewis had invited him to speak at the event. The lineup of speakers for the dedication contrasted sharply with the morning's program; there were no women.

In presenting the building to the trustees, Gurley spoke of his brother and their dreams for the renewed prosperity of the school. Gurley Hall was just the beginning. The school needed a building for music and art, a building for natural sciences, and a dormitory. Most important, however, it needed an endowment "by which all its grand facilities may be placed within the reach of the young girls here and elsewhere who have little besides intelligence, energy, and virtue, and who hunger for [an education]."[64] Peck accepted the building on behalf of the trustees. He heralded the founder, claiming, "She was not the founder of an institution only; she founded a new and fruitful conviction in the minds of men."[65] Next came King who eloquently reviewed the seminary's place in higher education: "From this fountain have flowed streams which have fertilized the soil out of which Vassar, Wellesley, Smith, Bryn Mawr and other distinctive schools for young women have sprung."[66]

It seems clear that Gurley, Peck, and even Olivia Sage envisioned that the school would remain a school and not become a college. Emily Wilcox, in contrast, hoped for the school to take the steps necessary to become a college. Other alumnae supported this goal and would express this desire often between 1891 and 1894. Mindful of the millions necessary to endow a college, the trustees continued to raise money to improve the *school*. Less than a month after the dedication of the Gurley building, the Troy papers reported another major gift to the seminary.[67] Anna M. Arnold Plum Quackenbush '35, wed and twice widowed to two prominent Troy businessmen, had agreed to fund an art and music building in memory of her daughter, Anna Plum '66, who had succumbed to spinal meningitis in 1887, the same year that William Gurley died. The younger woman's obituary stressed her interest in music, calling her "an excellent musician and a fine performer on the piano."[68] Within days of the Plum announcement, the board of trustees voted to demolish the old seminary building to make room for the new arts facility. Sold at auction for $150 to James E. Ryan, the building was scheduled to be removed by September 1.[69]

With the opening of Gurley Hall, the promise of Plum, and the work of the Emma Willard Association, the school's revitalization was assured. The activities of the EWA were widely covered in the press, bringing to the public outside of Troy renewed awareness of the founder and her role in the education of women. In addition to Elizabeth Cady Stanton and Olivia Sage, other graduates had begun to have public identities and were invariably identified as former students of Emma Willard. Certainly, the social high jinks of the Duchess of Marlborough were part of this fame, but other, more serious alumnae also claimed national attention. Among them were Louise Chandler Moulton '55, forgotten now, but at the time a widely published author of both poetry and literary criticism; Lucy Watson Bostwick '50, whose Margery Daw cookbooks were widely distributed and favorably reviewed; and Lydia Wood Baldwin '52, whose novel based on her experiences as a teacher in Reconstruction Virginia earned positive publicity.[70]

The Columbian Exhibition, scheduled to open in Chicago in May 1893, would be the next great venue for the EWA to showcase the founder and her legacy. Along with Juicy Fruit gum, Cracker Jacks, shredded wheat, and the Ferris wheel, the 27 million visitors to the Chicago World's Fair would be introduced to Emma Willard and her work.

A Thorough Preparation
for Any College

FOR THE EMMA WILLARD ASSOCIATION (EWA), the grand dedication of Gurley Hall in the spring of 1892 was just the first in a series of events in the 1890s designed to recapture the school's early grandeur. Rapid changes during the next three years would bring the trustee and alumna dream to fruition. By November, at the second annual banquet in New York, the usual reminiscences were accompanied by reports on the accumulating statue fund, the nearly completed scholarship being raised to help a young woman attend Middlebury College, and plans for an all-alumnae reunion at the Columbian Exposition in Chicago. In conjunction with her plans to hold a reunion at the Chicago fair, Florence Montgomery Taylor '66 had begun accumulating a list of the names, addresses, and basic vital statistics (husbands, addresses, death dates) of as many seminary graduates as she could locate. This project, along with the reunion plans, was quickly appropriated by Olivia Sage and the New York association.

Beginning in the winter of 1893, reports on the fair were matched by progress statements from a newly established biographical record committee. Under the leadership of Mary Hastings '45, Mary Mason Fairbanks '45, and Mary Skilton Palmer '48, the committee, which was organized regionally, sent out thousands of questionnaires and edited the responses for publication. Initially the project met with some resistance. Hastings reported to the EWA at their March meeting that some alumnae "do not desire to appear in any biographical record, seemingly thinking that their life stories were to be given publicity."[1] This was not surprising, in light of the Victorian code of propriety that held that a woman's name should appear publicly only three times, at her birth, marriage, and death. In the end, however, the committee convinced thousands of alumnae to participate. The compilation of their stories, first published in 1897 and in a second edition with addenda and errata in 1898, would eventually become the much heralded biographical record, *Emma Willard and Her Pupils.*

Most of the EWA meetings during the winter of 1892–93 were devoted to planning for the exhibition the association was organizing for the World's Columbian Exposition in Chicago, a long-heralded event scheduled to open in May. Americans had debated for years the proper way to celebrate the four hundredth anniversary of Columbus's "discovery" of America. After Congress had settled on the concept of a world's fair, New York and Chicago had vied with each other to host the event. Financiers and industrialists in both cities proffered money, but Chicago, eager to demonstrate the growth it had experienced since its devastating fire in 1871, raised the most.

Many of the Chicagoans who pushed to make their hometown the fair site had seminary ties. Cyrus McCormick's widow, Nettie Fowler McCormick '53, as well as merchant Marshall Field, husband of Nancy Scott '57, advanced money for the fair. Lyman Gage, a prominent Chicago banker and the husband of Sarah Etheridge '59, was credited with swinging the final vote in Chicago's favor when he raised several million dollars just in time to sway the congressional decision. The combined World Congresses to be held in conjunction with the Columbian Exposition were chaired by attorney Charles C. Bonney, husband of Lydia Pratt '48.

Prior fairs, including the Philadelphia Centennial in 1876, had showcased women's arts and achievements. Chicago, however, was the first to feature a women's building created by a woman and managed by women. Sophia Hayden, one of the few female architects in the country and the first woman to earn an architecture degree from the Massachusetts Institute of Technology designed the building, and Bertha Honoré Palmer, wife of one of Marshall Field's early partners, Potter Palmer, chaired the board of lady managers. As early as the spring of 1892, Olivia Sage had written to Bertha Palmer requesting permission to include an exhibit about Emma Willard at the fair, and Palmer had agreed. A year later, with the opening of the fair rapidly approaching, Charles Bonney called on Sage and promised that the Willard tribute would be cordoned off by "silken curtains" and a brass railing, and the floor would be covered by rugs.[2] He also assured her that an Emma Willard tribute would be part of the Educational Congress.

The EWA met monthly at the Sage home on Fifth Avenue to plan for the fair. Not only would Chicago provide an occasion for a social reunion, but it would also allow the alumnae to advertise the founder and their school. The final choice of Willard artifacts for the exhibition included portraits of Emma, Sarah, and John Willard; copies of all of the founder's writings, including "The Temple of Time"; photographs of the Willard home in Middlebury, the old seminary building, its apparatus room, lecture room, and library; and a watercolor of the old examination room. In addition, photographs of the new Gurley building, along with architectural drawings of Gurley and Plum Halls, would be displayed. There would be two framed "catalogs" of pupils from 1822 and 1824, and a copy of John Lord's *Life of Emma Willard*.[3]

Mary Hastings was placed in charge of the exhibit; Olivia Sage paid for her to travel to Chicago to ensure that the installation went smoothly. It was good she did. The association minutes record that Hastings found the Emma Willard exhibit assigned to the wrong room, some of the boxes of memorabilia were lost, the "display was at first poorly arranged and unattended,"[4] and the fair organizers often mixed up Emma Willard with Frances Willard, the famous temperance advocate. Mary Hastings, "a consecrated intelligence,"[5] was just the person to straighten things out. Her admiring association colleagues recorded that "by a sort of alchemy . . . she at length made order reign where confusion had rioted."[6] When Hastings was finished, the display was so attractive that over three hundred alumnae visited and signed the guest register; there is no record of the numbers of strangers who were also drawn to the exhibit. Alumnae welcomed nonalumnae. Indignant that some visitors "had never heard of Emma Willard," the association declared that their role at the fair had become "a Campaign of Education."[7]

Although the fair opened in May, the main events for the seminary alumnae were scheduled for "Education Week," a series of education-related events held in July. On July 17, Olivia Sage welcomed the alumnae to a reunion held in the Illinois pavilion. In her speech she gave a brief history of the EWA and reported on the statue and Middlebury initiatives. She also described the ongoing improvements to the campus. Although the EWA was dominated by women from the Northeast, and the alumnae were meeting in Florence Taylor's home state, as of this reunion, there was no doubt that Olivia Slocum Sage was regarded as the president of all alumnae.

After welcoming the reunion attendees, Sage introduced Mary Newbury Adams '57. Like Taylor, Adams was a lifelong midwesterner, but her mother had studied with Emma Willard in Middlebury. An ardent suffragist, she lectured on "Emma Hart Willard, an Important Factor in American History," drawing parallels between Willard's way of teaching and writing about history and the record of progress at the Columbian Exposition. Both, she maintained, demonstrated the advancement of civilization through "a telescopic view of all nations and religious customs and races."[8] For Adams, woman suffrage was simply the next logical step in this progression. No doubt aware of the significant affluence of her audience, Adams recommended finding the "means to prevent wealth from being destructive by educating women to learn how to use it for universal good of all."[9]

The first day ended with an invitation from another midwesterner, Jane Hart Dodd, niece of Emma Willard and former art teacher at the seminary, to visit the Cincinnati Room in the Women's Building, where Rookwood pottery was on display. Largely because of Rookwood, Cincinnati had gained an international reputation as a ceramics center. Jane Dodd and her daughter, Jessie Hart Dodd, were both ceramicists. Funded by Cincinnati heiress Maria Longworth Storer (whose nephew would famously marry Alice Roosevelt), Rookwood is still in operation today and claims to be "the first female-owned manufacturing company in the United States."[10]

The second day of the reunion began with the presentation of a paper by Jane Bancroft Robinson '71, former dean of women at Northwestern, who was prevented from attending because she was caring for a sick relative. Robinson's paper was titled "Emma Willard: The Results of Her Life and Work." In addition to tracing Willard's life, she wrote "personally" of her regard for Emily Wilcox's teaching, recalling the "wise, persuasive, stimulating words of dear Miss Wilcox, who made geometry so attractive to me."[11] Next on the agenda was Mary Wright Sewall, a suffragist and educator from Indianapolis whose mother, Mary Brackett, had studied in Troy in 1826. She urged that the fair be the start of a movement to memorialize great women. In a speech that foreshadowed the women's studies curriculum of the 1960s, she exclaimed about the foremothers of her generation: "Let us call the public attention of the world to their names! Let us set up their statues! Let us write their memoirs! Let us have their portraits hanging in our public libraries, in college halls and in museums."[12]

Wisely varying the pace of the day, Olivia Sage then took the stage to display some memorabilia. She shared with her audience an autograph album that Virginia Bullitt '37 had compiled. The album included a poem by Emma Willard that the founder had composed and inscribed in the book. For Sage, Emma Willard's words perfectly captured the mood of the Chicago reunion. In the poem, a woman, presumably Bullitt, is leafing through the album on a day far in the future and telling her children about her youth and schooling:

> A book she holds,
> And as its leaves she turns, name after name,
> She reads. 'These were my youthful friends,' she says,
> My school-day intimates—ever yet beloved. . . .
> And here you see her name who taught us all;
> She loved me well, and taught me much
> That I have taught to you. She, too, is dead.
> Perchance she watches those she loved on earth,
> And feels approving joy, that the good seed
> She sowed was not in vain—nor she forgot.[13]

Next Sage displayed a picture of Lydia Ely Vanderwarker '24, age ninety-five, and believed to be the oldest living graduate. She recounted the tragic event that brought Lydia to Troy; on her honeymoon, her husband had died, and the eighteen-year-old widow had subsequently enrolled at the school to train as a teacher.

After this interlude, the speeches resumed. Emily Wilcox, prevented from attending the fair by the final illness of her sister, had written a short history of the seminary, which Mary Van Olinda '60, read to the assembly. In her sketch, Wilcox highlighted the educational methods of the founder and celebrated the legions of women who had taught at the school. Its success, she believed, owed in large part to its faculty: "[A]ll through the years, even down to this present, it has had faithful teachers, to whom no small share of its excellent character and remarkable success have been due."[14] When Van Olinda had finished, the group moved on to the New York State Building where Mrs. Sage hosted a reception for the alumnae and their friends. Among the guests at the reception were Mr. and Mrs. Frederick Douglass, the first notice of any black Americans in attendance at a seminary event in a capacity other than servant. Unlike other black activists, Douglass had not boycotted the lily-white fair, preferring to work within the social structure. There is no record of how the alumnae reacted to his presence, but it was noted positively in the alumnae minutes. This reception brought the formal reunion festivities to an end.

The next day, however, Olivia Sage was once again on a dais when she presided over a session of the Educational Congress held in the Art Palace. She had agreed to do so because Elizabeth Cady Stanton had written a paper for the occasion. Stanton was absent, but her friend and colleague, Susan B. Anthony, read "Emma Willard, The Pioneer in the Higher Education of Women." In typically fiery, feminist tones, Stanton tartly dismissed those opponents of women's education who argued that ill health attended women who aspired to be educated. She wrote, "I doubt whether as many women die annually from writing essays . . . as from over-production, and yet no flags of danger are raised on the house-tops where mothers of a dozen children languish and die, or in workshops, where multitudes of feeble women labor from fourteen to sixteen hours a day."[15] She concluded that it should be the goal of all women "to secure to their daughters justice, liberty and equality in every position in life, and thus exalt the real woman as well as the ideal as an object of love and worship."[16]

There was one more treat in store for those alumnae who had remained in Chicago to hear Stanton's work. Seemingly on the spur of the moment, Nettie McCormick had invited her fellow seminary students to a reception at her palatial Rush Street home. The recording secretary of the EWA, Sarah Spelman '56, enthused unabashedly, "Not unlike a school girl's eager expectation of the Christmas holidays was our anticipation of the reception at Mrs. McCormick's."[17] Spelman described McCormick as the "Madonna Gloriosa of our sisterhood" and gushed about "lovely young girls in dreamy gowns presid[ing] at fairy-like tables."[18] Lest her hero worship appear unseemly, she was quick to explain why McCormick's wealth and position mattered: "Mrs. McCormick's reception was a demonstration of the fact that we have within the circle of our influence the wealth, culture, social position, intellectual power and moral force necessary to carry on an aggressive work for woman on the lines laid down by our illustrious teacher."[19] Spelman's words echoed Emma Willard's defense of education for "the daughters of the rich" when she asked, "Can a class of citizens be found whose influence over [the nation's] prosperity is greater?"[20]

Spelman ended her published account of the events in Chicago by noting that Mary Hastings, Emma Willard Scudder (who had died unexpectedly of pneumonia in May), Olivia Sage, and Harriette Dillaye were all looking for a grand mission that the energy of the EWA could accomplish. To Spelman, the mission was clear: "[the] ultimate hope and purpose" should be "a *University for Women*—WILLARD COLLEGE—on the site of the old Seminary." Her final plea was to "watch the dying for bequests that this glorious work may be begun."[21]

In Chicago, the school had the opportunity for broad exposure to Americans from all parts of the country. This was especially important if the boarding department was to reopen, which was now almost a certainty. In March, as the EWA planned for Chicago, the press had carried the news that Russell Sage had agreed to build the seminary a dormitory in honor of his wife. Questioned by a reporter, Sage replied, "My wife . . . declares that the report that I am to give away a building is true, so I guess it must be so."[22] The Troy papers rejoiced. A restored boarding department would bring business and prestige to the city. As one observer explained, "Commencement meant something in the years before 1872,

[when] whole families travel[ed] from every point of the compass to Troy." "The hotels," he noted approvingly, "did a rushing business."[23] The same reporter further exulted, "Again will the Trojans see the stylish New York girl, the stately studious Bostonian, the Quaker City maid, the dainty, indolent Southern girl, and the bright, bustling, Western girl, as part of their own population as long as the school year lasts."[24]

The notoriously secretive Russell Sage might feign ignorance of the project when speaking to a reporter, but in private he was deeply involved in all aspects of the planning for the new dormitory. He chose Marcus Cummings, Gurley Hall's architect, to design the building, which would be furnished with every modern amenity, including passenger elevators, "a novelty for school buildings." The initial plans called for "walls of buff-mottled brick, with terra cotta trimmings . . . [with] basement walls and door and windowcaps and sills of Belleville gray sandstone." [25] In a departure from the practice at the seminary, all of the beds in Sage Hall would "be single, it being deemed more healthful that pupils should sleep alone." To prevent students from feeling too isolated, however, the bedrooms would "open into parlors so the pupils will have parlor mates instead of roommates."[26]

Sage called a meeting in his Manhattan office for Cummings and Lewis Gurley, as well as the president of Western Union and the architect for the Western Union Building in Manhattan,[27] whom Sage apparently wanted to review Cummings's drawings. There was some disagreement about the timetable for the work. When Cummings said it could not be completed in 1894, Sage replied that he would simply hire more workers. Cummings countered that some of the work could not be rushed, and Sage eventually agreed to Cummings's timeline. A sign of his concern for all facets of the project was Sage's insistence on hiring a special inspector for the quarry in Perth Amboy where the bricks were to be made; he intended to have this employee "pass at the quarry upon every piece of the stone before it is shipped to Troy."[28] Newspaper accounts insisted that Russell as well as Olivia Sage had a "cherished desire" to "bring back the prestige of Troy as a boarding school."[29]

For the most part, Sage's contemporaries and his biographers have characterized him as a ruthless businessman and very reluctant phi-

lanthropist whose donations were designed to offset his piratical image. In 1893, just as plans for the new dormitory were being laid, the
United States endured a severe economic panic that led to the most
devastating depression the country had as yet encountered. Populist
politicians and the press held multimillionaire financiers like Sage responsible for the economic crisis because of their manipulations of
the gold market and reckless trading on the stock market, particularly
with regard to railroad stocks. Taxes and tariffs were hot topics in the
press. Striking a familiarly modern note, *The Troy Press* editorialized,
"This proposition to tax the poor man's breakfast table just about as
largely as that of the rich man to sustain the government meets with
strong opposition."[30] Philanthropy was one way for "the rich man" like
Sage to counter the criticism that he was indifferent to the needs of
others.[31] He may simply have wanted to please his wife. As historian
Ruth Crocker has concluded in her biography of Olivia Sage, the Sage
marriage was a partnership between disparate personalities who nevertheless worked together companionably on each other's causes.[32] An
interview a few years before his death supports this analysis. Sage included in his "'Rules for Giving'" the advice that "'A man . . . should
favor all well-managed charities for women."[33]

At the third annual luncheon of the EWA, the alumnae continued to
focus on raising money for the erection of an Emma Willard statue to be
placed on the old seminary grounds in close proximity to the new buildings. Olivia Sage had become a convert to the cause of woman suffrage,
and she invited Elizabeth Cady Stanton and Susan B. Anthony to speak at
the luncheon. For once the minutes did not reprint the speeches verbatim,
with Spelman recording only that the two women made "characteristic
addresses."[34] However, the report published Mercy Mann Peck's reminiscences in their entirety. Not all the members of the EWA were suffragists.
(Emma Willard Scudder, for example, great-granddaughter of the founder and an honorary member of the association after her mother's death,
opposed woman suffrage.)

The final speaker at the luncheon, Clara Stranahan, compared
Emma Willard with Mary Lyon, "as one who has had the privilege of being under the influence of both these distinguished teachers."[35] She con-

trasted the "brilliant courses of higher education at Troy" with "Mary Lyon's constant consecration to christianizing [*sic*] the higher education of woman."[36] She evinced a feminist view of women's accomplishments in organizing their portion of the fair. Referring to press accounts of arguments among the members of the national board of the Women's Building, she reminded her audience that the women were drawn from all sections of the nation and their achievements far outweighed their disagreements. After all, she commented, "when the slur of 'women disagreements' is cast, . . . those of [the national board] have never exceeded, never even equaled, those of the members of Congress."[37] The meeting ended with the singing of "Seminary Days," a song written by Evelyn Harvier and set to the tune of "Auld Lang Syne." The final stanza and chorus captured the universal spirit of reunions:

> Then let us all with joyous hearts
>   Our youthful days live o'er
> Turn back through years that time has sped,
>   To-day we're girls once more.
> Of Seminary days we sing,
>   Of Seminary days,
> We meet once more in memory of
>   Our Seminary days.[38]

The third report of the association ended with a form for making a bequest to the school—either as an annual or an outright gift. Their fund-raising was maturing.

Meanwhile in Troy, the results of the trustees' fund-raising continued to change the face of the campus. As the winter of 1893 faded into the spring of 1894, Anna M. Plum Memorial Hall was rising over Ferry Street. By September 1894, Plum was ready for pupils, and the trustees planned a dedication ceremony in conjunction with the first day of classes. According to the press, "the dedicatory exercises were, as designed, of an informal nature."[39] Perhaps because the plans for Sage Hall were already on the architect's drawing board and the statue fund was nearing its goal, they were anticipating a full-scale celebration in the spring when the dormitory was to be dedicated and the statue unveiled. In addition, Anna Arnold Plum Quackenbush '35, the building's donor, had died in May.

The ceremony, therefore, was brief, with a few musical numbers and an address by Lewis Gurley bracketed by prayers from two local ministers, one Episcopalian and one Universalist. Gurley recalled that at the dedication of Gurley Hall, he had spoken of the school's need for a dormitory and a building dedicated to the arts—and a scant two years later these needs were close to being met. On behalf of the trustees, he announced a major curricular departure, "the organization of a conservatory of music and a school of art, both to be located in [Plum Hall] and both . . . well equipped for the highest success and excellence."[40]

A female reporter for *The Troy Daily Press* toured the new building the day before the dedication. She met with Marion Sim, the principal of the conservatory, a local woman who had studied music in Europe and considered the popular Polish pianist Paderewski a personal friend. Sim welcomed the reporter into her office, "a private sanctum . . . all light in tone, even to the new Wissner piano."[41] Wandering through the building, she found "banjos, guitars, flutes, clarionets [*sic*], and mandolins. . . . I poked my head into all the corners and put my head into the cosy little practise [*sic*] rooms, each one seeming to be the fitting abode of genius."[42] She wandered upstairs to the art department and met its director, Charles M. Lang, a portrait artist with studios in Albany and New York.

Unlike the music rooms, the art rooms were not yet finished. Lang apologetically explained that "in place of the odd tables and stools upon which implements of the trade are now scattered in hopeless confusion, there are to be built neat desk-like appointments for the keeping of crayons and brushes and that heterogeneous collection of stubs and what not, which are the weapons of art in the hands of a clever workman." Overall, she concluded that "to be in the building is to immediately feel the charm and stimulus that brings out the best that is in us."[43]

A month after the opening of Plum Hall, Olivia Slocum Sage became the first female member of the board of trustees. Once again, the seminary was trailing the new women's colleges. Vassar, Smith, and Wellesley already had women on their boards, as did Mount Holyoke. Expanding the board of trustees to include women was just one more reason for Olivia Sage to support woman suffrage; it required a vote of the legislature, all men voted into office by men and not necessarily sympathetic to the needs of women's institutions.

At an April meeting of suffrage sympathizers held at the Sage home, Olivia had reminded her guests of the repeated negativity on the part of state legislators to bills concerning the Troy Female Seminary. She also recalled for her guests the initial rebuffs by the legislature of Emma Willard's pleas for public support of female education. The recent governance change had failed to pass the legislature on the first try. It took two votes to pass the proposed expansion of the seminary board from fourteen to seventeen members, a move intended to make room for four women. As an additional governance change, the board had asked for the elimination of the mayor of Troy as a board member. The rationale for this move, according to a New York paper, was that the mayor "was not always an educated man."[44]

Although the bill to change the composition of the board had passed on the second vote, it was vetoed by Gov. Roswell Flower, whose brother and business partner was married to Ida Babcock '71. The *New York Times,* in a lengthy article on the meeting, reported that "Mrs. Sage told the ladies about how the Governor had offended . . . and they said he was not to be elected again."[45] Women's views on politics were gaining more press. Throughout the spring of 1894 New York newspapers were filled with news of "society women" lining up on either side of the suffrage question, in large part because it was an election year.

By the fall, however, the annual meeting of the EWA focused once more on the construction of Sage and the plans for the school's revitalization. On October 18, Lewis Gurley, "who can boast of being the only man invited to the dinners of the association,"[46] addressed a crowd of over two hundred alumnae on the topic of women's higher education. He concluded by reading a letter from John Peck announcing that Olivia Sage would be joining the board of trustees. As he left the luncheon, Gurley, whose commitment to women's education was unimpeachable, nevertheless demonstrated the cavalier diminution of women common among even the most enlightened men of the era: "'Now girls . . . when this building . . . is dedicated next May, I hope to see you all in Troy.'"[47]

Two themes ran throughout the minutes of the meetings leading up to the May events. First was the continuing question of whether or not the seminary would become a college. As the secretary captured the debate, some took the position that a first-class preparatory school would "do the greatest good to the greatest number, while others held that only a College . . . would do fitting honor to the work of the great Teacher."[48] Second was an ongoing discussion of what to call the renovated school. In January the venerable former teacher Harriette Dillaye said bluntly, "It can scarcely remain Troy Female Seminary."[49] At the March meeting the association unanimously adopted the following resolution:

> *Resolved,*—That we look forward to the development of the Troy Female Seminary into a College or University for women, bearing the name of Emma Willard, and holding that superiority to all other similar institutions that the Troy Seminary held in her lifetime.[50]

In April they revisited the question. They had successfully raised $2,000 for the Middlebury scholarship, and a new scholarship fund for a student to study in Troy stood at a few hundred dollars. They recognized that a college or university would require an "endowment of millions" and the "intellectual leadership which will command the confidence of the country."[51] They resolved to join with the trustees to probe the feasibility of raising the kind of money and interest necessary to turn the school into a college.

Meanwhile, they made plans to go to Troy. As they had done at the time of the dedication of Gurley in 1892, the alumnae planned a reunion in conjunction with festivities surrounding the dedication of Sage Hall and the unveiling of the statue. On May 16 they descended on Troy "from all points of the compass. . . . sixty by the night boat, singly or in groups by the railroad."[52] This time, however, the alumnae were not entertained off campus. Instead they were welcomed in the library of Gurley Hall, where they were presented with badges and "armed with pink programmes" before heading outside where a special platform for the 250 visitors had been erected opposite the new statue of Emma Willard "draped in the flag she loved so well." The "dear, shabby old Seminary" was gone; in fact, the only landmark from earlier days was "Mrs. Willard's old home on the corner, looking strangely dwarfed and out of place among the beautiful and stately buildings which seem to have risen by magic from the old grey walls."[53]

Happily, the weather cooperated, and the first order of business, the unveiling of the statue, occurred under a sunny May sky. Designed by Alexander Doyle, the statue captured the founder in the prime of her life and was taken from the portrait by A. B. Moore, the portraitist whose painting of Emma Willard in vigorous midlife had been displayed in Chicago. Doyle was renowned for creating heroic statues, including many Confederate monuments in New Orleans and the Haughery statue in that city. In 1890 he had been commissioned to sculpt the marble statue of assassinated president James Garfield for the Garfield Memorial in Cleveland.

John Peck, secretary of the board, accepted the bronze tribute from the statue committee. He reviewed the founder's achievement in establishing the school in the face of social opprobrium, concluding that her ability to work within the "limitations then placed by custom on the sphere of women" demonstrated her "genius in leadership."[54] Predicting that "the uncanopied figure will face unkind elements unmoved,"[55] he foresaw that the statue would forever draw the attention of "the casual passer along these streets."[56]

After Peck spoke, Susan Colegrove MacArthur '44, the chair of the statue committee, introduced the morning's keynote speaker, John M. Taylor, president of Vassar College, who again reviewed Emma Willard's contributions to education. At the conclusion of Taylor's speech, the alumnae gathered around the statue for a group photograph and then returned to Gurley where the Troy alumnae hosted a luncheon. Pink was everywhere. The schoolrooms were curtained in pink draperies, the tables festooned with pink flowers, and the current pupils who served the lunch wore pink-and-white dresses. After lunch, the guests were entertained by a concert in Plum.

At three o' clock the crowd moved to the Presbyterian Church for the dedication of Sage Hall. Lewis Gurley presided over the afternoon session, which opened with an invocation by Rev. J. W. Ford. Again the speakers were all men. Rev. Melancthon W. Stryker, president of Hamilton, delivered a speech that was an amalgam of praise for the progressive people of New York State, a sermon on the grace of generous people, and, of course, a review of Emma Willard's contributions to women's education. Next, Lewis Gurley thanked the Sages on behalf of the board, promising that "the trustees are not unaware of the increased responsibility these gifts of Mrs. Quackenbush and Mr. and Mrs. Sage impose upon them." Somewhat mysteriously, he added that the trustees' plans for the future of the school would be "revealed in due season" and that "something has already been done."[57]

Gurley then introduced Chauncey Depew, a politician and wealthy businessman who was active in New York State Republican politics and had received considerable support for the Republican presidential nomination in 1888. In his speech, the future senator addressed the issue of great wealth and its potential for both good and evil, explaining that "in money making, as in everything else, there is construction and destruction." Countering the opinion of the press and liberal Democrats that the country was being overrun by unscrupulous, wealthy industrialists, Depew instead maintained "the number of successful and legalized robbers is not large in the community" and those "dangerous brigands" who did exist were controlled by "wise legislation."[58]

He recognized that "the press asks, the pulpit inquires, the platform orator wants to know what the rich man is doing with his money that he should receive for it the protection of the State."[59] In answer, he pointed to Vassar College, the University of Chicago, Cornell, and Columbia as institutions that owed their existence to the munificent gifts of wealthy industrialists. Sage Hall was simply another example of the "beneficent use and administration of money by a man in his own lifetime." According to Depew, Russell Sage had donated the money for the new dormitory "to show his appreciation of years of happy wedded life and of the value in the close companionship in marriage . . . of the educated woman."[60] Like every other speaker, he extolled Emma Willard's virtues, recalled the highlights of her life and work, and heralded her influence, which, he reminded his listeners, "did not stop here [but] crossed the ocean."[61]

Although not scheduled to do so, Russell Sage unexpectedly took the podium to confirm Depew's assertions. In a repudiation of his historical reputation, he spoke of his high regard for women in general and his wife and Emma Willard in particular. With that the dedication ceremonies ended, although an evening reception in honor of the Sages was later held in Gurley Hall. Not surprisingly, the day's festivities were reported verbatim in the Troy papers. At the conclusion of the lengthy account in *The Troy Daily Press*, a small paragraph revealed the changes to which Gurley had alluded. Emily Wilcox, who had taken no part in the day's dedication ceremonies, had announced her resignation. An anonymous trustee told a reporter that a new principal would be announced shortly, but "as to Miss Wilcox's reasons for resigning, he would say nothing."[62]

Neither Emily Wilcox nor Lewis Gurley left diaries or correspondence detailing the end of her employment after nearly forty years at the school, the last twenty-three as principal. In 1893 she had written to Olivia Sage, thanking her effusively. "Joy ever seeks to find expression," she wrote, "and so I cannot refrain from writing you of the great joy and happiness that Mr. Sage's gift brings to me."[63] Little did she know that Mr. Sage's gift would affect her employment. There is no record of any retirement agreement. In fact, although she was sixty, she did not—perhaps could not afford to—retire; according to the census of 1900, she was living with her sister-in-law in her birthplace, Middletown, Connecticut, and was employed as a schoolteacher. There is no record of her ever making a return visit to Troy or seeing the new campus on Mount Ida, even though she lived until 1915.

Reading between the lines of the minutes from the annual meeting of the EWA in the fall of 1895 presents the best—if somewhat condensed—record of the rapid changes that came to the school after the completion of Sage and the erection of the statue. Elizabeth Borst '71 addressed the luncheon. She briefly touched on the life of the founder but then heralded the work of Sarah Willard and Emily Wilcox. She referred indirectly to the fact that the school had a new name, Emma Willard, assumed for it by the alumnae. She suggested that the alumnae "assumed in changing [the school's] name the sponsorship of the school's future."[64] When Borst concluded her address, Olivia Sage introduced "Miss Mary A. Knox, Principal of the Emma Willard School."

Knox urged the "old pupils of the old Troy Seminary"[65] to enroll their daughters and granddaughters in Emma Willard. She then outlined the new curriculum that was being developed and explained that "the school aims, first, to give to students who desire it, a thorough preparation for any college."[66] Clearly, Emily Wilcox's dream of Willard College or University had ended with her resignation.

Mary Alice Knox was not the only new face on campus. In fact, when the school had opened in September, only one teacher, Mary Green, remained from the seminary days (and she would last only one more year). The new corps of teachers, explained Miss Knox, were "college graduates, who have had the advantage of a broad education."[67] Mary Alice Knox herself had earned a B.A. from Elmira College and had taught history at Wellesley for ten years. The daughter of a minister, she was the niece of Algerina Knox '44. While at Wellesley, she had been active in the settlement movement that so many women's college students and faculty supported.

In fact, it may have been Knox's participation in the settlement movement that led to her leaving Wellesley. Whether the Troy trustees knew it or not, she had been removed from the Wellesley faculty by the college's new president, Julia Irvine. Between 1894 and 1896, Irvine completely revamped the faculty. Her goal was to have a faculty focused on pure academics rather than on reform movements and community outreach.[68] Knox was "purged"[69] in the spring of 1895. Just as the school began seeking college-educated teachers, Wellesley sought professors with graduate degrees; Knox had only her bachelor's.

In Troy, a four-page flyer had been printed in lieu of the annual catalog. It outlined the curriculum and highlighted the new buildings and principal. The academic program was divided into three four-year segments: primary, intermediate, and academic. In addition to preparation for college, students could study art or music exclusively, and there was "a general course of study . . . [for] those who do not desire to pursue a collegiate course."[70] The flyer contained few details about the course of study, but the public was promised that there would soon be "another publication giving more particular information."[71] Some specific information was included, for example, the costs. In spite of the ongoing national economic crisis, the tuition for day students was set at $56 per year for primary and intermediate students and $80 per year for academic students, with additional charges for French, German, and chemistry. These charges represented a 100 percent increase over the year before and marked the first rise in tuition since 1872. As had been the case since Emma Willard opened her first school, music and art classes carried separate prices.

As dramatic as this increase must have seemed, the boarding charge was even more extraordinary. For a girl to be a boarding student cost her family $700 per year, an amount that included "board, room, with table and room furnishings, washing to the extent of one and one-half dozen pieces per week, pew rent in such church as parents may indicate, laboratory expenses and tuition in all branches except music and art."[72] Not one of the women's colleges cost that much, and neither did the men's colleges. Tuition, room, and board at Vassar hovered around $400, at Amherst the same. As late as 1910, students at Bryn Mawr, a college that attracted a significant number of affluent undergraduates, paid only $200 for tuition and another $300 to $400 for room, board, and fees.

Preparatory school tuition varied dramatically, depending on the amount of endowment or other support—most typically religious—that the school received. When Porter Sargent produced the first edition of his "authoritative" handbook of private schools in 1915, Exeter and Andover, well endowed, charged only $150 while newer institutions like Choate and Groton charged $950. There was a similar fluctuation among girls' schools, with Miss Hall's, Burnham School, and Dana Hall charging more than $1,000. Neither Emma Willard nor Miss Porter's submitted tuition figures to the first handbook, but the boarding tuition at Emma Willard that year ranged from $900 to $1,100, depending on the student's choice of room.

Clearly, schools charged whatever tuition they needed to operate; consequently, the program they offered needed to meet parental needs if they were to attract paying customers, especially if the costs were high. In 1895 the trustees had decided that parents wanted a college preparatory education for their daughters. Willard University had no future, but the Emma Willard School did. It would be a college preparatory school of the finest distinction and would continue to fulfill the founder's legacy by being the best in its class. Mary Alice Knox, ten-year veteran of college teaching, would be the appropriate person to guide the establishment of a new curriculum and the hiring of a college-educated faculty.

This decision paralleled a number of movements in education throughout the country. Perhaps most important was the publication of the *Report of the Committee of Ten*. In 1892 a conference was convened in Saratoga to establish "uniformity in school programmes and in requirements for admission to college."[73] Chaired by Charles Eliot, the president of Harvard, the committee included ten men, ranging from the U.S. commissioner of education, William T. Harris, to college presidents and professors from Michigan, Oberlin, Vassar, and the University of Missouri. High schools were represented by the principals of Lawrenceville, Albany High, and Girls' Latin in Boston.

For decades, college admission had been determined by examination of the entering students. Often the young men and women who sat for these examinations, which often took place after they arrived on campus, failed and were placed in the preparatory departments of the college. The Committee of Ten hoped to provide guidelines for secondary school curricula that would enable high schools to prepare students more successfully for college and allow colleges to get out of the remedial business. Since 1871 some state universities, beginning with Michigan, had provided for admission to college by certificate, meaning that they accepted students based on the certification of their secondary schools that they had completed a proscribed curriculum. The Committee of Ten wanted to encourage the certification process; over twenty years Michigan had found that "the standing of students admitted by certificate was considerably higher than the standing of students admitted by examination."[74] For wider use of certification to be possible, a better articulation between high school and college curricula was necessary.

Between its first meeting in Saratoga and its second meeting at Columbia in November 1892, the committee collected confidential curricular information from forty "leading" secondary schools and tabulated the results. They found that more than forty subjects were taught at all of the schools and another thirteen at a few schools. They criticized "wide diversity of practice with regard to the time allotted to [each subject]."[75] From this preliminary investigation, they decided to call nine conferences in specific academic areas with membership drawn from colleges and secondary schools. These conferences would make recommendations for their disciplines. Students who studied at secondary schools that adopted these curricula would then be admitted to college by certification of their high schools.

The nine conferences covered Greek, Latin, English, other modern languages, mathematics, physical science (physics, astronomy, chemistry), natural history (biology, botany, zoology, physiology), history, including civil government and political economy, and, finally, geography, which encompassed physical geography, geology, and meteorology. Each conference had ten members; of the ninety teachers and professors selected, only one woman, Abby Leach, professor of Greek at Vassar, was selected.[76] All ninety were white and Christian. Among the secondary schools represented were Exeter, Andover, Lawrenceville, Collegiate, Williston, William Penn Charter School, and Albany Academy. Girls' High in Boston, a public school, was the only girls' school providing a committee member; Vassar was the only women's college to do so. The committees had from December 1892 to April 1893 to complete their work.

Each committee was charged with answering a set of eleven questions. They were to "consider a school course of study extending approximately from the age of six years to eighteen years,"[77] and they first needed to decide the optimum age when a discipline should be introduced. Other questions had to do with the selection of topics to be covered, the number of years necessary for mastery and the best pedagogical methods. For each discipline, the committee also addressed "in what form and to what extent should the subject enter into college requirements for admission."[78] The most controversial questions posed to each committee were numbers seven and eight:

> 7. Should the subject be treated differently for pupils who are going to college, for those who are going to a scientific school, and for those who, presumably, are going to neither?

> 8. At what stage should this differentiation begin, if any be recommended?[79]

When all of the reports were in, the results showed a "unanimity . . . [that] is striking and should carry great weight."[80] Certainly, Troy was listening. Throughout the 1880s, the academic program at the seminary had included a primary and intermediate department, as well as a high school or "academic" course, but few girls seemed to follow the entire program. In the last catalog printed during Emily Wilcox's administration, the school enrolled 140 girls, but only 5 were listed as "members of the graduating class" for 1895.[81] The curriculum in the "Academic Department" was described as designed to "meet the wants of individual pupils" and "embraced as wide a range of subjects as can be consistently taken."[82] Among the subjects were algebra, geometry, physiology, botany, physics, chemistry, English, history (separate courses in French, English, Roman, and Greek), English literature, psychology, Latin, German, French, and physical culture. Clearly, this was the sort of scattershot program that the Committee of Ten disdained.

Mary Alice Knox was hired to change things, and she did. If a full catalog was ever printed to succeed the flyer announcing the school's reorganization, it has not survived. However, the catalog produced during the 1895–96 school year[83] clearly outlines the changes and definitely reflects Knox's familiarity with the work of the recommendations from the Committee of Ten. Boarders were to be admitted only to the high school, and the curriculum at that level would conform to college standards. Recognizing that not everyone would wish to go to college, those "who do not wish to undergo the strenuous educational work of the college" could take courses in the "department of graduate study"[84] at the school. These students could elect what they wanted after completing the academic course, and it was expected that they would most likely study history, literature, philosophy, modern languages, and science. If they were boarders, they had to elect at least twelve hours of class work per week. Other changes included the establishment of a school government and the opening of the kindergarten and the primary grades to boys as well as girls.

In spite of its elegance, Sage Hall housed only a few boarders in the fall of 1895. As late as mid-September, notices appeared in newspapers around the country advertising under the title "Troy Female Seminary" that "this famous school will be reopened as a Boarding School on September 25, 1895" and that inquiries should be directed to Mary Alice Knox, Emma Willard School.[85] No boarders came, but Knox was unperturbed. Reviewing her first year at the annual EWA luncheon in the fall of 1896, she recalled, "When I accepted the position of the principal of the school, one of the conditions I named was that I be allowed to run in debt for the first two, or even three, years." This was necessary, she pointed out, "in view of all that was to be accomplished."[86] She was also happy to report that in 1896–97 there were twelve boarders hailing from Connecticut, Rhode Island, Ohio, California, Michigan, and seven cities and towns throughout New York. Three were the daughters or granddaughters of alumnae, two had been recruited by trustees, and "a number made their decision on the merits of the school itself."[87] In September, Russell Sage had paid for furniture for the rooms on the third floor; Knox was supremely confident that she would be able to fill the dormitory soon. (Its capacity was about sixty boarders.)

High on Knox's list of things to be accomplished was the hiring of a new faculty. It seems likely that some of teachers simply retired with Emily Wilcox, but it is unlikely that any had the choice of staying on, with the exception of Mary Green. In her report to the EWA, Knox called the new faculty she had hired "stronger . . . both in numbers and character," and described faculty meetings that were "a genuine source of inspiration."[88] By "character," Knox undoubtedly meant educational attainment. The catalog for the year emphasized that "the teachers who have been secured for the Academic Department are finely prepared for their specialties."[89] Among them was Louisa M. Hannam, who had earned a Ph.D. from Cornell. Over the course of her administration, which lasted until 1902, Knox attracted several more teachers holding doctorates. Given that there were only 207 doctoral degrees awarded to American women prior to 1900, this showed remarkable recruitment on her part. In the academic department, under Mary Alice Knox, teachers holding bachelor's degrees began to be the norm rather than the exception.

None of these teachers would make Troy their ultimate professional destination. Hannam went on to become chair of the English department and dean of women at Colorado State Teachers' College. Winnifred Edgerton Merrill, the first woman to earn a Ph.D. from Columbia, taught mathematics in Troy for a few years and later opened her own girls' school in Mamaroneck. Ella Bliss Talbot, one of the earliest women to earn a Ph.D. in philosophy (she was a Sage Fellow at Cornell) taught one year in Troy before moving on to Mount Holyoke where she remained for three decades. Vida Moore, who had also earned a doctorate in philosophy, taught at Holyoke before Emma Willard and at Elmira for fourteen years after.

Elizabeth Hazelton Haight and Ada Woolfolk did not have their doctorates when they came to Troy, but Haight went on to earn one in classics, after which she became a revered professor at Vassar and the author of several well-received scholarly books, as well as small pieces for *The New Yorker*. At Vassar, Haight was legendary, not least for her feminism. The syllabus for her class on ancient myth included "one or more heroines along with every hero."[90] Woolfolk, whom Knox had met through the college settlements movement, never earned her doctorate but returned to social work, running Atlanta's Family Welfare Society during the New Deal. The Knox faculty also included Ada Brann and Julia Haynes. Brann, an 1884 Wellesley graduate who had helped establish the Barstow School in Kansas City before coming to Troy, coined the motto "To educate a girl is to educate a nation." Haynes was a gifted science teacher who regularly demonstrated her classroom techniques and experiments at national conferences.

Knox was aware of the talented faculty she had gathered, and she used them to help redesign the curriculum. From 1895 until her departure in 1902, she held weekly faculty meetings. There was an annual election of a faculty member to record the minutes of each meeting. (The art and music faculty were not required to be there; the primary and intermediate teachers were sometimes excused.) The minutes have survived and provide an inside view of the work of the academic department and an echo of the voices shaping the curriculum.

In the first year, in addition to fleshing out the academic curriculum, the faculty tackled grading, student government, library policies, absenteeism, homework, the school calendar, relations with the Regents, students struggling with academic work, and the exam schedule. Although the Wilcox administration had begun the practice of sending home progress reports, there appeared to be some confusion as to what an A really meant. The faculty decided at a meeting in October: A stood for Excellent, or work in the 90–100 range, B for good (80–89), C for Creditable (70–79), D for Weak (60–69), E for Deficient (50–59), and F was simply Bad. In January the faculty settled on a system of school government; every student would be a member, but there would be an executive committee composed of Knox, an elected faculty member, one student representative from each of the three intermediate classes, the freshman and sophomore class, and two each from the junior and senior classes.

Periodically, the faculty discussed students whose work fell in the D, E, and F range, and they also debated issues of calendar. Easter, as always, was problematic. Its inconsistent date made it difficult "to divide the second half of the year as evenly as possible."[91] Under Knox the school year started late in September and ended earlier in June than had been the case in the past. The Thanksgiving vacation was lengthened. (It had traditionally been only a day long.) Two new holidays were added: Washington's Birthday in 1897 and Memorial Day in 1899. The latter holiday was especially important in 1900 because, Knox reported at a faculty meeting, "Buffalo Bill will be in town that day."[92]

Knox no doubt anticipated absences by families attending the famous rodeo show. Absenteeism was a constant topic, as it had been for Emily Wilcox judging from the increasingly stern language in the catalogs. In the final catalog arranged by Wilcox, a section on "Parental Cooperation" stressed the importance of class attendance and urged parents to cooperate and to provide written excuses in cases of "unavoidable" absence. It was "only as parents help to support and carry out our principles that we can do our best"[93] in educating their daughters, wrote Wilcox. Knox took the attendance issue seriously and personally, at least for students in the upper grades. No pupils were allowed to return to class after an absence without a signed note from Mary Alice Knox, and parental excuses for "social engagements cannot be accepted."[94] She also circulated lists of students who missed the day before and the day after a vacation, noting which were excused.

One of the more vexing issues that the faculty tackled in their first year was the relationship between the school and the Board of Regents. In October the faculty expressed their desire not to administer Regents examinations "if the Trustees agree."[95] The trustee response is unknown, but Knox traveled to Albany to meet with state education department officials and returned with the response that the Regents were willing to give special examinations at Emma Willard that would comply with the school schedule. This did not satisfy the faculty, and after further discussion, presumably with state education, Knox announced that the examinations would be optional, that pupils could take them if they wanted to, but "the faculty need not hold each examination in mind in planning and carrying out their work, and that the students shall understand that the work of the school does not conform to the standards set by the Board of Regents."[96] In short, Emma Willard was an independent school and its faculty would not, in the vernacular of New York public schools, "teach to the Regents."

Throughout Knox's administration, and in subsequent years, much of the work of faculty meetings was taken up with curricular discussions. In the second year, two meetings a month were devoted to "means and methods"[97] of teaching. Each department presented its goals and pedagogy, and there was a good deal of conversation about the coursework in the intermediate division and how it prepared students for the work of the academic division. To a lesser degree the faculty also discussed the continuity between the studies in the lower and intermediate grades. College certification and the work of the Committee of Ten were constant reference points, although not always absolutes. For example, the Committee had recommended eight years of natural science; after a presentation by the Science Department, the faculty voted for six years.

The requirements for graduation were set at "sixty-four appointments for four years."[98] Work expectations were also decided: "from 6 to 6½ hours a day, 3 hours in school, and 3½ hours outside was as much time as the average student could profitably spend on intellectual work."[99] As the school made the shift to the new curriculum, there was some question about girls who had begun studying under one and finished under the other; Miss Knox and the science teacher, Julia Haynes, were left to decide how this would all work out. Meanwhile, the catalog elaborately describing courses and textbooks was ready for publication. In addition to being a recruiting tool, the catalog would be used to appeal to Wellesley, Smith, Vassar, and other colleges for the right of certification.

Commencement 1896 marked the completion of a successful first year for Mary Alice Knox. Olivia Sage traveled to Troy for the ceremony. President Raymond of Union College was the keynoter, and Lewis Gurley also addressed the crowd. He spoke of the changes: "One year ago . . . the Troy Female Seminary was closed and the school entered upon a new departure, with new leaders, a new curriculum, new aspirations and something of new apprehensions."[100] He was happy to report that the school was thriving. In addition to 200 academic students, there were 240 enrolled at the music conservatory and 100 in the art program.

The direction taken by Knox and the trustees contrasted sharply with the aims of Sarah Porter, who had written, "I do *not* want *one* college trained woman"[101] and whose pupils mocked attendance at Vassar, Smith, and Wellesley, singing, "To college, to college, we'll never go there."[102] In terms of academic rigor, Troy was once again the standard-bearer for girls' education. After years of worry and work, Gurley and Sage, along with the rest of the trustees and alumnae, could rest assured that they had preserved the founder's legacy.

No Lovelier Landscape
Than That from Ida Hill

AT A FACULTY MEETING IN 1900, Mary Alice Knox introduced the possibility of a student newspaper. The teachers responded enthusiastically, and *Triangle* was born. In its first years the publication featured original poems and short stories, student work copied from other school and college newspapers, alumnae news (especially weddings and debuts), jokes from the classroom, and reports of campus events such as graduation. Published three times a year, *Triangle* cost 20 cents a copy or 50 cents for a year's subscription; within a few years, it carried as many as nine pages of advertisements to help defray expenses. Alumnae were urged to subscribe.

Given the infrequency of its issues, it is not surprising that *Triangle* rarely had the scoop on any story, and in 1901 the December edition reported the important but relatively old news that Mary Alice Knox was leaving the school after seven years as principal. In fact, she had left in November. The editors of *Triangle* regretted her decision. They had "come to think of Miss Knox as a permanent part of the school ... so ... when we heard of her resignation, we were very much surprised."[1] They reported that there was "genuine sorrow" among the students at her leaving and that each girl visited the principal in her office to say goodbye personally. As a farewell tribute, the students presented Knox with an opal ring surrounded by diamonds. From the student vantage point, the principal's accomplishments included the formation of the glee, mandolin, and guitar clubs, the basketball team, the system of cooperative student government, and, of course, *Triangle*.

Mary Alice Knox had told Lewis Gurley in the summer of 1901

that she intended to leave Emma Willard at some point in the fall. Although no record of their negotiations remains, it is clear that the trustees reached some agreement with her about remaining at the school and serving as an adviser through the transition period. She received a salary until May 1902 (like the faculty, Knox was paid for nine months each year from September through May). In 1897–98, her salary had been increased to $400 per month; initially, she was paid $360 a month. Although her intentions had been made public in the summer, she did not leave until November. On October 15, she formally announced to the faculty that she "has resigned the principalship of the school and is to leave soon, holding herself ready to return on call if the need arises."[2] She explained that the board had decided the school would be run by a committee of faculty until a new principal could be hired.

Frances Lucas, a history teacher who had been elected as secretary of the faculty for the year, would preside over faculty meetings. Each teacher was responsible for "the management of the affairs of her own department," but "matters which in any way concern a general interest of the school" would be "brought before the faculty for discussion and decision by faculty vote."[3] In addition, Ada Woolfolk, English instructor, would oversee the residential program; Edith Bickham, Latin and Greek teacher, the academic program; and Ella Jones, head of the mathematics department, all disciplinary matters. All of these women were young, newly minted college graduates, Woolfolk and Lucas from Wellesley and Jones from Vassar. (The source of Bickham's bachelor's degree is unknown.) Of the four, only Jones would remain at the school more than a year after Knox's departure.

The faculty appear to have been as disappointed as the students to see Knox leave. At a faculty meeting on November 6, Lucas read a note of thanks from the departing principal for the flowers and letters of farewell she had received from the teachers. Shortly before leaving, she had hosted the residential students and their day student guests in Sage Hall for a Halloween party. As had been the case for several years, a highlight of the festivities was her reading of *The Yellow Wall Paper* to the assembled students with no light but the flames of the fireplace behind her. This tradition had become "famous . . . as a Halloween tale and is begged for each year" by the boarders. The next night the Glee Club serenaded the principal outside her apartment in Sage, singing "There Is a Tavern in the Town," with its appropriately poignant lyric, "Fare thee well for I must leave you."[4] Finally, on November 2, Mary Alice Knox boarded the train for Pelham, New York, where, the *Troy Press* reported, "She will spend part of the winter in rest and part in travel."[5] She eventually planned to open a new school, Briarcliff School for Girls, which she did in the fall of 1903, running it jointly with Mary E. Dow. Dow, who had worked with Sarah Porter, had succeeded Porter as the head of the Farmington school but had been forced out after two years by Porter's nephew, Robert Porter Keep. After only one year, Mary Alice Knox would leave Briarcliff School, founding Miss Knox's School for Girls in 1904. She remained head of this school until her death in 1911.

In her seven years at Emma Willard, Mary Alice Knox had built a faculty whose credentials were second to none in the girls' preparatory school world, garnered collegiate approval for an Emma Willard education by negotiating the admission of Emma Willard students by certificate to Vassar, Wellesley, Smith, and Cornell; restarted the boarding program; introduced a number of student activities to make residential life in particular, and student life in general, more appealing to teenage girls; begun a number of traditions, including the awarding of a school pin; raised Emma Willard's profile in Troy by "bringing eminent men to the city to give talks upon special subjects";[6] created closer ties with area independent schools, specifically St. Agnes and Albany Female Academy; developed the five-year reunion pattern; instituted a lunch counter to serve day students meals during the academic day; added a kindergarten to the primary program; and presided over an extremely successful art and music program.

Under her administration the system of public oral examinations was ended, but all graduating seniors were required to write and deliver orally a well-researched theme prepared under the guidance of a member of the department most applicable to the thesis topic. The Troy newspapers heartily approved this change, *The Troy Press* commenting that the examinations "differ from those of other days . . . [in that] the papers are now all prepared by system, and the answers being written give the pupil every chance to think clearly and slowly without the excitement of sudden questioning from the powers that be."[7]

In addition, the press regularly reported the names of the seniors and their thesis titles; some papers critically reviewed the essays. The 1897 list of seniors and their topics was typical:

> Alice Crandall, "A Study of Daniel Defoe's History of the Plague in London"
> Alice Darling, "The Idea of Fate in the First Six Books of the *Aeneid*"
> Frances Hardy, "The Quality of Visual Sensation"
> Ethel M. Irving, "The Psychological View of the Relationship Between Mind and Body"
> Clara Moore, "The Development of the Central Theme of the *Aeneid*: The Glory of the Roman Empire"
> Bessie K. Smith, "The Quality of Auditory Sensation"[8]

A committee composed of Knox, the English department chair, and the chair of the department most closely related to the thesis topic reviewed each theme for English, factual accuracy, and the extent to which the paper was clear to nonspecialists, criteria that had been debated and adopted by the full faculty. One afternoon during commencement week was set aside for the seniors to read their work to the faculty and invited guests.

During her tenure, Knox experienced significant changes in the board of trustees. While she was at Emma Willard, women first joined the board, with Olivia Sage leading the way. In 1897 Lewis Gurley died, and in that same year, Russell Sage took a seat on the board alongside his wife. A Gurley had been board president since 1882, and the legacy continued with William F. Gurley assuming his father's place as president. He would remain in this post until his death in 1915. Meanwhile, his brother-in-law and business partner, Paul Cook, served as board treasurer from 1879 to 1915, at which point he became board president. (It is not surprising to find William Gurley Cook among the few little boys enrolled at the school in the primary program.)

While Knox was in Troy, the United States recovered from the depression that had shadowed the early 1890s and engaged in the

Spanish-American War. Although student interest in the war seems to have been understandably far less fervent than what it had been during the Civil War, the conflict did not pass without notice. Florence Eddy, who lived around the corner from the school, provided an American flag to be flown on the northern side of Sage Hall, where it would be visible from Congress Street. In May when the local companies marched down Second Street to war, girls lined the balcony of Gurley Hall. According to a newspaper report, they "waved flags while their gowns in red, white and blue predominated."[9] The local news also covered a cotillion at the school in 1898 that had a military theme. Party favors included miniature Rough Rider hats, bugles, and knapsacks. The girls in attendance wore hat pins festooned with flags, and their dates sported tricolor boutonnieres. The band played "The Girl I Left Behind Me," a song favored by soldiers since the American Revolution, and as a closing number, "The Star-Spangled Banner."[10] Six months later a paper reported that a boarder had returned to school with a bull terrier named "Teddy" in honor of Theodore Roosevelt, the most famous Rough Rider.[11]

Although the students may have treated the war somewhat frivolously, it was a topic of hot debate among the alumnae, particularly among woman suffrage advocates, many of whom were pacifists. Never one to shrink from controversy and a strong supporter of women's right to vote, Olivia Sage invited Elizabeth Cady Stanton's outspoken pacifist daughter, Harriot Stanton Blatch, to address the annual meeting of the Emma Willard Association (EWA) in November 1898. As fervent a pacifist as she was a suffragist, Blatch, who had lived overseas, argued that women in Europe worked under extremely harsh conditions because of their nations' militarism. She argued that it was the "relentless working out of economic law" that "luxury has to be paid for, especially luxury in the form of soldier-straps." Referring to the expansionist views that had led the United States into the war, she asked, "Why need we follow in the wretched steps of Europe and be bitten with land hunger, we of all nations, stretching from Atlantic to Pacific?" She concluded, "If we must grow, let it be in the sphere of ideas—in matters of education, in prison reform," adding drily, "We might expand by making a few good roads in our country."[12]

Most EWA speakers were less controversial during the Knox years, with stereopticon shows of travels in foreign lands providing frequent and educational entertainment for the alumnae. Ministers and college professors spoke on topics ranging from "Womanhood" to "The Model Teacher" to "Domestic Economy and Life Insurance for Women." There were occasional flashes of humor. The Rev. Gordon Mackay, the Sages' pastor, began an address at the tenth annual banquet by remarking that if a person could not attend Emma Willard, "the next best thing was to marry a pupil of that school."[13] At another meeting, baritone Ericsson F. Bushnell, an opera singer, entertained with classical numbers and "a drinking song [that] was much enjoyed."[14] The association completed one major project at the end of the 1890s, the publication of the biographical record, and they began two others, the placement of busts of Emma Willard in the state capitol at Albany and in the hall of fame at New York University. Olivia Sage spent $7,000 to publish *Emma Willard and Her Pupils*, and she was the driving force in the negotiations about the statues with state officials and the university chancellor.

Knox, along with the Gurleys, shrewdly courted the Sages and their philanthropy. The couple was invited to Troy each spring for commencement, and in 1897 Olivia Sage was invited to be the graduation speaker. Her husband was in the audience, and the city closed Second Street to traffic during the ceremony. It was the fiftieth anniversary of Sage's graduation from the Troy Female Seminary, and she proudly displayed her diploma for the crowd. She asked rhetorically, "Am I a fossil, an antique?"[15] She answered her question with an emphatic no, although she stressed the old-fashioned virtues of good deportment, self-discipline, and religious faith as her primary values. She mentioned her friendship with Elizabeth Cady Stanton,[16] maintaining that, like Stanton, she believed that woman's work must be done in cooperation with men. Recalling the contributions of the recently departed Lewis Gurley, she said, "A perfected humanity must combine the most exalted qualities of both men and women." She implied that she still had much to give to her alma mater, quoting a bit of poetry to illustrate her obligation:

> Life is like an inn
> Upon a summer day;
> Some stay to sup
> And then away;
> They who longest stay
> Have the most to pay.[17]

At the conclusion of Sage's address, Fanny Seymour Patterson '66, a trustee and EWA officer, paid tribute to the EWA president and, on behalf of the alumnae, presented her with a diamond pin that she wore on all future school occasions. The pin was a replica of the one worn by all members of the EWA, but as the *New York Times* described it, it was far more lavish:

> larger and thickly studded with diamonds . . . somewhat in the shape of a shield, from the top of which appears the flame of the torch of learning. This is set with diamonds and diamonds encircle it at the bottom. Below is a band of the school pink in enamel, bearing the motto, "Fama Semper Vivat." The three initial letters of the association are set with diamonds, and four large diamonds mark the top, bottom, and each end. A smaller diamond is in the end of the torch. The stones are all very beautiful.[18]

The most glaring failure of Mary Alice Knox's administration was her inability to fill the boarding department. In spite of significant advertising during her administration, Mary Alice Knox never filled Sage Hall to capacity. Try as she might, she never managed to enroll more than thirty boarders. In 1895–96, for example, the school spent $265 on advertising, 4 percent of the $6,500 operating budget.[19] Nor did the inclusion of little boys in the primary program prove to be very successful. Only twice did the total number of boys top ten, and the overall primary numbers remained small. Although the catalogs indicated that the primary classes were intended to enroll twenty to twenty-five students per grade, the typical enrollment in the primary classes hovered around fifteen.

Enrollment was clearly a challenge. Notwithstanding the carefully outlined course of study, the school admitted a large number of "special" students. Among the categories of student between 1895 and 1902 were "Specials in Bible," "Ladies Taking Special Work," "Pupils Taking Single Lines of Work," "Regular Freshmen," "Special Pupils Ranked as Freshmen," "Regular Sophomores," Special Students Ranked as Sophomores," "Regular Juniors," "Special Students Ranked as Juniors," "Seniors," and "Graduate Students." Special students who wanted to board had to take twelve class meetings per week, but these could be in music and art.

That the school operated in the black throughout Knox's tenure was in large part attributable to the success of the art and music schools. In 1895–96, her first year, there were 443 students at the school, 97 in art, 240 in music, and 116 in grades 1 to 12. In her last year, 1901–2, there were 915 pupils total: 505 in music, 260 in art, and 58 in the high school, 70 in the intermediate, and 22 (including 6 boys) in the primary. There were fewer than thirty boarders, including a seventh grader from Kansas, in spite of the admissions requirement that all boarders be at least fourteen years old.

By 1902 the music and art departments offered their own diplomas. Music diplomas were given at the completion of three years of study that included specialization in an instrument or voice, four terms of music theory, and the successful passing of an examination in the history of music. An art diploma required four years of work, the bulk of it in drawing, but classes in anatomy and composition were also required. The art department existed for those "who wish to become artists or teachers" and "those who desire to study art as an accomplishment."[20] The art department and music conservatory had separate directors, but they reported to the principal of the school.

The faculty for both art and music was large and diverse, with more men employed in each than in the academic portion of the school. Throughout Knox's tenure, Marion Sim ran the conservatory and Emilie Adams the art program. Neither was a graduate of the school. Sim, a Canadian, was an organist who frequently performed at conservatory concerts and at other venues throughout Troy. The subjects offered by each division were extensive. In the music school, students could study piano, organ, violin, clarinet, cello, cornet, flute, mandolin, guitar, or banjo. In addition, there were classes in harmony, counterpoint, fugue, sight reading, and music theory and composition. Students studying instruments could play in an orchestra or ensembles, and concert performances were required of diploma candidates. Art students were offered drawing classes using casts and live models in addition to specialized coursework in oil painting, clay, portraiture, landscape and marine painting, crayon and pastel, watercolor, tapestry, leatherwork, embroidery, miniatures on ivory, painting on porcelain, woodcarving, design, glass decorating, and Venetian ironwork.

The academic course offered to the girls who wanted to attend college or at least earn a high school diploma conformed generally to the recommendations of the Committee of Ten, although Knox and her faculty made adjustments over time. Most changes were subject to faculty vote. For example, in 1899 the faculty voted to exempt girls who were preparing for college from taking psychology and science if they elected three languages. Another faculty meeting discussion resulted in the reduction in the number of periods that freshmen studied modern languages. They also voted on the quality of work necessary to justify certification for college. In 1898 the faculty pondered the "practice of permitting pupils to raise the hand during a recitation." As was often true during Knox's tenure, a compromise was reached, and it was "generally agreed that while the practice might be admirable in some cases, it should be regulated and controlled with great care."[21]

As is ever the case, weak students claimed a good deal of faculty time; they spent many meetings discussing adjustments to individual students' schedules to shore up their academic weaknesses. At several meetings there was discussion about how much extra help struggling students should receive without their families incurring additional costs. The faculty concluded in March 1900 that "incidental help which can be given in the morning hours shall not be regarded as tutoring, but that help which is given outside school hours—except in the case of boarding pupils—or which requires considerable time shall be so regarded."[22] Tutoring, by the faculty's definition, meant extra attention for which the student had to pay.

By the time Mary Alice Knox left the school, the curriculum had stabilized, and the requirements for a diploma had actually been reduced. In 1895–96 girls were required to carry eighteen units (called appointments) over four years. In 1902–3 there were only sixteen required appointments; language and mathematics had both been reduced by one. In all of the academic departments, the course of study was laid out for six years, beginning with the third intermediate or seventh grade year. For example, seventh grade Latin began with grammar and vocabulary and progressed to Caesar, Cicero, Vergil, culminating with Horace in the senior year. Greek was offered for three years only, but a senior elective allowed students who had not studied Greek to have "some knowledge of Greek."[23] French and German were the two modern languages that were offered, although the catalog for 1896–97 had promised that Italian would be offered "as soon as there is demand."[24] With Italian immigrants pouring into Troy, the language was associated with poverty and tenements rather than great works of art and Renaissance thinking.

The description of the aims and content of the English classes changed every year. Until 1900 the English curriculum was tied closely to the history curriculum, and English was viewed as the discipline that provided the basis for clear expression in student work across the curriculum. That year the faculty voted to separate the English curriculum from the history curriculum. By 1901–2 the English curriculum began with American literature in the seventh grade followed by a survey of English literature "from Chaucer to Tennyson to Browning."[25] Freshman year focused on Chaucer's *Canterbury Tales*, and sophomore year the pupils studied *Old English Ballads*, a book by Francis B. Gummere, a prolific Haverford professor whose English texts were widely distributed in American high schools. Junior year the course content was English drama, and the seniors focused on the "masterpieces" of nineteenth-century poetry.

Although the requirement in history was slight—just one year— students could choose from a number of history courses. The history of Rome, Greece, medieval Europe, the United States, and France were all possible choices. Ideally, students began their study of history in seventh grade, where it took the form of "biographical work."[26]

The principal no longer taught moral philosophy to the seniors, but electives were available in both psychology and philosophy, and the work in these areas, intended for older students, was a combination of seminar and individual study. After 1897–98 there was no longer a separate course in ethics.

Mathematics and science, the subjects so dear to Emma Willard in her pioneer curriculum, were offered but not stressed. Mathematics was available through analytical geometry, but students preparing for college focused on elementary algebra and plane geometry. In 1899–1900 a one-semester course in plane trigonometry was added to the curriculum because of its "practical value . . . in engineering, surveying and navigation,"[27] an interesting rationale given the extreme unlikelihood that any of the students were planning to pursue study or careers in these areas. Science was emphasized a bit more than mathematics. Courses were offered in chemistry, physics, biology, and botany, and pupils were assured that the proximity of Rensselaer Polytechnic Institute (RPI) ensured great advantages for scientific studies. Studies were intended to give pupils "an intelligent idea of foundation principles" and "careful training in scientific method."[28]

In addition to the requirements in the traditional academic areas, students who wished to earn a diploma were required to take a course in elocution. The description of the elocution course evolved over time. By 1900–1 it involved "breathing and voice exercises for the strengthening and development of the lungs and voice; drill in articulation, pronunciation, and production of tone; emphasis and inflection; pitch, movement, and volume; climax and rhythm; fundamental principles of expression both physical and psychical, including work in pantomime for practical demonstration."[29]

Although voice was the only required course outside the liberal arts, instruction in religion, including the Bible in history and literature, was available to students who wanted it. Special students and adult learners from Troy were invited to these lectures that were given throughout this period by Dr. T. P. Sawin, the minister at First Presbyterian Church, the religious institution bordering the school on the west side. From 1897 until the end of Knox's tenure, Sawin's Bible instruction was divided into three years, covering the literature of the Bible, the Book of Judges, and "narration, parable, oration and sermon"[30] in the New Testament. Given Emma Willard's refusal to allow Sawin's predecessor, Nathan Beman, to teach religion at the school, the invitation to allow Sawin to offer Bible classes shows a conservative departure from the strict nonsectarianism of earlier days. Knox herself was the daughter and sister of Presbyterian ministers.

Finally, the school offered extensive opportunities for sports and physical exercise. Beginning in 1897, boarders were provided with twenty free dancing lessons each year. The year 1897 also saw the school equip a gymnasium for Swedish gymnastics. Directed by Grace Waterman '91, a graduate of the Boston Normal School of Gymnastics, the new physical education program attracted praise from the press. In the stereotypical language of the time, the *Troy Press* approved the Swedish method because the Swedes were a people "noted for their splendid carriage, erect poise and graceful movements." The gym was outfitted with "wonderful looking contrivances," and Grace Waterman wore the correct outfit. She was "dressed in the correct costume, which in her case was composed of dark blue bloomers and blouse, scarlet belt, necktie and chest piece. Black stockings and low shoes with electric soles complete the outfit, and in this loose, comfortable and sensible dress, the motions may be accomplished."[31]

In addition, by 1900 "a field within easy reach of the school [had] been secured for the use of the students in the boarding department,"[32] who played tennis and basketball there. Basketball games between the boarders and the day students were routinely covered by the Troy papers; in a typical story, *The Troy Press* reported in October 1898 that "the basket ball [*sic*] team is getting very expert."[33] The expertise appears to have been more defensive than offensive because the boarders beat the day students 7–4. For two years the commandant of the Watervliet Arsenal, whose two daughters were Emma Willard students, provided the students and the faculty with the use of the "Arsenal golf links."[34] After Colonel Arnold was transferred, boarders were provided with memberships to the Troy Golf Club, which had a "fine golf course, excellent tennis courts, and a basket-ball ground . . . on a hill on the outskirts of the city." The school provided a "chartered car"[35] to transport students to the club. Cycling for women had come into vogue, and the school maintained "a school wheel"[36] for a teacher who chaperoned cycling groups. Fencing was added to the athletic program in 1899.

The growing interest in sports and games seems very modern. However, one aspect of the physical education program would horrify today's students. As a way of assessing students' physical progress, girls were weighed and measured for height and chest size. The results were reported in *Triangle* so that everyone in the school learned that the average weight gain for the year was 5 pounds, but that Miss Jenkins held the record with an impressive gain of 17 pounds. As far as lung capacity, which was what the chest measurements ostensibly sought to discover, the average one year was 10 cubic centimeters, with one student complimented for her spectacular 56 cubic centimeter gain.[37]

By far the most historically interesting sporting event at the school occurred in May 1902 when Constance Appleby visited and held a three-day seminar in field hockey, a British sport that was newly popular on women's college campuses. The sport had been played in England for hundreds of years when Appleby introduced it to the United States. In 1901 she embarked on a "missionary pilgrimage" to the "Eastern foci of feminine culture,"[38] introducing the sport at Vassar, Bryn Mawr, and Emma Willard, among other places. The school paid Appleby $20 for her three-day residency. According to *Triangle*, the students were enchanted by both Appleby and the new sport. "Miss Appleby," wrote the reporter, "is certainly a remarkable teacher, as she gave us all the points of the game in three days. She is really quite irresistible, being very witty and saying no rude or sarcastic things on our playing." The school quickly divided into two teams with faculty members Ella Jones and Helen Haight as the captains. The *Triangle* article concluded that the "game seems easy enough, but playing it is another matter entirely. . . . Before we learned to play, there were many whacks administered to the ankles."[39]

By the time Appleby visited the school, a new principal was in place; whether or not she arranged for the field hockey demonstration is unknown. Appleby's tour had begun in the fall of 1901 and could have been prearranged by Mary Alice Knox. Nevertheless, the issue of *Triangle* that reported on Appleby also spoke approvingly of the new principal, who had come on board in February. The faculty committee had found that running the school by triumvirate had not gone smoothly. Faculty meetings between November and February were increasingly devoted to disciplinary matters. At a meeting in early December, Ella Jones had reported that students were behaving in an unsatisfactory and disorderly manner in the assembly hall, corridors, and cloakroom. She had warned them they would lose the right of self-government if they did not shape up. She had done so at a school government meeting where she admonished the students about the "great disorder in the assembly room caused by the scholars walking heavily and collecting in groups and talking." In addition, "the library had not been quiet and voices had been heard in the cloak-room, in which the scholars were prohibited to congregate." These charges, she concluded, were "too serious to overlook."[40] A week later, Ada Woolfolk reported that the sophomore class was likely to finish only two thirds of the curriculum. In January, the faculty decided the school would supply paper for upcoming semester examinations to forestall cheating. According to the editors of *Triangle*, the lack of a principal had "created a feeling of unrest."[41]

It was probably with great relief, then, that the faculty learned in late January that Anna Leach had been appointed principal. Leach had an impressive pedigree. She had earned a B.A. from Wellesley, an M.A. from Vassar, and she had done graduate work at both Wellesley and Cornell. She had been an instructor at Drury College in Missouri, and she had overseen the Woman's College in Halifax, Canada, where she was credited with a jump in enrollment during her five years at the helm.[42] She had spent nine years prior to her arrival at Emma Willard as the Lady Principal of Elmira College. Elmira, a Presbyterian institution, enrolled about two hundred pupils during Leach's tenure, had four buildings, nineteen instructors, a yearly budget over three times the size of Emma Willard's, and an endowment of $25,000 for scholarships. Leach was well regarded in academic circles as evidenced by the use of her name in textbook endorsements. For example, in 1898 an advertisement for *The Forms of Discourse*, a speech text by William Cairns, a professor at the University of Wisconsin, carried an endorsement from Leach.[43] Leach was forty-nine and an experienced administrator when she arrived in Troy.

Anna Leach's sister Abby was even more distinguished academically than her older sibling. A longtime classics professor at Vassar, she had been the only woman associated with the Committee of Ten. At the time of Anna's appointment at Emma Willard, Abby had just finished a two-year stint as the president of the Association of Collegiate Alumnae, the forerunner of the American Association of University Women. Their younger sister, Edith, was a teacher in New York City. The Leach girls had grown up in comfort in Brockton, Massachusetts. Their father, Marcus Leach, owned a profitable shoe factory where their only brother, Wendell, worked. The Leaches traced their ancestry to Cornet Robert Stetson, who settled in Scituate, Massachusetts, in 1835. That both Abby and Anna were cognizant and proud of this ancestry can be inferred from their attendance at a reunion of the Stetson descendants in the summer of 1906.

On January 27, the faculty agreed that "a note be sent to Miss Leach on her arrival extending to her the cordial welcome of the faculty and assuring her of their hearty support and cooperation in the work of the school."[44] The alumnae and students were equally welcoming. *The Troy Record* reported that Frederick Orr, acting on behalf of the board of trustees, had introduced Anna Leach to the students at their morning assembly. She was greeted by "a storm of applause" and within hours "was at her desk."[45] On February 10, the trustees held a reception for Miss Leach, to which the juniors and seniors were invited. According to *The Troy Record*, which reported in advance of the event, hundreds of invitations were sent, and the "center table will be filled with a large mound of pink tulips and all the tables will be adorned with handsome silver candelabra with pink shades."[46] The next day the paper reported the reception's success, noting that Prof.

Abby Leach was in attendance and describing in detail the dresses worn by such local social luminaries as Fanny Patterson, Mrs. L. E. Gurley, and Mrs. William F. Gurley.[47] On Valentine's Day, the Troy chapter of the EWA followed suit and made her an honorary member of the association. In the March issue of *Triangle,* the editor reported that the "girls hailed with joy the arrival of our new principal, Anna Leach," and added sympathetically, "It must be very hard for her coming in the middle of the school year."[48]

As badly as Leach's tenure would end (she holds the distinction of being the only principal removed from office midyear), it had begun spectacularly. By June *Triangle* reported with caesarean flair that she "came, and saw, and conquered all our hearts at first sight." One of the reasons for their ecstasy was that she had erased the division between day students and boarders. The paper reported happily, "The rivalry between the boarding and day departments has been done away with— we are all Emma Willard girls now and not 'Boarders' and 'Days.'"[49] Throughout the next eight years, Anna Leach appears to have earned the respect and affection of her pupils.

There were more guest lecturers than before (including frequent visits by Abby Leach) and a new emphasis on current events. Beginning in 1905, a Saturday morning class devoted to this subject was inaugurated and met with student applause (at least from those students who wrote for *Triangle*). Middle-class and upper-middle-class white Protestant women—the mothers and older sisters of the Emma Willard students—were fueling the Progressive Era reform movements known as, and Leach exposed the student body to their thinking. One such visitor was Dr. Taylor Bissell of Vassar, who addressed the school on the work of the Consumers' League. *Triangle* erroneously ascribed to Bissell the motto of the league, which had been coined by liberal reformer Florence Kelley: "To buy is to have power, to have power is to have duty," but it was clear that the students took the sentiment to heart. The newspaper, foreshadowing the fair trade movement at the school in the twenty-first century, concluded, "We can refuse to purchase goods made under unwholesome conditions, and give our moral and financial support to those merchants who live up to a fair standard in the manufacture and sale of their goods . . . [who] make all their goods on the premises; who do not employ child labor; who do not require overtime."[50]

Not all the additions to student activities were intellectual. Leach introduced horseback riding, continued Knox's tradition of holding cotillions and elaborate Halloween parties, hosted "flower parties" for the students, and encouraged social events with colleges. She personally escorted boarders to a reception at the Chi Phi fraternity at RPI, and in the fall of 1905 arranged for boarders to attend a Williams-Colgate football game. She also launched a program of domestic science that included "theoretical and practical cooking,"[51] as well as sewing and household management. In addition, driving lessons were made available for boarders for an additional fee.

Anna Leach appears to have had a cordial relationship with the alumnae as well. She was a frequent guest at the association meetings in New York, beginning with the annual banquet in November 1902, the fall of her first full year on campus. The guests at that banquet were particularly illustrious and included President M. Carey Thomas of Bryn Mawr, President Mary Woolley of Mount Holyoke, Dean Ellen Fitz Pendleton of Wellesley, Dean Agnes Irwin from Radcliffe, Dean Laura Gill of Barnard, and Prof. Mary Augusta Jordan from Smith. Vassar was represented by Helen Hadley, a Vassar alumna whose husband Arthur was president of Yale. Leach told the assemblage that the "founding of scholarships is one of the best means for advancing the interests of the school." The college representatives spoke on the importance of good preparatory schools. As Agnes Irwin summarized it, "Without the schools, the colleges could not exist."[52]

Leach's comments and reports were well received by the alumnae. In January 1903, she attended a meeting where the minutes reflected that she very "clearly and minutely described the condition and needs of the school at the present time."[53] Over time the minutes of the association continued to include appeals from Leach for "practical needs of the day."[54] She repeatedly urged them to raise money for scholarships. Although they professed support for the needs of the school, as always they developed their own separate agenda. In 1904 they secured a space at the Louisiana Purchase Exposition in St. Louis. Once again a world's fair would have a display honoring the founder, and once again, Olivia Sage underwrote the exhibit. The membership of the EWA was affluent, and widowhood rarely changed their circumstances, but they were aware that "some former pupils of the old school [are] sadly in need of financial relief."[55] They committed to fund-raising for these unfortunate former classmates, establishing a relief fund for this purpose.

In addition, like the students, the alumnae listened to speakers who spoke on the various reforms of the Progressive Era and who urged them to contribute to numerous causes. In 1907 the Troy chapter hosted a luncheon for Jane Addams and learned of the work she was doing at Hull House, the famous settlement house she founded in Chicago. Speakers at the annual lunches in Manhattan included Yonkers native Mary Marshall Butler on the role that women could play in purifying urban America, Edward Van Zale on "Progress Is the Law of Life," a Dr. Palmer on "The New York Public Schools and What They Are Doing for the Little Foreigner," a Mrs. Beiermeister on "White Slave Traffic," and alumna Dr. Sarah McNutt '50 on "What Research Has Done for Drugs."

In spite of their interest in progress, the founding members of the association were aging. During Leach's tenure, Olivia Sage was often absent from the meetings either because of her own ill health or the ill health of her husband. He was in his mid-eighties and she in her mid-seventies when Anna Leach arrived at the school. Stalwarts and founders of the organization such as Clara Harrison Stranahan, and Evelyn Baker Harvier died in the first few years of the twentieth century. The latter's alumnae memorial recalled that she had been the one "to suggest the lovely pink rose to be the Association's color."[56] Sarah Willard died in 1906; her sister Mary followed in 1910.

Always and often, however, they reminded themselves of the words of their late secretary, Sarah Hoyt Spelman, who constantly urged that the meetings of the EWA not be simply reunions where the Troy Female Seminary alumnae looked back but also be opportunities to look forward. Cora Filley Searle '62, the new recording secretary, took Spelman's words to heart and turned them into a poetic charge for the EWA in 1903:

> To the cherished haunts of the olden time
>   Our eyes are backward cast; . . .
> But however dear are the visions,
>   We do not dare to stay,
> From out of the Gone, we must move on
>   To the duties that call To-day.[57]

She included this poem in the minutes, and having attended the most recent graduation at the school, urged her fellow alumnae to see that the "Golden Age" for Emma Willard School was not in the past, but in the future. She could scarcely have anticipated the stunning truth of her words.

Less than three years later, on July 26, 1906, Russell Sage, just six months shy of his ninetieth birthday, died, leaving the bulk of his vast fortune to his widow. Overnight, Olivia Sage, who had always been keenly interested in philanthropy, suddenly controlled the resources that would dramatically change the alma mater she loved. At the annual luncheon in 1903, the last one she attended prior to her husband's death, she had reminded the alumnae of "their gratitude to Alma Mater, which she thought stood next to that due to parents."[58] In 1905 she had published an essay, "Opportunities and Responsibilities of Leisured Women," in which she made it clear that women of wealth had a special obligation to use their money for good purposes. With an inheritance estimated at $70 million, she was indisputably a woman of wealth. She took this responsibility seriously. Fast approaching her eightieth birthday, she was eager to demonstrate her gratitude to her school by giving it a transformational gift. By Thanksgiving, just months after Russell Sage was laid to rest next to his first wife at Oakwood Cemetery in Troy, his widow contacted William F. Gurley and told him of her intention to donate $1 million to the school. Women's colleges had been the recipient of similar amounts, but this was the largest gift any girls' school had ever received.

Most of the negotiation with the school was carried out by Robert DeForest, Sage's chief financial adviser. He asked Gurley to submit a plan for the use of the million-dollar gift. Gurley immediately contacted M. F. Cummings and Son, a Troy architectural firm. Cummings, father and son, were highly respected architects, responsible for some of the most spectacular commercial and residential architecture in Troy and beyond. They had designed the three buildings on the Second Street campus in the 1890s.

In early December, Gurley wrote to DeForest outlining his general thinking about the use of Sage's gift. He told her attorney that he thought the school should move to a new site, the three newest buildings should be moved to that site, and a new gymnasium and large school building should be constructed. DeForest liked this plan. His letter of approval implied that there had been some earlier conversation about expanding the school at its Second Street location because he mentioned he had had reservations about spending hundreds of thousands of dollars to buy the Presbyterian Church grounds abutting the school property.

A week later Gurley submitted the preliminary plan and cost estimate created by Cummings. The architect[59] proposed moving the three newest school buildings, Gurley, Plum, and Sage halls, from their location in downtown Troy and the construction of several new buildings. Most prominent would be a single building housing a new assembly hall, offices, and upper-story dormitories. This building, projected to be four stories high above the basement, would cost nearly $160,000. Second, there would be a gymnasium with a swimming pool, projected to cost $44,550. In addition to these two main buildings, the new campus would have a power house, an engineer's house, a barn and tool house (with greenhouse), and "a gate lodge for gardener." All of these would cost approximately $20,000. There were estimates for grading the grounds and tennis courts, fencing, landscaping, installing heat, water, and electrical systems, and outdoor lighting. In summary, Cummings suggested that the whole plan would cost $446,565, the bulk of it, $369,730, to be spent on buildings and the rest on "improvement of grounds, power plant, heating and lighting."[60]

Gurley assured DeForest that he had no intention of spending the entire million on buildings and grounds. At least half the amount would be invested as an endowment, which Gurley assumed would provide $20,000 annually for "maintenance and repairs as well as make possible the increase of salaries necessary to secure and retain the best instructors."[61] He believed that several items in the architect's estimate could be removed if necessary, including the engineer's house, the barn and tool house, and the gatehouse, which would save around $40,000. However, he anticipated that new furnishings would add $30,000 to the initial costs. In addition, he proposed that the old site be made into a city park surrounding Emma Willard's statue at a cost of $5,000. Finally, he expected to pay about $50,000 for the new property.

Although Gurley never specified in these early letters where the school would be located, he already knew the land he wanted. At this point, no one but Gurley, DeForest, Cummings (and possibly Olivia Sage) knew anything of these plans. As Gurley explained to DeForest in early January, he was not telling anyone about the gift or the plans until he had purchased the property, not even the other members of the board. DeForest agreed completely with Gurley's assessment that the owner of the property in question would raise the price dramatically if he knew what was at stake. The seller was Charles W. Tillinghast, who had been a member of the board of trustees until his resignation in 1898. In addition to Tillinghast's property, there were a few adjoining parcels for which Gurley was also negotiating, and there was a gravel pit where the proposed power house would sit.

The lands in question were on the east side of Troy, an area that had become fashionable in the late nineteenth and early twentieth century as wealthy businessmen moved away from the polluted air and water that their factories had contaminated to the peace and cleanliness of Mount Ida. Troy newspapers featured pictures of the new mansions; for example, the home of collar manufacturer E. Harold Cluett was "located on a spacious property between Pine Woods and the Emma Willard School campus."[62] For generations the high ground to the east of the city had been a favorite destination for seminary students to hike and "botanize." In 1846, after reflecting on the sights she had seen throughout the United States and Europe, Emma Willard concluded that she had seen "no lovelier landscape than that from Ida Hill."[63] By 1906 a streetcar ran up Congress Street to Pawling Avenue connecting the homes on the hill with the businesses downtown.

By the end of January, Gurley had the property he wanted under contract. He acquired the Tillinghast property for $50,264, the gravel pit for $800, and two additional lots from a Mr. Harrison and a Mr. Cooper for just under $10,000. It was time to go public. As DeForest had noted earlier in the month, Olivia Sage did not want her gift to be anonymous. This was not ego on her part; as her most recent biographer has amply proven, she not only felt an obligation to distribute her own wealth, she also wished to set an example for others. She wanted to be a philanthropic leader as well as a philanthropist. But DeForest cautioned Gurley that when he told the press of the gift, he should "emphasize Mrs. Sage's personal relations of longstanding to the Emma Willard School as a reason for going in that direction, so as to differentiate it from other institutions to which she has no like relationships."[64] He sent similar directions to Palmer Ricketts, president of RPI, which had received a matching million.

Sometime in late January, Anna Leach was finally informed of Sage's gift because she wrote to the school's benefactor on January 28, 1907, thanking her. Noting that she "bowed in prayer" when Gurley informed her of "the noble gift," she was quite understandably stunned. She admitted, "I cannot altogether grasp the thought of all this just now."[65] The news came to Leach less than a week before it was public knowledge. On February 2, the *Washington Post* reported that Mrs. Sage had given $100,000 to her alma mater, and more was in the offing.[66] Within days, papers throughout New York and elsewhere had the full story of her million-dollar gift. In the April edition of *Triangle*, the editors praised Sage's generosity, declaring, "The Seniors and Juniors are not a whit less happy because they are not to share immediately in the good fortune that has befallen the school."[67] The editors apparently anticipated that the sophomores would study on the new campus; if they were right, the construction would be completed by the fall of 1908. They were off by two years. None of the high school students at the school in 1906–7 would study on the new campus, although the graduation ceremony for the girls who were freshmen at the time of the gift, the members of the class of 1910, would be held on the Mount Ida campus.

At the annual Emma Willard birthday celebration in February, Kate Upson Clark, a noted writer, delivered an address, "Solomon vs. The New Woman." More importantly, however, Cora Searle announced the gift from the woman the Troy chapter had dubbed "our fairy god-mother." Anna Leach was in attendance and paid tribute to Sage. A few months later, William F. Gurley spoke at the annual banquet and outlined the plans for the new construction. In the intervening time, it had been decided that it was impractical to move any of the old build-ings to the new site. Instead, the architects and Gurley had planned a comprehensive campus featuring a school building, a dormitory, and a gymnasium as well as a power plant. Gurley told the more than two hundred alumnae at the luncheon that the board had "purchased thirty acres of land two miles east of the city, fifteen minutes by the car lines." The downtown campus, he explained, has "not the facilities for a girl's school on a modern basis."[68] In particular, he pointed out that the school had lost students because "every parent wants a room on the second floor, with a southern exposure."[69] The new school would be different: "There will be two large buildings—the dormitory and the school build-ing. They will stand north and south, so that we hope the morning sun will strike about three-quarters of the rooms at the same time.[70]

The dormitory would be three stories high, and the rooms would not be uniform, although each one would have a closet "large enough to contain any young woman's wardrobe." The rooms themselves would come in "all shapes and sizes to suit every variety of female mind."

Gurley pointed out that another critical shortcoming of the cur-rent campus was the lack of "space for playgrounds or exercise." This problem would be solved by the extensive acreage and the new gym-nasium. The gym, a multipurpose facility, would be "convenient for plays and dancing, and will seat 600." In addition to being outfitted with gymnastics equipment approved by the nation's leading physical education teacher, Dr. Dudley Sargent, the gymnasium would have a swimming pool in its basement, making it the first girls' boarding school in the country with this advantage. Gurley concluded by giving the timetable for the project: groundbreaking in the spring of 1908 followed by eighteen months of construction.

Just as he had told DeForest, Gurley assured the alumnae that not all of Sage's gift would be spent on the buildings. He promised that the trustees intended "to save a good portion of Mrs. Sage's gift for an endowment fund."[71] The minutes of the meeting reflect that the alumnae discussed the curricular changes that the gift might inspire. Ellen Wentworth Goodwin '52 hoped that the new school would allow for "original research in the curriculum." She asked rhetorically, "What more fitting study for a true woman than that of the prevention and care of disease, the investigation of the stormy heavens and scores of kindred subjects?"[72] She also suggested that the EWA investigate whether or not the new campus might be designated a college.

Whether or not the school was losing pupils because of the lack of southern exposure in the dormitory rooms is hard to prove. However, it is clear it was not gaining boarders, in spite of Anna Leach's aggressive marketing in periodicals throughout the country; she continued the same ad strategy that Mary Alice Knox had used and with equally poor results. Between 1902 and 1907, the school continued to have hundreds of students enrolled in the art and music departments, and it never had more than twenty-nine residents in Sage Hall. The catalog for 1907–8 contained no student lists, but it did have a flyer enclosed that described the new buildings (highlighted features included "hot and cold shower baths," "a bowling alley," and "its own electric plant"). The next fall, there were forty-nine boarders. Clearly, the new campus was a draw.

In addition to describing the new campus, the catalog for 1907–8 announced that after 1908–9, "the scope of the school will be enlarged to meet still further the demands of those students who do not intend to go to college."[73] The number of seniors and the number of students going to college had remained small, and it appears that Leach had decided to cater to the desires of the majority of her clients. Between 1906 and 1909, thirty-five girls had gone to college, eight to Smith, six to Wellesley, one to Mount Holyoke, and twenty-one to Vassar (perhaps a reflection of Abby Leach's influence). Wells was the only college added during these years that agreed to accept students by certification, although beginning in 1903–4, the catalog promised that the school prepared students for Bryn Mawr, Barnard, "and all colleges for women."[74]

There had been little curricular change since Leach's arrival. Changes from year to year as reflected in the catalog had more to do with the addition of rules than with any substantive academic work. The one new course, "Foreign Travel," was an elective clearly intended for young women with the means to travel abroad. The course used photos and stereopticon images to familiarize students with European cities they were likely to visit in the future.

Many of the changes had to do with attendance. In 1903 the catalog emphasized that "All pupils are expected to remain in the school building until the hour of dismissal," and "The presence of all pupils the *first day following any vacation* is especially desired."[75] During 1904–5 new regulations concerning gym uniforms were announced: a local dressmaker could be hired to make the outfit, which was "an untrimmed blouse, skirt and trousers of navy-blue serge."[76] In 1906–7 parents were instructed to provide their daughters with raincoats, overshoes, and umbrellas. Up until that year, students applying to the music or art divisions made separate applications to the directors of those programs. Now they were to apply directly to Anna Leach. In 1907–8 the catalog insisted forcefully, "*No eatables be sent to the girls or brought to the school.*"[77]

The years 1907–8 and 1908–9 saw extraordinary faculty turnover. Nine new faculty members joined the school in the fall of 1907 and fifteen in the fall of 1908. The faculty stopped recording the minutes of their meetings in 1905, but the tone of the minutes during Anna Leach's early tenure was not unlike that of the catalogs. There were more directives and fewer discussions. The minutes tended to report what "Miss Leach" said. Among other things, she asked that the faculty "take some of the control in the Boarding department to see that lights are out and study hours kept (10/25/04)"; "reminded the teachers that it is necessary to dismiss classes promptly" (11/1/04); "did not like girls going to the Hart Library in the morning" (11/1/04); told the teachers they were to "have no communication with any parent without consulting her" (12/6/04); told the faculty that they were not to accept any "message . . . when delivered orally [by a student]" (12/13/04); told the faculty that "no student was to be excused from an examination until two-thirds of the time had elapsed" (1/17/05); reminded the faculty that "girls are *not* to put the books on the book shelves in the library" (2/7/05); informed the faculty that she had "noticed that books were very much marked by the girls" (3/14/05); asked each teacher to give her a written statement about the "work that has been accomplished and what remains" in each of her classes (5/16/05).[78]

Because of hindsight's proverbial accuracy, it may be reading too much into these minutes to suggest that autocracy was the root of Anna Leach's difficulties at the school. A more sympathetic view might be that the board's complete circumvention of her in important decision making drove her to greater dictatorship in those areas where she exercised control. It is impossible to know for sure. What is sure is that in February 1910, trustee Frederick Orr wrote to Gurley offering to serve as business manager on a temporary basis if "it is desirable to retain Miss Leach until the proper person is found to head the Administration." He suggested that he knew what he was getting into because he appreciated "the difficulties a person would encounter in working with her to avoid a friction that might cause an explosion."[79] Clearly, the board was aware of erratic behavior on her part. There are no extant student letters about any difficulty, but years later, Elizabeth Skinner '10, told fund-raisers who were soliciting her for a gift that her years at the school were not happy because the principal was "off her head."[80]

It took a year for the crisis to reach its climax. Leach's formal correspondence yields few clues to her frame of mind. Most of the extant letters are to parents and teachers. They are professional, warm, and coherent. On many of the letters she received, however, she scrawled partial and increasingly illegible responses. Possibly Caroline Warr, the secretary she hired in 1903, translated these into lucid responses. Whatever the circumstances, between 1908 and 1911, she wrote letters to parents and students about course selection and roommates, letters to faculty about contracts and dates they needed to be at school, letters to fathers about delinquent bills, and letters to agencies about the placement of school advertisements. In return she received affectionate letters from former students and parents. On October 4, 1908, Laura Bradley wrote from Oklahoma City about her daughter Agnes, "You certainly know how to care for the girls."[81] On February 3, 1911, Leach wrote sympathetically to Katherine Wellman's mother that Katherine's potential roommate for the following year might not be able to afford the more expensive room that Katherine wanted. (Rooms still had differential pricing, depending on their size.) She assured Mrs. Wellman that she would be speaking with the girls about rooming in mid-February.

It is doubtful that she held that meeting. On February 4, the board of trustees held a special meeting. According to the minutes, William Gurley called the meeting to discuss "the subject of Miss Leach's retirement from the principalship of the school, stating that it was imperative for the school that she resign."[82] He had been in contact with her sister Abby and referred to a letter she had written to him; its contents are unknown.[83] It was proposed and accepted that "further negotiations looking to the resignation and immediate withdrawal of Miss Leach be conducted between the executive and Miss Leach by a third party entirely disinterested."[84] The identity of the third party is unknown, but on February 6, Gurley signed a check for Anna Leach in the amount of $3,650 "for salary, house, board as per agreement."[85]

On February 23, ironically Emma Willard's birthday, at another special meeting of the board held at the Troy Savings Bank, Gurley read Miss Leach's letter of resignation and recommended that Eliza Kellas be immediately appointed principal at a salary of $2,500 per year. Only one trustee, Seymour Van Santvoord, raised serious objections. He denounced the "irregularity and illegality of the actions of the board in this whole affair . . . [and] wished to go on record as not voting for any resolution of a principal at this meeting."[86] Anna Leach had already left Troy because the board passed a resolution thanking Elizabeth Simpson for her service as acting principal.

That evening two Troy papers carried the news that Emma Willard had a new principal.[87] The wording in each announcement was the same, indicating it had been released to the press prior to the afternoon's board meeting. At the urging of Agnes Irwin, Radcliffe's dean, Eliza Kellas had been persuaded to interrupt her doctoral studies to go to Troy. She and the board agreed this would be a temporary arrangement. She remained for thirty-one years.

There Is Only One Miss Kellas

ON FEBRUARY 23, 1911, a driver from Dalton's Livery met the afternoon train from Boston. Eliza Kellas had arrived in Troy. After stowing her luggage, he assisted the forty-four-year-old woman onto the seat of the buckboard, clucked to his horses, and the new principal began her first ascent to Mount Ida. Although she had signed a contract a few days before, at least one board member cautioned, "This arrangement is tentative."[1] As the wagon swung onto Pawling Avenue from Maple, Eliza Kellas caught her first glimpse of the campus that would be her home for the next thirty-one years. During her tenure, hundreds of students would come to believe, as one succinctly put it, "Emma Willard *was* Miss Eliza Kellas."[2]

The search for a successor to replace Anna Leach had begun a few months earlier. Paul Cook, board treasurer, had turned to his sister, Emma Willard Cook '70,[3] for help. She contacted an old friend, Agnes Irwin, the first dean of Radcliffe and the former head of a successful girls' school outside Philadelphia. At some point in the process, Irwin traveled to Albany to meet with Cook and board president William F. Gurley. She apparently returned to Cambridge without making any definite recommendation, but in January she wrote to Cook that she had "not forgotten nor neglected my quest for a paragon." She assured him that she did not use the term *paragon* in jest, insisting "in all seriousness that is what you want." Irwin, who had served twenty-five years as the headmistress of the school that now bears her name, referred modestly to her experience when she wrote, "I think I understand the requirements of the position."[4]

The person Irwin had in mind had studied at Radcliffe while Irwin was dean and had recently embarked on graduate studies there. Forty years old when she entered Radcliffe as a sophomore English major in 1907, Eliza Kellas had already earned a degree in classical studies from Potsdam Normal School[5] in 1889. One of her Potsdam professors, Edward W. Flagg, in his recommendation to Radcliffe on her behalf, noted that her work in his classes in rhetoric, history, and English literature was "characterized by . . . earnestness, thoughtfulness and breadth."[6] After her Potsdam graduation, she had remained on the campus as an instructor for a year. A year later the New York Department of Education opened a new normal school in Plattsburgh, a north country town closer to her family's home in Mooers Forks. She transferred there, serving first as an instructor and later as preceptress (an office akin to that of college dean) and remaining at the school for a decade. For her biography of Eliza Kellas, Elizabeth Potwine collected stories from many students and contemporaries who knew Eliza Kellas at Potsdam and Plattsburgh. It is clear from these reminiscences that she was an able administrator and, above all, a gifted teacher. Potwine concluded that this gift for teaching was rooted in her "love for her work [and] interest in her pupils beyond the obligation of duty."[7]

Eliza Kellas's "obligation of duty" changed significantly in 1901 when her mother, also Eliza Kellas, died, and the widowed Alexander Kellas moved to Malone to live with his son John, an attorney. While she had resided and worked in Plattsburgh, Eliza had been able to visit her parents frequently in the rural village where she had grown up, the older daughter and second child in a family of four. Her father Alexander, born in Scotland, had emigrated to the United States with his parents when he was a small boy. Her mother was born in Ireland to Scots-Irish parents; her parents' Scots heritage was always a particular point of pride for Eliza Kellas. Sometime before 1860, her parents had married and moved to Mooers Forks, a small northern New York village on the Canadian border. In addition to her older brother John and younger sister Katharine, Eliza had an invalid brother, Alexander, who stayed at home and predeceased his parents.

The February day she rode from the train station to the Emma Willard campus in an open buckboard was bitterly cold with strong winds and the thermometer hovering near zero. However, growing up in northern New York had inured her to harsh weather. Wresting a living from a farm in Clinton County in the late nineteenth century was a backbreaking enterprise, but Sandy Kellas, as Eliza's father was known to his neighbors, was up to the task. He not only survived but prospered. A schoolmate of Eliza's remembered that Mr. Kellas "was ambitious for his children" and that their "clothes were of better quality" and their "home was better furnished"[8] than those of their neighbors. Alexander Kellas instilled in his children the values of hard work, thrift, and education along with Scottish pride, self-reliance, and personal reserve. Eliza, commented her childhood friend, "was a farmer's daughter who lived hard in the present while she planned wisely for her future."[9] Mr. Kellas's ambition for his children and Eliza's sage plans for her future centered on education. Like the young Emma Willard, Eliza Kellas had her father's support in her quest for the best education she could obtain. In the beginning, Eliza and her siblings attended the neighborhood country school; as they grew older, they traveled to Malone to attend high school at Franklin Academy. By 1880, Eliza, aged fourteen, was a high school student living with her brother John, twenty-five, in a boardinghouse in Malone.

With her mother's death and her father's relocation, Eliza probably felt a certain relief at being able to leave the north country, a landscape that she found both beautiful and stifling. During the decade she lived in Plattsburgh, she had spent many summer vacations traveling, even cycling through the British Isles with a fellow teacher. In 1901, however, she received the offer that enlarged her world enormously and gave her rich experiences to complement the Scottish values instilled by her parents. She was invited to serve as a companion to Mary Lyon Cheney, a wealthy widow who had been her friend and colleague in Plattsburgh in 1891 and 1892. Cheney came from a very different background, both educationally and socioeconomically. Three years Eliza's junior, she had grown up in Connecticut and had graduated from Wellesley. Her uncle, Andrew Draper, was the New York state commissioner of education. In 1870, when the federal census listed Alexander Kellas's assets as a very respectable $6,900, Mary's father, Edwin Lyon, a physician in New Britain, registered a net worth of $24,500, and the Lyon household, with just two children, included two servants.

Mary Cheney's husband Charles was a man of even greater means; his father had made a fortune in the transportation industry, starting a firm that would eventually become American Express. Tragically, the younger Cheney contracted tuberculosis within the first few years of his marriage and died, leaving his widow with three young children: two boys, Charles and William, ages seven and four, and Ruth,[10] a six-year-old girl. Eliza moved to Peterborough, New Hampshire, to serve as companion to her old friend and governess to her children. With the Cheney household, she traveled to Europe and Central America; she met Indian princes and members of the British royal family. She spent winters in Baltimore and New Orleans, she lived on a lemon ranch in Montecito, California, and at "East Hill," the Cheney family estate in Peterborough. At some point, she converted from the Presbyterian Church of her forefathers to Mary Cheney's more fashionable Episcopal Church (a religious switch that mirrored Emma Willard's action in the early years of the nineteenth century).

In 1905 Mary Cheney remarried. Her new husband was a Harvard professor. William Henry Schofield taught Norse literature and was founding chairman of the college's department of comparative literature. Eliza still lived with the Schofields (in the historic Longfellow House in Cambridge) for a few years after their marriage, but as the children grew older and needed her less, she resumed her studies at Radcliffe. She continued to travel during vacations, notably crossing Iceland on a pony with the Schofield/Cheney family during the summer of 1910, a trip undertaken in conjunction with Professor Schofield's sabbatical work. When this adventure ended, Eliza left the family in Europe and returned to Cambridge where she intended to earn a master's degree and then, according to Elizabeth Potwine, work in a settlement house in Boston.

Thanks to Agnes Irwin, Eliza Kellas's life veered sharply from this plan. After meeting with members of the executive committee of the board of trustees, she agreed to take the reins at Emma Willard School, a decision that Irwin applauded. Learning from Paul Cook that Eliza had signed on with the school, Irwin swore the trustees would not be sorry. "There is," she wrote, "only one Miss Kellas."[11] By April, it was apparent that Irwin's faith in Eliza Kellas was justified. According to *Triangle*, she had quickly earned the students' affection and respect. Although the paper marked the parting of Anna Leach by extending their "hearty good wishes . . . in whatever work she may engage," they focused more on their new principal, editorializing, "Although she has been with us but a few weeks, already we have felt the quiet strength and gracious charm of her personality."[12] All students were perhaps not as quickly taken with her as *Triangle* suggested. Doris Crockett '11, a senior that winter, recalled that initially, "We eyed her with suspicion,"[13] but she noted that even the seniors were won over by graduation. The faculty most definitely welcomed her. At the height of the controversy surrounding Anna Leach's resignation, the Troy newspapers had predicted sweeping changes in school personnel.[14] In reality, only two people left with Leach, Ella V. Jones, the mathematics department chair and a close associate of the outgoing head, and Sarah L. Doyle, the principal's secretary.

When Eliza Kellas arrived on Mount Ida, there was a great deal to be done. First, of course, she had to stabilize the mood on campus. In a final commentary on Anna Leach's departure, a Troy newspaper had reported authoritatively, "Miss Leach . . . was dethroned because of her temper. She is said to have an excitable way about her and would scale [*sic*] books and rulers through the school rooms and has been known to throw things at pupils."[15] The cool, thoughtful, and stately manner of Eliza Kellas must have been a refreshing change from the volatility of her predecessor.

The campus, dedicated the prior June, was far from complete. Finishing it must have been high on the trustees' agenda for the incoming head of school. In spite of its magnificence, many parts of the brand-new facility, most notably the library, were unfinished. There was a place for a clock on the gym tower but no clock. The grounds were barren, devoid of gardens and trees, and wooden boardwalks crossed the yet-to-be-landscaped lawns. While the new principal worried about these details, the students were already enjoying the more distinctive features of the campus. As reported in *Triangle*, "Journeying through the tunnels connecting the buildings affords a merry pastime."[16] In their class history, the class of 1913, sophomores during 1910–11, recalled the first year on the new campus as one of "daring adventures, like feasting in the tunnel, climbing the power-house tower, and covering ourselves with dust in the gymnasium attic."[17] For entertainment, there was "a fine new Victrola,"[18] on which the boarders could listen to such popular hits as "Come, Josephine, in My Flying Machine," "A Ring on the Finger Is Worth Two on the 'Phone,'" and Irving Berlin's scandalous "Everybody's Doing It Now." (The "It" was the turkey trot.)

There were 194 girls enrolled at the school, including 37 girls in the intermediate program and 26 in the primary. A total of 131 students were enrolled in the academic program, as grades 9 to 12 were called. Of those, only forty-four were boarders. (Six intermediate students also boarded, including the Herrera sisters from Panama.) Forty-one students in the high school had such uneven academic records that they were "unclassified," which meant they had not been assigned to a grade. There were thirty seniors, all white and Christian. One may have been Roman Catholic, but they were overwhelmingly Protestant—mostly Episcopalian, Congregationalist, and Presbyterian. All had been born in the United States, although one had Irish parents, two had a parent born in England, and one had parents born in Norway. Slightly more than a third came from homes with live-in maids; two also had resident chauffeurs and cooks. None of their mothers had professions; their fathers were businessmen, doctors, lawyers, and merchants.

No member of the class of 1911 received financial assistance; the cost for a day student was $150, and for a boarder, either $800 or $900, depending on the type of room she chose. Ten percent of the class had lost a mother or father before senior year. Eighteen were day students, and fifteen of those were from Troy. One lived on Pawling Avenue. Two were cousins. Senior boarders came from Connecticut, Indiana, Illinois, Washington State, Texas, and Pennsylvania—and, of course, New York State. In the class of 1911, three girls went to Vassar, five to Wellesley, and one to Albany Normal College.

When Miss Kellas arrived, no member of the faculty had been at the school longer than six years. However, among those teachers were a number of women who would become key members of the Kellas faculty, including Elizabeth Simpson, Ellen Manchester, Julie Mayser, Lea Surleau, Elizabeth Robson, Mary Wilson, Grace Handsbury, Lucy Hamson, and Mary Ida Hare. Within a year Janet Maxwell and Katharine Weaver, destined for legendary careers, would join their ranks. All of these women had college degrees, most earned at Vassar and Wellesley; the majority also held master's degrees. Unlike the faculty, the trustees had shown little change under Leach and remained stable under Kellas. In fact, for the most part, trustees did not retire; they died in office. Even Seymour Van Santvoord, who had protested the unorthodoxy of the board's removal and replacement of Anna Leach, stayed on the board for many years after the change in administration. John Hudson Peck was the last Willard relative serving on the board; his term of service had begun in 1882.

So, although Eliza Kellas faced challenges, she could count on the beauty of the campus, the stability of the board, and a well-educated and energetic teaching corps who would prove loyal to her and her management of the school. In addition, the school's major donor, eighty-three-year-old Margaret Olivia Slocum Sage, was still actively interested in her alma mater and other institutions for women, and she still had millions of dollars to give away. By 1911 she was donating almost exclusively to women's institutions. Two of her gifts in that year illustrate this pattern. She gave $150,000 to Vassar for the construction of Olivia Josselyn Hall, a dormitory named for her grandmother, and $300,000 to Cornell for a woman's dormitory named for her late husband's mother. Interestingly, given Sage's importance to the school, it seems that the board left it to Eliza to introduce herself to Sage. She wrote to her three weeks after her arrival in Troy, "Doubtless the Board of Trustees have informed you that there has been a change in the administration of this school and that I have become Principal."[19] She asked to visit with her the next week, a request that was denied because of Sage's fragile health.

In addition to all of these assets, Eliza Kellas also had the benefit of the school's location. In 1911 Troy no longer commanded the wealth that it once had, but it was nonetheless thriving. Its population of near-ly 80,000 people placed it in the top one hundred American cities. In anticipation of Troy's one hundredth birthday as an official municipal entity, scheduled for 1916, the Chamber of Commerce in 1913 pub-lished a pamphlet entitled *A New Troy*. A classic of Progressive Era ur-ban boosterism, *A New Troy* touted the city's parks, educational insti-tutions (RPI, Emma Willard, "two classical High Schools, Commercial High School, vocational schools . . . twelve kindergartens, a Catholic Seminary and Novitiate"), rail and river transportation, public library (50,000 volumes), three hospitals, four orphan asylums, an insane asy-lum, seventy-one churches, "beautiful Music Hall, fourteen other the-atre, vaudeville and moving picture houses," growing suburbs, "efficient police protection and modern fire apparatus, new combined telephone and two telegraph systems . . . , nine daily and weekly newspapers."[20] In terms of industry, the chamber boasted that Troy had more than 196 incorporated companies capitalized at $50 million and employ-ing 28,000 employees for an industrial production of $40 million per year. The collar, cuff, and shirt industry dominated the industrial land-scape, but Troy's products, destined for "all the markets of the world," included "laundry machinery, valves, knit goods, engineering instru-ments, weights and measures, bells, horseshoes, merchant iron, steel and malleable iron products, stoves, heaters, boilers, grates, iron tub-ing, rail joints, chains, brushes, ventilators, fans and blowers, fire brick, fire proofing, metal storefront bars, stamped tinware, paper, paper box-es, paint, electrical apparatus, street cars, motor trucks, oil-cloth, files, railroad signals, buttonhole machines, chains, flour, cordage, hydro-extractors, high-pressure hydrants, malt beverages and cigars." In brief, the Chamber concluded, "'Made In Troy' means worth."[21]

After stressing Troy's commercial advantages, the chamber laid out the steps Troy needed to take to remain a leader among twentieth-century cities. Prominent among these ideas were standards of urban progressivism such as clean politics, city beautification (including more parks and statues), municipal responsibility for improved infra-structure (including underground electrical wiring and updated sew-age and garbage facilities), and programs to combat youthful crime.

Two committees, one on municipal affairs and one on "civic art," tackled the biggest issues and presented their plans to the chamber. The committee on civic art was chaired by the city engineer, Garnet D. Baltimore, the first African American graduate of Rensselaer Polytechnic Institute (RPI). Although Baltimore's role was far from typical of the social integration in the city as a whole, the chamber's integrated leadership, perhaps more than anything else, marked it as forward looking.

The change in leadership at Emma Willard came at a propitious time; over the years Eliza Kellas would become as great a Troy booster as the city's businessmen, eventually becoming the first woman to hold the title "Citizen of the Year." In the meantime, however, she focused on leading the school, and she seems to have developed her administrative style very quickly. She was determined to imbue her charges with character and a sense of service, to develop them intellectually to the extent that they were capable, to teach them the value of hard work, to encourage them to pursue their education beyond Emma Willard, and to instill in them a reverence and respect for the founder. From the first she stressed Emma Hart Willard's commitment to women's education and shared with Willard a recognition of the critical role educated women could play as citizens of the world's greatest democracy. Key to her success was a thriving boarding department. When she arrived there were too many empty beds in Sage Hall. The new dormitory had room for a hundred students; only fifty beds were occupied.

Exactly how she increased the boarding population remains a bit mysterious. The simplest explanation is that she did it through the strength of her own reputation and the overall quality of the education she provided—both inside and outside the classroom. She did not do it by advertisement; the advertisements in national magazines so ubiquitous during the Willard, Knox, and Leach eras were reduced drastically in her first few years and disappeared almost entirely by 1920. She did not do it by lowering the price; over the course of her first ten years at the school, tuition nearly doubled. She did not do it by hiring professional recruitment officers or using placement agencies.[22] In short, it is clearer to see what she did not do than to see what she did do because so much of what she did was not quantifiable; by force of her personality and by modeling intellect and character, she carried Emma Willard's vision for girls' education into the twentieth century.

To help her, of course, she had "the most modern and finely equipped seminary in the country"[23] with which to attract prospective families. As noted earlier, the plan to move the three 1890s buildings to Mount Ida had proved prohibitively expensive, so everything at the school was new. Located 390 feet above sea level, the school was isolated from the dirt and disease that threatened the downtown site. The campus was a model of modern fireproofing; the Sage tower, which soared over 100 feet, was ringed by four giant gargoyles looming protectively over the buildings below. The tower, visible from multiple approaches, contained a water storage system that held 50,000 gallons of water and was connected to standpipes that could be activated at the first sign of fire. In addition, all of the floors were constructed of concrete and hollow tile designed to make them fireproof.

The interior of the residence hall was grand and gracious, replicating the style of a great manor house. The porte-cochère entrance on the southern end of Sage opened into a reception parlor and office that adjoined the living spaces for the teachers and the principal. Magnificent as the public rooms were, the faculty rooms were modest. Eliza Kellas, used to the spacious homes inhabited by the Cheneys, recalled that the narrow white bedstead provided for her in the principal's chambers made her feel as though she had landed in a convent.[24] (Nevertheless, she lived there nearly two decades.)

The living room and dining room were located in the far wing of the dormitory. Thirteen round tables filled the dining room, and a complete set of English porcelain engraved in gold with the school monogram was used at every meal. Adjoining the dining room were a housekeeper's apartment, kitchen, pantries, and various storerooms. The upstairs servants' quarters were provided with a private dining room, parlor, bedrooms, and bathrooms. The kitchen, itself, was "a large and airy room . . . strictly sanitary . . . [containing] the most modern equipped outfit that can be found in any institution or hotel system."[25] The basement of the dormitory housed the laundry facilities, a cold storage vault, vegetable cellars, a room specifically set aside for apple storage and a fruit cellar with shelving for three thousand cans of preserves. Supplies for the kitchen arrived through a tunnel from a power house on Elmgrove Avenue. The *Troy Record* noted approvingly that the tunnel system "will be used mainly for the carrying in of provisions [which] will avoid the entrance of supply carts upon the grounds of the school." Kitchen waste would go out the same way, "delivered directly to the power house, there to be consumed under the boilers, the purpose being to cremate all refuse."[26] The student rooms were located on the second and third floors of Sage Hall. Variously priced, these accommodations were arranged as single sleeping and study rooms; double sleeping and study rooms; or single sleeping, study, and bathrooms. At one end of the third floor there was an infirmary capable of housing six students with an apartment for a resident nurse.

Slocum Hall was the "school building." Students entered Slocum through the entrance on the north front facing Pawling Avenue. Day students, from primary through intermediate to high school, stored their coats in the basement under the assembly hall. The day students' lunchroom was also located in this area. Chemistry and physics classrooms, laboratories, and science teachers' offices were also placed in the basement. On the first floor of Slocum, in addition to the assembly hall, there were four classrooms for the primary grades, four for the intermediate grades, the principal's office, a meeting room for trustees, a teachers' room, and an office for the librarian. The library, with its parquet floors, massive fireplace, and soaring ceilings, was located at the northern end of the first floor. For a school that had long prided itself on being academically rigorous, it was fitting that the library was "the finest room of the institution."[27] In 1911 it had not yet been filled with books; to help remedy that solution, the class gift from the seniors in June was a fund for new library books.

The third building was the gymnasium. In addition to the gymnasium proper, there was a running track and a fencing room. The basement of the gymnasium contained a bowling alley, a swimming pool, three hundred lockers, "shower baths," and dressing rooms. To the east of the gym were playing fields designed for field hockey, outdoor basketball, and baseball (women did not yet play softball), and numerous tennis courts. One field was flooded in winter for skating. The gymnasium would prove to be a multipurpose facility during the first decades of its life, housing everything from concerts and theatrical events to graduation and reunion activities. Without question, this facility ensured that the school had the finest athletic facilities of any girls' school in the country. When the RPI class of 1887 presented their alma mater with a gymnasium in 1912, the *Christian Science Monitor* wrote a feature story on the "notable" athletic facilities at Troy's two leading private institutions. The *Monitor* noted that at "neither of these institutions is athletics allowed to interfere with intellectual training but . . . an earnest attempt is made to harmonize the two important fields of work."[28]

As impressive as the buildings were, the infrastructure was equally modern and awe inspiring. In the power house, the school generated its own electricity. The underground coal cellar had a capacity of 200 tons of coal, covered with ground-level coal chutes. Coal could be delivered directly from wagons to the cellar without the intermediary step of shoveling. (Nevertheless, two men were required to work twenty-four hours a day, seven days a week, shoveling coal from the cellar into the boilers.) The power house also contained the school well, which had the capacity to pump out hundreds of gallons per hour of the "purest water in the city."[29] The water was drawn into the pump room for distribution throughout the buildings; the beautifully tiled pump room was a model of sanitation. Other infrastructure innovations included the use of hot pipes along the edges of the gutters to prevent ice buildup on the roofs in winter, the electric illumination of the tunnels, and the installation of telephone lines to all the buildings. By 1912, as part of registration, parents received a special form asking for the family telephone number. And, as is always the case, new technology brought new rules. The 1911–12 catalog included this directive: "Students are not allowed to go to the telephone during school or study hours, nor can they be called from the dinner table."[30]

Covering the three buildings were carved gargoyles and etched mottoes, all intended to inspire and to place this extraordinary school for girls on the continuum of liberal arts education stretching back to the sixteenth century. The gargoyles were the most distinctive decorations, but there were also globes and animals and signs of the zodiac adorning the stone walls and cut around the windows and doors. Whimsical and expressive, the gargoyles represented the activities in the buildings they graced: those on Sage cooking, dining, and other residential pastimes, those on Slocum education and the arts, and those on the gymnasium games and sports. Latin phrases were inscribed at entrances and intended to motivate young scholars and inculcate love of learning, duty to country, and reverence for God.

Clearly, Eliza Kellas had significant material with which to attract more boarders, but even so, the pace of her success was extraordinary. By the fall of 1911, the dormitory was full. The *Troy Budget*, at the beginning of the school year, reported in amazement, "The lists have been closed for the last six weeks, something never before known, and pupils have been refused admission because there is no room." They ascribed this happy condition to "the ability of Miss Kellas [who] has proven a wonderful educator and manager."[31] To accommodate a larger number of students in Sage, twelve teachers had been moved out of the dormitory to the "White Cottage," a building south of the gym that had been outfitted as a teachers' residence.

The increase in boarders was not a one-year phenomenon. The residential population continued to grow for the next twenty years. Space was a chronic issue. In 1915 Eliza Kellas made her first appeal to the board of trustees for a new dormitory that could accommodate an additional one hundred students. Noting that there was no money left in the Sage gift that could be allocated for this purpose, the board voted that "when the funds of the school permit a new dorm be erected."[32] At Eliza's urging, the board discussed the need for more dormitory space in 1917 and again in 1919. On October 13, the minutes recorded the need for "a new dormitory to take care of at least 100 or more scholars" and that "Miss Kellas was very earnest in her request that this matter be taken up and carried to fulfillment."[33] A special meeting was called for a full board discussion of a new dormitory, and on October 27, 1919, the board unanimously passed the resolution that "a dormitory be erected immediately to take care of at least 110 new scholars."[34]

The proposed dormitory would not materialize for nearly a decade.

In the meantime, Eliza Kellas made do, moving more teachers out of Sage, rooming students in Slocum in the wing adjacent to the Assembly Hall, and adapting old structures on and near the school property for dormitories. In July 1913, she wrote to Lizzie Lee Pound '15, a prospective student from Alabama, "All the rooms in Olivia Sage Hall . . . are taken, and most of those in Slocum Hall. . . . We still have, however, in that building two places at $800 each . . . both rooms have unusually large windows, are light, airy and most comfortable."

Or Lizzie Lee could also room in a separate house, which her future principal explained had been used as a teachers' residence. This was Gray Gables, which she described in great detail: "This house is but a few rods from our main dormitory. It was built a year and a half ago and consists of twelve sleeping rooms, two sitting rooms and two bath rooms. It is lighted by electricity, heated by hot water and is modern in every possible respect. . . . In this house we shall put eleven girls with a chaperone, and the price of each room will be $900."

Whichever choice Lizzie Lee made, she was assured that "the girls in Slocum Hall and in the cottage have all the privileges of the girls in the main dormitory" and "in fact are together all the time with the exception of the quiet hours and at night after they retire."[35] Lizzie Lee came (after choosing the $800 room in Slocum) but only remained at the school for one year, leaving because of poor health, not inferior accommodations.

In May 1919, Eliza Kellas wrote similarly to the father of a prospective student from Colorado. His daughter was being removed from the waiting list and offered a place in Slocum, she explained, because "the last sixteen who apply live in Slocum Hall in which we have sixteen girls and two teachers."[36] Unlike Lizzie Lee Pound, this student, Jane Quackenbush '22, came and stayed, entering as a sophomore in 1919. There is no comprehensive extant record of where individual students lived, so it is impossible to know if living outside of Sage was viewed unfavorably. One of the school's most generous lifetime donors, Helen Snell Cheel '23, lived in Slocum at least one year and was president of Gray Gables as a senior. In a brief reminiscence that he wrote about Eliza Kellas, Bertrand Snell, Helen's father, recalled that after eating dinner with his daughter and the principal (a Potsdam classmate of his), "I walked with Helen across the campus to her rooming house,"[37] a casual reference that suggests the outlying student residences were very much accepted.

Students roomed in Slocum until the new dormitory was opened, but there is no record of where they bathed, and there are no separate yearbook references to girls in this area; it was perhaps seen as temporary. But from yearbook entries and occasional scrapbooks, it seems clear that the girls in the two outlying dormitories, Allenwood and Gray Gables, developed a special camaraderie. They certainly do not seem to have felt neglected. In 1920 a major March snowstorm apparently prevented the girls and teachers in the detached residences from reaching the Sage dining room. According to *Triangle*, the inhabitants of the "teachers' cottage" (a new one built in 1916 to replace the White Cottage) and "the senior house" were snowed in, and "heavily laden men ploughed their way through the deep snow with baskets of provisions."[38]

That "heavily laden men" could move more easily through the drifts than teenaged girls perhaps reflects an interesting and commonly accepted division of labor apportioned according to gender. However, this was a school whose head exhorted her pupils at commencement in 1913, "Women are doing splendid things to-day; in the social way, in reform work, in scientific research, in the business and professional world, they are taking their places beside their fellow men."[39]

Given the socioeconomic status of the student body, the decision to send workmen with meals for the snowed-in boarders and faculty was more likely a reflection of class than gender. After all, Eliza Kellas also instructed her pupils that red "was for strumpets," and only "washerwomen" stood with their arms crossed. In her mind and presumably the minds of the students, class differences existed. These could be transcended by education and behavior, but they most certainly did exist.

In spite of their grandeur, then, the new buildings lacked the dormitory capacity that Eliza Kellas felt the school needed to be successful. There was one other flaw, as far as she was concerned. She did not believe the infirmary should be included within the main dormitory. In an era when measles, scarlet fever, flu, and other contagious diseases too often led to pneumonia and death, she felt that ailing students should be completely removed from the boarding area. Given her fervor on this subject, it is no wonder that Eliza Kellas's first major fund-raising appeal to the alumnae was a plea for money to build a separate infirmary.

She had reason to be concerned. Outbreaks of contagious diseases disrupted school life significantly during her first few years as principal. Less than two months after she arrived, she had to add two weeks to spring break because of an outbreak of scarlet fever. In January 1916, with her students recently returned from the Christmas break, she mentioned to Olivia Sage's secretary, Lilian Todd, that she "dreaded vacations" because the girls brought so many germs back to school with them. There were, she noted, "four distinct diseases [measles, chickenpox, scarlet fever, and German measles], each girl quarantined with a special nurse." She enclosed a copy of her fund-raising appeal to alumnae, "a little circular asking the alumnae of the school to build an infirmary for us."[40] The day after she wrote this letter, she closed school, forcing the students to leave again for two weeks, "an exodus of Emma Willardites"[41] that resulted in a postponement of semester examinations until mid-February. The following fall, the opening of school was delayed two weeks because of an infantile paralysis epidemic that swept the Northeast in July and August, terrifying parents and delaying the opening of public and private schools and many colleges.

Of course, the biggest health threat came with the great influenza outbreak of 1918. Because of this worldwide pandemic, the opening of school was delayed until October in the fall of 1918, and the day school suspended classes even longer. Because of the late opening, the first issue of *Triangle* was postponed until December and, in the words of the editor, "arrived . . . surrounded on all sides by germs, and almost pushed out of existance [*sic*] by Work-to-Make-Up."[42] At one point cots were set up in the gymnasium to handle the number of flu cases. Eliza Kellas herself nursed many students through the disease, which was perhaps most terrifying because of its fatal impact on seemingly healthy young adults. In a black-bordered announcement of four alumnae deaths from the flu, *Triangle* mourned their loss, noting poignantly, "the girls were so young."[43] The flu victims included members of the classes of 1914, '15, and '17 and a nongraduate who would have been a member of the class of 1920, so their deaths were very real to their former schoolmates.

In spite of the challenges of finding space for the burgeoning boarding population and appropriate health facilities for students with communicable diseases, Eliza Kellas almost immediately began planning a grand centennial celebration of the founder's vision for girls' education. By 1913 she was focused on the best way to commemorate the one hundredth anniversary of Emma Hart Willard's revolutionary venture in Middlebury, Vermont. Shortly after presiding over her third commencement, she wrote to Olivia Sage, "we turn our faces toward the beginning of the one hundredth year." For the upcoming event, she hoped "to build upon [the] strong foundation" of "our glorious past."[44] She dreamed that every living student who had attended the Troy Female Seminary or Emma Willard School, including the nongraduates, would be present. Six months later, in January 1914, the board affirmed the principal's plans, voting that a two-day celebration be staged in October to mark the unprecedented milestone in American women's education. Although the budget for the celebration has not survived, it must have been significant; in response to a query about undertaking a new initiative at the school in 1914–15, Eliza Kellas replied, "The centennial celebration will be all we shall feel like undertaking financially."[45]

By all accounts the fall of 1914 was given up to preparations for the anniversary extravaganza. The historian for the class of 1917, in a chronicle of their sophomore year published in the yearbook, recalled, "We learned . . . what it meant to be at Emma Willard during a centennial celebration. For two weeks in school, we had a busy but unacademic life, amid sewing, hectic dressmaking and rehearsing."[46] In preparation for the big event, Mrs. Sage sent portraits of her husband and herself to be hung in Sage Hall (where they remain today). Lilian Todd, Mrs. Sage's secretary, who was fast becoming Eliza Kellas's friend, supporter, and confidante, assured her that the philanthropist liked her portrait. Understandably so, wrote Todd, as it makes her "younger looking [and] flatters her, which, however, is harmless. . . . It looks enough like her to be recognized as such."[47] Sage sent Todd to the school to supervise the installation of the paintings and remained interested in the centennial proceedings, ordering fifty of the commemorative spoons commissioned by the alumnae association ("disappointing"[48] was her verdict) and sending the school a plaque she had received from the Emma Willard Association (EWA) in 1893 for the memorabilia collection to be displayed in conjunction with the celebration. She had previously sent Eliza Kellas a desk belonging to Emma Willard that she had acquired at some point. Miss Kellas treasured all these artifacts; she hoped, she said, "to have all so arranged that they will withstand the ravages of time, and when the biennial of the school is celebrated, there will be a wealth of material from past ages."[49]

School opened on September 23, 1914, just two weeks before the scheduled festivities. Not only was every bed filled (118 resident students registered), but the school was putting the finishing touches on the Playhouse, a building designed to host student activities from dances to theatricals to roller-skating parties. The Playhouse was critical to the success of the anniversary festivities; located directly across the campus from Slocum, it had the capacity to seat hundreds and contained an auditorium that measured 60 by 110 feet, significantly larger than the Assembly Hall, which measured 55 by 42 feet. Equipped with electricity, the Playhouse was a one-story building with high ceilings and an open piazza along one side. According to the *Troy Budget*, "its acoustical properties are remarkably good."[50]

After months of preparation, the days of celebration arrived. Houses along Pawling Avenue were decorated for the occasion, and flags in honor of the school flew on public buildings. At 2:30 on Tuesday, October 6, by proclamation of Mayor Cornelius Burns, the fire alarm sounded one hundred times.[51] Simultaneously, nearly three hundred alumnae presented their pink admission tickets to the ushers at the doors of the Playhouse. According to the guest register, Abbie Whipple, a member of the class of 1847, was the oldest one present. After a prayer by St. Paul's pastor, Edgar Enos, William F. Gurley welcomed the alumnae. Mary Knox Robinson '56 responded on behalf of the New York chapter, and Margaret Ingram Silliman '65 spoke for the Troy branch. Then Mary E. Woolley, president of Mount Holyoke, delivered the keynote address,

"Emma Willard and Her Gift to Education." Various musical interludes, including the obligatory congregational singing of "Rock'd in the Cradle of the Deep," rounded out the program.

After this portion of the events concluded, the assemblage repaired to the lawn in front of Slocum. While her mother, Emma Willard Scudder, looked on, Emma Willard Scudder Keyes, great-great-granddaughter of the founder, unveiled the tablet commemorating the contributions of both her ancestor and Margaret Olivia Slocum Sage. Given by the Emma Willard Association, the impressive plaque, cast in the foundry of the famous Gorham Company, was intended "to tell for years the story of the beginning of this school and of her who was its founder, and then the other story of love and loyalty of one of its graduates."[52] William Gurley accepted the memorial for the board, and the crowd sang "Auld Lang Syne," long a staple of seminary reunions. Following this the guests gathered around a new sundial, positioned on the lawn between Sage and Slocum and dedicated to former principal Emily T. Wilcox. It was the gift of those alumnae who had studied under her at the Troy Female Seminary. Again Gurley accepted the tribute, and again the crowd sang, this time giving voice to the "Alma Mater."

Finally, the alumnae entered the new library where two more bronze plaques were waiting to be installed, one given by the trustees and one by Olivia Sage. The trustee gift paid tribute to the work of John and Sarah Willard, and the other honored three early teachers, Theodosia Hudson, Mary Hastings, and Harriet Dillaye, "in affectionate appreciation of their influence and service."[53] The afternoon concluded with a reception in the library. Most of the visitors attended dinners around the city hosted by the Troy chapter of the alumnae association, after which many returned to campus for a student production of *The Piper*, an award-winning play about Robert Browning's poetic hero of Hamelin that had had a successful Broadway run in 1911.

The next day the celebration continued. In the morning, the faculty and trustees in full academic regalia led a procession of students and visitors to the gym. After an opening prayer, this time by Presbyterian minister Adelbert Higley, the president of Smith College, LeRoy Burton, addressed the crowd. Extolling the virtues of "The Educated Person,"

Burton urged the students to "have opinions without being opinionated, to have ideas without being rabid."[54] William Gurley then paid tribute to Eliza Kellas, describing her as "a woman in whom the ideals of the Founder had been realized."[55] She responded characteristically that "the history of the school had been a great incentive for her work" and added that she could not have accomplished anything "without the ever-present loyalty and cooperation of the faculty."[56] Following the speeches, the alumnae repaired to different locations for luncheons arranged by class. By early afternoon they were back. Chairs had been set up on the lawn behind the gymnasium for the audience to view the culminating centennial event, a pageant illustrating the history of the school. Faculty, students, and a number of local alumnae participated.

Through a series of seven episodes and interludes, the spectacle covered Emma Willard's life and the founding of the school. To set the stage, Minerva, the Roman goddess of wisdom, accompanied by heralds, was seated on a dais where she could watch the story unfold and bestow her metaphorical blessing on the enterprise. Episode I, entitled "Captain Hart," stressed the founder's colonial heritage and her father's Revolutionary War service. Dozens of students dressed as Revolutionary War soldiers marched onto the playing fields, muskets, fifes, and drums at the ready, following the lead of librarian Elizabeth Kent '07 in the role of Samuel Hart. Six more "episodes" followed, covering Emma's childhood yearning for an education, her work in Middlebury, the founding of the school in Troy, Lafayette's visit to the seminary, the founder's visit to France, and a scene from the 1850s when John and Sarah Willard ran the school. The recording secretary of the Emma Willard Association wrote approvingly of these scenes of bygone days when there were no "slit skirts, 'tangoes' and 'turkey trots.'"[57] The pageant concluded with a final academic procession across the campus to the library.

Newspapers around the country repeated the Troy papers' coverage of the events, and a number of papers also featured a human interest story about a Troy Female Seminary graduate who turned one hundred along with the school. Born in Whiteboro, New York, Louisa Capron Thiers attended the school in 1827 and 1828. The centenarian currently lived with a daughter in Wisconsin and made great newspaper copy. A fervent supporter of woman suffrage, she remembered traveling by canal to Troy "in those days when girls were not supposed to have brains enough to learn more than a smattering of the three R's."[58] In one interview she neatly captured the changes that she and the school had seen over the hundred years of their existence:

> Contrast the early transportation facilities of sailboat and so forth with the airships, the steam and electric railways, the automobiles of today. The wonder of telephone and telegraph, of the wireless telegraph, the ocean cable, the great majestic ocean liners, have all come in my day. When I was a girl, we cooked by the open fireplace, in kettles hanging from cranes; we baked our bread in a brick oven. Look at the kitchen of today with its gas range and electric appliances, its fireless cookers with electrical attachments and all the rest of it.[59]

Mrs. Thiers's interviews were laced with references to the extraordinary education she had received in Troy. She realized that because she had attended Emma Willard's school, her education set her apart from most women of her era. Although the curriculum had changed greatly since Louisa Thiers's day, the academic program in the early years of the Kellas administration continued to set Emma Willard graduates apart from most of their contemporaries. Mary Alice Knox had begun the emphasis on college preparation, and Anna Leach had built a college-educated faculty. Eliza Kellas would continue this work. Although she maintained a curriculum broad enough to accommodate individual student needs and family preferences, she increasingly emphasized college preparation. By 1920, 50 percent of the class planned to attend college, and in 1929, fifty-eight of the seventy graduates continued their education beyond Emma Willard.

When Eliza Kellas joined Emma Willard, it still had a "day school" enrolling girls in the primary and intermediate grades. (Technically, boys were admitted to the primary classes, but rarely did a boy enroll.) Very few pages of the annual catalog focused on these years; in fact, most years the paragraphs devoted to dress regulations far outnumbered those outlining the curriculum for the younger grades. Most children entered the primary at age six, and after four years they were promoted to the intermediate department. To advance to the first intermediate (or fifth grade) class, a student had to have "the ability to perform simple work in addition, subtraction, multiplication, division, to read readily, to spell common words, and to write legibly from dictation."[60]

The work of the intermediate grades was explained in a bit more detail, the aim of those years being preparation for the high school. In addition to work in arithmetic and English, intermediate students had a two-year course in "nature study," followed by "simple experiments in botany and chemistry" in the third year (seventh grade) and a half year of physiology and a half year of physics in the fourth year. Intermediate students studied history and geography each year, and the fourth intermediate girls began the study of Latin. The tuition for the primary grades was $80 in 1911–12 and for the intermediate grades, $100. By the mid-1920s, the cost for a year of primary education had risen to $100, and the intermediate program had been divided into fifth and sixth grades at $175, and seventh and eighth grades at $200, the latter reflecting a discrete junior high school experience. (Junior high as a distinct educational period dates to 1909.)

In spite of the presence on the campus of fifty to seventy-five little girls, the high school, or "academic program," was the main focus of the school. The expressed "aim" of the school was unchanged during the first fifteen years of Eliza Kellas's principalship and reinforced her belief that the boarding population was the heart of the institution. According to the catalog, the central purpose of Emma Willard School was "to give a thorough education to the girls entrusted to its care; to surround them with a happy, healthful atmosphere, which shall develop the possibilities of each student to the fullest extent."[61] As had been the case since Emma Willard's day, there was acknowledgment that not all students studied at the same pace or wished to pursue the most rigorous curriculum. To that end, "the work of each student is considered individually, and when occasion demands, special arrangements are made for her. Emphasis is placed not only upon the ability to meet requirements of the College or of the General Course, but upon work well done and the gain in power to think and do."[62]

The general course and the college course had been developed by her two immediate predecessors, but in her first year, Eliza Kellas asked the trustees to add another program—the Advanced Course.

This was intended to provide graduates of other high schools with the work they needed to prepare for college, to study art or music, or to prepare in a scientifically based way for homemaking. The Advanced Course could also lead to a diploma that seems to have been the equivalent of a two-year college degree. In addition, a separate music or art diploma was still available. The Emma Willard Conservatory of Music continued to occupy Plum Hall on the downtown campus. Extensive art offerings were available on the Mount Ida campus, and nonresident students could elect to take these on a per course basis. Finally, Anna Leach had added a comprehensive two-year course in domestic science. Far from eschewing this seemingly nonacademic course of study, Eliza Kellas championed its value and refined it over time. In a letter to Olivia Sage in 1912, she referred to domestic science as a subject "with which I feel all girls should be familiar."[63]

The need for a broad curriculum that ranged from the most rigorous college preparation to elective coursework in a variety of areas had two rationales. First, the school was almost completely dependent on tuition revenues, and there were not yet enough young women desiring a college education to make an exclusively college preparatory school for girls economically feasible. Second, there were, after all, almost no admissions requirements. Whether or not the school was suitable for a student was left to her parents to decide, as long as she was white and Christian. Year after year, the catalog exhorted parents "not to make application for the admission of a girl who from lack of health, or ability, cannot perform the full duties of the school."[64] Parents were also responsible for deciding whether or not their daughters would undertake college preparation, a decision they were urged to make "as soon as possible."[65]

Although students often corresponded in advance with the principal about their intended course of study, they were usually not placed in courses until they arrived and could be tested. This possibly explains the number of "unclassified students" during Anna Leach's tenure. Under Miss Kellas, all students were classified, but they often spent more than one year in a grade. To determine a student's placement, the school asked prior principals to provide lists of texts, the material the applicant had covered, and to fill out a form about personal habits and academic potential. Not until the 1930s did the school routinely receive actual transcripts of grades as part of the application process.

The letters supporting a student's application were often brutally honest by the standards of today's letters of recommendation, which are invariably positive and written with an ever-present awareness of how the letter might stand up in some future lawsuit. For example, a letter of recommendation for one student included the information that she was "snobbish," "unwilling to listen to advice or correction," was "unreliable . . . [had] no sense of dependability," and was "fond of playing capital jokes, which often become harmful to others and destructive to property." In response to the question of whether or not the student had school spirit, the response was "apparently none."[66] Another student was recommended in spite of her "belligerent" attitude and yet another was described as "commonplace, ill-bred, and absolutely unattractive."[67] All three of these students entered, graduated, and remained loyal and grateful to their alma mater and to Eliza Kellas.

Clearly, the school had to have a curriculum that would suit students of widely varying ability and attitudes toward learning. There was only one sure reason to reject an applicant: her faith. In 1902–3 the first catalog produced under Anna Leach contained a new section: "Religious Life." According to this brief paragraph, "The school is undenominational, but positively Christian in its influence."[68] Unlike the school of the nineteenth century, where Jewish girls were enrolled at least until the 1890s, early twentieth-century Emma Willard reflected the same anti-Semitism that was sweeping the college world in the first two decades of the 1900s. A "commonplace, ill-bred, and absolutely unattractive" Protestant was far more desirable than a highly recommended young woman whose family was Jewish.

In response to an appeal by a "good Presbyterian" recommending the daughter of a Jewish friend, Eliza Kellas wrote, "It is a Christian school, and some years ago, owing to certain circumstances, it was deemed wise to decide to admit those of but one faith." She explained that "a private school is a business enterprise and were [we] to admit pupils of the Jewish faith our other pupils would gradually withdraw."[69]

In Porter-Sargent and other school and camp directories of the 1910s and 1920s, an institution's willingness to enroll Jewish students was invariably noted. In his extraordinary history of anti-Semitism at colleges during these years, particularly at Harvard, Yale, and Princeton, Jerome Korabel provides ample evidence that sadly confirms that colleges and schools across the Northeast shared Eliza Kellas's conclusion that the admission of Jewish students meant risking the withdrawal of Christian students. Abbott Lawrence Lowell, president of Harvard, feared "that the sheer number of Jews would cause the flight of the Protestant elite and thereby 'ruin the college.'"[70] There is little comfort, however, in knowing that Emma Willard trustees and Eliza Kellas's willingness to practice religious discrimination put them in good company. How much nobler if they had been prepared to take a less popular route; the voice of the crowd, however, held sway. As Eliza Kellas wrote to George Diener, "I am extremely sorry that it is necessary for us to take this stand but until public opinion changes very materially we have no choice in the matter."[71]

Although every full-paying white Christian young woman was admitted—at least until the beds were full—there was no guarantee that she would remain at the school more than one year. The catalog was precise on this point: "The right is reserved of requesting the withdrawal of a pupil who for any cause is a detriment to the school."[72] That few were ever asked to leave and few even left of their own accord is a testament to the quality of the community that Eliza Kellas forged at the school. Through the development of athletics, the fostering of clubs and student government, and the initiation of enduring traditions, she created a distinctive school culture that defined an Emma Willard girl for three decades and more. She did this in spite of a world war, a devastating depression, and her simultaneous tenure as a college president.

The Biggest Influence on My Life

THE YEAR OF THE EMMA WILLARD centennial was a watershed year in world history. In August 1914, just months before the students and alumnae glorified Captain Hart's role in the American Revolution, another war broke out in Europe. In contrast to the Revolution, this war initially seemed not to touch Americans. It was a war based on age-old familial and territorial squabbles; after all, the immediate cause was a Serbian's assassination of the Archduke Franz Ferdinand, heir to the Hapsburg throne. In the ensuing alignment of nations, King George V of England and Kaiser Wilhelm II of Germany took opposite sides. They were first cousins, grandsons of Queen Victoria. Certainly, this seemed like a family squabble, far removed from the United States.

Viewed in the high beams of hindsight, the Great War was in fact a world conflagration that introduced the tools of modern conflict, from airplanes to chemical weapons to machine guns and howitzers. It was the first major war in which more soldiers died in combat than from disease, in spite of the fact that the last year of the war coincided with the influenza outbreak of 1918. Of the fifteen million people killed, about a third were civilians. Girls studying world geography in 1914 learned the outlines of four empires, German, Russian, Ottoman, and Austro-Hungarian, that would dissolve in defeat at the end of the war.

Although the war at first seemed far away from Mount Ida, Eliza Kellas and the school felt its impact almost immediately. Lila Shepard '14, a Canadian girl who had studied in Troy for two years, shipped to Europe as a nurse during the first winter of the war. She corresponded extensively with her former principal. She had packed her Emma Willard French text in her trunk, and she wrote that "nearly every night [I] go over those horrid irregular verbs."[1] Assigned to a Canadian hospital tent in France, Lila treated some of the war's worst casualties. She had no time to cry, she wrote, because of the "endless procession of stretchers with their still grey blanketed figures . . . and horrible wounds."[2] Working very close to the front lines, she wrote of holding limbless, sightless boys in her arms while they died. One autumn day, her nursing station was bombed. Two German planes appeared suddenly overhead, "like great birds of prey," and dropped bombs on the hospital compound. Lila was especially horrified that this human destruction "happened at ten o'clock on a bright, sunny morning in the twentieth century."[3] In spite of the horror around her, she managed to fall in love, and in one of her letters, she asked Miss Kellas for romantic advice. Her beau was a Canadian officer who was Roman Catholic, and her Protestant parents opposed the marriage. In addition to asking Eliza Kellas for advice, she also asked her for a loan to travel to England for the ceremony. Although only her side of the correspondence exists, the wedding took place, presumably with help and encouragement from Miss Kellas.

In many of her letters, Lila urged Miss Kellas to involve the students in aid for the Allied cause, even though "I must always remember you are neutral."[4] She requested that the students make small linen bags for the troops and fill them with cigarettes, tobacco, and cigars. They eagerly complied. More important than this effort, however, was the work of Emma Willard alumnae, who became involved in aiding the Allies well before the official declaration of war in April 1917. The German invasion of neutral Belgium at the start of the war in August 1914 outraged world opinion. In the United States, stories of German atrocities in Belgium stimulated both relief efforts for Belgian refugees and work on behalf of French and British soldiers, in spite of Wilson's official call for neutrality.

Chief among the alumnae contributions was their participation on the Surgical Dressings Committee of the United States, an organization of women that collected clothes for Belgian relief and made surgical dressings to be sent to British, French, and Canadian military hospitals in Europe. The Surgical Dressings Committee report for December 1914 recorded that boxes of clothing for Belgian relief were "the contribution of the teachers and the pupils of the Emma Willard School."[5] In Troy, the Surgical Dressings Committee was led by Mary Tappen McQuide '86, who very quickly became the chair of the entire New York State branch of the organization; what began in Troy had spread quickly to thirty-seven cities throughout the state. Because McQuide initially drew her membership from the Emma Willard Association in Troy, the Troy chapter was officially "The Emma Willard Chapter of the Surgical Dressings Committee." The *Troy Times* noted in early 1916 that it was "not generally known that Troy is perhaps the foremost city in the country in organizing and prosecuting this work."[6]

Once the United States entered the war in 1917, Emma Willard's volunteer efforts on behalf of the Allies increased, and the impact of the war on the school intensified. The alumnae continued to raise money, collect dressings, and knit clothing. Margaret Cook '99, stationed in France with the YWCA, supervised "hostess homes" in Europe, hotels for "French bride work," and places of "refuge for any American women doing war work."[7] Eliza Kellas was "eager to make every girl feel that she has a part in winning the war."[8] The students continued to sew and knit bandages, socks, and scarves for the soldiers, but they also contributed money to the cause. In 1918 they raised nearly $5,000 for the Students' Friendship War Fund, a project of the YMCA that sent volunteers to work in prison camps. (Miss Master's School raised $5,700 for this cause, Hotchkiss $6,000, Wellesley and Vassar $15,000, and Yale $41,000.) The class of 1917 and the class of 1918 both raised funds to support an American military hospital in France. A grateful wounded French soldier wrote to Miss Kellas thanking her: "A la tête de mon lit, existe une plaque, 'Emma Willard School.'"[9]

In May 1918, the Emma Willard Association (EWA), with student help, raised several hundred dollars by holding an entertainment at the school; admission was ten cents. The "Pageant of the Allied Nations" consisted of a series of tableaux depicting each nation fighting with the United States through stereotypical characters. For example, Russia was represented by dancing bears, Italy by opera, China by laundry-men, and England by Morris dancing. An advertisement in the program called for volunteers for the Farmerettes and urged students to spend the summer working on one of the farms near Troy, promising somewhat disingenuously, "Farming takes no more strength than playing tennis or golf."[10] The Farmerettes were part of the Woman's Land Army, a voluntary woman's organization designed to provide the labor needed to produce food as men mobilized for service. Emma Willard also faced a labor shortage, and the students pitched in to fill the gap. One observer noted that students "mowed the lawns, and weeded, and kept the place immaculate, carried chairs for the outdoor entertainment, and have filled in wherever possible, in the most cheerful manner." She noted, however, "Miss Kellas will not permit them to work at this sort of thing more than a half hour at a time, because they are so unaccustomed to it."[11] Miss Kellas also did her part. When her old friend Congressman Bertrand Snell stopped by the school in the summer of 1918, he found the principal in an apron, armed with a mop. She explained that it was "impossible to hire anyone to clean and put the buildings in proper shape for the opening of school, and she had spent the greater part of the vacation doing that work."[12]

Students and faculty felt the impact of the war in food rationing and inflation. Some efforts were voluntary. A month after war was declared, the students gave up their spring dance. "Realizing that our little bit might be of great help . . . in giving up our dance we were in some measure at least doing something to help."[13] In another sign of wartime austerity, the class of 1918 did not carry roses at graduation. Three months later, at a party they hosted for the underclasswomen, the seniors "Being blessed with a patriotic spirit . . . limited our refreshments to a strictly war-time dish—apples."[14]

Other, more significant sacrifices were ordered by the government. Strict food rationing meant that beef could no longer be served as often as the school dietitian wished. Initial regulations stipulated that there could be no beef served on Sunday, Tuesday, or Friday, a rule modified later in the war. As substitutes, liver and tongue were added to the school menu. Food prices skyrocketed. From the fall of 1917 to January 1918, the price of butter rose a penny a pound (and the school consumed thirty pounds of butter daily). The price of chicken rose from 27 cents to 35 cents a pound. Oysters, haddock, bluefish, cod,

This is one of the few actual photographs of Emma Hart Willard. She disliked most photos of herself, preferring the less realistic portrayals of portraits. This was probably taken just after the Civil War.

Although this modest frame house in Berlin, Connecticut, has been modernized and expanded, it retains characteristics of the original Hart homestead. Located on Lower Lane, it was the farmhouse occupied by Samuel Hart and his wife, Lydia Hinsdale Hart, when Emma and her youngest sibling, Almira were born.

This flyer advertises the Waterford Female Academy, the second site of Emma Willard's school and her first venture in New York. Waterford Female Academy was the first school for girls chartered by the New York State legislature.

Waterford Female Academy.

Incorporated by the Legislature of the State of N. York. The studies comprehended in the Plan of instruction in this seminary are

Reading, English Grammar, Geography, (ancient and modern) and Arithmetic.   at pr. Quarter, of 12 weeks, - - - - - - $ 6,00

Additional charges for the following studies will be made, Viz. For Rhetoric, History, Writing, Elements of Geometry, Logic, Natural Philosophy, Elements of Criticism, Moral Philosophy, and the Philosophy of the mind. - - - - - $ 2,00

Music, - - - - - -	10,00
Drawing and Painting, - - -	4,00
French Language, - - -	4,00

Dancing, if required, at a price not exceding 5,00 No pupil can be received for a less term than one quarter. Board will be furnished at $ 2,25 pr. Week, and the Quarter, Bills must be paid the one half in advance, the other half at the end of the Term.

The Students will be expected to furnish themselves with Beds and the necessary covering ; or an additional charge will be made for the accomodation.

The advantages to be derived from this institution are unquestionable—the situation is healthy and pleasant, the Teachers able and accomplished, and, whilst unceasing efforts will be directed to insure the great object of instruction, the character of the Seminary will recommend itself to the attention of the Public.

N. B. The next term will commence on the 3d, day of May.

By order of the Trustees
JOHN KNICKERBACKER, Jnr. Secretary.
WATERFORD, March 11, 1820.

Amos Eaton, co-founder in 1824 of the institution that would become today's Rensselaer, was instrumental in the development of early science education at the school. Not only did he prepare a special series of science lectures for the students at the seminary, he also tutored Emma Willard's sister, Almira, in botany and chemistry.

This marker for Sarah Pierce's Litchfield Academy in Litchfield, Connecticut, bears testimony to the competing claims of early girls' schools. Sarah Pierce's school opened before Emma Willard's, and, like Willard, she taught chemistry and mathematics to her pupils. However, the Litchfield School did not survive for long after Sarah Pierce's death in the 1830s.

The wallpaper in the Lafayette Alcove in Sage Hall depicts the historic visit of the Marquis de Lafayette to the Troy Female Seminary in 1824. A young Emma Willard curtsies to the visiting hero in the lower left portion of the picture.

This is an early illustration of Mrs. Willard's school, probably drawn before the Erie Canal brought the traffic and trade that boosted the city's economy and spurred its phenomenal growth.

The Seminary's fame spread in part because of newspaper accounts of the public examinations held at the end of each term and attended by parents and interested citizens, mostly male. Girls stood and answered questions posed by a panel of examiners who were most often professors and ministers whom Emma Willard invited to participate.

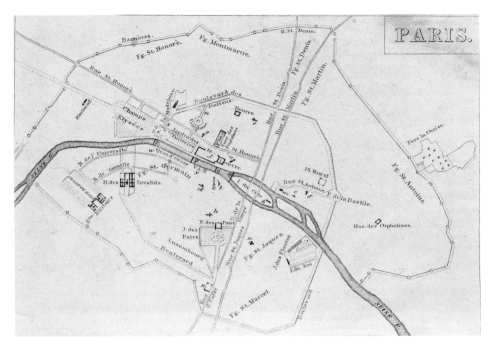

Emma Willard included this map of Paris in her Journal and Letters from France and Great-Britain. She drew extremely well and always included maps and charts in her geography and history textbooks. She donated the proceeds from the sale of this volume to the founding of a school for girls in Athens, Greece.

By 1835 the Seminary had been enlarged, and a new federal courthouse had been built across Second St. from the school, evidence of Troy's growing regional importance.

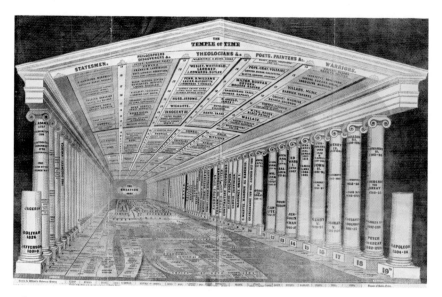

One of Emma Willard's most famous graphic depictions of history, the "Temple of Time" was awarded a gold prize at the Great Exhibition in London in 1851.

A huge crowd greets Troy soldiers who have been fighting for the Yankee cause. The welcoming arch spans Second St. near present-day Monument Square just a few blocks north of the school.

After the Erie Canal opened, river traffic on the Hudson between Troy and New York increased dramatically. The city's waterfront was filled with piers and warehouses, and boats of all descriptions plied the water along Troy's shore.

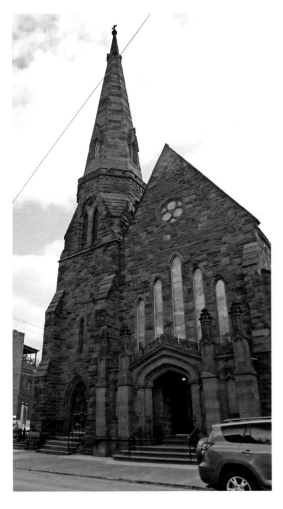

A devout worshipper at St. John's Church on First St. for much of her adult life, Emma paid for a new steeple for the church with insurance money she received after a favorite niece, Jane Lincoln '37, was killed in a railroad accident near Burlington, New Jersey, in 1855.

This photo shows an early science laboratory. In the early to mid 19th century girls who graduated from the school often had a better science education than the classically trained young men who were graduating from liberal arts colleges.

Jane Bancroft '71 was the first Troy student to earn a doctorate, receiving a Ph.D., from Syracuse University in 1877. She later served as dean of women at Northwestern University before her marriage to George Robinson. In 2010, Johns Hopkins University, in conjunction with a local hospital, announced the establishment of the Jane Bancroft Robinson, a $75M fund to provide grants for programs intended to serve impoverished populations.

Lily W. Price '72 attended the school during the same era as Jane Bancroft. After inheriting a fortune from her first husband, she married the impoverished eighth Duke of Marlborough and thus became Winston Churchill's aunt. Although she moved in very different circles from Jane Bancroft, she was considered to be intelligent and well-educated. She managed her money and her British estate herself—and wisely.

In the late 19th century, Troy earned the nickname "Collar City" because of the thriving collar and shirt industry. At one point 90% of the detachable collars worn by American men were manufactured in Troy. As was true in the Manhattan garment industry, the vast majority of the workers were women; the supervisors were male.

In 1891 the alumnae organized as the Emma Willard Association, elected Margaret Olivia Slocum Sage as their president, and held regular meetings and banquets in New York City. This menu card from the sixth annual banquet of the association is typical—and reflects the social position of the women who formed the E.W.A.

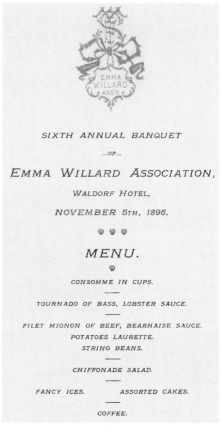

SIXTH ANNUAL BANQUET

...OF...

EMMA WILLARD ASSOCIATION,

WALDORF HOTEL,

NOVEMBER 5TH, 1896.

❀ ❀ ❀

MENU.

❀

CONSOMME IN CUPS.

TOURNADO OF BASS, LOBSTER SAUCE.

FILET MIGNON OF BEEF, BEARNAISE SAUCE.
POTATOES LAURETTE.
STRING BEANS.

CHIFFONADE SALAD.

FANCY ICES.   ASSORTED CAKES.

COFFEE.

A very wealthy woman after she married Russell Sage, Margaret O. Slocum '47 had taught school for years before marrying the financier when she was 41. She never forgot the education she had received nor the hardships she had endured living on a teacher's salary. Her many gifts to her alma mater reflected both.

In 1895 the alumnae gathered in Troy for two reasons. Thanks to a gift from Russell Sage, a new dormitory, Russell Sage Hall, had opened, enabling the school to resume operations as a boarding school. On the same day Sage Hall was dedicated, the Alumnae Association unveiled a statue of Emma Willard.

The new dormitory had a formal dining hall where teachers and boarders ate their meals. Dining room waitresses served three meals a day, and students sat at tables set with linens, china, and silver.

When Sage Hall opened in 1895, it joined Gurley Memorial Hall and Anna M. Plum Memorial Hall to form a new downtown campus. The old seminary building was torn down, and the Alumnae Association renamed the school in honor of the founder.

These happy girls are piled onto a bed in Sage Hall on the downtown campus just after the turn of the twentieth century.

When the board of trustees began negotiating for land for a new campus, they turned to the east side of Troy where wealthy citizens were beginning to build big homes that would remove them from the industrial pollution in the air and water of downtown Troy. These three little girls are playing in a field on the site of the Mount Ida campus. All three would graduate from the school in the early 1920s.

When Constance Appleby toured women's colleges in the early 1900s to introduce American girls to field hockey, she visited Emma Willard and held a workshop on the sport. In this photograph Emma students practice the techniques that Appleby taught them. The field was located somewhere within walking distance of the school.

This panoramic view of the construction of Sage and Slocum was perhaps taken from the roof of the new gymnasium.

With the walls of the gymnasium rising in the background, a craftsman carves gargoyles to adorn the new building.

In 1910 the gymnasium included state-of-the-art gymnastics equipment and an elevated running track along the wall.

Eliza Kellas took over the school in 1911. She was a relatively young woman at that point, but when she retired in 1942, she was 78 years old.

Union Station was one of the largest, most ornate railroad stations in the country when Troy was at its economic peak.

In the early years, Emma Hart Willard accepted students ranging in age from eight to thirty. By the late nineteenth century, the school had a primary, intermediate and high school division, with most of the "little girls" coming from Troy and the surrounding area. At formal meetings, students were seated from youngest to oldest, with the smaller pupils in the front.

In 1914 the school celebrated its 100th anniversary. A big part of the celebration was a pageant in which students played a number of roles, including Revolutionary soldiers under the command of Emma's father, Colonel Samuel Hart.

Ellen Manchester wrote the first Revels, which was performed in January, 1916. Although the show has changed greatly over time, the jester has been a central character from the first.

June Day, which evolved into May Day, was one of the many traditions started by Eliza Kellas. This performance, although undated, probably took place around 1920.

After World War I and throughout the 1920s, more and more families sought admission to the school for their daughters. Eliza Kellas pushed the trustees to add a dormitory, and when the new dormitory was built in 1928, it was named in her honor.

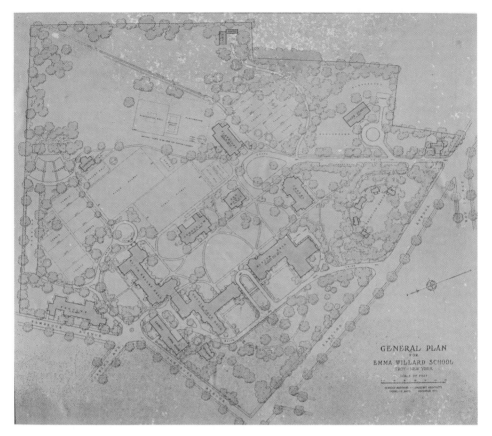

When the Playhouse burned down, the board of trustees commissioned a master plan for future campus needs. Unfortunately, by the time this plan was complete, the Great Depression had the nation—and the school—in its grip.

During World War II, an advanced art class painted murals on the walls of Slocum basement. Like this one, the murals reflected the assault on democratic institutions by the fascist totalitarian governments against whom the U.S. troops were battling.

In spite of the Depression, Eliza Kellas insisted on going ahead with plans for a new, modern science building, citing the school's historic commitment to science education for young women. Weaver Hall, named for longtime science chair, Katherine Weaver, opened in 1937.

The Class of 1950 was the first class to graduate under the renowned "Correlated Curriculum" that was the hallmark of the Wellington-Lay administration. Their senior skit reflected their awareness of their special status as the first to experience the new curriculum.

Having a young, male principal with a young wife and young children was a novelty on the campus. Not since John and Sarah Willard ran the school in the 1840s and 1850s had such youth and family life graced the campus.

The library had long been the center of academic life, and the school had outgrown the library space in Slocum. Bill Dietel and the trustees raised the money for a new state-of-the-art facility that could house the book collection as well as new audio-visual technology, the music department, and, eventually, the fine arts.

The 1960s were in full swing, but things remained very formal at Emma Willard. Under Bill Dietel's leadership, however, the civil rights movement came to the campus through his positive outreach to black families and insistence that students be made aware of the national movement for black equality.

These students were allowed to go to Ohio to work on Carl Stokes' successful campaign to become the mayor of Cleveland and thus the first black mayor of a major metropolitan city.

H-209   CHORAL MASTERPIECES
        Mr. Cunningham   2 units
            A survey of the choral tradition in Western music from its beginnings
        with early polyphony through the new forms of the Italian Renaissance and
        Reformation Baroque and concluding with 19th and 20th century developments;
        specific examples from the major forms (mass, motet, cantata, oratorio) will be
        studied. There will be several opportunities for students to demonstrate
        their knowledge in writing.
            2nd - M,W,F   open to: 10/11/12

H-214c ECONOMIC ACTION
        Mr. Moon   2 units
            A project oriented course to analyze specific economic problems and
        identify solutions. Skills developed in the Fall and Winter will be used to
        encourage independent, well considered judgements and action plans on policy
        issues such as natural resource and population control, the local economic
        environment and other topics. While much of the work will be done individually,
        periodic reports will be made to the group.
            Prerequisites: THE ECONOMIC FUTURE (H-214b).
            4th - W,F   open to: 11/12

H-218   FRANCE IN THE EIGHTEENTH CENTURY
        Staff   2 units
            French culture in the age of the Enlightenment; the thirst for freedom
        and the rise of the democratic spirit; the decline of the monarchy under
        Louis XV and Louis XVI and the early days of the Revolution. The rococo
        style in the arts; satire, idealism and emerging romanticism in literature.
        Assignments in reading, listening and viewing. One short research paper will
        be required.
            (Note: Enrollment in this course is not limited. This course will
        meet as a large group.)
            Prerequisites: None; FRANCE IN THE SEVENTEENTH CENTURY (H-217) is strongly
        recommended.
            1st - M,Tu,Th,F   open to: 11/12

H-223   HOW IT WORKS: AN INTRODUCTION TO TECHNICS
        Mr. Homan   2 units
            This course is an experimental approach to a proposed full year course in
        industrialism. In it, the student will be introduced to significant inventions
        and new processes as they have appeared during man's history. No doubt we
        will start with the wheel. Emphasis will be placed on the effect of these
        various break-throughs in technique. Visual aids will be used generously as
        well as working models wherever possible. The course is envisioned as operating
        on a credit/no credit basis. There will be occasional written exercises.
            7th - Tu,Th   open to: 10/11/12

In the 1970s, the school adopted an almost entirely elective curriculum. This page from
the voluminous course catalogue shows the breadth of offerings.

Since the conversion of the gymnasium into a chapel in the 1950s, the school had gone many years without a dedicated athletic facility. Title IX legislation spurred an increased interest in sports among young women, and the school responded by building a new gym.

During the early 1980s Harvard researcher Carol Gilligan conducted a study of female adolescent moral development at the school. Here she confers with Bob Parker.

EMMA WILLARD SCHOOL
ROBISON FAMILY TIMING SYSTEM

READY
SET
CELEBRATE !

In 1997, thanks to the generosity of Helen Cheel '23 and others, the antiquated swimming pool in the basement of the chapel was finally replaced with a swimming pool appropriate for competition.

In the first years of the twenty-first century, the campus has received a multi-million dollar makeover. The first floors of the dormitory have been redesigned for multiple student uses, and great care and attention have gone into preserving and restoring the historic architecture. The gargoyles that guard the tower were removed and the stone parapets repaired. Here a gargoyle soars back to his perch high above the school.

mackerel, halibut, flounder, shad, Pollock, finnan haddie, and smelt, all cheaper than chicken, became staples of the school diet. When the United States entered the war, the kitchen was feeding 137 students a day, 20 teachers, and 40 residential staff members. These people consumed on average 234 pounds of meat a day, 90 gallons of milk, and 17 quarts of cream. In October 1917, the school purchased 1,451 pounds of beef for $299.67, and in October 1919, 792 pounds for $317.70. The total cost of food rose from $21,668.98 in 1917 to $27,093.75 in 1919. Nor was food the only area hit by inflation during—and immediately after—the war. Total costs including food, power, ice, and coal rose 20.89 percent from 1917 to 1918 and another 18.89 percent from 1918 to 1919. Tuition rose from a maximum of $1,100 in 1917–18 to $1,200 in 1918–19 to $1,400 in 1919–20.[15] Day prices also rose; high school day students paid $175 per year in 1919–20.

The end of the war brought great rejoicing. On Armistice Day, Miss Kellas called off classes and most uncharacteristically instructed the students "to yell, so we proceeded to obey all afternoon."[16] Her elation was tempered by sorrow. She had suffered a personal loss during the war when Billy Cheney, the youngest of the three children she had cared for before coming to the school, had been killed in an aviation training flight in Italy. He was nineteen years old, on leave from Harvard. His mother was comforted, she wrote to her old friend, by knowing that he had done his part, a sentiment shared by many as they counted the cost of the war. In this vein the editors of *Triangle* declared triumphantly that "the most frightful struggle in history is over" and "Right has triumphed over Might."[17]

However, not all students believed the postwar truism that this had been a "war to end all wars." The same issue of *Triangle* contained a short story by E. L. '19. (The author was probably Elinor Lodge, a day student whose father was a chemist and whose brother was an army officer.) "Gassed" was the grimly realistic story of a man who committed suicide after working in a chemistry laboratory to create poison gas during the war. He explains to the narrator that he is very pessimistic about the future and does not believe the recent war will end war because "they've got university professors, nice kindly lookin' sort of men, chemistry students, and druggists, hundreds of fellows just like me who come from little towns all over the country . . . working, studying and plotting in cold blood to invent a new and more effective form of agony."[18]

While Eliza Kellas shielded her students socially from much that was modern and radical, she did not do so intellectually. Instead she allowed them to hear lectures from people whose opinions might not have pleased the students' fathers, the vast majority of whom voted Republican.[19] For example, in the spring of 1919, students heard five lectures on "Problems with the Peace Conference," given by Dr. Henry Huntington Powers, a professor at Cornell and the president of the Bureau of University Travel. Powers pointed to the Arab world as an area of future concern, predicting that the persecution of Jews worldwide would destabilize world peace sometime in the future. A few years later, she took the entire school to see the silent film classic *The Big Parade*, the first Hollywood attempt to show the horror of trench warfare and to call into question the value of the heroic sacrifices made during the Great War.

In January 1918, Eliza Kellas had written to a friend that "there won't be much left of me when peace comes." Food shortages, tight budgets, personal loss, and the general strain of living through a major war all contributed to her weariness, but there was one major reason for her exhaustion. In 1916, at the urging and with the support of Olivia Sage, she had created a college for women on the grounds of the old female seminary. In later years she regarded this as the accomplishment she valued "most highly,"[20] but in 1915 when Olivia Sage asked her to build and lead Russell Sage College, she was reluctant to take on the project.

Much of the work of developing the plans for the college fell to E. Lilian Todd, who, as secretary to the increasingly feeble Mrs. Sage, controlled the information that her boss received. Todd, an unusual woman, became one of Eliza Kellas's greatest champions. An airplane inventor in an era when few men entered aeronautic engineering, Todd was self-taught and had come to Olivia Sage's attention when Sage backed the trial run of one of Todd's airplanes, eager as always to support a woman's project. Shortly thereafter, Todd left aviation to work as Sage's secretary. Requests for Sage's philanthropy were filtered by Todd and the DeForest brothers, the elderly philanthropist's financial and legal advisers; Todd often pressed women's causes in opposition to the desires of the DeForests. She was particularly forceful in getting Mrs. Sage to act on Emma Willard's needs.

In 1915 Eliza Kellas was desperate for a new dormitory; she wrote to Todd that "I have my heart set on that dormitory."[21] Apparently, she had appealed to Mrs. Sage for the funding, but Sage suggested that she use the buildings on the downtown campus, particularly Russell Sage Hall, already outfitted for dormitory use. Todd had to explain to Sage that it was "quite a long ride even in the trolley car."[22] Although Todd realized that Sage Hall on Second Street was unsuitable for an Emma Willard dormitory, she realized that Sage was anxious about the building and wanted it to continue to serve some educational purpose. The YWCA was pressing the board to sell it to them for $25,000, much less than it was worth, and several members of the board with ties to the Y were supporting the transaction. Although Plum Hall still housed the Emma Willard Conservatory of Music (a thriving enterprise technically managed by Eliza Kellas), Gurley Hall was empty after being rented for two years to the city for use as a public school.

In a conversation with Eliza Kellas while she was on campus as Mrs. Sage's representative to the centennial, Lilian Todd had discussed the use of the buildings. In the spring of 1915, she reminded the principal that "You spoke to me of wishing to start some sort of classes in those buildings . . . something that would bring certain forms of education within the reach of girls who could not afford to go to the main school."[23] Perhaps because she herself had been the kind of girl who would have profited from this sort of school, Todd had taken this idea to Mrs. Sage and convinced her this was the perfect use of the old buildings. Mrs. Sage agreed to fund a college similar to Simmons and Pratt, one with a clientele who expected to be self-supporting, and a curriculum that would combine vocational and liberal arts courses. After all, she herself had been self-supporting for the twenty years between her graduation from the seminary and her marriage. She insisted, however, that Eliza Kellas be president of the new college. Writing to Miss Kellas, Todd acknowledged that she knew the educator was "not prepared to take up this school now" but cautioned that it was "now or never, and I think you would prefer to accept Mrs. Sage's offer even at some inconvenience, than to lose the opportunity it may present."[24] Reluctantly, Eliza Kellas agreed, calming alumnae with the message, "I am not leaving Emma Willard School. There will be absolutely no change in my relations with the school or the girls."[25]

The new college was managed by the Emma Willard board of trustees, and the school charter was amended to join the two institutions. In making her gift, Olivia Sage announced her "belief that the new school will fill a useful and important field and that its conduct by the Emma Willard School will extend the usefulness and scope of that institution."[26] At first, Mrs. Sage gave the new project only $250,000, but at Todd's urging, she almost immediately raised that amount to half a million dollars; within a few years, Emma Willard had contributed another half a million, so the initial stake for the college was a million dollars. It was not nearly enough. As Todd explained to De-Forest, tuition alone would never offset expenses because "the income derived from a school of this sort cannot be large because the pupils will be unable to pay high tuition rates."[27] The target population for the new college was young women who planned to work to support themselves. As a contemporary journal had reported, mimicking Whitman, there was a growing population composed of the "ordinary, everyday-go-to-work girl who . . . runs to catch a trolley-car, jostles you in the subway, and patronizes what . . . she calls the 'movies.' It is in fact the goddess of the typewriter, the fairy of the newspaper office, the grace of the telephone that I sing."[28]

On December 23, 1915, Olivia Sage sent the Emma Willard trustees the formal offer of her gift. She named the new college the Russell Sage School of Practical Arts and stipulated,

> The Emma Willard School shall appropriate and set apart for the use of the new school the old school site and buildings in the City of Troy.
>
> The standard of work and study at the school shall be at least equal to the standard maintained at . . . Simmons . . . and the Pratt Institute
>
> Miss Eliza Kellas shall be . . . Directress of the school at an

appropriate salary which shall be in addition to the compensation she is now receiving from the Emma Willard School.

I make this offer in the belief that the new school will fill a useful and important field and that its conduct by the Emma Willard School will extend the usefulness and scope of that institution.[29]

She would subsequently agree to changing the name to Russell Sage College as long as the institution continued to provide "instruction of high character in practical arts."[30] The curriculum for the new college was divided into Secretarial Work, Household Economics, and Industrial Arts. The course in secretarial work included foreign language and English in addition to practical subjects like accounting, typewriting, and stenography. Miss Kellas found no conflict between the liberal arts and vocational studies. She wrote, "There exists between the liberal and the vocation aim no real contradiction; none between the cultural and the practical aim . . . liberal education is vocational; and vocational education, at its best, is liberal."[31] In spite of Miss Kellas's ability to craft a point of intersection between the school and the college, it was an unequal partnership. The school was wealthier, as were its pupils. The tuition at the school was much higher than the tuition at the college, its endowment greater. From the first, Russell Sage College enrolled far more Roman Catholic and Jewish girls than were admitted to Emma Willard. In 1920 Father Leo Clark of St. Mary's urged a reluctant Eliza Kellas to allow a Newman Club on campus because of the "goodly number of Catholic girls."[32] Local Jewish girls also found the college to be a hospitable place. In general, according to Lilian Todd, Troy embraced the new college more fervently than they did the school. In a memorandum to Mrs. Sage, she commented that in Troy "everybody was speaking of you as if you were a deliverer . . . they speak of it as the 'Resurrection of Troy' by you. . . . They do not feel the same way about the school on the hill—those girls could be paid for anywhere by their parents."[33]

Although not considered a problem at the time, wealthy Emma Willard alumnae were persuaded to support the new college. For example, the Troy EWA quickly established an annual scholarship for a day student at Russell Sage, and Mrs. Cyrus McCormick (Nettie Fowler '53) and Mrs. Sage both provided tuition aid for deserving young women to attend the college. (Sage, of course, also donated to scholarships at the school, but there is no record of McCormick ever doing so.) As the school prospered and the college struggled, the trustees made periodic gifts to the college, including a nearly $50,000 loan that was forgiven when the college was unable to repay it during the Depression.

In spite of its financial issues, Russell Sage College was an immediate success. Projected to open with 60 students, there were 170 on opening day, 1916, an opening delayed by two weeks because of a record-breaking outbreak of polio in the state.[34] Not only did it attract the young women it was created to educate, it numbered among its first class two graduates of Emma Willard and Vassar who wanted to learn the practicalities of domestic science. In spite of the many differences between the two institutions, over the years, many young women with Emma Willard diplomas would enroll at the college.

In agreeing to take on the presidency of Russell Sage, Eliza Kellas clearly hoped to please Olivia Sage enough to convince her to build the dormitory that the school still needed. However, Russell Sage College turned out to be the great philanthropist's last major project. In the fall of 1918, she died, most likely a victim of the influenza, although it counted fewer elderly victims than most diseases of its kind. Todd, who had absorbed the class consciousness of her boss, wrote unfeelingly to Eliza Kellas that the culprit was "one of the maids . . . who had been everywhere cleaning and shaking her dust cloth around, and coughing all over the place."[35] This unfortunate woman, with no option than to work in spite of her illness, died. Mrs. Sage took ill shortly thereafter and died on November 4. She was buried in Oakwood Cemetery in Syracuse next to her parents, not her husband, who rested next to his first wife at Oakwood Cemetery in Troy. No one from the school attended the funeral.

Miss Kellas was left with the charge of the two schools and no possibility of a dormitory from Olivia Sage. Until 1928, she continued in both roles. In December 1927, the Emma Willard School charter changed once again, and the two institutions were separated, with each one having a separate board of trustees and separate finances. The Russell Sage students were ecstatic. They had resented the use of the name Emma Willard School on their college diplomas, reasoning that it weakened their degree in the eyes of future employers. Furthermore, as capable as Eliza Kellas was, she did not have the advanced degree that was almost de rigueur at colleges by this time.

Miss Kellas's ability to supervise both institutions was aided immeasurably by the presence of her sister Katherine, who joined her in Troy in 1916. Five years younger than Eliza, Katherine had followed in her sister's academic footsteps, earning her first degree at Potsdam Normal School three years after Eliza graduated. She later went to the University of Michigan, where she completed her B.A. and M.A. before returning to Potsdam as preceptress. (Kellas Hall at Potsdam is named in honor of both sisters.) In 1916, as plans for Russell Sage College accelerated, board president Paul Cook wrote to Katherine Kellas urging her to take a position at the college. For $2,000 and rooms in Sage, she agreed, becoming the dean of the college, an office she held until 1928 when she resigned along with her sister and assumed the role of assistant and then associate head at the school. She held the latter position at her death in 1941.

Dubbed "Miss Katherine" by students from the late 1920s through the early 1940s, she handled much of the academic minutiae, including scheduling. Her reputation was mixed. Some saw her as a softer, more approachable version of her sister, others as a spy for her sister. A formidable pair, the two sisters together were known, in a parody of schoolgirl Latin, as "the Kellae." Katherine Knowlton McLane '23 remembered "Miss Katherine . . . at the pre-dinner gathering in the living room, putting a friendly arm across our shoulders, which we interpreted as a gesture designed to find out if we were wearing the proper underwear."[36] To her colleague Ellen Manchester, she was modest, retiring, and intellectually stimulating, a professional whose "presence inspired young and old alike to practice the gracious art of consideration."[37] On balance, most students viewed her with affection. Louise Porter Thomas '30 captured her strengths in "Miss Katherine Kellas," a memorial poem:

She lived with dignity.
In order and in graciousness she wrought
The pattern of her busy days and sought
The common good with just and single mind—yet
    Not aloof from us, but always kind,
Ready to laugh should some gay thing befall.
And we who came and went will long recall
How quick her memory would be at meeting
One who returned; how warm her greeting.[38]

As absorbing as was the work of establishing the college, as she had promised, Eliza Kellas never lagged in her attention to the school. She spent the majority of the day on the Mount Ida campus perfecting the school culture that she had honed in her first five years at Emma Willard, a school culture that bore her imprint for the remaining quarter century of her tenure and beyond. Eliza Kellas firmly believed that the academic ability of her pupils was, for the most part, fixed before they came under her charge—and was a function of native intelligence, genetic background, and talents unevenly distributed by a wise, all-knowing God. As a consequence, some students could be prepared for college and some could not, no matter how hard they or their teachers worked. She fervently hoped that all of her graduates would go on to some form of higher education, but she was very hardheaded and realistic about the possibility that not all of them could— or should—expect admission to Smith, Vassar, or Wellesley, the most popular choices in the 1920s and 1930s.

Single herself and by any estimation a successful professional woman, she nevertheless reminded her students that college educated or not, their most important roles in life would be those of wife and mother. For years the catalog expressly stated that the school made an "earnest effort . . . to give the pupils such advantages and training as fit her for social life and her own home."[39] The domestic science curriculum was aimed at young women who would someday run a household. By 1916, the course in domestic science had expanded to include sewing ("to cultivate in each pupil a proper sense of discrimination in the value of materials"), food science ("the dietetic and economic value of foods" as well as physics, chemistry, physiology, and bacteriology "in relationship to cooking"), and household science (which included "choosing a site for a home" and "the selection of furnishings . . . [both] aesthetic and economical").[40] In 1918 the "Homemaking Course" was a carefully proscribed two-year curriculum with coursework based on science (food and nursing) and psychology (child study). Domestic science as a separate curricular choice was a part of the school's offerings throughout the 1920s; girls who opted for this had to take courses in English and mathematics as well.

Students in the domestic course and in the general course actually took more science than students enrolled in the college preparatory curriculum. In addition, the general course students were required to take history of art and, during the 1920s, they could elect a course called "Foreign Travel," which focused on Paris—and presumably prepared them for a year or two of travel to round out their education. The college preparatory curriculum, in contrast, adhered closely to the requirements of Vassar, Smith, Wellesley, and their sister institutions. From World War I until World War II, college preparation focused on basic science and mathematics, four years of Latin, three years of a modern language, four years of English, ancient history, and a year of American history. The reading load in English was heavy and traditional: juniors were required to read *Quentin Durward, As You Like It, Mill on the Floss, Bleak House, The Rivals, The House of the Seven Gables,* and *David Balfour*, in addition to poems, short stories, and some novels of their own choosing (from a list provided by the school), and selections from *The Atlantic Monthly*. As the numbers of college preparatory students increased both numerically and proportionally throughout these two decades, the demand for a separate course in domestic science ended, and the numbers in the general course dwindled. In 1935 the latter was revamped during the Depression to stimulate enrollment by meeting the needs of a wider range of students.

Miss Kellas carefully distinguished between the liberal arts colleges and all other forms of higher education. When Mrs. E. A. Fessenden, mother of Elizabeth Fessenden '32, requested that Elizabeth be placed in advanced mathematics and science classes, Miss Kellas responded that Emma Willard was "a college preparatory school and we give the courses required by the students who are entering college . . . our greatest task is the preparation of girls for college, and while those subjects may be offered, they are not required." She pointed out that Elizabeth was planning to go to Cornell, "not to a college."[41] Furthermore, Kellas questioned the wisdom of Elizabeth's preparation for Cornell, which in her mind was far too narrow. Elizabeth, she cautioned the girl's mother, was in danger of "becoming one-sided. She needs more history, more languages—in fact more general culture."[42]

Elizabeth, like hundreds of Eliza Kellas's students, stayed in touch with her principal after she got to college. From Cornell (where she arrived after spending seven years at Emma Willard, one of the dozens of college preparatory students of that era required to repeat their junior years), she wrote to Miss Kellas that she was absolutely prepared in French and that her Cornell course, in fact, duplicated "word for word" what she had learned in high school. She found herself "struggling" in chemistry, however. She did not blame Emma Willard and its lack of advanced science courses. Instead, she ascribed her difficulties to the sexist climate at the university, commenting, "My roommate and I are the only girls in the class as women chemists are a rather scarce article here."[43] In spite of the dearth of female chemistry students, Elizabeth Fessenden not only graduated from Cornell with a degree in chemistry, she pursued a long career as an analytical chemist and in 1996 earned a Lifetime Achievement Award from the EWS Alumnae Association for her pioneering work in environmental science.

For Eliza Kellas, Fessenden's perseverance in the face of her struggles, rather than her academic prowess, defined her as the right kind of Emma Willard girl. Whether or not her girls went to one of the colleges she prized so highly, to a more technical program at a university, to a nursing or secretarial course, to a two-year "finishing school," traveled, or simply stayed home until marriage—and some graduates of the 1910s, 1920s, and 1930s chose each of these options—Eliza Kellas wanted them to complete what they had begun. The mother of sophomore Elinor Dutcher '33, who had "grown fast and tires easily" and then "had an operation for appendicitis [that] set her back," heard from Miss Kellas that "[Elinor] will have to work hard to accomplish what she wants to do, but then most of us do."[44] As she insisted to Mrs. Dutcher, "It is by the combination of our natural ability and our power of application that we succeed in what we undertake."[45] Eliza Kellas could do little about her students' natural ability, but she could improve their character, and that would increase their chances for success. During the Kellas years, a talented, dedicated faculty taught the history, English, mathematics, science, languages, and arts required by colleges. At the same time, Eliza Kellas taught self-discipline, rigorous habits, humility, ethics, spirituality, fair play, duty, leadership, hard work, and integrity—of course, all these values, in her view, were best understood when viewed through the lens of Christianity as presented in the Protestant Bible.

For Eliza Kellas, what her pupils did with their lives after Emma Willard was far less important than how they lived those lives. Her graduates became presidents of their classes at Smith, Vassar, and Wellesley, teachers, doctors, writers, historians, artists, musicians, chairs of Red Cross chapters and other charities, board members, philanthropists, mothers of large and small families, and wives of local civic leaders and national political figures, including ambassadors and cabinet secretaries. These accomplishments mattered, but not nearly as much as how they conducted themselves.

It is almost impossible to exaggerate the importance of Eliza Kellas herself in the development of her pupils' character. She modeled everything she espoused, and her students were acutely aware of the standard she set and the many ways in which they fell short. Her maxims were legendary and remained vivid, long-lasting memories. Many of them were etched in the rule book and reinforced visually on the minds of their readers. Famous among those was the edict, "A lady never throws anything from the window, including her voice." Others came in daily conversations about behavior and in weekly homilies that supplemented the required chapel services on campus. Nearly twenty years after she graduated, Isabelle Adie '32 listed her favorites:

When in doubt, don't.
Do not be bounded by your own four walls.
Do you think Grace Coolidge *knew* that someday she would be First Lady?[46]

Many Kellas imperatives had to do with conducting oneself properly. She valued good posture, shipshape room care, precise diction, and a neat personal appearance; they were all part of the code of conduct that was characteristic of the model ladies she expected her students to become. For example, she exhorted them that "A lady never carries anything heavier than a jewel case." Only in tenements were articles placed on windowsills. It was a Kellas dictum that "No lady ever lifts her hands above her waist in public,"[47] a rule that prevented such unseemly behavior as powdering one's nose in front of others. Proud of her own chestnut mane, which she wore piled on top of her head, adding to her already considerable height, she reminded her students that "a woman's hair is her crowning glory."[48] Slang was invariably corrected. One student who asked permission to telephone her "folks" was told, "You may always have permission to telephone your parents, Jeanne, but never your folks."[49]

Taken all together, the maxims and rules contributed to a community "designed for refined, earnest, trustworthy girls."[50] The school community counted far more than any one individual. Eliza Kellas had no patience for self-expression, which she disdained as "a growing trend [that] has been dinned at us until we are weary."[51] Whether the topic was integrity or the proper way to sit or dress, Miss Kellas's advice seemed to emanate from on high. As a member of the class of 1919 recalled, "Even in her little talks in the study hall when she told you such things as what it is to be a lady, she had the truth and power of an oracle."[52] As Carolyn Hull Curry '28 recalled, "She set before us ideals of behavior, of achievement, of living that always aspired to the best."[53]

She might disdain self-expression, but Eliza Kellas valued self-development. As in everything else, the principal expected her students to adhere to high standards of dress and hygiene, and she also expected them to monitor themselves in these respects. In the 1920s, students were asked to maintain a "Daily Record of Health Habits," checking each day their adherence to sixteen daily routines, including "Slept with window open," "Kept feet well protected," "Hastened to remove damp clothing," ""Drank at least six glasses of water," "Spent one hour out-of-doors or exercising," "Took neither tea nor coffee," "Maintained good posture," and "Did not worry."[54] The dress code changed slightly from year to year, but it was always detailed and specific. Precise clothing regulations applied to everything from coats to underwear. By 1913 Miss Kellas had settled on a navy blue serge suit with a red tie designed by Peter Thompson, a clothier noted for outfitting schoolgirls and college women everywhere. Parents were advised that "The skirt and waist of this suit must be fastened together making it a one-piece suit."[55] In warmer weather a linen version of the outfit was allowed. Silk underwear was forbidden, probably because it would not survive the school laundry, which already had to deal with "Bust Supporters," "Corset Waists . . . Corset Covers [both gauze and cotton] . . . Linen Collars . . . Cotton and Woolen Drawers . . . Kimonos . . . [and] Petticoats (White, Colored and Flannel)."[56]

The Peter Thompson "middy" was the standard uniform until 1932, although women's fashions changed dramatically in the Roaring Twenties. During that decade, skirts rose from the floor to the knee, and stylish pumps replaced lace-up shoes. A boyish silhouette topped by bobbed hair became the ideal look. On Mount Ida the uniform skirt got a little shorter, but it was still "a bit stodgy,"[57] especially when compared to the flapper costumes advertised by Troy department stores in the pages of *Triangle* and the *Gargoyle*. Hairdos, however, one of the few things outside school control, showed the influence of current fashion. Bobbed hair, which evolved from the shorter styles worn by working women during the war, was popularized by F. Scott Fitzgerald in his first *Saturday Evening Post* story, "Bernice Bobs Her Hair." Bobs became *the* look for the modern girl. By 1925 every senior at Emma Willard sported the new look.

Eliza Kellas might not have indulged her pupils, but she most certainly cared deeply for them. Not only did she provide them with tireless guidance, she also worked tirelessly on their behalf. When Suzanne Whidden Ward '40 woke up in the hospital after an emergency appendectomy, Eliza Kellas was sitting by her bed. Priscilla O'Connell Kinney '39 remembered 6 A.M. tutoring sessions from the principal she called "the biggest influence in my life."[58] In 1924 Eliza Kellas remained at school during the Christmas vacation because, "just before school closed, one of the girls developed scarlet fever and was obliged to be here in quarantine . . . necessitating standing by the ship."[59] To stand by the ship was just one of her duties; additionally, she was "educational director, financial manager, dormitory supervisor, as well as mother pro tem and spiritual advisor of 250 resident pupils."[60]

Her advice did not stop with graduation. Miss Kellas's correspondence with alumnae was legion, and over time she lent them money, advised them on jobs and marriage, offered child-rearing suggestions, and supported them in difficult times. Learning that a former pupil was suffering from an abusive husband, she helped her secure a divorce and find a job. Eking out a living in New York during the Depression, another alumna wrote to her former principal, "One thing that . . . helps a great deal in my work is your telling us that although one may be disappointed, she must never be discouraged."[61] A young alumna in college, struggling with depression, wrote to her, "This is the first time I have unburdened myself to anyone . . . you, more than anyone can understand."[62] Extant letters to academic deans and directors of residence regarding Emma Willard students during their collegiate years document the sweep of her concern for the students she always called "my girls," no matter how old they were. Expecting her first child, Adeline Aldrich '19 sent the news to Miss Kellas with the observation that "When the time comes, I hope there will be someone as wise and understanding as I had to supervise her education so that what she learns will become for her, as it did for me, an enduring basis for happiness and growth."[63]

Of course, there were those who chafed under the strictures. As Miss Kellas recognized, "The change from a home in which one is the center . . . is more difficult for some pupils than others."[64] However, even those who hated the confinement seemed to take something good from their association with Eliza Kellas. The Hollywood actress Emily Lawrence, who attended the school as Emily Abel '33, commented wryly fifty years later that the school was "good for me—as good as a needed dose of milk of magnesia."[65] Throughout her life, however, whether she was working in Hollywood or on a USO tour of Europe with Katherine Cornell, she maintained a correspondence with her principal, at one time writing, "Your familiar words . . . haunt my life."[66]

Miss Kellas's active guidance was the primary force in molding student character, but she shaped her students' value system in another way as well. She encouraged their development as leaders and good citizens by instituting a great number of student activities designed to foster a student community that prized leadership, cooperation, a sense of duty, sound decision making, and philanthropy. She emphasized competition among the four high school classes and made the senior year so special that all underclasswomen aspired to be seniors one day. Student leaders readily adopted the credo of senior responsibility that she espoused. A typical *Triangle* editorial, for example, noted, "Of course it's hard not to talk in Study Hall; of course the proctor who reports us . . . seems awfully mean. . . . Do you think she likes to report anyone? She's just shouldering her responsibility."[67]

To reinforce the status of the senior class, Miss Kellas almost immediately established multiple senior traditions. Among these were the "senior annual," *Gargoyle*, the Senior Feast, the Senior Dance, the Senior Play, the Emma Willard birthday lunch for the seniors given by the alumnae association, Ivy Day, step-singing, June Day, and the seniors' ownership of the triangular piece of lawn in front of the gymnasium. Seniors—often with Eliza Kellas at their head—led the popular and frequent snake dances, a dormitory ritual that followed special meals, especially the annual October 4 celebration of the principal's birthday. The seniors chaired the school government, served as dormitory proctors and academic monitors, and they headed school government, the Athletic Council, the Mandolin Club, the Glee Club, and the Christian Association. The editor in chief of *Triangle* was always a senior. At least once a week, Miss Kellas met with the resident members of the senior class after dinner in the Yellow Parlor,[68] which was actually the sitting room for the faculty who lived with her in the suite of teachers' rooms on the first floor of Sage. Eliza Kellas set the tone and agenda for the year; senior class officers were elected early in the fall to avoid undue influence from the outgoing senior class that might not jibe completely with the principal's plans. As she explained it, "The preceding class passes on to the incoming Seniors a great many ideas that perhaps would just as well be omitted."[69] Each year Eliza Kellas favored the senior class, and, for the most part, they returned the sentiment. Thirty-one volumes of the yearbook were produced between its inception in 1912 and her retirement in 1942. Over half of them were dedicated to her.

In addition to making senior leadership central to school culture, Miss Kellas also emphasized competition. She instituted Field Day and Prize Day. Field Day occurred in November and culminated in field hockey and basketball games that pitted the juniors against the seniors. From 1918 on, the two classes alternated wearing purple and green, and the victors received large silver cups to commemorate their triumph. Senior honor was at stake. Chronicling her senior year Field Day, Elesa Scott '27 wrote in her scrapbook, "Oh the thrill! Seniors won both hockey and basketball."[70] Eliza Kellas believed that competition, whether in games, classes, or elections, taught sportsmanship and fair play to winners and losers alike, and the range of prize-worthy activities revealed the various areas of school life in which students could strive to be best. On the first Prize Day in 1912, awards were given for prowess in tennis and track and for maintaining perfect attendance records. In 1913 Eliza Kellas herself provided a cup for highest overall scholarship, and Olivia Sage provided a $50 gold piece for the greatest improvement in English. Other alumnae over the years funded awards in German and French. In 1923 Helen Snell '23 carried off a bowling trophy, and her classmate, Clementine Miller, captured the prize for the highest score on the General Information Test.[71] Over time, awards for neatness, posture, and outstanding achievement in most academic disciplines were added.

In 1915, in conjunction with the new emphasis on athletic competition, Eliza Kellas began the tradition of bestowing the EW award on a small group of senior girls. At its inception, the EW was an athletic award, given for "promotion of athletics, school and class spirit . . . to seniors only."[72] The process for selecting the EW winners was spelled out in the bylaws for the Athletic Association, published in 1919. According to Article II,

> The E.W. shall be a general award, given by the athletic department. The selection of the E.W.'s shall originate first with the nomi-

nations of the senior class; secondly, to be approved by a committee ·of three, consisting of the president of the student Government, the president of the Student Association, and the president of the Athletic Association; thirdly, to be approved by a committee consisting of four academic teachers and the head athletic instructor.[73]

The award evolved from athletics to more general citizenship over time. An edition of *Triangle* in 1920 explained that the EW was given to "girls of the senior class not only for athletic ability but also for splendid spirit and influence in all school activities."[74] By 1923 the winners had to meet "certain requirements in Athletics, Scholarship, Spirit, Poise and Self-Control, Influence and Neatness."[75] By 1926 there was a point system, with 25 points each being awarded for athletics, school spirit, and influence, 15 points for poise and self-control, and 10 points for neatness.[76] By 1940 the award had assumed its modern form in most respects. EW winners were "based on cooperation in upholding and supporting school standards and activities, positive contributions as in character, personality and leadership; and adequate scholarship, both in fulfilling academic requirements and making a sincere effort."[77] Meanwhile, the school had joined the national Cum Laude society in 1928, thereafter inviting the leading senior scholars into Cum Laude membership. The EW and membership in Cum Laude became and remain among the most prestigious awards at the school.

Like EW and Cum Laude, many other traditions started by Eliza Kellas early in her tenure have survived into the twenty-first century. By far the most beloved of these traditions has become a senior ritual, although it did not start out that way. In 1915 Eliza Kellas asked English instructor Ellen Manchester to create "a Christmas fête in the old English manner." Miss Manchester immediately recognized that the "Gothic assembly hall and library furnished a perfect setting." Hoping to create "that blend of the secular and religious which was the essence of the ancient celebration,"[78] Miss Manchester created a pageant with three episodes. First came the Boar's Head Procession, next the Procession of Wise Men, and third, the Yule Log Procession.

The cast for the first Revels included a herald, torchbearers, minstrels bearing a boar's head and a plum pudding, the Lord of Misrule,

King Wencellas [sic] and his page, twelve Morris dancers, the bearer of the star, the wise men, each with his own page, four shepherds, Father Christmas, four Yule log pages, and a Yule log sprite. The Glee Club played many of the parts; of forty-four girls in the cast, twenty-five were Glee Club singers. The full cast included students in ninth through twelfth grades. Seniors played the herald, one of the torchbearers, a bearer of the plum pudding, and one of the Yule log pages. Juniors played the Lord of Misrule, King Wencellas, the bearer of the star, most of the Morris dancers, Father Christmas, and a number of pages. Two freshmen played pages for the wise men.

Carols dominated the show. The boar's head procession entered the hall singing "God Rest Ye, Merry Gentleman," followed by "Good King Wencellas," which introduced the arrival of that king. In the second episode, the Wise Men entered singing "We Three Kings," and the cast sang "Adeste Fideles," "What Child Is This," "The First Noel," and "From Far Away We Come to You." A line in the chorus of the last of these carols, "Minstrels and maids, stand forth on the floor," signaled the Morris dancing. Finally came the Yule log procession. After circling the hall, the pages pulled the Yule log to the library where the log was actually cast into the fireplace. Cast and audience were then treated to a feast and more caroling, and Eliza Kellas pronounced, "Tonight something has been started, which will, I believe, become a school tradition.[79]

No words were more prophetic. A year later, Revels had already become "an established custom."[80] In 1917 a second performance was added to accommodate the parents and alumnae who wanted to see the show. That same year the lord and lady of the manor house and their guests made their first appearance. In 1918 the Mummers were introduced: lantern bearers, the King of Egypt and his daughter; St. George, the Turkish knight, and the doctor took the stage, to be joined two years later by the hobby horse. Four years after that Beelzebub joined the cast, and in 1926 Cleverlegs, an encephalitic village idiot, provided comic relief for an audience used to humor based on disability and difference. (Vaudeville shows routinely used ethnic dialogue and stereotypes to entertain; the humor section of *Triangle* regularly included jokes about African Americans and Irishmen, casually referred to "darkies" and "Paddy.")

Cleverlegs aside, Revels quickly became synonymous with Emma Willard in December, as "bound up with thoughts of Christmas as hanging up a stocking."[81] In 1923 Julia Melcher '18, one of the first heralds, wrote to the editors of *Triangle* that she always thought of Revels at Christmas and wondered "who is carrying our horn and if she forgot her words as [I] did and sang the first verse over and no one noticed it."[82] The editors agreed that "Revels are really beyond description."[83] Eight years later, a new generation of editors concurred: "There are no words to describe Revels."[84] Yet they tried. An editorial in 1933 characterized Revels as "an illumination of our school spirit." Revels was "the very spirit of artistic loveliness" with its music, dancing, color, and history. Maintaining that "an appreciation of beauty is an Emma Willard characteristic," the editors found that "our inherent as well as our cultivated love of beauty is centered and finds an outlet in Revels." While acknowledging that Revels celebrated a Christian holy day, they suggested that the significance of its spirituality came in its fusion with art, a blend "of high ideals and standards" that would "become [their] own when we too must leave these 'gray arched walls.'"[85] Revels, initially a Christmas show for the boarding population, became an annual tradition, with roots that were both strong enough and flexible enough to withstand cultural changes from generation to generation.

In the twenty-seven performances under Miss Kellas's reign, seniors dominated the cast, but girls from sixth grade on had roles, and some girls took part for more than one year, often in the same role. The first Revels after Miss Kellas retired was the first time that the senior class "as a whole participated."[86] In the early years, the cast was limited to boarding students, with the exception of the sprite. Early audiences, like early casts, were restricted to boarders, and freshmen were limited to attending the dress rehearsal. Not until 1929 and the expansion of the Assembly Hall did the entire school view the production together. Beginning in 1926 alumnae often performed, usually as soloists. The cast was not secret and was posted by early November. Until 1941, Miss Kellas chose the girl to play the bearer of the star, a part whose importance stemmed from its religious symbolism. There was no guarantee that a student would have a part in the play, so the cast list was anticipated with much trepidation. In a letter to her parents in the fall of 1937, a senior exclaimed, "Oh! I am in Revels. I was afraid I wouldn't be."[87]

Since the Kellas era, graduation has vied with Revels each year as the most significant event in the school calendar. Commencement is actually composed of a whole series of events, most of them created by Eliza Kellas. Senior dinner was—and is—a nostalgic ritual that kicks off the final week of events. Typical of the Kellas years was the dinner in 1927, carefully documented in her scrapbook by Elesa Scott. All of the seniors, save three who languished in the infirmary with mumps, assembled together before entering the dining room. In the teens and twenties, the dinner was "a most secretive affair,"[88] with the juniors and the faculty bidding farewell to the seniors at the door to the dining room; inside the graduating class feasted on an eight-course dinner served by the kitchen staff; Miss Kellas joined them at the end of the meal. From the first, however, it was a sentimental occasion; as Scott confided in her journal, "We all wept."[89] Senior dinner was followed by the Ivy Day[90] exercises, the occasion for passing leadership from the seniors to the juniors. That same day, step-singing, a tradition borrowed from the women's colleges, reinforced the passing of leadership. Like senior dinner, it was a time for nostalgia and emotion. Elesa Scott recorded, "We gave our steps to the seniors of next year. Very weepy business."[91]

From 1916 on, June Day was the next activity in the commencement week. With a senior queen and court and underclasswomen dancing around maypoles (originally one apiece for each of the younger classes), it was a recognizable ancestor of today's May Day celebrations. Centered in front of the gymnasium, June Day featured a queen chosen by Miss Kellas for her "grace and charm of manner and speech, and whose influence in school affairs has always been for the best and highest."[92] As is the case today, the ceremony involved "much flitting about on the triangle."[93] The triangle, itself, evolved from being a piece of land cared for by the seniors to a piece of land owned exclusively by the seniors. By 1917 it played a critical role at graduation with Miss Kellas and the senior class forming a line at the base of triangle to receive the rest of the school and senior guests, a forerunner of today's "Wailing Wall." Protecting the triangle so it would be ready for graduation was initially a senior responsibility. As explained in one yearbook, "If ever an underclassman trampled over even a minute corner of the triangle, a senior was without doubt the first to scream her disapproval. 'Wait 'til you're a senior, and then you'll know what it is to want the campus looking nice in the spring!'"[94] When a landscape architect suggested to Miss Kellas in 1930 that the triangle's edges be rounded as part of a new campus design, she firmly refused; the geometric shape had too much sentimental value to disturb.

The final commencement tradition throughout the first two decades of Miss Kellas's tenure was the senior dance. Underclasswomen were packed off for home after the graduation ceremony, and Miss Kellas hosted a dance for the seniors and their male guests. Who the guests were and what senior families did while the graduates danced are lost details, but what is known is that for the seniors the evening was magical and sentimental. A *Triangle* reporter described it as something "which each graduate holds in her memory so dearly—the last gathering of her entire class in the familiar living room"[95] Eliza Kellas greeted the senior guests personally, and she remained in attendance until the dance ended at midnight, at which point the girls and their dates were given an hour in Sage Living Room to say their good-byes.

In spite of the many rules imposed on Emma Willard students during the Kellas decades, social interaction with young men was both encouraged and arranged by the principal. According to Elizabeth Potwine, Miss Kellas was unique in this way. "Far more than other headmistresses of her generation," wrote her biographer, "she welcomed young men at the school."[96] In contrast to the impression made by many other single headmistresses, an aura of wistful romance clung to Miss Kellas. Although it was perhaps apocryphal, she was believed by many students to have lost a fiancé to pneumonia in the Spanish-American War. The silver tea service that she used with the seniors was an early wedding present; with the wedding plans destroyed, the donor told her to keep the tea set as a reminder of her lost love.

Whether that story was true or a schoolgirl invention, Eliza Kellas seemed to share with her students an enjoyment of those occasions when boys and men appeared on campus, even though there were never quite enough young men to go around. Yearbook after yearbook and many issues of *Triangle* celebrated these occasions, although the general dearth of young men on Mount Ida was annually mourned as well. In the very first senior annual, the Class Alphabet contained the following couplet: "I is for Interest and J is the Joy/We take in one thing and that thing is a boy."[97] In 1918 the "Class Ballot," an early form of senior superlatives, included "Manhater," and "Greatest Lover of the Masculine,"[98] and in 1939 the editors of *Triangle* moaned, "When it comes to Prom week-end, it's more likely to be you and your second cousin opportunely dug out of mothballs."[99] For generation after generation, the scarcity of boys on campus meant that "a comparatively insignificant pair of pants from nowhere in particular can pack the audience into all available windows and balconies."[100] When the Union College Glee Club arrived for a joint concert and dance, the students "donned their best frocks as they were to see real men," but, alas, there were two times as many girls as "men."[101]

Often, as with the Union College event, social occasions revolved around joint concerts with glee clubs, either from prep schools or colleges. In addition to Union's choral group, Miss Kellas periodically arranged concerts with the Williams Glee Club, the Deerfield Glee Club, and the Hotchkiss Glee Club. In an era when many young women married shortly after high school, hosting college men was not as unusual as it would be today. In 1922, for example, Miss Kellas invited a group of West Point seniors who were on a tour of the Watervliet Arsenal to stop by the campus for "supper and a dance."[102] The cadets took trolleys to the school and marched from the trolley stop on Pawling Avenue up to the Sage porte cochere, much to the delight of the waiting girls. On another occasion, the Emma Willard students eagerly awaited the arrival of some Amherst college men. According to *Triangle*, "We were ready long before the first rickety Ford coughed its way up Mount Ida—but the boys will never know that!"[103]

As long as Eliza Kellas ran the school, girls were allowed to leave the campus for two weekends a year—neither of which could be taken in January, February, or March for fear of students returning with germs—

but in 1939 she temporarily changed the academic calendar, putting Saturday classes on Monday "until the end of football season," a convenience for "weekenders."[104] As encouraging as she was about fostering opportunities for social events on campus, Miss Kellas also closely monitored her girls' behavior. Katherine Eisner '41wrote to her mother that prior to a dance with Deerfield, the principal had called them together to forbid "dancing cheek to cheek because she didn't like the idea of us snuggling up to strange boys." In spite of this prohibition, the dance was a success—the boys were seniors, "not short and scrawny."[105] Given that visiting boys were paired up with their "dates" by height, a group of vertically challenged young men was never popular!

Eliza Kellas may have been more lenient about coeducational opportunities than her counterparts, but her carefully controlled social activities, well-regulated school routines, and homilies stressing old-fashioned verities about truth, integrity, religion, and duty contrasted sharply with the world of the 1920s outside Emma Willard. In *Tender Is the Night*, his first best-selling novel, F. Scott Fitzgerald characterized the younger generation as "a new generation . . . grown up to find all Gods dead, all wars fought, all faiths in man shaken,"[106] a cynical view most definitely not shared by Eliza Kellas. She was, however, well aware of the hazards of the new decade. Cigarettes, which before the war had been considered disreputable even for men, doubled their sales in the 1920s, and by 1926 tobacco companies directly targeted women. Lucky Strikes, for example, urged newly diet-conscious women to "Reach for a Lucky, instead of a sweet." Radio and moving pictures created an unprecedented media culture that often contradicted the teachings of home and school; nevertheless, bowing to change, Miss Kellas outfitted the school with a radio and a movie projector for weekend entertainment. By 1938 *Triangle* reported that there was even a radio on the field hockey field so that "substitutes could listen to the Yale game."[107] Periodically, the entire school traveled together to Troy to see first-run films of the principal's choosing.

Eliza Kellas worried most about the effects of the automobile, a machine sociologists Robert and Helen Lynd famously dubbed a "house of prostitution on wheels."[108] In 1919 only 10 percent of car interiors were closed; by the end of the decade 85 percent were closed, providing a degree of unchaperoned intimacy that young people had not previously experienced. In an era of unprecedented prosperity, the price of cars declined. There were seven million automobiles on the road in 1919 and over three times that in 1929. In 1912 a *Gargoyle* advertisement offered a car for $1,275, "complete with top and windshield."[109] In 1929 a Model T cost an easily affordable $300. After taking a group of girls to a conference at the Northfield School, Miss Kellas noted, "Chaperoning girls today is very different from what it was ten years ago. . . . The automobile is a source of great anxiety."[110] Moral temptations aside, the car was also dangerous. Car deaths per thousand rose from two in the 1910s to nearly thirty in the 1930s. Alice Judd '30 was one of the victims. Home for Christmas vacation of her junior year, as her mother later wrote to Miss Kellas, Alice was on "her first 'date' with a boy"[111] when the accident happened. Alice, her date, and several other teenagers from leading families in Kenosha, Wisconsin, were killed when a train hit three cars filled with young people. Less than three years later, William Glover, who had directed the music conservatory since 1908, was killed in a one-car accident on the outskirts of Troy.

Anxious as she was about the social and technological changes that roiled the United States after World War I, Eliza Kellas exposed her students to an impressive variety of modern thinking in art, literature, and scholarship. Reviewing modern poets in *Triangle*, Carol Derby '21 noted that critics might call the new poetry "discordant," but she argued that "there is real music to be found in contemporary poetry. This is the poetry of youth, of youth in love with its own country and time. . . . Like the stuffy clothes of the Victorian Era, the trailing skirts and boned bodices, are the old forms and meters . . . this is an age of short-skirted simplicity."[112] Although Miss Kellas kept her students in uniforms some considered old fashioned, she allowed them to study poetry that was most definitely twentieth century. Emma Willard students heard poetry readings by Robert Frost, Vachel Lindsay, Amy Lowell, Carl Sandburg, Stephen Vincent Benét, and his sister Laura, class of 1903, and Edna St. Vincent Millay. They also heard speeches by Thornton Wilder, who had just won the Pulitzer Prize for *The Bridge at San Luis Rey* and Cornelia

Otis Skinner, who celebrated independence for young women in her best seller, *Our Hearts Were Young and Gay*.

They heard both modern and classical music. The Troy Music Hall was already renowned as a concert venue. Traveling by trolley and later by bus, they attended concerts by Nikolai Sokoloff, Jan Paderewski, and Vladimir Horowitz—and the von Trapp Family Singers. As one alumna reminisced, "What a sight it must have been—a fleet of trolleys lighted up to the gills, filled with girls of all shapes and sizes, floating down the length of Pawling Avenue."[113]

Students also heard presentations by explorers—Sir Wilfred Grenfell, who introduced electricity and education to Newfoundland; Donald MacMillan who brought radios and airplanes to the Arctic; James Breasted, who was featured on the cover of *Time* for his archeological work, including his exploration of the newly discovered tomb of King Tut; Admiral Byrd, who came with his dog Igloo and regaled them with tales of the South Pole; and, one of the few featured women, Amelia Earhart.

Although local ministers spoke at the campus services on Sundays and at the year-end baccalaureate, nationally renowned religious leaders, many of them controversial, spoke at other times during the year. Among these were labor supporter Reinhold Niebuhr, anti-Zionist rabbi Samuel Goldenson, and liberal Protestant theologian Henry Sloane Coffin. These clerics were not the only speakers to present controversial topics for student consideration. Eunice Avery, a popular lecturer on college campuses, was a frequent campus speaker. In 1935 she warned of the danger inherent in American ignorance of the Japanese culture. There would be a price to pay, she cautioned, for the U.S. restriction on Japanese immigration and imposition of limitations on her navy because these actions had "offended [Japanese] honor."[114] In 1940, nearly two years before the United States entered World War II, she lectured on the horrors of concentration camps, describing the Nazis, whom many conservative Americans admired, as "retarded men—adult physically while their minds remained in the undeveloped stage of piracy."[115]

For Eliza Kellas's students, there were to be no walls around ideas. The important thing was to learn to discriminate, to learn the "difference between . . . wisdom and foolishness, and between what is genius and what is artificial."[116] By the 1920s, the vast majority was heading to college, and she wanted them to be prepared for the intellectual challenges that waited. As an incentive to undergraduates, messages from girls in college were read at assemblies and published in *Triangle*. Beginning in 1920, the first assembly opened with telegrams from alumnae at Smith, Vassar, and Wellesley. The girls at college sent back advice. In 1929 Elise Armitage '29 wrote, "Classes are so different! We go about with notebooks and pencils and take notes on lectures. . . . We have time unendingly. . . . Last year's routine was a help in getting me arranged."[117] At Mount Holyoke, Louise Porter '30 promised that "Instead of feverishly trying to memorize . . . you learn in college the fundamental truths."[118] Throughout the 1920s and 1930s, the school catalog included a list of references drawn mostly from the presidents and deans of the women's colleges. When she could get them, however, Miss Kellas included endorsements from college personnel outside that narrow band. In the late 1930s, for example, Dean Homer L. Dodge, the head of the Physics Department and Dean of the Graduate School at the University of Oklahoma, was added to the list. Nearly seventy years later, his daughter Alice '38 would endow faculty chairs in science and literature in honor of him and her mother, Margaret Wing Dodge.

In 1932 the school began listing college acceptances in the annual catalogs, and in 1933 Miss Kellas first reported College Board results to the board of trustees; she also noted curricular pressure from "the demands of the colleges." Although she would have liked to see more students enrolled in art courses, "the strongest colleges do not accept work in art for entrance credit."[119] One recent graduate urged the students not to be swept up in the preparation for college: "Don't keep your eyes merely on the goal; enjoy school life while you have it."[120]

As college preparation became more intense, Emma Willard students were comforted by the fact that Eliza Kellas and her school were nationally recognized. Writing from Vassar, Sallie Hooker '31 commented smugly, "Emma Willard students look superior while many look bewildered."[121] Louise Porter '30 concurred, "In that hectic first week when the freshmen are comparing notes and finding that every third person was a valedictorian of her class (and the others for the most part were salutatorians), you will discover with a thrill of pride how much respect the name of Emma Willard commands among your classmates."[122]

Miss Kellas was responsible for the reputation the students valued. Her school and her graduates shared a discrete set of values that bore the recognizable imprint of an Emma Willard education. As important as this accomplishment was, it was not her sole achievement. She was also responsible for reorganizing and revitalizing the alumnae association, steering the school through the nation's most severe economic depression, and reconfiguring the physical campus.

In Spite of Present Conditions

In the fall of 1936, Emma Willard students celebrated a dual anniversary: Eliza Kellas's seventieth birthday and the twenty-fifth year of her leadership. In spite of the jubilation surrounding the occasion and her willingness as always to lead the annual snake dance in her honor, the mood of the principal was somber. The mood of the country was too, with people mired in the seventh year of the Great Depression. For years the school's income had not covered expenses without serious operational economies. At seventy, Miss Kellas recognized that she was already past the age of retirement, but she could not leave her school in its imperiled state, no matter how exhausting its challenges. By 1936 the severe fiscal situation was compounded by increasingly menacing news from European dictatorships and the totalitarian regime in Japan. During the final years of her principalship, Eliza Kellas ably piloted Emma Willard past the obstacles presented nationally by the financial crisis, internationally by the coming of a second world war, and locally by an aging physical plant, significant turnover on the board of trustees, increasing demands for financial aid, and industry-wide pressure to modernize budgeting and enrollment practices.

Miss Kellas's concern for even the smallest details of her students' academic and personal lives was legendary, but she was just as vigilant in her care for the campus as she was for its inhabitants; as a *Triangle* editor concluded, one could "see her work in every tree that grows upon the hill and in every girl who makes a success of her life."[1] She was particularly conscientious about the grounds. After her death, "Old Charlie," a school gardener, recounted, "Miss Kellas knew the location of every tree on the place . . . in the summer time one could find [her] walking over

367

the grounds sprinkling grass seed from her pocket as she dreamed and planned for her school."[2] Her meticulous surveillance extended beyond the grounds to the plant, where the chief engineer marveled at her encyclopedic knowledge about the heating and water systems.

From the first, she had viewed the campus she inherited as incomplete. Separate infirmary and additional dormitory spaces topped her inventory of projects, but there were many other items on the list. She was also concerned about the lack of dedicated visual arts and science facilities, the cramped performing arts space, the lack of equipment for horseback riding, and the inappropriateness of educating primary school girls in the same building as high school students. She worked tirelessly to get the board of trustees to share her vision for campus development and traveled extensively to raise money from alumnae to fund that vision.

Ten years after her arrival, the first new construction was added in the maintenance area along Elmgrove Avenue. In 1921 the laundry was moved out of the cellar of the dormitory and into a new space adjacent to the power house, freeing the area in Sage basement for informal student activities. Five years later, a new infirmary joined the laundry on the northern edge of the campus. Early in her tenure, Miss Kellas had moved the infirmary from Sage into a separate cottage that had formerly housed faculty, but it did not have a permanent home until Overbridge opened in 1926. Funded by alumnae gifts and profits from the investment of the endowment in the booming stock market, Overbridge was a compact stand-alone three-story building that matched the exterior of Sage and was outfitted to serve as a small convalescent hospital.

These were relatively small changes. Far bigger was the addition of a new dormitory. At a meeting of the board of trustees in March 1927, eight years after the trustees had voted to add a second large dormitory to the campus, trustee Julia Howard Bush '91 moved that construction on the new dormitory finally begin. Eliza Kellas Hall opened in September 1928, "a beautiful material manifestation of the constructive work"[3] that had filled the principal's life (although when the dormitory opened, that work was far from over). The construction had taken over a year. Built to house 120 boarding students, the dormitory was made of the same gray stone as Sage, Slocum, and the gymnasium, which meant, according to one observer, that it had "no appearance of startling newness."[4] There was another reason that the new building fit so easily into the campus. It was designed by Fred Cummings, architect of the original three campus structures. Only the lack of gargoyles distinguished Kellas from its older companions.

A porte cochère on the eastern end of the three-story building marked the front entrance. Once inside, visitors found a formal waiting room. Beyond were dormitory rooms and a corridor leading to the main living room, dining room, and reception room "where periodicals and newspapers may be found." The corridor had been furnished with gifts from the class of 1923 and included "cabinets of dark walnut." The living room had hardwood floors covered with "rugs of greens and crowns . . . tables of rare form, chairs with velvet upholstering in browns and greens, a fine piano and many small chairs of wood." The color scheme continued in the wallpaper, which extended above dark wainscoting in a pattern of "leaves in browns and greens." The new dining hall was "very large and sunny" and connected to Sage dining room by an updated kitchen and serving rooms. Most of the student rooms were located on the second and third floors, and they were arranged in suites that accommodated two or three students. Some rooms had private baths, and the halls were covered with rugs that were "heavy and of fine value."[5] The basement contained a large playroom and twenty music rooms, each containing a piano.

Just inside the front door was a suite of rooms initially intended to house guests. However, in June 1928, Eliza Kellas gave up the presidency of Russell Sage College, and her sister resigned as dean of the college. The guest suite became Eliza Kellas's apartment, and Miss Katherine, now associate principal of the school, moved into the principal's former rooms in Sage. For many years, seniors would have the privilege of living in the new dormitory with their principal.

The *Troy Times Record* approvingly reported that "as far as possible Troy firms have furnished the equipment and have done the work on the building," and the paper noted that "a host of artisans"[6] working all summer ensured that the building would be open when fall semester classes resumed on September 26. The Emma Willard project was only one manifestation of regional growth. Troy businesses in general were experiencing incredible expansion. At the same time that the *Record* reported on the dormitory's progress, they also covered an enlargement of the Ford plant on Green Island that promised to bring five hundred additional jobs to the area. There were few empty storefronts in Troy. Traffic was so heavy in the downtown commercial areas that the city voted to make most of the main streets one-way thoroughfares in 1928.

In spite of the signs of prosperity and the prospect of a new dormitory, Eliza Kellas spent an anxious year during the dormitory construction. The first piece of work, undertaken in the summer of 1927, was the renovation of the kitchen and the construction of new service quarters in the area of the building that would eventually connect the two dormitories. In August, she worried that the building would not be ready in time for the arrival, not only of students, but also of kitchen and dormitory staff. The latter would not only work in the new facility, but they would also be housed in the section connecting the new building with Sage. Miss Kellas confided her fears to William Shields, who as board treasurer monitored the financial side of the project.

She explained that she had urged Cummings to finish the kitchen and maids' quarters first because those people understandably needed to arrive before the students. Cummings, however, was excited about framing the dormitory; as she saw it, "His mind is focused on the entire building."[7] Her needs were more pressing. A new dietitian was expected on the first of September, and "and on the eighteenth our entire army of help will report, ready for work." She had spoken with the project engineer, who suggested that the kitchen and servants' quarters be put in the hands of another company to finish up, but that of course would add additional cost. In her conversations with Fred Cummings, she found the architect to be "very comforting and very soothing," but she distrusted his placating words. She wrote Shields, "I have dealt with him before, and I know that the fact that the domestic quarters will not be ready does not trouble him very much . . . no matter how amiably he may talk about it, he is not doing anything to see that the kitchen and the living quarters for the help are ready." She was turning to Shields for help as she did "not know just what to do."[8]

What she did know, she assured him, was that "in a month we should have a kitchen and living quarters for our help in proper condition."[9] Her concern illuminates the situation at the school near the end of the 1920s. In an era of unprecedented prosperity, Emma Willard's students came largely from wealthy homes. In 1970, when asked on a reunion questionnaire to rate the importance of the "opportunity to be with disadvantaged students" during her time at Emma Willard, a member of the fiftieth reunion class wrote dismissively, "There were none."[10]

Just as the graciousness and splendor in the details of Sage had mirrored the luxurious surroundings of the upper classes in Edwardian America, the new dormitory purposefully included features and services that affluent white families would expect. As Miss Kellas explained to the board treasurer, "If our school is not properly run this year, we shall not need the new dormitory, because the kind of people to whom we cater will not put up with inconveniences, lack of proper service and attention, and the other difficulties that attend lack of domestic service." Mindful as she was about the expectations of her students and their families, she was also aware of the needs of the women who would serve them. The maids' quarters were far from finished, and she was very concerned about the amount of work remaining "to make [them] habitable for self-respecting maids."[11]

One way or another—and no doubt in large measure because of the vigilance of Eliza Kellas during the vacation months—the school opened smoothly in 1927. A year later, the new dormitory was finished on time for the start of the fall semester. On September 28, 1928, a record number of pupils gathered in the Assembly Hall to hear Eliza Kellas welcome them to the 115th year; there were 257 residential students enrolled. The board had already decided to name the new building in the principal's honor, but in recognition of her willingness to remain in Troy throughout two summers to oversee the project, they also gave her a munificent present. They voted to give her $3,000 for European travel during the summer of 1929.

Before Eliza Kellas set sail, however, another building project was underway. For years, the Assembly Hall had been an inadequate space, incapable of seating the entire student body and faculty for Revels. And, although it housed weekly church services for the boarders, the hall did not have an organ. With a larger student body and ledgers reflecting a comfortable excess of income over expenses, on May 12, 1929, the board authorized an addition to the assembly hall. Again, Cummings and Son was the architectural firm, and again the board treasurer, William Shields, negotiated the contracts. Using Cummings's blueprints, C. M. McLean and Sons, a Binghamton firm, undertook the work of extending the Assembly Hall by a third. The cost was $86,000, and the project included the installation of an organ and new lighting throughout Slocum Hall.[12]

The work took all summer and was still incomplete when the students returned in the fall, perhaps because Miss Kellas was not there to supervise. Along with her traveling companions, her sister Katherine and their close friend and faculty member Janet Maxwell, Eliza Kellas arrived home from England on Cunard's *Carinthia* on September 9. She had spent over two months in Europe. It would prove to be her last real vacation.

The arriving students, again in record numbers that matched the prior year's enrollment, were unperturbed by the incomplete Assembly Hall. For them, the delay was a bonus because it meant an extra trip off campus each week because "we are all attending the churches in Troy."[13] By Thanksgiving, however, the new hall was ready, and on December 17, the members of the class of 1933 were the first freshmen able to watch Revels with the rest of the school, "our new Assembly Hall just finished in time for the occasion."[14] Their predecessors had complained that as ninth graders, "Our youth condemned us to the Dress Rehearsal."[15] In the new space, concluded the editors of *Triangle*, "Revels seemed more gorgeous than ever."[16] In June, the new organ was featured at baccalaureate services that were held for the first time on the campus.

Just as work was being completed on the enlarged Assembly Hall, another, initially less positive, change occurred. On November 29, the Friday night after Thanksgiving, the Playhouse, the large wooden recreational building located on the hill southeast of the gymnasium, burned to the ground. The Troy Fire Department responded, but to no avail. When their hoses could not reach the water mains on Pawling Avenue, they tried unsuccessfully to attach them to the swimming pool in the basement of the gym. In spite of this failed attempt, the flames were confined to the Playhouse, and the students watched the blaze from their dormitory windows.

Rather than view this loss as a complete tragedy, Eliza Kellas and the board of trustees chose to see it as an opportunity. Within two weeks, Edgar H. Betts, board president, had contacted Olmsted Brothers, the most famous landscape design firm in the country. Betts explained to James Dawson, one of the firm's partners, that the board wanted the architectural firm to complete a survey of the entire campus before any decision was made about replacing the Playhouse. "We have in mind," he wrote, "several new buildings for the school at some future time and wish to study the whole project before building anything."[17] By the week after Christmas, Dawson had visited the campus, and Miss Kellas had taken him on a complete tour of the buildings and grounds. He assured Betts that for $1,500 to $2,500, the firm would be able to draft a comprehensive study of the campus. On January 15, Betts told Dawson to proceed.

The Olmsted plan for the campus would not be completed for a year, and in the meantime, the board decided to go ahead with the construction of a new Playhouse. The Olmsted firm supported this initial move and also urged the immediate purchase of "cheap-looking houses" on the southern boundary of the school to protect against "undesirable conditions."[18] The houses were not purchased, but plans for a new Playhouse were developed, the board authorizing $85,000 for the project at their May meeting. Construction began a month later, and the new facility was ready for student use in the spring of 1931. Once again, Cummings was the architect, but there were definite struggles between the local and New York City–based architectural firms. Primarily, they disagreed on the layout of the new building with respect to the land where it was to be constructed. By starting the work without a final consultation with Olmsted, Cummings prevailed.

Other campus changes accompanied the building project. School roads were reconfigured, and the power plant was upgraded by the installation of a steam exhaust and an ash hoist. In her principal's report to the board in the fall of 1930, Eliza Kellas was most enthusiastic about the latter. Not only would these improvements save up to a ton of coal a day, they would improve the air quality. She noted, "the dust and dirt from the power house has [sic] been most objectionable both to the neighbors who live on Elmgrove Ave. and to the people who live in the dormitories . . . [it has been sometimes] necessary to do a whole week's laundry a second time."[19]

Saving on coal and laundry had become more important in the months since the Playhouse fire. By the time the new building was underway, the ripples from the great stock market crash in October 1929 had begun to permeate all aspects of the economy. Emma Willard School was far from immune. Nevertheless, when the Olmsted drawings arrived in January 1931, they embodied all of Eliza Kellas's fondest dreams for the campus. Among others, they included provision for a separate grade school, a dedicated chapel building, an art and music facility, improved faculty housing, a stable, and a number of amenities designed to enhance the program including a sylvan theater, two additional hockey fields, and a toboggan slide.

Although all of these were exciting, the prospect of a separate grade school must have particularly delighted her. In her most recent principal's report to the board, she had urged that such a building be erected on Merry Mount, the wooded land south of Slocum where Allenwood stood. The classrooms for the first eight grades, then housed in Slocum, were "very crowded," with the first and second graders forced to share the same room. Young children, she believed, "should have a freer school life than we can possibly give them while they are housed in the same building and on the same floor as the high school students."[20] Ideally, she told the board, the first eight grades should have their own building with separate classrooms for each level, a small assembly hall, a reading room, lunchroom, playroom, and music room. With regard to the last, she reminded the trustees that "music and play enter quite largely into the training of little children."[21]

Although the new Playhouse was completed two months after the

Olmsted drawings were delivered to the school, the grander plan was not to be. As J. D. Langdon, one of the men hired by Olmsted to survey the campus, had confided to his employer about the school's resources, "Cummings says they have about $400,000 out at interest and can't make it stretch to what they want to do."[22] Langdon's—and Cummings's—numbers were a bit off, but their general perception of the school's inability to undertake any expensive building projects in 1930 was accurate. As early as the prior fall, the board specifically recognized that fiscal matters had begun to monopolize the principal's time. Eliza Kellas's management had gone beyond the academic. In a resolution passed at the October meeting, the board expressed "to the Principal, Miss Kellas, its appreciation of the results of the work of the past year both educational *and financial* [author's emphasis]."[23] The Depression's negative impact on enrollment and the endowment would dominate the work of the board and the principal for the rest of the decade.

Eliza Kellas prided herself on the operation of a school whose budget balanced and whose excess of revenue over expenses, particularly tuition revenue, allowed for campus enhancements, programmatic initiatives, and a very generous faculty-to-student ratio. As the reality of the Depression set in, the principal reported to the board that since 1918 (the end of World War I), tuition has covered "all expenses of living, instruction, and maintenance of the school,"[24] and that $1,423,520.82 in excess revenue had been added to the endowment, in spite of the school's significant support for Russell Sage College.

The key, of course, was enrollment, and in the first few years of the Depression, it held firm. At Eliza Kellas's urging, the board even voted to increase the boarding tuition for 1930–31. It had held steady at $1,600 for nearly ten years. The price was raised to $1,800, with an increase of $50 at each level of day tuition, bringing the cost for senior day students to $250. As she explained her reasoning, "No school in the country has as much to offer . . . best teachers . . . staff, dorms . . . first-rate . . . food of a very high character . . . no fees except music lessons, church, infirmary."[25] In support of her argument that tuition was too low, she offered information about the tuition rates at schools she considered competitive: Madeira and Baldwin charged $1,700, Miss Hall's, $2,000, and

Spence between $2,300 and $2,500. (At the time, Baldwin and Spence had boarding programs.) In spite of the price increase, the enrollment in the fall of 1930, with 254 boarders, was just two students shy of the record enrollments of the prior two years.

However, a dramatic change in enrollment began in 1931, and the board dropped tuition back to $1,600 in anticipation of a shortfall in students. Without crowding, the dormitories could accommodate 250 boarders. The extra four to six students in 1928, 1929, and 1930 had been squeezed into former faculty apartments and larger suites. In the fall of 1931, however, for the first time, there were unfilled beds as the boarding population shrank below 250 to 244. Eliza Kellas had watched helplessly as several students withdrew from enrollment during July and August. As she told the board, "Owing to the economic depression, the past summer was one of the most anxious we have had in the last twenty years."[26]

Over the next few years, the situation did not improve. In her report to the board in early 1932, the principal anticipated an even more difficult year. On February 6, 1933, she informed the board that for the "first time in twenty-two years, the Residence Department of the school has not been filled to capacity." According to her analysis, as she explained to the board, in times of economic pressure, "parents feel it imperative to send their boys to preparatory school and college [and] as fewer girls will enter college . . . private schools for girls are expecting a harder year."[27]

Characteristically, she had gauged the academic climate correctly. In 1932–33, the residence numbers fell to 202, a slide that would finally end in 1938–39 when the boarding population sank to 147. Among them there was only *one* boarding freshman, and Eliza Kellas pronounced 1938–39 the "hardest year experienced since [the school] moved to the present location."[28] A decrease in primary students also occurred, but it was not nearly as dramatic, with the total population in grades 1 to 8 sliding from 111 in 1931–32 to 94 at the end of the decade. (The nadir for the lower school was reached in 1936–37 when the enrollment stood at 82.) In spite of the relative stability of the primary enrollment, however, the lower grades were in jeopardy. In 1937–38 the first grade had eleven students, but there were ten or fewer pupils in grades 2 through 5, with only four girls enrolled in grade 3. In October 1938, with a budget projecting expenses of $279,000 and income of $272,000, Eliza Kellas suggested discontinuing the primary because it was a "drain on the resources of the school."[29]

Meanwhile, the day population in the high school actually increased. Economic pressure outweighed the desire to remain an overwhelmingly residential school. In 1930–31 in a high school numbering 300 students, only 46 were day girls. In 1938–39, the high school population totaled 224, and 77 of those were day students. From a small minority of 15 percent, the day student total had jumped to a full third of the school. In an attempt to fill beds and realize income, the school encouraged girls in the fifth through eighth grades to board; although never very successful, in 1938–39 there were sixteen middle school girls housed in the dormitories.

Accommodating greater numbers of day students and younger boarders undoubtedly put a strain on school programs, but another effect of the Depression created an even greater set of problems. The number of one- and two-year students increased, often creating a senior class disproportionate to the rest of the school. The peak came with the class of 1938 that had 103 graduates. Having so many older students presented social issues in the dormitory, challenges for college admission, and scheduling issues for both faculty and students. The biggest problem, however, was that each year Eliza Kellas was forced to find a great number of students just to replace the outgoing senior class. The problem persisted until the end of her tenure. In her final fall, she reiterated to the board that "the turn-over each year is too great."[30]

For years, word of mouth among the alumnae had been the chief source of new students, and to aid her in recruitment during these difficult times, Miss Kellas turned to the alumnae again. She was direct in explaining the problem. One alumna responded that she had heard from her mother that "you are rather worried about the school—the attendance has fallen down so."[31] Another, responding to a letter from her former principal, wrote that she was sorry "its contents was not more cheerful." She was living at home in Ohio and knew "five people with children the right age" but was "not sure of the financial situation"[32] of the families. In addition to writing to her former pupils, Eliza Kellas contacted them in person. She reported to the board in June 1933 that she had visited all of the alumnae chapters except the ones in California. She was proud of the ways her former pupils were dealing with the crisis, noting that "all seem to be courageously and patiently doing their part in their homes and in the communities in which they live. . . . Failure of banks, loss of position, cuts in salary and so on have altered their plans, but their pluck and optimistic spirit were most inspiring."[33]

Proud of them she might be, but she also heard from them about the Depression. The same week Franklin Roosevelt signed the banking act that led to the Bank Holiday, Elizabeth Butler '32, studying sociology at New York University, wrote that she had seen a man "peddling Hershey bars . . . who looked as though he were a man of considerable intelligence, formerly a business man."[34] She also commented about the Bank Holiday, recalling that "so many people were caught with just a little bit of money in their pockets."[35] Another alumna, a sophomore at Vassar, informed Miss Kellas that she was going home to the University of Iowa because her father had suffered a heart attack as well as business losses. She wrote about her hometown: "Waterloo's last bank closed last week."[36]

Closer to home, the Depression hit at members of the board of trustees, most of whom were among the wealthiest citizens of Troy. When board treasurer Frederick Orr died after serving as a trustee for forty-three years, his sixty-nine-year-old widow Evelyn found herself in economic trouble. Emma Willard helped her out. She wrote to her husband's successor, William Shields, thanking him. She explained that as a result of this "awful Depression," her trust fund was "gone," and she "could not even find a market for my diamonds." She had wanted to sell or mortgage her property in Round Lake but had been unsuccessful. Then she received word from her attorney that "Emma Willard School will take care of it." She thanked Shields for "your wonderful kindness in securing the mortgage loan on my Round Lake home [which has been] a Life Saver."[37]

Securing a mortgage was not as unorthodox as it might sound; the school's investment portfolio included several mortgages on properties in the greater Manhattan area; throughout the Depression, the finance committee reported on the ability of the homeowners to meet their obligations, and in 1936 the business manager was sent to inspect the properties. Orr was not the only trustee whose finances were hit. When longtime trustee C. Tillinghast Barker died in 1938, his obituary noted the decline in his fortunes; Barker, whose grandfather was an early trustee and whose family had owned some of the property purchased for the Mount Ida campus, had "in his youth abundant wealth," but "in more recent years, his fortune gone, his home with its beautiful furnishings and treasures of art and travel [had been] closed."[38]

Additional board support for fellow trustees included their action when William B. Frear, a trustee for sixteen years, died an "untimely" death in 1933. Trustee Albert Cluett moved that Frear's daughters, at the time students in the lower school, be supported "until graduation."[39] The board did not accept his widow's attempt to donate the family home on Pawling Avenue to the school; the finance committee thought the taxes on the property were too high, and the school had no use for it. (The building was fated to become a Rensselaer Polytechnic Institute [RPI] fraternity house and a magnet for generations of misbehaving students.)

In 1934, with the boarding population hovering around 160, the school hired a field secretary "to organize the Alumnae" in order to "increase the registrations." In spite of this help, Eliza Kellas continued to be the primary force in sustaining enrollment. In 1935 she visited alumnae groups in Baltimore, Buffalo, Rochester, Syracuse, Scarsdale, Orange (New Jersey), Philadelphia, Scranton, Washington, D.C., Boston, Hartford, Chicago, Grand Rapids, Akron, Cincinnati, Toledo, Terre Haute, Kansas City, Cedar Rapids, Des Moines, Denver, and Lincoln (Nebraska). In Baltimore she attended the annual meeting of the National Association of Principals of Schools for Girls, where the declining enrollments among the member schools were the chief topic. In conjunction with the meeting, Hazel Nelson Roper '16 hosted a tea for her former principal. The daughter-in-law of Secretary of Commerce Daniel C. Roper, she was one of the few alumnae supportive of the Roosevelt administration's efforts to fix the economy. (Eliza Kellas, herself, disapproved of the president and his policies.) All of this travel, particularly for a woman nearing seventy, was, she admitted, "an expensive process, both physically and economically."[40]

Tuition was not the only source of school income, and it was not the only revenue supply hit hard by the Depression. During the 1920s the board of trustees had become increasingly active investors in the stock and bond markets. In 1929 the Dow surged to 398 with unemployment at 3.2 percent; by 1939, the high for the year was 155 with unemployment at 17.2 percent (which was even lower than the previous year's record 19 percent). The great economic expansion of the 1920s meant that Emma Willard's board bought and sold stocks and bonds at significant profits. The investment report for 1921–22, for example, reported the sale of stocks and bonds for $46,325.02. This represented a profit of $10,395.64 over the purchase price. This sort of return on investments added $39,910.69 to the endowment in 1926 and $57,341.92 in 1927. The endowment topped $1 million for the first time in 1930; by December 1940, it was $748,207.25. The initial impact on investments was not disastrous. As late as 1932, the treasurer reported to the board, "In spite of present conditions, . . . at the end of the year the income of the school from securities would not be more than $1,500 lower, due to cut dividends, and that no bonds in the possession of the school had defaulted."[41] This situation would worsen, however.

Losses on investments were only one reason the value of the endowment declined. Over the course of the Depression, the school spent the total return from its investments most years, and endowment dollars as a percentage of the budget rose significantly. The high point was reached in 1934–35 when the $31,810 realized from the endowment represented 10.34 percent of the budget. During the eleven years between the crash of the stock market and 1940, the average percentage of the budget funded from the endowment was 7.69 percent.

During the Depression, prices fell, so some operating expenses were reduced, which certainly helped the principal balance the books. During the decade of the 1930s, the annual cost of operating and caring for the physical plant declined from $63,091.90 in 1930 to $52,946 in 1939, with the lowest cost, $49,074.99, occurring in 1934. The lower enrollment, of course, had some impact on these costs, but the plant itself demanded attention that it had not needed in the 1920s. Slocum and Sage were twenty-five years old in the middle of the decade, and their infrastructure was aging. Broken lead pipes, leaking water mains, walls that needed repointing, and windows that needed recaulking filled the reports from the building committee of the board. Near the end of the 1930s, problems with the water pressure meant that "baths cannot be drawn on the second and third floors [at least] once a week."[42] Furthermore, the "loose fit of sash" in the 449 windows in Sage (none had been recaulked since they were installed) was a "contributing factor to the heat loss"[43] in the building.

As with everything else at the school, it was Eliza Kellas who dealt most directly with plant issues. She did not shy from the responsibility, reminding the board of the "demands of the school on the Principal's time" because she "has never had a well-trained man in charge of the buildings and grounds."[44] Through judicious temporary repairs and the support of the staff and faculty, she kept expenses down without sacrificing student comfort. In 1937 longtime plant supervisor John Kapps retired. Miss Kellas had described him as "willing and agreeable," but she fretted because "he knows little or nothing about trees, shrubs, hockey fields, tennis courts or other sport . . . necessities."[45] She was pleased when Willard Egy Jr., a 1935 West Point graduate with an engineering background, replaced Kapps.

The one area where economies would not work, and the area that put equal pressure on the assets and liabilities sides of the school's balance sheet, was scholarship aid. Although the school had offered tuition assistance to pupils since Emma Willard's time, scholarship recipients had always been a tiny fraction of the whole student body. The vast majority of students paid full tuition. The most likely candidates for financial aid had traditionally been daughters of clergymen, daughters of alumnae who found themselves in straitened means, and daughters of military officers. Emma Willard had begun the practice of aiding the first two groups, and Olivia Sage had added the third. Most tuition assistance was provided by alumnae, and very few dollars were allocated for this purpose from the operating budget. The two established scholarships were the one funded by Olivia Sage in honor of three of her teachers (Hudson-Dillaye-Hastings) and the scholarship established by Admiral Ludlow in memory of his wife.

Because of the Depression, families who would never have considered financial assistance in the past found themselves unable to pay the bills. When the board voted to award diplomas to eighty-one members of the class of 1932, they were informed that there were "a few financial difficulties that might have prevented some of the members of the class from graduating, but they have been taken care of."[46] Six months later, at the start of the second semester in February 1933, Eliza Kellas reported that nearly $4,000 in boarding tuition was outstanding from the first semester, and over $1,500 was owed by day students. Additionally, a few day students still owed money for 1931–32. The board wisely authorized Eliza Kellas to offer aid in the form of discounts, in short to "use her own judgment in offering scholarships to worthy students."[47] The 1931–32 catalog was the first to devote significant space to the subject of scholarships. By 1935–36, although the tuition was still $1,600, when all the discounts were accounted for, the average income the school received per boarding student was just over $1,420.

The correspondence between Eliza Kellas and parents struggling to pay the bills reveals a fundamental shift in the scholarship policy of the school. Although endowed scholarships were still extremely important and allowed "girls of high ideals and ambition to profit from what the school has to offer,"[48] Miss Kellas recognized that financial assistance to any qualified, needy girl helped keep the beds filled and spread the costs over a larger student population. Consequently, when a father whose investment securities firm was threatened to the point that he could not pay his daughter's tuition for the second semester of her sophomore year, Eliza Kellas kept her on, in effect providing a 50 percent reduction for the year, and she subsequently offered a partial scholarship for the following year. (In the end, he refused, and the student finished at her public school.)

If financial aid was new for the principal and the board, it was also a new—and shameful—thought for some parents. Amy Pfau Butler had had one daughter graduate from the school but was uncertain whether or not she and her husband could pay their younger daughter's tuition, especially with the older girl still in college. In the summer before the younger daughter's junior year, Eliza Kellas made an offer of a partial scholarship. Writing to the principal that "I didn't know there was such generosity in the world," Mrs. Butler explained that she could not respond to the offer until she had had time to discuss it with her physician husband (temporarily away on medical business). In contrast to the response of many of today's award recipients whose initial response is often to bargain for more, the Butlers needed to consult to figure out "just how much we can accept." Even more astonishing in light of the current Lake Woebegon attitude that "all the children are above average," Amy Butler wrote to Miss Kellas, "If the girls were brilliant or even above average, I would feel justified in accepting it."[49]

In addition to allocating school money for scholarship assistance, Eliza Kellas also used her own money to aid students. Beginning in 1937–38, she refused to accept a salary, telling the board that she wanted the money to be used for scholarships. (Her salary at the time was $7,500 a year.) She gave more than her salary, however, and when she retired, one of her regrets was that she would no longer be able to afford such generosity. As she reported at one of her last board meetings, "I have helped a good many girls not only by turning in my entire salary for several years but I have also used some of my regular income."[50] Moving off campus in retirement, she noted, would preclude her continuing this practice; when she refused a pension, the board decided to deposit the money that would have gone to her in a scholarship fund in her honor.

For the most part, however, the trustees focused on day students. Virtually all of the trustees were local, and most were bankers, lawyers, and businessmen who were well aware of the severe economic downturn in the Troy economy. They formed a committee to investigate day student aid and eventually established criteria for day student scholarships. They determined that a candidate should have "need for aid" and her "ability should be as to suggest that at graduation she would be representative." There was no suggestion that aid would help diversify the student body; in fact, the opposite was true. According to the board's criteria, any day student receiving aid "should come from a background that would make her congenial with the other pupils."[51] This stipulation suggests that their concern was personal; they were hedging against an increasingly uncertain future when they and their colleagues might no longer be able to afford the school for their daughters. Day student assistance remained minimal, although the push for day student aid got a lift from three local alumnae who died during the Depression decade. Edith Sampson '95, Jessie MacDonald Gibson '90, and Mary A. Hall '84 all left money in their wills to support day students.

Some of the trustee focus on day students undoubtedly stemmed from their concern with the school's image in relationship to the city, particularly as the decade wore on. At its lowest enrollment, Emma Willard still had over a hundred young women in residence whose families could afford a private school education in spite of the Depression. At one point Edward Pattison, a trustee and civic leader, suggested taking a select number of ninth and tenth grade girls from Troy and Lansingburgh schools gratis to fill out Emma Willard's classes and to help with overcrowding in the public schools. Not only would this improve public relations, but he argued, these students would "occupy seats left vacant by the present low registration in the high school . . . [and] the operations of the school would be more nearly in balance from the bookkeeping standpoint than they are from the tentative budget."[52] Ever conscious of the school's relationship to the community, Pattison also wrote to the commissioner of assessment and taxation, asking that the listing of the school's property value be reduced from $6 million to $2 million. Because the school was a tax-exempt organization, Pattison knew that its value on the tax lists made no real difference, but he also knew that "on the other hand there is an element unfavorable to Emma Willard School because of the public impression that it creates as to the wealth of the school, and this has been a real handicap."[53]

To the casual observer, the school certainly did appear wealthy in the 1930s. Students in fashionable riding gear galloped on their own and school-owned horses along the trails east of the campus leading to the Country Club of Troy, where Eliza Kellas had a special membership paid for by the trustees. When the Troy Orphan Asylum considered selling the point of land across from the Pinewoods entrance to a developer as a site for a gas station, the trustees bought it for $4,000. In

1935 concrete sidewalks were laid throughout the campus, replacing the wooden boardwalks that had been there since 1911. In 1936 the Emma Willard Conservatory of Music moved from Plum Hall on the Russell Sage campus to the basement of Kellas. That same year, visiting lecturer John Erskine, president of Juilliard, warned the students that the proliferation of recorded music signaled the death knell for professional musicians. He lectured the students that the proliferation of records meant that live concerts were in danger of extinction. Nevertheless, the conservatory continued to sponsor concerts featuring world-class musicians, including Josef Hofmann, billed as the world's "greatest living pianist." However, in the eyes of Trojans outside Mount Ida, perhaps the most ostentatious manifestation of the school's separation from their lives was the major construction project undertaken in 1936 that concluded in 1937 with the addition of a new science building. Named for Katherine Weaver, who had chaired the science department since 1910, the new building faced Kellas on the southern side of the campus in a woodsy area known as the Allenwood Orchard.

Although most of the Olmsted plan had been shelved at the onset of the Depression, Eliza Kellas still had dreams for the campus. In March 1936, she made a special report to the board of trustees on the need for a science building, predicating her plea on the false premise that "Emma Willard School was the first school for girls in which the natural sciences were taught." She also recognized that the cost, which she estimated would be $125,000, might be prohibitive. Beautiful as it was, the campus did have one drawback when it came to adding to the buildings. "It is a matter of genuine regret," she told the board, "that the type of architecture selected for this school makes building very expensive."[54] Although the buildings and grounds committee supported her wish for a separate science facility, the board voted—as they had at the time of the Playhouse fire—to consider the science building within the context of all of the school's needs.

Consequently, a long-range planning committee was appointed consisting of board president Edgar Betts, Dwight Marvin, editor in chief of the *Troy Record*, Ruth Harvie, wife of a local physician whose children were in the primary grades, Eliza Kellas, and William O.

Hotchkiss, president of RPI. They weighed the need for new science laboratories as well as a separate lower school building, new arts facilities, a pension system, faculty salaries, and the addition of a resident psychiatrist before reporting to the full board on April 7. They found that English, foreign language, mathematics, social studies, drama, and music were being taught in well-appointed rooms, and that the craft room in the Playhouse and two small "graphic arts" studios provided the studio arts with sufficient space. Better science classrooms, however, were an "imperative need."[55] Not only were the laboratories inadequate; their location in the basement of Slocum meant that noxious fumes filled the building almost weekly.

The committee also recommended developing a pension plan for both faculty and staff and raising the salaries of both groups. In response to their report, the board voted to take $140,000 from the endowment to build a two-story gray stone building dedicated to science instruction. The decision was not unanimous; three trustees voted against the proposal. For the first time, the trustees selected an out-of-town architect, choosing the Massachusetts firm of J. R. Hampson that had recently built the academic building at Deerfield and new gymnasiums at RPI and Williams. Hampson agreed to do the project for $160,000; in the end, it ran a mere $300 over budget. In addition to science classrooms, the building housed a "larger, better lighted, better ventilated lunchroom"[56] for the day students, who were still separated from the boarders for the noon meal.

The building was ready for classes in the winter of 1937, and the editorial for the March issue of *Triangle* was devoted to the new addition. Echoing the oft-repeated, although fallacious claim that "Ours was the first school for girls in which science was taught," the editor praised the building for being "in general harmony with our other campus buildings." She described the new laboratories in detail:

> Each laboratory—light, spacious, and well-equipped—has its own preparation room with work-desk for the teacher, cabinet for storage, and rolling table. In the physics laboratory special equipment includes box curtains, through which, on the brightest day, the laboratory can be converted into a pitch black room in which experiments with light can be performed. A novel kind of switch-

board offers the convenience of all types of current, not only in the physics laboratory, but throughout the building. Just off the biology laboratory is a sunny conservatory, where plants and animals used in biological experiments may be kept. Another feature of the new bldg. is the science library, which has attracted many by the beauty of its high-paneled walls (on which appears the familiar pattern of the Tudor Rose).[57]

As was their custom, the Troy newspapers reported on the campus changes, noting that the building had a tunnel "to be used during the winter months as a passage" to Slocum and that modern radiators were concealed in the walls. Both *Triangle* and the *Troy Record* made special note of the lunchroom for the day girls, and both used the term *cafeteria* to describe the two-room area "with complete lunch counter, dish washing and other facilities, all in monel metal."[58] Both publications also noted that one laboratory was to be devoted to domestic science, which was having one of its periodic resurrections as a subject demanded by some parents. In the end it was never outfitted for this purpose because Eliza Kellas concluded that "it is decidedly better to do well what is attempted than to have too large a number of departments."[59]

In her continuing efforts to "do well" in her final few years as principal, Miss Kellas turned her attention and the attention of the trustees to the personnel recommendations made by the long-range planning committee. It had long been her hope to have "a definite policy of appointment and term of service," and she proposed to the board that new faculty be given two one-year contracts, during what she called their "trial period," then a three-year contract, after which they would be "eligible for a final or permanent appointment" dependent on "a favorable periodic evaluation." She also supported a sabbatical plan that would allow for "a semester at full pay for study or travel."[60] In 1935 the school had joined the financial services organization TIAA-CREF, but she favored optional participation by new faculty prior to their fifth year at the school.

Just as she was aging, so were her faculty and staff, and they had not had time to invest enough in the pension plan to provide adequate retirement income. Throughout the 1930s, when teachers retired, the board voted individually—and inconsistently—on their parting settlements. Léa Surleau returned to Europe in 1932 after twenty-seven years as chair of the French Department; in 1936 Louise Inslee left the primary after twenty-eight years, and Elizabeth Simpson retired after thirty years, twenty-seven of them as Latin Department chair. Each received a year's salary. That same year Elizabeth Robson resigned from the Latin Department after thirty years to get married, but there was no board action. A year later Gretchen Van Buren, a twenty-eight-year veteran of the lower school, left to get married and was awarded a year's salary. As a general rule, most longtime teachers received a year's salary; Lucy Hamson, who retired for health reasons in 1938, and Grace Waterman '91, who left her physical education post in 1940, both got a year's pay.

Replacing these women with others of their dedication would not be easy. Fewer women were going to college, and fewer women were training as teachers. To address this problem, Eliza Kellas introduced an internship program in the fall of 1940, a plan she adopted from "some of the strongest schools for girls."[61] For $300 plus room and board, young graduates of Wellesley, Vassar, Smith, and similar colleges could be prepared for teaching. The first intern, a "cadet teacher"[62] in French with a B.A. and M.A. from Wellesley, arrived in the fall of 1941.

Some of the impetus for greater regulation of salaries and pensions may have come from outside observers. In 1936–37, the school underwent its first formal evaluation by the Middle States Association of Schools and Colleges. Furthermore, from 1932 to 1938, Eliza Kellas was one of twelve women and the only representative of a girls' boarding school to be part of a massive study on the best methods for evaluating secondary schools. The project, which involved dozens of men from colleges and universities as well as high schools, was an "intensive effort to discover the characteristics of a good secondary school and the procedures by which regional associations can most effectively stimulate schools to continuous growth."[63] Although the schools that participated were anonymous, Eliza Kellas proudly reported to the board that at the meeting of the Middle States Association where the results of the survey were presented for the first time, "the chairman of the commission told the Emma Willard delegates that the chart representing the best school was the chart of Emma Willard School."[64]

At the same time that Miss Kellas and the board were attempting to regulate the contracts and salaries of the faculty, they were also review-ing the same benefits for staff. The trustee who became most involved in this process was a new member of the board, John Amstuz, who had joined the board in 1937. A native of Switzerland, whose first language was German, he was a mechanical engineer at an abrasives factory, and he brought a systems approach to problem solving. He and his wife, also a Swiss native, were neighbors of the school.

In 1939 Amstuz surveyed the staff and suggested to Willard Egy, the youthful plant manager, "more efficient methods of procedure." There were six men on the maintenance staff between the ages of 65 and 72, and he proposed "a definite retirement policy" and the need for "under studies for all key men near the retiring age."[65] He also sug-gested that Egy develop job record cards, that the accounting office keep track of wages and hours for Egy, and that policies regarding maximum hours, overtime pay, vacation time, sick leave, and required physical examinations be instituted.

Amstuz's report to the board provides an unusually clear picture of the maintenance and grounds staffing. Charles Beaucheau, the chief engineer since 1910, earned $46 a week. Five other men worked in the power house with him, an operation that continued twenty-four hours a day, seven days a week. His son Roy, a steam fitter, electri-cian, and plumber, earned $30 a week, as did two of the four firemen responsible for shoveling the coal into the heating system. The other two earned $28 a week. The janitorial staff numbered five, four men and one woman. One man was responsible for cleaning Weaver, one for the gym, and two men and one woman were assigned to Slocum. The men made between $22 and $24 a week, but Mrs. Galvin, the sole woman, earned only $15. Three groundsmen earned the same as the janitors; two were paid $22 a week and one $24. Oliver Filkins, sixty-two, earned $27.50 a week for handling the mail, parcel post, doing minor repairs, and assisting as a janitor in the Weaver cafeteria and Slocum. A painter/carpenter named Walker earned $24 a week, and the night watchman, William McDonald, earned $25.

After analyzing the labor force at the school, Amstuz proposed that the watchman work a 72-hour week, the men in the power house a 48-

hour week, and the janitorial and grounds staff a 44-hour week. He also proposed that a wage scale be adopted. The starting salary for common laborers, watchmen, and *women* (emphasis added) was set at 40 cents an hour, and the wages for skilled workers such as electricians and plumbers at 85 cents an hour. His plan adjusted the salaries as well as the hours for the current staff. Beaucheau was to receive 96 cents an hour for a 48-hour week instead of the 85 cents an hour he was receiving for the sixty-plus hours he was used to working. Mrs. Galvin's salary was raised to 40 cents an hour; she was the only member of the janitorial staff to get a raise, but at $17.50 a week, her paycheck was still much smaller than that of the male janitors alongside whom she worked.

While the board wrestled with personnel policy, the school geared up for another anniversary. The year 1939 marked the 125th anniversary. In spite of the Depression, Eliza Kellas planned a celebration to match the 100th anniversary in 1914. She found an anonymous donor to underwrite the costs, the only hint to that person's identity that he or she was "a personal friend" of the principal. Miss Kellas directed the whole celebration, and according to Dwight Marvin, "there was not a flaw in the fabric."[66]

The birthday celebration was originally scheduled for the spring, but the class of 1939 objected to sharing their graduation with the anniversary, and it was moved to October. The opening of school was moved to September 19, a week earlier than usual, to compensate for the time students would spend preparing for and participating in the celebration. Starting school a week early cannot have been popular, but students earned one major concession in honor of the festivities. For the anniversary weekend, wrote an astonished observer, the "school is relaxing its restrictions and allowing the girls to wear silk stockings."[67] Scheduled for October 6 through 8, the program began on Friday night with student musical and theatrical performances and the first screening of a promotional motion picture about the school. Saturday morning, the school hosted an educational roundtable, which was followed by reunion luncheons and the placing of a wreath on the statue of Emma Willard in downtown Troy. In the afternoon, a pageant at Knickerbacker Junior High in Lansingburgh featured students, faculty, and alumnae playing the parts of important figures in the school's history. John Amstuz played Lafayette.

After the pageant, the five hundred alumnae joined faculty and local citizens at a dinner at the Hendrick Hudson Hotel in downtown Troy. Mildred McAfee, president of Wellesley College, was the dinner speaker. The alumnae announced a gift to the school: a garden "in honor and appreciation of Eliza Kellas . . . leader, teacher, friend."[68] The oldest alumna in attendance had graduated in 1873, and the one who traveled the farthest came from California. On Sunday morning the celebration concluded with a service at the Presbyterian Church. Methodist bishop G. Bromley Oxnam, a socially progressive minister who had served as president of DePauw University, reflected on world politics and the economic turmoil, sermonizing that "peace cannot be built upon economic injustice."[69] The weekend cost slightly over $2,300.

At the May board meeting where she outlined the plans for the fall celebration, Miss Kellas addressed the issue of her eventual retirement. According to the minutes, she was "unable to say at this time how much longer she would be able to serve the school as principal."[70] The enrollment was still low, projections for future growth were unfavorable, and only by the strictest budgeting was she able to keep the books balanced. Furthermore, war had broken out in Europe, and the United States was being inexorably drawn to the side of the Allies.

One month after the anniversary celebration, the student body traveled to the Troy Music Hall to hear the von Trapp Family Singers, whose escape from Austria at the time of the Anschluss would become the stuff of Hollywood legend. One month later, a *Triangle* article about Emma Willard students and faculty traveling in Europe over the previous summer reported that Elizabeth Grigg, a French teacher, had had "an encounter with a German submarine."[71] Meanwhile, Eliza Kellas was trying to temper the views of Ingrid Siering '41, a German student who "believed absolutely in the Nazi ideas and activities."[72] By early 1940, the students were again involved in the kinds of war work that had been a part of school life during World War I. Their first project was knitting socks and scarves for the beleaguered French who had fallen under German occupation.

It is possible that Eliza Kellas would have stayed at the school indefinitely. On December 7, when the Japanese attacked Pearl Harbor, she gathered the resident students together and "told us of our tremendous task and explained the opportunity that will be ours when this war is over to help create a better world."[73] It would have been totally consistent with her sense of duty for her to remain at the school for the duration of the war. However, on Christmas Eve, just two weeks after Pearl Harbor, her sister Katherine died. The principal sent terse telegrams to her friends announcing, "My sister passed away today. Funeral Sat. 2:30 Kellas Hall."[74] In fact, the younger Miss Kellas's viewing was held in Kellas Hall, but her funeral took place at First Presbyterian; unlike her sister, she had not converted from the religion of their Scottish ancestors.

Katherine Kellas had been in poor health all fall. For the first time, she had missed Thanksgiving dinner and Revels. Her death left her sister bereft of her longtime companion and best friend. In January Eliza Kellas wrote to alumna Grace Brandow '19, "The days ahead seem dark and lonely, but I do feel that her friends as well as mine will help me still to live a useful life." She thanked another alumna for the flowers that had been sent from the alumnae association, insisting that "the love and sympathy of my girls will help me to go on."[75]

Shortly after school resumed, however, she apparently changed her mind about continuing to work. On January 27, at the first meeting of the board of trustees for 1942, she announced her retirement. She hoped to leave at the end of the school year but promised that she would stay on until the board found a suitable replacement. The trustees formed a search committee to look for her replacement. Edgar H. Betts, the board chair, George Van Santvoord, headmaster of Hotchkiss, and William Hotchkiss served on the committee along with Alison Cook Cook '14, Paul Cook's daughter who had been elected the first alumna trustee by the alumnae association in 1940. The committee also consulted Alison Cook's husband Sidney, dean of the New Jersey College for Women.

There is no record of the number of candidates considered for the position. By the end of April 1942, the search had concluded. Anne Wellington, the secretary to the board of admissions[76] at Wellesley College, was appointed the ninth head of school. She was not a stranger. She had visited the school to recruit students for Wellesley. Furthermore, she had done her undergraduate work at Vassar at the same time as several members of the faculty. Thirty years Eliza Kellas's junior, she was offered a three-year contract and a $5,000 salary. A native of Belmont, Massachusetts, where her father's family had colonial roots stretching back eight generations, she had worked as secretary to the dean of Radcliffe College prior to going to Wellesley as an assistant in the admissions office. She was a Unitarian and a Republican. A graduate of Belmont High School, she had spent a postgraduate year at Cambridge Latin to prepare for Vassar. Except for summer jobs as a camp counselor during college, she had never worked directly with adolescent girls.

The school she inherited had not yet returned to the prosperity of the 1920s. In 1941–42, the boarding population stood at 154, five of whom were eighth graders. Enrollment for her first year was expected to be lower, and, in fact, the residential numbers plummeted to 126. The board was projecting a deficit for 1942–43 of over $50,000, the largest ever. Income was expected to bring in $265,611, approximately half the amount the board believed was necessary for a successful school operation.

Perhaps Anne Wellington's biggest challenge, however, was the presence of her beloved predecessor. The editors of the *Troy Record* could say that "it has been a privilege to have lived in the same city with Miss Kellas,"[77] but Anne Wellington was not so sure. Eliza Kellas was still vice president of the board of trustees, and although she had taken an apartment off campus, she was constantly around. At the first board meeting in the fall, Wellington delivered her principal's report after the rest of the board business was concluded; she was not invited to be there for the earlier portion of the meeting. Eliza Kellas, in contrast, attended both the executive committee meeting and the full board meeting. Although it irked her that the former principal was ever present,[78] in her board report Wellington graciously acknowledged that "Miss Kellas very kindly remained in Troy to make the first weeks easier by answering the many questions of the new principal," and commented that "socially her path was made pleasant by the lovely tea which Miss Kellas gave in September."[79]

In addition to unfilled beds and unsolicited advice, in her first few months at Emma Willard, Anne Wellington had to deal with labor shortages created by the war and changing expectations for the post–high school careers of the young women who had historically attended the school. The job of principal had really been split between the Kellas sisters, and as she tackled the various challenges, she realized that she, too, needed help. By October, she had introduced the board to the concept of a co-headmistress, and to the person she wanted to hire, her friend and lifetime companion, Clemewell Lay.

That Sensitive Balance Between Tradition and Innovation

AMERICANS IN THE YEARS AFTER World War II were uneasy. They had fought a long, costly war for democracy, a war that had heightened awareness that too many people in the United States still lived as second-class citizens or worse. They had defeated the totalitarian forces of the Axis, but in doing so had unleashed the most fearsome weapon humanity had ever known. They had borne witness to the Holocaust, perhaps the modern world's most horrific example of humankind's capacity for evil. With the creation of the United Nations, the United States somewhat reluctantly had taken on a central role in world politics. Their erstwhile ally, the Soviet Union, had almost immediately become their chief enemy, and the world was rapidly dividing into two halves, communist and free.

For most ordinary citizens, the end of the war brought a desire for domestic normality coupled with a constant, vague anxiety about the fragility of world peace and the threat of nuclear war. Nevertheless, many returning veterans found a society positioned for unprecedented prosperity. The booming car industry fueled the growth of suburbs, and industry's release from wartime production stimulated the manufacture of consumer goods. Marriage ages declined, and birthrates increased. High rates of inflation as the 1950s approached were offset by plentiful employment and healthy annual increases in the gross national product. The war had decisively ended the economic conditions that had plagued the country during the Great Depression.

Private schools had historically been bastions of prewar white Christian verities. As novelist John P. Marquand described them, they were places where "there was someone . . . to tell me what to do, someone who knew absolutely what was right and what was wrong, someone who had an answer to everything."[1] Now prep schools were at a crossroads. As one analyst saw it, "the most disturbing charge which is made against them" is that they provide "undemocratic education." In the aftermath of the war, the "new emphasis . . . on democracy and the rights of common men, the concern with race and religious prejudice" constituted a "threat to a kind of education which for the most part has been the privilege of well-to-do white, Protestant families."[2] The threat extended beyond charges of elitism. Inflation had hit educational institutions hard. Salaries were not the only area of fiscal concern. At private schools and small liberal arts colleges, the cost of everything from field hockey sticks to Bunsen burners, from electricity to insurance had increased dramatically. Endowments had not kept pace. At Williams College, for example, the endowment per student in 1939 was $455; by the end of the 1940s, it had dropped to $400. In the 1920s an $8 million endowment had generated $400,000 annually at a rate of 5 percent. In the late 1940s, it took $12 million dollars to generate the same amount, given the rate of return of 3.5 percent.[3]

Most institutions took a two-pronged approach in fighting the charge of elitism. First, and most obviously, schools and colleges planned to increase the number of students coming from nontraditional backgrounds. The GI Bill had single-handedly driven this change for colleges by widening educational access for returning veterans who had not dreamed of college before the war. For independent schools, the expansion of scholarship programs and more widespread student recruitment were critical to a similar transformation. Second, private schools began to shift their emphasis from private to independent. Private schools in contrast to public schools connoted exclusion. Independent schools, as opposed to public schools, had the freedom to develop curriculum, hire faculty, tackle questions of religion and morality, and build student character through residential life programs, athletics, and other extracurricular activities. In short, independent schools had the potential to beat their public school competition in the delivery of a higher quality education.

Anne Wellington and the board of trustees were committed to diversifying the student population and sought gifts for scholarships whenever possible. In keeping with this goal, the enrollment of girls of different faiths and the relatively early first steps toward student ethnic diversity demonstrated the school's determination to eschew WASP elitism. Then, as now, the faculty was far less diverse than the student body, but in the fall of 1950, the first nonwhite teacher joined the faculty. Grace Yang, a native Chinese woman and unmarried career teacher, was a product of the prestigious McTyeire School in Shanghai, Mount Holyoke, and Columbia Teachers' College. In other words, with the exception of her ethnicity, she was very much like the women who had taught at the school for years. In 1957 a Hawaiian of Japanese ancestry, Miyoko Sugano, joined the English Department as a sabbatical replacement.[4] However, with a small endowment and inflation as acute in Troy as elsewhere, the school lacked the resources necessary for any real change in the composition of either the student body or the faculty.

Instead Emma Willard took its most transformative postwar step with the creation and adoption of a new curriculum. The positive reaction from the educational world, the popular media, the faculty, the students, and prospective families ensured the school's relevance and solidified its place as an intellectual leader among its peer institutions. As the *Washington Post* proclaimed, "Education Gallops Upon a Trojan Horse."[5] On June 10, 1950, ninety-eight seniors received their diplomas. They were the first of more than twenty classes to complete the heralded "correlated curriculum" that the faculty had designed to meet the needs of high school girls in the Atomic Age. As the graduation speaker, Rev. Charles Noble, told the assembled parents and students in 1950, "The school has kept abreast of the times without losing the distinction which has characterized its history."[6]

Wellington and Lay had contemplated revising the curriculum shortly after Lay joined the administration, but the end of the war and new thinking about the ideal American high school education stimulated them to action in 1946. As had been the case in the 1890s, Ivy League and other elite colleges led the charge. In 1945 Harvard published *General Education in a Free Society*, a study of "universal education" undertaken by twelve professors chosen from two of the university's faculties, Arts and Sciences and Education. All twelve were men, but they included Radcliffe president and Emma Willard trustee Wilbur K. Jordan. According to James Bryant Conant, Harvard's president, their report added to the "veritable downpour" of books on the future of American collegiate education after the war. The Harvard report was limited not to Harvard or even to colleges, but laid out a blueprint for an ideal education across all levels. The impetus for the report was the concern that although increasing numbers of students were attending high school, the education they were getting lacked coherence and in no way guaranteed that they would become thoughtful, productive citizens. As Conant explained,

> Even a good grounding in mathematics and the physical and biological sciences, combined with an ability to read and write several foreign languages, does not provide a sufficient educational background for citizens of a free nation. For such a program lacks contact with both man's emotional experience as an individual and his practical experience as a gregarious animal. It includes little of what was once known as 'the wisdom of the ages' and might nowadays be described as 'our cultural pattern.' It includes no history, no art, no literature, no philosophy. Unless the educational process includes at each level of maturity some continuing contact with those fields in which value judgments are of prime importance, it must fall far short of the ideal.[7]

In his contemporaneous critique of women's higher education, Mills College president Lynn T. White struck a similar note, arguing that education in and of itself was not "good." As an example, he cited Mussolini's construction of schools for "Sicilian peasants" because a rudimentary literacy was necessary to convert the Italian masses to fascism.[8]

In contrast to the men at Harvard, White focused specifically on women's education. In fact, he castigated women's colleges in the Northeast for aping men's colleges and failing to meet the unique needs of their female students. He singled out Radcliffe for special scorn as an institution in "curricular bondage to Harvard"; further, he pointed out, Radcliffe had not appointed a woman professor to its faculty until 1948.[9] Nevertheless, for the women at Emma Willard, the Harvard imprimatur was the educational equivalent of the *Good Housekeeping* seal of approval. That the Harvard study played a large role in Emma Willard's development of a new curriculum was reinforced by the inclusion in the preface of statements from Emma Hart Willard and *General Education in a Free Society*. From the founder came this statement: "I look forward to what should be in education rather than back to imitate defective systems." From Harvard came the caution to balance the new with the best of the old: "Education can therefore be wholly devoted neither to tradition nor to experiment. . . . It must uphold at the same time tradition and experiment."[10]

Since Miss Kellas's time, the faculty who chaired the academic departments at the school had met in a body called the cabinet, and it was this group that Wellington and Lay asked to develop a new curriculum. All of the members of the cabinet were veteran teachers. From their ranks a curriculum committee evolved, chaired by Elizabeth Potwine, the head of mathematics. Ellen Manchester, English Department chair, Mary Wilson, History Department chair, and Katherine Weaver, Science Department chair, comprised the rest of the committee. Eliza Kellas had hired Potwine, who at sixty-eight was the oldest of the group and the only one without a degree from either Wellesley or Vassar. (She was a Mount Holyoke graduate.) Kellas's predecessor, Anna Leach, had hired the others. Mary Wilson's tenure had begun in 1908, the year after she left Vassar with both her bachelor's and master's degrees. She was sixty-four. Ellen Manchester and Katherine Weaver had joined the faculty in 1910; both had earned their bachelor's degrees at Wellesley, although Weaver was two years younger than Manchester, who was Wilson's age. Weaver, Manchester, and Potwine, like Clemewell Lay, had all earned graduate degrees at Columbia. All of these women were revered for their teaching. Speaking about Katherine Weaver more than fifty years after her graduation, one of her former students, who had a doctorate in microbiology, commented, "Teaching was in her genes, it just poured out of her soul."[11] What was true for Weaver in science was true for the others in their disciplines, according to the hundreds of students they taught.

Interestingly, in light of the increasing awareness of America's global role, the Harvard report had downplayed the need for foreign language in a general secondary school curriculum, and no one from the Language Department sat on the Emma Willard committee. Actually, the Harvard group went so far as to dismiss language study as having little role in the development of good non-college-educated American citizens. Foreign language, they concluded, was "of far less use to young people who do not go beyond high school than music, the arts, English or a study of American literature."[12] In spite of Harvard's emphasis on fine arts and music, no teachers from these disciplines were included on the school committee. Nor was any administrator a permanent member of the committee, although Clemewell Lay served ex officio. She would later describe the curriculum work as her "chef d'oeuvre" at Emma Willard.[13] According to Potwine, it was Lay who served as the chief advocate for including significant work in music and the fine arts. In turn, Lay described Potwine as "an especially clear thinking individual who speaks and writes well and whose personal fortitude equips her to take the slings and arrows in debate with equanimity and enables her to hold [a] committee to the main endeavor."[14]

The women who wrote the new curriculum were well aware of their seniority. At her retirement in 1950, Ellen Manchester remarked that when Wellington and Lay proposed the idea of a new curriculum, she was "at a stage in my career when the inclination might have been strong to follow a well tried pattern, [but] I was challenged to take a fresh approach and realize anew the vitality of education."[15] For Potwine, devoted as she had been to the discipline of mathematics, it was not "easy to discard the accepted ritual of mathematics and replace it with the big and vital idea."[16] She later wrote that she was able to do so because the committee as a whole valued the "spirit of unity, of cooperation, of change which does not overthrow, of growth which does not supersede."[17] For "Kitch" Jordan, the boldness of the new curriculum rested on three things: that it was "hammered out on the anvil of discussion by the faculty,"[18] that it was a "new approach . . . devised by older teachers,"[19] and that it was free of the "'tyranny of the college boards."[20]

For Anne Wellington, the support of her friend "Kitch" Jordan was extremely important. Not only was he able to consult regularly with the faculty committee, he also provided a voice of affirmation on the board of trustees. From the first, Jordan was enthusiastic about the "scheme of education" in which "those who are liberally educated . . . share directly and richly in a common cultural heritage." As a member of the trustee education committee, he reported regularly on the committee's work, and when the plan had been in operation for some time, he steadfastly maintained that it was "one of the most important experiments in secondary education in this last generation."[21]

Jordan also provided a collegiate stamp of approval. There was some trepidation about how colleges would evaluate applicants who had studied under the new curriculum, and from 1950 on, the headmistresses made elaborate reports to the board, the alumnae, and to parents celebrating the school's college placement record. These were designed to assuage any fears that the new curriculum provided less than adequate college preparation. In 1959 Wellington told a *Newsweek* reporter that when it came to soliciting college opinion about the change, "We told them. . . . We didn't ask them."[22] She was guilty of selective memory at best, for she certainly made sure that Radcliffe's chief administrator approved every step of the way, and she assured the board in 1948 that college admissions offices had been consulted.

The committee laid out an ambitious schedule. They began their work in the spring of 1946 with the understanding that the new curriculum would be implemented in the fall of 1947. In fact, the work was finished by February 1947. A special edition of the *Bulletin* published that month described the "Emma Willard Plan of Education" for alumnae and prospective families.[23] The new curriculum was initially designed to be a three-year course. Although the report did not mention it, the continuing low enrollment in the freshman and sophomore classes, compared to the numbers in the upper classes, probably drove this decision. The administration wanted to change the lingering Depression-era pattern of enrolling a student body disproportionately composed of juniors and seniors. By offering a cohesive curriculum beginning in the tenth grade, more families might be encouraged to send their daughters as sophomores. The growth in the sophomore class eventually occurred, but it was not until 1956–57 that the sophomores outnumbered the juniors and seniors for the first time. Curriculum—or burgeoning youthful population? The number of children between the ages of 5 and 14 grew from 24.3 million in 1950 to 35.5 million in 1960. The phenomenon of the teenager as a separate entity was underlined in 1959 when singer Pat Boone hit the best-seller list with *Twixt Twelve and Twenty*.

In outlining the new curriculum, the committee report began with an explanation of the reasons the change was necessary. First, the school, in line with the recommendations from the Harvard study, hoped to reverse the recent trend where secondary school curricula had become overly specialized and covered "too much ground," none of it thoroughly. Second were the pressures of the modern age. The first half of the twentieth century had seen an explosion of information so tremendous that the modern world could be equated with "a vast telephone exchange where hundreds of jangling calls are coming in, and there is no one to make the connections." In light of this information overload, the world was "losing—ha[d] perhaps lost—a right sense of values . . . those intangibles inherent in our tradition, our code of honor and acceptance of moral obligations." This "heritage of values" was drawn from "our classical and Christian tradition."[24]

The curriculum was unabashedly Western and Christian in its ethical point of view, but it took this position as a common starting point from which students could better understand other cultures, systems of government, and beliefs. In its focus on the heritage of timeless principles stretching back to Greco-Roman times, the curriculum mirrored the values that Emma Willard had depicted in her award-winning illustration, *The Temple of Time*. Clemewell Lay summarized it as "being a truly creative learning experience in which students develop a sense of values and some compassion, become excited about the roots of our American democracy, learn to evaluate their reading, discuss with some literacy both music and art . . . and realize from their work in science the terrible urgency to understand even more . . . if we are to survive." Taken all together, she concluded, the curriculum was "Life."[25] John Amstuz, who became president of the board of trustees in 1950, saw the curriculum as "preparing young people to enter the complex world with courage, understanding, and faith in our American way of life."[26] An early student in the course recalled that it gave her the "ability to see the whole of a problem . . . and not get bogged down in one area so that one loses sight of the multiple facets of a situation."[27] An education editor at the *Herald Tribune* likened it to the postwar curriculum adopted by Amherst College in 1947, writing that both "permit subjects and departments to join hands so that education emerges as a meaningful pattern rather than as a conglomerate of unrelated courses."[28]

As the *Tribune* pointed out, the key to the new curriculum was coordination among departments with a single area of concentration uniting the work of the sophomore, junior, and senior years. The sophomores, juniors, and seniors all enrolled in a correlated course in English, history, music, the fine arts, drama, and religion. Beginning in the fall of 1947, the sophomore course was organized around the study of the medieval and Renaissance periods. In 1948 the correlated course included the juniors who focused on modern European history, and in 1949 the correlation was completed with the addition of a senior course focused on American history. Sophomores in 1947–48, the class of 1950, became the first class to be completely "correlated," an accomplishment they celebrated in a senior skit titled "Correlation Belle" that featured a character they named "Guinea Pig." Beginning in 1958 freshmen took correlated courses centered on ancient history, a logical outcome of the requirement that all ninth graders take Latin. The class of 1962 was the first to have been correlated all four years.

From the beginning, the new curriculum required all sophomores, juniors, and seniors to take history, music, art, and religion, and all sophomores and juniors to take mathematics and science. Although the school had long been heralded for its science curriculum and often, although erroneously, touted as the first school to teach girls science and higher mathematics, this was actually the first science *requirement* at the school. The tenth and eleventh grade science courses were designed to provide "a *general education* in science, not to be confused with *general science*,"[29] a course traditionally taken by ninth graders in most American high schools. The sophomore science course was focused on biology and organized around the theme of "man as living organism," and the juniors studied physical sciences organized under the umbrella of "man in his relation to the physical world."[30] The new courses in mathematics, required for sophomores and juniors, were also topical. Wrote Potwine, who had taught mathematics in conventional order for over forty years,

> The course will be entirely new, differing in sequence of topics and in presentation from traditional courses. . . . The subject matter of the tenth and eleventh years satisfies the minimum requirement in geometry for college entrance and extends the study of algebra to the use of logarithms and the slide rule. . . . The reason for a girl's study of mathematics differs in several respects from her brother's. The values for him are in large measure in the facts and skills acquired; for her they are more likely to be in the overtones, the by-products which persist after the last theorem has been proved—and forgotten.[31]

For seniors whose interests lay in mathematics or science, there were electives along more traditional lines that were designed to prepare them for college work in these fields. Counting languages, which were elective after freshman Latin, a third of the new curriculum was elective. Half of the senior year was elective; Lay commented that "the variety of offerings is almost heady."[32] Choices ranged from "Preface to Ethics," where students read Plato, Dostoevsky, and Kierkegaard, among others, to music composition to theater to "Modern Problems," an elective required for international students because it would "aid them in understanding American affairs . . . and the Western concept of democracy versus the Russian."[33]

Nevertheless, the core was clear; in establishing the content of the courses, the curriculum committee stated directly that "the first essential is the study of the humanities and social studies,"[34] which they defined as written and oral English, literature, music and fine arts, and religion all coordinated with history. To the critics who feared that girls interested in mathematics and science would be shortchanged, Anne Wellington always pointed out that two members of the "guinea pig" class entered Harvard and Yale medical schools immediately after graduating with honors from Vassar and Radcliffe, respectively.[35] Furthermore, the mathematics curriculum, with its emphasis on concepts over rote memorization, predated the 1960 report from the Committee on Mathematics of the College Entrance Examination Board, which led to the widely adopted "New Math" curriculum.

The correlated curriculum also called for changes in pedagogy. Textbooks, although still available, were no longer universally used and, in fact, for the most part were "largely discarded."[36] To meet academic needs beyond texts, the library became an even more important center for student research and study. During the first decade of the correlated curriculum, the number of volumes in the library more than doubled. Faculty, under the supervision of Clemewell Lay, worked with the librarian to ensure that the library had the materials necessary to support the curriculum, particularly in art, history, and religion. Extensive outside reading lists were provided for every class. Lay believed that the outside reading provided additional stimulus for the more gifted students who benefited from the intellectual challenge, given that all tenth, eleventh, and twelfth graders took basically the same classes. As she explained, "The abler the student, the farther she reads, a method which automatically allows for differences in the levels of ability."[37]

There was also an increase in "the use of sensory aids—films, records and radio."[38] In addition, the lecture, as a main means of communicating information, was generally replaced by more hands-on learning. Mindful, however, that note taking was a skill that would be needed in college, the entire student body attended art history lectures by visiting Williams College professor Whitney Stoddard, one of the preeminent art historians of the twentieth century. (His daughter Elizabeth was a member of the class of 1957.)

In spite of the awareness of "note taking" as a necessary skill for future college students, the correlated curriculum in many ways veered from the increasing—and, in some cases, new—emphasis on college placement prevalent at many girls' schools during the 1950s and early 1960s. For some schools, college preparation was a relatively new phenomenon. At Foxcroft, for example, it had not been unusual for fewer than a third of the graduates to go on to college in the 1930s, and Miss Porter's had not shifted from its emphasis on "finishing" until after the war. Allegra Maynard, the second headmistress of Madeira, had been at the school since 1931 and had seen the transition on her campus. Now girls aimed for college, and it was "'fashionable to do well.'"[39] In the early 1950s, Westover still reserved 20 percent of its spots for students who were not planning to attend college.

Increasingly, however, college admissions drove the curriculum at girls' boarding schools. At Abbot, which had long shared Emma Willard's commitment to serious academic preparation, 100 percent of the students went on to college. Abbot girls were reputed to "scorn the "'empty-shell' preppies . . . who] have blond hair and wear Lanz dresses and talk about boys and diets."[40] At Abbot, however, the teachers worried that the emphasis on college admission meant that students "just want to know the right answer for the test."[41] The growing emphasis on college preparation meant that girls' school curricula were increasingly narrow and "crammed with vocab, algebraic formulas, and obscure points of American history—the fragmentary ammunition of test-taking." This pattern contrasted sharply with Emma Willard, "one of the few . . . to insist that its students not lose sight of the overall pattern of what they are studying."[42] The school adhered steadfastly to its singular curriculum in spite of the mounting college pressures.

These pressures came mostly from the increasing importance of test scores in determining college admission. The College Board had moved away from dictating secondary school curriculum and was now almost exclusively a testing organization; they had formed the Educational Testing Service (ETS), a not-for-profit corporation, in 1947. Although the board maintained that the "tests should measure what teachers taught but should not influence what or how they taught,"[43] the colleges' increasing use of achievement tests, first introduced by the College Board in 1937, counteracted that policy.

From 1947 to 1961, Wellington and Lay made no curricular changes specifically to meet college expectations, but they were acutely aware of the changing patterns in college admissions occasioned by the explosion in the numbers of teenagers and in the numbers of teenagers wanting to go to college. Over the course of the 1950s, 94 percent of seniors went on to college, 58 percent to four-year women's colleges, 27 percent to coeducational colleges and universities, and 15 percent to two-year colleges, almost all of which were women's institutions. As early as 1952, in response to tighter admission at northeastern colleges traditionally attended by Emma Willard graduates, they assured alumnae that students had undergone a "change in attitude." Emma Willard students now considered a much wider range of colleges. A senior was no longer swayed by the "fact that her roommate and everyone else on her corridor is going to Vassar,"[44] somewhat dubious support for the wider range assertion.

The changing landscape of college admissions meant another change beyond the inclusion of new institutions on graduates' wish lists. Over the course of the decade, "the numbers of well-qualified people made available to students for college counseling"[45] greatly expanded. Parents then—as now—had sometimes unrealistic goals for their daughters, in spite of the school's (and the media's) communication about changing admissions practices. Gertrude Watkins, the director of guidance from 1944 to 1961, penned a typical note to Wellington about a phone call from the mother of a senior. She had called "wondering why we couldn't get J—into Vassar!!"[46] (The student in question had entered the school as a junior with all D's on her transcript and had not scored over 400 on either part of her SAT, a horrifying profile by twenty-first century standards but one that would not have automatically precluded admission to Vassar in the 1930s.)

The rhetoric from the school on the subject of college admission sounded more and more modern as the 1960s approached. Wellington wrote about the "ever-mounting desire . . . for admission to colleges with well-known names" and "the frenzy attending college admissions,"[47] which she ascribed to the growing trend among seniors to make multiple applications. (Gone were the prewar days when families indicated on the application to Emma Willard the name of the one college where their daughter was already registered.) In 1958, in response to their rapidly expanding applicant pools, a group of highly selective colleges introduced a system of "early decision." Lay explained to the board that the new program would "affect only the ablest,"[48] and she estimated that just thirteen girls in the rising senior class fit that category. Reporting on the decisions for the class of 1958, she remarked that "there is an occasional upset which [is] magnified by the students."[49] College admission was becoming a source of student tension and stress, in spite of "every effort to . . . keep the girls from becoming too disturbed by the tightening admissions policies."[50] In another decade the college placement record would become an important factor in admissions, but for the time being, the value of an Emma Willard education outweighed future considerations. Lay wrote confidently, "Students recognize the quality of their instruction and say with conviction, 'If I should not get into the college I most want, I have already had a good liberal education.'"[51]

One aspect of "a good liberal education" was the opportunity to hear from a rich variety of outside speakers. Visiting lecturers had long been a source of instruction, entertainment, and, particularly at the weekly vespers services, inspiration. Throughout the 1950s, every attempt was made to augment and enhance the correlated curriculum with outside speakers. As the 1950s went on, the list of speakers more often included women. The poets May Sarton and Marianne Moore, as well as perennial favorite daughter Laura Benet '03, read their work at the school. Although fathers still dominated, mothers began to be featured as well. Katherine Elkins White, mother of Frances '51, made headlines in the *New York Times* when she was elected mayor of Red Bank, New Jersey. Not only was she a woman, but she was a Democrat in a Republican borough. Two months after her election, she addressed the girls on the topic "Women in Politics," sending the message that this was an acceptable career choice. When Susan Crary graduated in 1956, her mother, Catherine Snell Crary '36, a Barnard history professor, spoke at the post-commencement luncheon. On a lighter note, students heard from Josephine Lowman, mother of Cherry Lowman '52 and a nationally syndicated columnist who was an early diet and exercise maven.

In spite of these changes, the vast majority of outside speakers who came to the campus between the inception of the correlated curriculum in 1947 and the retirement of the headmistresses in 1961 were white male members of the clergy. The weekly vespers services continued to be required of all students, and religion was a key component of the curriculum. For Americans in general in the 1950s, the anxiety generated by the Atomic Age, as well as the threat of "godless communism" combined to propel them toward religion. As historians have pointed out, this form of American faith was not Protestant and exclusionary but a communal belief stemming from the fact that all American Protestants, Catholics, and Jews believed in one god. To have faith in one all-powerful God was part of defining what it was to be an American. In 1952, in *Zorach v. Clauson,* the Supreme Court declared that Americans "are a religious people whose institutions presuppose a Supreme Being," in 1954 the phrase "under God" was added to the "Pledge of Allegiance" recited in public schools, and in 1955 the words "In God We Trust" were added to paper money. In 1952, 1953, and 1954, the Revised Standard Version of the Bible topped the best-seller list. Atheism was equated with communism.

This was the climate in which the correlated curriculum was designed, and it was also the climate in which the conversion of the gymnasium into the Alumnae Chapel was completed. Both were of a piece with 1950s American thinking. As Elizabeth Potwine commented, "This was the fundamental correlation: the recognition of the values in our civilization that are permanent and should carry over into the life of the individual and the society of a new era."[52] To critics who questioned the value of teaching religion and history in the Atomic Age, she replied that there was no better time to ground future voters in their western Judeo-Christian heritage. Reviewing Revels, *The Troy Times Record* connected the school's study of the past with the present from a different perspective: "Capturing the spirit of the carefree era when the heads of King Henry's wives fell as freely as apples from autumn trees, the students took the 'Revels' audience out of the atomic age for a few merry hours into a more happy world."[53]

The class of 1950 was not just the first class to graduate under the correlated curriculum; they were also the first class whose commencement took place in the completed chapel. The chapel had been dedicated the prior June after the stained glass windows and balcony were installed. Although the iconography in the chapel was decidedly Christian, the dedication ceremony was very much in keeping with the language of universal faith as a cornerstone of

American citizenship (and also very masculine). The congregation dedicated the chapel

> to the worship of the universal Father of us all . . . to the training of youth in faith and knowledge and to the summoning of youth to a life of service [and] to the unfinished tasks of human welfare, to the establishment of justice, to the conquest of ignorance and fear, to the abolition of war, and to the consummation of the Brotherhood of all men under God . . . [and] in loving memory of all those who have gone before us in this beloved place of learning, and of all those whose hearts and hands have served in the enrichment of the lives nurtured in their youth by this school.[54]

Harriet Morgan Tyng, the director of the Willard Day School and a published poet, contributed "The Chapel," a poem that highlighted the role of the chapel in a troubled world. She urged the students to look at the chapel's walls and "Find faith in their simplicity of line/Their sturdiness of stone/Rising in contrast to the crude design/Of the world you have known."[55] For Ellen Manchester the chapel physically formed the third point in the campus triangle with Sage and Slocum and metaphorically provided the third element in the triangle of "Truth, Fellowship, and Faith" represented by the three buildings. Above all, she said, the chapel provides "that sensitive balance between tradition and innovation on which true progress rests."[56]

Small numbers of Jewish and Roman Catholic students enrolled steadily throughout the 1950s. Perhaps in response to the war and the revelation of Hitler's atrocities, in 1947 Revels lost some of its Christian focus when the nativity scene was dropped from the pageant. That same year saw the crowning of the first Jewish May queen. It was not until a decade later, however, that the catalog specifically acknowledged the enrollment of students who practiced faiths other than Protestant Christianity. The catalog for 1957–58 noted, "Although the school was founded in the Protestant Christian tradition, students from other faiths are enrolled."[57] The rules allowed students to attend their own services as long as these did not conflict with the two all-school required services held on the campus each week.

On Saturday mornings, a brief chapel service was conducted by students. Several times a year Lucile Tuttle, who had grown up in India with missionary parents, led traditional hymn sings. Other programs varied from informational talks on subjects such as "Christmas in Czechoslovakia" to presentations on community service opportunities including national projects like the March of Dimes and local work at nearby Vanderheyden orphanage. Additionally, there were programs on Jewish and even Islamic traditions. The Sunday afternoon services, however, remained monolithically Christian and Protestant; in a comprehensive listing of vespers speakers between 1943 and 1960, there was one woman, one African American, and no rabbi or priest. There were, however, numbers of very liberal Protestant theologians including Henry Sloane Coffin and André Trocmé, who, along with his wife, had provided refuge to numbers of persecuted French Jews. Although the lack of diversity is striking from a twenty-first century perspective, in 1957 the Middle States team conducting a ten-year evaluation of the school commended the school for its versatility in working with students of varied faiths.

Religious services were not the only aspect of the correlated curriculum that moved beyond the classroom. The whole point of the correlated curriculum was to produce the citizens the world needed to solve its problems. It was not enough for students to study the historic and ethical principles that underpinned America's greatness and had led to the nation's position of world leadership. The academic needed to be merged with the extracurricular, and students needed to "make use of the democratic principles studied in the classroom."[58] An elaborate system of school government was designed to ensure that every girl at some point had an opportunity to participate, and most had an opportunity to lead. In an article in *Harper's,* a reporter comparing and contrasting several girls' schools concluded that because of the correlation between the academic and the extracurricular at Emma Willard, "the activities of the school seem far more coherent than at any other school I visited."[59] She grouped Emma Willard with Brearley and Abbot as the only girls' schools more interested in developing leadership than preparation for a "dubious future of membership in a social class."[60]

Public speaking was an important corollary to leadership training. All students enrolled in the correlated curriculum were expected to learn to speak in front of a group. All seniors were required to write an original speech on the topic "I Speak for Democracy" for an annual national contest sponsored by the Veterans of Foreign Wars. In 1957 Deborah Allen, a senior from Massachusetts, was one of four national winners and adorned the cover of *Look* magazine with her state's handsome young junior senator, John Fitzgerald Kennedy, by her side. No other Emma Willard girls advanced to the national level, but in 1961 the visiting English-speaking Union scholar, Briony Sharman, won first place in the New York State division.

To provide enough leadership opportunities for every student, a complicated array of councils and committees was established under the umbrella of school council. Most elections were held in the spring, but some offices were reserved specifically for new students, who were elected in the fall. For example, the position of vice president on the Work Council was held for a new senior boarder, as was the co-captaincy of the intramural Green Team. Junior and sophomore representatives to Work Council were also chosen in the fall and limited to new members of those classes. In addition to the traditional class officers, proctors, and newspaper and yearbook staffs, students were elected to Slocum Council, the Welfare Committee, the Day Welfare Committee, the Athletic Council, the Cooperative Tea House Committee, class song leadership, Campus Players, Sage Council, Chapel Circle Council, Kellas Council, the business committee, the social committee, and the Day Girl Council. Heads of the various councils comprised the School Council, which met with the headmistresses or Lucile Tuttle, a larger-than-life figure in student lore who came to the school as director of admissions in 1953 but held a variety of senior administrative positions before her retirement in 1968.

One of the more important student groups joining the campus in conjunction with the new curriculum was UNEW, acronym for the United Nations at Emma Willard, a group whose main purpose was "to establish habits of thought regarding ways by which the mature citizen helps to keep the peace."[61] Wellington and Lay considered the United Nations to be the capstone of international citizenship, and UNEW provided a global forum at the school. All students were members, with international students often providing the programming for the group by telling the rest of the school about their native countries. Reporting to the board in the fall of 1950, Wellington emphasized that the new students included a number of international students. Among them were American Field Service students from Holland and France, Josephine Bisharat '51, the daughter of a Palestinian sheik, and freshman Diane Sze '54, the first Asian student to spend her whole high school career at Emma Willard. Throughout the 1950s, by the use of scholarships and by hosting visiting foreign students, sometimes for only a few weeks' stay, the school exposed students to the cultures of other nations. The emphasis on globalism contrasted sharply with the practice at other girls' schools. A *Harper's* reporter applauded the international awareness on the Troy campus and ruefully lamented that students at a girls' boarding school in Virginia stayed "in touch with the world by watching President Kennedy's helicopter pass overhead from time to time."[62]

Diane's father, Dr. Szeming Sze, was the medical director at the United Nations and instrumental in the founding of the World Health Organization. Throughout the early 1950s, he facilitated the school's annual field trips to UN headquarters in New York. A number of students were Dr. Sze's guests the day that Warren Austin, the U.S. ambassador to the UN, spoke about Gen. Douglas MacArthur's analysis of the intentions of the Chinese communists with regard to Korea, an analysis that soon led to President Truman's famous removal of the general's command. The students were most likely unaware of the day's significance, but the visit—and subsequent visits—were designed to impress on them the legacy of democracy that connected "individuals capable of writing the Constitution . . . and 175 years later of creating the United Nations."[63]

Because the faculty was teaching new material in new ways, they attended a number of seminars and workshops. In the fall of 1950, Charles Mott, General Motors founder and father of three Emma Willard students, funded a series of faculty lectures. His gift provided education professors from the University of Michigan who addressed the faculty on a variety of educational issues including "Teachers' Mental Health." On another occasion faculty attended a seminar on nuclear fission designed by Rensselaer Polytechnic Institute (RPI) and Union professors to explain atomic theory to area teachers. In the fall of 1956, the school hosted its own teachers' conference. The attendees at the weekend event were invited to spend the night on campus. (Seniors who gave up their rooms for the visitors were granted an extra weekend off campus.)

In spite of the emphasis on Western democratic traditions, the school endeavored to introduce students to other parts of the world. This goal was given a tremendous boost in 1958 when a grant from the Johnson Trust funded a multiple-year project in non-Western study. A week-long seminar on the Middle East involving speakers, workshops, and UNEW presentations was held in 1958–59. The next year the topic was Africa, and in the final year, the topic was the Soviet Union. In preparation for the session on Russia, Lucile Tuttle and Louise McKeon, chairs of the English and History Departments, made a two-week trip to the Soviet Union that was underwritten by the gift from the foundation. Dianna Strong '62 credited the area studies program with transforming her life. She recently recalled "the beautiful LARGE hand-painted map of the area [being studied] at the top of that exquisite double marble staircase in Slocum, and all the great speakers, artists, dancers. . . . As an impressionable young girl from Northern Connecticut, who had never even been on a train, *this area studies program opened my eyes to the world.*"[64]

Strong is just one of legions of graduates who regard the correlated curriculum as a seminal educational experience. Dozens of women who went on to earn graduate degrees at prestigious universities have steadfastly maintained that their Emma Willard education was the high point of their scholastic career.

The first decade of the correlated curriculum coincided with great growth in the school's enrollment. In the fall of 1946, the school had enrolled 220 boarders; by 1954 the number was 260, and by the end of the decade the number hovered around 290. Day student numbers remained static by design, never exceeding fifty. In 1955 record enrollments in both the ninth and tenth grades signaled that the school had reached a turning point in its quest to balance younger and older classes. The sophomore class that year numbered eighty-eight residential students, and there were thirty-two ninth grade boarders. Applications doubled during the same period, and selectivity increased dramatically. For example, 150 boarders applied for 1953–54, and only 9 were refused. Of the 276 applications for 1957–58, 89 were refused.

At the same time that enrollment increased, financial aid decreased. The prosperity of the decade undoubtedly contributed to the decline in requests for financial aid. In 1954–55, nearly 19 percent of the 260 boarders received financial aid. In 1957–58, only 14.6 percent of the residential population received some form of scholarship; the next year, only 12 percent of the 291 boarders received aid. At that point, three day students received assistance, and the total budget for scholarships stood at $32,800. In 1950 parents paid $1,900 in boarding tuition; at the end of the decade the tuition had risen to $2,700. In general, the school's tuition was lower than that at other girls' boarding schools and higher than the tuition at leading boys' schools such as Exeter and Andover.

In spite of burgeoning enrollments, hikes in tuition, and reductions in financial aid, the budgets during the 1950s rarely balanced. An exception was the 1951–52 budget, which showed a surplus of income over expenses of $9,000. Trustee George Van Santvoord, headmaster of Hotchkiss, found this feat remarkable at a time "when most schools are running a deficit."[65]

Budget woes were not limited to private schools. In 1952 the board noted that to save costs, area public schools were cutting back on after-hours programs such as scouting, and some trustees suggested that Emma Willard might provide space for such organizations as a way of giving back to the wider community. There was recent precedent for extending a helping hand to the public sector. Classes for seventh and eighth graders from Public School 16 had been held in the chapel since January 1949 when their school was the victim of a fire that destroyed the building.

Maintaining cordial relations with Troy's citizens was a primary reason for the continuation of the Willard Day School. The trustees believed that the school provided a service for the city because it was the only independent nondenominational option for young children in Troy. Nevertheless, the school had struggled ever since its move to Cluett House and its reinvention as a coeducational institution. In years when the high school broke even or showed a small surplus, the deficit from the Willard Day School tipped the balance into the red. In 1946 Harriet Morgan Tyng, a respected educator, was appointed director, but things did not improve. In 1951 a preschool class of three- and four-year-olds was added, but the $6,000 deficit that year marked a new high. By 1955 the trustees concluded that the construction of a new school on the site of the burned-out School 16 and the development of new parochial schools throughout the city had filled the demand for elementary education. Since the move to Cluett, the school had cost $130,000 in operating losses and renovation expenses. Between 1951 and 1955, the number of students had decreased from 140 to 81. The board decided to phase out the school over five years, eliminating the kindergarten in the fall of 1956 and other grades subsequently. In 1956 the school opened with only fifty-six students, and the buildings and grounds committee recommended that the day school be closed "at the earliest possible time."[66] Willard Day School closed in June 1957. The budgets for its last three years showed deficits of $21,000, $14,000, and $10,000. Wellington concluded, "The community is not able to provide the financial support for the kind of education the school is morally obligated to provide."[67]

The deficits in the day school were not the only persistent budget issues. On the eve of the 1950s, a subcommittee of the board focused on the high school budget. They estimated that the school needed $50,000 in additional income to run the programs it wanted, to recruit the caliber of faculty to match the quality of retiring senior teachers, and to diversify the student body by the addition of more international students. In their *Report of the Subcommittee of the Development Committee of Emma Willard School*, John Amstuz, Earl Newsom, and William Avirett outlined the five "tools" available to the board and administration: increase tuition, manage current resources more efficiently, appeal to parents and alumnae for support, focus on sustaining a "full quota" of 250 boarding students, and procure endowment dollars from foundations. They concluded that more efficient management, by which they meant cost saving in the administration, was impossible, so they focused on the others, lumping development and admissions together. They recommended that tuition be kept competitive with other girls' boarding schools and that scholarships be increased. They found that management efficiencies were unlikely to make a significant dent in the deficit and urged the board to raise more money rather than try to trim expenses. They urged an immediate and ongoing appeal to parents and alumnae for annual support, with the caveat that such appeals can become "abuse." As they cautioned the board, any fund-raising efforts had to enhance the prestige of the school, not detract from it. In fund-raising, as in all else, "The constant goal of . . . the School should be to maintain and expand the reputation of the School as offering absolutely top quality in educational and service facilities; a School which selects for its student body those exceptional girls who are to become leaders among those of their generation—without regard to race, creed, color, or economic status; a school so widely recognized in those terms that it maintains a constant waiting list of applicants."

This would be most effective if directed at specific projects such as scholarships, faculty salaries, or program. They also focused on admissions, arguing, "If Emma Willard School is to maintain its reputation as *the* School of quality, it is not enough that our curriculum be the best; that its teaching staff be the best; and that services offered to students as they grow to health and character be the best. The *students,* also, must be the most promising girls of their generation—inside and outside our national borders."[68]

To carry out their recommendations, they proposed that Clemewell Lay be relieved of all duties other than those related to development and admissions. Under Lay's direction, and with the help of professional marketing counsel, the administration and the trustees developed a sophisticated and ambitious long-term fund-raising plan designed to raise nearly $4 million by 1964, the 150th anniversary of the school's founding. Trustees William Avirett, Earl Newsom, and John Amstuz were critical to the success of the plan. Avirett, the former education editor of the *Herald-Tribune*, was a nationally regarded expert on American education and the husband of Helen Weiser '17 and father of Margery '38. Earl Newsom, father of Barbara Newsom '48, had begun life as an English teacher before forming a pioneering public relations firm in Manhattan. Amstuz brought his philanthropic commitment and a keen eye for systems analysis.

In 1951 the school adopted the recommendations of the development committee that included immediately raising the tuition by 10 percent, adding three to five parent trustees (all fathers) to the board who would aid in fund-raising efforts, establishing a Fathers' Committee, and setting 1964 as the end date for a capital campaign. In addition, Lay was charged with reorganizing the alumnae so that they might be more helpful in both fund-raising and admissions. In 1955 the school used the winter issue of the *Bulletin* to announce the goals of the capital campaign to the alumnae at large. By 1964 the school intended to raise $3,705,800, of which $2,500,000 was earmarked for "salaries that beckon able teachers" and the enrollment of "more students . . . from differing economic groups." Other needs ranged from a new arts facility to "unsqueaky, more comfortable chairs"[69] for the Assembly Hall. (This last was the first goal to be met; new chairs filled the Assembly Hall when students returned in September 1955.)

If the goals of the capital campaign were to be met, the alumnae had to be energized. Between 1946 and 1951, parent gifts were nearly double that of the alumnae. In 1954 Alice Stone Trainer '29, alumna trustee, inaugurated a new tradition in reunion giving when she motivated her classmates to give a 25th reunion gift, a practice that other classes subsequently adopted. In spite of Trainer's efforts, during the early years of the campaign, parents remained far more supportive than alumnae. To further alumnae efforts, in 1955 Evelyn Gabel Enteman '32, the president of the Alumnae Association, was granted ex officio membership on the board of trustees. This elevated status of the alumnae association president "coincided with unprecedented advance in the participation of the alumnae in support of the school."[70] There was a one-third increase in alumnae giving between 1954–55 and 1955–56, with an unprecedented 1,230 alumnae giving nearly $35,000. In 1958–59 annual fund-raising reached $100,000 for the first time. (In contrast, Miss Porter's School had no annual fund prior to 1970.)

Although there is little doubt that reenergized alumnae leadership led to the improved fund-raising results, the increase in giving also coincided with the publication of an elaborate campaign brochure. In 1954 every alumna received a copy of "The Highest Privilege . . . The Greatest Responsibility," a brochure highlighting the fund-raising needs of a campaign that had been named "The Second Century Fund." The brochure compared Emma Willard's endowment to those of Exeter, Andover, and Lawrenceville. At $2,500 per student, the school nearly matched Lawrenceville's $3,000 but did not come close to Exeter at $25,000 or Andover at $20,000. "Inspired Teaching" and "Variety of Students," led the list of needs, which also included money for sabbaticals, which the brochure proclaimed "of greater worth than rubies to all teachers," support for speakers, and at the end of the list, $12,800 for audiovisual equipment.[71]

The arts facility was the first major segment of the campaign to reach completion. In 1954 the school had purchased a second Cluett estate bordering school grounds. For $125,000 the school acquired Worfield Manor, the home of Nellie Cluett. The purchase price included the main building, "a house of great distinction," over 20 acres, a gatehouse, a garage with an apartment, a gardener's cottage, and one other outlying staff house. Nellie Cluett, who was eighty-four at the time of the sale, retained the right to inhabit the property for the rest of her life. To purchase the house, the board borrowed the money at 3.5 percent. For Wellington, the acquisition promised to be the perfect site for a future arts center. Given the importance of the arts in the new curriculum, such a facility was badly needed. She reminded the board of the centrality of the arts in the Emma Willard Plan of Education and their inadequate location in a number of basement studios in Kellas, Weaver, and Slocum.

By the time Nellie Cluett died in September 1959, $80,000 from the Second Century Fund had been used to pay off the Cluett property loan. The plans for the new arts center immediately proceeded, and in 1960 a clever foldout brochure featuring the newly refurbished building urged alumnae to "Open the Door to the New Emma Willard Arts Center." The Music and Theater Departments declined to move to the new space, but the fine arts faculty happily filled the studios created from the library, dining room, sunroom, and other beautifully lighted spaces in the old mansion, which the board designated as Wellington-Lay in honor of the headmistresses.

The two women had presided successfully over campus expansion, curricular change, steady enrollments, and the creation of modern fund-raising and college counseling departments. At the same time, however, there was another side to the school during the Wellington-Lay era that was not as positive. For many students the school had too many rules, too many regulations, and it restricted ordinary teen-age social life to an extraordinary degree. One alumna from the 1950s expressed an opinion widely held by students from the era when she wrote, "I was there under the reign of the Misses Wellington and Lay. We all loved the course, individual teachers, our friends, the music and the sports, but our common bond was to rage about our wardens."[72]

The handbook of rules, developed when Anne Wellington first got to the school, grew lengthier and lengthier throughout the reign of the headmistresses, and it was ultimately divided into separate day and residential pamphlets. In 1961–62 the handbook opened with the assurance that "We do not have an elaborate set of rules," but the 94-page residential guidebook suggested otherwise. (One mother, dropping off her sopho-more daughter in 1955, exclaimed to her husband that she had had far fewer rules at her all-girls' boarding school in the 1930s than there were at supposedly modern Emma Willard.) There were rules for everything from makeup to meals to the possession of cameras and girdles, from shopping in Troy to attending church, from dancing to dieting. There were nine fundamental rules. Some of these were standard at most prep schools. For example, the use of alcohol and cigarettes was forbidden. Plagiarism was also a fundamental violation, as was dishonesty in sign-ing on and off campus or in borrowing materials from the library. Less common as "fundamental" were rules requiring that students stay in their rooms after lights out and forbidding students to pose for pictures in which their school affiliation was identified.

Over the course of the 1950s, each of the following strictures appeared in one or more handbooks (and the first one was a fundamental rule):

> A student . . . is not to meet, travel with, accompany or converse with any boy or man . . . when off campus unchaperoned.

No one is permitted in bowling alleys or similar recreational halls.

Students must have breakfast at school before going to church off campus. (This rule posed a special hardship on Roman Catholic students wishing to take communion.)

NO CORSAGES on Easter Sunday.

When visiting with day students, boarders cannot use the facilities of the Country Club.

Knitting is not permitted in Slocum Hall.

Shirts must always be tucked in.

Borrowing gym clothes is a serious offense.

Lipstick and nail polish are not to be used while studying in one's room.

Flashbulb pictures may not be taken on bedroom floors without the special permission of the headmistresses.

Only seniors are permitted to drink coffee.

No student can telephone home until after the second weekend of the year.

No diets for REDUCING purposes are permitted.

Students are required to eat the following: at breakfast, cereal or any other item served and fruit; at lunch, soup and salad or a main dish and salad, bouillon when served; at dinner, meat, fish or other item, vegetables and dessert.

In catalogs for prospective families and in their reports to the board of trustees, the headmistresses frequently stressed the many opportunities that the school provided for meeting boys. A 1952 *Bulletin* article about social life on campus declared cheerfully, "No week-end at Emma Willard passes without a troupe of neatly brushed young men on our doorstep to sing, to dance, to skate, or to join in any of the many activities which make up the typical Emma Willard weekend." The article assured alumnae that "the Emma Willard student of 1952 does not gaze wistfully through her iron fence to catch a glimpse of the pleasures which rightfully belong to her age and her nature."[73] Annual headmistresses' reports to the board quantified the number of boys hosted at dances and other campus events; the peak came in 1954–55 when eight hundred young men visited the school.

As was the case with every other aspect of student life, these dances were strictly regulated. When a large group from one boys' school visited, the boys were paired with their Emma Willard escorts by height, a practice that often left a short senior with a visiting freshman. "Blind date" dances, a phenomenon in the early years of the decade, were discontinued when a horrified Anne Wellington found that "These men would walk out on their dates if they did not like [them]."[74] Social evenings with RPI students were also discontinued, although they had been a tradition at the school since the 1840s. According to Wellington, "The girls found the budding engineers less attractive than other dates, and boys preferred Russell Sage College and Skidmore girls who could date during the week."[75] From student accounts in *CLOCK*, it appears that "date dances," where girls, usually juniors and seniors, got to invite male friends to campus for dances in Sage Living Room, were the most successful. In an odd twist for a consciously feminist school, but a reflection of the strictly defined gender roles operating in most male-female relations at the time, the boys were allowed to smoke on campus. For the most part their smoking was confined to a specific area designated for this purpose, but for a time, the administration allowed them to smoke during the dances in the living room. The practice was discontinued because "boys (many of whom did not know how to smoke) danced with lighted cigarettes in their hands near the girls' inflammable dresses" and chaperones found "burning cigarette ends . . . under couches."[76]

By far the largest and most anticipated coeducational social events of the year were the proms, and for many years, there were two, one hosted by the junior class and one by the seniors, one in the fall and one in the spring. (In 1956 the seniors substituted three "date dances" for their prom, an indication that in spite of the hype surrounding the prom, it was not the most popular dance of the year.) Proms were usually two-day events, and for several years, the names of the girls' dates and their schools or colleges were published in *CLOCK*. At a typical 1950s prom, the prom goers and their dates were treated to a film in the Playhouse on Friday night. The prom itself was held on Saturday night, and after it ended at midnight, dates stayed on for an hour while Gracie Bartholomew, the flamboyant school accompanist, played the piano and the teenagers sang along.[77] *CLOCK* always covered the prom in depth. In November 1950, the editors maintained that "the only event comparable to the arrival of the Emma Willard Prom would be the arrival of the atomic bomb."[78]

The same edition of the paper carried a cartoon by Polly Ormsby '51 depicting dancers and the caption, "I have observed that the number of chaperones varies inversely with the square of the distance between the two dancers."[79] The implication—that proms were strictly regulated—was underlined by subsequent *CLOCK* articles. In 1955 an article, "Reminders for Prom Weekend," cautioned prom goers to "say good-byes in Sage quickly. Remember! You don't look as nice in the brighter light as you did in the dimmer living room. Don't give him time to realize it."[80] This admonition gave an oddly demeaning twist to the handbook rule that "farewells must be said in the dormitories." In 1956 the newspaper reminded the students that "Behavior on the dance floor is to be *above reproach*."[81] (By the end of the decade, the newspaper's reenforcement of school rules led to student protests that the school paper was nothing but an arm of the administration.)

It was Wellington's hope that the emphasis on good citizenship and leadership would translate into obedience. When it didn't, she reported the more serious infractions to the board. In 1952 she reported that two students had run away, an infraction she labeled "French leave."[82] In 1954 eight juniors were suspended, and one withdrew when "a supposedly trustworthy tradesman" and a "kitchen boy"[83] provided them with alcohol. In her report for 1955–56, she noted that she had "majored in seniors as never before," adding that the class "found it almost impossible to govern themselves."[84] In 1958 the problem was the sophomore class; many of them had been found smoking in the dormitory. In addition, two freshmen and a junior had been suspended for buying beer at the A&P and bringing it back to the campus. In 1959 a young science teacher and a junior eloped; the student's guardian knew of the relationship in advance, a minor consolation for Wellington. That year the head's report to the board included a separate section on "Student Problems,"[85] which included shoplifting freshmen, smoking juniors, and general classroom cheating. It is, of course, highly likely that there were far more rule violations than the administration discovered; certainly alumnae memories indicate this was so. In 1959, however, Wellington ascribed the problems to a small group of students whose philosophy was "to see 'what you can get away with.'"[86]

Many students saw it differently. They viewed the headmistresses as unnecessarily restrictive and totally out of touch with the times. Some of their parents agreed. The father of a student who had been repeatedly disciplined for small infractions (and did not return for her senior year) wrote to the headmistress that in his opinion "a very large age gap has grown between administrators and those they administer." As for the school government system that Wellington felt was the key to building "a spirit of responsibility to be where they should be, to do what they should do,"[87] he suggested that the leaders were handmaidens of adult authority. The faculty, he alleged, supported student leadership composed of "persons who are not the natural leaders in the youthful society—more 'prissy' members."[88] His charge seems somewhat dubious given that the leaders were elected by the students, but there is no doubt that once elected, they were expected to behave as rule enforcers. Students took an oath of office, swearing to "spread good will throughout the school . . . and to back the Headmistresses and Emma Willard School on all occasions."[89] As part of their plan for developing responsible citizens, the school encouraged self-reporting of infractions.

The house parents, Gertrude Watkins, and Lucile Tuttle, spent an inordinate amount of time keeping track of the smallest transgressions on a "house card record"—and when the list grew long enough reported them to Wellington on a specially printed form titled "Special Report." For example, one hapless young woman had a rap sheet that listed the following instances of misconduct: "Sept. 24, talked out of window during Sunday 'Quiet Hours'; Oct. 4, in bathroom after 5 minute bell, uncooperative when spoken to; Nov. 11, bed not made by 10:30 on Sunday; Nov. 17, out of room during room care; Dec. 4, caught at desk with flashlight, second time; Dec. 14, riding in laundry hamper on corridor; Jan. 15, bed linen not changed."[90] As a result of all these transgressions, she was placed on probation, which meant, among other things, she had to sit by an adult in chapel and could only use the telephone to call her parents.

At the same time, however, some of what the Guidance Department did was remarkably modern. By the mid-1950s, they administered the Mooney Problem Checklist, which asked students to identify any problems that were "troubling" them by underlining items having to do with their future vocational plans, their behavior, their relationship with their parents, their feelings about boys and dating, and their self-image. Choices included "ashamed of the home we live in," "too fat," "thoughts of suicide," "wondering how far to go with the opposite sex," and "finding it hard to control sex urges." Students were then asked if they wanted to talk to someone about the areas concerning them. Given the last two categories, in particular, it is no surprise that many girls answered, "Only my close friends." One student drily noted, "There are a lot more things wrong with me than I have marked, but they just don't trouble me."[91] At least on paper, the administration was willing to grapple with a host of teenage problems, and their reports on individual students often reflected familiarity with psychology. As early as 1956, a student was being evaluated for "autistic ideation."[92]

As remote as the administration and many of the faculty seemed to the students, there is no doubt that the headmistresses and the faculty wanted, for the most part, to be liked as well as respected. For several years, the faculty entertained the students the night after the spring administration of the SAT. After the Willard Day School closed, the school outfitted the basement of Cluett with comfortable furniture, games, and a piano. A working fireplace and supplies of marshmallows and apples were intended to make "Hearthside" a cozy meeting place for faculty and students to relax together, and it received favorable reviews in *CLOCK* and *Gargoyle*. Most remarkable in student eyes was Wellington's institution of the first Headmistress's Holiday, which she threw on her birthday in February 1955. The holiday was a surprise day off that she repeated annually from then on, although always on a different day. Classes were canceled, and, in Wellington's words, the day was marked by "a complete absence of regulation and routine." She explained to the board that "food was available for protracted hours in the morning, and a variety of recreation planned for the entire day." The results for the students, she concluded, were "slight fatigue, maximum happiness, a tremendous boost for general school morale," and perhaps most satisfying to her, "the verified suspicion that the headmistresses and teachers were, after all, 'human.'"[93]

Human they were, and by 1960 the headmistresses were ready to retire. Wellington would turn sixty-five in February 1961, and Lay a few months later. Student restlessness was undoubtedly part of the reason. Wellington told the board that it was a daily challenge to live with "300 volatile young women."[94] The unfinished capital campaign may have been another reason, however. The year 1964 was rapidly approaching, and the campaign was not even halfway to its goal. In 1960–61 the school's annual budget totaled a million dollars for the first time. In 1960 the school hired Marts and Lundy to assist in bringing the fundraising to conclusion. Among other things, they recommended targeted mailings to "LYBUNTS," donors who had given in the past but had not given in the current year. Perhaps Marts and Lundy made another recommendation as well—that the school hire a male head.

The trend toward male heads of girls' schools was growing. According to a *Newsweek* article, fund-raising was a major reason for the movement toward "male head mistresses." The article stated baldly, "Money-raising is an important part of a school head's job . . . and men can do this better than women."[95] The reporter singled out Van Santvoord Merle-Smith for special mention; the first male head of Foxcroft, Merle-Smith was related to several Emma Willard graduates. Whether or not Wellington and Lay thought the school needed a male head is unknown, but Wellington told the board that she felt a new administration should be in place before the 150th anniversary. She urged the board to join with her successor in a "bold new undertaking," the "establishment of a comparable boys' boarding school on the more remote unused school property."[96]

Once again, the search for a new head was entrusted to a small group of trustees. There was no faculty or student input. When the school resumed after the winter break, John Amstuz announced to the students and faculty that the new principal had been hired. According to the *Bulletin*, "excitement reigned" when he told the assembly "it is a couple—Mr. and Mrs. William Dietel." Although Bill Dietel was the contractual head, his wife, Linda Remington, was a member of the class of 1948, and when not caring for their four children, all of whom were under ten, she would be "associated with her husband in the administration of some of the activities of the school." Amstuz pointed out that Linda was only the second "student to be affiliated with the administration,"[97] citing Sarah Lucretia Willard's tenure as principal—and completely ignoring Emily Wilcox '56. A senior in the audience reported in her diary that "Miss Wellington said that since no one had given her any kind of welcome when she arrived, she wanted to make sure he got a BIG welcome." The student also confided to her diary that she hoped the new principal would change the rules, particularly the reporting system, because "who would want their kids to grow up in an atmosphere where if you went to the bathroom without your slippers you have to report yourself."[98]

The headmistresses prepared to move to an apartment near the Wellington homestead in Boston. Meanwhile, the board authorized $12,000 for Dietel's initial salary ($4,000 more than Wellington's final salary) and $15,000 to renovate Gorham House and make it a suitable residence for a family. Before leaving, the headmistresses wrote a detailed month-by-month memorandum to their successor, telling him what to expect in his new position. Their calendar of advice included the following monthly notations:

> October—"the month when younger girls try smoking"
> November—"approve Revels cast. The class decides whether or not to keep the cast a secret."
> December—"send Revels invitations to Troy guests. Although some profess to having seen Revels too many times, they still like to be invited."
> January—"Miss Hogben makes a model of the graduation dress and presents it to [you] for approval."
> February—"This is the time when sophomores try to persuade their parents that they should go to another school. This phase passes."
> March—"Do not allow time off for college visits."
> April—"Budget. Music department requests usually need to be cut down."
> May—"Hand out letters from colleges to seniors in the privacy of Sage Suite. Make sure counselors are there. The faculty need constant reminders not to make suggestions about colleges."

The comprehensive list, nearly twenty pages long, covered every aspect of the new head's job. They cautioned him that Flame Ceremony was "not an occasion for a light type of presentation" and should not feature "guitar players and corridor crooners." In the spring he should ask School Council "to watch out for the usual year-end aberrations of their classmates [because] some matter of small concern can touch off emotional reaction during the last trying months of uncertainty about college and mixed feelings about leaving school." There were detailed instructions for handling "French Leaves," which they assured him usually happened "right before or right after dinner."[99] Under no circumstances should he call the police. To his credit, the thirtysomething new principal appreciated the advice they gave him. He attended the May meeting of the board of trustees and told them, "after talking with several heads of school, he believes his experience is rare, indeed, that few—if any—have received the help from predecessors that he is receiving."[100]

On the list of duties Wellington and Lay left Bill Dietel was the instruction that he should check the *Gargoyle* before it went to the printer and watch for "references in veiled language" on the senior pages. Whether or not they checked the 1961 yearbook is unknown, but if they did, they learned in advance that it was dedicated to the two of them. The language in the tribute was not "veiled," nor was it effusive. The seniors dedicated their book to the headmistresses "because of your knowledge that order is necessary."[101] The Vassar alumnae quarterly profiled their retiring graduate. Wellington shared the alumna spotlight with Laura Benet and Josephine Bisharat, both Vassar graduates—and both Emma Willard alumnae.

When he announced the new school head, Amstuz had paid tribute to the departing headmistresses. After they left, he told the students, "their spirit, their work will live on in these halls."[102] Their work, yes, but a spirit of reform had come to Mount Ida with the new principal—not just reform within the protective gray walls, but also a spirit of reform in the world at large. Bill Dietel would ensure that the turbulence of the 1960s would not pass by Emma Willard students undetected.

A Master Headmistress

For his inauguration on January 20, 1961, John F. Kennedy asked Robert Frost to read a poem. In honor of the occasion, Frost wrote "Dedication," which he was unable to deliver because the glare from the bright winter sunshine obstructed his vision. Had he read his poem, the nation would have heard Frost praise the new president's "young ambition eager to be tried." Frost's feelings about Kennedy's inauguration paralleled the mood at Emma Willard. Just a few months after Kennedy's inauguration, William Moore Dietel was installed as the eighth head of school. A decade younger than the new president, Dietel differed from his predecessors as sharply as Kennedy contrasted with the eighty-six-year-old Frost and the retiring president, seventy-three-year-old Dwight Eisenhower. The administrations of both Kennedy and Dietel would be marked by turbulence, exuberance, change, resistance to change, extraordinary hope, and extreme despair. Both men had wives who were classy, smart, attractive girls' school graduates who created their own leadership roles. Additionally, both had young photogenic offspring who humanized their offices. Finally, both tenures ended under the shadow of tragedy. In the end, each left a legacy of promise and possibility for their successors to fulfill.

On October 15, 1961, over a thousand guests thronged the Playhouse for Bill Dietel's installation as principal of Emma Willard. The first head of school to hold a doctorate, Dietel was a young scholar with as much or more experience as a faculty member than as an administrator. After earning his undergraduate degree at Princeton, he had completed his master's and doctoral degrees at Yale. While in graduate school, he taught history at the University of Connecticut at

Stamford and at the University of Massachusetts at Amherst. When George Van Santvoord recruited him for the headship, he was an assistant dean and assistant professor of humanities at all-male Amherst College. Over the course of his tenure at Emma Willard, he would turn to Amherst time and again to recruit both faculty and administrators.

Eugene Wilson, Amherst's now legendary dean of admissions, delivered the keynote address at the installation. Titled "Emma Won't," the speech was a blend of admiration for the Emma Willard curriculum and advice for the students. The *Plan of Education* had often been described as a high school version of the Amherst curriculum. Wilson recognized the similarities and spoke authoritatively about the toll that an interdisciplinary curriculum took on a faculty. In an "integrated course of studies," he explained, faculty have to do "hard teaching" because "where subjects know no boundaries . . . the dedicated teacher [is forced] to widen constantly his [*sic*] horizons of knowledge."[1] He also celebrated Emma Willard's single-sex status, heralding "these wonderful manless years." If they were typical of the young Americans recently polled by Gallup, most of his teenage audience expected to marry by twenty-two and eventually have four children; at the time, a discouraging 40 percent of young women who entered college dropped out prior to graduation. Probably aware of these statistics, he warned, "You girls are too anxious to get your man."[2] He was delighted, however, that Emma Willard had gotten her man and predicted that "he will be a master headmistress."[3]

In his speech accepting the leadership of the school, Bill Dietel struck a compromise between progress and the past. He had, after all, trained as an historian, and he ably demonstrated his awareness of the school's place in history at the same time that he celebrated the future. He referred to the founder's famous iconography, *The Temple of Time*, whose "columnar walls . . . indicate by the ever widening gap between them that the limits of human interest and vision are forever expanding." Emma Hart Willard, he maintained, "never made the mistake of confusing her interest in the past experiences of mankind with the importance of living in the present." He saluted the *Plan of Education* as a continuation of the founder's ethos: "Instead of glorying in past accomplishments, [it] set forth to try out new educational ideas."

Overall, he concluded, he was excited to be at a school where "tradition is honored, but reverence is reserved for God."[4]

The choir echoed the day's themes, singing "God Send Us Men Whose Aim 'Twill Be." The aim, according to the hymn's various stanzas, was to have men whose goal was "not to defend some ancient creed" but to be "alert and quick" and to act "with hearts ablaze"—fighting words for a new era. Anne Wellington and Clemewell Lay, seated on the dais during the installation, must have been somewhat conflicted at the prospect of this brave new—and masculine—world. At their final commencement, just three months earlier, the speaker had described them as "Puritans who behave like Cavaliers." Puritan or Cavalier, they probably felt they were being replaced by a swashbuckler.

Whenever the modern world enters a new decade, there is an awareness of change and possibility, and the world at the beginning of the 1960s was certainly no exception. In the spring of 1961, Yuri Gagarin orbited the earth in his Soviet spacecraft, and a month later American astronaut Alan Shepard became the second man in space, although his "flight" was shorter and less spectacular. The space race was on, with profound implications for science and mathematics teaching all across the United States. During the summer, as Gorham House was being renovated to accommodate the growing Dietel family, the Soviets built a wall across Berlin. Faced with escalating Cold War tensions, in 1961 Kennedy proposed the Alliance for Progress and the Peace Corps. Under Patrice Lumumba's leadership, Africa began the painful process of shedding colonial rule.

Culturally, 1961 was mixed. Emma Willard students dreamed of looking like Audrey Hepburn in *Breakfast at Tiffany's* and swayed to "Moon River." At the same time, however, in the Café Rouge they gyrated to Chubby Checkers's new dance, the twist. The library featured best-sellers including *Catch-22* and *Franny and Zooey*, the former a caricature of the absurdity of authority and the latter a condemnation of modern life's phoniness, harbingers of the student attitudes in the movements from the middle to the end of the decade. And the Pulitzer Prize for Literature was awarded to Harper Lee for *To Kill a Mockingbird*, her now classic portrayal of racism in a small southern town. Over the course of the decade, Bill Dietel would expose his students to all of the issues raised in 1961.

In his first year, however, it was the faculty who commanded his attention. In November he told the board of trustees that he had been persuaded to come to Emma Willard because of his excitement about the curriculum. "I accepted the principalship believing that you all wanted and were willing to work for the *Plan*," he told them. Its signal strength, in his opinion, was that it was "flexible [and] self-generating." Nevertheless, he voiced a serious concern. The "Heart of the Plan—past, present, and future—is the faculty." For the curriculum to continue to be strong, the faculty had to be strong, and Dietel believed that the keys to a strong faculty were good pay and competitive benefits. To hire new teachers, it would be necessary in some cases to pay them more than what was being earned by old and loyal teachers, and as older teachers retired, they needed financial protection. Furthermore, the emphasis on mathematics and science fueled by the space race meant that "in some disciplines . . . the supply is so limited, salaries must go way up."[5]

The faculty that Bill Dietel inherited from his predecessors was overwhelmingly female, white, single, and significantly older than their new boss. Seventeen teachers had been at the school for more than twenty years, and of those, eleven were veterans of thirty years or more. There were eleven department chairs, two of whom were men. (Russell Locke chaired music and Arthur Homan, history.) The female chairs ranged in age from Dorothy Kirkland, the seventy-year-old chair of the speech and theater department to Marigwen Schumacher, the thirty-four-year-old chair of modern languages. Schumacher was an anomaly. The average age of the rest of the chairs was fifty-five. The administration matched the faculty; there were Lucile Tuttle, assistant to the head; Mary Alice Chapman, who was effectively the dean of students without the title; and Marjorie Pickard, the guidance counselor responsible for college placement. All three were in their late fifties. The residence staff was even more mature; the oldest was seventy-two and the youngest fifty-six. Six of the eight had been born in 1900 or earlier.

Only a third of the faculty earned over $3,000, and the top salary did not reach $7,000. A comparative study of faculty salaries that Dietel presented to the board in the spring of his first year demonstrated that in contrast to the leading boys' schools, the salaries at Emma Willard were "pitifully small" even for teachers "of the highest order."[6] On average, the minimum salary at boys' schools was $8,000, and salaries of $10,000 to $12,000 were not uncommon. As he explained to the board, he not only wanted to increase compensation for the current faculty, but also to change the age and composition of the faculty. His goals were to build a younger faculty and to increase the number of men with families. (Locke and Homan were the only men on the faculty when he arrived.)

To meet these goals, he assured the board, would mean money, especially for young faculty who would expect an annual raise. Like other heads of school in this era, he believed in paying married men with families more than their female counterparts, married or single. The school taught girls that they were equal to boys in intelligence but not necessarily in economic opportunity. Beyond money, however, the school would need to have better faculty accommodations. In 1961–62, nine faculty lived in Cluett, twelve in Northcroft, four in a small house on the corner of Pawling and Spring Avenues, and six in Underbridge. A comprehensive report to the board in the fall of 1962 detailed the extent of the problem. Unmarried female faculty lived in single rooms, "often less than ten by eighteen feet" in size. They shared bathroom facilities, and what little cooking they could manage was done on hot plates "in a most hazardous fashion." None had access to washers or dryers. In short, the principal deplored the "unattractive and uninspiring character of the rooms in which the vast majority of our dedicated teachers live."[7]

Over the course of his tenure, Bill Dietel met his early goals. When he left Emma Willard in 1970, the percentage of men on the faculty had grown dramatically, the average age of the faculty had dropped below forty, and the number of unmarried female teachers had been cut in half. The percentage of the faculty living in campus housing had dropped from 73 to 61 percent, but no one lived in a single room; all had access to private baths and kitchens. The starting salary had risen to $8,100, well above the top salary in 1961. Perhaps as a result of the change in the faculty's age and gender, the average tenure for a faculty member had declined from thirteen to five years, although four of his hires, Jack Betterly, Jack and Marcia Easterling, and Françoise Chadabe, became legendary figures, the last three teaching well into the twenty-first century. Two thirds of the faculty had master's degrees in 1961; that number had risen very slightly by 1970, but 4 percent of the faculty in 1970 held doctorates. Effecting these changes required foresight and energy, the foresight to see what was needed and the energy to raise money and recruit the new personnel. In addition, however, transforming the faculty so profoundly also required changing the attitudes and the composition of the board of trustees.

The board Bill Dietel inherited was not nearly as wealthy, nor in fact as farsighted, as would be necessary to bring about change of the magnitude he envisioned. For the most part, the major players were local. Since 1821 when Troy's leading citizens offered to refit the Moulton Coffee House for Mrs. Willard, membership on the school's board of trustees had been the purview of the male members of Troy's upper socioeconomic strata, and, very occasionally, a few of their wives who also happened to be alumnae. In the nineteenth century, these men often had wealth commensurate with their prestige, but Troy's relative wealth had declined precipitously in the twentieth century, as had the relative wealth of its business class. Since the death of Margaret Olivia Slocum Sage in 1918, the school had received no six-figure gifts from trustees. The trustees were loyal supporters of such causes as the annual School Fair, which usually raised a few thousand dollars, social events for students, and the occasional scholarship appeal, but they had neither the capacity nor the inclination to make large gifts. They had not supported the Second Century Fund, the Wellington-Lay capital campaign, to the extent that professional fund-raisers felt was necessary for a successful effort.

Eliza Kellas had raised money from alumnae for the various projects she undertook; trustee support for her work came, for the most part, in the form of encouragement and applause, not dollars. Except in the case of alumna trustees, term limits were not imposed, and board tenures lasting two or three decades were not uncommon. Anne Wellington had tried to widen the view of the board by enlisting trustees who were husbands and fathers of graduates and current students and who came from outside the capital district. She had successfully recruited educators such as Radcliffe president Wilbur K. Jordan and marketers and publicists like Earl Newsom and William Avirett. Although these men gave her invaluable assistance in their areas of expertise, they did not make the kind of capital gifts that Dietel knew the school needed to survive in the second half of the twentieth century.

The regular members of the board of trustees in 1961–62 consisted of seventeen men and three women. Within a few weeks of working with the board, Bill Dietel quickly figured out that there needed to be a change of leadership and a far greater alumnae presence. Additionally, the bylaws needed to be revised to ensure that new trustees could be added in a timely way. As Dietel recalls, "There were no major donors among the board's leadership. It was really a social obligation for a certain segment of Troy society."[8] The first obstacle to this amount of change was the board president, John Amstuz, who had been a trustee since 1939, had served the school tirelessly, and had donated to and raised money for his pet project, the conversion of the gymnasium to a chapel. He had also been the head cheerleader for the Wellington-Lay administration. Anne Wellington had returned his admiration. As long-term faculty member Russell Locke succinctly summarized the relationship: "Anne thought John Amstuz hung the moon."[9]

In 1961 Amstuz was chair of both the Emma Willard board and the board of Troy's rapidly growing Hudson Valley Community College. At sixty-six he was retired from the Behr-Manning Corporation but held a position as a deputy commissioner of the New York State Department of Commerce. The vice president of the board was George Van Santvoord, who had long family ties to Troy and was the retired head of Hotchkiss. The treasurer of the board was Terrence Gordner, also treasurer of the Behr-Manning Corporation, whom Amstuz had personally recruited. Other local members of the board included Robert G. Betts, whose male ancestors had been trustees since the mid-nineteenth century; Lewis Froman, the president of Russell Sage College; two local attorneys, Bruce Hislop and Edward Pattison; Gene Robb, publisher of the *Albany Times Union*; banker Ogden Ross; and businessman Charles Dauchy. The three alumnae were Helen Bull '08, longtime companion of Julia H. Bush '92, who had been given Bush's seat when she retired from the board; Evelyn Gabel Enteman '32; and Dr. Katharine Cook Gordinier '23, another trustee with a decades-long family connection to the board.

In their push to raise money for the Second Century Fund, Wellington and Lay, with Van Santvoord's help, had recruited a number of fathers for the board, and in 1961–62, there were seven such trustees, all of whom were businessmen, attorneys, or both, and all of whom lived outside of Troy (but exclusively in the Northeast). There were also, however, four alumnae representatives (as opposed to regular trustees who were alumnae) on the board, and the president of the alumnae association was an ex officio member. Two of these representatives and the association president would become key supporters of the Dietel administration, personally and financially: Clementine Miller Tangeman '23, her classmate Helen Snell Cheel '23, and Irene Mennen Hunter '35. Inspired by their leadership, Dietel concluded that the majority of the board should be alumnae. As he wisely wrote, "Surely we, who are committed to the education of women, should find in them the knowledgeable, sensitive, and wise leaders of its governance."[10]

The support of Tangeman, Hunter, and Cheel gave the development effort a critical push. With their encouragement, Dietel undertook a modern development campaign aimed at raising the money needed for both physical improvements to the campus and the establishment of a larger endowment. In the fall of 1961, the million-dollar endowment produced too little money to ensure that the budget would balance, even when every bed was full. Reporting to the board in her position as president of the Alumnae Association, Irene Mennen Hunter '35 underscored the importance of an aggressive development effort. "Only personal solicitation has any effect whatsoever," she told her fellow trustees, and organizing such an effort required a professional development staff for which "no expense should be spared."[11] All alumnae efforts, she believed, should focus on the school's needs. She proposed that reunion and the annual Emma Willard Day celebration (which the association had sponsored each fall for nearly a decade) should always have the same theme, and that theme should reflect the fund-raising priorities of the school.

Following Irene Hunter's lead, the school hired Marts and Lundy to counsel the development office and William Lanxner as assistant to the principal in charge of the Second Century Fund. The fund-raising effort still carried the name of the anniversary program launched by

Wellington and Lay, even though its focus had changed. Within a year, not only the focus, but the amount to be raised and the name of the program had changed. Marts and Lundy urged a four-prong approach to development: an annual fund, a program of planned giving, an "occasional capital fund," and "a continuous program of large gifts for major projects." They also urged the reorganization of the volunteer staff with a recommendation that reflected conventional sexist thinking about fund-raising. They recommended that the Development Council, the name given to the fund-raising steering committee, have "a male member of the board . . . appointed as chair with an alumna as co-chair,"[12] an arrangement that is particularly ironic in light of the fact that the first two alumnae to serve as co-chairs were the leading donors to the campaign. In phase 1, David Knowlton[13] and Clementine Tangeman held the chair and co-chair posts; they were followed by Craig Severance[14] and Helen Snell Cheel '23.

In April 1962, a committee of trustees presented the "Sesquicentennial Anniversary First Statement of Needs," which proposed that the fund-raising effort focus on dormitory renovation, endowment for faculty salaries and scholarships, a new art facility, the renovation of Wellington-Lay as faculty housing, and a library. Emphasizing that the school "has not been traditionally a finishing school nor a school for the daughters of the wealthy," they predicted that in the future the school would need "as diverse a student body as possible."[15] They also noted that the Music Department needed to be moved from the basement of Kellas and that the school needed a new gymnasium and a modern pool.

Bill Dietel's priorities clearly influenced the committee's report. Along with faculty housing, a new library and a new arts facility had quickly risen to the top of his construction agenda. He reminded the board that the 1960s had brought "a revolution in librarianship" and in librarians. New libraries operated on an honor checkout system, and the librarian was no longer "a Scrooge-like factotum" guarding the books. Emma Willard had outgrown the library in Slocum, and he wanted to replace it with a library capable of housing at least 35,000 volumes, double the number it then held. He also advocated for a modern library with up-to-date audiovisual equipment, language laboratories, study carrels, and faculty offices with provision for smoking. Privately, he also hoped to replace Mary MacLear with a younger, preferably male, librarian. He concluded, "In education, there is no substitute for great teaching; but a great library is equally indispensable."[16]

During 1962–63, the development staff and board of trustees worked to refine and quantify the list of fund-raising priorities. To this end, the board hired nationally renowned architect Edward Larrabee Barnes to draw up a master plan of campus needs. The immediate needs, as Barnes conceived them, undoubtedly on the advice of the principal, were faculty housing, a new fine arts facility, and a new library. Future needs included improved entrances and traffic patterns, a new gymnasium, a new music facility, an additional science wing, and a thirty-bed dormitory. At the May board meeting, with Barnes's preliminary report in hand, the development committee proposed that a fund-raising campaign be started in the fall. Called the "150th Anniversary Development Program," the campaign sought $1 million to endow faculty salaries, $500,000 for scholarships, $700,000 each for new arts and music facilities, $500,000 for a library, $100,000 to renovate Wellington-Lay as faculty housing, $340,000 for new faculty residences, $60,000 for improvements to the chapel, and $700,000 for other plant improvements.

The physical needs alone totaled $3 million. At a special meeting of the board in September, Barnes unveiled his master plan. Enthusiastic about the design, but leery of their ability to raise the full $3 million, the development committee proposed that the board authorize a campaign to raise $1.5 million by December 31, 1964. At that point Clementine Tangeman issued a game-changing challenge to her fellow trustees: raise the goal to $3 million, and she would supply the first $500,000.[17] With that leadership gift, Tangeman began the transformation of the Emma Willard board of trustees.

From then on, trustees from the alumna ranks who, for the most part, lived outside the capital district of New York, would provide the leadership and resources needed for a thriving modern school. At the November meeting of the board, the development committee reported that the trustees had already contributed $600,000—20 percent of the goal. Inspired by this news, Helen Cheel announced on the spot

that she was adding another $100,000 to her already significant dona-
tion in honor of "her father's long and close friendship" with Eliza
Kellas and her "enthusiasm for the present principal."[18] Clementine
Tangeman, Helen Cheel, and their classmate Elsa Mott Ives became "a
triumvirate of angels from the Class of 1923."[19]

Clementine Tangeman's leadership was not by any means limited to
her philanthropy, important as that was. In 1962 John Amstuz's health
had begun to fail, and George Van Santvoord had stepped in as acting
president of the board. In 1964 Amstuz died. The board moved boldly in
the direction Dietel wished them to go. As he explained to the alumnae,
"It is a curious and ironic fact that, with few exceptions, the boards of
trustees of independent girls' schools are in the hands of non-graduates,
fathers, and male friends of the school."[20] It was time for Emma Willard
to break that pattern. Clementine Tangeman was selected to be the first
female president of the board and assumed office July 1, 1965.

Tangeman's association with Emma Willard had begun when she
entered the school as a junior in 1921. Born in Columbus, Indiana,
she and her brother J. Irwin Miller had inherited great wealth because
of the success of Cummins Engine, their father's company. They were
taught from their earliest days that the wealth they enjoyed carried
with it the duty and obligation to give back to society even more than
they had received. Trusteeship—of churches, schools, colleges, and
nonprofit organizations—was a family tradition, both at home in Columbus and beyond. In addition to the Emma Willard board, Tangeman had served or would later serve on the boards of Butler University, the Christian Theological Seminary, Smith College, her second
alma mater, and the national boards of the American Red Cross and
Girl Scouts. She shared Bill Dietel's concern that the Emma Willard
board needed greater geographic diversity, more trustees with the capacity for leadership giving, and a membership with greater experience with and sophistication about governance. As he fondly recalled,
"Clemmie was pretty disturbed when she came on the board and discovered how parochial this crowd was."[21] Undaunted, she presided
over a board that gradually added more alumnae, instituted bylaws
reforms that brought its practices into line with those of other suc-

cessful nonprofits, ably managed the growth of the endowment,[22] and met or exceeded the construction and fund-raising goals of the Sesquicentennial Plan. She flew Bill Dietel to Columbus on the Cummins corporate jet so that he could meet with her brother and his associates; working with her, he found, was equivalent to "earning a mini-MBA."[23] She was savvy about fiscal policy, institutional management, and people. A tireless fund-raiser, she was joined in this work by Donald V. Buttenheim, who served as first vice president of the board, and Irene Mennen Hunter's husband, trustee James "Bing" Hunter, both of whom crisscrossed the country asking for donations from parents and alumnae alike. Both Buttenheim and Hunter had three daughters at the school in the 1960s; Buttenheim's sister, Martha, was a member of the class of 1929.[24] Over four decades later, enfeebled by age and illness, Buttenheim radiated excitement when he exclaimed, "We changed things. We went after the money, and we got it."[25]

Clementine Tangeman once explained her philosophy of volunteerism this way: "Find a cause that challenges your imagination and kindles your enthusiasm, then give it your best thought and effort and stick with it." In the 1960s and early 1970s, Emma Willard was her cause. Slowly, but surely, and with greater rapidity than in any prior fund-raising campaign, the school collected the money to meet the goals Bill Dietel had established. In less than a decade, the face of the campus changed dramatically. New faculty housing came first. Because of her leadership on the board and in the fund-raising campaign, the trustees voted to name the fifteen-unit faculty housing complex for her. The Tangeman apartments, opened in 1966, were designed primarily for single faculty. Women who had lived for years in cramped spaces with little privacy and few amenities now had their own kitchens, a laundry facility, and a living space with sweeping views of the lower campus.

However, to meet his goal of increasing the male presence on the faculty, Dietel wanted housing for married men with families. As he told the board in 1964, there are "far fewer unmarried women and an increasing number of married men with families."[26] With Tangeman underway, the board hired Graham Williams, a local architect and Rensselaer professor,[27] to convert the Cluett gatehouse and three outbuildings known as the "Mews" to faculty housing. The chauffeur's house, two garages, and the gatehouse were ready for faculty families by September 1966. The effort to raise money for faculty chairs in honor of retired faculty Ellen Manchester, Mary Wilson, Elizabeth Simpson, and Elizabeth Potwine had foundered, so the board decided to name the renovated spaces for them. In addition, the board authorized the creation of a faculty apartment on the first floor of the Cluett mansion.

The Mews and Tangeman were dedicated in October 1966. Graduates from the decade of the 1920s were invited to the event, along with Mary Wilson and Katherine Weaver. (Weaver laboratories had received a $20,000 makeover the year before). *CLOCK* reported that the alumnae were "stunned"[28] by the changes on the campus, especially the presence of men on the faculty. By all accounts, they were approving as well as amazed. As the push for more housing continued, alumnae gifts fueled the construction. In 1967 a modern house was built on Elmgrove Avenue next door to Gorham House, and in 1969 the "Duplexes opened." Individually named for the families of the alumnae who funded them,[29] they were occupied first by French teacher John Foster, chemistry teacher Thomas Nelson, English teacher Jack Pasanen, and English teacher and librarian Richard Zajchowski—four young men with young families. All together faculty housing had cost a million dollars, but when it was completed, the school had "the most extensive housing program for teachers and staff developed by any independent secondary school for girls in the country."[30]

Before the faculty housing was finished, the board decided to go ahead with the construction of a new library and music facility even though the funds for these buildings had not yet been secured. On March 14, 1966, the trustees excused Bill Dietel from an executive session where they voted, at Tangeman's suggestion, to name the new library for him. He had returned to the classroom that year, and in a message to the alumnae, he emphasized the importance of his teaching, noting that as an administrator he had "been away from the heart of the school" and had nearly lost "the perspective of the teacher."[31] Being back in the classroom restored that perspective and also reinforced for him the value of the library. In naming the library for him, the board recognized his scholarship, his teaching, and the value he placed on the library as the center of an academic community. As he promised the alumnae, "It is our intent that no student should leave this school without loving books."[32]

A year and a half later, the new library was finished, although the board was forced to borrow $100,000 to complete the project. On Saturday, October 14, 1967, a line of 155 girls carried nearly twenty thousand volumes from the old library in Slocum Hall to the new library across the campus. Faculty met them and shelved the books; the Dewey Decimal system was discarded in favor of the Library of Congress classification. In addition to a new way of enumerating the collection, the library had brand-new audiovisual equipment and seminar rooms and played a whole new role in student lives. The evening study halls that had regulated student life since the days of Eliza Kellas were abolished. Instead students were allowed to study in the library, a rule of silence applying only to the second floor. There were new microfilm readers. Writing about them, librarian Richard Zajchowski foreshadowed the challenges facing libraries in the Internet era: "For those of us used to the 'cool media,' the fun of thumbing through back issues of *Life* may seem to outweigh all the practical advantages of microfilm; but for our students raised on 'hot media,' the TV-like experience of the micro-reader provides a much more normal viewing experience."[33]

The Music Department got a new home at the same time as the library. Under the leadership of Russell Locke, who had joined the faculty in 1952, the choral music program was an extraordinary program housed in dismal basement space in Kellas. As Dietel wrote to Helen Cheel, "When I think of the years the music people have spent in that old basement, I marvel that Russell . . . did not leave long ago."[34] Funded primarily by Cheel, the Snell Music Building was named for her mother, a donor to the project, and her late father, Bertrand Snell, the northern New York congressman who had been a lifelong friend of Miss Kellas. Once again, Edward Larrabee Barnes was the architect, although I. M. Pei had bid on the project. The Barnes plan left room for a visual arts building to adjoin the library on its eastern end.

On May 12, 1968, the entire community gathered to dedicate the new spaces. Helen Cheel presented Snell to Russell Locke, and Clementine Tangeman presented the library to Dick Zajchowski. Practice rooms and study areas were named in honor of various faculty members and alumnae including Charlotte Main, Carolyn Hull Curry '28, and Helen Hutchins.

These three women, chairs of the Mathematics and English Departments and secretary to the principal and board of trustees, respectively, had all died unexpectedly. Hutchins had worked for three administrations when she dropped dead of a heart attack in the spring of 1962; she "understood the rectitude, the fidelity to details" of Miss Kellas, "welcomed the growth of the school" under the headmistresses, and "enjoyed the enthusiasm, humanity, and adventurous plans" of Bill Dietel.[35] Hutchins was in her sixties, but Curry and Main were a decade younger. Curry also died of a heart attack; Main spent a few weeks in the hospital before succumbing to breast cancer. Their deaths are stark reminders that well into the second half of the twentieth century, heart disease and breast cancer were almost always fatal to women.[36]

The new construction during the 1960s stood out, but interior renovations and new uses for old spaces also claimed thousands of dollars. In 1969 a world-class Noack organ was commissioned for the chapel; three years earlier, the building had been graced with a new roof. The organ was donated by Clementine Tangeman's nieces, Margaret Miller '61, Katherine Miller '64, and Elizabeth Miller '68, in memory of their uncle Robert Tangeman, who had died in 1964 shortly before his widow assumed the board presidency. During the summer of 1967, modern fire detection equipment was installed in the dormitories along with the addition of several fire escapes; fifty student rooms were repaired and repainted, and ten bathrooms were replumbed. This first phase of dormitory renovation cost $500,000. Phase 2, begun in the summer of 1969, cost another $500,000, $400,000 of which was borrowed on a four-year note. Interest in horseback riding fell dramatically in the 1960s, and in 1968 the school discontinued riding on campus. The maintenance department moved to the former stables, and Hearthside, the recreational lounge area in the basement of Cluett, moved to the first floor of the Laundry, where the Maintenance Department had been housed. In 1969 Cluett was renovated once again, this time as a dormitory for twenty-six students. The Assembly Hall was outfitted with new furniture and named Kiggins for sisters-in-law Evelyn Kiggins '25 and Kathryn Schafer Kiggins '21.

The physical enhancements to the campus were only one sign of the school's success. Enrollment during this decade mushroomed. Although the maximum capacity in the three dormitories was 294, the school routinely packed 300 boarders into Hyphen, Sage, and Kellas. There was perennial tension between wanting—and needing—more income and crowding three girls into rooms meant to be doubles. When the enrollment exceeded capacity in August 1968, Dietel wrote, "Bill Beebe [the business manager] will like this, but the people responsible for housing the young will be fit to be tied."[37] For Dietel, the additional income was only one positive outcome of the burgeoning applications. He also anticipated increased selectivity as a result of the growing numbers of applicants. When the number of applicants jumped significantly for the 1966–67 school year, he told the board, "The student body should be far more promising academically within five years than has been the case in the past." He was very candid in his assessment of student talent:

> We have had in the past twenty years our share of able girls, but again, candor demands that we not confuse what we believe to be the excellence of the student body at large with the reality. . . . a survey of the College Board scores of our graduates . . . and similar national testing devices would not leave the impression that a significant minority much less the majority of our graduates were a vastly superior group. . . . To put this another way, we are not Exeter, nor are we Andover. . . . I do not think there is an Exeter or an Andover in girls' schools, but Emma Willard School aspires to the same kind of reputation for excellence that marks these two boys' schools. [38]

Whatever the goal—student ability, faculty excellence, library volumes, or endowment—Dietel nearly always compared Emma Willard to Andover and Exeter, and Emma Willard usually came up short. He clearly valued Emma Willard and her alumnae, but he was an Exonian himself.[39] He also understood the invidious nature of such comparisons. As he wrote to a trustee who had inquired about measuring statistics against data from other schools, "It is very difficult to decide [what list to use]. If you want to be the best [it is] bound to mean places with a great many more resources." To compare with lesser institutions meant taking "a false satisfaction in how we are progressing."[40]

The comparison between Exeter and Emma Willard was drawn more finely in the winter of 1964 when Dietel hired Darcy Curwen, the retired chair of the Exeter English Department, to be a visiting instructor. Curwen wrote an article for the *Bulletin* comparing his former students at Exeter with his students at Emma Willard. He concluded that "a boy graduating from Exeter is better schooled in his courses of study than is a girl graduating from Emma Willard," but he also pointed out that this was a matter of depth rather than breadth in the curriculum. Art, music, and religion were "minor luxuries" almost unknown to the Exeter boys who had Latin "shoveled into them." In short, "The usable breadth of the Emma Willard upper classes is as impressive as the general depth of the Exonians." He found that Emma Willard had more rules (Exeter's consisted of "liberty tempered by expulsion") and was "more civilized." He complained that the girls took too many notes and were "self-defeating about colleges and husbands." He wondered why "so many fine intelligent women married less fine, less intelligent men" and why so many "prep school boys think themselves God's gift to womankind."[41] Curwen returned for several years, and a room in the new library complex was dedicated to him posthumously.

Academic comparisons aside, contrasting Emma Willard and Exeter—or any other leading boys' school for that matter—from a financial vantage point was truly disheartening. At the same time that Dietel and trustees such as Tangeman, Cheel, Buttenheim, Hunter, Knowlton, and Severance were raising unprecedented amounts for construction, they realized that money also needed to be raised to augment the endowment. Every bed was filled, and the tuition was high and kept going higher. In 1962–63 the boarding tuition was $3,000, and it remained there until 1966–67 when it jumped 10 percent. Two years later, it had jumped another $300 to $3,600. (Day student tuition rose from $800 to $1,100 during the same period.) In contrast, Exeter's tuition in 1969 was $2,500, and the tuition at Wellesley College was $3,100. Among comparable girls' schools, Emma Willard's tuition fell in the middle of the pack, with Dana

Hall at the low end with a $3,500 price tag and Rosemary Hall at the high end, charging $4,000. Among these girls' schools, Emma Willard was the largest, yet the income from tuition did not begin to cover costs.

By the sixth year of his administration, Bill Dietel viewed the financial stability of the school as the most critical issue facing Emma Willard. His school was not alone. At the end of 1966–67, he devoted his column in the *Bulletin* to the "financial crisis which grips the independent secondary schools of our country." He reminded them that tuition, even at the relatively high Emma Willard rate, did "not completely pay for the education of the student."[42] The money earned from the endowment subsidized each girl's education. By the late 1960s, Emma Willard's endowment had climbed to $2 million. Only nine girls' boarding schools had endowments over a million dollars. Ethel Walker was wealthiest, with an endowment that topped $5.5 million, and Emma Willard was in sixth place, ahead of St. Timothy's, Westover, and Madeira but behind Foxcroft, Miss Porter's, the Masters School, and Abbot. In contrast, seven boys' schools had endowments topping $10 million with Exeter leading the pack at $65 million, followed by Andover, St. Paul's, Choate, Lawrenceville, Deerfield, and Loomis. Miss Porter's operating budget showed that they were spending nearly $6,000 per pupil; Emma Willard, in contrast, was spending just over $4,000 per pupil. To enrich the program at Emma Willard and meet the demands of the physical plant would take many more endowment dollars.

For most of the 1960s, preliminary budget reports projected deficits ranging from $21,500 to $145,000. By trimming costs, final budgets most years squeaked into the black, usually helped by an infusion of cash into the annual fund. Faced with a possible deficit of nearly $60,000 in 1965, Dietel informed the board that most girls' schools were running deficits and, consequently, most balanced the books in the end with annual giving. The only solution to this kind of financial uncertainty was to build the endowment to a point where it would provide significant, steady revenue for annual operations. In the fall of 1962, the endowment had provided $50,000 to the operating fund for the first time; at the end of the decade, the endowment accounted for double that amount, but it was still not enough.

In the spring of 1967, Dietel predicted that the school would most likely run a deficit budget for the following academic year. He assured the trustees that there was "no need for panic," but that there was "a need for concern." He presented a five-year forecast showing that, short of cutting staff or program, a balanced budget could only be achieved by an endowment that provided $125,000 for 1967–68, $141,000 for 1968–69, with increases each year until 1971–72 when the income from the endowment would need to top a quarter of a million dollars. The board agreed that "the long term solution . . . lay with much greater endowment." In the short run, however, the executive committee of the board recommended that planning begin immediately to balance the budget in 1968–69 by reducing "faculty and staff without sacrificing the quality of the education,"[43] an oxymoron for any responsible school administrator.

If greater endowment was the key to survival, then the solution was to raise more money. In December 1967, the school had passed the $3 million mark in capital fund-raising. The director of development, Albert Smith, was critical to the success of this effort; he was, in Dietel's words, "the first really professional fund-raiser at the school."[44] Smith resigned in July 1968, just as the school launched a new campaign, this time seeking $9.5 million, $5 million for endowment and additional money for further plant renovations, the art wing of the library complex, and a new gymnasium. This campaign was titled the Emma Willard School Capital Program. Again the principal pressed the case for endowment with the alumnae, arguing in the *Bulletin* that a larger endowment was "a matter of survival."[45] In spite of his plea, alumnae giving hovered near 30 percent, although Miss Porter's and Westover could count on 50 percent of their alumnae for contributions, and Abbot, Foxcroft, and Madeira all had higher percentages of alumnae donors than did Emma Willard. Among the well-endowed boys' schools, only Lawrenceville's alumni fell below 40 percent participation. The new campaign, however, focused more heavily on leadership gifts than on broad donor appeal. Within the first year, over $3 million was raised, with 60 percent of the total coming from trustee gifts. In spite of this generosity, trustee giving was a million dollars short of the 28 percent that trustees on average provided for campaigns at comparable institutions.

If Dietel was disappointed or frustrated by trustee giving, in other respects, he had their full support. Nowhere was this more important than in his—and their—commitment to diversifying the student body. Wellington and Lay had broken the color barrier the fall after Linda Remington Dietel graduated from Emma Willard, but true diversity was elusive. In 1965 Dietel told the board that although the school did not discriminate on the basis of race, religion, or national background, "in truth the vast majority of the girls come from what can only be described as upper middle-class families, however great the geographic distribution." In fact, he reminded them, "Roman Catholics, Jews and Negroes are in a distinct minority."[46] The few black girls who had attended the school since 1948 had come from distinctly middle-class and upper-middle-class backgrounds. As Peter Schrag, a trustee and writer for the *Saturday Review of Literature*, wrote to Dietel, if the school only admitted black students "who are otherwise no different from the normal Emma Willard girls, there is hardly any point in doing it . . . unless we get something other than pleasant middle-class kids who are going to make it anyway . . . there is hardly much point in the fuss."[47]

While Bill Dietel was principal of Emma Willard, James Meredith entered the University of Mississippi, Martin Luther King Jr. delivered the "I Have a Dream" speech at the Lincoln Memorial, Sidney Poitier became the first black actor to win an Academy Award, four young black girls were killed by a bomb in a Birmingham church, three white civil rights workers died at the hands of virulent racists in Mississippi, Lyndon Johnson pushed the Civil Rights Act through Congress, riots tore up Los Angeles, Detroit, Newark, and a host of other cities, Bill Cosby became the first black actor to star in a primetime television show, Robert Weaver became the first black member of the president's cabinet, Malcolm X was killed, Stokely Carmichel and the Student Nonviolent Coordinating Committee (SNCC) proclaimed "black power," Thurgood Marshall was appointed to the Supreme Court, Carl Stokes was elected mayor of Cleveland, the Supreme Court struck down state statutes outlawing interracial marriage, Martin Luther King was assassinated, and Richard Nixon presented Duke Ellington with the Medal of Freedom. James Baldwin wrote *The Fire Next Time*,

William Styron received a Pulitzer for *The Confessions of Nat Turner*, Maya Angelou wrote *I Know Why the Caged Bird Sings*, the films *In The Heat of the Night* and *Guess Who's Coming to Dinner* tackled previously taboo subjects for Hollywood, Motown hits flooded the top-ten charts, and the Jackson Five went on tour for the first time.

In 1961–62 there were no black seniors on campus, in 1963, there was one, in 1964, none, in 1965, 1966, and 1967, there were two, in 1968, there were five. The messages of the civil rights movement resonated with Bill Dietel's sense of fairness and decency. In addition, Clementine Tangeman came from a family with long ties to social justice, and board member Alexander Aldrich, who had marched in Selma, led his fellow trustees in actively supporting additional scholarships and inviting an African American to join the board. As Jane Steinberg pointed out in "The Boarding School Mystique," an article in *Mademoiselle* that compared Emma Willard most favorably with other girls' schools, Emma Willard had *"always* been forward-minded (but quiet about it)." After a visit to the school, Steinberg concluded,

> All social and economic backgrounds are represented. . . . There is no typical Emma Willard girl—no two of a kind, no possible stereotype to be drawn in terms of any school image or dogma. . . . Emma Willard has *always* been open to a socially diverse student body. One gets from the girls an impression of good humor, good minds, and a prevailing gentleness—which is not at the expense of spirit. Emma Willard girls are every bit as polite and friendly as Miss Porter's girls, but good manners at Emma Willard seem spontaneous and natural—not so much like conditioned obedience.[48]

Given this reputation for inclusion and eclecticism, Emma Willard was the right place for students from groups who had been excluded from prestigious boarding schools in the past, particularly African American students. However, because of the deep economic inequalities fostered by decades of harsh segregation, most of the students the school hoped to attract would need significant financial assistance. In 1962–63, sixty-two girls received approximately $79,000 in financial aid. Dietel told the board that he hoped to raise enough money to endow another $70,000 in aid annually. His eventual goal was to enroll a student population in which 10 percent were African

American. Not surprisingly, the pressures on the school's budget from deferred maintenance, scholarships, and construction ultimately precluded his reaching this goal fully, but he made impressive strides. However, the lack of Emma Willard scholarship funds was offset by the school's participation in A Better Chance (ABC), a program begun in 1963 by a consortium of independent schools to help students of color gain access to a better education than was usually available in their segregated, underfunded neighborhood schools. For example, in 1965–66, the school granted $95,000 in aid, $20,000 of which came from ABC. Majority students celebrated the availability of aid and its consequences. Jane Wales '66, editor of *CLOCK*, wrote that the school is "saved from being just one of a legion of conventional girls' schools because of our large proportion of scholarships." She concluded optimistically, "Already way out of line with our income, our scholarship program is still not a patch on what we hope it will grow to."[49]

Unfortunately, by 1968–69, the school's portion of the financial aid budget had shrunk from $75,000 to $53,000 as money was taken from the financial aid budget to balance the books. From trustee correspondence and school records, it appears that individual donors often picked up the tab for deserving but financially disadvantaged students whom Dietel brought to their attention. The situation was aggravated in 1968 when ABC reduced its funding, leaving schools to decide whether or not to continue support for the ABC students already in their midst. Dietel asked the faculty whether they wanted to continue with these students, even if it meant other sacrifices. He wrote to a supporter, "Every voting member of the faculty, which included housemothers and gym teachers" agreed to increasing the school's portion of aid. These included Janet Maly, the first faculty representative to the board of trustees and a gifted mathematics teacher who spent several summers teaching mathematics to ABC students on the Mount Holyoke campus.

Dietel was a far cry from a classic knee-jerk liberal. He was a thoughtful humanist, and he understood that Emma Willard was "a white school which has some negroes [*sic*] in it." He informed the board, "We are part of the white establishment, and the fact that there are ten negroes [*sic*] on the campus does not change this fact."[50] Given the economic realities limiting the numbers of disadvantaged black students the school could assist, it was clear to Dietel that "our role is not to educate negroes [sic] and poor whites but to help educate the white community to their responsibilities . . . to use their power to achieve greater social justice as fast as possible."[51]

To this end, he widely broadened the education of all Emma Willard students. In 1963 he arranged for provocative southern novelist Lillian Smith to be a writer-in-residence. He approved the transformation of the Chapel Circle to the Civil Rights Group and allowed them to work among the impoverished, mostly black children living in the Taylor Apartments, a substandard housing development in downtown Troy. Carl Stokes, the first black man to head a major American city, visited the campus several times, and a team of four girls, two white and two black, went to Cleveland to work on his mayoralty campaign; they stayed at the home of Martin Sutler, Emma Willard's first African American trustee, and the father of Sherry '67 and Susan '70. Students heard opposing voices on civil rights; the school transported them to Albany to hear George Wallace and to RPI to hear Eldridge Cleaver. Prior to becoming the Civil Rights Group, the Chapel Circle attended NAACP meetings in Troy, supported the activities of SNCC, and went to RPI to hear Bob Dylan, whose protest songs became anthems for the civil rights movement. When the Kerner Commission report was issued, Dietel bought copies for every member of the faculty and student body. He convened interscholastic conferences on black political leadership in 1967 and human rights in 1968.

All of this served to meet his objective of educating the majority white student body to their responsibilities. In the spring of 1968, Susan Hunter '68, president of student government, speaking at a meeting of the board of trustees, "stressed how much the white students have learned from their Negro sisters."[52] A year later, one of Hunter's classmates anonymously paid the tuition for a black day student, renewing it each year for four years. Pictures in yearbooks at the end of the decade show interracial rooming, a phenomenon unheard of at most schools and many colleges. Black students were elected to prestigious student offices including class presidencies as early as 1963; in 1968 the first black May Queen was crowned. Given the paucity of their numbers, they obviously won these elections with the support of many white classmates.

There were no African American housemothers, and only one black teacher—and she left after two years.[53] Margaret Miller '61, teaching in an inner-city school in New Haven, wrote to Dietel, "I hope you have some black teachers or housemothers . . . who really feel the contradictions of being a black student in a middle class white school."[54] He was trying. To get "more Negroes on staff," he sent a letter to "all Negro alumnae and their parents." The effort was frustrating. Equally frustrating was the slow pace of change beyond Emma Willard. Bill and Linda Dietel, Nelson Rockefeller supporters, watched the 1968 Republican National Convention and were "terribly discouraged." He concluded, "If I were one of the poor or a Negro, . . . I think . . . that I would be tempted to give up all hope."[55] Linda Dietel had taken an active role in civil rights in Troy, serving on the city's newly formed commission for human rights. Local housing and education were both severely segregated, and in the late 1960s, city officials were just beginning to recognize the "depressing facts of housing" for Troy's "8000 Negroes."[56]

It is clear that Bill Dietel's commitment to civil rights transformed the campus for white students—but at what cost to the black students? From articles in *CLOCK*, literature in *Triangle*, and pictures in the yearbook, the young black women at Emma Willard appear strong, resilient, and proud. Over the course of the decade, their hairstyles evolved with the movement; straightened formal coiffures gave way to striking Afros. The leadership of Chapel Circle had been almost exclusively white, as had the initial leadership of the Civil Rights Group. Denise McCaskill '70 and Venessa Barabino '70, two African American students, took over in 1969; they changed the name to Masikizano, Swahili for "understanding." When Carmichel radicalized SNCC, Barabino did not hesitate to editorialize in *CLOCK*, "Separation is not a threat to the white community . . . it is a comprehensive resort for Black survival in a country that seems inherently segregated." In "My White Brother," a short story published in *Triangle*, Franciena King '68 wrote movingly, metaphorically, and sympathetically about what she had given to the white students she knew at Emma Willard, "I could give him something no riot, no sit-down, no government could give—a part of me . . . a place in my colored world . . . I could see him searching for a way of freeing himself from his prejudices. He struggled, stuttered, fumbled for words. I looked at him and smiled. He knew that I knew he was trying. I forgave him for my people."[57]

Civil rights, of course, was only one wave in the ocean of change that washed over the United States in the 1960s. The population grew 15 percent during the decade, topping 200 million by 1970. In 1967 *Time* magazine chose the youth of America (defined as people under twenty-five) as its man of the year. The baby boomers were on the cusp of adulthood and were changing the culture. The number of young women earning a bachelor's degree increased more than 100 percent over the course of the decade, and the number earning PhDs increased nearly 200 percent. Richard Nixon whined, "On every hand we find old standards violated, old values discarded, old principles ignored,"[58] but the thwarting of convention, the violation of taboos, and the toppling of false gods energized the young. Betty Friedan accelerated the women's movement with the publication of *The Feminine Mystique* in 1963, and in 1968 she declared authoritatively, "No girl child born today should responsibly be brought up to be a housewife."[59] During a decade dominated by their music, the Beatles moved from a floppy-haired boy band singing simple songs of love to a serious peace-loving, politically charged musical group that celebrated experimentation with drugs and Eastern mysticism. Vietnam became the longest war in American history; the U.S. military dropped more bombs on that small Asian country than they had dropped in all of World War II. American students protested the war in ever-increasing numbers. Clashes between authorities and demonstrators, visible in thousands of homes during the Democratic National Convention in 1968, climaxed with the shooting of four student protesters at Kent State in 1970.

Change crept into the highly regulated world of Emma Willard. In 1963 a student defined happiness as "walking in front of the dress checker with no stockings on and not getting caught" and "having to tie your 'sturdies' only once a day."[60] In 1969 the uniforms shifted to wash-and-wear material, but they were still uniforms. Washers and dryers were installed in Sage basement, and laundry service was discontinued. A disgruntled student wrote to the newspaper editor, "Emma Willard students have been given the glorious opportunity of sorting, presoaking, washing and ironing all their own clothes. . . . Now every Emma Willard girl can climb toward matrimony secure in the knowledge that she is a competent laundress."[61]

Although uniforms remained, there was some relief from strict regimentation. Beginning in 1964, students were allowed to wear sneakers in study hall and their own clothes to dinner on Wednesday nights. Housecoats were permitted at Sunday breakfast. Madras, however, was forbidden on dressy occasions. By 1966–67 students could wear their own clothes to Sunday dinner or chapel, as long as they did not wear "a sport-type shift or beach dress."[62] Midway through that year, hats and gloves were no longer required for Sunday chapel. As Dietel explained to the School Affairs Committee, "God really does accept us just the way we are."[63] In the spring of 1968, seniors were allowed to wear their own clothes but had to wear them "with sturdy browns and socks during the school day"[64] and were never allowed to wear sandals with their uniforms, even during nonacademic time. God might accept hatless, gloveless parishioners, but Emma Willard had standards.

A 1965 *CLOCK* cartoon captured classic adolescent righteousness about rules. A student is seated with hair over her face, and the caption reads, "There's a war in Viet Nam, there are problems down South, they're rioting in Africa, and starving in Spain, and you tell me to get the hair out of my eyes."[65] The *CLUCK*, a satirical issue of *CLOCK*, took a lighter view of dress regulations. They editorialized,

> The board of CLUCK is proud that Emma Willard is America's last bastion of old time womanhood. In all too many American secondary schools, aggressive, nomad girls toddle around in loafers and sling-backs, destroying their femininity and their arches in the pursuit of vulgar pleasures. Their lips, dyed foul pinks and oranges, their eyelids smeared, and their hair uncombed, their undernourished forms encased in fitted skirts and flowered blouses, they sully their image as America's future wives and mothers by constant companionship in study and sport with the other s-x. Not we. Stringy, spotty, and pasty, broad of rump and rumpled of wig, we clop about in the womanly dignity of sturdies. No *Too Early Spring* for us. It is not our

part to follow high school marriage and college baby with graduate school divorce. When at last, disciplined in mind and muscle, we burst from the frowsy cocoon of the Emma Willard 'uni,' our wings will be stronger, our colors fresher, than those of all competing butterflies. Or, anyway, that's what Mother told us.[66]

In general the rules had relaxed in Bill Dietel's first two years, but they remained fairly constant for the rest of his tenure. School Council was responsible for the introduction to the annual handbook, noting in 1963–64, "We do not have an elaborate set of rules . . . we do not smoke, we do not drink, and we do not leave the campus except as the regulations for leaves permit."[67] Nevertheless, the handbooks were still several pages long and covered all manner of topics, including lights out, bath rules, phone rules, bulletin board rules, room decorating rules, dining room rules, automobile and taxi rules, and dating rules. At one point or another, students were not allowed to meet boys in downtown Troy, they were not allowed to ride bicycles on Spring or Pawling Avenues, sit on windowsills, have cleaning fluids or prescription drugs in their rooms, chew gum anywhere but the dormitories, or sit on the lawn on the Pawling Avenue side of the campus.

One of the biggest changes came in 1967–68 when students were allowed to skip chapel as long as they attended services elsewhere. Interestingly, permission for this change was granted by the board of trustees, but Robert Hammett, chaplain and religion instructor, proposed it to them. As early as 1964, Bill Dietel had suggested allowing students to attend their own services, but the board disagreed. Not until 1969–70 was chapel made completely optional. Students had agitated for this publicly since 1966 when letters to the editor and editorials called for the change. The same movement was underway at Miss Porter's when the *Mademoiselle* reporter visited the Farmington campus in 1966. The editors of the MPS newspaper declared, "People beyond the age of fifteen should not be compelled to go to church."[68] Girls' boarding schools were not the only places questioning organized religion and a belief in an all-powerful God. On April 8, 1966, the headline on the cover of *Time* wondered, "Is God Dead?" and students on school and college campuses in greater and greater numbers answered resoundingly, yes.

Anti-authoritarianism and political protest movements were not the only trends that moved from college campuses to secondary schools. Marijuana, long a part of the counterculture, was becoming mainstream, and in 1966 LSD and acid rock made their first widespread appearance. In 1967 CLOCK published an editorial supporting the legalization of marijuana, and the school handbook for 1968–69 explicitly mentioned drugs: "There are stringent Federal and New York State laws concerning drug use, including marijuana and LSD. The school is largely obligated to give full support to these laws."[69] Although the government had ordered health warnings to be posted on cigarette packs in 1964, smoking among teenagers was on the rise. A student poll of other schools found that less than a third of girls' schools forbade smoking in 1967. A CLOCK reporter questioned whether Emma Willard's objection stemmed from health concerns, morality issues, or the danger of fire.[70] Both the principal and his wife smoked, as did 60 percent of the faculty. Jack Betterly, an outspoken history teacher, who would be a vocal critic of eight administrations during his long tenure at the school, agitated for faculty smoking at combined faculty/student occasions. In a memorandum to Dietel, he suggested that ashtrays be made available at school functions, "Not for students but for faculty. We are adults and we smoke—they are not and they don't. It is that simple."[71] Yearbook pictures often captured faculty, especially male faculty, with pipes and cigarettes in hand.

For several years students took a variety of smoking proposals to the administration, to the board, and to the Parents' Association. According to an anonymous CLOCK poll, by 1969, 32 of 70 seniors who responded were smokers, as were 23 of 83 juniors, 26 of 80 sophomores, and 12 of 40 freshmen.[72] Six months later a second poll found that 18 percent of the seniors and juniors who filled out the questionnaire claimed to smoke pot frequently, as did 10 percent of the sophomores and 2 percent of the freshmen. Another 14 percent of the seniors claimed they smoked pot infrequently, 13 percent had tried hashish, 9 percent had experimented with LSD, and 11 percent were pack-a-day cigarette smokers. Junior statistics were similar, with 12 percent of the class claiming the pack-a-day habit.[73] In the spring of 1970, just a few weeks before Bill Dietel left the school, the Faculty/Student Concerns Committee recommended that students be given the right to smoke with parental permission, although they were forbidden to smoke anywhere on campus or on the streets of Troy. Ironically, this initial permission to smoke passed at the same time that the school celebrated the first Earth Day and students formed the first Emma Willard environmental concerns group, the Pollution Concerns Committee. It was the same month that *CLOCK* headlined, "Drug Problem Acknowledged, Raid Possible."[74] Drugs might be a problem, but alcohol was something else altogether. In 1969–70 seniors were granted the privilege of drinking wine at class dinners and with faculty in their homes. The spring before, wine was served for the first time to faculty and students at the honors dinner.

Although much was changing, much was also staying the same. Revels was always Revels and always magical, although the play underwent minor script and character changes in accordance with the personality of each senior class. In 1964 the school began the tradition of releasing seniors from classes for a full week before Revels, and beginning in 1966, the most recently graduated class was invited to the show. In 1969 long retired Revels creator Ellen Manchester sent an annual fund gift to Bill Dietel with the note, "Christmas Revels will change, but it must never lose its joy."[75] Christmas Vespers continued to showcase the choir and to be uncompromisingly Christian; in 1964 the congregation lit candles for the first time. May Day occurred much the same as always, although the venue moved from the inner campus to the lawn behind Wellington-Lay. The Flame Ceremony continued to highlight student leadership, Cum Laude and EW were awarded to outstanding seniors, and graduation was the ultimate annual celebration. In 1968 graduation moved outside for the first time, although students had been petitioning for the change for a few years. During the 1960s, Headmaster's Holiday remained a popular tradition, although its name morphed into Principal's Playday. The critical mass of men on the faculty meant that by 1962 the holiday added a new wrinkle, a faculty/student basketball game. The School Fair remained a perennial favorite, but in the 1960s, the profits from the fair supported scholarships, not the chapel. In 1965 the fair raised $4,000 to fund ABC students, and in 1966, $6,500, which was matched by a gift from the Rockefeller Brothers Fund, the largest single contribution they made to any school, boys' schools included.

At least as early as 1963, there was a movement on campus to allow students to get their rings in their junior year. The *CLOCK* editor— a senior—wrote in opposition to the idea, claiming that only seniors could feel "the right spirit of the occasion," that the ring pledge was "the symbol of individual responsibility as part of the united class."[76] A year later, a poll showed, not surprisingly, that over 90 percent of the juniors felt they should have their rings junior year. Junior Jane Wales '66 editorialized that it would "add to the emotion [of the occasion] because the outgoing seniors will give the rings."[77] Not until 1970 did the juniors get their way; that spring they received their rings on the night of the Flame Ceremony. They stood in a circle in Kiggins while the seniors bestowed their rings on them, the ritual emphasizing "the changing of leaders, not the departure of seniors."[78]

A few current traditions appeared for the first time in the 1960s. Gift giving at the holidays was ritualized as Peanuts and Shells, Fathers' Day was replaced by Family (now Parent) Days, Dance Workshop was organized, and students were finally given vacation time at Thanksgiving. Senior skip day began in 1967, and the first senior prank was pulled off in 1968. Early in the decade the junior/senior prom occurred each year as it had for decades; in 1965 *CLOCK*, as was its tradition, listed the names and schools or colleges of the eighty-seven young men who had accepted invitations to the prom. By 1968, however, the idea of a prom evoked so little interest that the event was replaced by a semiformal dance. A limited social life, to the chagrin of students, was a continuing tradition at the school. As one *CLOCK* editor summed it up, "Why should [an Emma Willard student] fret over her social life when she really has not got one? She need not be concerned with what she will wear tonight for her date; someone tells her what to wear, and there will be no date."[79]

Mostly dateless, perhaps, but still healthy adolescent young women, and one of the more striking additions to the program in the 1960s was the addition of lectures and workshops on sex education—outside the traditional "reproductive unit" in biology classes that had embarrassed science teachers and students alike for generations. This time around sex education was taught by a combination of married men, married women, and young single women. Bill Dietel was one of the teachers, and he approached the new morality of the 1960s candidly. The pill, the IUD, and other new forms of birth control were transforming the sexual habits of unmarried women, and American attitudes about premarital sex were changing. In his first "sex lecture" to the student body, Bill Dietel told the students that there were "four causes for sexual experimentation which should never be: boredom, embarrassment, lack of a way out and fear of seeming afraid."[80] He did not tell them not to experiment. His speech was followed by grade-level meetings with the school's consulting adolescent psychiatrist, Dr. Lenore Sportsman. She told the girls that the new morality was defined by "fidelity rather than chastity."[81] The following fall the sex education discussions were led by Chaplain Robert Hammett, Mary Carter, a widowed housemother, Julie Smith, a young guidance counselor who had recently graduated from Skidmore, and Nancy Blackmun, another young guidance counselor who was in her first year at the school. According to Damien O'Leary'67, who reported favorably on the talks, "The adults involved have come to realize that we will not be shocked by anything they have to say."[82] A year later the sex lectures were broadened into human relations lectures and covered a range of topics including drugs, abortion, homosexuality, and sexually transmitted diseases. A mock version of Revels that December had the sprites waving plaques that said "Support Planned Parenthood." And the first senior prank in the spring of 1968 played off sex education, providing a little humor "after so many months of serious and intense discussion about sex."[83]

The times, as Bob Dylan reminded them in song, were most definitely "a-changin.'" By 1968 many of the traditionally single-sex colleges, especially the all-male institutions, were examining whether or not to become coeducational. Bill Dietel had recently met the new head of Andover, who told him that Abbot wanted "to join forces."

He thought it "a fine dream, but I think it only that."[84] Perhaps he was being disingenuous to soothe the fears of his correspondent, an ardent supporter of her alma mater. He certainly knew that coeducation was more than just a dream on many campuses, and the topic was a hot one at Emma Willard. A month after he wrote about the proposed Andover/Abbot merger, the Emma Willard trustees discussed coeducation at their fall board meeting. Richard Day, Exeter's headmaster and the parent of an Emma Willard junior,[85] was among the experts appearing before the board; two years later he welcomed the first female students to the venerable academy. In the spring of 1969, Dietel wrote, "the question most commonly asked by alumnae" is "when is Emma Willard going co-ed?" While there was not yet a definitive answer on Mount Ida, Dietel was "grieved to report"[86] that his alma mater, Princeton, had decided to admit women.

He suggested that the question of coeducation had been raised before, but that this time the conversation was quite different. "What is new," he wrote, "is the current conviction of many educators that co-education, especially for high school juniors and seniors, is essential to social, intellectual, and emotional development."[87] If this was true, then single-sex education was negative. To study the possibility of co-education at Emma Willard, Dietel appointed a committee composed of faculty and Linda Dietel. Jack Betterly, history instructor, was chair; Rebecca Kern, who had chaired the Physical Education Department for fifteen years; Margaret Gormly Pratt '32, a science instructor; and Bob Prior, a French teacher who had been a housemaster at Rugby, also served. With the exception of Kern, all had been educated in single-sex schools and/or colleges. In their report the committee noted that the obvious advantages to coeducation were the positive impact such a move would have on enrollment and fund-raising. The disadvantages, however, were the layout of the campus, especially the dormitories and playing fields, neither of which were particularly suitable for adolescent boys, and their basic belief that coeducation was not the right step for Emma Willard, given its leadership in girls' education.

The year 1968 has long been regarded by historians as a watershed year. The various movements that had roiled the country—civil rights, feminism, antiwar protests, and the youth movement—garnered full attention as the presidential election consumed the nation's attention. The fight for student rights on college campuses had evolved from freedom from institutional authority to freedom to be part of institutional authority. As one shrewd observer put it, the "legacy of academic liberalism"[88] meant that faculty and administrators everywhere felt an obligation to listen to students and include them in decision making. On campuses everywhere, the protests against great universal injustices such as racism, sexism, and oppression were coupled with student protests against school and college rules they found unnecessary and outdated. Emma Willard was no exception, although the biggest protests lagged about a year behind those on college campuses.

Between 1968 and 1969, students at Emma Willard smoked cigarettes, used drugs, drank alcohol, and protested "petty rules" like the administration's dictum that students not eat on walks between campus and a local store. Sarcasm dripping from her pen, "an upset, disillusioned, and disappointed senior" asked rhetorically if a student who bought an orange popsicle was really supposed to put it in a bag, walk back to her room, and proceed "to drink her melted popsicle from the paper bag."[89] Student requests to attend the "Vietnam Moratorium" in downtown Troy were matched by requests for more liberal dating rules. Lucile Tuttle, who had served as the chief administrative rule enforcer for many years, retired in the spring of 1968, and she was replaced by thirty-one-year-old Benjamin Shute as dean of students, the first man to hold that position. The same issue of the newspaper that carried the news of Tuttle's retirement also contained an editorial about cohabitation among college students; the editor concluded, "acting *in loco parentis* is commendably diminishing."[90]

The changing student attitudes toward authority were wearying for administrators, especially the principal. At the end of 1968–69, Bill Dietel wrote to a friend, "I am so relieved to think this year is finally finished. . . . It grows harder every year to know what to do with adolescents who seem so disturbed by the world they live in."[91] In fact, he had decided to resign, although it would not be made public until the fall, and he would remain as principal until June 30, 1970. He had many reasons for leaving. In addition to student unrest, the faculty had become "increasingly restive with [the] constraints" of the correlated curriculum, and "pressure from the parents was increasing . . . to assure the acceptance by their daughters into the best colleges in the country." He and the faculty knew that "the bottom half was not going to make it to the Heavenly 7." In addition, coeducation "was no longer talk but had become a reality,"[92] and in his view, the school—and all girls' schools—faced "a battle for financial survival [that would be] the major problem for as far into the future as I can see." As head, he would be "forever torn" between running the school, which he loved, and fund-raising, which was less appealing to him. As he summarized it for a former board member, "Very frankly, I am weary."[93]

Underlying all of these very real reasons was profound sorrow. In January, shortly after the students returned from their winter holiday, a sophomore boarder had killed herself on campus. A new student that year, she had been identified as troubled by her faculty and houseparent; however, after an evaluation, the school's consulting psychiatrist felt she was no danger to herself. Tragically, this was a misdiagnosis. Parents of other students wrote incredibly supportive letters to Bill Dietel, but as he said many years later, her death "took the starch out of me."[94]

Dietel's plans to resign were kept very quiet until October 1969. At a special meeting of the faculty the evening of October 9, he told his colleagues he had resigned. The next day he told the students. Although some of them had recently chafed under his rules and restrictions, he was, in general, their beloved "Daddy D." (This moniker, universally employed by alumnae of the Dietel era, did not appear in any student publications while he was head of school.) As reported in CLOCK, "The reactions of the students, ranging from dry-eyed shock to tearful sadness, reflected their admiration and love for Mr. Dietel."[95]

The transition was perhaps eased by the board's decision to let Dietel devote himself to fund-raising for several months during his final year. It was also most assuredly helped by Dietel's recognition that the school would go on without him. In a letter to the former headmistresses announcing his plans, he reminded Wellington that she had once told him, "When schools become so closely focused upon the head, they run grave risks for the well-being of the institution in the long pull." He continued, "People . . . think I have some special magic without which Emma W can't function. We know that isn't true."[96] He actively advised the search committee, which was headed by trustee Harold Higgins.

Seen from the perspective of the twenty-first century, the search for Bill Dietel's successor was appallingly sexist. Shortly after the resignation was made public, Barbara Colbron, the headmistress of Spence, nominated two members of the Spence faculty, "if your search committee is interested in considering woman candidates."[97] Dietel responded, "They are not opposed to taking on a woman head but they certainly do want to be sure that such a person can carry all the responsibilities which fall upon a single person."[98] Interviewed by *CLOCK*, English instructor Jack Pasanen confidently told the student reporter that "a woman could not handle the job by herself," and it was "unlikely that the Search Committee will find a married woman whose husband would want to have a headmaster as a wife."[99]

Assisting Higgins with the search were board vice president Don Buttenheim, the faculty trustee Janet Maly, and Helen Cheel '23. With the help of a search consultant from Spencer Stuart, Higgins drew up a list of qualities for the "Ideal Applicant for the Position." A man, age thirty to thirty-seven, who was "happily married," was the preferred candidate. His unpaid wife needed to be "outgoing, friendly, and able to command respect of students, faculty and staff." The candidate himself was expected to provide "academic leadership for the school,"[100] and, if possible, should hold a doctorate. Bill Dietel told Anne Wellington that he was sure the committee would take the best person, man or woman, "but their first preference is someone under the age of thirty-five and a married man from the University."[101] Put in its best light, those seeking the new head wanted to replicate Bill Dietel. However, it is hard to dismiss Higgins's decision to vet lists of alumnae to see which ones might have husbands who would be available for the job. Nor is it easy to read Dietel's nomination of one candidate that included the information that "one of [his] strongest points is that he has an exceptionally able wife."[102]

The committee met its goals in April 1970, with the appointment of Dennis A. Collins as the new principal. He was young; not yet thirty, he was the second youngest person and third man to head the school. He was married, had a baby daughter, and he came from the university world, having most recently served as a dean at Occidental College in Los Angeles. Meanwhile, the year wound down for the Dietels, who were planning an extended stay in England before relocating to Connecticut.

Change was everywhere. In the alumnae office, a new school symbol, internally dubbed "the squashed bug," replaced the old Willard crest. Ten faculty announced their resignations; the ones remaining were busy working on the new curriculum they would implement in the fall. A popular dean of students, E. C. Speers, had just finished a very successful first year in the job. Students were looking forward to the abolition of uniforms; as a *CLOCK* headline put it, "Trend Is to Unregimented Life."[103] Privately, Dietel had misgivings about all the change. He had written to Richard Davis, his counterpart at Miss Porter's, that he saw "something destructive about [students'] attitude of wanting to change everything willy-nilly."[104]

In April the Playhouse was demolished to make way for the new visual arts building. The 1970 *Gargoyle* opined:

> Change . . . disrupting tradition,
>> yet tradition in itself
>> Inherent in this change is contrast
>> The transition from old to new
>> A symbol of progress. [105]

In an interview with the yearbook editors, Bill Dietel told them that the future of Emma Willard and the future of independent schools was "bright if funded."[106] He knew what he was talking about. For nine years he had initiated programs, built new buildings and renovated old ones, hired first-rate faculty, expanded the scholarship program— and yet, there was never enough money to do all that he wanted to accomplish. From 1964–65 to 1969–70, all but two of the annual budgets showed balances in the red. Although he was leaving the headship, over the course of the next forty years, Bill Dietel's fund-raising efforts on behalf of the school would be significant and unwavering.

These Will Not Be Easy Years

THE DECADE OF THE 1970s did not share the exuberance and optimism of the 1960s. Between 1970 and 1980, the country suffered its first peacetime gasoline shortage, admitted defeat in a major war, and witnessed the first presidential resignation and the appointment of the first chief executive who had not been elected to either the presidency or the vice presidency. The celebration of the country's bicentennial was overshadowed by national self-doubt. In an article on the country's birthday for the school's alumnae magazine, veteran mathematics teacher Janet Maly commented that her patriotism had taken quite a blow since her childhood. Then, she was "proud to be an American," but she had come to see that her generation's "smugness was only matched by our naiveté."[1] A colleague in the history department dated the decline to the middle of the 1960s. It had been, he told the *Bulletin* reporter, "a hard ten years—the Kennedys dead, King dead, the drug boom, the 'generation gap,' Vietnam, Cambodia, Watergate."[2]

The idealism that had fueled so much of the "anti" movements of the prior decade seemed to be missing by 1970. The new attacks on old forms of morality did not have the moral force of the earlier movements for diversity and equality. The Vietnam War and the criminal actions of the Nixon administration had combined to destroy faith and trust in leadership. By 1976 double-digit inflation and 8 to 9 percent unemployment, the highest since the beginning of World War II, created a financial uncertainty that matched the cultural uneasiness. The promise of the civil rights movement appeared to be hopelessly mired in the seemingly unbreakable patterns of residential and economic segregation. Fed up with compromise, angry black leaders urged segregated solutions whose unintended effect sometimes exacerbated the situation. Northeastern cities, plagued by urban decay, were crippled by soaring criminal rates. The economic and social goals of the women's liberation movement gave way to the siren of sexual revolution, a far less easily defended position for most American women over thirty.

The 1970s tested Emma Willard as well as the nation. Unmanageable budgets, uneven leadership, an unprecedented admissions challenge created in large measure by elite boys' schools admitting girls, a culture of permissiveness among both students and adults, a revolution in women's athletics, increased parental and student demands about college placement, alumnae and parental philanthropic interests that ranged far beyond boarding schools, and an aging plant, leaking and peeling after years of deferred maintenance—all of these problems faced Dennis Collins, the young incoming principal. On Sunday afternoon, October 4, 1970, he accepted the mace of office from board president Clementine Tangeman. A graduate of Stanford, where he had earned both his B.A. and his M.A., Collins was a West Coast boy through and through. He had graduated from a public high school in Seattle, Washington, before going to Stanford as a Heritage Leadership Scholar. Fluent in French, Italian, and Spanish, he had served as a dean of admissions and then dean of students at Occidental College between 1965 and 1970.

That Emma Willard had chosen another man to head the country's oldest school for girls evoked little comment. In part, of course, this was a reflection of and a credit to Bill Dietel's successful administration. However, the reaction also reflected a national trend. Across the country, girls' schools were increasingly headed by men. The Headmistresses Association of the East, a prestigious organization founded in 1911, had only three men among its membership in 1954. By 1972 forty of its ninety-six members were men. Once the nearly exclusive province of girls' schools and the women who ran them, the organization not only added men, but after 1960 it began electing heads of coeducational schools.

In his inaugural address, Collins quoted Bennington College president Edward J. Bloustein, who had remarked that administering a school or college in 1970 was tantamount to "playing chess on the open deck of the sinking *Titanic*."[3] Collins was not, however, referring to the multiple problems facing the school. Instead, he meant the shifting landscape of American education and the groundswell for fundamental curricular change. In addition to Bloustein, he cited Charles Silberman, who had recently published *The Crisis in the Classroom.* Silberman, like many other educators at the end of the 1960s, believed that American schools stifled free, creative thought. Had he known about the elective curriculum being implemented on Mount Ida, he would have heartily approved. The school's new plan of education jibed nicely with his contention that if students were provided with a rich academic environment, their natural intellectual curiosity would sustain their focus and lead them to an education.

The other speakers also highlighted the nation's profound need for educational reform, invariably concluding that the new, largely elective course of study established the school once again as a pacesetter in secondary school curriculum development. As she handed him the mace of office, Clementine Tangeman urged Collins to make sure that "Emma Willard remains a school of experimentation, innovation, and excellence,"[4] implicitly referring to the new curriculum that the board and the faculty had enthusiastically endorsed the prior year. The afternoon's keynote speaker, Robert S. Ryf, sounded the same theme, declaring that the new curriculum was "at once sound and innovative."[5]

Ryf, vice president of Occidental, titled his address, "The Trouble with Education Is . . ." However flawed he found the current system of education, he celebrated Emma Willard as one of those "places where education in its most profound sense is always the paramount value."[6] Collins reiterated Ryf's message, quoting nine men and never once mentioning the founder. He urged the crowd to "rejoice that we have initiated a radical reordering of the classroom experience." The new curriculum in his view was "less preoccupied with order than with the growth of creative, humane, and sensitive students who thrive on the activities of the mind and intellectual growth."[7] He specifically highlighted two aspects of the program: "joint inquiry," which he defined as teachers as learners, an arrangement in which the "faculty will simply be the more mature students," and independent off-campus experiences, cautioning, however, that the practical had to be linked with on-campus learning because "mere uninterpreted experience is not enough." He alluded only briefly to one of the critical challenges facing the school: coeducation. He urged his audience to consider the question, "'If we were to become a coeducational institution, would we be a better place?'" To please those on both sides of the question, he hastened to add, "I have yet to declare myself on this issue."[8]

Surely unbeknownst to him, the school Dennis Collins inherited in the fall of 1970 was about to encounter the steepest decline in admissions since the dark days of the Great Depression. In Bill Dietel's last year, the school enrolled 369 students, of whom 315 were boarders—a record high. This would be the peak, however. At Collins's inauguration, the size of the school was slightly smaller; the 365 students on hand to welcome their new principal included 313 boarders and 52 local girls. However, in the spring of 1970, the director of admissions, Beverley Marvin, had begun to prepare the board for changes in the admissions picture. She had shown the board comparative admissions statistics at several boys' and girls' boarding schools, highlighting that both types of schools had decreasing applications and were forced to fill up to a third of their residential spaces between May and September. She cited several reasons for the change: rising tuition, the growing popularity of coeducation, many schools' remote locations far "from where the action is," a general "disenchantment with institutions," and the "tendency for students to have a greater voice in the choice of school."[9]

Two months later, she reiterated that Emma Willard would not be full until at least July and that she expected this to be the case "for several years to come." Twenty-nine boarders enrolled during the summer of 1970; during the summer of 1966, that number had been two. In 1971 two boarders enrolled a week after classes started, an "exception" that would prove to be the rule almost every year for the rest of the twentieth century. Marvin warned the board of another change: To "maintain its existence," the school would have to attract "children in large numbers from families who have never shared or supported a boarding school existence."[10]

Lest the trustees think that Marvin was merely justifying the disappointing numbers coming out of her office, they had only to turn to the national press for confirmation that Emma Willard's admissions woes were shared by other schools. The week before the class of 1970 graduated, the *New York Times* reported on the declining enrollment at girls' boarding schools. For the *Times* reporter, the reasons went beyond those cited by Marvin. She suggested that the social cachet of boarding school was "irrelevant in these stressful times" and that behind the numbers was a "complicated social question." In short, by increasing scholarships to enable girls from disadvantaged families to attend (a practice boarding schools had borrowed from the Ivy League and Seven Sisters colleges), the schools were "squeezing out . . . students from the middle class, leaving an enrollment made up of the dazzlingly affluent and the poor." Although she could get no parents to go on record as saying it, she talked to "mothers who are put off by the bringing in of what they describe as 'lower class kids,'" an additional challenge for schools trying to balance their growing scholarship ranks with tuition revenue from families who could afford the full price tag.

This situation, at least, did not apply to Emma Willard, which the article described as "the oldest and one of the most academically demanding" of the boarding schools; at Emma Willard, the reporter noted approvingly, the student body actively raised money for scholarships. Other problems for the boarding schools, however, could apply to Troy. These included the "drug problem" (a faculty meeting in the fall of 1970 included a movie on drugs and how to identify students with substance abuse problems), the general improvement in suburban public schools, and, as worrisome at Emma Willard as elsewhere, a change in college admissions. Beginning in the 1960s, colleges sought to diversify their student bodies, and "the boarding school girl is often passed over for one from the slums." An unnamed spokesperson at the school interviewed for the article confidently and inaccurately stated that the school had "more applicants than we can take care of" but admitted "they aren't up to our usual standard."[11] Clearly, the movement toward coeducation by a number of leading boys' boarding schools was beginning to be problematic for Emma Willard. Exeter, Taft, and St. Paul's all admitted girls in 1971, with Andover and a host of others following in the next few years.

At the time of Collins's inauguration, although the size of the school remained nearly the same as it had the year before, there was— or should have been—some cause for alarm at the fact that the number of ninth grade boarders had dropped from 44 to 24. A year later, however, not only was the ninth grade residential population still small (28), there were only 284 boarders overall, for a total school population of 349. By September 1972, there were 266 boarders and 54 day students, and in 1973 the entire school population was only slightly larger than the boarding population had been two years earlier: only 232 of the 284 students were boarders. In September 1974, the beginning of Dennis Collins's final year on campus, the school population nudged above 300 again, but only because of an increase in the number of day students. (By 1976, there were 85 day students in a student body of 316.) The other troubling trend was the uneven distribution of students across the four grades. Attracting ninth graders remained challenging, and to meet enrollment projections, students were admitted for one or two years or as postgraduates, inflating the size of the junior and senior classes. The class of 1973, for example, numbered 126, an all-time high. Because the number of new students the school enrolled during the early 1970s hovered between 80 and 90, a class of this size guaranteed a smaller school the following year.

The enrollment of a student body that was 10 percent African American was the one area where a goal had been set and very nearly met. In 1971 there were sixteen black students on the campus, and by 1976 there were thirty, a significant increase and at 9 percent of the student population close to the 10 percent goal set in the 1960s.[12] Throughout the 1970s, race relations on the campus were tense, but the issues were addressed openly in a number of forums including meetings between black students and the trustees and black students and the administration. Influenced by national attitudes, the Afro-Am student group was increasingly exasperated and separatist. They complained to the trustees that faculty had trouble telling them apart, told them "to appreciate how lucky [we] are,"[13] and treated them condescendingly: "When a black student makes a mistake, it's not viewed as just her mistake alone, but a characteristic of all black people."[14]

More than one white student publicly defended the black students' frustration, with one of them telling *CLOCK*, "We can no longer expect the blacks to be patient with us."[15] To a large extent, race relations were intertwined with generational politics. When the African American students asked for a separate section of the dormitory, the school consulted their parents. Regardless of their backgrounds, parental responses to dormitory segregation were negative. Dr. Nathan Scott, a professor of theology at the University of Chicago, wrote an elegant letter denouncing the idea; his sentiments were echoed exactly by a note from a mother whose painful penmanship and poor grammar were undoubtedly products of her inferior segregated educational opportunity. There were no full-time faculty members of color, although the school hired an African American counselor who lived on campus with her family. By the 1970s, there were 7,600 black students in schools affiliated with the National Association of Independent Schools (NAIS), but only 250 teachers of color. Among the white faculty, there were those who viewed black student activism with dismay. Arthur Homan suggested to Collins, "There are enough forces working . . . to destroy the girls' secondary boarding school without our encouraging a dissident minority to further weaken the fabric."[16] The school also faced the economic reality that the 9 percent of the student body who were African American girls commanded 26 percent of the total financial aid budget. In a tightening admissions world, where the school sought to attract majority as well as minority applicants from a wider variety of backgrounds, the recruitment of African Americans in larger numbers was costly as well as controversial.

The admissions situation was also exacerbated by a growing rate of attrition. In Collins's first year, the school lost forty-two students for personal and disciplinary reasons. The class history written by the class of 1971 noted thirty-one students who had been members of the class but were not there to graduate. For the class of 1972, this number was thirty-five. During the 1972–73 year, thirty girls left the school, seventeen of them because they were expelled. Between 1973 and 1982, the average annual attrition was 15 percent, in line with other boarding schools but significantly higher than had been the case in the past. In addition to student violations of school rules, general student restlessness accounted for this trend. Learning in mid-August that a member of the senior class had decided not to return, Marvin told Collins, "There is a serious rebellion on B's part against parents, school, home, country, etc."[17] Outside of expulsion or academic failure, the reasons for attrition were never easily categorized. Collins informed the trustees that he was anticipating 15 percent attrition for the foreseeable future; most frustrating was that 40 percent of the girls who were leaving were going because there was "not enough structure" at the school, but 60 percent were going because there was "too much."[18] Whether students or parents were making the decision probably accounted for the difference. A counselor at Renbrook, one of the junior boarding schools that had historically sent their students on to boarding high schools, told Beverley Marvin that he had more and more parents who were leery of boarding schools that had loosened up too quickly. It was a mistake, he told her, to "let the stoppers out too quickly," especially when schools "more and more are needing to account to parents for their guidance and rules."[19] The curriculum was not the only place where Emma Willard "let the stoppers out." In keeping with the philosophy of student choice at the heart of the elective curriculum, Emma Willard had thrown out uniforms, abolished sit-down dinners, no longer required student attendance at lunch and dinner, provided weeknight transportation to the local mall, extended the experiment for voluntary chapel, and allowed individual corridors to vote when to enforce "lights out."

In hindsight, of all the privileges granted to students in the 1970s, the most ill advised was the permission to smoke. Just before Dietel left, the school had granted students the right to smoke in a designated outside area. Soon, however, they were petitioning the new administration for an indoor smoking area as well. After all, explained a *CLOCK* editorial, "There is nothing more unpleasant than sitting in three inches of mud and water smoking a waterlogged cigarette."[20] During the summer of 1970, a new student center was created on the ground floor of the former Laundry. Smoking was prohibited in the dormitories, but security officers routinely found girls in violation of this rule. As the log recorded, "1:45 a.m.: Girls were seen running out of P.O. Box area. They seem to keep their cigarettes in their boxes and come down at all hours to smoke."[21] Throughout his tenure, Collins waged periodic war with student smokers over the state of the smoking area. After closing the smoking area once again, he called a special assembly to discuss the condition of the smoker. His notice, however, recognized that there were a number of addicted, habitual smokers: "Those who would find it impossible to get by between now and noon tomorrow without a cigarette" could "indulge" in Sage Browsing Room, a lovely book-lined parlor on the first floor of the dormitory.[22] Students who were caught smoking in the dormitories were usually suspended but not often expelled.

Adolescent smoking, of course, was only one aspect of the permissive atmosphere enveloping schools in the 1970s. In the summer of 1973, the school moved the indoor smoking area into the old sewing room in Sage basement. To safeguard the buildings, a fireproof door was put on the tunnel closest to the smokers. Rumors about and evidence of illicit drug use in the Laundry occasioned the move. Drug use in boarding schools was on the rise and increasingly publicized. Emma Willard addressed the issue by relocating the smoking area and initiating a host of programs with both guidance counselors and outside professionals.

Numerous girls were suspended and expelled, but the drug problem on Mount Ida never reached the spectacular heights it did at other schools. In his first year, Collins shared with the counseling staff and senior administration a letter he had received from Donald H. Werner, headmaster of Westminster, at that point an all-boys' school. Westminster had discovered that "a quarter of the student body has been involved in some fashion with drugs," had expelled five boys, suspended twenty-six, and placed twenty-one students on "final probation." Of the fifty-four boys who confessed, thirty-six had tried marijuana for the first time at home, and sixteen had supplied marijuana that they obtained at home. Werner spoke for most school administrators when he acknowledged sadly, "Drugs make an atmosphere of trust impossible . . . turns classmates into informers, faculty into policemen, users into evaders of all but the most limited and special fellowship."[23] The headmistress at Madeira, Barbara Keyser, shared with Collins a letter she had sent to the parents of her students, letting them know that Madeira would turn illicit drug users over to the police.[24] John Heyl, an Exeter student cast in *A Separate Peace*, told the *New York Times*, "[Drug use] has become part of my generation. We smoke joints before dinner, at parties, walking down Main Street in Exeter."[25] At least one parent wrote to the principal complimenting him on the supervision in the dormitories and the evident lack of drugs on the campus.[26] Nevertheless a *CLOCK* poll, with returns from 65 percent of the student body, revealed that 57 percent smoked marijuana. A total of 39 percent of those admitted to smoking the drug on campus, 19 percent claimed that they had been introduced to it at school, and 43 percent of the respondents had never tried it.[27]

The identification of drugs with prep schools and a naive parental belief that keeping their children close to home would keep them away from drugs compounded the admissions issues for Emma Willard and other boarding schools. If, at his inauguration, Dennis Collins was not fully aware of the admissions challenge ahead of him, he clearly recognized the problem by the end of his first year. As his first class prepared to graduate, a class, he wrote Clemewell Lay, that had had "more than its share of sorrows," over 50 percent of the residential spots had yet to be filled for 1971–72. He wrote to one trustee, "These are challenging days."[28] Internally, he soon referred to the admissions picture as "horrendous."[29] His sympathetic predecessor wrote him that the declining admissions statistics were "a hard blow to the solar plexus."[30] Dwindling numbers of applications, a lower yield on acceptances, and a soaring attrition rate logically led to another shift in admissions, one that had far-reaching consequences for school culture. Fewer and fewer applicants were rejected. For the fall of 1971, only 7 of the 166 applications were denied; for 1972, the number of applications dropped to 163, the number of rejections to 6. By 1977, only two applicants failed to gain acceptance.

Interestingly, the "come one, come all" aspect of the admissions crisis did not greatly concern the administration. In the fall of 1971, Marvin frankly told the board that the admissions office was "accepting a wider range of ability than we have had in the past."[31] However, Marvin—and Collins—were certain that this would not pose a significant problem. In a brief paper titled "Implications of the New Curriculum for Admissions," the decades-old question for Emma Willard admissions, can the applicant "survive academically here?," was deemed "irrelevant" because the elective nature of the curriculum meant "we will be able to plan a program for any student who applies."[32] The new curriculum, implemented in 1970–71, was believed to have sufficient breadth to engage and educate a very wide range of student ability. Collins claimed an additional bonus for admissions: "Because of . . . [the plan's] emphasis on term electives, we will be able to admit students during the year."[33] Dropping requirements to increase the numbers of acceptable students in the admissions pool was a solution to declining enrollment at schools outside Troy as well. Speaking to the *Times* reporter, Ethel Walker's spokesperson admitted they were using curricular innovation to address admissions issues; to that end, she said, "there will be more elective courses."[34] Dobbs and Northfield were also reported to be dropping some requirements as a way of attracting more applicants.

If admissions stood to gain from the elective curriculum, that was simply an attractive side effect. The impetus behind the new plan was truly innovative curricular change for a new generation of students, and that change had been put in motion by Bill Dietel. One faculty member, who enthusiastically endorsed election, maintained twenty years later that "the curriculum between 1968 and 1974 was dominated by Bill Dietel, even in his absence, and represented an attempt at radical reform spearheaded by a charismatic . . . and powerful headmaster."[35] Dietel had begun to change the curriculum as early as 1964–65 when he moved the school to a three-term schedule, added a greater number of senior electives, and appointed Edwin Kitzrow as academic dean, but he wanted a more sweeping and comprehensive overhaul of the educational program.

In the 1960s, the space race and the Cold War put pressure on American public high schools to upgrade what and how they taught. In 1965 Dietel had informed the board that "curricular innovation was no longer coming from independent schools," and he welcomed the competition from innovative public schools because such competition "serves to remind us all that complacency has no place in the thinking and planning for the future of Emma Willard." He was keenly aware of the vast resources being channeled into science and mathematics education by public schools and the government. Recognizing that Emma Willard could probably not compete in this arena, he maintained that "it may be well that our genius is and should be confined to the work in the arts and humanities and that we should not be either ashamed or despondent over our failure to be innovative and experimental in other areas as well."[36] In fact, he hoped that Emma Willard would be a "pacesetter" in secondary school curriculum development.[37]

By 1967 he and Kitzrow, along with a faculty committee, had modified the amount of correlation, particularly in the younger grades, and had renamed correlation among art, music, and humanities the Culture of the Western World, a program that was "interdisciplinary, not interdepartmental."[38] The committee, in line with Dietel's emphasis on playing to the school's curricular strength, further emphasized that "humanities should receive strong and central emphasis in the Emma Willard program of education."[39] Elsewhere in the independent school world, particularly among the boys' schools, curricular discussion was stimulated not only by Cold War politics, but also by the changing patterns in college admissions and the concern that older high school students in the late 1960s were, if not more mature, then certainly more restless than their predecessors.

Assembled from Andover, Hill, Lawrenceville, and Exeter, a group of male faculty representing the classics, mathematics, physics, and English undertook a study of the last two years of high school and the first two years of college. Their work, ultimately published by the College Board, concluded that the "liberal education of late adolescence requires a reorganization of faculty and curriculum into task-oriented—which is to say student-oriented—units."[40] Maintaining that the boys in their schools were fully prepared for college by the end of eleventh grade, they proposed that the senior year be devoted to internships, which they defined as "individually oriented programs"[41] ten to eleven weeks long. They castigated the "chaos of contemporary college admissions," accusing the colleges of having an "equipoised sense of self-interest and of social conscience"[42] (a somewhat more genteel way of saying that colleges were choosing students from "the slums" over students from boarding schools). As a consequence, their students had to attend a wider variety of colleges, which made the articulation between preparatory school and college curriculum increasingly "disjointed."[43] Even more concerning was the "withering effect on an adolescent's self-esteem"[44] that came from negative college decisions. Internships had the power to counteract this negativity by aiding students' emotional growth. Internships let "them choose, with wise and sympathetic advice, the times for reflection, play and work."[45]

In August 1967, Bill Dietel convened a faculty committee, chaired by Richard Zajchowski, librarian and English teacher. The committee included Janet Maly, Marjorie Pickard, the college counselor, English teachers Edith Prescott and Jack Pasanen, Latin teacher Marigwen Schumacher, history teacher Mark Johnson, and assistant principal Ben Shute. In June 1969, the committee delivered its recommendations to Dietel, and in September the full faculty voted its approval. Kitzrow told the board that the faculty as a whole approved the curriculum as "appropriate to the students we teach and the times in which we live." The new curriculum was a radical departure for Emma Willard—or for any traditional liberal arts boarding school. It was designed, according to Dietel, to provide "a pathway through the Seventies."[46] To that end the new plan of study was "for the most part a 'contentless curriculum.'" In fact, the committee emphatically declared, "We reject the notion that a liberal arts education consists of a prescribed sequence or distribution of courses."[47]

Dietel told the alumnae, "Whatever else one might say about the 1960s, in the realm of secondary education this was a time of shifting attitudes toward the learning process, the role of the teacher, the importance of required courses, and the governance of educational institutions."[48] Bearing this change in mind, Dietel had charged the committee with developing a "plan of education which will be broader in its concerns both for the intellectual and the emotional development of young people."[49] The central premise of the new curriculum was "the assumption that the best education for each student at Emma Willard will be an individual one; that each student should pursue a course of study that takes into account her needs, interests and abilities."[50] Noting that students had a wide variety of styles and speeds of learning, and what was good for one girl was not necessarily best for her classmates, the committee asserted that "once a student has mastered the mathematical and verbal skill necessary for her academic program, there are as many shapes and varieties of liberal education as there are students."[51] In keeping with their charge, the committee broadened the definition of curriculum to include the residential program and the "interaction of students" with each other. They emphasized that "education does take place in and out of the classroom, and that worthwhile educational experiences are not limited to the classroom, the campus, or even the local community."[52]

The academic departments were reorganized: under the new plan there would be seven equal divisions: Communication, Humanities, Language, Science, Mathematics, Arts, and Physical Activities. No course would be given more weight than any other; to guide student choice, units would be assigned to courses according to the amount of work and time demanded. Internships and off-campus independent study would receive academic credit in the same way. Students would be responsible for planning their own program of study, although they would be assisted in these efforts by guidance counselors. Under the new curriculum an Emma Willard education would "transmit knowledge necessary for further study and knowledge which will enrich the student's life and broaden her understanding of herself and the world in which she lives." In addition, the new curriculum would "encourage each student's search for self-knowledge and personal identity,"[53] a fitting goal for a curriculum in an era dubbed "The Me Decade."

There were a few requirements, but even these had great flexibility built into them. All new students would be enrolled in "Analysis, Perception, and Thought" (APT), a course taught by members of the Communication division. The aim of APT was "the development in all entering students of an analytical, perceptive, and critical attitude of mind." This would be accomplished by having students read "many kinds of expository prose from various subject matter areas" and examples of various literary genres. In addition, APT emphasized "articulate speaking, logical thinking, and responding critically." Nothing in the course would be "taught as separate units of study."[54] Instead, all of the skills would be interwoven.

Along with APT, new students would be required to take a writing course. Depending on student ability, this course could take from three to six terms (one to two years). The Mathematics and Physical Activities divisions demanded the only other requirements. Without identifying algebra, geometry, or any other traditional mathematical courses, the report recommended that entering students take mathematics for six to nine terms or until they had developed "the understanding and appreciation of mathematical concepts . . . and the skills necessary to . . . pursue further work in mathematics, science and other fields." Finally, all students were required to "pursue a physical activities program" in ninth and tenth grades, and it was recommended that they do so all four years. In keeping with the central philosophy of the new curriculum, each student's physical activities would be "designed to accommodate her individual needs and her athletic ability."[55]

Except for the handful of required courses, all courses were essentially electives. Thus traditional courses such as French I, Biology, and U.S. History were technically electives because no student was required to take them. Each division also developed electives according to faculty interests. Student course selection was taken very seriously. The guidance staff was increased, and students met in small groups to explain their choices to their peers and counselor. The alumnae were informed that current Emma Willard students "must go through the procedures of course selection that many college students do," and that a typical student-to-student dialogue might go like this: "If you can't get into H-101, you might give A-140 or L-311 a look."[56] (Because the first of these courses was a humanities course, the second an arts course, and the third a foreign language course, it is easy to see how the selection of courses could be criticized as lacking cohesion.) In spite of the multiple divisional offerings—over two hundred courses for three hundred students—the new curriculum also featured tutorials. If a student wanted to pursue a subject or topic that was not offered, she just had to arrange it with a willing faculty member. Tutorials were taken seriously; in the words of the curriculum committee, "We propose that tutorial instruction be available to students as part of their regular program. To initiate a tutorial, the student, with the approval of the teacher with whom she wishes to work, would discuss her intention with her guidance counselor, who would clear it with the teacher's division chairman. The tutorial should be listed on the student's record."[57]

Whether or not such a curriculum would have ever worked is debatable, but given the times, it was doomed to failure. First of all, it was extremely expensive. Implementing the new curriculum cost money at a time when revenue from tuition was declining dramatically. Designing a curriculum based on individual student desires meant many small classes and a larger faculty and a larger guidance department than would have been necessary with a core curriculum. Additionally, the off-campus emphasis meant that revenue was lost when students took terms away. Because there were so few requirements, strong students discovered that they could accelerate and graduate in three years, again a loss of tuition. In addition, each time a teacher offered a new topic, the library had to order new books and materials to support the course. At the ten-year evaluation, midway through the decade, the visiting team noted that Emma Willard's per pupil library expenditures were more than double that of comparable schools.

Second, although it was a curriculum that had room for students with weaknesses in one area or another, many, if not most, weaker students lacked the skills and motivation to navigate the curriculum successfully. They often needed more structure, not less, to shore up their academic lives. Jack Easterling, a masterful teacher who taught both traditional and topical electives in literature and art history, has summarized the situation clearly: "The elective curriculum would have been perfect for a student body that the school was no longer attracting.[58] As one measure of the declining student ability, it is illuminating to point to the average SAT scores of the senior class, which dove precipitously. Between 1969 and 1976, the average verbal score dropped from 500 to 400, which was lower than the national average. A year later the scores had declined again, and the college counselor worried that the class of 1978 was "being unrealistic about colleges"[59] because the scores for 1978 were lower than those in 1977.

Although Dennis Collins had celebrated curricular innovation in his inaugural address, as a former college admissions officer, he worried about the impact that the new curriculum would have on college placement. Where a school's seniors headed after graduation was an increasingly important factor in families' selection of a preparatory school. Those on the faculty who embraced the innovation of the new curriculum had an easy solution: Emma Willard should no longer call itself a college preparatory school. They, however, were not responsible for the budget; nevertheless, this argument, begun in 1970–71, flourished among a vocal minority of the faculty until the mid-1980s when it was emphatically put to rest by the adoption of the *1984 Curriculum*.

Some students shared Collins's concern. In 1972 a senior wit mused in *CLOCK*, "If I can convince them that Elementary Hindu chanting and Beginning Earth Science connect in my mind in a sort of metaphysical sense, I can talk them into anything."[60] The president of CREW, the school government that had been organized at the same time as the new curriculum, complained to the board of trustees that students felt that there were "not enough basic, traditional courses, and some seniors worry about whether they have the requirements to get into the college of their choice." She also felt that "the counselors do not have enough time to counsel students."[61] Even with an enlarged guidance staff, the ratio of counselors to students was 1:75.

Three months into his first academic year, Collins appointed the chairman of the curriculum committee, Dick Zajchowski, to a new position, director of academic affairs. From the memoranda he sent Zajchowski, it is clear that Collins monitored the curriculum and tried very hard to ensure its rigor. The grading scale and unit weight for tutorials were supposed to be set in advance, but teachers often changed those criteria midway through a course to assist students who had overloaded their schedules. Faculty also overused the grade of "Incomplete" for the same reason. When 45 students earned 75 grades of "Incomplete," Collins decreed that the grade be given only with administrative consent. He also declared that changing tutorials once they had begun was "completely unacceptable."[62] Marjorie Pickard, the college counselor, was nearing sixty, had served in the navy during World War II, and was widely viewed as an old school stickler for structure who set up roadblocks for the new curriculum. She was often at cross purposes with seniors wanting to take courses she considered poor college preparatory material. Collins, however, often sided with her, telling Zajchowski that "we are obligated to our students to make rather hard-nosed assessments of the senior programs." He didn't "blame Jerry Pickard for being distressed,"[63] citing as an example the student who wanted to "wipe out a literature sequence for creative dramatics."[64] Implicit in this statement was a sense that theater was inferior to literature, an attitude that was anathema to the champions of the new curriculum and its egalitarian view of divisions.[65]

Another innovation was faculty freedom to decide whether or not to grade their classes on a traditional A-B-C scale or on a credit/no credit basis. Collins was concerned that students were not being graded rigorously enough, asking at one point, "Have we got out of the business of failing students?"[66] (In fact, by faculty vote, the grade of F was discontinued. Students who failed to pass received a grade of NC, or no credit.) Collins also worried that the counselors were too effusive in the recommendations they wrote to colleges. When a counselor wrote a letter that he deemed "too positive," he commented, "As we continue to cause colleges pain by our curricular experimentation, it is imperative that we be known abroad as a school that tells it like it is."[67] It was a hallmark of his administration that he closely supervised the college admissions process; assisting the seniors with their choices was "a prime interest."[68]

By the end of the first year of the new curriculum, a number of veteran faculty questioned its soundness, including Janet Maly. As faculty trustee, she reported on its shortcomings to the board. She told the trustees that she feared the school was moving away from academics and becoming "an institution for social change." As a member of the curriculum committee, she admitted ruefully that it was "harder to implement visionary ideas than it is to have them in the first place" and suggested that the school needed to put more requirements in place. She also raised an issue that would remain for fifteen years at the heart of the controversy between those faculty who liked the open, freewheeling elective curriculum and those who wanted more structure: "Should the courses a teacher likes to teach necessarily be the best courses for him to teach?"[69] For example, if the English Department wanted to teach electives using works by new noncanonical authors but offer nothing from Shakespeare, Austen, or other classic writers, what, if anything, did that say about the worth of an Emma Willard diploma?

Given the number of courses and the lack of cohesion within disciplinary offerings, it was increasingly difficult to know whether or not good teaching was happening. It was impossible for division chairs to critique all the classes for which they were responsible. On top of that, the school hired a number of adjunct teachers to staff some electives. Most of these faculty were young, although a few were local retirees, and some had not yet graduated from college. For example, Lucy Lentz, a senior at Smith, taught a half-term course, "The Role of Women in the Bible," in the winter of 1972. Even more remarkable a Yale *junior*, Rick Warren, taught a short course on poetry in the winter of 1973. An Antioch master's candidate taught a six-week women's studies course, and the sister of a student, herself just out of college, taught a course in black history. Under Bill Dietel, the school had welcomed visiting teachers, artists, writers, and experts in a host of other areas; budget pressures precluded the continuation of the visitor-in-residence program at its impressive former level.

CLOCK interviews with the visitors contain critical and revealing observations about the school. The Antioch student found Emma Willard "balancing itself awkwardly between being a formal and an informal school,"[70] and the Yale man's "one disappointment is that there is no real course in 'expository writing,' which would give a student an idea of the principals [*sic*] of clear writing."[71] (Apparently, spelling was not stressed either.) An experienced teacher, the wife of the school's attorney, who substituted for an English instructor on sabbatical, compared her classes with classes she had taught at Albany Academy for Girls and concluded that teaching at Emma Willard was harder because she was not used to classes with "students from such varied academic backgrounds."[72]

At least one senior member of the Mathematics Department bluntly told the principal, "I think we are constantly lowering our standards." Because of the lack of structure in the new curriculum, she felt that "students are misled into believing that superficial knowledge means understanding."[73] To be sure, some students thrived under the elective curriculum. These were extremely gifted young women whose academic and career paths were certain and who elected courses, tutorials, and internships that impressed college admissions offices and later launched them into highly successful careers, often in fields they had been exposed to through term electives or off-campus experiences. However, there were simply not enough of them. Their peers knew why: they assured the board of trustees that most of the "very smart girls" they knew were going to coeducational schools. On balance, the adoption of the elective curriculum meant "a change in emphasis from a very competitive academic program"[74] to a less consistently rigorous one at a moment in history when the "most academically demanding" of the girls' schools was losing its share of the boarding school market.

Not surprisingly, worry about the annual budget consumed much of Dennis Collins's time during his four years at the school. The school year 1969–70 had ended in the red by approximately $60,000, and in 1970–71, the board anticipated a shortfall of over $100,000. As the trustees planned for 1971–72, it was clear that tuition would have to go up, even if admissions recovered, which was unlikely. Only 44 boarding students had enrolled as of March 15, and the school needed 120 residential students to remain the size it was. The administration considered freezing salaries, cutting staff, outsourcing the laundry, and reducing financial aid. The projected budget included additional costs created by adding a medical benefit for the faculty and a 10 percent increase in retiree pensions. The last was a small part of the school's annual expenditures, and ranged from $15 a month for retired French teacher Lydia Brunaud to $87 for the former director of residence Gladys Lott and $125 for each of the headmistresses who were living in a retirement community in California.[75]

In the early 1970s, the annual operating budgets topped $2 million, and over 70 percent of the budget was funded by tuition (compared with less than 50 percent in 2012). In 1970–71, at $4,100 for boarding students and $1,950 for day students, the tuition was high compared to the competition. Nevertheless, the board voted to raise the tuition for

1971–72 to $4,350 for boarders and $2,075 for day students. Among the girls' boarding schools, only Rosemary Hall charged more; most had reached $4,000, but just. Abbot, Dana Hall, and Westover all cost $4,100. Exeter, in contrast, charged $2,800. A trustee long-range planning committee convened in 1966 had anticipated annual tuition increases of $100; it was now clear that the increases would exceed that. The board appointed a new Master Planning Committee, chaired by trustee Harold Higgins. Entirely male, the committee included Collins, the business manager, Franklin "Fred" Moon, local trustee Ernest Warncke, and assistant headmaster Ben Shute. Even with the tuition hike and an austerity budget that froze the salaries of senior faculty and staff, the school faced a $270,000 deficit for 1971–72. According to Higgins's committee, the deficit would reach a half a million dollars by 1975, and within seven years, the school's endowment would be nonexistent unless there was a dramatic change. Higgins told the board "the trend of recurring deficits has to be thought of cumulatively as a persistent and growing drain on the permanent resources of the School."[76]

The summer issue of the alumnae magazine was devoted to the school's finances. In "The Principal's Page," Collins wrote of "staggering" financial pressures, which he defined as "rising prices and operational expenses, overwhelming demands on philanthropic dollars, an economy in flux, a society in turmoil, and changing educational patterns."[77] In the cover article, Fred Moon and the development director, H. Mark Johnson, maintained that the school could not reduce expenses any more than it had without hurting the quality of the program. They argued that "'economies of scale' don't work when the product is human growth and development. . . . We haven't the luxury of considering a move to a smaller or cheaper labor force. Excellence simply won't permit it."[78] Only endowment growth would assure survival.

By adhering to an austerity budget, spending some restricted funds on operations, amortizing some plant loans internally, and spending an unusually high amount of unused student fees, the actual deficit for 1971–72 was reduced to $100,000. But 1972–73 loomed as another year where expenses would far outpace revenues. Clearly, the school needed other sources of revenue. The endowment stood at $2.1 million when Collins became principal. Bill Dietel's final year as principal had been the best fund-raising year in the school's history, but the $9.5 million capital campaign that had been launched during Dietel's tenure had proved more successful in raising money for specific projects than for endowment.

Chief among these was the new arts center. The arts center, designed to bracket the library on the opposite side from the music building, was estimated to cost $900,000. When ground was broken for the new facility in the spring of 1970, the building fund was short by nearly $200,000. Fund-raising for the project continued, spearheaded by trustee Walter Maguire, who had donated the bulk of the money for the arts building. His daughter Megan was a member of the class of 1973, and Maguire wrote potential donors that he and his family "firmly believe that money dedicated to education today can best be used at the secondary school level, and at this particular point of time, in women's secondary schools."[79]

Although the Maguire Arts Building opened in November 1971, the campaign in general was stalled. At the end of Collins's second year in office, the endowment, at $2.5 million, had barely grown. As was true for most girls' schools, the endowment provided only 6 percent of the annual operating budget; at boys' schools, the figure was 10 percent. Emma Willard's endowment per pupil, however, was less than that at Westover, Miss Porter's, Abbot, and Madeira. On the positive side, annual gifts to Emma Willard underwrote 13 percent of the budget, compared to 8 percent at girls' schools in general, with the result that Emma Willard was slightly less dependent on tuition than was average for girls' schools: 75 percent at Emma Willard compared to the 80 percent average at all girls' schools. The potential for capital fund-raising was there.

In the spring of 1972, Clementine Tangeman called a special meeting of the board to focus on raising money for the endowment and to reactivate the stalled campaign. Browning and Associates were hired to advise the board. There was a standoff at the meeting between the board chair and the professionals. Mrs. Tangeman made it clear that it was "essential that women be involved." The campaign counsel told the board that in their experience, however, "very few women solicit big money effectively."[80] Happily, Clementine Tangeman and a new member of the board of trustees, a familiar face on the campus, Linda Remington Dietel, would ultimately prove them wrong.

In the fall the development committee of the board recommended that a new capital campaign be undertaken. Board vice president Donald Buttenheim led the charge for a renewed commitment to raising endowment dollars. Declaring emphatically that "the future of the school is wholly dependent upon the development of endowment,"[81] he moved the establishment of a capital campaign whose goal would be a $15 million endowment. By June, the endowment had reached $3.5 million. Once again, however, external economic conditions challenged the fund's growth. By September 1973, the fund had dropped below $3 million. Nixon's impeachment, war in the Mideast, and the attendant energy crisis contributed to a recession. In 1973 the rate of return for the Dow was negative 13 percent and at Emma Willard, negative 22 percent. The New York Stock Exchange lost 19.6 percent.

In addition to dire necessity, there was another reason for the board of trustees to focus on long-range planning and fund-raising for the endowment. In September 1971, the trustee committee on coeducation had delivered its report to the board. Chaired by Joel and Avery Brooke, parents of Sarah '71, the committee had included faculty members, a student, parents, and alumnae. They concluded that "now is not the time" for the school to admit boys, even though 95 percent of the students favored doing so. Sixty-eight percent of the alumnae said they would send their daughters to the school if it was coeducational, but fewer than half would send a son to their alma mater. Parents who responded were almost equally split; 25 percent favored coeducation, 27 percent favored remaining an all-girls' school, and 29 percent had no preference. Among the schools that the committee regarded as competition, Abbot and Andover and Rosemary Hall and Choate had developed coordinate structures. To go coed by joining with a boys' school was not an option for Emma Willard, however, because there was no logical partner in the vicinity. The committee considered the possibility of pulling up stakes and moving to a boys' school campus. (Taft and Hotchkiss were both considered.) They concluded, however, that "Selling out and moving away seems almost inconceivable to Emma Willard people."[82] Concord and Shipley had voted to admit boys, and Dana Hall, Foxcroft, Madeira, Masters, Miss Porter's, and Westover had all voted to remain girls' schools. Although many of the boys' schools had opted for coeducation, others, including Groton, Hotchkiss, and Deerfield, had chosen to remain all boys (for the time being).

At the very least, coeducation would mean building a gym, re-configuring the dormitories, and staffing the school differently. Girls' school faculty generally assumed very different duties from those in boys' schools, and the committee found that some of the Emma Willard faculty "find girls' schools more satisfactory partially or wholly because they do not feel comfortable with . . . dormitory and athletic duties."[83] The committee also contended that coeducation had not been an entirely successful experience for women on college campuses. They singled out Yale and Princeton as being "essentially male institutions," commenting that "In formerly all-male colleges, the girls have found that they were not received with quite the open arms and minds they expected."[84] The committee felt that the school should wait and continue to "evaluate schools that have gone co-educational."[85] Their recommendation was put to a vote of the full board on November 8, 1971, and passed unanimously. The decision was reported to the students at a special assembly; some were dismayed, but the overall reaction was positive. To sweeten the decision, the board and school administration pledged to find more "functional alternatives"[86] to single-sex education—in other words, more ways to meet adolescent boys.

In 1972 Edgar Sanford, headmaster of the Thacher School whose daughter Diana was a sophomore, wrote to Dennis Collins suggesting a one-term exchange between the two schools. Located in California, Thacher was an academically strong school with a comprehensive riding program and a campus set among orange groves, canyons, and mesas that was strikingly different from Emma Willard. By the fall of 1974, forty students from each campus were studying at the other school. Two faculty members accompanied the girls, and one of the first chaperones from Thacher was Susan Smith Griggs '64, the wife of a Thacher instructor. In spite of the tuition differential (Thacher cost

$3,800; Emma Willard cost $4,350) and the fact that the Thacher boys found the Emma Willard work "easier," the exchange was a success.[87] It only lasted until 1977, however, because Thacher's board voted to admit girls. Undaunted, Emma Willard followed the Thacher experience with an exchange in the South at all-male Woodberry-Forest. Although the school had hoped the exchange might help attract applicants from the South, it was not completely successful, in some measure because of Emma Willard's more progressive attitude toward civil rights. In 1978 Deerfield became the exchange school, remaining so until that school, too, voted to become coeducational. At least one alumna, Nancy Frederick Sweet '45, had the unusual experience of having a son, David, Deerfield '81, attend her school.

Ironically, the exchanges with boys' schools coincided with a burgeoning sense that Emma Willard, rather than apologize for being a girls' school, should wholeheartedly endorse feminism. A curriculum review committee in 1974 concluded, "Because Emma Willard is a school for young women, we believe that we must become more self-conscious about the special needs of young women in our society. We should, for example, give special attention to fields which have traditionally not been open to women, and we need to give thought to ways in which we can assist the development of self-esteem and self-confidence in our students."[88] The committee reaffirmed the elective curriculum but repurposed it as particularly germane to girls.

One hallmark of the elective curriculum had been the inclusion in the humanities offerings of courses on women's studies and black studies, both of which were relatively new at the college level and rare on the secondary level. In 1972 Emma Willard surveyed twenty-five girls' schools on institutional responses to the feminist movement and found it was the only school with a faculty Women's Rights Group and one of only two schools with a student group. Eleven schools had some sort of women's rights course, but Emma Willard had the most, with three term courses on the subject. Miss Porter's was more typical, with a six-week elective titled "Women's Lib."[89] A *New York Times* article on the role of men in girls' schools found that "A stronger feminist attitude has been shown at Emma Willard [than at other girls' schools]. . . . There have been visits from representatives of the National Organization for Women and from a theater group that discussed changing life-styles and alternatives to marriage." Collins reported to the paper that he had "a woman's rights group of faculty members ages 23 to 63."[90]

Internally, he was perhaps not as comfortable with this turn of events as he sounded. The group, chaired by Edith Prescott, sought an audience with Collins and other male administrators to discuss "a tone on this campus which discriminates against women and career aspirations," male faculty who put "lesser demands on students because they are female," "discourage girls' career goals," and even show "amusement" at girls in mathematics and science. Collins refused to set up a meeting between the Women's Rights Group and the five senior male administrators. To his credit, he called for a full faculty meeting that could make "a non-personal assessment of how well we are doing in assisting students in their self-actualization—particularly as women who will move out and beyond Emma Willard to take positions of responsibility in the broader community."[91] He also supported the women's group in their desire to host a conference on women's rights, and for three days in March 1973, nearly two hundred outsiders attended "Toward Equity for Women." Betty Friedan was a featured speaker. If as Janet Maly had feared, Emma Willard was becoming an institution for social change, at least it was change that fit the lives of its main constituency, its female students. And Maly was a founding member of the faculty women's committee.

Courses with self-conscious feminist themes grew in number and enrollment throughout the decade. Edith Prescott spoke at national conferences about the inclusion of women's studies and women's groups at the secondary level; her course, "Status of Women," was a standard-bearer for incipient women's studies programs throughout the independent school world. Inevitably, students began to share the growing feminist consciousness on the campus. One of the most articulate of them wrote about her disappointment with the gender roles she encountered during her term at Thacher. Selected for a one-week camping trip led by the headmaster, she was shocked when they stopped to make camp the first night, and he announced that "the guys" would pasture the burros and the "gals" would set up the kitchen and start dinner. When I heard the term "guys and gals" and our appointed jobs, I felt like running the ten miles home in the dark. . . . I hadn't come on this trip to play house-wife, and I would have liked to pasture burros over kitchen duty anytime. After we had done our jobs, the boys came striding back as if they had just cleaned the Aegean stables. They told us what an ordeal it was trying to tie the burros up. The burros seemed pretty calm to me, but I nodded my head. . . . Our job had entailed hauling water, collecting firewood, starting a fire, rummaging through packs for food, and trying to make what was inedible at least digestible. I realized that at some point I was going to have to politely protest our little suburban set-up.[92]

She did protest; the head told her, "I don't really know if I am ready for co-education." Silently, she "whole-heartedly agreed."[93]

In the fall of 1973, Dennis Collins received an offer to become the founding head of the San Francisco University High School. He resigned, effective June 30, 1974. The new venture matched the young headmaster: the new school was "established by a youthful board of trustees and community activists . . . in response to a deeply felt need for an innovative, co-educational, independent secondary school in the Bay area . . . who shared a vision of a school that would be a model of equity and excellence."[94] An enthusiastic *CLOCK* reporter wrote that the curriculum at SFUHS would be more structured than the one at Emma Willard because the new school "must sacrifice the luxury of experimentation that Emma Willard can enjoy, because of its long-standing reputation."[95] On Mount Ida, Collins's tyro administrative skills had been honed by dealing with budget deficits, admissions shortfalls, and faculty dissension over curricular change. With his wife and two young daughters,[96] he returned to the comforts of California, coeducation, and a structured curriculum in the summer of 1974. His brief four-year tenure, although unprecedented at Emma Willard, was symptomatic of the decade in which private schools all over the Northeast were seeing an "increasingly rapid turnover among headmasters."[97]

The growing feminist consciousness on the campus undoubtedly influenced the board's decision to appoint a woman as the next head of school. The search committee included four trustees, among them the chair, Patricia Tolles Smalley '58, her alumna colleague, Polly

Ormsby Longsworth '51, and parents Russell Ford and Joel Brooke, as well as the faculty trustee, French instructor Deirdre Simpson. For the first time in the history of the school, the new head would be chosen by a group that was mostly female. In early January 1974, the search committee solicited opinions from students and faculty. Both groups "stressed the importance of trying to look for a woman," and both groups also "urged that a person who had been a teacher (not necessarily an administrator) in a secondary school, as opposed to a college, should have the position." Some at the meeting suggested that a husband/wife team might solve the conflict of a single person trying to juggle the internal and external demands of the job, a reaction to student complaints about Collins's "being off campus much of the time."[98]

In the spring, the board announced the appointment of Dr. Frances Roland O'Connor. A native of Milton, Massachusetts, O'Connor was a former member of the progressive order of the Religious of the Sacred Heart of Jesus that administered girls' schools throughout the United States and the world. She had earned her undergraduate degree at Manhattanville, at the time a Roman Catholic college for women, her master's at Boston College, and her doctorate at the University of Massachusetts where she wrote her dissertation on curricular innovations in the secondary school curriculum. She had been a mathematics teacher and administrator at a number of schools that were part of the coalition of Sacred Heart Schools, which defined themselves as independent and were members of the NAIS. They stressed strong college preparatory academic programs and were committed to ethnic, religious, and socioeconomic diversity. Before her appointment as head of Emma Willard, O'Connor had served as assistant head of Newton Country Day School and head of Stuart Country Day and Stoneridge Academy. During her time at Stoneridge, she had worked with disadvantaged students of color in housing projects in the Washington, D.C., area. The first issue of *CLOCK* expressed student delight with the new principal, reporting that the "fairly typical" initial response was "She's fantastic."[99]

On October 12, 1974, Frances R. O'Connor was installed as the twelfth head of school. Donald Buttenheim, who had succeeded Clementine Tangeman as board president in 1973, presented her with the mace of office. Elizabeth Johns Ruckert '29 welcomed her on behalf of the alumnae. The keynote address was delivered by Charles Longsworth, president of Hampshire College, which had opened just four years earlier. Its individualized, multidisciplinary curriculum shared similarities with the elective curriculum at the school. Furthermore, Longsworth was married to search committee member Polly Ormsby Longsworth '51. Carol Davis '75 spoke on behalf of the student body, and Russell Locke spoke on behalf of the faculty. In a characteristically arch and witty speech, he captured the faculty's issues for the new head: "We speak in diverse tongues and accents, and at great length. . . . We function in the classrooms and the committee room, on the highways as bus drivers, in the dormitories *in loco parentis* and in the corridors with mops and brooms *in loco janitoris*. We are poor, and our spouses toil so that we may enjoy a few pathetic little luxuries, but we have the kind of nobility that poverty bestows upon the truly enlightened."

Locke also took aim at the curriculum: "[We teach] ancient history and futuristics, criminal justice and Jemima Puddleduck. . . . Spring offers the vacation in the far west with full academic credit [and] we know few bounds in the presentation of traditional materials in new and fascinating relationships. . . . It is remarkable that no one has yet taken advantage of the close proximity of the trampoline and the sacraments for a truly transcendental experience.[100]

O'Connor's response was sober. Maintaining that "money never could, and never can buy quality education, and the lack of it, by itself, cannot prevent it," she nevertheless highlighted the problematic financial situation at the school. "These will not be easy years," she told her audience. As for the curriculum, she predicted that the pendulum would swing back in the direction of structure, asserting, "The seventies have taken us beyond our desperate need for innovation just as the sixties took us beyond our stubborn clinging to tradition."[101]

As a former nun and veteran of Sacred Heart schools, O'Connor was used to a dominant female presence in administration. She appointed Deirdre Simpson, the faculty member on the search committee, to be the dean of students; the prior year the school had operated without anyone in this position. Ben Shute, the second in command under Collins, resigned as O'Connor came in. Two years would pass before his position was filled; in 1976 Susan Edwards was named associate principal. The director of admissions and the director of college counseling were women, and the role of dean of the faculty "was assumed by the principal."[102]

O'Connor's biggest initial concern was the budget. As a trained mathematician, she spoke confidently and accurately about quantitative matters, and the board welcomed her analysis of the perilous financial situation. The books at Emma Willard, like those at half of the schools in NAIS, showed an operating deficit for 1973–74. The deficit of $233,995[103] was larger than the prior year's $200,000 shortfall and showed astronomical growth since 1970–71 when the deficit was $43,250. To correct the imbalance, the rate of withdrawal from the endowment continued to rise, routinely ranging from 8 to 9 percent instead of the 5 to 6 percent regarded among schools and colleges as a healthy management figure. On a positive note, the student population was incrementally larger than it had been the year before, with the total topping 300, 241 of whom were boarders. Nevertheless, the budget projected a $400,000 deficit for 1974–75.

In December the board held a special meeting on the budget. O'Connor proposed replacing one person in the business office with a computer, phasing out Latin and German by 1976–77, reducing the faculty in the arts by a half-time instructor, eliminating a librarian and one secretary, raising tuition, and lowering faculty benefits by halving the school's contribution to the TIAA retirement fund, holding faculty raises below the projected rate of inflation (anticipated to be 7 percent), changing the withdrawal formula for endowment spending, and pursuing more aggressive fund-raising. The board accepted all of her recommendations, although one hard-nosed trustee would have gone even further. He questioned any raise at all for faculty members in a year when "there are no raises on Wall St."[104]

It is hard, even from the vantage of hindsight, to envision any solution to the fiscal crisis other than budget tightening and expense reduction. Short of an extraordinary gift to the endowment, O'Connor had few options for increasing revenue besides raising tuition. For

1974–75, boarders were charged $4,550 and day students $2,125, increases that, although significant, did not come close to the anticipated rate of inflation. In an inflationary economy, it was impossible to reduce expenses without cutting programs. In large measure, fuel, food, maintenance, janitorial, and security costs were fixed; elective offerings and teaching loads were not.

For the next four years, O'Connor and the board struggled to balance the budget. The tuition rose almost every year. By 1978–79 boarders paid $5,900 and day students $2,730. The boarding tuition was over $1,000 more than students paid at Exeter and Andover. Salaries at Emma Willard and at girls' schools in general remained stubbornly low. Coeducational schools, which now, of course, included the most heavily endowed of the preparatory schools, paid the best, with salaries in the top quartile ranging from $18,500 to $23,200. At girls' schools the range was $16,800 to $17,300, and at Emma Willard, the most highly paid teacher made $16,400. In contrast, the average public school teacher in New York State commanded a salary of $15,950 in 1977–78.

In the fall of 1977, O'Connor prepared a five-year financial forecast, using 1978–79 as year one. She proposed increasing the enrollment to 400 by 1982–83, with a 75:25 ratio of boarders to day students, a $100,000 annual addition to the operating budget for deferred maintenance, annual faculty raises of 7 percent, and a financial aid budget equal to 10 percent of the operating budget.[105] In addition to greater tuition revenue, she projected $15,000 from summer programs, which had netted $12,000 the previous summer. That same season, Girlsummer, a day program for younger girls, began; although the program lost money its first two years, it eventually became a revenue source and an admissions feeder for day students. O'Connor also proposed enhancing revenue by selling school-owned property that was not contiguous to the main campus. To reach the goal of a 5 percent spending rate from the endowment, she also proposed fund-raising to raise the endowment principal to $10 million by 1982–83.

When she presented her five-year budget projection to the board of trustees, O'Connor stressed the urgency of working to make the plan a reality and asked the board to commit to raising $2 million a year for the next five years for endowment, a goal her ambitious young director of development, Don Myers, supported. She warned the board that the school had "two years to insure the Emma Willard program and philosophy as we know it. . . . With no change [in revenue] we must cut the budget by $500,000 by 1979–80 to achieve a 5% withdrawal rate." Specifically this would mean "In addition to teaching, the faculty would have to counsel, to run the dorms, and to run the athletic program. Then we would not have to hire a counseling staff, an athletic staff or a dormitory staff . . . [faculty] who elect to remain will have less time to develop courses, less time for tutorials and independent studies. . . . To cut the budget 20% means giving up the elective curriculum."

Alternatively, she told the board, the school could continue to spend at the 8 to 9 percent withdrawal rates of the last few years, which would eventually mean closing of the school. She concluded emphatically, "Emma Willard will go in style and with a program that is truly excellent, but it will go."[106]

In fact, her financial plan was not achieved, and, of course, the school did not go out of business. Admissions nudged up slowly; applicants were rarely rejected, and the school's reputation inevitably declined. Alumnae daughters and sisters, a quarter of the student body in 1973, fell to 7 percent of the population in the fall of 1978. The rate of withdrawal from the endowment topped 8 percent in 1976–77 and 1977–78, finally falling to 6.5 percent in 1978–79 when the boarding enrollment jumped from 247 to 275. The endowment did grow, reaching the $10 million goal in 1981. Overall, the fund-raising program was comparatively successful. Under Myers's leadership of the development office, the annual fund topped $300,000 for the first time. Careful management by the investment committee of the board helped the endowment weather difficult markets. In the first quarter of 1977, the endowment had dropped 5.8 percent, but the Dow dropped 7.5 percent. Between 1977 and 1978, Emma Willard's endowment grew at a modest 2.3 percent; the Dow, in contrast, lost 12 percent.

In spite of the fragile economic situation at the school, O'Connor pushed ahead on the one large facilities project that remained to complete the campus master plan of the late 1960s: the construction of a new gymnasium. Since 1971, the school had had no sports facility, and gym classes had been accommodated haphazardly, as noted by Locke in his reference to the trampoline in the chapel. The dance program was well served by a magnificent space that had been created on the second floor of Slocum Hall through the conversion of a large study hall into the Strong dance studio, the gift of a family with long ties to the school.[107] Two successive admissions directors, however, reported that the lack of a gymnasium was a definite deterrent to enrollment among prospective students. Beverley Marvin had urged Dennis Collins to reinstitute riding, and in 1976 Director of Admissions Susan Edwards reported to the board that 75 percent of the accepted students who did not enroll cited the lack of a gymnasium as the main reason.

Although in many ways in sync with progressive education, the school was most definitely out of step with the national trend in girls' physical education. In 1972 Congress approved an extension of the Higher Education Act of 1965 that included this groundbreaking provision: "No person in the United States shall, on the basis of sex, be excluded from participation in, be denied the benefits of, or be subjected to discrimination under any education program or activity receiving Federal financial assistance."[108]

Known as Title IX, these few words "brought a cultural shift in the United States, blasting gender discrimination in education."[109] The area most profoundly affected was women's athletics. Although the National Collegiate Athletic Association (NCAA) opposed the legislation, there was no turning back. Colleges and universities complied with the law, for the first time granting their female students increasingly equal access to fields, coaches, equipment, uniforms, and opportunities for competition. The movement quickly encompassed high schools, where girls sought the same opportunities.[110] When Title IX passed, the girls at the recently coeducational prep schools moved, albeit not without some male opposition, into the gyms and onto the playing fields at institutions with sports legacies and state-of-the-art athletic facilities. A picture of Taft girls playing soccer appeared in the *New York Times* in 1974. The vision of strong, healthy, active young women breaking a gender barrier implicitly challenged the girls' school raison d'être.[111]

Raising money for the gymnasium had been a slow process; the cost of the facility was estimated at over $900,000. Stimulated by the hope that a new gym would be a spur to admissions, the board voted in May 1976 to go ahead with construction, although there was only $673,000 in the building fund. The bulk of the money had come from Elsa Mott Ives '23, who had been named an honorary trustee in 1975 after years of dedicated service on the board. The daughter of Charles Stewart Mott, a founding partner of the General Motors Corporation, Elsa Ives donated $200,000 to the project, which was matched by a gift from the foundation that bore her father's name, and over $100,000 from her sister Aimee Mott Butler '21, a member of the class of 1921. Two of Elsa Ives's granddaughters attended the school in the 1970s, Kathleen Kleinpell '75 and Virginia Mott Kleinpell '78. Truly a family gift, the gym was named for Charles Stewart Mott, only the third building on campus named for a man.

In addition to the Mott funds, the Troy-based Howard and Bush Foundation had given the school $330,000 to endow the gymnasium with the stipulation that the new facility would be made available to the public. In order to proceed with the building, the board voted to borrow $285,000 from the foundation money, with the intention of paying it back over five years. In actuality, the school was unable to pay for the building until 1984. Various cost-saving ideas were proposed to trim the budget. Architect and parent trustee Graham Williams advised the board not to install a less expensive floor, but the money for bleachers and equipment storage rooms was unfortunately cut from the plan. The gymnasium was ready for use in the fall of 1977, five years after the passage of Title IX. In the spring, O'Connor hired a new young director of athletics, Judy Bridges. According to the school paper, she was immediately popular with the students, who praised her "pleasant attitude and sense of humor."[112] Over the course of the next few years, she would introduce a competitive interscholastic sports program, at the same time working with the arts division to maintain balance in the curriculum between sports and the arts. An able athletics director, she would eventually become a highly successful dean of students, holding that position longer than any other person in the school's history.

The dedication of the Mott gymnasium was probably the high point of O'Connor's tenure at the school. Sadly, however, the budget crisis was not the lowest. If women's athletics was a national trend that stimulated positive change at the school, there was another national cultural shift that had a deleterious effect on the campus. There was a pervasive atmosphere of permissiveness that, taken to its extreme, promoted the idea that little, if any, sexual activity should be censored. In the 1960s, the school had taken a progressive stand on sex education. In spite of conservative critics charging sex education as anti-American and anti-Christian, it had become widespread in public and private schools by the 1970s. Increasingly, however, the curriculum was changing from an informational program largely intended to combat unplanned teenage pregnancy, to courses in "human sexuality," designed, according to the Centers for Disease Control and Prevention, to "facilitate mental health through improved social relationships."[113] In 1979 about 70 percent of teenage girls reported having a sexual relationship by the age of nineteen, and three of the decade's best-selling nonfiction books were "sex manuals."[114]

Male–female relations on campus were uneasy. In 1977 a feminist editorial in *CLOCK* charged that there were "too many male mentors." *CLOCK* counted 83 women and 27 men on the faculty and staff but bemoaned the fact that "men head the finance department, admissions office, humanities, science and language departments, disciplinary committee, development, and the assemblies committee." It was clear to the editor that the school had "fallen into the trap of our patriarchal society."[115] The same edition of the school newspaper sounded an even more disturbing note when a reporter mentioned that the "single male faculty members satisfy the fantasies of the young women of Emma Willard."[116] Unfortunately, some faculty–student relationships had moved beyond fantasy.

On May 2, 1978, O'Connor called a special meeting of the faculty to tell them that she had discovered evidence of "sexual intimacy between teachers and students." This was, she emphasized, "not one unfortunate event, but several; not one teacher, but several; not one student, but many." She chided the faculty for "playing games . . . games that castigated people for being conservative . . . and exalted them for being liberal and free thinking." She concluded, "If there have to be two camps in this

School, let it be those of us who feel the calling of an educator to be a privilege and a responsibility against those who want it to be an amusement and ego builder."[117] Two weeks later she reported to the board that she had fired one male faculty member, accepted the immediate resignation of a second one, and was working to secure another resignation. In the twenty-first century, with sexual harassment policies and the penalties for their violations quite clearly defined, it is unnerving to imagine a school culture where the basest violations of professional ethics were tolerated by at least some of the adult community. Nevertheless, as the recent allegations at Horace Mann have made clear, schools in the 1970s were not always safe places for students. At their best—as was the case at Emma Willard—administrators boldly addressed the issue and took action; at their worst, as seems to have been the case at Horace Mann, administrators ignored rumors of sexual misconduct among the faculty.

In speaking with the trustees, O'Connor used a broad brush in her definition of the moral lapses of the faculty, linking the sexual misbehavior of a few men with "faculty insubordination," which she defined as undermining the authority of counselors, house parents, and administrators, refusing to do required tasks, and canceling classes or missing them altogether. Linda Dietel, as always, calm, wise, and well informed about the wider educational landscape, told the board, "I don't know of a school, college or university which hasn't had a serious moral, morale or personnel problem in the last several years."[118] Certainly, sex and girls' boarding schools were being linked in the public mind as never before. Miss Porter's garnered unwelcome national attention in 1976 when a newborn baby was found dead in a dormitory room, and in 1980 Jean Harris, the headmistress of Madeira, who had twice been a candidate for head of Emma Willard, shot and killed her lover. This event and Harris's subsequent trial were covered by newspapers ranging from tabloids to the *New York Times*.

The board voted to affirm the content of O'Connor's speech to the faculty, and trustees were asked to work only with O'Connor and the senior administration and not to reach out to individual faculty members. The faculty, for their part, had become increasingly unhappy and had reached out to the board to complain about O'Connor's leadership and policies. In particular, they were angry that O'Connor had fired three women in their fifties who had served the school for decades. A lack of trust permeated the campus, snaking through the student body as well as the faculty. O'Connor, by most accounts, had an autocratic administrative style. She did not deny this. Writing about her leadership to a faculty member, she commented, "I like participatory decisions and lots of discussion, but that's a luxury at this point."[119]

By 1978 O'Connor had already decided to resign, effective June 30, 1979. Although many faculty who taught at the school during this era believed that she was ruthlessly unconcerned about the impact of her financial decisions on the faculty, she was, in fact, neither unaware of nor unconcerned about the human price of her belt-tightening policies. After one series of budget cuts, she confided that she knew the year had been "hard on faculty" and regretted halving retirement benefits, providing minimal salary raises and the fact that "several of their colleagues were let go."[120] For administrators in small institutions, financial decisions are often accompanied by wrenching human costs that appear to give lie to school rhetoric about community values. Making such decisions with a minimum of community disruption requires that the administrators have the trust of those who work for them, and they, in turn, must demonstrate they trust those people. O'Connor did not have enough time to gain the trust of the faculty before she had to make tough budget choices. By 1978 at Emma Willard, Linda Dietel "ached for the school she loved"[121] and recognized that beyond financial woes and faculty misbehavior, the "deeper problem . . . was the lack of mutual trust within the school."[122] O'Connor's resignation gave Dietel and her fellow trustees hope that with a new decade, a new head could heal the community and continue the positive momentum in admissions and development that might someday lead to a financially stable school.

Listening to Voices
We Have Not Heard

As had been the case at the start of the 1960s and 1970s, the new decade brought a new principal. Robert C. Parker would guide Emma Willard into the 1980s, a decade marked not by the tyranny of totalitarian control predicted by George Orwell, but rather by a national preoccupation with consumerism at home and American supremacy abroad. At the end of the era, feminist poet Adrienne Rich, looking back at "those years," summarized them as a time "people will say, we lost track/ of the meaning of *we*, of *you*/ we found ourselves/ reduced to *I*."[1]

During the decade, Pac-Man, aerobics, Smurfs, minivans, camcorders, Prince Charles's marriage to Diana Spenser, Michael Jackson's moonwalking, Madonna's fishnet stockings, and E.T.'s glowing finger each received more publicity than the American bombing of Libya. Ubiquitous "Baby on Board" signs heralded the boomer generation's embrace of parenthood. The 1980 assassination of Beatle John Lennon shocked the United States more than the assassination of Indian prime minister Indira Gandhi four years later. However, in spite of the preoccupation with popular icons, superficial changes, and commercial fads, the decade witnessed transformative and meaningful changes. Women made high-profile news: Sandra Day O'Connor was appointed to the Supreme Court, Geraldine Ferraro ran as vice president on a major party ticket, and Sally Ride flew through space.

African Americans, too, made progress in terms of their acceptance by white America; Jesse Jackson captured over 20 percent of the popular vote in Democratic primaries in 1984, although he failed to win the presidential nomination he sought. *The Cosby Show* joined *The*

Jeffersons on prime-time television. In the 1970s, the Jeffersons had presented a world where black and white Americans lived and laughed together, which was a departure from the Watts neighborhood occupied by Redd Foxx on *Sanford and Son,* but the lyrics from the show's catchy theme reinforced George and Louise Jefferson's anomalous "movin' on up" and emphasized that they were out of their element on the white Upper East Side of New York City. Bill Cosby and his family, in contrast, represented an upper-middle-class professional family that happened to be African American. The Cosbys took professional careers, college education, and the material trappings of upscale urban life in stride, if not for granted.[2] By the end of the decade, Douglas Wilder was governor of Virginia and Colin Powell chairman of the Joint Chiefs of Staff, both firsts for black Americans.

The decade saw its share of scientific and technical firsts as well. In 1980 Ted Turner launched CNN, the nation's first all-news cable network, which, because of its unprecedented twenty-four-hour coverage, revolutionized the way Americans reported and received the news. A year later the United States launched *Columbia*, the first reusable space station, a breakthrough that cemented American dominance in the space race. Soon after, the Strategic Defense Initiative, dubbed "Star Wars" by President Ronald Reagan, bolstered American hegemony in the Cold War. All of these scientific advances depended heavily on the decade's extraordinary improvements in computer technology. In 1981 IBM introduced the first personal computer, launching a revolution in American homes, workplaces—and schools.

That same year, scientists made an important medical discovery with far-reaching cultural implications. In 1981 they identified the virus that was killing otherwise healthy young, gay, male Americans. When movie star Rock Hudson died from AIDS in 1985, not only the actor emerged from the closet, but so did homosexuality in unprecedented ways. Mainstream audiences flocked to Broadway to see the Tony-winning musical *La Cage aux Folles.* Although there were many battles still to be fought in gaining respect and full rights, gay Americans reaped an unexpected benefit from the horrific AIDS epidemic.

No one on campus had the power to predict all that would transpire during the upcoming decade, but there was a definite sense of optimism and change. In his first interview with *CLOCK*, Bob Parker promised the reporter, "This new decade ushers in . . . a new era in the life of Emma Willard."[3] Parker, who had yet to be officially installed as principal, had been appointed in February. A graduate of Groton School, he had earned his B.A. at the University of North Carolina and his master's degree at Middlebury. After beginning his career at then all-male Brooks School, from 1966 he had taught at his high school alma mater, chairing the English Department, serving a stint as dean of students, and, once the school went coed, coaching the girls' varsity crew. He was always at heart a teacher and coach; in fact, he clearly warned the search committee, "If you are looking for a fund-raiser, you are knocking on the wrong door . . . I am an English teacher."[4] Perhaps he was not an experienced fund-raiser, but he was a man of vision and exuberant vitality who energized the campus and the alumnae.

A consummate boarding school man, Bob Parker's vision of a school had been shaped to a great degree by his experience first as a student and second as a teacher at Groton. The school had been founded in 1884 by legendary headmaster Endicott Peabody. An Episcopalian priest and proponent of the Victorian value of "muscular Christianity," Endicott aimed to fit Groton's boys—most of whom were wealthy and privileged—for a life of service. When Bob Parker was at the school as a student, John Crocker, Peabody's immediate successor, was still in charge. He had admitted the first black student to the school in 1951, and during Parker's schooldays, Crocker championed the civil rights movement, even marching with his students alongside Martin Luther King Jr. Daily chapel and daily sports were part of every boy's routine.

In light of Emma Willard's curricular and extracurricular swing toward the nonconventional during the 1970s, it is not surprising that the search committee was attracted to a man schooled in tradition who put an emphasis on community building, but who also had vision. Chaired by trustee Jim Welles, father and husband of Emma Willard alumnae,[5] the committee included past board president Donald Buttenheim and two other trustees, John Esty and Kendra Stearns O'Donnell '60, as well as two faculty members, Jack Easterling and Adeline Scovil. Parker, along with two other finalists, was interviewed in early December 1978, and he quickly emerged as the committee's top choice. The salary he was offered was $4,000 more than what O'Connor was paid in her last year. Parker had a wife and two daughters; the old habit of paying married men more than single women died hard.

Officially, the board had no preference for a man or woman, and just wanted, as Linda Dietel put it, "the best person for the job."[6] Surprisingly, a majority of the faculty and students, when polled by *CLOCK*, had no preference either; however, both groups rated "sense of humor" and "concern for adolescents"[7] as important qualities for the new leader. As one teacher recalled years later, the new head would be "crucially important in reestablishing the civilities of institutional life,"[8] after a period of low morale caused predominantly by controversial administrative reactions to economic strictures and shifting educational and social values. As one administrator who bridged the O'Connor/Parker years has recalled, "There was almost a lost decade [before] Bob came to Mount Ida."[9]

The old oak tree that had stood in the center of campus between Sage and the chapel had been dying for years, and its deterioration from leaf anthracnose fungus was all too symbolic of the malaise that suffused the campus. The decision to plant a new oak on the occasion of Bob Parker's installation as principal was emblematic of hope and the future. A poem, dedicated to the tree and printed on the back of the installation program, captured the sense of renewal:

> Here is the earth again, turning
>   the seasons stretch to catch another year
> as dry leaves fall on cold grass
> burning
> bright on the edge of winter –
> the oak we stood below to watch
>   the snow has gone . . .
>   How green, how green, the Stately Groves of Academe.[10]

On October 14, 1979, the Emma Willard community gathered to honor the new tree and to welcome the new principal. Parker's former colleague, Peter Camp, assistant headmaster at Groton, highlighted his friend's strengths as an educator: "He knows that at least fifty percent of a private school student's real education takes place outside the classroom, and respects that notion while demanding of himself and others professional excellence, superior teaching skills, and sensitive counseling." Camp predicted that Parker would "live the message that life is precious, that love is essential, that trust becomes real only when there are those who can be believed as well as those who believe."[11]

The student speaker, Petra Perkins '80, remarked that "so far . . . [Mr. Parker] has done a fantastic job."[12] He had only been at the school a few months, of course, but in his opening convocation speech, he had told the students that, among other things, their "sense of assurance" had impressed him. Echoing that theme as she welcomed him on behalf of the alumnae, Susan Hunter '68 apprised the new principal, "Emma Willard School taught me to be critical, to examine, to consider and weigh various perspectives, and, most importantly, to draw my own conclusions."[13] Speaking for the faculty, Marcia Easterling, an experienced and versatile history and Spanish teacher, alluded to the difficult times just past but highlighted the "remarkable, if at times hard pressed, loyalty to this institution of not only the faculty, but of students, alumnae, parents and friends alike."[14]

Linda Dietel presented Parker with the mace, symbol of the office of principal, lauding his "desire to build on the heritage which has shaped this school." In addition to his "great good sense and good humor," she noted that he had the "courage to look to the future, to ask hard questions and to dream dreams."[15] In accepting the mantle of office, Parker reflected that Dietel had promised him that being principal of Emma Willard was "a heavy task, but a joyous one." In his acceptance speech, he stressed the challenges facing young women in a changing world and an emerging global community. It was his goal, he said, to give girls the "confidence to make choices, and the skills to follow through on them." Most important, he noted, was to keep "firm in our minds the value of both the caretaking and the achieving roles and the importance of making both a part of our lives."[16]

These words were far from randomly chosen. Bob Parker had been at Groton in 1975 when the school first accepted girls, and he had coached the girls' varsity crew team there. As Groton adjusted to girls on campus, Parker was intrigued by the differences he found in teaching and coaching Groton girls as opposed to Groton boys, particularly in the way they made decisions. He found similar differences when he compared Emma Willard girls with Groton boys. He was particularly fascinated by the contrast between the two groups when it came to making choices and explaining the rationale for those choices. In his quest to understand this difference more clearly, he read an essay in the *Harvard Educational Review* by Carol Gilligan entitled "Woman's Place in Man's Life Cycle."[17]

A psychology professor who focused on moral development, Gilligan hypothesized that the ways people make decisions and choices are heavily influenced by gender. This was problematic for women because the theories of moral psychology used to explain the life cycle of adult humans were based on the lives of men. For this reason, those theories gave greater weight to considerations of autonomy and rules than to intimacy and attachment in evaluating what constituted mature decision making. The *Harvard Educational Review* article, which would become the first chapter of Gilligan's revolutionary work, *In a Different Voice*, captivated Parker. He called Gilligan to ask her what she could tell him about how girls make choices and why they seemed to him so different from the ways his former male students had operated. He was floored when she told him that so very little work had been done on normal female moral development that there was not even enough to warrant one chapter in a general textbook on moral psychology.

That was the bad news. The good news was that Gilligan aimed to change the field, but she was lacking a human database to test her theory. Parker promised her the Emma Willard student body—if he could raise the money for a research project. Together with the author,[18] Gilligan and Parker designed a research proposal and pitched it to the Geraldine Rockefeller Dodge Foundation. In May 1981, the foundation gave the school $40,000 to fund Gilligan's research for two years; in 1983 the foundation renewed the proposal for an additional two years at the same funding level. In October 1981, Gilligan came to the campus to explain to the student body what she intended to do; when a junior in the audience asked her what she could possibly learn by studying the decisions that she and her fellow students had made, Gilligan knew she was in the right place. Even at Emma Willard, where the education was squarely focused on young women, there were girls whose voices had not yet been heard.

Emma Willard appealed to the Dodge Foundation on the grounds that a school with its long legacy of "understanding and educating female adolescents" was the "logical place to begin substantive research." The many boys' schools that now accepted girls, it was suggested, defined gender equality as "the opportunity to integrate into boys' programs." For the school, the research was an opportunity to investigate how students make choices about advisors, disciplinary decisions, course selection, and roommates. For Gilligan, the research would provide a way to measure how girls solve the moral dilemmas they face, particularly how they weigh "caring and friendship against achievement and success."[19] Built into the proposal were opportunities for faculty to meet with the researchers at the end of each school year in order to lend their perspective on the findings. This kind of collaboration between the researchers and the school was as innovative as Gilligan's hypothesis and the research method she employed.

In November 1981, Gilligan arrived on campus with her team of twelve researchers, who were mostly advanced graduate students. Over the course of a few days, the visitors interviewed a random sample of seventy-two students, ranging in age from freshmen to seniors. Among other questions, the girls were asked the "moral dilemma" question—to describe a situation when they were unsure what action to take, to report what they chose to do, and to explain why they made the choices they had. Asking the girls to define their own moral dilemmas marked Gilligan's research as dramatically different from standard research in moral psychology, nearly all of which had used male research subjects and had posed a set dilemma. For example, Lawrence Kohlberg used the classic "Heinz dilemma": Was it wrong for a man to steal a drug he could not afford in order to give it to his dying spouse? Kohlberg's widely accepted scale of moral psychology, a scale intended to show which people's decision making was most evolved, was constructed based on responses to Heinz's conundrum.

It was standard wisdom among psychologists that moral development could be measured in this way; Carol Gilligan believed, in contrast, that the traditional scales excluded a perspective that was gender dominant but not gender specific. In making decisions, most women, she postulated, used an ethic of care in making decisions, as opposed to the more hierarchical ethic of justice mapped by Kohlberg, Erik Erikson, and other male psychologists. Those who emphasized the ethic of justice easily dismissed as moral relativism or simply muddled thinking those whose decision making utilized an ethic of care. By interviewing girls over time, Gilligan hoped to validate her theory with data that showed that people making decisions by using an ethic of care have a "way of organizing the world that has a logic and consistency all of its own."[20] The Emma Willard study would be "the first coherent, long-range attempt at charting the ways in which girls' moral development takes place."[21] Aiding Gilligan in this effort was Dr. Nona P. Lyons, who had designed the coding scheme that would be used to evaluate student answers to their self-generated moral dilemmas, the central component of the interviews.

Although students generally welcomed the researchers and enjoyed participating in the study, there was inevitably some friction between the researchers and their subjects. Trouble erupted, for example, when the students learned that Gilligan proposed to tape judicial hearings to analyze the decision-making considerations of both the defendant and those who sat in judgment on her case. Irate *CLOCK* editors consulted an attorney who told them that legally the proposed taping was neither "legal nor illegal," but it certainly represented a case where "student rights were being 'worn away.'"[22] True to her liberal academic roots, Gilligan immediately backed down, assuring the students through a letter to the editor that she had rethought the situation and would not tape the hearings.

By listening to student and faculty reactions as they went along, the researchers crafted a collaborative project with the school. In the end, their results found a widespread audience among both independent and public school educators, and the Dodge Study was clearly the defining effort of the Parker administration. In 1989 the school published *Making*

Connections: The Relational Worlds of Adolescent Girls at Emma Willard School. In addition to chapters on the study at Emma Willard—"Listening to Voices We Have Not Heard," "Unfairness and Not Listening," "Competencies and Visions," and "Reflections"—the book also contained a number of chapters that suggested ways in which the Dodge Study could illuminate further research into such areas as eating disorders, racial identity formation, sexual behavior, and girls' relationships with their mothers.[23]

For the Emma Willard faculty and for Bob Parker, the implications of the Dodge Study for curriculum and nonacademic life were of utmost importance. Gilligan, herself, refused to make any wholesale claim that the study provided a blueprint for curricular change, but the faculty who were involved in the workshops about the study almost immediately saw critical implications for their work in the classroom and as advisors. So did Bob Parker. At the end of his second year at the school, he reminded the faculty that declining admissions numbers was the largest problem facing the school, and he firmly asserted that "curriculum will not change our admissions picture."[24] Critical as he was of the current curriculum, he drew a clear distinction between what was taught and how it was taught. He greatly valued the faculty and their teaching: "In your wildly diverse ways, you perpetuate the dream of our founder to develop each student to her fullest according to her potential."[25] Nevertheless, the more he learned about girls from the Dodge Study, the more he believed the curriculum needed to change.

Before the curriculum could be revised, however, other measures could be taken that would make the school more attractive to the right kind of girls. Parker moved immediately to improve weekend programming; to establish an on-campus chaplaincy and hire a chaplain[26]; to expand sports offerings; to redesign the dining program, including both more nutritious food and more frequent community dinners; to introduce a peer counseling program with an emphasis on human sexuality and drug education; and to hire resident advisors to increase the numbers of adults in the dormitories. He put most of these innovations in place within two years, although the addition of varsity crew, lacrosse, and track—all of which he actively encouraged—had to wait for facilities improvements.

As is often the case, student reaction to change was swift and not always positive. For example, the introduction of the Rodale diet, which emphasized organic, locally grown foods, met with a great deal of student resistance. When the new food was the "Issue of the Issue" for the school newspaper, the responses focused on one theme: the introduction of tofu into school menus. Typical comments included "They're going a little overboard with the tofu," "The tofu can be forgotten," and "They could cut down on the tofu stuff."[27] The return to required chapel was even less popular. After experimenting with no chapel in the early 1970s, the school had reinstated some required services in 1974 and increased the requirement in 1979. Parker refined the policy. By 1983 all students, boarding and day, were required to attend four services a year including Christmas vespers. Boarders had to attend two additional services per term, although these could be off campus at a church or synagogue of their choosing. Some students, however, still had "personal objections to chapel at a liberal learning institution."[28] *CLOCK* editors questioned whether or not the administration's goal—encouraging students to reflect on their spirituality—was being accomplished when 15 percent of the student body professed to attending chapel only to sing in the choir and a third of the students attended only to avoid detention.[29]

Cautioned by Gilligan that the Dodge Study was just beginning and could not yet support cognitive implications, Parker did not act as rapidly on curricular change. Consequently, he proposed postponing any significant revision of curriculum content, asserting that "innovative teaching and advising are more important than innovative curriculum development."[30] Nonetheless, he had already made some changes. Frustrated by the lack of coherence in the elective curriculum and aware that parents were less interested in "elective choice [than in] academic excellence,"[31] Parker and Academic Dean Jack Easterling had begun tightening the curriculum in 1980, with the assistance of a curriculum steering committee. The number of periods in the academic day had been reduced from ten to eight, and the arts department had introduced sequencing to ensure that students in more advanced sections had learned the necessary skills and techniques.

Most important to the two men, both of whom were English teachers before (and while) they were administrators, an English Department had been organized, and new year-long courses for freshmen, sophomores, and juniors were *required*. The changes were welcomed by the majority of the faculty, although, according to *CLOCK* editorials, the student body chafed at what they viewed as restrictions.[32]

The students were not only upset by the increased academic requirements. They were also resentful about the tightening of dormitory rules. Disturbed by the number of disciplinary cases, Parker and his dean of students, Kurt Meyer, added a number of new regulations intended to account for student whereabouts. By the spring of 1982, he reported to the board, "Students will tell you there's a different feel to the campus."[33] Perhaps, but at least according to *CLOCK* reporters, that new "feel" was not all good. The abolition of certain senior privileges—particularly the right to "roam" through the dormitories after hours on weekdays—and more general restrictions about study hours (which were now to be spent in one's own room) led to charges of an "inhuman attitude" toward students.[34] One four-year senior concluded, however, that although "he is clamping down on the rules . . . he is pulling the school up by its bootstraps."[35]

Perhaps there was no wider administrative–student gulf than over the issue of MTV. Bob Parker loved music and he loved technology; he played his trumpet at every opportunity, and he incorporated computers into his advanced composition course before any other English or humanities course at the school used computer technology. He could not wait to install a fax machine in the head's office. However, he was most definitely not fond of television, which he believed was destroying English skills. He railed against "the language of television," decrying the low level of the vocabulary used in most programming. "The speech patterns children pick up [from television] are graceless, banal, and utilize perhaps 20% of the total resources of the language."[36]

MTV—and the amount of student time consumed by the trendy new music channel—became a source of tension between the administration and the student body. In the fall of 1982, MTV viewing was limited to Sage television room, but by 1984 the administration had banned it altogether in spite of student cries of "censorship."[37] Not all students disagreed with the decision, however. One newspaper article decried the mindlessness of the "incessantly repeating loop."[38] Another wrote facetiously, but pointedly, that "Conversations, meals and meetings have felt the effects of this latest phenomenon. A few nights ago . . . one of my colleagues ran from the table and the dining room in the middle of a sentence. I thought she was choking, but . . . it was the magnetic force of the Rolling Stones . . . she had already seen them play four times that day, singing the same song . . . watching mouths move unsynchronated to the music."[39]

Parker may not have liked television, but he did value entertainment, and early on in his tenure, he solicited support for a speakers' series. As a result, the school enjoyed the 175th Anniversary Series Lectures, a program that brought noted scientists, politicians, journalists, athletes, and artists to the school. In addition to making an evening presentation to the entire student body, the visitors met with students over meals and in the classroom, remaining on campus for a minimum of twenty-four hours. Not since Bill Dietel's days had the students been exposed to such a rich array of lecturers. The series began in November 1982, with a debate between journalists William Rusher and Leslie Gelb on the nuclear arms race. The second lecture featured Dr. Emily Vermeule, a Harvard art historian, who spoke on Greek history and art in the Bronze Age. The year finished with Dian Fossey, a prominent zoologist who worked with the gorillas of Rwanda. Over the course of the next few years, the school welcomed Nobel laureate and physicist Rosalyn Yalow, Children's Defense Fund leader Marian Wright Edelman, historian James McGregor Burns, computer scientist Sherry Turkle, mountaineer Arlene Blum, jazz pianist Marianne McPartland, Olympic swimmer Donna deVarona, and actor Alan Weeks. The lectures were a popular break from routine and dubbed by one student as "one of Emma Willard's most precious gems."[40] Day students as well as boarders were required to attend, but a policy of "light homework," designed by Easterling for the nights when 175th lectures occurred, made these required events more palatable.

If the students chafed at restrictions, Bob Parker chafed at inaction. In the second year of the Dodge Study, he was ready to force curricular change. He appointed Easterling as chair of a faculty curriculum committee; the faculty elected the six other members. None of the few remaining champions of the elective curriculum were elected. Among other goals, Parker charged the committee to be attentive to the ramifications of the Dodge Study and to make sure the new curriculum "self-consciously serves the adolescent female in both content and methods of instruction." He also charged them with writing a "broad liberal arts" curriculum that had "appropriate" coursework for different age levels, a schedule supporting an academic day and week with a reasonable pace and intensity, combined a commitment to the arts with a regular program of physical education, and provided room for varied learning technologies. In recognition of the growing international student population at the school, he called for the inclusion of instruction in English as a Second Language and urged that the curriculum ensure knowledge of other countries and cultures. It should be, he wrote, "a distinctive part of an Emma Willard education that students leave having a greater knowledge of the world than do most high school graduates." The committee was not to limit its work to the classroom but should also review student activities and residential life, keeping in mind that Emma Willard was and would remain "predominantly a boarding school."[41]

His charge implicitly critiqued the curriculum he had inherited. The new curriculum was to be "distinguished more by how it is taught than by special intricacies of its own design," should have "college placement standards automatically included," and permit "no student to avoid a challenge in subjects in which she perceives herself to be weak." The committee was to "take into account the student body's academic abilities, educational background, and the pressures of popular culture," and the final report should include "a well-developed plan for making each academic department strong and effective." Finally, the curriculum should be designed in such a way as to ensure that "mastery of verbal and mathematical skills . . . [are] a distinctive part of an Emma Willard education."[42]

After months of deliberation, the committee's report was placed before the faculty for three days of discussion and a vote on each separate recommendation. The twenty-five-page report outlined changes in both the academic and nonacademic areas of school life. It "reconfirm[ed] Emma Willard's commitment to a strong liberal arts curriculum" but retained "an unusually wide range of elective courses." The latter were important because "the opportunity for student decision-making is vitally important." In a veiled reference to the biggest weakness of the elective curriculum, the committee noted that "while independence and individual growth are stimulated by varied new experiences, adolescents will be most encouraged to try such experiences if they are given a select range of choices from which they *must* choose." The committee recognized that "adolescents need adult mentors in order to make both academic and non-academic choices," and the report called for "more frequent and more varied contacts between adults and students."[43]

The committee outlined new distribution requirements that were "considered standard by American colleges and universities." These included four years of English and humanities literature courses; the study of at least one foreign language through the third level; the study of mathematics through the third level; two years of laboratory science; one year of humanities from the area of art studies, philosophy, religion, and social sciences; two years of history, one of which must be taken in eleventh or twelfth grade; two years of arts courses in four years, divided among performing and nonperforming arts; and four years of physical education. Some of the committee's work was referred to ad hoc faculty and student committees, which were charged with completing their work by June. Among those was a student/faculty committee on community dinners, faculty committees on writing standards, and "a bibliography of written and visual materials on women and a report on pedagogical techniques that specifically serve adolescent females."[44] In the end, the faculty voted overwhelmingly to accept the report. As Parker informed the board, "the faculty . . . enthusiastically endorses the amended report as a new curricular design for the school and pledges itself without reservation to its speedy, creative and wholehearted implementation."[45] In fact, the final vote was 59 to 1.

The student body was not as enthusiastic. As was their practice, the trustees dined with students at their February meeting. They reported much "whining about the curriculum."[46]

In general, students voiced concern "about the direction Emma Willard is headed for the future," specifically worrying that it would become "only a college preparatory school."[47] Used to a great deal of freedom in their academic choice, they resented the "no tolerance" class cut policy implemented by Easterling in 1981–82, the English sequence, and the additional physical education requirement. For students who had been allowed a collegiate model of two class cuts per term, Easterling's escalating system of penalties beginning with the first class cut was "overkill."[48] As for the increased gym requirement, it was clear evidence to some students that the administration was trying to "drag the school back to a more conservative curriculum."[49] Students deftly turned administrative rhetoric to their advantage. In a letter to the editor, the president of the class of 1983 protested, "Although the school is *for* students and in existence because of students, it seems as though events on campus . . . revolve around the approval and decisions of the faculty and administration."[50]

In the time-honored way of smart students, the protesters used administrative language to their advantage, arguing that the new curricular directions contradicted admissions literature. As evidence, they quoted the recently published admissions prospectus, "To Achieve." In that publication, the school had boasted, "The regimented march through a rigidly sequenced set of courses that is typical of so many high schools is not part of Emma Willard."[51] One senior, concluding that the changes would not impact her Emma Willard studies, focused her objections on process: "Let those in power stop teasing and provoking the powerless by letting them believe if they complain loudly enough, they will be heard. I would rather have it understood that the curriculum is faculty domain."[52] Student angst aside, the *Curriculum of 1984* was introduced in September of that year.

The greatest student protest focused on the committee's recommendation that the school schedule shift from trimesters to semesters. In part, this was a response to "a widespread concern about the hectic pace of life at the school."[53] For most of the faculty the semester system made sense because it would "provide fewer examination and marking periods and longer blocks of time for the mastery of course materials."[54] To students, it meant cutting elective choice by a third.

The faculty on the committee, guided by Easterling, had another, more profound reason for switching to a semester schedule. Under the new curriculum, "each course in each department" was to "allow time for each student to have some inquiry and research work."[55] This innovation required serious, sustained oversight of the faculty by both the academic dean and department chairs, a level of administrative control that had not existed during the years of elective curriculum and was resented by a minority of the older faculty for whom their classrooms had been their kingdoms. To help standardize pedagogy and the criteria for acceptable student performance, two documents were adopted by the department chairs: *Writing Standards Across the Curriculum* and *Points of Classroom Practice*. The latter required that all courses in all subjects consciously include "the female perspective."[56] During 1984–85, several faculty meetings were devoted to departmental presentations about how they were meeting this criterion.

Although Parker firmly believed that curricular innovation did not, in and of itself, affect admissions, he also believed that the way teachers interacted with students at a boarding school, both in and outside the classroom, made a difference in a family's willingness to send a child to the school. Overall, the committee had designed exactly the kind of program he sought: "streamlining the present curriculum, augmenting the physical education program, and strengthening the non-academic and residential programs at the School."[57] However, in spite of the new approach, admissions remained stubbornly problematic.

When Parker assumed office, the school had 272 boarders and 78 day students. The next year there were 273 boarders and 90 day students. As of 2012–13, the student population has never reached that level again. Between 1980 and 1985, the boarding population fell from 273 to 196, although the day population remained relatively stable. In large measure, shrinking the student population was a calculated move, led by Parker and approved by the board of trustees. In 1981 the board authorized $70,000 for Parker to hire a marketing firm to look at the Emma Willard admissions situation. Jan Krakowski, principal of Kane, Parsons & Associates, conducted the market research and made a sobering report to the administration. Although the researchers called families with teenage daughters in affluent zip codes having high percentages of students who attended independent schools, fewer than 25 percent recognized Emma Willard by name. Even in the New England area, the region most receptive to boarding schools, recognition never reached 50 percent.

Furthermore, Krakowski analyzed the admissions statistics at the school and found that although there had been modest gains during the O'Connor years, "a high proportion have been marginal students" entering in the eleventh or twelfth grades, that admissions goals had been achieved by "compromise[ing] educational quality," that the numbers of students ranking in the lowest and highest tenths of the student body had remained fairly constant, but the "middle group has shifted sharply downward." Parents did not want their children in school with "problem children," nor was "stress on electives and curricular freedom . . . advantageous."[58] The numbers of teenagers in the population had declined significantly from the highs of the late 1960s and early 1970s; 1980s parents wanted their children to be taught by experienced faculty, to be exposed to arts and culture along with a rigorous college preparatory education.

Parker reported the market research to the board—along with an action plan. He reminded them that he had already put a few changes in place: required chapel and a tightening of the curriculum with the addition of the year-long English requirement. However, he admitted, in the past two years that the school "took students who were destined not to last" because of their behavior, emotional, and drug problems and "marginal academic ability."[59] He reminded the board that in 1980–81, seventy cases of student rule-breaking were heard by the Faculty-Student Judiciary—and, of course, those were just the students who were actually caught.

He outlined a five-prong solution: first, commit to rejecting marginal students, even at the cost of empty beds; second, institute a merit scholarship program to attract a number of academically talented girls; third, improve residential life by reconfiguring the dormitories so that families could serve as houseparents; fourth, revise the curriculum so that the academic program was "second to none"[60]; and fifth, develop new recruiting strategies that would increase Emma Willard's visibility and reach new nontraditional sources of students. The new board president, Kendra Stearns O'Donnell '60, who had succeeded Linda Dietel on July 1, 1980, heartily endorsed the plan, even at the risk of deficit budgets.

In retrospect, the move seems incredibly bold. Parker was not a spendthrift. He recognized the unorthodoxy of the course of action he proposed. Anticipating the impact of his plan on the endowment, he assured the executive committee of the board, "For those of us who were raised to believe that there could be nothing so unthinkable as to invade endowment principal, the figures . . . are sobering indeed." He asked the board to consider carefully "whether we feel the expenditure of these funds justifies the erosion of the endowment."[61] For the next few years, the deficits were often staggering, but O'Donnell consistently reminded the board that "the principal reason for the deficit is the new admissions policy."[62] At least one board member disagreed with the budget, calling it the "height of irresponsibility"[63] to abandon the 5 percent spending formula.

In the spring of her final year at Emma Willard, O'Connor had presented a five-year projection demonstrating that to maintain the traditional spending formula, the school would have to enroll 400 students, 300 of them boarders, by the fall of 1980—and the size of the school would have to remain at 400 after that. With tuition accounting for more than 60 percent of the operating budget, even in 1980–81, with a school population of 363, there was an excess of expenditures over income of nearly $60,000. Complicating the admissions picture was the reality that tuitions rose every year. Increases ran between 6 and 9 percent, with day tuition increasing more slowly than boarding tuition. The tuition for 1985–86 increased by 8.8 percent and pushed the boarding fees over $11,000. Still, the deficits increased as the school enrolled 251 boarders in 1982, 223 in 1983, 215 in 1984, and 196 in 1985. For 1982–83, the deficit approached $400,000, and for 1983–84 the deficit was nearly $240,000, and the board approved a budget for the next year that potentially included a $300,000 shortfall. The total operating budget for those years ranged from slightly over $4 million in 1982–83 to over $5 million in 1985–86. Allocating certain expenses "below the line," a kind of accounting "smoke and mirrors," helped keep the spending formula under 10 percent, but the withdrawals still fell in the 7 to 9 percent range. Allocations below the line were completely legal, but they unnerved those trustees who believed in the fiscal discipline of adhering to a strict 5 percent withdrawal formula.

In spite of the stubborn admissions figures, the budget for 1984–85 balanced. In addition to removing certain large items from the operating budget, this balance, in large measure, was the result of two factors: the unprecedented growth in the endowment and a strong fund-raising campaign. The performance of the board's endowment managers regularly outpaced the market, and the market in the early 1980s was strong. In the second quarter of 1983, for example, each of two fund managers showed increases of 27 and 29 percent while the Dow Jones rose 22 percent. In July 1980, the endowment surpassed $7 million. By 1985, the number was $18,067,000.

Included in that amount was $3,980,995 in new gifts. Not only had the annual fund reached ambitious new heights, but the board had committed in 1980 to a capital fund-raising campaign in anticipation of the school's 175th anniversary. In the first phase of the 175th Anniversary Program, the goal was to raise $8.5 million, with a second and final phase that would bring the total to $30 million by 1989. Once again Bill and Linda Dietel took leadership roles in the fund-raising effort. Bob Parker praised the former principal's "heroic"[64] effort in personally contacting four hundred donors who could potentially give between $5,000 and $50,000. Meanwhile, the annual fund, which had never reached $300,000 in the 1970s, reached a half million dollars in the early 1980s and continued to increase each year.

Parker took many steps to save money. He closed Cluett and Northcroft, two outlying dormitories, even though their relatively positive houseparent-to-student ratios meant they fit his vision for dormitory staffing. He also increased summer revenues, adding a successful Elderhostel program in 1981 and encouraging the growth of Girlsummer, which became a steadily reliable profit-making enterprise. Where he did not stint was on faculty salaries and benefits. For 1985–86 the budget he recommended to the board showed an aggregate increase of

17 percent for faculty salaries and benefits, more than twice the proposed increase in tuition. He wanted more teachers to live on campus, and the board, at his urging, purchased houses along the perimeter and land on Central Avenue for faculty housing. He routinely rejected applications from teachers who already lived in the Capital District or the surrounding area. He wanted them in campus housing. In a typical response to a job applicant who hoped to commute from western Massachusetts, he wrote, "Your situation in the Berkshires puts you out of distance from [consideration] by Emma Willard." [65]

Bob Parker's desire to have teaching faculty live in the dormitories caused one of the few rifts between him and the faculty who had long opposed the "triple threat" model of boys' boarding schools. A survey of five other girls' boarding schools in 1980 revealed that only one, Stoneleigh-Burnham, was organized with 100 percent teaching houseparents. Westover had two, Dana Hall one, and half the houseparents at Ethel Walker taught. Miss Porter's, like Emma Willard, had a completely separate residential staff. Parker hastened to assure a *CLOCK* reporter, "I would never ask a full-time teacher to run a dorm."[66]

Parker may have had a traditional view of faculty as teacher/coach/resident staff member, but he was committed to a diverse faculty, and he was committed to promoting women. When the National Association of Independent Schools (NAIS) produced a new booklet, "A Career in Independent School Teaching," Parker was highly critical of its photographs. He pointed out that no faculty of color were pictured, the two administrators depicted in the pamphlet were both men, and there were five "action shots" of male teachers and of the three female teachers featured, one was in an elementary classroom and two were passive. He wrote to the NAIS president, "[T]his booklet is aimed at young people. Let's not pass on to them our own, ingrown, thoughtless biases."[67] Parker was also sensitive to the needs of working women, and he worked with several young mothers on the faculty to establish the school's first on-site day care, a cooperative parent venture subsidized by the school.

Midway through the decade, the school faced a host of challenges and opportunities. In spite of missed admissions goals and nearly annual encroachments on endowment principal, fund-raising was positive. The faculty felt energized by the Dodge Study and the new curriculum. With Parker's support for an increased budget, the athletic program had expanded with the addition of a competition track, a parcourse, and a new playing field. Always mindful of school culture, Athletic Director Judy Bridges had built a program that combined interscholastic competition with healthy individual fitness. As the *Bulletin* assured the alumnae, "What Judy Bridges has not done . . . is create a major athletic power. Sports are not the major focus of the school culture . . . but under [her] watchful eye, more and more Emma Willard students are suiting up."[68]

Meanwhile, the Leadership Scholars program, merit scholarships underwritten in part by a grant from the Dr. Scholl Foundation, enticed several outstanding young women to attend Emma Willard; to a girl, they earned admission at the most selective colleges and universities including Stanford, Yale, Chicago, and Wesleyan. Trustee leadership was dynamic, and after 1984, the combination of Jack Easterling as academic dean and Judy Bridges as dean of students proved to be a powerful force in checking attrition and ensuring healthy, productive student outcomes. Finally, there was a dawning realization at the board level that a significant part of the entire Emma Willard enterprise had been steadily growing, was financially secure, and was in danger of becoming a larger part of the school than the high school. This was the Emma Willard Children's School (EWCS).

The Children's School had opened in 1972 as the "Nursery School Pilot Program," under the direction of Bob Hammett, whose contract as chaplain had been reduced to part-time status with the diminution of the chapel requirement. Many of the first nineteen students at the Children's School were faculty offspring. The program enrolled 3- and 4-year-olds, three days a week. Within six months of its opening, a faculty committee proposed making the pilot a permanent program with a goal of enrolling twenty children in each of the two age groups in 1972–73. The school would not only serve its constituents but could provide a laboratory for early childhood education. The plan was enthusiastically embraced by the faculty and the student body. In 1972–73, EWCS nearly met its enrollment goal, with thirty-six preschoolers enrolled. Eight of the children received financial aid, with one full award paid for by the student council from its fair proceeds. Meanwhile, Effie Hogben, the tireless campus seamstress, made drapes and slipcovers for the children's classrooms in Wellington-Lay.

In spite of this support, things were rocky at first. In 1974–75, in spite of enrolling nearly seventy students, EWCS ran a deficit over $10,000, and the board appointed an advisory committee to oversee the new initiative. In 1975 Hammett resigned, and the school hired Alice Meyer, wife of mathematics teacher Kurt Meyer, to run the school. In 1977–78, the school broke even for the first time, and by 1981 there were more than a hundred students enrolled in preschool and kindergarten classes. In May, the school successfully petitioned the board to add grades 1 to 3. First grade started in the fall of 1982 and second grade in 1984. Third grade was added in 1985. In the spring of 1983, the EWCS budget showed an excess of revenues over expenses of $14,000, and they had 118 children enrolled for the fall and were projecting 127 for the fall of 1984. When Alice Meyer resigned in 1984 to accompany her husband to his new post at the Thacher School, Marlisa Parker, the principal's wife, and an experienced early childhood educator who had been substituting at EWCS regularly since 1979, was appointed Children's School director. The board of trustees had recently established a separate Children's School committee with trustee Robert Kafin at its helm.

For the remainder of Parker's time in office and for a decade after that, the role of the Children's School on the Emma Willard campus was unsettled. On the one hand, Emma Willard had had a long history of enrolling young children. However, with just a few exceptions, these children had always been girls. The Children's School was coeducational, and as the parents of the very successful program pushed for the addition of classes beyond third grade, the administration and board wrestled with the question of whether or not the argument for single-sex girls' schools might be negatively impacted by a successful coeducational middle school. Second, there were arguments about resources: who had first access to the school vans, for example, high school field trips or Children's School field trips? Were the Children's School surpluses really surpluses? Their maintenance, kitchen, and utility expenses were difficult to isolate, and there was a nagging feeling on the part of some high school faculty and trustees that the real surpluses were not as large as advertised. Faculty with children on reduced tuition at EWCS enthusiastically supported the program. Faculty members with no children or grown children were not so sure. Originally, the EWCS staff were second-class citizens in terms of their salaries and benefits. Marlisa Parker pushed hard to ensure that the elementary school teachers were paid on the same basis as the high school teachers. And, when low enrollment at the high school might have necessitated staff cuts, part-time work at the Children's School staved these off. In 1985, for example, four teachers taught quarter time at the Children's School, providing art, Spanish, computer science, and physical education classes.

Always, there remained the central question: Was Emma Willard one school or two? Officially, the answer was one, but from a practical standpoint, the answer was more convoluted. In terms of mission, the preschool had been an easy fit; Emma Willard was a woman's institution with a long history of training women who entered the workforce. As more and more women in the Capital District worked outside the home, EWCS provided a service that the public needed: high-quality programming for children who were too young for public school and whose parents did not want to park them with a babysitter.

Justifying the elementary grades was more problematic. When pressed, however, EWCS turned to an address the founder had delivered in 1853. In a discourse for the Rensselaer County Teachers' Association, Emma Hart Willard had written that it was "educationally a great mistake [to neglect the education of the youngest scholars]. . . . Suppose the gardener were to neglect his plants in the first stages of their growth because at that moment they were of no use? . . . Do we not see that to insure the ultimate growth and full development of the plant, attention is the most indispensably requisite in its earliest stages? Neglect it then . . . and it becomes beyond the power of any future cultivation to redeem it. Even so, it often happens to the minds of little children."[69]

Willard went on to encourage teachers of young children to incorporate "clapping and singing" and "healthy modes of frequent exercise" into their school day. This jibed perfectly with the oft-repeated

EWCS philosophy that "children's work is children's play." Here again, however, there was friction with the philosophy of "the big school" as the Children's School dubbed the high school. Applicants to the high school took standardized tests and were selected on their ability to handle the curriculum. Children's School applicants were admitted on a strict first come, first served basis. If the school were to expand beyond elementary school, would there be eighth grade girls who were not prepared to handle the work of the high school—and what would that mean? Citing sound educational research, director after director at EWCS adamantly refused to test the school's young applicants.

As all of this was being debated and discussed, there were three important milestones on the school's horizon. First, Emma Willard was scheduled to undergo its ten-year evaluation in 1987; at Parker's insistence, the board had voted to switch accrediting agencies from the Middle States Association to the New York Association of Independent Schools. Parker was a trustee of the latter. The year 1987 would mark the 200th anniversary of the founder's birth. Then, two years later, the school would celebrate its 175th birthday. In anticipation, the board convened a Strategic Planning and Policy Council under the leadership of trustee Keven R. Bellows '55. The committee, composed of trustees, faculty members, and Dodge researcher Nona Lyons, delivered their report in May 1985.

The council focused on the high school, confirmed the school's single-gender status once again, and committed Emma Willard to remaining "an essentially residential school for young women in grades 9–12, with a student population of approximately 350." This population was to be "diverse" and include both a mix of domestic and international boarders and a number of day students that would not exceed 40 percent of the total student body. The admissions effort was charged to make "special efforts" to ensure that "most students are admitted in grades 9 and 10" and promised a continuation of "the historic commitment to a strong program of financial aid." The school would also strive for a diverse faculty and would offer "salaries and perquisites . . . [which] will be competitive." Noting that the plant had suffered during the years of deficit budgets, when the major maintenance line items were often postponed, the strategic plan called for "plant development [to] proceed according to a master plan for use, restoration, expansion and maintenance." They specifically recommended, "Improving educational facilities, redesigning the residential areas, preserving the historic buildings, increasing space for faculty living, addressing the requirements of a diverse program of physical activity, and developing maximum year-round use of the plant."

Echoing the Dodge Study and Parker, the council called for a commitment to women's leadership: "Recognizing the need at the present time for women to assume greater leadership roles, the administration will actively develop leadership skills among the women in the community and seek its own leaders among women of talent and ability." Women were highlighted in the section on curriculum as well, with the committee recommending that the new curriculum be underpinned by an "enlightened understanding of the educational needs and the patterns of development in young women."

To realize all of these goals, the school needed to commit to "financial equilibrium," which could only be accomplished by securing a "substantial endowment." The alumnae would naturally play a role in increasing the endowment; in fact, the council called for a relationship between the alumnae and the school that would be "mutually beneficial and enriching." A second, more controversial, way to meet the strategic planning goals was the development of a "sustained, professional marketing and public relations campaign."[70]

The stage was set for the school to take even bolder steps. In May 1985, the same month that the strategic plan was unveiled, Jane Fonda '55, easily the school's most famous twentieth-century graduate, returned for her reunion. Now a fitness guru, she helped Parker christen the new track and field, and she committed to participating in the 175th anniversary ceremonies in 1989. Two weeks later, the school attracted widespread positive media attention when a rogue black bear took up residence in a tree on the front of the campus and had to be removed by environmental officers. As students and faculty left for the summer, the mood was generally positive.

However, just as school was gearing up for the 1985–86 academic year, tragedy struck. Bob Parker was diagnosed with cancer. He underwent surgery in early October. Doctors had feared he had pancreatic cancer, but it was in fact a diffuse large cell non-Hodgkin's lymphoma. After a prolonged stay at Albany Medical Center, he began a twelve-week regimen of chemotherapy that knocked out his immune system so he had to stay away from students and faculty because of the risk of infection. He remained in daily contact with his senior staff, particularly the author, who served as his associate head, and the business manager, Dana Wright (the first woman to hold that position at the school).

As he recovered from his treatment, he wrote optimistically to the trustees, "The track record of this particular protocol in producing the desired result is excellent."[71] At the beginning of February, he returned to his office. His optimism continued. He wrote to Clementine Tangeman that he was back at work and "confident we have won the battle."[72] On campus, both the faculty and students rejoiced at his return, and the highlight of the winter occurred two weeks before spring break when the adult community staged a spoof of Revels. Jack Easterling was a most convincing devil who promised "endless tests and no vacations." Bob Parker had a starring role. He wrote exuberantly to an alumna, "Yours truly, bedecked in a long satin gown, wig, furs, heavy makeup, and L.L. Bean boots presided as the Lady of the Manor."[73] In the spring, he and the Inner Choir greeted Gilbert de Lafayette, a descendant of the marquis, when he landed at the Port of Albany, much as his famous ancestor had done. And, like the more famous marquis, the modern Lafayette visited the school, dining with faculty and students.

Parker was not there for the dinner. His cancer had returned. He officiated at graduation and reunion and then headed for Vanderbilt University Medical Center in Nashville for a cutting-edge treatment that involved a bone marrow transplant. Although he returned to the campus in August, it was soon apparent that the treatment had failed. On August 20, 1986, he resigned as principal, citing the need to focus on his health. On September 19, with the school year barely under way, he died at Gorham House. Over a thousand people attended his memorial service, which was held on the triangle outside the chapel. The next edition of the alumnae magazine was devoted to his tenure.

In words and pictures, it captured his vigor and energy. Jack Easterling noted, "Bob loved the whole throbbing variety of his job because of all the pieces and parts of the School, especially the people."[74] Alumna Sarah Shove Edwards '47 remembered that his was "an energy that gave rather than depleted."[75] The most poetic tribute came from a man who knew him as a colleague and teacher of boys at Groton. Todd Jesdale wrote that as far as he was concerned, "[H]e continues here—teaching and thinking and listening, moving through the strips of light, through the golden leaves. He is undefeated for me, moving through some different light, through another water, his great vitality with the boys who rowed his shell, his Odyssey and Beowulf, with his friend who still loves him."[76]

At his memorial service, Barbara Jones '39, the director of the Council for Religion in Independent Schools, praised Bob Parker realistically. "Bob," she cautioned, "was not perfect—his person was too definite and his hopes too rich for patience."[77] Nevertheless, the board of trustees had formed a search committee to look for his successor, and inevitably Parker's shadow would provide a standard against which the candidates would be weighed and measured.

If You've Been to Emma Willard, You've Been to the Mountain

ALTHOUGH MANY TRUSTEES and most senior administrators felt it would be prudent to postpone Emma Willard's ten-year evaluation in light of Bob Parker's illness, the principal, himself, was determined that it go on as scheduled, whether or not he would be able to participate in the process. Honoring his wishes, the school welcomed the evaluating team in the winter of 1987. The committee's report highlighted Parker's loss, and it noted that much of what he had wanted to do remained unfinished at his death. In recognition of the work of the 1985 Strategic Planning and Policy Committee, the committee suggested the plans he had had for the school reflected enough broad constituent support that they could and should move ahead under new leadership. Their report, presented to the school in March 1987, concluded, "Tragically, many of his plans were unfinished at his death, but his leadership was sure, and left the mechanisms for fulfilling his vision firmly in place."[1]

On Parker's agenda, and supported by the board of trustees, were the completion of the 175th Anniversary campaign, continued efforts to increase the school's visibility in the admissions marketplace, the publication and dissemination of the Dodge Study findings, and the review and refinement of the 1984 curriculum. Just weeks before his cancer diagnosis, Parker wrote to Jameson Baxter '61, vice president of the board of trustees, that his hopes for the second phase of the capital campaign were threefold. First, he hoped "to build a residential community" by providing enough housing for 70 to 80 percent of the faculty to live on campus. Second, he wanted to increase the residential staff so that the ratio of adults to students in the dormitories would approach 15:1, although he knew that breaking the grand historic buildings into smaller units would be "expensive."[2] Finally, although the endowment had grown dramatically during his tenure, he wanted to raise even more money for this purpose. Emma Willard, he contended, needed to rank in the top ten boarding schools in terms of endowment per pupil to reach its other goals: more competitive faculty compensation packages and the ability to meet all applicants' financial need. He also recognized that beyond faculty and scholarship endowments, the school needed unrestricted endowment to have "that margin of flexibility to respond to change, to be proactive."

As a "perfect example" of the use of unrestricted endowment funds, he pointed to the board's decision in 1984 to build a new track and playing field. In the 1984 Summer Olympics, Carlie Geer '76 had won a silver medal in rowing, and at that moment, "the board . . . saw the importance of athletics for girls and realized the gap they had to fill in short order."[3] Of course, crew was his favorite sport,[4] and happy as he was with the track, he dreamed of building an Emma Willard rowing program on the Hudson. He also told Baxter that a pool and another athletic field should be part of the campaign.

In addition to being the vice president of the board, Baxter was the chair of the search committee charged with finding a new head of school to take office on July 1, 1987. At the end of April, the board announced the appointment of Philip Sedgwick Deely. A graduate of Berkshire School and Hobart College, Deely had earned his master's degree in history at the University of Chicago. He had taught at Simon's Rock and Foxcroft, where he served as chair of the History Department and was elected president of the faculty. For nearly a decade prior to coming to Emma Willard, he had worked at the Ethel Walker School, where he had broad administrative experience, serving as academic dean, associate head, and one year as acting head. In choosing Deely, the board saluted his commitment to and experience in girls' schools, his youth, and his family. His wife was also a teacher and had chaired the Theater Department at Walker's. They had two young children: a daughter, eight, and a son, two, both of whom would enroll in the Children's School. In announcing Deely's appointment, Kendra

O'Donnell described him as a "seasoned administrator, well-versed in the issues surrounding the education of young women."[5] Deely was also a genuine, funny, caring man who understood that the Emma Willard community was still in mourning for Bob Parker.

What Deely failed to understand, however, was that the board of trustees wanted a dynamic head to tackle its problems right away. On July 1, 1987, the board leadership had changed. Kendra O'Donnell had made history when she was appointed the first female principal of Phillips Exeter Academy, one of the oldest, most prestigious independent schools in the country. Because of her new duties, she had resigned from the board, and Jameson Baxter had stepped into the presidency. At a meeting of the trustee executive committee in September, Deely listed his priorities for his first year. Chief among them were to get to know Emma Willard, to get to know Troy, to travel for development, to assist with admissions initiatives, and to work on ongoing projects. His agenda offered little in the way of new initiatives, but instead focused on building upon those plans that Parker had left unfinished. As he told a *CLOCK* reporter on his first visit to the campus after his appointment, "I don't think it's good policy to step in to a stable, well-run organization and start changing things overnight."[6]

His strategy, although understandable, would not work for a school that had essentially been on hold for two years. The 175th campaign needed to be jump-started. The budget was not balanced; for 1987–88 the drawdown on the endowment exceeded 6.5 percent. On the bright side, in spite of the encroachments on principal, the endowment had continued to grow, topping $26 million in the spring of 1987. However, maintenance of the historic campus had been deferred time and again and had accumulated to such a significant degree that the board voted to segregate $4 million of the endowment to tackle the most critical facilities issues.[7] In addition, admissions had yet to recover from the decision to shrink the boarding population. Most unsettling was the reality that the quality of the student body had not improved significantly, at least by quantitative measurements. In 1987–88 the school enrolled 189 boarders and 83 day students for a total population of 272, the lowest resident figure since the Great Depression, and still the admissions office had rejected less than 10 percent of the applicant pool. The numbers of students scoring at the high end of the SAT and PSAT had grown with the introduction of the Leadership Scholars; for example, in the class of 1986, four students scored over 700 on both the mathematics and verbal portions of the SAT, and twelve members of the class of 1987 scored over 700 on the mathematics section. Average scores, however, remained stubbornly close to the 500 mark, and the average PSAT score actually slid between 1987 and 1990.[8]

Trustees, alumnae, and, to a certain extent, the people in the admissions office pointed to the school's location in Troy as a big part of the difficulty in recruiting students. In this respect, Deely's commitment to "getting to know Troy" was heralded as a positive step. He joined Russell Sage president Sara Chapman, an Emma Willard trustee, on the Image Committee for Troy, an initiative to promote the city's downtown. Troy had changed dramatically since the end of World War II. Norman Rockwell's famous painting of a neighborhood of people leaning out the windows of their well-maintained brownstones to cheer a returning soldier was modeled on a block of Fourth Street in South Troy. When the veterans had returned home in 1945–46, Troy's population topped 75,000; by 1980 it had lost a quarter of those citizens, and more were leaving every year.

In the immediate post–World War II years, Troy had been a shopping destination for its citizens and for people in the small towns and villages in eastern Rensselaer County. One historian captured the feel of the city in 1947:

> River Street between Franklin Square and Fulton, and Third Street from Fulton to Congress was the heart of downtown (or "uptown" if you lived south of Ferry Street). The shopping strip contained over forty apparel stores, the city's four major department stores (Frear's, Denby's, Peerless, Stanley's), four '5 and 10's' (Woolworth's, Grant's, H.L. Green's, and Kresge's), thirteen shoe stores, thirteen beauty salons, six jewelers, seven restaurants and luncheonettes, candy stores, florists, book stores, three theatres, and dozens of other specialty stores.... Retail stores selling women's wear were numerous: Weinberg's, Muhlfelder's, the Up-To-Date, Knitcrafts, the People Store, and Lord & Tann. Fashion Furs, Hasso's and Broughton's were the major furriers. Among the popular children's clothing stores were the Young Folks, Kranson's, the Qual-

ity Shop and Kings Children's Store. All sold children's wear produced at Troy's Tiny Town Togs and the Trojan Maid. Among the men's apparel available at Chasans, Snappy's, Wells & Coverly, and the Morris Store were products made by Trojans in Troy's clothing factories: Cluett's, Berk-Ray, Kelly Clothes, Standard Manufacturing, M. Nirenberg, Wultex, and others. . . . Thirty-two retail bakeries, including the Public View, the Crystal, and the Capital, provided fresh baked goods daily. Depending on the particular Troy neighborhood you lived in, fresh produce was brought to your door by vendors such as the Carey Brothers, Mike Esposito, Gus Speciale, Anthony Patti, and others. Freihofer's baked goods were still delivered by horse and wagon; milk, eggs, ice, poultry and other items were also available from door-to-door vendors who made shopping a bit easier for city folk.[9]

Troy lost industry and population in the 1950s and 1960s, and it lost its edge as a retail center for the area when suburban malls began to attract customers to their locations across the Hudson. By 1970 the county desperately needed more revenue, and the city budget was running enormous annual deficits, even though it had shifted to a city manager system to streamline municipal services. In the early 1970s, a host of construction projects promised "a face-lifting that should have started half a century ago"[10] but in fact had the opposite effect. In 1972 the Congress Street Bridge connected the city to Route 7, providing access to suburbs in Latham and other towns in Albany County. In 1974 the Hoosick Street Bridge enabled traffic to connect easily with the arterial leading to Interstate 87. Instead of enhancing Troy, however, these transportation improvements drew people from the city. Many businesses closed, and nearly 3 percent of Troy's downtown housing stock stood empty.

In response, city planners envisioned a mall in the central part of the city that would rival the suburban malls springing up around the Capital District. Under the guidance of the Troy Urban Renewal Agency and with the help of state and federal funding, the city planned a mall that would provide up to 10 acres of shopping in the area bounded by State, Federal, River and Sixth Streets, and plenty of free downtown parking. The new mall would be anchored near Monument Square by a new city hall. Scheduled to open in 1977, the construction for the new shopping complex necessitated the removal of scores of old houses and stores.

Some historic structures would be saved: the brownstones on the western side of Fifth Avenue between Fulton and Broadway, the dwellings on Second Street between Broadway and Fifth, the post office, the Troy Savings Bank, the Cannon, Frear, Rice, and Chasen buildings, Proctor's Theater, and Harmony Hall. Everything else in the area would be razed. The city secured federal funds for the work involved in knocking down buildings and relocating displaced businesses and residents. The New York State Urban Development Corporation (UDC) agreed to fund the $90 million construction project.

Much of the site work had been completed when the UDC encountered financial difficulties and abandoned the project. Troy was left with 3 acres of unoccupied land in the downtown area and the need to find a developer to build the mall. The city advertised for backers in the *New York Times,* and "developers came and went like guests at a party"[11] while a large hole stood in the middle of downtown Troy. Finally, a local businessman and builder, Carl Grimm,[12] agreed to finish the project, albeit on a much more modest scale than had been envisioned originally. On November 22, 1978, the Friday after Christmas and the traditional start to the holiday shopping season, Denby's, a local department store, opened its doors in a new location in the Uncle Sam Atrium Mall. On March 22, 1979, Patricia Harris, the secretary of Housing and Urban Development, officially cut the ribbon that opened the mall completely. In spite of the hype, the shopping center never realized the traffic its planners had projected. Consequently, it never produced the sales tax revenues that Rensselaer County so badly needed. Denby's closed within five years and was briefly replaced by another local department store, Carl's, headquartered in Schenectady. No national chain ever appeared. By the end of the 1980s, however, the mall's future, if any, was as an office complex. Students at Emma Willard had virtually no reason to go into Troy except to perform community service. As one commented in a *CLOCK* article, "I Hate Troy," "Realistically speaking, fine architecture is not enough to redeem a city, especially in the eyes of students."[13]

The admissions office began touting Troy for its location as a hub from which people could easily reach other places—three hours from

New York City and an equal distance from Boston. Although admissions materials referred to the independent study opportunities available in the state government offices in Albany, little was said about Troy beyond a brief mention of the school's proximity to Rensselaer Polytechnic Institute. In spite of his membership on the Troy Image Committee, Deely was—unfairly—seen as forswearing Troy. On weekends, he took his family to their home in western Massachusetts, and he hosted both administrative retreats and a full faculty meeting in that region. On October 4, 1987, just weeks into his first school year, a freak snowstorm dropped two feet of snow on Troy and knocked out the power on campus. In a spirit of camaraderie, the faculty, staff, and students—without electricity and without hot water—shoveled walks and cleared fallen trees to clean up the campus. Deely was not there because he could not be. He was trapped by the storm at his home in Tyringham, Massachusetts.

He had hardly returned to the campus when another blow struck; the stock market, which had performed so strongly in the first part of the decade, took an extraordinary dive. On Monday, October 19, the Dow Jones Industrial Average fell almost 23 percent in response to falling prices worldwide. In retrospect, the crash was more of a corrective to an overheated market than a real economic collapse; the Dow Jones had grown phenomenally in the months prior to October. Nevertheless, the worldwide economic jitters hardly helped the admissions effort. In the winter of 1987–88, Director of Admissions Mary Jo Driscoll reported that the number of students taking the Secondary School Admissions Test, the most common measurement of interest in boarding schools, was half what it had been in 1982–83. By September 1988, only 259 students were enrolled, and only 168 were boarders. The projected deficit for the 1988–89 academic year was $380,000, which represented a nearly 7 percent drawdown from the endowment, two percentage points above the board mandate of 5 percent. There was some comfort in knowing that among girls' schools, there had been a 17.2 percent aggregate decline in admissions over the past four years, a significantly higher loss than the 10 percent experienced at Emma Willard.[14] However, not a few trustees wondered if girls' boarding schools were going the way of dinosaurs.

On campus during Deely's first year, students were edgy. He had closed the smoking area and banned all student smoking, a move that the faculty overwhelmingly approved. He also banned the senior practice of "blacklisting" underclasswomen who violated the senior triangle. When the rising senior class protested, he cited a new state law prohibiting hazing. Meanwhile, the school geared up for the celebration of the 175th anniversary, a planning process that left the class of 1988 feeling left out. As one of them editorialized, "As members of the 174th class, we recognize the importance of the 175th anniversary. But we feel we have been overlooked."[15] Members of the celebrated class of 1989 tried to smooth the waters by responding that "We couldn't be the 175th if you weren't the 174th. Thank you."[16]

For the school, the 175th anniversary meant three things: a major fund-raising opportunity, the chance to take the Dodge Study findings on the road in a series of seminars, and a huge celebration at Reunion. Given the economy, the fund-raising was slow going, and Deely had not yet had the time to cultivate the kinds of relationships with alumnae donors that might have ensured the campaign's success. An all-alumnae survey in 1988 received an extraordinarily positive response, and the trustees were eager to capitalize on the findings with ever more aggressive fund-raising. Alumnae described themselves as "forthright," "communicative," "challenging," and "committed to their institutions."[17] Clearly, they were fertile ground for increased school support. As for the Dodge Study, Deely accompanied Lyons, Gilligan, and various faculty members to seminars in Albany, Washington, D.C., Boston, New York City, Chicago, Minneapolis, San Francisco, and Los Angeles, but his role was minimal because he had not been at the school during the research.

While the school planned for the big 175th celebration in May, Deely was forced to make difficult economic choices. Because of continuing admissions shortfalls, he had to reduce the faculty and restrict course offerings, most notably by removing German from the curriculum. Teachers who resigned or retired were not replaced; one English teacher was let go, and Kathleen McNamara, a young, highly effective English teacher, was reduced to half time and assigned to the admissions office. Electives were sharply curtailed. Positive coverage in the popular teenage magazine *Sassy* made students feel good, but it had no noticeable impact on admissions. In general, the faculty was not in a celebratory mood.

The hoopla around the party met with mixed student response as well, which was muted when an alumna donor provided a dinner cruise on the Hudson for the whole student body while the alumnae and faculty partied on campus. The fun was preceded by two days of seminars on a variety of topics focused on women's achievements. The presidents of Vassar, Russell Sage, and Bard sat on an introductory panel about the future of education. Kendra O'Donnell, nearing the end of her second year as principal of Exeter, spoke on "Women's Work: Unfinished Business," and Madeleine Weigel Ludlow '72 moderated a panel on "Women and Mathematics." The first Alumna Life Achievement Award, created in honor of the anniversary, was presented to Jane Fonda '55. Amid speeches and fireworks, the alumnae and friends of the school toasted 175 years of Emma Willard's vision.

The senior class worried that the anniversary would overshadow their graduation. Jane Fonda was scheduled to be the commencement speaker. Mused one, "I've heard rumors that graduation is going to be some 'shin-dig'; protestors, news coverage, every single alumnae [sic] who is still alive. Some may even pop up from the grave, the way the talk is going."[18] Graduation Day 1989 dawned under leaden skies that gave way to a torrential downpour during the outdoor ceremony. The crowd was too large to move into the gymnasium. Parents and seniors draped themselves in plastic garbage bags, and drenched academic robes leaked blue and black dye on the faculty and their commencement finery. Jane Fonda, alone of the participants and resplendent in a white suit, remained dry throughout the proceedings as first the senior class president and then Deely held a protective umbrella over her.

At Phil Deely's installation, his friend and fellow educator, Peter Buttenheim, had characterized him as "a *gentle man*," explaining, "In an age of little breeding, Phil has manners. In a period of greed, Phil is selfless. In a time of indifference, Phil is caring."[19] He might have added that in the face of fiscal crisis, Deely never lost his sense of humor or his core belief that educational institutions were different from businesses. Just prior to building his first budget for the school, he sent the trustees a tongue-in-cheek budget statement from the manager of the New York Philharmonic:

> For considerable periods, the four oboe players have nothing to do. Their number should be reduced and the work spread more evenly over the whole of the concert, thus eliminating peaks of activity. All twelve first violins were playing identical notes—this seems unnecessary duplication. Much effort was expended in the playing of semiquavers—this seems an excessive refinement. It is recommended that each note be rounded up to the next quaver. No useful purpose is served by repeating on the horns a passage which has already been played by the strings. It is estimated that if all redundant passages were eliminated, the whole concert time of two hours could be reduced to twenty minutes, and there would be no need for an intermission.[20]

Unfortunately for Deely, the board of trustees did not believe that humor and self-effacement were the qualities needed to lead the school during this period of fiscal challenge. Furthermore, the faculty was restive, worried about the decline in admissions and future reductions in staff, and they were increasingly unwilling to give Deely any more time to figure out ways to meet the mounting problems. The boarding enrollment seemed to be in free fall. Although the decline was in large part a casualty of the significant downturn in the high school population nationally, the board was aware that some schools were able to attract students. A few weeks after graduation, the executive committee of the board met and decided that a change of school leadership was in order. For the second time in three years, the school would enter the fall with an acting head. It would also enter the school year with a student population of 236, the lowest total enrollment since the 1930s.

The board of trustees quickly formed a search committee with trustee Keven Bellows, manager of the 1985 strategic planning effort and architect of the 1988 alumnae survey, at its head. In April, after a national search and several months of deliberation, Robin A. Robertson was appointed principal. Robertson held a doctorate in anthropology and was a professor and administrator at Southern Methodist University. For the six years prior to her appointment at Emma Willard, she served as SMU's associate dean of general education. An active anthropologist whose academic work focused on ceramics and pottery in Mayan culture, Robertson was actually working on site at an archeological dig in the Mayan ruins of Belize when her appointment was announced. She had two young daughters, the older of whom, Alayne Friedel '96, was in middle school. Lara, the younger, would enter second grade at the Children's School. Robertson's husband, Serge Kappler, was a tenured professor of philosophy at SMU. In 1995 he would join the administration at Emma Willard as the head of the school's expanding technology department.

A graduate of a public high school in Delaware, Robertson had earned her bachelor's degree summa cum laude from the University of Pennsylvania and her master's and doctorate from Harvard. She had had little personal experience with single-gender education. However, she was an articulate, passionate feminist who had been an outspoken advocate for her female students and colleagues at SMU. During her tenure, she would often tell students about the role her mother, a university dean, played in raising her consciousness about the challenges faced by professional women because of gender bias in the workplace. To the board, her chief qualification was that she had "spent her entire professional career in education, as a scholar, a teacher, and as an administrator."[21] Her accomplishments at Dedman College, SMU's division of general education, were impressive: She had been "responsible for the articulation and implementation of the undergraduate liberal arts curriculum, admissions and enrollment planning for the school of general education, the creation of the University's honors program, and management of career planning."[22] She had experience recruiting and evaluating faculty and soliciting both corporate and individual donors for the college's support. Robertson herself believed her arrival at Emma Willard had an inevitability about it. As she told the students during a May visit to the school, "I got my first glimpse of the campus through the gates, and I said, 'I'm home.'"[23]

In contrast to Deely, Robertson was quick off the mark in September 1990. Her immediate goal was to energize the campus by reinforcing and instituting traditions, beginning with a weekly all-school singing of the "Alma Mater" and a return to senior teas where students were required to dress well, use and learn good manners, and even play croquet on the grounds of Gorham House, the principal's residence. "A sense of the appropriate" became a Robertson dictum and was, in fact, the title of her address at the second opening convocation over which she presided; it quickly became apparent to faculty and students that on formal occasions, form mattered almost as much as substance to Robin Robertson.

Robertson's inauguration as principal on October 6, 1990, was marked by ritual pomp and circumstance. Her family, dressed in the Robertson plaid of their Scottish ancestors, added a personal touch to the ceremony. Dr. Theodora Penny Martin, a professor of education at Bowdoin College, delivered the keynote address, the first woman so honored. A former high school English teacher, Martin was a feminist scholar and the author of *In Our Own Voices*, a well-received history of women's study clubs in the second half of the twentieth century that drew on the work of feminist historian Anne Firor Scott who had used the Emma Willard archives for her research. Martin connected quickly with the students in the audience, at least some of whom were "touched and emotionally moved"[24] by her speech. For her part, Robertson accepted the mace of office with characteristic enthusiasm and verve and a speech designed to underline her reputation as a scholar. "On Education" was highly theoretical and cited classic works and classic authors: Homer and Shakespeare, Bach and Cézanne, Trevelyan and Mozart. A brief allusion to Lady Macbeth offered the only mention of a female figure. Oddly enough, given her often-voiced awareness of sexism in education, and in marked contrast to her two male predecessors, she never mentioned the founder.

A significant section of her speech was dedicated to the important role of mathematics and science in a rigorous education. Once formally installed in her new position, Robertson set to work on curricular revision, one of her two immediate major initiatives (fund-raising was the other). She urged Academic Dean Jack Easterling to increase the graduation requirement in science. She also asked him to work with the department chairs to expand the number of and enrollment in Advanced Placement (AP) courses. Easterling and a significant portion of the faculty were not keen on following this path, particularly as it meant abandoning curricular freedom, a hallmark of independent school education. The AP curriculum had many critics in the independent school world; they argued that it demanded a formulaic course of study prescribed by an outside agency and left little room for creativity and innovation. For Robertson, who had spent many years evaluating the high school transcripts of students attending SMU, most of whom came from public high schools throughout the southern and southwestern United States, the AP represented rigor. She was also well aware that AP was shorthand for academic excellence in parents' minds. To advance the idea of the AP, as well as other curricular change, she asked Easterling to chair a curriculum review committee and charged it with a thorough review of the curriculum that had been instituted in 1984 and modified somewhat by the faculty. She urged the committee to be bold in its thinking.

The curricular review began during the spring semester of 1991; Easterling was aided in his work by a committee of seven faculty elected by their colleagues.[25] To initiate the discussions, Robertson asked the committee to respond to a fourteen-point charge she had prepared. Before starting their work, they interviewed faculty and staff and surveyed young alumnae about their experiences in college. Meanwhile, Robertson encouraged the Science Department to add AP Chemistry to their offerings for 1991–92. Queried about this by the *CLOCK* editor, she told her that "insuring that students leave [the school] with outstanding test scores"[26] was one of her priorities. The committee was not as concerned with test scores, as was clear when they delivered their report in December 1991. Their "overarching conclusion," to the principal's dismay, was that "there is not a need for major curricular revision."[27]

Furthermore, the report "was not organized to answer [the principal's] . . . fourteen questions point for point."[28] Easterling had taken a somewhat independent approach to the review. Rather than overhaul the curriculum, he told the faculty, he had centered the committee's work on assessing ways the current curriculum with some modification could best solve "the problem of the school's attracting and retaining the most able students while at the same time helping the less able students."[29] And, rather than focus exclusively on academics, the committee framed its recommendations in response to five "themes" that had emerged in their discussions with faculty, students, and young alumnae:

> The first and most overriding theme is that a boarding school such as this one is a twenty four hour per day institution. Although its principal emphasis must always be academic, its curriculum must attend to and plan for the whole of the student's life, not only her academic work. Second, there is the wide recognition of the heterogeneity of our student body—in ability, interest, and background—and with this recognition the demand that this heterogeneity be addressed without compromising principles. Third, external demands and expectations from colleges, parents, and students themselves exercise and will exercise an ever more dominant influence upon all aspects of the academic program. Fourth, co-curricular programs have grown in their importance and have demanded greater amounts of student and faculty time. Fifth, as a result of all of the above, faculty, administration, and staff now need more guidance to address increased complexities in almost every area of the school.[30]

The report laid out no startling new curricular directions; nor did it recommend the addition of any specific mathematics or science courses. As for the AP program, it was mentioned briefly in a section recommending that each academic division "investigate and adopt structures or pedagogical techniques which will allow it to challenge and serve the *full* range of its students." AP showed up on the list of "structures and techniques" but as one of many things including those that were designed for the less able students—for example, "remedial sections" and "learning centers."[31] In addition, the committee recommended that the academic divisions should "encourage students capable of advanced work" that they defined as "AP or other."[32] In short, they gave no wholesale endorsement to the AP program.

For the most part, the academic recommendations focused on improving communication within departments and across the faculty as a whole with an eye toward doing a better job of serving students who came to the school from heterogeneous academic backgrounds and possessed a wide range of skills. The report also cited the growing use of computer technology and supported its integration into the classroom "wherever feasible."[33] Finally, the committee recommended that a separate group be formed to assess the strengths and needs of the English as a Second Language program, which had grown somewhat haphazardly in response to the increasing numbers of international students on campus—in large measure their recruitment a reaction to low domestic numbers as opposed to intentional planning for a global residential community.

Nearly half the report concentrated on students' out-of-classroom lives. Contrary to a growing faculty perception that students were stretched too thinly in their extracurricular commitments, the committee concluded that there was no action needed "to remedy overcommitment."[34] Those few students who took on too much, either academically or in their out-of-class pursuits, would profit by better advising, not broadly restrictive school policy. In addition to greater student supervision on the part of individual advisors, the report called for increased involvement by the faculty who advised student activities, as weekend chaperones encouraging attendance at area cultural events, at sit-down dinners, and as mentors helping students run the multiple clubs and organizations on campus. The faculty did not react well to some of these recommendations, particularly the additional community dinners and two proposed all-school community service days that cut into precious class time. For her part, Robertson vetoed committee recommendations that faculty be paid for more time-consuming extracurricular assignments (such as coaching or advising a student publication) and that the school hire class deans to monitor student advising and academic scheduling by grade level.

In general, the principal was dissatisfied with the report. It was not the imaginative, groundbreaking wholesale revision of the curriculum that she had envisioned. Phil Deely had waited too long before making any bold moves, but Robertson had perhaps moved too quickly and decisively to change a curriculum that was not even a decade old. Under Easterling's leadership, the faculty believed they had modified the *1984 Curriculum* to fit the needs of the student body quite well. Asking for a review before she had experienced the curriculum in operation for a full year felt dismissive. However, undaunted by this setback and determined to make changes, she pushed for two specific curricular modifications: the addition of chemistry and English III as required courses for all students. After a series of heated faculty meetings, both proposals passed in 1992.

The changes did not make the students happy. As they had in 1984, they protested the restriction on individual choice created by the new requirements. *CLOCK* editorialized that requiring "diehard" juniors to take English III instead of the electives in writing and literature that were historically favorite courses was "needless" and "disappointing and unnecessary."[35] As she would do often during her administration, Robertson met directly with the students in an open forum to let them air their questions. The result was mixed with some students applauding her because "she made the effort" and others distrustful of "elegant speech skills" that they believed she used "to circle the topic many times."[36] As for the chemistry requirement, students protested this as well, but they were more concerned about the gap between rhetoric and reality in the makeup of the science department. When a popular female science teacher resigned and was replaced by a man, they pointed out that administrators "constantly speak of equality in science and mathematics," and a science department with only one woman in it was a "contradiction of our beliefs."[37]

Students might be unhappy, but Robertson firmly believed the school was on the right track. She reported to the board of trustees that in her view, the focus had changed for the better. The school in the past had "concentrated more on the weaker student, leaving the stronger student to fend for herself," and the new requirements ensured that the school would "focus equally on the stronger student."[38] Robertson hoped to attract the type of student found in the honors track at top suburban high schools, in short, the type of students she had recruited for the honors program at SMU. To that end, restrictions on student choice in the curriculum were coupled with increasing rules in the dormitory and a change in the office of the dean of students when Judy Bridges returned to serving as athletic director in the fall of 1992 and was replaced by veteran Spanish instructor Marilyn Hunter. A student sit-in the day before semester exams in February 1993 and the publication of an underground newspaper, the *Alarm Clock,* were manifestations of student unrest. For Robertson, the sit-in and other student uneasiness could be explained as a result of "weaker students experiencing a sense of anxiety and mistrust"[39] in reaction to her emphasis on strengthening the curriculum and tightening behavioral expectations.

The continuing admissions challenge was at the center of the dispute between the administration and students. Robertson believed that a more rigorous curriculum would attract greater numbers of academically able students. In contrast, Easterling and many of the faculty believed that the curriculum had to serve the students who had historically been attracted to the school and were actually enrolled in the early 1990s—a group representing a wide range of talents and abilities. Bolstering this view was a report from Director of Admissions Mary Jo Driscoll, who described disheartening findings from the Coalition of Girls' Boarding Schools (CGBS). As a group, these schools were "battling the perception that girls' schools are less challenging." The perception was clearly—and unfortunately—backed by statistics: at coeducational schools, "the SSAT averages were 20 points higher than at girls' schools."[40] The CGBS had surveyed the parents who had inquired about a girls' boarding school for their daughters and found that less than half of these parents "rank their daughters in the top 10% of their class." Thus, concluded Driscoll, to meet enrollment goals, "we must continue to recruit girls of lower ability [when] we want to be in a position to reject the girls who are accepted by the [less selective girls' schools] of the world."[41]

Robertson and the board, particularly those board members with marketing experience, refused to accept this conclusion. Keven Bellows urged the board to hire a marketer with whom she had worked in conjunction with Girls Inc., a national advocacy organization for girls with a history stretching back to 1864. Bellows recommended Glenda Ruby of Glenda Ruby Associates in Manhattan, who proposed a bold national advertising campaign that she promised would transform the market position for Emma Willard and, by inference, girls' schools in general. It was crucial, she told the trustees, that the school make a positive case for single-sex education for girls. She argued that the primary target for this argument should be fathers, and to that end, she urged the publication of "position statements" on the op-ed pages of the *New York Times* and *Wall Street Journal*. For $120,000 in 1991–92, the school could buy three such advertisements in each of the two national newspapers plus a few additional ads in "spot markets," cities and suburbs where the demographics showed households with high incomes and preteen girls. For Emma Willard, which had long shared the reluctance to advertise prevalent among girls' boarding schools, the decision to accept Ruby's recommendation was breathtakingly bold. Convinced that audacious action was called for, Robertson led them all the way.

Ruby created three statements for 1991–92. With Robertson's consent, and aware of the growing educational conversation about the limitations of coeducation for young women, Ruby fashioned a particularly aggressive position statement for the first run. Male prep school alumni and administrators all over the country nearly choked on their coffee when they opened their copies of the *Times* and the *WSJ* on the mornings of September 26 and 27, 1991. Staring out at them from the op-ed pages was a confident young woman under the bold banner: "Why the St. Grottlesex education you enjoyed might not be the best for your daughter." The accompanying copy picked up the American Association of University Women (AAUW) theme that gender bias hurts girls' self-esteem and suggested bluntly, "even when girls do achieve, they feel their achievement is an anomaly." The next two ads did not strike at coeducational schools quite as directly, but they still made a strong case for girls' boarding schools. The second ad advised parents: "How to Make Certain Your Daughter Connects with the Most Important Person She'll Ever Know. Herself." The statement asserted that coeducation perpetuated sexual stereotyping and consequently concluded that a girls' school was a far better environment for young women to maximize their strengths and talents. The third ad pushed the idea that the students who attended girls' schools were strong, independent young women: "Stars. Scholars. Presidents. Editors. Champions. Our girls are all these things. And will be." The headline was underlined by the message, "Every day we remind them of the marvelous limitless possibilities the world presents an educated young woman. And vice versa."

Emma Willard alumnae response was overwhelmingly positive. A typical response came from Madeleine Weigel Ludlow '72. She wrote, "I was at my desk reading the *Wall Street Journal* when I saw the 'Grottlesex' headline and thought, 'This is fantastic! This is so exciting!' Then when I saw it was *my* school, I was just beside myself."[42] In the long run, the ad campaign probably had less impact on admissions than it did on alumnae pride (and consequent financial support) and Emma Willard's visibility in the independent school world. To assuage nervous trustees (a few of whom had gone to St. Grottlesex schools and more who had relatives connected with those institutions), Robertson pointed out the ads' effectiveness, at least in terms of publicity. By the beginning of 1992, she reported that she had "met with Ellen Goodman, columnist with the *Boston Globe*, and the school has been approached by "Sixty Minutes," Jane Pauley, *Town and Country*, and *Working Woman*."[43]

These advertisements also created a stir in the independent world, particularly among girls' schools who generally believed that the entire group of schools benefited from the publicity. Margaret Bonz, head of the Ethel Walker School, wrote Robertson that among her alumnae, "everyone was abuzz about your ad," and added, "Friends at Miss Porter's and Madeira say the same."[44] Single-sex education for girls was gaining new visibility and more positive press in general, and the Emma Willard campaign fueled this development. A new organization, the National Coalition of Girls' Schools, had formed in 1991 to provide mutual support for one another and general advocacy for girls' schools. Not surprisingly, there was widespread appreciation for the ad campaign among this group. The ads also dovetailed nicely with groundbreaking research published by the AAUW in the spring of 1991. This landmark work, "Shortchanging Girls, Shortchanging America," gave new support to the argument that single-sex education for girls was both positive and valuable. The AAUW study was based on a national survey that assessed "self-esteem, educational experiences, interest in mathematics and science, and career aspirations of girls and boys ages 9–15."[45] Carol Gilligan, along with Janie Victoria Ward, one of the team of Dodge Study researchers, advised the project that concluded gender bias against girls permeated the nation's schools and limited young women's aspirations in significant harmful ways.

The one group (other than educators at coeducational schools) who questioned the advertisements was the student body. One commented that the *Alarm Clock* was in part a response to "over emphasis on advertising."[46] In response to the ads, students protested that the admissions office "puts pictures of certain types of girls in ads and promotional materials," and that "they are choosing to portray Emma Willard students the way the admissions office wants them seen."[47] Student consternation was particularly directed at the administration's use of a single image to complement each ad. Describing the choice of subject as a "marketing ploy," students objected to photographs that "unfairly project a poster girl who does not exist [and] does not represent the majority of girls here."[48]

The position statements continued to run throughout the 1990s, and, when Ruby's contract ended, admissions personnel at the school wrote a couple of new ones that imitated her style. Meanwhile, there was change in the admissions office. In 1993 Driscoll resigned, and a new director of admissions took over in the spring of 1994. William Dennett, who had had a long and respected career in college admissions, most recently as the dean of admissions at Denison University, succeeded her. However, in spite of position statements, curricular adjustments, and personnel changes, admissions remained a stubborn challenge. Fortunately, however, the trend was upward. September 1991 proved to be the low point. In 1992 there was an increase of seventeen boarders, the biggest positive jump since 1978. Day student enrollment also increased, topping a hundred throughout most of the decade of the 1990s. The total number of students rose slowly, finally hitting three hundred in the early years of the twenty-first century.

The continuing struggle to meet admissions goals of course had a direct impact on the budget. In November 1990, board president Jameson Baxter reviewed the fiscal situation for the board. The 1990–91 budget reflected a $200,000 deficit for the year, and a similar deficit was anticipated for the following year. Baxter counseled fiscal prudence, warning her fellow trustees that they needed "to insure that we do not institutionalize our pattern of deficit spending." She insisted, "We must always know that the total expenses which we expect to incur can be covered by reasonable revenues"[49] and reminded them that the strategic plan they had agreed to in 1988 called for fiscal balance by 1993–94. The endowment in 1990 was nearly $21 million and had more than doubled during the decade of the 1980s because of the strong market growth. Baxter was a gifted financier, a shrewd manager who had served on numerous for-profit and not-for-profit boards of trustees. From 1989 to 1994, she simultaneously served as the chair of the board of Mount Holyoke College, her second alma mater. She had broken a number of gender barriers in the world of investment banking and would continue to do so well into the twenty-first century. Her financial acumen was widely respected. In 1990, as she outlined the fiscal discipline she believed the school needed to follow, she made one uncharacteristically erroneous prediction. She cautioned the board that they could not expect the market gains of the 1980s to be "replicated in the 1990s." In fact, the endowment would double in the five years between 1992 and 1997 in large part because of the boom in technology stocks. At the end of the decade the endowment was valued at $61 million.

The increases in the endowment cushioned tuition shortfalls, but the board and the administration were concerned about launching a capital campaign without being able to show a balanced spreadsheet to prospective donors. The strong endowment performance, however, allowed the school to cover extraordinary expenses such as the advertising campaign and major deferred maintenance projects outside the operating budget, making balance—at least on paper—more achievable. In addition, Robertson insisted that her senior administrators budget stringently, and, along with her business manager, Paul Campbell, she created operating budget scenarios that varied according to the success with which tuition goals were met. Budgeting was increasingly tied to educational policy decisions. For example, she froze the salary pool in the winter of 1993[50] until all vacant positions had been filled to guarantee that the dollars she needed to recruit experienced new faculty would be there throughout the hiring season. This ensured flexibility and guaranteed that departments would not be forced by finances to settle for younger inexperienced teachers. An academically sound policy, it rankled somewhat among current faculty, who were used to having their raises set prior to hiring new people.

Spurred on by budget realities and facilities needs, Robertson moved just as quickly on fund-raising as she had on curriculum. At her second board meeting, she laid out the skeleton for an aggressive capital campaign. She hoped to raise $4 million for faculty salaries and a like amount for scholarships. For a gift of $500,000, a donor could endow a faculty chair, for $250,000, a scholarship. For $7 million a modern addition to the science building could be added—and its maintenance endowed. A new swimming pool, attached to the Mott Gymnasium, was projected to cost $5 million to build and endow, and the completion of the dormitory renovations, including the construction of a faculty apartment in the "tower rooms" in Sage, would total $1.5 million.

Robertson's initial fund-raising goals complemented her focus on making the curriculum mirror the honors courses at top public high schools. She hoped to raise faculty salaries to be able to recruit the best possible teachers and to increase the financial aid budget and thus the academic qualifications of the student body. These, of course, were classic fund-raising goals at Emma Willard. Added to them was her desire not only to repair and renovate the existing buildings, but to build new ones, particularly for science, athletics, and the performing arts. Science and sports facilities were typically better at coeducational schools with which the school hoped to compete more effectively for top students. She also hoped to tackle all of the deferred maintenance identified in the 1989 "Major Maintenance Matrix," a multimillion-dollar master plan identifying campus facilities needs from roofing to outdated mechanical and plumbing systems, from leaded windows to classroom furniture. The renovations in the dormitories were well underway, funded by a half million dollars raised in Bob Parker's memory and an additional amount from the segregated deferred maintenance funds approved by the board. The architect of the dormitory master plan was Graham Williams, whose courtly, gentle manner matched his loyalty to the institution. He approached any changes in the original buildings with caution, viewing the historic architecture as "a sacred trust."[51]

Robertson immediately proved to be an extraordinarily effective fund-raiser who connected well with alumnae both in person and through the countless handwritten notes she penned to them. Alumnae responded positively to her enthusiastic claims for their school. She invariably expressed sorrow at not being an alumna herself, and she shared her pride in her daughter, Alayne, who entered the school as a freshman in 1992. After all, Robertson explained to groups of admiring graduates, "If you've been to Emma Willard, you've been to the mountain, and it is yours."[52] In her first year, the annual fund exceeded its goal, and by 1993–94, the fund topped $1 million, the first girls' boarding school to accomplish this goal. By 1993–94, Jean Grimmer, an experienced fund-raiser, had taken over the reins of the development office. Grimmer, who had become director of development in the spring of 1992,[53] coordinated the campaign. Victoria Thompson Winterer '61 had agreed to chair the effort. In addition to pushing initiatives like the inclusion of the annual fund in the capital campaign, Grimmer, working with Winterer, eventually pushed the board to raise the goal of the campaign to $30 million. Grimmer also oversaw the revitalization of the alumnae association and the shift in reunions from May to June, a move calculated to bring more alumnae back to campus.

By the summer of 1993, the silent phase of the campaign had ended, the prospectus had been written, and the initial goal had been set at $22 million. On November 12, 1993, hundreds of alumnae and friends of the school gathered at the Waldorf-Astoria for the kickoff dinner for the *Campaign for Emma Willard*. Jane Fonda, the main speaker, whipped up the crowd by appealing to the special legacy she shared with the women gathered before her. Proudly she announced, "We had backbone, and boy can you see it in this room tonight."[54] The goals for the campaign included $4.2 million for an addition to Weaver, $2.5 million for dormitory renovations, $5 million for a gymnasium addition that would include a competition-size pool, $4.5 million for faculty salaries, and $4 million for financial aid. For the first time, the capital campaign contained two very important elements. The science, dormitory, and pool projects each included millions of dollars as endowment for the future needs of the building. Secondly, the overall goal would "count" all Annual Fund dollars raised between 1992 and the end of the campaign, an amount estimated to be nearly $4 million of the $22 million total.

The first really big boost for the *Campaign for Emma Willard* came in 1994 when Helen Snell Cheel '23 pledged $3 million for the new swimming pool. Almost simultaneously, Irene Mennen Hunter '35, along with her husband and children,[55] agreed to fund a new wing of the science center. The construction of the new science center gave Robertson an opportunity to revolutionize at least one segment of the curriculum. Piggybacking on the AAUW conclusion that girls are most often shortchanged in mathematics and science courses, she determined that the Hunter Science Center would "change the paradigm for science education" through the design of its classrooms and through the pedagogical techniques employed in those classrooms. Architects Billie Tsien and Tod Williams used Robertson's ideas to create a science building that featured fractal towers that "eliminated the distinction between lectures and laboratories." The new building was fully computerized, with each classroom equipped with student computer stations for computer-based laboratory work. To connect Hunter and the older classrooms in Slocum and the library to the Internet, the school built a campus network of fiberoptic cabling at the same time Hunter was being constructed; Robertson's husband, Serge Kappler, supervised this technology work. The Internet was intended to be used as a research tool, something that was "being done nowhere else [in the country] at the secondary level." Taking as a given that the twenty-first century would see an explosion in technology that would require girls as well as boys to be familiar with computer science, Robertson claimed that Hunter would "demystify" the Internet for girls and "increase their comfort level with computers."[56]

In October 1995, parents were invited to visit the school, as had been traditional for many years. This year was special, however, because they would attend the groundbreaking for the Hunter Science Center. Students objected to the fact that they were required to stay through the ceremony on Saturday morning, even if their parents were not there. (A two-day Long Weekend had been attached to the occasion, and students understandably wanted to maximize their time off campus.) Once again, *CLOCK* was quick to identify the gap between administrative rhetoric and student reality. First of all, having a Tuesday off to substitute for a Saturday "was just not the same." Second, they pointed out, construction on the site had already begun, so that "save for ideology, the groundbreaking is bogus."[57] For the most part, however, faculty, trustees, and parents were delighted with the event and the promise for an upgraded science education represented in the new building.

Hunter Science Center opened in the fall of 1996, and in May 1997, the whole school gathered for *Curiosity and Confidence: Girls Claiming Science*. Sara Lee Lubin Schupf '58 chaired the two-day symposium that featured Jane Fonda as a keynoter, many alumnae scientists from the '50s to the '80s, Maxine Singer from the Carnegie Institute, and the president of Radcliffe College. Over 250 science educators attended the event, along with the entire faculty and student body. The symposium met with widespread student enthusiasm even though it required attendance at lectures on a Saturday. It was, wrote one, "true to the school's history of advancement of women's education."[58] Students were receptive to the new science building, but they were even more excited about another construction project that kicked off two days after the symposium. On Monday, May 19, Helen Cheel, driven in a golf-cart-turned-yacht, led the entire student body to the site of the groundbreaking for the Cheel Aquatics Center, scheduled to open in the fall of 1998.

The board of trustees had begun proceedings for a bond issue to raise money for the pool when the nonagenarian Cheel accelerated the payment of her pledge. The spectacular pool was designed by Williams and Tsien, the same architects responsible for the science center. Architect and trustee Erica Ling '75 praised it as "a truly handsome and memorable space and quite intimate for such a big building."[59] Planned for high school competition, it would enable the school to field another varsity team in addition to providing space for recreation and exercise. Interest in interscholastic competition had grown steadily throughout the 1980s. For years the admissions office had cited the lack of competitive sports in general and of a swimming pool in particular as reasons Emma Willard often lost top candidates to coeducational schools. These schools, especially the former boys' schools, historically had better athletic facilities. In 1990, in a move calculated to strengthen competition, the school had petitioned to join the Colonial Council and was accepted. When school opened on September 15, 1991, the athletes had already been back for two weeks of the first preseason athletic tryouts and conditioning. It was immediately

debatable whether or not membership in the highly competitive Colonial Council League was a boon to students. The league schedule
meant many more contests per team, and faculty questioned the toll
this was taking on students whose exhaustion was obvious in class and
who were clearly suffering an increased number of injuries. The more
intense competition also meant cutting more girls from team rosters,
which caused hurt feelings at a school where everybody had once had
a chance to play. Even with leaner, more competitive teams, Emma
Willard lost far more games than it won, causing widespread student
discouragement about the school's place in league standings. To some
faculty, the admissions effort, with the compliance of the principal,
was remaking the school for a marketing image, rather than marketing the school. In 1991 Robertson cautioned the trustees that there
was "a profound difference between a corporation and an educational
institution,"[60] and yet, for much of her tenure, students and faculty
challenged the marketing techniques she employed as being at odds
with "internal reality."[61]

In the first six months of 1997, the *Campaign for Emma Willard*
came to a triumphant conclusion, surpassing the $30 million mark by
June 30. At the same time, the school prepared for its ten-year evaluation. As was customary, the administration, faculty, and board of
trustees reaffirmed the school's mission statement. Adhering to Emma
Hart Willard's vision, the mission restated her educational values
within the context of the waning twentieth century:

> Cognizant of the challenges facing young women in the world,
> Emma Willard School is first and foremost committed to developing
> in each student the habits of an intellectual life that will provide her
> with the competence and courage to shape that world. It offers an en-
> vironment where active, participative learning balances individual
> achievement with team work; it promotes the development of lead-
> ership, responsibility, and cooperation, and it directs each student
> to develop personal values and ethics that will endure in an increas-
> ingly complex global society. It combines personal achievement with
> service to others, both within and beyond our community. . . And
> in the firm belief that spiritual, emotional, and intellectual growth
> and physical well-being are ever interdependent, the School seeks to
> instill life-long habits of physical health in all its students.

> In the tradition of Emma Hart Willard, the School is committed
> to remaining a single-gender, primarily residential high school. . . .
> Today, we celebrate the contributions of women and value the female
> perspective in human affairs.[62]

"The female perspective" was not always embraced by the students. An outspoken member of the class of 1995 complained in *CLOCK* that the emphasis on women writers in the English curriculum went too far. After all, she asserted, "Most of the 'classics' of Western . . . literature were written by men, and though this statement may induce apoplexy in some, it's true."[63] Two years later, one of her classmates, forced to read "some dumb feminist book in my political science class" at Brown University, wrote to a former faculty member, "I thought I got my fill of that junk at Emma Willard."[64] Student disdain aside, the trustees, the administration, and the majority of the faculty supported the mission statement including its emphasis on the "female perspective." At the same time, the board of trustees developed a strategic plan to guide the school into the twenty-first century. In spite of the success of the capital campaign, the strong growth in the endowment, the addition of new facilities for science and athletics, the improved admissions outlook, and the increased visibility of the school and girls' education, the board was unwilling to rest. As board chair Linda Glazer Toohey '66 explained to her fellow alumnae, "For other schools, these basics would be sufficient conditions for success. For your school, they are only necessary conditions. Emma Willard has never settled for basics."[65]

By the spring of 1998, Robin Robertson could look back at nearly a decade of dynamic change at the school. She was not only responsible for successful fund-raising, but in the course of the campaign, she was responsible for urging the board to establish a number of awards that would become annual traditions at the school. Among these were the Clementine Miller Tangeman Award, given to individuals "for service to their communities and Emma Willard"; the John Willard Award, designed to reward men whose service to Emma Willard was outstanding; the Madelyn Glazer and Linda Glazer Toohey Award for Faculty Excellence; and the Jameson A. Baxter Award for the senior whose career at Emma Willard reflected Baxter's commitment to taking responsibility for one's own education. The first winners of the adult awards were Vicky Winterer for her work on the campaign, Donald Buttenheim for his service to the board as trustee and fundraiser, and Kathleen McNamara, an English teacher who modeled excellence in her classrooms, her advising, her work in the dormitories, and her deft supervision of *CLOCK*. Robertson also encouraged the board to name William Dietel the first principal emeritus in recognition of his continuing interest in and active campaigning on behalf of the school. In turn, the trustees had officially changed Robertson's title to head of school as a reflection that her role in external relations went far beyond that of principal, a title that had traditionally meant first among the faculty.

In 1998 Jack Easterling decided to return to the classroom, and mathematics instructor Nathaniel Conard replaced him as academic dean. In 1997 Hunter had returned to teaching Spanish full time, and Judy Bridges had once more assumed the office of dean of students. Jean Grimmer had retired at the end of the campaign. Not only had Robertson built and maintained a strong administrative team, but she had assisted in the successful transition in board leadership when Linda Toohey replaced Jameson Baxter as board chair in 1994. Robertson had also provided leadership for Troy. The city had not shared the school's prosperity, but Robertson had worked with the Troy Redevelopment Corporation, which consisted of Troy's non-tax-paying not-for-profits that were attempting through voluntary contributions to help relieve the city's financial distress.

At the board meeting in February 1998, the development committee of the board presented a draft of a plan for the next campaign that would include raising money to repair the deteriorating leaded-pane windows, a technology endowment, and a performing arts center. In what was perhaps an early signal of the direction in her thinking, Robertson told the board of her "reluctance to build a performing arts center" and urged them "to make the most efficient use of the School's present facilities before contemplating adding additional square footage."[66] In the fall, when an opportunity arose for her to head coeducational Milton Academy, she took it. In February 1999, as the second semester got underway, she announced her departure to the student body, telling them that she "finished a major piece of work" and that it was "time for change."[67]

As she left the school, the board of trustees, alumnae, and faculty donated money to outfit a laboratory in the new science center in Robertson's honor. Her years of service were celebrated as "a dynamic era in the life of an extraordinary school."[68] She had raised "the awareness of Emma Willard in the national arena" and had created an "expanded and cleaner physical profile"[69] for the campus. Cheel Aquatics Center and Hunter Science Center stood on either side of the campus, monuments to her efforts. She had drawn hundreds of alumnae back to campus and redefined alumnae activities. Most of her best work had involved outreach. Robertson had worked indefatigably to sell the idea of Emma Willard to alumnae and other donors. The results were new facilities, new scholarships, and campus-wide technology.

Much remained to be done, however, and the dawning of the new century afforded an ideal moment for change and a propitious time for the school to embrace both challenge and opportunity. Board president Linda Toohey announced to the community that the trustees had decided to hire an interim head, launching a national search for Robertson's successor to take office on July 1, 2000. A handful of male former heads of coeducational schools visited the campus to interview for the job. In addition, one former female head of school, with extensive experience in the administration of girls' schools, was considered. The unanimous favorite of the faculty, students, and staff who met her, Trudy E. Hall was appointed interim head of school for the 1999–2000 academic year.

Charting the Way for Others to Follow

IN THE SPRING OF 1999, signs of prosperity abounded on Mount Ida. A multimillion-dollar bequest from the estate of Louise Lueder '31 meant that the school could begin seriously planning for the long, painstaking process of restoring the historic leaded-glass windows on the three original buildings and Kellas, a project that would not only improve the campus aesthetically but would also ensure greater energy conservation.[1] At $63 million, the endowment was larger than that at any other girls' boarding school. The faculty was energized by the prospect of new leadership, and the students had enthusiastically participated in the search for a new dean of students, slated to take office at the same time as the interim head. In his second year as academic dean, Nat Conard had "built a strong base of support with the faculty and [had] the confidence of the students."[2] Retention was high, a fact attributed by Robin Robertson to Judy Bridges, who had served yet another stint as dean of students but was returning to full-time athletic director in the fall. Admissions was on target to continue the upward trend of the prior three years. The school would open in September with 178 boarders, the largest residential population since 1987.

In addition, the combination of Serge Kappler's expertise and Helen Cheel's philanthropy meant that the campus boasted state-of-the-art technology on the eve of the new century. Fiberoptic cabling ran throughout the academic buildings, every teacher had been issued a personal computer, administrative functions were fast becoming automated, the school had an address on the Internet, and the library was well on its way to complete automation. When school ended in June, crews swarmed the dormitories, installing the cables necessary to provide every room with a telephone—to the amazement of even the youngest alumnae. Conard kept a prudent eye on academic technology, mindful of the siren call of gadgetry that could cost thousands and be outmoded in a matter of months. At the height of the enthusiasm for more and better technology, he cautioned the board that the "investment in computers must be mission-driven, not acquisition-driven."[3]

As school began in September, it seemed likely that Trudy Hall's interim year would contain few surprises. The search for a permanent head was underway, and she assured the senior administrative team that she would pursue the conventional course of interim heads: Hers would be a caretaker year, not a year for policy initiatives or change. The new dean of students was young and, in sharp contrast to Hall, had had no experience in girls' schools. The acting director of development was also young and relatively inexperienced. Consequently, much of the interim head's time in her first few months was consumed with mentoring her younger administrative colleagues. Fortunately, she could rely on Nat Conard, who had the academic program firmly in hand and was a particularly able, efficient, and popular administrator. Students were especially pleased by his rearrangement of faculty assignments and schedules in the Science Department, a reorganization that allowed for greater elective work in that area.

During the interview process, Hall had been told that a major problem at the school was "an unresponsive administration,"[4] and as a result, she consciously reached out to the faculty and the students. On a Friday in mid-October, she hosted an impromptu wine and cheese gathering for the adults in the community. She also used the "Faculty Column" in *CLOCK* to encourage the student body to join with her to "talk about the real issues of culture, ethics, responsibility and morality," assuring them that she wanted to hear "student voices."[5] Mark Doty, an acclaimed poet, was the first all-school speaker of the year and charmed faculty and students alike with his verse, his humor, and his warmth. Students also welcomed a new Faculty-Student Interaction Committee, an arm of School Council formed to address communication issues. Four teaching interns, three of whom were made possible by endowed gifts solicited in the *Campaign for Emma Willard*,[6] enlivened the playing fields, dormitories, and classrooms.

By mid-fall, as the search committee brought candidates through the school, it became increasingly clear to both the faculty and the trustees that the interim head was a significantly stronger candidate than any of the other contenders they had interviewed. By early December, the search committee had unanimously concluded that Trudy Hall should be the sixteenth head of Emma Willard. On December 14, her appointment, "effective immediately," was announced to the student body by board president Linda Toohey. Alumnae Chapel rang with cheers and applause. Acknowledging the acclaim, Hall told the assembly that her appointment was evidence that "dreams do come true." She also highlighted the significance of the date, noting that taking office at the end of a century meant "connecting our legacy with our visionary future."[7] Because she had grown up in Inlet and High Falls, New York, and was a graduate of St. Lawrence University, her return to New York State was a homecoming. She had earned master's degrees at Harvard and Duke and had worked at an international school in Saudi Arabia and the coeducational Savannah Country Day School. However, most of her career had been spent in administration at girls' schools, including Culver Girls Academy, Stoneleigh-Burnham, and Miss Hall's School, where she had served as head for four years. Just prior to her interim year at Emma Willard, she was the associate head of Hutchison School, one of the largest girls' schools in the country.

Hall had little time to bask in the glow of her new office; almost immediately, the problem-solving and decision-making skills she had honed during her career were put to the test. A crisis emerged almost simultaneously with her appointment. For over five years, the Children's School had been losing enrollment, particularly in the elementary grades. The two directors following Marlisa Parker continued Parker's open admissions policy, a policy that Robertson did not like. To her, first come, first served meant that the school was in danger of acquiring a reputation for taking too many "special needs" children. As Teresa Snyder and her successor, Joy Irish, were fond of saying, early childhood educators view all small children as having special needs; some are just more obvious than others. Like Parker before them, both women were passionate about a philosophy of education that supported David Elkind's concerns in his book *The Hurried Child* about the price American schools, society—and children—were paying for pushing too hard. Rather than focus on reading scores and scales of numerical mastery, Snyder and Irish focused on the Children's School motto: "Children's work is children's play."

In 1991, a group of Children's School parents, dismayed that Emma Willard would not expand the elementary program past third grade, had founded a new school, the Robert C. Parker School. In honoring Emma Willard's former principal, they recognized his support of the Children's School as "a learning environment where children developed mutual respect, a love of learning, and an expectation that learning is exciting, interesting, and fun."[8] In 1997 the Parker School added lower grades, with the eventual goal of enrolling students in grades pre-K to 8. This decision had an immediate impact on enrollment at the Children's School. Parents chose Parker because their children could remain at the same school for all of elementary and middle school and were not forced to change schools after third grade. By 1997–98, the enrollment at the Children's School, which had topped 225 students in 1990, had dropped to 158, with most of the loss in the elementary grades. At the same time, however, the school had become more integrally bound with the "big school." The third graders had an annual role in Revels, and girls at the high school who had attended the Children's School viewed themselves as "real diehards." Four members of the class of 2000, anticipating their senior roles in Revels, reminded *CLOCK* readers that this would be their second performance; dancing as third graders had been their first.[9]

The loss of income from underenrollment understandably disturbed the trustees, at least some of whom did not want the high school to cover shortfalls in lower school tuition. Robertson took them on; no small part of her objection to the Children's School admissions policy had been her commitment to seeing the two schools as one, and the variation in admissions policies between the high school and lower school seemed wrong to her. She insisted that the board cover the shortfall, arguing, "If the School regards the Children's School as a divisional program within the larger school in times of plenty, it should do so in difficult times as well."[10] The board agreed but also decided to commission an independent audit of the status of the Children's School and the advisability of continuing it. Privately, Robertson and some trustees met with administrators at the neighboring Doane-Stuart School to see if there might be some sort of bridge between the third grade at the Children's School and the fourth grade at Doane-Stuart.

A team from Independent School Management (ISM) delivered their report in time for the February 1998 board meeting. They concluded that the Children's School faced stiff competition in the Capital District and that without significant renovations to Wellington-Lay and Cluett, it would lose out to Parker and other schools in the quest to enroll first through third graders. They advised the board that it would be "prudent to concentrate on the School's mission as a primarily residential high school for girls."[11] The board voted to close grades 1 to 3, a decision that cost $175,000. The school would remain open, but only for children ages three to five, just as it had been when it started in 1972. A group of former Children's School parents and faculty immediately laid plans for opening a new school just a few blocks from the campus; they named it for Susan Odell Taylor, a beloved Children's School teacher who had died in 1997.

In light of the ISM recommendation to concentrate on the mission of the high school, in the fall of 1998, Robertson asked the board to reaffirm the existence of a preschool program on the campus. She found justification for the school in the fact that as "a woman's institution," Emma Willard could provide a service to "dual-income families and single working women." This fact, she maintained, made the preschool program "most assuredly compatible with the mission of the high school."[12] Furthermore, for 1999–2000, she decided to enhance the early childhood program by combining the faculty on-campus daycare program with the preschool program. The daycare could then expand to include children whose parents were not on the faculty. The combined programs had an enrollment goal of fewer than 90 children for September 1999.

As a consequence, when Trudy Hall assumed the headship, the Children's School had been transformed from an early childhood program to a relatively small infant and toddler program. Unfortunately, under New York State law, infant programs were regulated much differently from elementary schools. At some point in the late fall, an anonymous person tipped off the state that Emma Willard School was running an unauthorized, unlicensed infant daycare program—and the state responded by ordering that the school close the program immediately. When she should have been enjoying her first Revels and looking forward to a winter break, Hall—along with board president Linda Toohey and Susan Dake, the trustee chairing the committee with oversight for the Children's School—were forced to meet with frantic parents, many of whom were Emma Willard faculty and staff members, arbitrary state officials, curious members of the local press, and panicky Children's School teachers. Often accompanied by Toohey or Dake, Hall met with every affected constituency and worked long hours throughout the winter holiday to help families of displaced children find quality daycare programs before school resumed in January. In the end, the fiasco positively showcased the organizational talents and administrative skills of the new head.

Not only her skills but also her style were immediately apparent as the second semester began with her firmly in the head's role. Although initially planned as a May event, Hall's formal installation was postponed until fall to accommodate her wish that it be part of a bigger occasion—a symposium on women's leadership. On October 5, 2000, "Values and Vision" brought together students, alumnae, the faculty, and women leaders from the fields of higher education, science, medicine, the arts, athletics, religion, business, finance, government, law, technology, and volunteerism for a discussion of women's leadership and its implications for the new century. Television journalist Linda Ellerbee was the keynoter, speaking with humor and authenticity on feminism and the rules for survival in a changing world. "Think tank" panels invited the audience to participate in conversations about women's leadership in a variety of fields.

The day culminated with Hall's formal installation, which took place downtown at the historic Troy Music Hall. Welcomed by Evette Stair '01 on behalf of the student body and Jack Easterling on behalf of the faculty, she accepted the mace of office from James Morley, who had succeeded Linda Toohey as president of the board of trustees in July. He pointed to the day's symposium as emblematic of Hall's leadership style, one that "brings everyone into the process of defining priorities and executing plans."[13] For her part, Hall accepted her new office by pledging her allegiance to the historic vision of Emma Hart Willard. She informed her audience that they would not be hearing her vision for the school because "After 186 years, Emma Willard's vision needs no improvement or alteration." Her charge, she explained, was "to lead the founder's school."[14] She did, however, indicate the specific directions in which she hoped to lead the institution: a comprehensive curriculum review that would bring the academic and residential sides of the school together in unprecedented ways and a renewed effort to preserve the historic buildings on the campus. In a foreshadowing of the ambitious fund-raising campaign that would soon begin, she announced a million-dollar challenge gift from Susan Hunter '68, a gift that would ensure Emma Willard was on the "leading edge of technology education."[15]

The curriculum review Hall sought was launched in February with Nat Conard and Kathleen McNamara co-chairing the effort. An assessment of student attitudes conducted in the spring of 2000 had found that students were extremely satisfied with their academic life but very dissatisfied with the social aspects of their lives. In addition, the residential program needed restructuring so that the adult-student interaction in the dormitories could match the quality of the teacher-student interaction in the classrooms. The windows project had begun, but restoring the windows was just one part of physical campus needs. The masonry, the plumbing, and the heating and electrical systems all needed attention.

These initiatives would cost money, and it was apparent that Hall would need to lead a major capital campaign. She engaged the board and the faculty in a strategic planning process to assess the needs of the school and prioritize the goals for a capital campaign. She was assisted in these efforts by a new director of advancement, Larry Lichtenstein.

In May 2002, the board approved *The Plan for Emma Willard's Third Century,* a blueprint for an unprecedented $75 million capital campaign and for the school's future. Based on several principles, "A Tradition of Educational Excellence for Girls," "Leadership," "Academic Rigor," and "Curriculum," the plan had several goals:

> Emma Willard's curriculum will remain a standard for excellence and will model balance among
> humanities, the sciences, foreign languages, athletics, the arts, and technology.
> Emma Willard's library will be a vital learning resource at the heart of the academic enterprise.
> Emma Willard School will match its rigorous academic program with a student life experience of the highest quality.
> Emma Willard will strengthen and celebrate alumnae connections to the school and each other for the benefit of all.
> Emma Willard School will preserve its historic campus, renewing and adapting facilities to meet program needs.
> Emma Willard School will build financial strength commensurate with its needs and aspirations.

As the planning proceeded, however, the stock market presented a jarring challenge. The $63 million endowment slid downward in the years immediately following Hall's installation, a decline that Douglas Hart, the chair of the board investment committee, analyzed as "the worst three-year decline in the market since the 1940s."[16] Not until the fourth quarter of 2003 would the endowment return to $60 million and continue to grow. Undaunted, the school hired Sasaki Associates to analyze the current uses of space in the historic buildings and to propose renovations to the community spaces that would enable the architecture to assist in the goal of bringing the residential side of the school into harmony with the academic side. The adaptive reuse of the historic campus was the underlying goal for the new plans.

Fund-raising during Hall's tenure had gotten its start with the Hunter technology challenge, and in 2002 a gift from Sue Kruidenier Edwards '41 boosted the school's ability to expand the residential staff and enhance the programming in that area of school life. Edwards criticized her experience at Emma Willard in much the same way that the current students had recently done; she had been served extremely well academically, she recalled, but her social experiences had been limited at best and negative at worst. She was eager to correct this imbalance for the third-century generation, and her gift seeded a farsighted student activities program that would become a model for residential curricula among independent schools. At the same time, athletics, another important nonacademic side of student life, was enhanced by the renovation of the track. The facility was the gift of the Robison Foundation, two of whose directors were alumnae, Elissa Robison Prout '52 and Barbara Robison Stegmaier '41.

These gifts, although not part of an official capital campaign, were important to Hall and the development staff as they contemplated a major fund-raising effort. The biggest lift to those planning the campaign came from the Avenir Foundation, whose president is Alice Dodge Wallace '38. Conard had created a detailed analysis of the state of faculty compensation, demonstrating that Emma Willard's salaries fell well below the median for independent schools. Lichtenstein presented the statistics to the president of the Avenir Foundation, highlighting in particular the unfavorable contrast between faculty salaries at Emma Willard and those at coeducational schools such as Exeter, Andover, and Deerfield, which had formerly been all boys. Influenced by her father, a university administrator and physics professor, Wallace had long been committed to assisting those who chose an academic life over more lucrative professions. To that end, her first major gift to the school had been the establishment of the Avenir Scholarships, which provided financial assistance for the daughters of educators. In 2004, the Avenir Foundation established a $10M endowment to assist in the funding of faculty salaries and benefits, the largest single gift for this purpose ever received by a girls boarding school. In addition to the endowment an initial amount was provided to facilitate immediate implementation of the plan to increase faculty compensation. One fourth of the endowment was designated to endow two faculty chairs named in honor of her parents: the Homer L. Dodge Chair in Science and the Margaret Wing Dodge Chair in Literature. Unlike earlier instructorships, these two were fully funded at the point of inception.

An ambitious campaign seemed to be within reach, and the campaign planners were ready to reach out to all of the school's constituencies. Two alumnae, Ann Beach '76 and Diane Mercer '61, had agreed to co-chair the national fund-raising effort in its initial stage; in the public phase, Mercer's co-chair would be parent Nancy Alexander.[17] The endowment had recovered and had surpassed $70 million, the enrollment was the highest in twenty-three years, and, with Conard's announcement that he was leaving Emma Willard to head the Pingry School in New Jersey,[18] Hall had the opportunity to restructure the administration to position it for the work that would come with developing the programming made possible by the new resources. Christopher Kimberly, a young science teacher, was named director of faculty development, and Jack Easterling returned to the administration as dean of the faculty. Lisa Schmitt was added to the administration as interim dean of curriculum and design. Hall's goal was to "tie strategic initiatives with operating initiatives more logically."[19] For its part, the board had appointed a task force to identify trustee leadership. Morley, an expert in educational finance, had proven to be an indispensable sounding board for Hall in her first few years, but he was stepping down in July. The task force recommended that Mariana Leighton '55 succeed Morley. Leighton was an experienced educator who had headed the independent Calhoun School in Manhattan. She had served an earlier term as an alumna trustee in the 1980s and was well respected and well liked by veteran faculty and administrators. Tragically, her tenure as board chair would be cut short by her death in April 2008.

In the spring of 2005, however, as Leighton prepared to take on the board leadership, the trustees authorized the hiring of two architectural firms to carry out the construction of the new student life spaces that Sasaki Associates had envisioned after meeting with various school constituencies including the students and faculty. The trustees moved boldly ahead on the largest building project since the building of the Mount Ida campus between 1908 and 1910. In part they based their decision on the robust endowment, but they had another reason for their timing. On May 21, 2005, former trustee and magnanimous benefactor Helen Cheel had died. Over time her philanthropy had made it possible for the school to build the music wing and the aquatics center, renovate the day student center, wire the campus, and provide numerous scholarships. In the eighty-two years since her graduation, her support for Emma Willard never wavered. In paying tribute to Cheel, Linda Toohey focused on her faith in the generations of Emma students who had come after her: "Without even knowing you, Helen realized that in every class that came through this school, women of true substance and integrity could be fostered."[20] Helen Cheel's final gift to her alma mater was a bequest of $16.5 million, another unprecedented gift for a girls' boarding school. In February 2006, with the endowment clearing $100 million for the first time, the board voted to borrow $32 million through a bond issue to redesign the first floors of Sage and Kellas, refit the laundry as office space, turn Gorham House into a faculty residence and guesthouse, and create a new home for the head of school in Wellington-Lay.

"Re-imagining space" on the historic campus would not only cost millions of dollars, but it would also require careful orchestration of students and faculty as their multi-building home was renovated while they lived there. Eric Niles, who had served as dean of students since 2003, was charged with working as the liaison between the construction project and the campus, and Judy Bridges moved into the dean's office once again. Aware that her administration had become synonymous with change, Hall chose change as the topic for her opening convocation speech in 2006. "*Change*," she told the students, "whether it is used as a noun or verb . . . is impossible to utter . . . without provoking an emotional reaction." "This six-letter word," she continued, "can evoke tears, prompt sneers, instigate trouble, and induce high blood pressure."[21]

When the changes in the buildings were revealed to the students in May 2007, they evoked a most positive reaction. There was a new kitchen, a new dining room, a new student center, a new study space, and new offices for student services and admissions. Best of all, the new spaces were all located on the first floors of the two dormitory buildings. The goal of integrating social and academic spaces had been achieved in a way that architect and alumna Erica Ling dubbed "brilliant."[22] Over the course of the next year, a new dormitory, nicknamed the Bridges, would open in the old health center building and a new health and wellness center, named in honor of Keenan Kelsey '62, opened in Sage basement. Informal student spaces would be enhanced by the 2e-Café, named in honor of former board president Linda Toohey, her daughters, Megan and Elizabeth, and her mother, Madelyn Levitt Glazer. The former television room in Kellas Hall was remodeled as a meeting and dining space and named Wadsworth in honor of its donor, Michal Colby Wadsworth '65. In short, by 2007 the social spaces used most by students and faculty had been transformed.

Other changes were not as popular. Kimberly had instituted a new schedule in 2006–7. There was less free time for some students, and the lunch period was shortened significantly. Nevertheless, the new class timetable provided time for longer class blocks, a seminar program that addressed the developmental stages of students at each grade level, and a substantial block of time each week for student/faculty community service. The latter two programs were administrative responses to the faculty's development in 2003 of the "Sixteen Outcomes" they hoped for an Emma Willard education and the "Nineteen Standards of Faculty Excellence" agreed on in 2004. The curricular review had culminated in the identification of five core values for an Emma Willard education developed by the Curriculum Design Task Force in 2005.

By the fall of 2008, the new schedule had been refined, and students and faculty had adapted to the longer classes and new seminar and community service programs. Although major gifts had fueled a good part of the capital campaign, there were still more dollars to be raised to meet the $75 million goal. Dubbed "The Emma Willard Idea" in 2007, the campaign energized the entire alumnae body with its theme, "Empower a Girl, Transform the World." A symposium on "Women, Power, and Responsibility" brought home the theme as women who had made significant differences in the lives of others shared their stories with students, parents, and alumnae. From BBC world journalist Katty Kay to Christel DeHaan, founder of schools for disadvantaged children on four continents, to Ann Cotton, the entrepreneur behind CAMFED, the international campaign for female education, the panelists inspired their listeners and demonstrated the relevance of Emma Willard's vision in the twenty-first century.

Students resonated to the symposium and the themes of globalism and service. They had been stimulated by the community service program and a series of speakers who had come to the school. Faculty and students participated in Civitas Mosaic, a program to promote global citizenship. Over the next few years, Greg Mortenson, Nicholas Kristof, and Sheryl WuDunn challenged admiring crowds of students and alumnae to extend education to areas of the world where girls did not have schooling. School trips during spring break moved beyond language immersion to work in orphanages in Mexico and Ethiopia, and Habitat for Humanity projects in inner-city areas of the United States. The students heard from alumnae such as Neelam Mehta '93, whose ClickAid program provided used computers to children in areas where technology was lacking, and Elizabeth Colton '66, who developed the International Museum of Women, an online museum to "celebrate and advance the lives of women worldwide."[23] Generous donors enabled students from Afghanistan and countries created from the former Soviet Union to enroll at the school. In 2008 the Davis family, whose United World College Fund provided financial support for international students wishing to study in the United States, expanded the program to high school students. Thanks to Gale Lansing Davis '63, Emma Willard was the only girls' school included in the program; in September, the first Davis Scholars, girls from Vietnam, Croatia, Bolivia, and Botswana, enrolled.

Hand in hand with the commitment to globalism and service came a schoolwide dedication to sustainability and environmental conservation. Faculty and students embraced Fair Trade, trays were removed from the dining room, recycling became a watchword, and the director of dining services provided locally grown foods wherever possible. To make student philanthropy and outreach even more realistic, trustee Michal Wadsworth, along with her husband Jim, funded an extraordinary initiative. She provided a student group, called Phila, with substantial annual funding that was theirs to give away to the charity or charities of their choice. Students were and are trained to solicit and evaluate proposals, make site visits, and decide the final appropriations.

In 2008 Emma Willard was healthy and thriving. That October, when the bottom fell out of the world economy, the school felt its impact in a severely diminished endowment, although the trustees found solace in the investment committee's report that "Emma Willard is faring better than most schools in the economic downturn."[24] Nevertheless, the reduced income from the endowment necessitated some pruning of programs and personnel. Shortly after the crash, Hall reminded the board that the fiscal reality created by the economic crisis meant that the school must turn "a laser-like focus on the question of programmatic relevance."[25] She and the board faced the challenge with planning rather than panic, initiative rather than retrenchment, and bold ideas rather than recycled themes.

While other schools reacted with short-term plans, Emma Willard strategized for the future. In February 2010, the board approved *A Bicentennial Call to Action*, focused on the school's upcoming 200th birthday. After reaffirming the fundamental principles of *The Plan for Emma Willard's Third Century*, the document called for the school to

> Be the benchmark for excellence in girls' education worldwide.
> Achieve fiscal sustainability.
> Develop and deliver a curriculum responsive to the needs of girls in a rapidly transforming, increasingly diverse world.
> Be a dynamic learning community that intentionally fosters the habits of an intellectual life both on Mount Ida and beyond.[26]

Hall and others were well aware that 2014 was rapidly approaching. To ensure that the vision for the school extended beyond the bicentennial celebration and also included voices from all of the school's constituencies, Hall convened a task force to project out to 2020. As Meg McClellan, co-chair of the 2020 group, saw it, their task was "to create a distinctive and sustainable program for Emma Willard that allows us to make smart, consistent decisions about the future."[27]

The future is hard to predict, of course, but Hall knew that responsible educators invariably try to imagine what their students will need in ten, twenty, or thirty years. Otherwise, long-range planning has no focus—or is focused on the wrong things and not on the students for whom it is designed. In 1818 Emma Hart Willard had famously declared that "education should bring its subjects to the perfection of their moral, intellectual and physical nature in order that they may be of the greatest possible use to themselves and others." Her words will provide a framework for education at her school in 2020 as readily as they did two hundred years ago.

The challenge for the 2020 group and everyone else at the school is how to define moral perfection for girls who have grown up with reality television and cable news and for whom rap music and dirty dancing have always been part of the mainstream.[28] Equally challenging is the definition of intellectual perfection for young women who are completely at ease in cyberspace but who have only the most tenuous grasp of the metaphoric significance of classic texts and the literary canon. And what of physical perfection? Is it achieved through team experiences that pit fully equipped six- and seven-year- olds against each other in highly structured contests regulated by paid officials, intense coaches, and parental audiences who put extraordinary value on elementary school athletic success?

The cultural landscape of the first quarter of the twenty-first century shifts yearly if not more frequently. Parents who grew up in the 1970s and 1980s experienced change, but not the rapid change that roils their daughters' lives. Members of the class of 2020 at Emma Willard will rarely if ever have written in cursive or learned to tell time, and they may never have purchased or used a postage stamp. One of the biggest challenges for the curriculum at Emma Willard—and elsewhere—will be to teach them to distinguish information from knowledge. For the students of 2020, film, fax machines, and answering machines will be museum pieces, and email an inferior, ponderous form of communication. They already write faster with two thumbs than their parents do with ten fingers; other gaps between the generations will most certainly emerge. Increasingly, they know who is calling them before they answer the phone, and they must be taught to decide wisely when to answer. Their mothers—and grandmothers—spent hours after school chatting on the phone. In contrast, they are in constant contact with their friends. Their mothers' diaries were secret; theirs are exposed to the public.

And, furthermore, what will be the impact of multiculturalism on their intellectual growth? They are accustomed to women running the American State Department, a black man being president, classmates in head scarves, and "coming out" in their world is far removed from debutante parties. By 2020 over a quarter of all children under eighteen in the United States will have at least one immigrant parent. For students at Emma Willard in 2020, the Soviet Union, Burma, Tiananmen Square, Czechoslovakia, East and West Germany, and a federal budget under $1 trillion will be historical facts in a textbook. They will travel far more extensively than their parents did in their high school years, but they will never be out of touch with their families while they travel. Already, their parents can instantaneously view what they view and are able to eyeball them in real time at least once a day; for the most part, the only limitation on their communication is the impact of disparate time zones on parental sleep.

The future cannot be predicted, but one thing can. As educators wrestle with the impact of change on curriculum, school structure, pedagogy—especially as these things apply to teenage girls—Emma Willard School will be in the vanguard. It is the legacy of the founder that at each turn in American educational history, beginning with the foundation of her original school in a time of war and national fragility, her school has taken the lead in the education of young women. Her school owns unparalleled longevity but it can also claim much more. From the annals of institutional history comes a heritage of masterful pedagogy tracing back to the legions of women who went out from Troy to form their own schools, a legacy of curricular innovation spanning Willard's emphasis on applying rather than memorizing information to the correlated curriculum, the Dodge Study, and the newly created *Signature Program*. The school also claims a historic commitment to science that serves it well in the midst of rapid technological change—from Amos Eaton's lectures on science for young ladies to the research mentoring program that brings Emma Willard girls into nanotechnology laboratories, the route has been well defined. Most important, from the school's earliest days, the student body has been vibrant and dynamic. From Willard's time until now, a commitment to those with fewer resources, a willingness to expand beyond the cultural norm of other schools, albeit within the context of the time, and a vision that the education modeled in Troy should extend worldwide are the building blocks that ensure Emma Willard School's survival and leadership in a multicultural world.

At two hundred, Emma Willard School remains true to the founder's vision. Because of her work and the work of the women and men who succeeded her, the school remains, as it was in 1814, a model of educational excellence for girls, women's leadership, innovation, and daring. Its work remains the same as it has always been—"charting the course for others to follow."[29] In "Prophetic Strains," Emma Hart Willard foretold the day when women's voices would be celebrated. She surely would have celebrated her twenty-first-century school, one of whose poets captured the modern voice of the Emma Willard woman:

> She speaks when she's spoken to
> But speaks before she's asked
> And she'll keep up her soliloquy
> Until she's spoken, outspokenly, and spent.[30]

Chapter Notes

Foreword

1. Katharine Knowlton McLane '23 to Robin Robertson, Fall 1997, Emma Willard School Archives.

An Influence Which Will Be Enduring

1. Emma Willard, personal diary, April 6, 1870, Emma Willard School Archives (hereafter EWSA).
2. Emily Wilcox to Emma Willard Dodd, April 16, 1870, EWSA.
3. "Mrs. Emma Willard," *Troy Daily Times,* April 16, 1870.
4. All figures pertaining to trustee assets in this section were culled from U.S. census data at http://www.ancestry.com.
5. Statistics about Troy were taken from Arthur Weise, *Troy's One Hundred Years: 1789–1889* (Troy: W.H. Young, 1891).
6. "Funeral of Mrs. Willard," *Troy Budget,* April 19, 1870.
7. Ibid.
8. Thomas Coit, *A Sermon in Reference to the Death of Mrs. Willard* (Troy: W.H. Young and Blake, 1870).
9. *Troy Daily Times,* April 16, 1870.
10. "Obituary," *New York Times,* April 19, 1870.
11. "Mrs. Emma Willard," *Harper's Weekly,* May 7, 1870, 290.
12. Sarah Josepha Hale, "Mrs. Emma Willard," *Godey's Ladies Book,* September 1870, 276.
13. "Mrs. Emma Willard," *Harper's Weekly.*
14. Celia Burleigh, "Mrs. Emma Willard on the Woman Question," *Woman's Journal,* April 1871.

Patriot Breast

1. Almira Hart Lincoln Phelps, "A Reminiscence," *American Ladies Magazine,* December 1836, 530.
2. Emma Willard to William Cogswell, December 21, 1841, 2, typescript, Emma Willard School Archives (hereafter EWSA).
3. Helen Buss Mitchell, "The North and South Meet: Almira Hart Lincoln Phelps and the Patapsco Female Institute, 1841–56," PhD diss., University of Maryland, 1990, 13.
4. Emma Willard, *Abridged History of the United States or Republic of America* (New York: A.S. Barnes, 1850), 108.
5. Willard to Cogswell, December 21, 1841, 1.
6. Alfred L. Holman, ed., *Hinsdale Genealogy: Descendants of Robert Hinsdale of Dedham, Medfield, Hadley and Deerfield* (privately printed by Alfred Hinsdale Andrews, 1906), 78.
7. Ibid., 62.
8. Henry Fowler, "Educational Services of Mrs. Emma Willard," *The American Journal of Education,* March 1859, 125.
9. John Lord, *Life of Emma Willard* (New York: D. Appleton, 1873), 16.
10. Fowler, "Educational Services," 126.
11. Quoted in Ibid., 127.
12. Quoted in Lord, *Life,* 31–32.
13. Emma Willard, *History of the United States or The Republic of America* (New York: A.S. Barnes, 1845), frontispiece.
14. Almira Hart Lincoln Phelps, "Our Picture Gallery," *Philadelphia Home Weekly,* February 20, 1867.
15. Fowler, "Educational Services," 127.
16. Quoted in Emma Lydia Bolzau, "Almira Hart Lincoln Phelps: Her Life and Work," PhD diss., University of Pennsylvania, 1936, 15.
17. Phelps, "Our Picture Gallery."
18. Bolzau, *Phelps,* 31–32.
19. Quoted in Mary Kelley, *Learning to Stand and Speak: Women, Education, and Public Life in America's Republic* (Chapel Hill: University of North Carolina Press, 2006), 156.

20.Quoted in Margaret Nash, *Women's Education in the United States: 1780–1840* (New York: Palgrave MacMillan, 2005), 20.

21. Quoted in Alma Lutz, *Emma Willard: Daughter of Democracy* (Boston and New York: Houghton Mifflin, 1929), 20.

22. Ibid., 16.

23. Ibid., 21.

24. Jedediah Morse, *The American Universal Geography* (Boston: Isaiah Thomas and Ebenezer Andrews, 1801), preface.

25. David N. Camp, *History of New Britain, with Sketches of Farmington and Berlin, Connecticut, 1640–1889* (New Britain: William B. Thomson, 1889), 226.

26. Quoted in Lutz, *Emma Willard*, 26.

27. John H. Lockwood, *Westfield and Its Historical Influences, 1669–1919*, vol. 2 (privately printed, 1922), 209.

28. Ibid., 210.

29. Quoted on the Williams College Web site, *www.williams.edu/home/history/*.

30. Lockwood, *Westfield*, 208.

31. Samuel and Lydia Hart to Emma Hart, n.d., EWSA.

32. Willard to Cogswell, December 21, 1841, 1.

33. Ibid., 4.

34. Benjamin Rush, "Thoughts Upon Female Education" (Philadelphia, 1787); reprinted in Rush, *Essays, Literary, Moral and Philosophical* (Philadelphia: Thomas and William Bradford, 1806), 82.

35. Quoted in Lord, *Life*, 24.

36. Ibid., 38.

37. Ibid., 36.

38. Ibid., 39.

39. Samuel Hart to John Willard, October 18, 1809, EWSA.

40. Lutz, *Emma Willard*, 39.

41. Samuel Swift, *History of the Town of Middlebury in the County of Addison, Vermont* (Middlebury: A. H. Copeland, 1859), 250.

42. W. Storrs Lee, *Stagecoach North: Being an Account of the First Generation in the State of Vermont* (New York: Macmillan, 1941), 49.

43.Ibid., 181.

44. Quoted in Lord, *Life*, 25.

45. Swift, *Middlebury*, 251.

46. Hart to Willard, October 18, 1809.

47. Ibid.

48. Hannah Bull to Emma Hart, June 19, 1809, EWSA.

49. Quoted in Lutz, *Emma Willard*, 43.

50. Hart to Willard, October 18, 1809.

51. Ibid.

52. Quoted in Lord, *Life*, 47.

Female Education, the Subject That Interests Me Most

1. Emma Willard to Mr. and Mrs. Tappan, March 12, 1815, Emma Willard School Archives (hereafter EWSA).

2. Kenneth Degree, "Malfeasance or Theft? What Really Happened at the Middlebury Branch of the Vermont State Bank," *Vermont History* 68 (Winter/Spring 2000): 18.

3. James Madison to John Willard, April 19, 1808, New York Historical Society.

4.Emma Willard to Nancy Whittlesey, February 5, 1813, EWSA.

5. Henry Fowler, "Educational Services of Mrs. Willard," *Memoirs of Teachers, Educators and Promoters and Benefactors of Education, Literature, and Science*, ed. Henry Barnard (New York: F. C. Brownell, 1859), 133.

6. Willard to Tappans, March 12, 1815.

7. John Willard to Gustavus Willard, July 23, 1815, EWSA.

8. Willard to Tappans, March 12, 1815.

9. Advertisement, *Vermont Mirror*, April 6, 1814.

10. Fowler, "Educational Services," 133.

11. Quoted in Alma Lutz, *Emma Willard: Daughter of Democracy* (Boston: Houghton Mifflin, 1929), 57.

12. Thomas Woody, *A History of Women's Education in the United States* (New York: Octagon Books, 1980), 21.

13. Emma Willard, *An Address to the Public; Particularly to the Members of the Legislature of New-York, Proposing a Plan for Improving Female Education* (Middlebury: J.W. Copeland, 1819), 6.

14. Ibid., 35.

15. Margaret Nash, *Women's Education in the United States, 1780–1840* (New York: Palgrave Macmillan, 2005), 53.

16. "Female Academy," *The Star* (Raleigh, North Carolina), January 21, 1814; "The Female Academy at Pittsfield," *The Berkshire Reporter*, May 5, 1814; "Goshen Female Academy," *Orange County Patriot*, June 21, 1814; "School for Young Ladies," *Middletown Gazette*, January 13, 1814.

17. Charles Beecher, ed., *The Autobiography, Correspondence, Etc. of Lyman Beecher* (New York: Harper and Bros., 1866), 226.

18. Quoted in Lynne Templeton Brickley, "Sarah Pierce's Litchfield Female Academy," PhD diss., Harvard Graduate School of Education, 1985, 288, n. 87.

19. Emily Noyes Vanderpoel, ed., *More Chronicles of a Pioneer School, from 1792 to 1833, Being Added History of the Litchfield Academy Kept by Miss Sarah Pierce and Her Nephew, John Pierce Brace* (New York: The Cadmus Bookshop, 1927), 147.

20. William Paley, *Natural Theology or Evidence of the Existence and Attributes of the Deity Collected from the Appearances of Nature* (London: Hallowell, 1826), 330.

21. Mrs. Phelps, *Botany for Beginners: An Introduction to Mrs. Lincoln's Lectures on Botany* (New York: Huntington and Savage, 1849), 12.

22. Mrs. Phelps, *Natural Philosophy for Beginners: Designed for Common Schools and Families* (New York: F. J. Huntington, 1840), v.

23. Willard, *Improving Female Education*, 22.

24. Ethel Stanwood Johnston and Eva Johnston Coe, *American Samplers* (Boston: Colonial Dames, 1921), 230.

25. John Lord, *Life of Emma Willard* (New York: D. Appleton, 1873), 38.

26. Helen Buss Mitchell, "The North and South Meet: Almira Hart Lincoln Phelps and the Patapsco Female Institute, 1841–56," PhD diss., University of Maryland, 1990, 7.

27. Emily Noyes Vanderpoel, ed., *Chronicles of a Pioneer School from 1792 to 1833* (Cambridge, MA: University Press, 1903), 290.

28. Ibid., 319.

29. Ibid., 80.

30. Brickley, *Sarah Pierce's Litchfield*, 6.

31. Ibid., 73.

32. "Order of Exercises," Atkinson Academy flyer, September 24, 1818.

33. Quoted in Lord, *Life*, 38–40.

34. Ibid., 41.

35. Emma Willard to Elisha Treat, March 2, 1815, EWSA.

36. Benjamin F. Willard to John Willard, n.d., New York Historical Society.

37. Emma Willard to Sally Russ, September 14, 1818, EWSA.

38. Ezra Brainerd, *Mrs. Emma Willard's Life and Work in Middlebury* (prepared originally for the Emma Willard Society of New York; reprinted by Middlebury College, 1918, 44.)

To Endow a Seminary for Females

1. "List of the Names of the Young Ladies Who Boards [sic] at Mrs. Willard's," *Mary Lydia Treat Family Papers*, Henry Sheldon Museum, Middlebury, Vermont.

2. Benjamin Willard to John Willard, n.d., New York Historical Society.

3. Emma Willard to Mrs. Benjamin Tappan, March 1815, Emma Willard School Archives (hereafter EWSA).

4. Emma Willard to Hannah Davis, April 11, 1818, EWSA.

5. Benjamin to John Willard, n.d.

6. Emma Willard to Hannah Davis, March 16, 1818, EWSA.

7. Willard to Davis, April 11, 1818, EWSA.

8. Emma Willard to Zebulon Rudd Shiperd, April 13, 1817, EWSA.

9. William T. Willard to John Willard, May 28, no year, New York Historical Society.

10. Henry Fowler, "Educational Services of Mrs. Willard," *Memoirs of Teachers, Educators and Promoters and Benefactors of Education, Literature, and Science*, ed. Henry Barnard (New York: F. C. Brownell, 1859), 134.

11. Ibid., 133.

12. Emma Willard to William Cogswell, December 21, 1841, 5.

13. Fowler, "Educational Services," 134.

14. Ibid., 136.

15. Willard, *Improving Female Education*, 5.

16. Ibid., 6.

17. Ibid.

18. Ibid.

19. Ibid., 7.

20. Ibid.

21. Ibid., 8.

22. Ibid., 10.

23. Ibid., 8.

24. Ibid., 9.

25. Ibid., 24.

26. Ibid., 9.

27. Ibid., 10.

28. Ibid.

29. Ibid., 12.

30. Ibid., 10.

31. Ibid., 11.

32. Ibid., 12.

33. Ibid.

34. Ibid., 13.

35. Ibid., 14.

36. Ibid., 15.

37. Ibid., 15–16.

38. Ibid., 16.

39. Ibid., 17.

40. Ibid.

41. Ibid., 18.

42. Ibid.

43. Ibid., 18–19.

44. Ibid., 20.

45. Ibid., 20–21.

46. Ibid., 22.

47. Ibid., 22–23.

48. Ibid., 23.

49. Ibid., 24.

50. Ibid., 25.

51. Ibid., 24–25.

52. Ibid., 25.

53. Ibid., 32–33.

54. Ibid., 34.

55. Fowler, "Educational Services," 135.

56. Willard to Cogswell, December 21, 1841, 8, EWSA.

57. Ibid.

58. Ibid.

59. DeWitt Clinton to Emma Willard, December 31, 1818, EWSA.

60. Emma Willard to Sally Russ, March 26, 1819, EWSA.

61. Christopher Kilby to Charles Kilby, March 14, 1819, EWSA.

62. Ibid.

63. "Waterford Female Academy," flyer, April 30, 1819, EWSA.

64. Sydney Ernest Hammersley, *History of Waterford, New York* (Waterford: privately published, 1957), 181.

65. William Willard to John and Emma Willard, July 25, 1819, New York Historical Society.

66. "A Spectator," *Plough Boy*, January 1, 1820.

67. "From the Waterford Recorder, September 12, Waterford Female Academy," *The Albany Gazette*, September 22, 1820.

68. "Waterford Female Academy," *The Albany Gazette*, January 23, 1821.

69. Willard to Cogswell, December 21, 1841, 9, EWSA.

70. Ibid., 12.

71. "The Petition for Endowing a Female Seminary," *The Plough Boy*, April 8, 1820.

72. Grace Phillips to her parents, May 20, 1820, EWSA.

73. Grace Phillips to her parents, July 12, 1820, EWSA.

74. Ibid.

75. Murray Rothbard, *The Panic of 1819: Reactions and Policies* (New York: Columbia University Press, 1962), 12.

76. Ibid., 18.

77. Lord, *Life of Emma Willard* (New York: D. Appleton, 1873), 87.

78. Ibid., 92–93.

We Have Concluded to Go to Troy

1. Arthur Weise, *Troy's One Hundred Years: 1789–1889* (Troy: W. H. Young, 1891), 29.

2. Ibid., 30.

3. *Laws of the State of New York Passed at the Sessions of the Legislature Held in the Years, 1789, 1790, 1791, 1792, 1793, 1794, 1795, 1796, Inclusive*, Vol. 3 (Albany: Weed, Parsons, 1887), 233.

4. George Baker Anderson, *Landmarks of Rensselaer County, New York* (Syracuse: D. Mason, 1897), 235.

5. Ibid., 238.

6. Evan Cornog, *The Birth of Empire: DeWitt Clinton and the American Experience, 1769–1828* (New York: Oxford University Press, 1898), 106.

7. Benjamin Silliman, *A Tour to Quebec in the Autumn of 1819* (London: Sir Richard Phillips, 1822), 23.

8. "An Awful and Destructive Fire," *Troy Northern Budget*, July 4, 1820.

9. Quoted in Weise, *Troy's One Hundred Years*, 87.

10. Emma Willard to Lydia Hart, quoted in John Lord, *Life of Emma Willard* (New York: D. Appleton, 1873), 93.

11. "Mrs. Willard's Academy," *The Plough Boy*, May 26, 1821.

12. "MRS. WILLARD HAVING…," flyer, April 18, 1821, Emma Willard School Archives (hereafter EWSA).

13. Ibid.

14. Willard to Cogswell, December 21, 1841, 13.

15. "Troy Female Seminary," *Troy Post*, May 8, 1821.

16. Emma Willard to Mary Heywood, May 13, 1820, EWSA.

17. *Catalogue of the Troy Female Seminary for the Term Ending August 31, 1822*, EWSA.

18. Information regarding courses, calendars, and curriculum was provided in an annual "catalog," although the first three years of these were single-sheet flyers listing only the names of pupils and teachers. The information in this paragraph and the two following was distilled from the catalogs issued during the first few years in Troy.

19. *Troy Female Seminary*, September 8, 1825, EWSA.
20. Merab Bradley to Jonathan Dorr Bradley, March 15, 1823, EWSA.
21. *Troy Female Seminary*, July 1829, EWSA.
22. *Catalogue of the Members of the Troy Female Seminary for the Academic Year commencing September 9, 1827 and ending August 6, 1828*, 8, EWSA.
23. Willard to Cogswell, December 21, 1841, 13.
24. *Troy Female Seminary*, 1825.
25. *Catalogue of the Troy Female Seminary for the Two Terms preceding August 9, 1826.*
26. Grace Phillips to Gerish Barret, June 19, 1822, EWSA.
27. Ibid.
28. Merab Bradley to Jonathan Dorr Bradley, July 1, 1822, EWSA.
29. Emma Cordelia Clark to Mrs. Jerome Clark, October 25, 1823, EWSA.
30. Daniel Parker to Emma Willard, September 1, 1829, EWSA.
31. Emma Cordelia Clark to Mrs. Jerome Clark, June 16, 1822.
32. Emma Cordelia Clark to Grosvenor Clark, December 7, 1823, EWSA.
33. Phillips to Barret, June 19, 1822.
34. Grace Phillips to parents, July 29, 1822.
35. Grace Phillips to parents, June 1822.
36. Emma Willard to Samuel Southard, November 10, 1827, EWSA.
37. Cornelius Van Ness to Emma Willard, October 23, 1824, EWSA.
38. Clark to Clark, October 25, 1823.
39. Emma Cordelia Clark to Mrs. Jerome Clark, April 10, 1824, EWSA.
40. Daniel Parker to Sarah Parker, December 28, 1829, EWSA.
41. Lucy Huntington to Henry Huntington, December 2, 1825, EWSA.
42. Elizabeth Mansfield to Mary Ann Mansfield, March 9, 1823, EWSA.
43. Eleanor Worthington to Thomas Worthington, December 19, 1825, EWSA.
44. Thomas Worthington to Emma Willard, September 2, 1825, EWSA.
45. Elizabeth Mansfield to Mary Ann Mansfield, May 1822, EWSA.
46. Elizabeth Mansfield to Mary Ann Mansfield, March 9, 1823, EWSA.
47. Mansfield to Mansfield, May 1822.
48. Clark to Clark, April 10, 1824.
49. Emma Willard to Gideon Grainger, March 4, 1826, EWSA.
50. Sarah Parker to Daniel Parker, July 3, 1829, EWSA.
51. Parker to Lincoln, December 7, 1829.
52. *Catalogue of the Members of the Troy Female Seminary for the Two Terms ending August 7, 1823*, EWSA.
53. Phillips to Barret, June 19, 1822.
54. Emma Willard to Mills Olcott, October 6, 1826, EWSA.
55. Merab Bradley to William Bradley, March 15, 1823, EWSA.
56. "Troy Female Seminary," *The Ladies' Garland*, October 30, 1824.
57. Mary Treat to Elisha Treat, August 24, 1829, EWSA.
58. Daniel Parker to Emma Willard, June 29, 1829, EWSA

The Mothers of the Next Generation

1. Emma Willard to William Marcy, December 20, 1836, Emma Willard School Archives (hereafter EWSA).
2. Emma Willard, *History of the United States, or Republic of America: With a Chronological Table and a Series of Progressive Maps* (New York: A.S. Barnes, 1852), 371.
3. "Troy Female Seminary," *Connecticut Mirror*, April 10, 1826.
4. Bayard Tuckerman, ed., *The Diary of Philip Hone, 1828–1851* (New York: Dodd, Mead, 1889), 189.
5. "Little Short of Madness," *American Heritage* 59, no. 4 (Winter 2010): 43.
6. Mrs. A. W. Fairbanks, ed., *Emma Willard and Her Pupils* (New York: Mrs. Russell Sage, 1898), 78.
7. Ibid., 102.
8. Ibid., 74
9. "Canal Trade of Troy," *Hampshire Gazette* (Northampton, MA), December 28, 1825.

10. "The City of Troy," *The Monthly Repository and Library of Entertaining Knowledge*, Vol. 2 (New York: Francis Wiggins, 1832), 153.

11. Peter L. Bernstein, *Wedding of the Waters: The Erie Canal and the Making of a Great Nation* (New York: W.W. Norton, 2005), 183.

12. "Grand Canal," *New-York Mirror and Ladies' Literary Gazette,* December 27, 1823, 175.

13. Thomas Curtis Clarke, "Water-Ways from the Ocean to the Lakes," *Scribner's Magazine* 19, no. 1 (January 1896): 106.

14. Pnina G. Abir-Am and Dorinda Outram, eds., *Uneasy Careers and Intimate Lives: Women in Science, 1789–1979* (New Brunswick, NJ: Rutgers University Press, 1989), 88.

15. Jared Sparks, ed., *The Library of American Biography*, Vol. 7 (Boston: Hilliard, Gray, 1837), 283.

16. Richard Peters, ed., *The Public Statutes at Large of the United States of America from the Organization of the Government in 1789 to March 3, 1845...,* Vol. 4 (Boston: Charles C. Little and James Brown, 1850), 78.

17. Emma Willard to the Marquis de Lafayette, September 10, 1828, EWSA.

18. *Gray Matter*, May 19, 2008, forwarded by e-mail to the author, May 20, 2008.

19. "The Nation's Guest," *Niles's Weekly Register*, October 2, 1824.

20. Ibid.

21. Ibid., 71.

22. Ibid., 72.

23. Ibid.

24. Ibid.

25. Willard to Lafayette, September 10, 1828.

26. Emma Clark to Grosvenor Clark, December 7, 1823, EWSA.

27. Emma Willard, "Memoir of Dr. John Willard," Addison County Medical Society, November 7, 1846, 3–5.

28. Ibid., 6.

29. Ibid., 11.

30. Ibid., 3.

31. Merab Bradley to Jonathan Dorr Bradley, July 1, 1822, EWSA.

32. William T. Willard to John Willard, September 15, 1824, *John Willard Papers*, New York Historical Society.

33. Emma Willard to Louisa Baker '22, November 8, 1825, EWSA.

34. Mary Treat '26 to Elisha Treat, June 20, 1825, *Elisha Treat Family Papers*, Sheldon Museum, Middlebury, VT.

35. Emma Willard to Jared Mansfield, October 15, 1825, EWSA.

36. Emma Willard to Alden Partridge, December 15, 1825, EWSA.

37. Emma Willard to Thomas Worthington, June 21, 1826, EWSA.

38. William T. Willard to John and Emma Willard, February 10, 1824, *Papers of John Willard,* New York Historical Society.

39. William T. Willard to John Willard, September 20, 1824, *Papers of John Willard,* New York Historical Society.

40. William T. Willard to John Willard, October 14, 1824, *Papers of John Willard*, New York Historical Society.

41. William T. Willard to John H. Willard, September 8, 1824, *Papers of John Willard*, New York Historical Society.

42. Willard to Willard, October 14, 1824.

43. John H. Willard to Mary Treat and Elizabeth B. Hart, March 7, 1827, *Papers of Elisha Treat*, Sheldon Museum, Middlebury, VT.

44. John H. Willard to Mary Treat, February 12, 1828, *Papers of Elisha Treat*, Sheldon Museum, Middlebury, VT.

45. Emma Willard to Thomas Twiss, October 7, 1826, EWSA.

46. Thomas Twiss to Emma Willard, October 16, 1826, EWSA.

47. Thomas Twiss to Emma Willard, January 5, 1827, EWSA.

48. Emma Willard to Thomas Twiss, n.d., EWSA.

49. Thomas Twiss to Emma Willard, January 23, 1828, EWSA.

50. Mary Treat to Elisha Treat, August 24, 1829, EWSA.

51. Mary Treat to Elisha Treat, December 11, 1829, EWSA.

52. Peter J. Knapp to the author, e-mail message, October 2, 2008.

53. Quoted in John Lord, *Life of Emma Willard* (New York: D. Appleton, 1873), 100.

54. Ibid.

55. John H. Willard to Mary Treat, March 31, 1828, *Elisha Treat Papers*, Sheldon Museum, Middlebury, VT.

56. Willard to Treat, February 12, 1828.

57. Treat to Treat, August 24, 1829.

A Peculiar Kind of Woman

1. Although Mary Ulrich was listed as coming from Russia in the published catalog, she signed the register as living in Fishkill, New York.

2. Almira Lincoln to Mary Treat, September 22, 1830, Emma Willard School Archives (hereafter EWSA).

3. Mary Treat to Elisha Treat, August 24, 1829, EWSA.

4. Emma Willard, *Journal and Letters, from France and Great-Britain* (Troy: N. Tuttle, 1833), iii.

5. Emma Willard to Samuel Southard, September 11, 1830, EWSA.

6. Mary Treat to Elisha Treat, December 11, 1829, EWSA.

7. Mrs. Almira Hart Lincoln Phelps, *Lectures to Young Ladies* (Boston: Carter, Hendee and Co., 1833), 2.

8. Willard, *Journal and Letters*, 9.

9. Mike Seccombe, "Historian Looks at Americans in Paris," *Vineyard Gazette*, July 14, 2009.

10. Emma Willard, *History of the United States, or Republic of America* (Philadelphia: A. S. Barnes, and Co., 1843), vi.

11. Willard, *Journal and Letters*, 14.

12. Emma Willard to the Marquis de LaFayette, September 10, 1828, EWSA.

13. Willard, *Journal and Letters*, 100.

14. Ibid., 41.

15. Ibid., 148.

16. Ibid., 149.

17. Ibid., 153.

18. Ibid., 100.

19. Ibid., 104.

20. Ibid., 69.

21. Ibid., 110.

22. Ibid., 134.

23. Ibid., 131.

24. Ibid., 163.

25. "Mrs. Willard's Journal and Letters," *American Ladies' Magazine* 7, no. 2 (February 1834): 88.

26. Willard, *Journal and Letters*, 233.

27. Ibid., 166.

28. Ibid., 116.

29. Ibid., 142.

30. Ibid., 188.

31. Ibid., 280.

32. Ibid., 316.

33. Ibid., 380.

34. Ibid., 382.

35. Phelps, *Lectures*, 307.

36. Mary Gordon to Henry Gordon, April 21, 1830, EWSA.

37. Phelps, *Lectures*, 151.

38. Ibid., 68.

39. Ibid., 109.

40. Jane Burritt '39 to William Brown, April 4, 1836, EWSA.

41. Phelps, *Lectures*, 142.

42. Ibid., 244.

43. Ibid., 240.

44. Ibid., 171.

45. Ibid., 172.

46. Ibid., 197.

47. Ibid., 207.

48. Ibid., 250.

49. Ibid., 251–52.

50. Mrs. Hamilton Peck (Anna M. Johnson '44) to Mary Fairbanks, May 28, 1894, EWSA.

51. Phelps, *Lectures*, 293.

52. Pamelia Archer '38 to Stevenson Archer, June 20, 1836.

53. Phelps, *Lectures*, 37.

54. Ibid., 305.

55. Ibid., 40.

56. Frances Emerson '32 to Sarah Dutton '33, March 15, 1833, EWSA.

57. Angelo Repousis, "The Trojan Women: Emma Hart Willard and the Troy Society for the Advancement of Female Education in Greece," *Journal of the Early Republic* 24, no. 3 (Fall 2004): 445.

58. Harriet Russell '39 to William Russell, November 22, 1837, EWSA.

59. Emma Willard, *Advancement of Female Education: Or, A Series of Addresses, in Favor of Establishing at Athens, in Greece, a Female Seminary* (Troy: Tuttle, 1833), 9.

60. Repousis, "The Trojan Women," 476.

61. Emma Willard, *Memorial to the Trustees of the Troy Female Seminary*, April 21, 1833, 3, EWSA.

62. Ibid., 4.

63. Ibid.

64. Ibid., 6–7.

65. Ibid., 5.

66. Ibid., 12–13.

67. Ibid., 15.

68. Ibid.

69. Ibid., 28.

70. Ibid., "Additional Memoirs"

71. Ibid.

72. Ibid.

73. Ibid.

It is Time . . . [to] Enlarge Their Sphere

1. Emma Willard, *Advancement of Female Education: Or, a Series of Addresses, in Favor of Establishing at Athens, in Greece, A Female Seminary Especially Designed to Instruct Female Teachers* (Troy: Norman Tuttle, Printer, 1833), frontispiece.

2. Emma Willard to Thomas Twiss, September 30, 1832, Emma Willard School Archives (hereafter EWSA).

3. John Lord, *Life of Emma Willard* (New York: D. Appleton, 1873), 142.

4. Harriet Russell to her brothers, November 3, 1837, EWSA.

5. "New Boarding School," *Vermont Gazette* (Bennington), March 10, 1818.

6. Henry Fowler, "Educational Services of Mrs. Emma Willard," *Memoirs of Teachers, Educators and Promoters and Benefactors of Education, Literature and Science*, ed. Henry Barnard (New York: F. C. Brownell, 1859), 153.

7. Emma Willard to A. W. Holden, September 5, 1846, quoted in James A. Holden, "Emma Willard, a Sketch and a Letter," *Educational Review* 61 (April 1916): 392.

8. Anne Firor Scott, "The Ever Widening Circle: The Diffusion of Feminist Values from the Troy Female Seminary, 1822–72," *History of Education Quarterly* 19, no. 1 (Spring 1979): 8.

9. Emma Hart Willard to Mary Ann Hadley, November 15, 1839, EWSA.

10. Emma Willard to Sarah Dutton, n.d., EWSA.

11. Emma Willard to William Whittingham, June 27, 1833, EWSA.

12. Emma Willard to Harriet Hart, December 28, 1837, EWSA.

13. Lord, *Life*, 136.

14. Elizabeth Heartt to Sarah Dutton, April 9, 1834, EWSA.

15. Emma Willard to Lydia Sigourney, January 1, 1846, EWSA.

16. Ibid.

17. Fairbanks, *Emma Willard and Her Pupils*, 42.

18. Ibid.

19. Karen Roberts, ed., *New Year in Cuba: Mary Gardner Lowell's Travel Diary, 1831–32* (Boston: Massachusetts Historical Society and Northeastern University Press, 2003), 79.

20. William Hart to Freedom Hart, October 17, 1839, EWSA.

21. "Dr. Weller's Female Seminary," *Nashville Banner and Whig*, December 22, 1834.

22. Statistics taken from the annual reports of the Troy Female Seminary to the Board of Regents, EWSA.

23. Jane Burritt to William Brown, July 17, 1837, EWSA.

24. Frances Emmons (on behalf of Emma Willard) to Sarah Dutton, May 20, 1833, EWSA.

25. Emma Willard to Sarah Dutton, May 2, 1833, EWSA.

26. Ibid.

27. Ellen Strong Bartlett, "Emma Willard, a Pioneer of Education for Women," *The New England Magazine 25* (September 1901–February 1902): 571.

28. Susan Schulter, "Emma Willard and the Graphic Foundations of American History," *Journal of Historical Geography* 33, no. 3 (July 2007): 545.

29. "Report of the Directors of the American School Agents' Society," *American Annals of Education and Instruction for the Year 1833*, Vol. 3, ed. William C. Woodbridge (Boston: Allen and Ticknor, 1833), 525.

30. "Miss Beecher's Essay on the Education of Female Teachers," *American Annals of Education and Instruction for the Year 1835*, Vol. 5, ed. William Woodbridge (Boston: William D. Tichnor, 1835), 277.

31. Catharine E. Beecher, *The True Remedy for the Wrongs of Woman; With a History of an Enterprise Having That for Its Object* (Boston: Phillips, Sampson, and Co., 1851), 240.

32. Sarah Lucretia Willard to Emma Willard, May 1, 1846, EWSA.

33. George Frederick Miller, *The Academy System of the State of New York, New York*, reprint ed. (New York: Arno Press, 1969), 171.

34 The seminary's population fluctuated dramatically by modern standards. In the years prior to the Civil War, the number of pupils topped 400 six times, hitting an all-time high of 532 in 1853. In 1862 the school census was 245.

35. Anonymous, "Notes of a Northern Excursion," *The Southern Rose* 4, no. 25 (August 6, 1836): 197.

36. Jane P. Lincoln (on behalf of Emma Willard) to Sarah Dutton, November 23,1833, EWSA.

37. *Catalogue of the Members of the Troy Female Seminary for the Year Commencing September 21, 1831 and Ending August 1, 1832 Together with the Terms of Admittance &c.*, F. Adancourt, printer, 8, EWSA.

38. Sarah Willard's salary remained $2,000 until her retirement in 1872. Of course, her husband was pocketing the profit from the school annually. The largest profit came in 1854: $5,405.97. There were also years when the school's budget ran in the red; the low point was 1872 when losses totaled $2100.01.

39. *Catalogue of the Members of the Troy Female Seminary for the Year Commencing March 4, 1835 and Ending February 17, 1836*, no printer listed, 10, EWSA.

40. Ibid.

41. Ibid.

42. *Report to the Regents*, 1839, passim.

43. *Classification* was a nineteenth-century term for placement.

44. Emma Willard to Harriet Hart, June 10, 1833, EWSA.

45. Quoted in Henry Barnard, "Detached Thoughts on Studies and Education," *The American Journal of Education* 33, no. 26 (1873): 437.

46. [Sarah Hale], "Troy Female Seminary," *American Ladies' Magazine*, December 1835, 708.

47. Ibid.

48. Ibid.

49. Mary Williams to her uncle, September 30, 1837, EWSA.

50. Jane Burritt to William Brown, July 19, 1836, EWSA.

51. Charles Davies, *The Common School Arithmetic Prepared for the Use of Academies and Common Schools in the United States, and Also for the Use of the Young Gentlemen Who May Be Preparing to Enter the Military Academy at West Point* (New York: N. and J. White, 1833), 122.

52. The English course was a curriculum in contrast to the classical course, which prepared young men for college and contained little more than Latin, Greek, and arithmetic. The English course was popular at girls' academies and increasingly popular at boys' schools with those young men who planned to go into trade or technical fields.

53. Sarah Crocker to her mother, July 12, 1835, EWSA.

54. *Catalogue of the Members of the Troy Female Seminary for the Year Commencing September 15th, 1830 and Ending August 3rd, 1831,* F. Adancourt, printer, 15, EWSA.

55. Ibid.

56. *Catalogue of the Officers and Pupils of the Troy Female Seminary February, 1838,* Tuttle, Belcher, and Burton, printers, 16, EWSA.

57. Mary Elizabeth Williams to her mother, June 10, 1837, EWSA.

58. Mary Huntington to her mother, June 20, 1832, EWSA.

59. Hale, "Troy Female Seminary, 705–6.

60. Sarah Crocker to a friend, August 20, 1834, EWSA.

61. Virginia Anderson to her mother, July 12, 1834, EWSA.

62. Mary Elizabeth Williams to her uncle, February 20, 1837, EWSA.

63. Chloe Cole to Daniel Hyde Cole, February 22, 1834, EWSA.

64. Ann Phelps to Charles Phelps, March 3, 1837, EWSA.

65. Jane Burritt to William Brown, February 13, 1836, EWSA.

66. Jane Burritt to William Brown, April 4, 1836, EWSA.

67. Jane Burritt to William Brown, May 28, 1836, EWSA.

68. Ibid.

69. Emma Willard to Alonzo Paige, February 17, 1837, EWSA.

70. *Catalogue of the Troy Female Seminary, 1849–50,* missing title page, 25, EWSA.

Who Proved the Truth of Her Mother-in-Law's Creed

1. Anonymous, "Northern Excursion," *The Southern Rose,* 4, no. 25 (August 6, 1836): 197.

2. A search in newspaperarchive.com on the terms *female seminary* and *female academy* between 1830 and 1850 returned articles about or advertisements for schools in Delaware, Maryland, North Carolina, New York, Iowa, Wisconsin, Ohio, Pennsylvania, Illinois, Maine, Indiana, Rhode Island, and Texas. With the exception of Troy, none of these schools is still in operation.

3. Thomas Woody, *A History of Women's Education,* vol. 1. Reprint (New York: Octagon Books, 1980), 395.

4. "Memoir," Emma Willard to Board of Trustees, Troy Female Seminary, April 21, 1833, 23, Emma Willard School Archives (hereafter EWSA).

5. Harriet Russell to William Russell, June 1, 1838, EWSA.

6. Sylvester D. Willard, ed., "Dr. Christopher C. Yates," *Annals of the Medical Society of the County of Albany, 1806–1851, with Biographical Sketches of Diseased Members* (Albany: J. Munsell, 1864), 290.

7. Christopher C. Yates, *Observations on the Epidemic Now Prevailing in the City of New-York; Called the Asiatic or Spasmodic Cholera; with Advice to Planters of the South, for the Medical Treatment of Their Slaves* (New York: George P. Scott and Co., 1832).

8. "Winfield Scott Yates," *New York Mirror: A Weekly Journal Devoted to Literature and the Fine Arts,* March 2, 1833.

9. *Criminal conversation* is an outmoded legal term for adultery. Yates won the case, which was later reversed on a technicality having to do with the three-man panel adjudicating it.

10. "Winfield Scott Yates," *New York Mirror.*

11. "Winfield Scott Yates," *The Treasury of Knowledge and Library of Reference, Containing a Million of Facts or Common Place Book of Subjects of Research and Curiosity in the Arts and Sciences, History,*

Genealogy and Literature; Embracing Sketches of Jewish History, American History, and History of American Literature; Also, American Biographies, or Original Biographical Sketches of Distinguished Americans, Vol. 3 (New York: C. C. Childs, 1850), 406.

12. Charles Sidney Bluemel, *Stammering and Cognate Defects of Speech*, Vol. 2 (New York: G. E. Stechert and Co., 1913).

13. Willard, "Yates," 289.

14. Ibid.

15. Anna Johnson to Mrs. A. W. Fairbanks, May 28, 1894, EWSA.

16. Mary Elizabeth Williams to her uncle, June 16, 1837, EWSA.

17. John Lord, *Life of Emma Willard* (New York: D. Appleton, 1873), 186.

18. Jane Burritt to William Brown, October 15, 1837, EWSA.

19. In a letter to his father, Freedom Hart, prior to the elections in the fall of 1838, William Hart noted, "I suppose Cousin John expects to get a good Whig out of me." William Hart to Freedom Hart, October 17, 1838, EWSA.

20. "Wedding Week," *Troy Whig*, September 18, 1838. See also "Married," *Troy Northern Budget*. September 20, 1838.

21. "Hymeneal," *Vermont Phoenix*, September 28, 1838.

22. Almira Hart Lincoln Phelps to Emma Willard, May 4, 1838, quoted in Lord, *Life*, 183.

23. William Hart to Freedom Hart, October 17, 1839, EWSA.

24. Henry S. Cohn, "Connecticut's Divorce Mechanism: 1636–1969," *The American Journal of Legal History* 14 (1970): 37.

25. For more information about the Yates's divorce proceedings, see Lucy F. Townsend and Barbara Wiley, "The Divorce of a Domestic Educator: The Case of Emma Willard Yates," *Review Journal of Philosophy and Social Science* 27, nos. 1 and 2 (2002):3–25.

26. Emma Willard to Harriet Hart, March 25, 1841, EWSA.

27. Emma Willard to Lydia Sigourney, August 23, 1839, EWSA.

28. Ellen Jane Thompson to Mary [last name unknown], May 30, 1841, EWSA.

29. *Register #1: 1831–1852*, St. John's Episcopal Church., 155.

30. Norris Wilcox was married to Harriet Hart, daughter of Emma's brother Jesse. In 1841 he was not only involved in his wife's aunt's divorce proceedings but was also an official representative in New Haven at the *Amistad* trial.

31."Another Divorce Case in High Life," *Wisconsin Enquirer*, September 21, 1839.

32. "Review of New Books," William E. Burton, ed., *The Gentleman's Magazine and Monthly American Review* 4, no. 2 (February 1839): 124–25.

33. "Mrs. Emma Willard Yates," *New York Sunday Morning News*, February 17, 1839, EWSA.

34. Quoted in Nancy Iannucci, "The Founder and the Bounder," *Emma: The Bulletin of Emma Willard School* 63, no. 3 (Fall 2005): 75.

35. "Miscellany," *The Brooklyn Eagle*, July 1, 1845.

36. Emma Willard to Alonzo Paige, June 17, 1843, EWSA.

37. William Hart to Freedom Hart, October 17, 1839, EWSA.

38. She often signed official documents Sarah, but her husband and mother-in-law called her Lucretia, a name she once confided to her mother-in-law, "I would not give . . . to a child because it is not generally liked." Sarah Lucretia Willard to Emma Willard, May 1, 1846, EWSA.

39. Among the weddings that took place in St. George's was the illegal union of Frederick Augustus, Duke of Sussex, Queen Victoria's favorite uncle. The Hudson-Robinson marriage is recorded in John H. Chapman, ed., *The Registry Book of Marriages Belonging to the Parish of St. George, Hanover Square in the County of Middlesex*, Vol. 2, 1788–1809 (London: no publisher, 1888), 281.

40. Willard to Cogswell, December 21, 1841, 13.

41. Sarah Crocker to Sarah [last name unknown], August 20, 1834, EWSA.

42. Rob Shields, *Places on the Margin: Alternative Geographies of Modernity* (London: Routledge, 1991), 124.

43. Anne Firor Scott, "The Ever Widening Circle: The Diffusion of Feminist Values from the Troy Female Seminary, 1822–1872," *History of Education Quarterly* 19, no. 1 (Spring 1979): 17.]

44. Eliza Hunt Apthorp to Emma Willard Scudder, May 9, 1892, EWSA.

45. Jane Burritt to William P. Brown, May 28, 1836, EWSA.

46. Mrs. A. W. Fairbanks, *Emma Willard and Her Pupils* (New York: Mrs. Russell Sage, 1898), 223.

47. Ibid., 353.

48. Ellen J. Thompson to Mary [last name unknown], May 30, 1841, EWSA.

49. Margaret Ann Freligh to her mother, May 25, 1842, EWSA.

50. Fairbanks, *Emma Willard*, 353.

51. Sarah Lucretia Willard to Emma Willard, May 1, 1846, EWSA.

52. Lydia Sigourney to Emma Willard, n.d., EWSA.

53. John H. Willard to Emma Hart Willard, March 16, 1844, EWSA. This house on the corner of Ferry and Second Streets would be Emma's home until her final illness. It was torn down to make room for the current Russell Sage College library.

54. Emma Willard to Harriet Mumford Paige, September 10, 1846, EWSA.

55. John H. Willard to Emma Willard, September 6, 1847, EWSA.

56. Emma Hart Willard to Harriet Kirby, September 4, 1845, EWSA.

57. *Catalogue, 1849–50*, 22, EWSA.

58. Helen Phelps to John Phelps, February 24, 1843, EWSA.

59. Sarah Lucretia Willard to Emma Willard, May 1, 1846, EWSA.

60. In 1865 Emma mentioned that two of her granddaughters had spent the summer in Newport where they had "a house and carriage furnished by their father." Emma Willard to Mary Whittlesey, September 10, 1865, EWSA.

61. Mary Elizabeth Williams to her mother, August 24, 1837, EWSA.

62. Marian F. MacDorman and T. J. Matthews, "Recent Trends in Infant Mortality in the United States," *NCHS Data Brief No. 9* (October 2008). Retrieved September 7, 2010, from www.cdc.gov/nchs/databriefs/db09.pdf.

63. Gail Collins, *America's Women: 400 Years of Dolls, Drudges, Helpmates and Heroines* (New York: HarperCollins, 2003), 135–36.

64. Fairbanks, *Emma Willard*, 190.

65. Maria Patchin to Thaddeus Patchin, November 24, 1840, EWSA.

66. Maria Patchin to Charlotte Patchin, September 21, 1840, EWSA.

67. Fairbanks, *Emma Willard*, 151.

68. Emma Willard to Harriet Hart, July 20, 1848, EWSA.

69. Fairbanks, *Emma Willard*, 300.

70. Emma Willard to Harriet Mumford Paige, April 3, 1848, EWSA.

71. Harriet Russell to William Russell, February 27, 1838, EWSA.

72. Mary Elizabeth Williams to her uncle, December 1, 1836, EWSA.

73. Susan Storer to Sarah Storer, June 11, 1846, EWSA.

74. Emma Willard, *History of the United States, or Republic of America* (Philadelphia: A.S. Barnes, 1845), 374.

75. Maria Patchin to Aaron Patchin, June 22, 1832, EWSA.

76. Emilie and Eliza Read to Mrs. H. H. Read, June 22, 1849, EWSA.

77. Mary Huntington to Bethia Huntington, June 28, 1832, EWSA.

78. "The Cholera from The Troy Press," *The Huron Reflector* (Norwalk, Ohio), September 4, 1832.

79. "Cholera," *Weekly Wisconsin* (Milwaukee), May 30, 1849.

80. "Died," *New-York Evangelist*, July 10, 1841.

81. Henrietta Collins to Finette Armstrong, January 9, 1843, EWSA.

82. Emma Willard to Harriet Hart, May 12, 1841, EWSA.

83. Ellen Thompson to Mary [last name unknown], May 30, 1841, EWSA.

84. Spencer C. Tucker, ed., *U.S. Leadership in Wartime: Clashes, Controversy and Compromise*, Vol. 1 (Santa Barbara, CA: ABC-CLIO, 2009), 223.

A Band of Sisters

1. All statistics from the reports to the New York State Board of Regents are taken from the school's report for the year cited. Copies of these reports can be found in the Emma Willard School Archives EWSA.

2. The new building included a gymnasium, the first at the seminary and probably the first at any girls' school.

3. *Report of the Trustees to the State Board of Regents*, June 30, 1858.

4. Anna Shankland Kellogg diary, April 9, 1857, *Anna Kellogg Collection*, EWSA.

5. Mentioned from 1839 on in the annual *Report of the Trustees to the State Board of Regents*.

6. Margaret Freleigh to her mother, May 25, 1842, EWSA.

7. Susan Storer to her mother, June 11, 1846, EWSA.

8. Kellogg diary, September 11, 1856.

9. *Catalogue of the Troy Female Seminary, Anna Kellogg Collection*, EWSA.

10. Mrs. A. W. Fairbanks, *Emma Willard and Her Pupils* (New York: Mrs. Russell Sage, 1898), 504.

11. Ibid., 585.

12. Ibid., 364.

13. *Report of the Trustees to the State Board of Regents, January 28, 1841*, repeated for many years in catalogs beginning with *Catalogue of the Officers and Pupils of the Troy Female Seminary for the Year Beginning March 2, 1842 and Ending February 22, 1843* (Troy: N. Tuttle, Printer, 1843), 19.

14. Anna Bedell to Mott Bedell, January 28, 1848, EWSA.

15. Nettie Fowler to Eldridge Fowler, September 17, 1852, *Nettie Fowler McCormick Collection*, MSS 1B, Box 1, Wisconsin State Historical Society (WSHS).

16. Fairbanks, *Emma Willard*, 454.

17. Ibid., 487.

18. Ibid., 614.

19. Kellogg diary, May 23, 1857.

20. "Additional Remarks," *Report of the Trustees to the State Board of Regents, January 28, 1842.*

21. Fairbanks, *Emma Willard*, 509.

22. *Report of the Trustees to the State Board of Regents, January 30, 1850*. It is important to note that although the students at the seminary could study mathematics, science, Latin, and other subjects that girls elsewhere did not, they also could elect an "ornamental" curriculum.

23. Emma Willard to Eliza Neely, April 13, 1855, EWSA.

24. Mrs. Emma Willard, "The Schoolmistress," *New York State Teacher*, May 1855, 237.

25. Ibid.

26. Ibid.

27. "Sudden Death of a Young Lady—Suicide," *New-York Daily Times*, April 14, 1855.

28. Willard, "The Schoolmistress," 237.

29. Sarah Hendricks to her brother, December 4, 1853, EWSA. (Sarah's great-great granddaughter is Ethel Kennedy, widow of Robert F. Kennedy.)

30. Emma Willard, *Last Leaves of American History, Comprising a Separate History of California* (New York: A. S. Barnes, 1853), 242.

31. Two of Fremont's descendants, Parker Hamilton Poling '95 and Tandy Hamilton '00, recently graduated from the school.

32. Emma Willard, *Late American History, Containing a Full Account of the Courage, Conduct, and Success of John C. Fremont; By Which, Through Many Hardships and Sufferings He Became the Explorer and the Hero of California* (New York: A. S. Barnes, 1856), preface.

33. Emma Willard to Miss Foster [no first name], November 5, 1848, quoted in Lord, *Life of Emma Willard* (New York: D. Appleton, 1873), 228.

34. Emma Willard, *Last Periods of Universal History* (New York: A. S. Barnes, 1855), 2.

35. Fowler, "Educational Services," 163.

36. Emma Willard to Harriet Mumford Paige, June 25, 1853, EWSA.

37. Lord, *Life*, 218.

38. Nettie Fowler diary, June 1, 1853, *Nettie Fowler McCormick Collection*, MSS MSS4B, Box 1, WSHS.

39. Kellogg diary, May 12, 1857.

40. Jane Shepard to her mother, September 12, 1856, EWSA.

41. Minnie Otis to her cousin, October 20, 1859, EWSA.

42. Jane Shepard to her mother, September 12, 1856, EWSA.

43. "Additional Remarks," *Report to the Regents, 1841.*

44. Nettie Fowler to Eldridge Fowler, January 8, 1853, *Nettie Fowler McCormick Collection*, MSS 1B, Box 1, WSHS.

45. Nettie Fowler to Eldridge Fowler, April 20, 1853, *Nettie Fowler McCormick Collection*, MSS 1B, Box 1, WSHS.

46. Jane Shepard, September 12, 1856, EWSA.

47. Ibid.

48. *Catalogue of the Officers and Pupils of the Troy Female Seminary for the Academic Year Commencing September 18, 1850 and Ending July 23, 1851* (Troy: A. G. Johnson, Printer, 1851), 22.

49. Diploma awarded to Mary Phillips, 1849, EWSA.

50. Nettie Fowler diary, May 31, 1853, *Nettie Fowler McCormick Collection*, MSS 4B, Box 1, WSHS.

51. Kellogg diary, June 17–18, 1857.

52. Keziah Lewis did not live to graduate. She died in the spring of a fever. So many students were sick that the examinations at the end of the spring term were canceled.

53. *Catalogue of the Officers and Pupils of the Troy Female Seminary for the Academic Year Commencing September 10, 1851 and Ending July 14, 1852* (Troy: A. G. Johnson, Printer, 1852), 28.

54. Ibid., 29.

55. Ibid., 27.

56. Samantha Otis to her cousin, October 9, 1859, EWSA.

57. Susan Storer to Sarah Storer, June 1, 1846, EWSA.

58. Emma Willard to William and Nelly Hart, January 8, 1856, EWSA.

59. Kellogg diary, November 2, 1856.

60. Nettie Fowler to Eldridge Fowler, June 5, 1853, *Nettie Fowler McCormick Collection*, WSHS.

61. *Catalogue of the Officers and Pupils of the Troy Female Seminary for the Academic Year Commencing September 8, 1852 and Ending June 29, 1853* (Troy: A. G. Johnson, Printer, 1853), 29, EWSA.

62. "Aunt Patience," *Ohio Cultivator*, April 15, 1850.

63. Louise L. Stevenson, *Miss Porter's School: A History in Documents, 1847–1948* (New York: Garland Press, 1987), 162.

64. Ibid., 165.

65. *Catalogue for 1852–53*, 31.

66. Ibid., 23.

67. Ibid., 29.

68. Sarah Crocker to her mother, July 12, 1835, EWSA.

69. Kellogg diary, June 15, 1857.

70. Stevenson, *Miss Porter's School*, 36.

71. Ibid., 174.

72. Ibid., 208.

73. Ibid., 213.

74. Ibid., 35.

75. Ibid., 229.

76. Ibid., 166.

77. Ibid., 62.

78. Ibid., 169.

79. Ibid., 188.

80. Kellogg diary, December 6, 1856.

81. Ibid., December 1, 1856. Mr. Sinsabaugh, the proprietor, must have admired the seminary girls who patronized his shop. His daughter Sarah studied at the school from 1866 to 1870.

82. "Additional Remarks," *Report to the Board of Trustees, 1841*.

83. *Catalogue of the Officers and Pupils of the Troy Female Seminary for the Year Commencing March 6, 1839 and Ending February 19, 1840* (Troy: N. Tuttle, Printer), 4.

84. *Catalogue*, 1852–53, passim.

85. "Additional Remarks," *Report to the Board of Trustees, 1841*.

86. Jane Shepard to her mother, September 12, 1856, EWSA.

87. Ibid.

88. Otis to her cousin, October 9, 1859.

89. "Additional Remarks," *Catalogue, 1840–41*.

90. Richard Baldwin to Charlotte Baldwin, November 16, 1851, EWSA.

91. Fairbanks, *Emma Willard*, 365.

The House Is Divided

1. Jane Shepard to mother, September 12, 1856, Emma Willard School Archives (hereafter EWSA).

2. Ermina Merrick to Nettie Fowler, November 11, 1853. MSS 2B, Box 3, *Nettie Fowler McCormick Collection*, WSHS.

3. Mary Huntington to her mother, June 1, 1832, EWSA.

4. Maria Patchin to Thaddeus Patchin, September 15, 1831, EWSA.

5. "Noted Theologian Dead," *New York Times*, November 21, 1913.

6. James F. Holcomb and Helen H. Holcomb, *In the Heart of India* (Philadelphia: Westminster Press, 1905), v.

7. Harriet House, "Sight-Seeing in Bangkok," in *Siam and Laos as Seen by Our Missionaries*, ed. Mary Backus (Philadelphia: Presbyterian Board of Publication, 1884), 82.

8. Ibid., 84.

9. Mrs. Helen Harriet Howe Holcomb, *Bits About India* (Philadelphia: Presbyterian Board of Publication, 1888), 12.

10. Ibid., 272.

11. Mongkut is the king celebrated in *The King and I*.

12. Quoted in Nancy Wooloch, *Women and the American Experience* (New York: Alfred A. Knopf, 1984), 127.

13. Henry Fowler, "Educational Services of Mrs. Emma Willard," *Memoirs of Teachers, Educators and Promoters and Benefactors of Education, Literature, and Science,* ed. Henry Barnard (New York: F. C. Brownell, 1889), 167.

14. John Willard even paid pew rent at Grace Church in Manhattan.

15. The one exception was Mormonism, which Emma Willard called in her U.S. history textbooks "one of the most extraordinary impostures of the age." She called Joseph Smith "obscure, uneducated" and, in a striking example of her feminism, argued, "His laws . . . give his followers licence [*sic*] to commit every crime; especially that they degrade and demoralize women" (*Abridged History of the United States* [New York: A. S. Barnes and Co., 1852], 332).

16. Mrs. A. W. Fairbanks, *Emma Willard and Her Pupils* (New York: Mrs. Russell Sage, 1898), 102.

17. John Lord, *Life of Emma Willard* (New York: D. Appleton, 1873), 116.

18. Ibid., 113.

19. Ibid., 116.

20. *Report to the Regents of the State of New York, 1861*, 21.

21. Drew Gilpin Faust, *This Republic of Suffering: Death and the American Civil War* (New York: Alfred A. Knopf, 2008), 172.

22. Ibid.

23. *Regents Report*, 1861, 21.

24. *Catalogue of Amherst College for the Year 1892–93* (Amherst: Amherst College, 1893), 67.

25. Oscar Fay Adams, *Some Famous American Schools* (Boston: Dana Estes and Co., 1903).

26. Quoted in Frederick W. Jordan, "Between Heaven and Harvard: Protestant Faith and the American Boarding School Experience, 1778–1940," PhD diss., Notre Dame University, 2004, 161.

27. Ibid.

28. *Alumni Horae* 11, no. 2 (July 1931): 63–64.

29. Fairbanks, *Emma Willard*, 693.

30. Rachel Kellogg to Anna Kellogg, March 18, 1857, The Anna Kellogg Collection, EWSA.

31. Statistics taken from *Quinquennial Catalogue of Officers and Students of Mount Holyoke College, South Hadley, Mass., 1837–1895* (South Hadley: Mount Holyoke, 1895), 281.

32. Deborah Waters to Mary Hastings, December 6, 1859, EWSA. Lucy B. Jones was the health officer at the seminary, Aurelia Hopkins '44, Caroline King '46, and Mary Smith '51 were teachers. Mr. Arms may have been Seneca Arms, a bookkeeper.

33. "The Revolver," November 15, 1859, quoted in Louise L. Stevenson, *Miss Porter's School: A History in Documents, 1847–1948* (New York: Garland Press, 1987), 123.

34. Emma Hart Willard to Dr. Washington, June 5, 1861, EWSA.

35. Isabel McKennan to her sisters, September 25, 1860, EWSA. Isabel was the daughter of Pauline deFontevieux '37, the French girl Emma Willard had "adopted" in 1830.

36. Stevenson, *Miss Porter's*, 159.

37. Sarah Willard to Emma Willard, November 8, 1860, EWSA.

38. Willard to Washington, June 5, 1861.

39. Sarah Willard to Olivia White, March 4, 1861, EWSA.

40. Isabelle McKennan to Maddie [last name unknown], April 25, 1861, EWSA.

41. Quoted in Stevenson, *Miss Porter's*, 186.

42. McKennan, April 25, 1861.

43. Emma W. Willard to Emma Willard, May 17, 1861, EWSA.

44. Quoted in Lord, *Life*, 260.

45. Ibid., 260–61.

46. Ibid., 253.

47. Willard to Washington, June 5, 1861.

48. Emma Willard, *History of the United States, Or, Republic of America* (New York: A. S. Barnes, 1856), 468.

49. Emma Willard, *Via Media: A Peaceful and Permanent Settlement of the Slavery Question* (Washington, DC: Charles H. Anderson, Bookseller, 1862), passim.

50. Quoted in Stevenson, *Miss Porter's*, 190.

51. Emma Willard to Sarah Willard, February 20, 1861, quoted in Lord, *Life,* 261.

52. Fairbanks, *Emma Willard*, 356.

53. Ibid., 603.

54. Sarah Lucretia Willard to John Willard, 1864, *Emma Willard Family Papers*, Box 8, Amherst College Archives.

55. Emily Virginia Mason, "Memories of a Hospital Matron," *Harper's Magazine*, October 1890, 482.

56. Quoted in Lord, *Life*, 277.

57. Sarah Lucretia Willard to John Willard, May 24, 1864, *Emma Willard Family Papers*, Box 8.

58. Mary Willard to Emma Willard, August 2, 1861, EWSA.

59. Emma Willard to Mary Whittlesey, September 10, 1865, EWSA.

60. Sarah Willard to John Willard, April 4, 1870, *Emma Willard Family Papers*, Box 8. Sarah must have left Emma and the new baby, Heywood, to get to her mother-in-law's side before she died.

61. Ibid., 42.

62. "The Household . . . Moderate Terms," *Harper's*, August 3, 1872, 606.

The Task of Reviving a Dying Institution

1. Walter A. McDougall, *Throes of Democracy: The American Civil War Era 1829–1877* (New York: HarperCollins, 2008), 563.

2. M. Emilia Rockwell, *A Home in the West, or, Immigration and Its Consequences* (Dubuque, IA: Dubuque Express and Herald, 1858).

3 For example, Francis Woodbridge, son of Eliza Cass Kercheval Woodbridge '39, served with the Seventh Infantry and was critical to the campaign to subdue the Nez Perce.

4 Bonney and her organization are widely credited with influencing Congress to pass the Dawes Act.

5. Thomas Woody, *A History of Women's Education in the United States*, vol. 1, 3rd ed. (New York: Octagon Press, 1980), 545.

6. Ibid., 546 (statistics derived from chart).

7. Emma Willard, *An Address to the Public; Particularly to the Members of the Legislature of New-York, Proposing a Plan for Improving Female Education* (Middlebury: J.W. Copeland, 1819), 5.

8. Ibid.

9. *Catalogue of the Troy Female Seminary, 1871, With Appendix Containing Mrs. Emma Willard's Plan of Female Education Published in Middlebury, VT, in 1818* (Troy: William H. Young and Blake,1871), 17, Emma Willard School Archives (hereafter EWSA).

10. *Fortieth Annual Report of the Board of Education, Together with the Fortieth Annual Report of the Secretary of the Board, 1875–76* (Boston: Albert J. Wright, State Printer, 1877), 84.

11. L. Clark Seelye, *Early History of Smith College, 1871–1910* (Boston and New York: Houghton Mifflin, 1923), 9.

12. *Catalogue of the Officers and Pupils of the Troy Female Seminary for the Academic Year Commencing September 20, 1871 and Ending June 26, 1872* (Troy: William Blake and Young, 1872), 15, EWSA.

13. No title, *Daily Picayune* (New Orleans), August 11, 1871.

14. Miscellaneous invoices, Box 6, *Emma Willard Family Papers*, Amherst College Archives.

15. In October John Willard made a $100 donation to the relief fund for families affected by the great Chicago fire, a gift whose magnitude belied any personal financial suffering.

16. "The Troy Female Seminary—An Appeal from the Trustees," November 10, 1871, *Troy Public Library Historical Scrapbook Collection* (hereafter TPLHSC), Vol. 171, 31.

17. Ibid.

18. Ibid.

19. Ibid.

20. Almira Lincoln Phelps to John Willard, May 27, 1872, Box 6, *Emma Willard Family Papers*, Amherst College Archives.

21. Gustav Schirmer to John Willard, June 19, 1872, Box 6, *Emma Willard Family Papers*, Amherst College Archives.

22. Dr. William Baker to John Willard, January 14, 1869, Box 6, *Emma Willard Family Papers*, Amherst College Archives.

23. Scudder House at St. Paul's School bears his name.

24. Horace Peck to John Willard, Box 6, *Emma Willard Family Papers*, Amherst College Archives.

25. *Catalogue 1871–1872*, 14–15, EWSA.

26. Ibid., 18.

27. Ibid., 17.

28. Kemp, the last of the old guard mayors, had been elected after Carroll. He was followed by Edward Murphy Jr., Edmund Fitzgerald, and Dennis Whelan. The new mayors, although businessmen like their predecessors, tended to be brewers, not bankers.

29. "The Troy Female Seminary," *Troy Daily Whig*, May 5, 1873; TPLHSC, Vol. 171, 81.

30. "The Changes of '72 in Troy," *Troy Northern Budget*, April 1, 1872; TPLHSC, Vol. 171, 40.

31. Ibid.

32. "Sale of Troy's Greatest Relic," *Troy Budget*, February 10, 1872; TPLHSC, Vol. 171, 38.

33. Ibid.

34. *Circular*, 1872, EWSA.

35. Mrs. A. W. Fairbanks, *Emma Willard and Her Pupils* (New York: Mrs. Russell Sage, 1898), 626.

36. "The Female Seminary Once More," *Troy Daily Times*, July 1, 1895.

37. "Notes," *Troy Daily Press*, June 17, 1873.

38. *Circular*, 1873, EWSA.

39. Emily Wilcox to Sarah Willard, n.d., EWSA.

40. *Annual Report of the Troy Female Seminary to the Board of Regents for the Year Ending June 27, 1870,* passim.

41. *Circular*, 1873–74, EWSA.

42. Ibid.

43. Paul H. Mattingly, *The Classless Profession: American Schoolmen in the Nineteenth Century* (New York: NYU Press, 1975), 83.

44. Fairbanks, *Emma Willard*, 626.

45. I was unable to find either the paper or its topic.

46. *Report to the Regents*, 1866, 18, EWSA.

47. Fairbanks, *Emma Willard*, 52.

48. Ibid.

49. Ibid., 627.

50. *Troy Female Seminary, 1881–1882* (no publisher, 1882), 10, EWSA.

51. Ibid., introductory page.

52. "The Plan Falls Through," *Daily Telegram*, February 18, 1886; TPLHSC, Vol. 178, 133.

The Best Work Women of Wealth Can Do

1. "Pictures of the Past," *The Troy Press*, n.d., *Troy Public Library Historical Scrapbook Collection* (hereafter TPLHSC).
2. Arthur James Weise, *Troy's One Hundred Years* (Troy: William H. Young, 1891), 404.
3. "The Decadence of Troy," *The Troy Press*, February 13, 1889.
4. *Tariff Hearings Before the Committee on Ways and Means, 1893* (Washington, DC: U.S. Government Printing Office), 874.
5. Weise, *Troy's One Hundred Years*, 410.
6. Ibid., 405.
7. *Tariff Hearings*, 868.
8. Eric Homberger, *Mrs. Astor's New York: Money and Social Power in the Gilded Age* (New Haven: Yale University Press, 2002), 204.
9. "Already a Sensationalist," *The Troy Press*, October 18, 1888, TPLHSC.
10. "How Lillie Is Entertaining Lady Campbell," *Morning Telegram*, November 3, 1888.
11. "The American Duchess at Blenheim," *The Troy Northern Budget*, November 4, 1888.
12. "An Unhappy Duchess," *The Troy Northern Budget*, November 25, 1888, TPLHSC.
13. "Too Bad," *The Troy Press*, November 28, 1888.
14. "Russell Sage: Says That He Loves Money and the Whole World Loves It Also," *The Troy Daily Times*, November 9, 1888.
15. Weise, *Troy's One Hundred Years*, 374.
16. "Death of John H. Willard," clipping, TPLHSC, Vol. 139, 88.
17. Mercy P. Mann to William Gurley, April 16, 1872, *William Gurley papers*, Emma Willard School Archives (hereafter EWSA).
18. William Gurley to Mercy P. Mann, April 17, 1872, *William Gurley papers*, EWSA.
19. Ibid.
20. Ibid.
21. The school ledgers are not yet formally catalogued but are housed in the EWSA.
22. "Financial Statement of Troy Female Seminary," enclosure, TPLHSC, Vol. 178, n.p.
23. "William Gurley Dead," *The Troy Press*, January 11, 1887, TPLHSC, Vol. 20, 3.
24. *Troy Reunion and Report of the Emma Willard Association*, December 1895 (Brooklyn: Collins and Day, 1895), 42, EWSA.
25. Class year unknown.
26. Mrs. Foster Bosworth, "A Graceful Tribute to the Memory of Troy's Illustrious Educator," clipping, January 5, 1889, *Emma Willard School Scrapbook Collection*, 1890–99, 5, EWSA.
27. Emma Willard Statue Association, flyer, October 1890, EWSA.
28. Baker was married to Leon Harvier, a successful actor. She was also an actress at one point but by 1889 was described as "the leader of a quite influential literary clique" ("Brief Comment: Doings of the Literary World," *Current Literature: A Magazine of Record and Review* 2, no. 3 [March 1889]: 270).
29. Belle McArthur Perry, *Lucinda Hinsdale Stone: Her Life Story and Reminiscence* (Detroit: Blinn, 1902), 161.
30. Ibid., 3.
31. Anna Howell Clarkson, *A Beautiful Mind and Its Associations* (New York: The Historical Department of Iowa, 1903), 333.
32. Harriet Dillaye to Mary Hastings, February 17, 1892, EWSA.
33. Olivia Sage to Nettie McCormick, November 9, 1891, *Nettie Fowler McCormick Papers*, Series 2B, Box 51, WSHS.
34. Louise L. Stevenson, *Miss Porter's School: A History in Documents, 1847–1948* (New York: Garland Press, 1987), 153.
35. "Troy's Female Seminary: First Annual Reunion of the Alumnae Association," *New York Times*, October 16, 1891.
36. *The Emma Willard Association of Troy Female Seminary: Report of Its Organization and First Reunion, October 15, 1891* (New York: J. J. Little and Company, 1892), 14, EWSA.
37. "Troy's Female Seminary," October 16, 1891.

38. *The Emma Willard Association . . . Report . . . 1891*, 36.

39. Ibid.

40. Ibid., 52.

41. Ibid., 48.

42. Ibid., 29.

43. "Troy's Female Seminary," October 16, 1891.

44. *The Emma Willard Association . . . Report . . . 1891*, 29.

45. "Laying the Corner-Stone," clipping, June 3, 1891, Vol. 190, 20, TPLHSC.

46. "Telegraphic Brevities," *New York Times*, March 21, 1891.

47. The YWCA building still stands; the rooms where the alumnae met and had tea now house Daisy Baker's, a popular local restaurant.

48. "Seminary Day," *The Troy Daily Press*, June 8, 1892.

49. *Reunion of the Emma Willard Association and Dedication of the Gurley Memorial Hall, Troy, June 8, 1892* (New York: J. J. Little and Company, 1892), 8.

50. Ibid., 9.

51. Whether or not the scholarship recipient was to be a graduate of the seminary was not clear. Because there are no records in the 1890s of any TFS graduates going to Middlebury, it would seem unlikely this was a criterion. This first scholarship attempt, although clearly honoring the seminary's roots, fell wide of the mark in terms of reviving the school's reputation or finances.

52. Martha Read had married Alexander Mitchell, Milwaukee's leading citizen. The current Milwaukee airport is named for their grandson, William "Billy" Mitchell, credited with founding the U.S. Air Force. Her granddaughter, Ruth Mitchell, Billy's sister, was imprisoned in a Nazi concentration camp because of her sympathies with Serbian resistance fighters.

53. This was the early name for the Albany Academy for Girls.

54. *Reunion of the Emma Willard Association . . . 1892*, 32.

55. Ibid.

56. Ruth Crocker, *Mrs. Russell Sage: Women's Activism and Philanthropy in Gilded Age and Progressive Era America* (Bloomington: Indiana University Press, 2006), 153. As Crocker ably demonstrates, between 1891 and 1893 Stanton kept up a cordial relationship with Sage that would ultimately lead to her "conversion" to woman suffrage.

57. *Reunion of the Emma Willard Association . . . 1892*, 44.

58. Ibid., 40.

59. Ibid., 41.

60. Ibid., 44.

61. Ibid., 43.

62. Ibid., 48.

63. Hall was a local businessman noted for his poetic contributions to Troy events. His wife, Margaret Lane Hall, was a member of the class of 1847.

64. "Seminary Day," 7.

65. Ibid.

66. Ibid.

67. "Mrs. Quackenbush's Gift," *Troy Daily Press*, July 21, 1892.

68. "Anna M. Plum," *The Troy Daily Times*, February 9, 1887.

69. "The Willard Seminary Building Sold," clipping, Vol. 173, 189, TPLHSC.

70. Lydia Wood Baldwin, *A Yankee Schoolteacher in Virginia* (New York: Funk & Wagnalls, 1884).

A Thorough Preparation for Any College

1. "Sage's Structure," *The Troy Daily Press*, March 9, 1893.

2. Ibid.

3. *Third Annual Report: Chicago Reunion of the Emma Willard Association of the Troy Female Seminary, November, 1893* (Brooklyn: The Brooklyn Eagle, 1893), 10–11, Emma Willard School Archives (hereafter EWSA).

4. Ibid., 11.

5. Ibid.

6. Ibid., 11–12.

7. Ibid., 12.

8. Ibid., 16.

9. Ibid., 17.

10. "Milestones in Rookwood History," retrieved May 11, 2011, from rookwood.com/timeline.html. Jane Hart Dodd's daughter, Jessie Hart Dodd, was also a ceramicist and studied and lived in Philadelphia with her first cousin, Jessie Wilcox Smith, whose mother, Katherine DeWitt Wilcox Smith, studied in Troy in 1844. Jessie Wilcox Smith was easily the most successful illustrator of children's books in the United States in the early years of the twentieth century. The edition of *A Child's Garden of Verses* that she illustrated has never gone out of print. The artistic ability that Emma Willard demonstrated in her many drawings of maps and charts seems to have had strong genetic roots.

11. *Third Annual Report . . . 1893*, 33.

12. Ibid., 37.

13. Ibid., 38.

14. Ibid., 53.

15. Ibid., 66.

16. Ibid.

17. Ibid., 67.

18. Ibid., 68.

19. Ibid.

20. "The Petition for Endowing a Female Seminary," *The Plough Boy*, April 8, 1820, 358–59.

21. Ibid., 59.

22. "That Sage Seminary Building," *The Troy Daily Press*, March 4, 1893.

23. "Emma Willard Statue," *The Troy Daily Press*, March 4, 1893.

24. Ibid.

25. "Sage's Structure," March 9, 1893, 1.

26. Ibid.

27. The Western Union building, constructed in the 1870s, was for a short time the tallest building in Manhattan and the first office building to contain elevators. It was also aesthetically grand, with mansard roofs and many extra features, particularly on its top floors. Workers transmitted telegrams from its offices twenty-four hours a day, seven days a week, and the building was always lighted.

28. "Sage's Structure," March 9, 1893.

29. "Emma Willard Statue," March 4, 1893.

30. "All is Chaos," *The Troy Daily Times*, July 18, 1893.

31. In 1891 Sage had been the object of an assassination attempt, which he allegedly foiled by pulling a clerk in front of him as a human shield. The assassin blew himself up accidentally, and the clerk was disabled for life. Sage did not voluntarily provide any relief for the injured man, who sued him. Nor was this the only suit brought against him. On July 19, 1893, the last day of the Chicago reunion, newspapers carried word of a former housemaid's suit against him for "seduction under promise of marriage" ("Russell Sage Sued by a Woman," *The Troy Daily Times*, July 19, 1893).

32. Ruth Crocker, *Mrs. Russell Sage: Women's Activism and Philanthropy in Gilded Age and Progressive Era America* (Bloomington: Indiana University Press, 2006), passim.

33. George L. Howard, "Russell Sage as a Philanthropist," *Broadway Magazine*, September 1904, 26.

34. *Third Annual Report . . . 1893*, 71.

35. Ibid., 90.

36. Ibid., 91.

37. Ibid., 92.

38. *Third Annual Report . . . 1893*, 93.

39. "Music and Art," *The Troy Daily Press*, September 13, 1894.

40. Ibid.

41. Ibid. This office is currently a part of the suite of offices used by the president of Russell Sage College.

42. Ibid.

43. Ibid.

44. "Its First Woman Trustee," *New York Herald-Tribune*, October 19, 1894, 7.

45. "Equal Suffrage for Women," *New York Times*, April 15, 1894. Flower was not reelected. He was succeeded by Republican Levi P. Morton, whose first wife's mother was Sarah Hinsdale Kimball '20, a relative of Emma Willard who studied under her at Waterford.

46. "Emma Willard Association Reunion," *New York Times*, October 19, 1894.

47. *Report of the Emma Willard Association, Troy Reunion, Unveiling of the Emma Willard Statue and the Dedication of Russell Sage Hall* (Brooklyn: Collins and Day, 1895), 36 EWSA.

48. Ibid., 40.

49. Ibid., 42.

50. Ibid., 43.

51. Ibid., 44.

52. Ibid., 5.

53. Ibid.

54. Ibid., 7.

55. Ibid., 9.

56. Ibid., 8.

57. Ibid., 23–24.

58. Ibid., 26.

59. Ibid.

60. Ibid., 27.

61. Ibid., 30.

62. "The Principal Resigns," *The Troy Daily Times*, May 17, 1895.

63. Emily Wilcox to Olivia Sage, March 6, 1893, Box 1, Folder 2, Margaret Olivia Slocum Sage Collection EWSA.

64. *Report of the . . . Unveiling*, 67. Although the EWA took credit for changing the name of the school—and the new name was used after May 1895—the official name change was not approved by New York State until 1910.

65. Ibid., 70.

66. Ibid.

67. Ibid., 71.

68. "Between 1894 and 1896 . . . community outreach," Patricia Ann Palmieri, *In Adamless Eden: The Community of Women Faculty at Wellesley* (New Haven: Yale University Press, 1995), 46.

69. Ibid., 51.

70. *Emma Willard School*, flyer EWSA.

71. Ibid.

72. Ibid.

73. *Report of the Committee of Ten on Secondary School Studies with the Reports of the Conferences Arranged by the Committee*, 2nd ed. (New York: American Book Co., 1894), iii.

74. *Report of the Commissioner of Education for the Year 1894–95*, Vol. 2 (Washington, DC: U.S. Government Printing Office, 1896), 1172.

75. *Committee of Ten*, 5.

76. Her sister, Anna Leach, would succeed Mary Alice Knox as principal of Emma Willard in 1902.

77. *Committee of Ten*, 6.

78. Ibid., 6.

79. Ibid.

80. Ibid., 12.

81. *Troy Female Seminary, 1894-95* (Troy: William H. Young, 1894), 12. Interestingly, there were a few students from out of town who boarded with local families. In 1894 these included girls from Geneva and Saranac, New York; Germantown, Pennsylvania, and Fort Scott, Kansas.

82. Ibid., 20.

83. The catalog titled 1895–96 set forth the calendar and curriculum for 1896–97, the one titled 96–97 the calendar for 97–98, and so on.

84 *Report of the . . . Unveiling*, 70.

85 "Troy Female Seminary," *The Watchman* [Boston], September 19, 1895. The same ad appeared in *The New York Evangelist*, *The Independent*, and *The Christian Advocate*.

86. Henry McMillen, "A Sumptuous Spread," *The Troy Press*, November 6, 1896.

87. Ibid.

88. Ibid.

89. Ibid.

90. Donald Lateiner, "Elizabeth Hazelton Haight, 1872–1964," *The Classical World*, November 1996, 155.

91. *Informal Record of the Faculty Meetings of the Emma Willard School*, February 26, 1896, 27, EWSA.

92. *Faculty of the Emma Willard School, Minutes*, May 25, 1900.

93. *Troy Female Seminary, 1894–95* (Troy: William H. Young, 1895), 24, EWSA.

94. *Annual Catalogue of the Emma Willard School, formerly The Troy Female Seminary, 1895–96* (Troy: E. H. Lisk, 1896), 11, EWSA.

95. *Informal Record of Faculty Meetings*, October 22, 1895, 5.

96. Ibid., December 4, 1895, 12.

97. Ibid., September 30, 1896, 49.

98. Ibid., March 4, 1896, 28.

99. Ibid., 27.

100. "The Emma Willard School," *The Troy Press*, June 10, 1896.

101. Nancy Davis and Barbara Donahue, *Miss Porter's School: A History* (Farmington, CT: Miss Porter's School, 1992), 21.

102. Louise L. Stevenson, *Miss Porter's School: A History in Documents, 1847–1948* (New York: Garland Press, 1987), n.p.

No Lovelier Landscape Than That from Ida Hill

1. "Editorial," *Triangle*, December 1901, 1, Emma Willard School Archives (hereafter EWSA).

2. *Faculty of the Emma Willard School: Minutes*, October 15, 1901, EWSA.

3. Ibid.

4. "News," *Triangle*, December 1901, 7–8.

5. *Troy Daily Press*, November 2, 1901.

6. "At the Emma Willard School," *Troy Daily Press*, April 23, 1898.

7. "Notes from Emma Willard School," *Troy Daily Press*, January 28, 1899.

8. *Informal Record of Faculty Meetings*, March 10, 1897, EWSA.

9. Clipping, *Troy Public Library Historical Scrapbook* 184 (May 2, 1898): 63.

10. "A Dance at the Seminary," *Troy Daily Press*, December 13, 1898.

11. "News from Emma Willard School," *Troy Daily Press*, June 8, 1899.

12. *Eighth Annual Report, Constitution, By-Laws and List of Members of the Emma Willard Association* (Brooklyn: Styles and Cash, 1898), 12, EWSA.

13. *Tenth Annual Report, Constitution, By-Laws and List of Members of the Emma Willard Association* (Brooklyn: Brooklyn Eagle, 1900), 10, EWSA.

14. *Twentieth Annual Report, Constitution, By-Laws and List of Members of the Emma Willard Association* (Brooklyn: Eagle Press, November 1910), 9, EWSA.

15. "Mrs. Sage's Reminiscences," *New York Times*, June 20, 1897.

16. Interestingly, many upper-class women found Stanton to be unruly, undisciplined (at least in her eating habits), and irreligious.

17. "Mrs. Sage's Reminiscences," June 20, 1897.

18. Ibid.

19. *Cash Ledger, Troy Female Seminary*, 1895–96, EWSA.

20. *Annual Catalogue of Emma Willard School, Formerly the Troy Female Seminary, 1896–97* (Troy: E. H. Lisk, 1897), 16, EWSA.

21. *Faculty Meeting Minutes*, January 25, 1898, EWSA.

22. *Faculty Meeting Minutes*, March 6, 1900, EWSA.

23. *Annual Catalogue of Emma Willard School, Formerly the Troy Female Seminary, 1900–01* (Troy: Troy Times Art Press, 1901), 18, EWSA.

24. *Emma Willard School Catalogue, 1896–97*, 19, EWSA.

25. *EWS Catalogue, 1900–01*, 26, EWSA.

26. Ibid., 28.

27. *Annual Catalogue of Emma Willard School, Formerly the Troy Female Seminary, 1899–00* (Troy: Troy Times, 1898), 32, EWSA.

28. Ibid., 34.

29. Ibid., 39.

30. *Emma Willard School Catalogue, 1896–97*, 28.

31. "Seminarians Instructed in Gymnastics," Troy Public Library Historical Scrapbook (TPLHS), 183, 46.

32. *Annual Catalogue of Emma Willard School, Formerly the Troy Female Seminary, 1898–99*, 12, EWSA.

33. "At the Emma Willard School," *The Troy Daily Press*, October 9, 1898.

34. *Emma Willard School Catalogue, 1896–97*, 11.

35. *Emma Willard School Catalogue, 1898–99*, 12.

36. "Back to Their Studies," *Troy Daily Press*, September 23, 1896.

37. "News Around Campus," *Triangle*, May 1906, 61, EWSA.

38. Caspar Whitney and Albert Britt, eds., "Field Hockey as a Woman's Sport," *Outing* 45 (October 1904–March 1905): 477.

39. "News," *Triangle*, June 1902, 25, EWSA.

40. *Secretary's Book of the Cooperative Government Association of the Emma Willard School*, 113, EWSA.

41. "Editorial," *Triangle*. June 1902, 1.

42. Information taken from "In the Schools of the State," *American Education* 5, no. 6 (February 1902): 360.

43. Endorsement, Henry N. Hudson, ed., *Romeo and Juliet* (Boston: Ginn and Company, 1898), 189.

44. *Faculty Minutes*, January 27, 1902, EWSA.

45. "At Emma Willard School" *Troy Record*, February 9, 1902.

46. "In Honor of New Principal," *Troy Record*, February 10, 1902.

47. Information taken from "New Principal Greeted," *Troy Record*, February 11,1902.

48. "Editorial," *Triangle*, March 1902, 1, EWSA.

49. "Editorial," *Triangle*, June 1902, 1, EWSA.

50. "Editorial," *Triangle*, April 1910, 34, EWSA.

51. "Domestic Science," *Triangle*, November 1909, 2, EWSA.

52. *12th Annual Report, Constitution, By-Laws and List of Members of the Emma Willard Association, 1902* (Brooklyn: Eagle Press), 5, EWSA.

53. *13th Annual Report, Constitution, By-Laws and List of Members of the Emma Willard Association, 1903* (Brooklyn: Eagle Press), 4, EWSA.

54. *14th Annual Report, Constitution, By-Laws and List of Members of the Emma Willard Association, 1904* (Brooklyn: Eagle Press), 15, EWSA.

55. *Report, Emma Willard Association, 1910*, 7.

56. *15th Annual Report, Constitution, By-Laws and List of Members of the Emma Willard Association, 1905* (Brooklyn: Eagle Press), 5, EWSA.

57. *Report, Emma Willard Association, 1903*, 10.

58. Ibid.

59. The architect for this project was primarily Fred Cummings, Marcus Cummings's son. Mark, the elder Cummings, had retired from active practice and was living in Vineyard Haven. He consulted periodically with his son, and all the drawings were stamped "Marcus F. Cummings and Son."

60. Marcus F. Cummings and Son, *Estimate of Costs—Emma Willard School*, December 18, 1906, EWSA.

61. William F. Gurley to Robert DeForest, December 19, 1906, EWSA.

62. Picture and caption in *TPLHS* 17 (1910), 49.

63. Abba A. Goddard, ed., "A Letter," *The Trojan Sketchbook* (Troy: Young and Hart, 1846), 163.

64. Robert DeForest to William F. Gurley, January 30, 1907, EWSA.

65. Anna Leach to Margaret Olivia Slocum Sage, January 28, 1907, EWSA.

66. "Gifts by Mrs. Sage," *Washington Post*, February 2, 1907.

67. "Editorial," *Triangle*, April 1907, 1, EWSA.

68. "Praise Mrs. Sage for $1,000,000 Gift," *New York Times*, November 15, 1907.

69. *17th Annual Report, Constitution, By-Laws and List of Members of the Emma Willard Association, 1907*, 13, EWSA.

70. "Praise Mrs. Sage," 9.

71. *Report, Emma Willard Association, 1907*, 14.

72. Ibid., 21.

73. *Ninety-Fourth Year of the Emma Willard School, 1907–08* (Philadelphia: Charles Elliott Co.), 10, EWSA.

74. *Ninetieth Year of the Emma Willard School, 1903–04*, no pub., 13, EWSA.

75. *Eighty-Ninth Year of the Emma Willard School, 1902–03* (Troy: Henry Stowell and Son), 25, EWSA.

76. *Ninety-First Year of the Emma Willard School, 1904–05*, no pub., 28, EWSA.

77. *Emma Willard School Catalogue, 1907–08*, 26, EWSA.

78. *Faculty Meeting Minutes*, passim.

79. Frederick Orr to William Gurley, 1910, EWSA.

80. *Development Office Report on Meeting between Walter Maguire and Elizabeth Skinner*, 1971, "Elizabeth Skinner, *Alumnae files*, EWSA.

81. Laura Bradley to Anna Leach, October 4, 1908, EWSA.

82. *Trustee Minutes*, February 4, 1911, EWSA.

83. There was perhaps a family trait that explains her volatility. Abby Leach was described in a biographical sketch as "distressingly inflexible" and "inspiring admiration rather than affection." Her biographers concluded that her "career was marred by her inability to get along with Grace Harriet McCurdy" (another iconic classics professor at Vassar). Edward T. James, Janet Wilson James, Paul S. Boyer, *Notable American Women, 1607–1950* (Cambridge: Belknap Press of Harvard University Press, 1971), 380.

84. *Trustee Minutes*, February 4, 1911.

85. "Check no. 543," *William F. Gurley Papers*, EWSA.

86. *Trustee Minutes*, February 23, 1911, EWSA.

87. "Willard School's New Principal," *Troy Daily Press*, February 23, 1911; "Emma Willard School," *Troy Record*, February 23, 1911.

There Is Only One Miss Kellas

1. Paul Cook to Agnes Irwin, February 20, 1911, Emma Willard Archives (hereafter EWSA).

2. Robin MacKenzie Johnson, "A Celebration Remembrance: Miss Eliza Kellas," *Emma Willard Bulletin*, Spring 1989, 6.

3. As Emma's name suggests, the Cook family had a long association with and affection for the school. Paul's mother, Mary Halsey Thomas Cook, was a member of the class of 1840 and taught at the seminary from 1842 to 1846. His father also taught at the school in the 1840s. Paul's father, George, was the state geologist for New Jersey, and as Paul would do later, earned a degree from RPI. Both men met their seminary wives while studying in Troy. Paul's sister, Sarah, graduated in 1868. His first wife, Esther Gurley '71, was the daughter of William Gurley. Paul joined her father's firm and joined his father-in-law as a board member at the seminary in 1879. In a letter to Olivia Sage (January 12, 1917, EWSA) Paul Cook explained his connection with the school: "My heart is in the Emma Willard School for my own Mother was educated there and my sisters were also and I have had five daughters graduate there and now two granddaughters are under Miss Kellas's care."

4. Agnes Irwin to Paul Cook, January 11, 1911, EWSA.

5. Potsdam Normal School is now the State University of New York at Potsdam. When Eliza Kellas entered Radcliffe in 1907, her sister, Katharine Kellas, was the preceptress at Potsdam. She had started there in 1901 and would remain until 1917 when she joined her sister in Troy as the dean of Russell Sage College.

6. Edward W. Flagg to Radcliffe, February 6, 1907, Schlesinger Library, Radcliffe Institute, Harvard University.

7. Elizabeth B. Potwine, *Faithfully Yours, Eliza Kellas* (Troy: Emma Willard School, 2000), 36.

8. Edith V. Brill to Elizabeth Potwine, *Elizabeth Potwine Collection*, EWSA.

9. Ibid.

10. Ruth was a teenager when Eliza Kellas left to go to Emma Willard, but she did not attend the school. Nevertheless, she wrote to Elizabeth Potwine that Miss Kellas was a strong influence on her childhood, and as Ruth Cheney Streeter, she became the first director of the women's division of the U.S. Marine Corps Reserve in 1943.

11. Agnes Irwin to Paul Cook, February 22, 1911, EWSA.

12. "Editorials," *Triangle*, April 1911, 1.

13. Doris Crockett, *untitled reminiscences*, EWSA.

14. "The Scene of a Commotion," clipping, *Emma Willard School Scrapbook*, 1911, EWSA.

15. Ibid., untitled clipping,.

16. "School Notes," *Triangle*, February 1911, 29.

17. Marie Longendyke '13, "Class History," *Gargoyle*, 1913, 40.

18. "Fine New Victrola," *Triangle*, February 1911.

19. Eliza Kellas to Margaret Olivia Slocum Sage, March 17, 1911, EWSA.

20. Troy Chamber of Commerce, *A New Troy* (Troy: Troy Press), 1913, 34.

21. Ibid., 35.

22. The first agencies for schools and camps appeared around this time. The first edition of Porter Sargent was published in 1915.

23. "Emma Willard Buildings Practically Completed," *Troy Record*, June 3, 1910.

24. Potwine, *Faithfully Yours*, 79.

25. *Troy Record*, June 3, 1910.

26. Ibid.

27. Ibid.

28. "Notable Schools of Troy, New York, Pioneers and Finely Equipped," *Christian Science Monitor*, November 6, 1912.

29. *Troy Record*, June 3, 1910.

30. *Emma Willard School in its 98th Year* (Boston: A. W. Elson, 1912), 38.

31. *Troy Northern Budget*, September 10, 1911.

32. *Minutes, Emma Willard Board of Trustees*, May 16, 1915, EWSA.

33. *Minutes*, October 13, 1919, EWSA.

34. *Minutes*, October 17, 1919, EWSA.

35. Eliza Kellas to Lizzie Lee Pound '15, July 25, 1913, EWSA.

36. Eliza Kellas to William D. Quackenbush, May 2, 1919, EWSA.

37. Bertrand Snell, "Eliza Kellas," EWSA.

38. "School Notes," *Triangle*, June 1920, 16.

39. "Graduation at Emma Willard," clipping, Emma Willard Scrapbook, EWSA.

40. Eliza Kellas to E. Lilian Todd, January 19, 1916, EWSA.

41. "School Notes," *Triangle*, March 1916, 26.

42. "Editorial," *Triangle*, December 1918, 5.

43. "Alumnae Notes," *Triangle*, March 1919, 41.

44. Eliza Kellas to Margaret Olivia Slocum Sage, June 16, 1913, EWSA.

45. Eliza Kellas to Margaret Olivia Slocum Sage, June 17, 1914, EWSA.

46. "Class History," *Gargoyle*, 1917, 71.

47. E. Lilian Todd to Eliza Kellas, June 4, 1914, EWSA.

48. E. Lilian Todd to Eliza Kellas, September 9, 1914, EWSA.

49. Eliza Kellas to E. Lilian Todd, June 22, 1914, EWSA.

50. "100 Years of Work," *The Northern Budget*, September 6, 1914.

51. The only sour note was a complaint in the *Troy Record* that "the statue of the founder . . . has been overlooked, not a piece of bunting, a flower or a flag being in evidence." "An Oversight," *Troy Record*, October 7, 1914.

52. Emma Willard," *Troy Times*, October 6, 1914.

53. Ibid.

54. "The Centennial Celebration," *Twenty-Fourth Report of the Emma Willard Association* (Brooklyn: Brooklyn Eagle Press, 1914), 24.

55. Ibid.
56. "Conclusion of Exercises," *Troy Times*, October 7, 1914.
57. *Twenty-Fourth Report, E.W.A.*, 26.
58. "Mrs. Louise K. Theirs 100 Years Old Today," *Milwaukee Free Press*, October 2, 1914.
59. "Centenarian Is Interested in European War," *Evening Wisconsin*, October 2, 1914.
60. *Emma Willard, Ninety-Eighth Year*, 35.
61. Ibid., 11.
62. Ibid.
63. Eliza Kellas to Margaret Olivia Slocum Sage, November 16, 1912, EWSA.
64. *Emma Willard School One Hundred and Sixth Year* (Philadelphia: Elliott, 1920), 37.
65. *Catalogue, 1911–12*, 17.
66. Application materials, alumna file, 1916, EWSA.
67. Application materials, alumnae files, 1911 and 1928, EWSA.
68. *Catalogue, 1902–3*, 12.
69. Eliza Kellas to George T. Diener, September 5, 1911, EWSA.
70. Jerome Korabel, *The Chosen: The Hidden History of Admission and Exclusion at Harvard, Yale and Princeton* (Boston: Houghton Mifflin, 2005), 88.
71. Kellas to Diener, September 5, 1911.
72. *Catalogue, 1911–12*, 12.

The Biggest Influence on My Life

1. Lila Shepard to Eliza Kellas, March 28, 1915, Emma Willard School Archives (hereafter EWSA).
2. Lila Shepard to Eliza Kellas, Fall 1915, EWSA.
3. Ibid.
4. Lila Shepard to Eliza Kellas, July 21, 1915, EWSA.
5. "Report of the Emma Willard Chapter of the Surgical Dressings Committee," December 24, 1914, EWSA.
6. "Social Activities," *Troy Times*, January 6, 1916.
7. "Alumnae Notes," *Triangle*, November 1919, 30.
8. Eliza Kellas to E. Lilian Todd, January 1, 1918, EWSA.
9. Note included in a letter from Francis Otis to Eliza Kellas, June 13, 1918, EWSA. Translation: "At the head of my bed is a plaque, 'Emma Willard School.'"
10. Program, "Pageant of the Allied Nations," May 3 and 4, 1918, EWSA.
11. E. Lilian Todd, *Report on Emma Willard School*, June 19, 1918, EWSA.
12. Bertrand Snell, "Eliza Kellas," EWSA.
13. *Gargoyle 1917*, 88.
14. *Gargoyle 1919*, 111.
15. Prices were still being set according to the size of the room a girl occupied; minimums for each of these years were $200 lower than the maximums.
16. *Gargoyle 1919*, 111.
17. "Right Has Triumphed Over Might," *Triangle*, December 1918, 4.
18. E. L.'19, "Gassed," *Triangle*, November 1919, 8.
19. This generalization is predicated on the assumption that the students generally voted like their parents. In every straw poll for president between 1920 and 1940, inclusive, the students overwhelmingly picked the Republican candidate—as did the faculty. Eliza Kellas was on record as a member of the Republican Party.
20. "Miss Eliza Kellas Chosen Leading 1937 Troy Citizen," newspaper clipping, *Emma Willard School Scrapbook 1936–38*, EWSA.
21. Eliza Kellas to E. Lilian Todd, May 12, 1915, EWSA.
22. E. Lilian Todd to Margaret Olivia Slocum Sage (MOSS), June 1, 1915, EWSA.
23. E. Lilian Todd to Eliza Kellas, May 10, 1915, EWSA.
24. E. Lilian Todd to Eliza Kellas, November 16, 1915, EWSA.
25. Eliza Kellas to Grace Brandow '19, early 1916, EWSA.
26. MOSS to Emma Willard Board of Trustees, December 23, 1915, EWSA.

27. E. Lilian Todd to Robert DeForest, November 26, 1915, EWSA.
28. *New York American*, 1914, quoted in Time-Life Books, *This Fabulous Century*, vol. 2 (New York: Time, 1969), 35.
29. MOSS to the Emma Willard School Board of Trustees, December 23, 1915, EWSA.
30. MOSS to the Emma Willard Board of Trustees, September 17, 1917, EWSA.
31. "B.S. Course, Department of Practical Arts," *Bulletin of Russell Sage College: Catalogue 1921–22* (Troy: Russell Sage College), 1921, 26.
32. Father Leo Clark to Eliza Kellas, November 27, 1920, EWSA.
33. E. Lilian Todd to MOSS, October 1916, EWSA.
34. Emma Willard did not open until October 4.
35. E. Lilian Todd to Eliza Kellas, November 10, 1918, EWSA.
36. "Memories," Katherine Knowlton McLane '23, EWSA.
37. "Miss Katherine Kellas," *Triangle*, March 1942, 5.
38. Louise Porter Thomas '30, "Miss Katherine Kellas," ibid., 8.
39. *Emma Willard School in Its Ninety-Eighth Year* (Boston: A. W. Elson Co., 1911), 12.
40. *Emma Willard School In Its One Hundred and Fourth Year* (Boston: Elliott, 1917), 25.
41. Eliza Kellas to Louise Fessenden '32, June 11, 1931, EWSA.
42. Ibid.
43. Elizabeth Fessenden '32 to Eliza Kellas, October 27, 1933, EWSA.
44. Eliza Kellas to Enid Dutcher '33, June 24, 1930, EWSA.
45. Ibid.
46. Isabelle Adie '32 to Anne Wellington, June 12, 1950, EWSA.
47. Johnson, "A Celebration Remembrance," 6.
48. Ibid.
49. Jeanne Skerry '41 to mother, April 1943, EWSA.
50. "For the Residents of the Emma Willard School," 1927–28, EWSA.
51. "Miss Eliza Kellas Chosen Leading 1937 Troy Citizen."
52. Frances Faust Moore '19, "Emma Willard During the War, and Other Memories," *Triangle*, March 1936, 9.
53. "A Celebration Remembrance," 6.
54. "Daily Record of Health Habits," *Papers of Elisabeth Miles Crow '27*, EWSA.
55. "The skirt . . . one-piece suit," *Emma Willard School in Its One Hundredth Year, 1913–14* (Belmont, MA: A. W. Elson), 1913, 37.
56. "List to Be Sent to Laundry," *Crow Papers*, EWSA.
57. "Memories," McLane.
58. Priscilla O'Connell Kinney '39 to Trudy Hall, July 31, 2000, in file, "Priscilla O'Connell," EWSA.
59. Eliza Kellas to Grace Brandow '19, January 3, 1924, EWSA.
60. *Principal's Report to the Board of Trustees*, November 17, 1930, EWSA.
61. Elizabeth Rose '32 to Eliza Kellas, February 23, 1937, EWSA.
62. Mary Elizabeth Campbell '24 to Eliza Kellas, February 18, 1926, EWSA.
63. Adeline Aldrich '19 to Eliza Kellas, December 24, 1940, EWSA.
64. Eliza Kellas to parents of a student, 1933, EWSA.
65. Emily Abel '33, *1972 Reunion Questionnaire*, EWSA.
66. Emily Abel '33 to Eliza Kellas, January 17, 1942, EWSA.
67. "Editorial," *Triangle*, December 1924, 2.
68. Today this is the admissions waiting room.
69. Eliza Kellas to Joan Goodrich Lang '35, July 17, 1934, EWSA.
70. Elesa Scott '27, *Scrapbook 1926–27*, EWSA.
71. The General Information Test was a current events test sprung by surprise on the students periodically throughout the year, most often on Saturdays.
72. *Gargoyle 1915*, 116.
73. "Athletic Notes," *Triangle*, December 1918, 20.
74. "Athletic Notes," *Triangle*, March 1920, 17.
75. *Gargoyle 1923*, 125.

76. *Gargoyle 1926*, 140.
77. *Gargoyle 1940*, 90.
78. Ellen Russell Manchester, "Yule Log Revels," *Emma Willard Alumnae News*, 1931, 26.
79. Ellen Russell Manchester to Dorothy Kirkland, March 18, 1960, EWSA.
80. "School Notes," *Triangle*, January 1917, 18.
81. "The Story of Revels," *Triangle*, December 1938, 8.
82. "Letters to the Editor," *Triangle*, June 1923, 3.
83. "School Notes," *Triangle*, March 1923, 21.
84. "School Notes," *Triangle*, March 1932, 21.
85. "Editorial," *Triangle*, December 1933, 1.
86. *Gargoyle 1943*, 68.
87. Alice Dodge '38 to Homer and Margaret Dodge, November 1937, *Papers of Alice Dodge Wallace*, Boulder, Colorado.
88. "School Notes," *Triangle*, December 1918, 15.
89. Scott, *Scrapbook*.
90. Today this ceremony is known as Flame Ceremony.
91. Ibid.
92. "School Notes," *Triangle*, June 1921, 21.
93. Scott, *Scrapbook*.
94. *Gargoyle 1940*, 86.
95. "School Notes," *Triangle*, November 1920, 18.
96. Elizabeth Potwine, *Faithfully Yours, Eliza Kellas* (Troy: Emma Willard School, 2000), 28.
97. *Gargoyle 1912*, 70.
98. *Gargoyle 1918*, 125.
99. "School Notes," *Triangle*, June 1939, 23.
100. Ibid.
101. "School Notes," *Triangle*, June 1921, 22.
102. Eliza Kellas to Grace Brandow '19, May 24, 1922, EWSA.
103. "School Notes," *Triangle*, June 1925, 23.
104. "School Notes," *Triangle*, June 1939, 23.
105. Katherine Eisner '41 to mother, Spring 1941, EWSA.
106. F. Scott Fitzgerald, *Tender Is The Night* (New York: Charles Scribner's Sons, 1921), 304.
107. "School Notes," *Triangle*, December 1938, 29.
108. Quoted in Frederick Lewis Allen, *Only Yesterday*, 1931, Kindle edition, loc. 1396–1402.
109. *Gargoyle 1912*, 81.
110. Eliza Kellas to Grace Brandow '19, July 4, 1933, EWSA.
111. Eva Judd to Eliza Kellas, January 14, 1929, EWSA.
112. Carol Derby '21, "America Sings," *Triangle,* March 1921, 6.
113. "Memories," McLane.
114. "America's Destiny Linked with China, Japan, by Speaker," newspaper clipping, January 28, 1935, *Emma Willard Scrapbook*, EWSA.
115. "Speaker Describes Nazi Leaders' Minds as in State of 'Piracy,'" newspaper clipping, January 22, 1940, *Emma Willard Scrapbook*, EWSA.
116. *Gargoyle 1942*, 5.
117. "From Wellesley," *Triangle,* December 1929, 24.
118. "Mount Holyoke," *Triangle,* December 1930, 21.
119. *Principal's Report to the Board of Trustees*, November 13, 1933, EWSA.
120. "Mount Holyoke," December 1930.
121. "From Vassar," *Triangle,* December 1931, 18.
122. Mount Holyoke," December 1930.

In Spite of Present Conditions

1. "To Miss Kellas," *Triangle*, June 1942, 6.
2. Ibid., 5.

3. Evelyn Fry '37, "Changes on Our Campus," *Triangle*, March 1936, 5.
4. "Emma Willard Residence Hall Nearly Finished," *Troy Record*, September 18, 1928.
5. Ibid.
6. Ibid.
7. Eliza Kellas to William Shields, August 16, 1927, Emma Willard School Archives (hereafter EWSA).
8. Ibid.
9. Ibid.
10. Anonymous, *Reunion Questionnaire*, June 1972, EWSA.
11. Kellas to Shields, August 16, 1927.
12. *Papers of William F. Shields*, EWSA.
13. "School Notes," *Triangle*, December 1929, 21.
14. *Gargoyle 1933*, 93.
15. *Gargoyle 1932*, 101.
16. Ibid., 25.
17. Edgar H. Betts to James Dawson, December 12, 1929, EWSA.
18. James Dawson to Eliza Kellas, March 8, 1930, EWSA.
19. *Principal's Report to the Board of Trustees*, November 17, 1930, EWSA.
20. Ibid.
21. Ibid.
22. J. D. Langdon, *Report to Olmsted Brothers*, May 1, 1930, EWSA.
23. *Minutes of the Emma Willard Board of Trustees*, October 6, 1930, EWSA.
24. *Principal's Report to the Board of Trustees*, November 13, 1933, EWSA..
25. *Principal's Report to the Board of Trustees*, December 30, 1929, EWSA.
26. *Principal's Report to the Board of Trustees, 1931–32*, EWSA.
27. *Principal's Report to the Board of Trustees*, February 6, 1932, EWSA.
28. *Principal's Report to the Board of Trustees*, October 23, 1939, EWSA.
29. *Principal's Report to the Board of Trustees*, October 10, 1938, EWSA.
30. *Principal's Report to the Board of Trustees*, October 27, 1941, EWSA.
31. Eleanor Alford '31 to Eliza Kellas, August 25, 1932, EWSA.
32. Eloise Blinn Trowbridge '27 to Eliza Kellas, January 21, 1932, EWSA.
33. *Principal's Report to the Board of Trustees*, June 9, 1933, EWSA.
34. Elizabeth Butler '32 to Eliza Kellas, March 9, 1933, EWSA.
35. Ibid.
36. Eleanor Alford '31 to Eliza Kellas, July 20, 1932, EWSA.
37. Evelyn Orr to William Shields, January 12, 1933, EWSA.
38. *Minutes of the Emma Willard Board of Trustees*. May 9, 1938, EWSA.
39. *Minutes of the Emma Willard Board of Trustees*, September 11, 1933, EWSA.
40. *Principal's Report to the Board of Trustees*, May 13, 1934, EWSA.
41. *Treasurer's Report*, January 11, 1932, EWSA.
42. *Minutes of the Emma Willard Board of Trustees*, October 23, 1939, EWSA.
43. *Report on Sage Hall, 1940–41*, EWSA.
44. *Principal's Report to the Board of Trustees*, May 10, 1937, EWSA.
45. Ibid.
46. *Principal's Report to the Board of Trustee*, June 16, 1932, EWSA.
47. *Minutes of the Emma Willard Board of Trustees*, May 9, 1932, EWSA.
48. *Emma Willard School Catalogue, 1939–40*, 36.
49. Amy Pfau Butler to Eliza Kellas, August 14, 1932, EWSA.
50. *Principal's Report to the Board of Trustees*, May 8, 1939, EWSA.
51. Ibid.
52. *Minutes of the Emma Willard Board of Trustees*, October 1, 1938.
53. Edward Pattison to Stanton Lee, October 18, 1940, *Papers of Edward Pattison*, EWSA.
54. *Minutes of the Board of Trustees*, March 25, 1936, EWSA.
55. *Report of a Meeting of the Special Committee on the Development of the School*, April 7, 1936, EWSA.

56. *Report of the Principal for 1936–37*, EWSA.
57. "The Science Building," *Triangle*, March 1937, 14.
58. "Science Building at Emma Willard Ready for Fall," *Troy Record,* July 21, 1937.
59. *Principal's Report to the Board of Trustees*, October 27, 1941, EWSA.
60. *Principal's Report to the Board of Trustees*, January 22, 1940, EWSA.
61. *Principal's Report*, October 27, 1941.
62. Ibid.
63. *Evaluation of Secondary Schools: General Report on the Methods, Activities and Results of the Co-operative Study of Secondary School Standards* (Washington, DC: Cooperative Study of Secondary School Standards, 1939), v.
64. *Principal's Report*, January 9, 1939, EWSA.
65. *Power House Report*, January 1940, 16, EWSA.
66. *Minutes of the Board of Trustees*, December 12, 1939.
67. T. D. H., "Ann Arbor Town," newspaper clipping, *Emma Willard School Scrapbook*, 1938, EWSA.
68. "125 Years at Emma Willard," newspaper clipping, *Emma Willard School Scrapbook*, EWSA.
69. Ibid.
70. *Minutes of the Board of Trustees*, May 8, 1939, EWSA.
71. Pat Connally '41, "Emma Willard Abroad," *Triangle*, December 1939, 17.
72. "Recommendation for Smith College," *File of Ingrid Siering*, EWSA.
73. "School Notes," *Triangle*, March 1942, 30.
74. Eliza Kellas to Grace Brandow '19, December 24, 1942, EWSA.
75. Eliza Kellas to Helen L. McCook Jordan '14, December 1942, EWSA.
76. This position was analogous to today's position of dean of admissions.
77. "Miss Kellas Retires," newspaper clipping, *Eliza Kellas Collection*, EWSA.
78. In a visit with the author in July 1986, Anne Wellington recalled how frustrated she was by Eliza Kellas showing up in Slocum almost daily with constant advice about how things were done at Emma Willard.
79. *Principal's Report*, October 12, 1942.

That Sensitive Balance Between Tradition and Innovation

1. John P. Marquand, *H. M. Pulham, Esq.* (New York: Little, Brown, 1941), 71.
2. Russell Lynes, "Can The Private School Survive?" *Harper's Magazine*, January 1948, 39–41.
3. James Phinney Baxter, "Inflation Hits the Colleges," *The Atlantic*, March 1948, 59–62.
4. Miyoko Sugano would return to Hawaii where she became a professor at the University of Hawaii and the author of books on native Hawaiian women and their literature. She also writes poetry.
5. "Education Gallops Upon a Trojan Horse," *Washington Post,* June 13, 1948.
6. "Emma Willard School Conducts Commencement," *The Troy Record*, June 12, 1950.
7. Harvard University, *General Education in a Free Society* (Cambridge: Harvard University Press, 1945), viii.
8. Lynn T. White, *Educating Our Daughters: A Challenge to the Colleges* (New York: Harper Brothers, 1950), ix.
9. Ibid., 60.
10. "The Plan of Education of Emma Willard School," *Bulletin of Emma Willard School* 5, no. 2 (1947): introduction.
11. Jane Reuhle '51 to the author, November 19, 2008.
12. Benjamin Fine, "Education in Review," *New York Times*, July 29, 1945.
13. Clemewell Lay, "Wellesley College 50th Reunion Questionnaire," Spring 1969, *Alumna File: Clemewell Lay '19*, Wellesley College Archives.
14. Clemewell Lay and Anne Wellington, *The Emma Willard Plan of Education* (Troy: Emma Willard School, 1961), 96.
15. Ellen Russell Manchester, "Remembrance of Things Past," *Bulletin of Emma Willard School*, November 1950, 8.
16. Fred M. Hechinger, "Emma Willard School Finishes First Year of New Study Plan," *New York Herald-Tribune*, June 6, 1948.

17. Elizabeth Potwine, "Change Which Does Not Overthrow," *Bulletin of Emma Willard School*, September 1952, 11.

18. Wilbur K. Jordan, "A Review of the 'Emma Willard Plan of Education,'" *Bulletin of Emma Willard School*, December 1961, 10.

19. *Minutes of the Emma Willard Board of Trustees*, March 8, 1953, Emma Willard School Archives (hereafter EWSA).

20. Jordan, "A Review," 10.

21. Ibid.

22. Herman R. Allen, "The Young Ladies Buckle Down to Work," *Newsweek*, February 9, 1959, 55.

23. "The Plan of Education of Emma Willard School," *Bulletin of Emma Willard School*, February 1947, Part 2.

24. Ibid., 4–5.

25. Lay, "50th Reunion."

26. Lay and Wellington, *The Emma Willard Plan*, 10.

27. Ann Marie Reid Cromwell '51 to Frances O'Connor, September 17, 1977, EWSA.

28. Fred M. Hechinger, "Amherst Plan on the High School Level," *Herald-Tribune*, September 4, 1954.

29. Lay and Wellington, *The Emma Willard Plan*, 35.

30. "Plan of Education," *Bulletin of Emma Willard School*, January 1950, 8.

31. Ibid.

32. Lay and Wellington, *The Emma Willard Plan*, 56.

33. Ibid., 41–42.

34 ."Plan of Education," January 1950, 6.

35. They were Sally Esselstyn and Phyllis Bodel. Both had distinguished careers, and the Phyllis Bodel Childcare Center at Yale University was named for Bodel in recognition of her groundbreaking work with regard to women and medical careers.

36. Hechinger, "Emma Willard School Finishes First Year," June 6, 1948.

37. Lay and Wellington, *The Emma Willard Plan*, 63.

38. "Plan of Education," January 1950, 3.

39. Allen, "The Young Ladies," 54.

40. Phyllis Lafarge, "A Warm-Hearted Guide to Certain Girls' Schools," *Harper's Magazine*, April 1963, 6.

41. Ibid., 7.

42. Ibid.

43. John A. Valentine, *The College Board and the School Curriculum: A History of the College Board's Influence on the Substance and Standards of American Education, 1900–1980* (New York: The College Board, 1987), 71.

44. "School Aids Students in College Selection," *Bulletin of Emma Willard School*, May 1952, 4.

45. Anne Wellington, "The 1950 Decade in College Admissions," *Bulletin of Emma Willard School*, September 1960, 15.

46. Gertrude Watkins to Anne Wellington, 1953, *Anne Wellington papers*, EWSA.

47. Wellington, "The 1950 Decade," 15.

48. *Report of the Co-Headmistress to the Board of Trustees*, March 10, 1958, EWSA.

49. *Report of the Co-Headmistress to the Board of Trustees,* May 12, 1958, EWSA.

50. *Report of the Headmistress to the Board of Trustees*, November 14, 1960, EWSA.

51. Lay and Wellington, *The Emma Willard Plan*, 19.

52. Ibid., 99.

53. "Emma Willard Students Stage Yuletide Revels," *The Troy Times Record*, December 16, 1950.

54. *Dedication of the Alumnae Chapel and the John Amstuz Balcony, Emma Willard School*, program, June 11, 1954, EWSA.

55. Harriet Morgan Tyng, "The Chapel," *Bulletin of Emma Willard School*, May 1950, 2.

56. Manchester, "Remembrance of Things Past," 10.

57. *Catalogue of Emma Willard School, 1957–58*, 18.

58. *Report of the Headmistress to the Board of Trustees*, October 9, 1950, EWSA.

59. Lafarge, "A Warm-Hearted Guide," 8.

60. Ibid., 8.

61. *The Bulletin of Emma Willard School: Catalogue Issue*, January 1960, 22–23.

62. Lafarge, "A Warm-Hearted Guide," 8.

63. Lay and Wellington, *The Emma Willard Plan*, 99.

64. Dianne Strong '62 to Diane Mercer '61 and the author, e-mail message, June 27, 2007.

65. *Minutes of the Board of Trustees, Emma Willard School,* October 13, 1952, EWSA.

66. *Minutes of the Board of Trustees, Emma Willard School,* November 12, 1956, EWSA.

67. *Report of the Headmistress to the Board of Trustees,* November 12, 1956, EWSA.

68. *Report of the Subcommittee of the Development Committee,* December 1949, EWSA.

69. "Second Century Fund," *Bulletin of Emma Willard School*, February 1955, 2.

70. *Report of the Headmistress*, November 12, 1956, EWSA.

71. *The Highest Privilege . . . The Greatest Responsibility, EWSA.*

72. Cromwell to O'Connor, September 17, 1977.

73. "Deerfield, Choate, Berkshire, Darrow Boys Join Emma Willard for Concerts and Dances," *Bulletin of Emma Willard School*, May 1952, 1.

74. "Information Given to the New Principal," 1961, *Anne Wellington Papers*, EWSA.

75. Ibid.

76. Ibid.

77. From 1927 to 1959, Gracie, who had studied at the Emma Willard Conservatory of Music, accompanied everything from vespers services to Revels performances. When the author was first hired by Emma Willard in 1980, she met a man in his fifties who had attended Emma Willard dances with his prep school. His only memory: Gracie Bartholomew at the piano. She also entertained fathers at Fathers' Weekend by playing drinking songs for them to sing.

78. "Prom," *CLOCK*, November 24, 1950, 4.

79. Ibid.

80. "Reminders for Prom Weekend," *CLOCK,* November 18, 1955, 2.

81. "Date Dances," *CLOCK*, May 11, 1956, 4.

82. *Report of the Headmistress to the Board of Trustees*, March 10, 1952, EWSA.

83. *Report of the Headmistress to the Board of Trustees,* May10, 1954, EWSA.

84. *Report of the Headmistress to the Board of Trustees,* November 12, 1956, EWSA.

85. *Report of the Headmistress to the Board of Trustees,* March 8, 1959, EWSA.

86. Ibid.

87. *Report of the Headmistress to the Board of Trustees,* May 12, 1958, EWSA.

88. Father of a member of the class of 1959 to Anne Wellington, August 21, 1958, EWSA.

89. *Handbook of Emma Willard School 1952–53*, 20, EWSA.

90. *Special Report*, alumna file, EWSA.

91. "Mooney Problem Checklist," various alumnae files, EWSA.

92. "Memorandum," alumna file, EWSA.

93. *Report of the Headmistress to the Board of Trustees,* November 14, 1955, EWSA.

94. *Report of the Headmistress to the Board of Trustees,* November 14, 1960, EWSA.

95. Allen, "The Young Ladies," 56.

96. *Headmistress to the Board of Trustees*, November 14, 1960.

97. "Excitement Reigns at School When Announcement Is Made," *Bulletin of Emma Willard School,* March 1961, 2–3.

98. Ruth Kramer Ziony '61 to the author, e-mail message, October 12, 2008.

99. "Information Given to the New Principal," EWSA.

100. *Minutes of the Emma Willard Board of Trustees*, May 8, 1961, EWSA.

101. "Dedication," *Gargoyle 1961*, 5.

102. "Excitement Reigns," 3.

A Master Headmistress

1. "Inauguration of Mr. Dietel as Headmaster Attended by Over One Thousand Guests," *Bulletin of Emma Willard School*, December 1961, 4, Emma Willard School Archives (hereafter EWSA).

2. Ibid., 5.

3. Ibid., 3.

4. Ibid.

5. *Report of the Principal to the Board of Trustees*, November 13, 1961, EWSA.

6. *Committee for Sesquicentennial Anniversary First Statement of Needs*, April 15, 1962, EWSA.

7. *List of Needs*, Fall 1962, EWSA.

8. Conversation between William M. Dietel and the author, September 26, 2008.

9. Conversation between Russell Locke and the author, December 20, 2011.

10. "Adsum Absentibus," *Bulletin of Emma Willard School*, June 1965, 5.

11. *Minutes, Emma Willard Board of Trustees*, November 13, 1961, EWSA.

12. *Minutes, Emma Willard Board of Trustees*, May 14, 1962, EWSA.

13. Knowlton was the brother of Katherine Knowlton McLane '23 and father of Lee Knowlton Parker '58 and Kathrina Knowlton West '63.

14. Craig Severance was the father of Michael Severance Joy Hauser '62 and stepfather of Evelyn Tulp Norton '65 and Claire Tulp Poole '72.

15. *Committee for Sesquicentennial Anniversary First Statement of Needs*, April 15, 1962, EWSA.

16. *List of Needs*, Fall 1962, EWSA.

17. *Minutes, Emma Willard Board of Trustees*, September 23, 1963, EWSA.

18. *Minutes, Emma Willard Board of Trustees*, November 11, 1963, EWSA.

19. Robert C. Parker to the author, July 1980.

20. "Adsum Absentibus," *Bulletin of Emma Willard School*, June 1965, 5.

21. Conversation between the author and William M. Dietel, May 4, 2009.

22. Between 1960 and 1967, the school's portfolio outperformed the Dow by a third.

23. Dietel conversation, May 4, 2009.

24. The girls were Deborah Buttenheim '64, Judith Buttenheim '68, and Nancy Buttenheim '70; Elizabeth Hunter '63, Barbara Hunter '66, and Susan Hunter '68.

25. Conversation between Donald Buttenheim and the author, March 6, 2006.

26. *Minutes of the Emma Willard Board of Trustees*, March 4, 1964, EWSA.

27. Williams was married to Patty Ide Williams '50. Their daughters are Wendy '74 and Amy '78, and their granddaughter is Hannah Haight '12. He later served on the board of trustees.

28. Barbara Williams, "Alumnae Stunned by Changes," *CLOCK*, November 4, 1966, 1.

29. Thom House, Hapgood House, McKennan House, and Boshart House.

30. "Faculty Housing at Emma Willard," *Bulletin of Emma Willard School*, Summer 1969, 1.

31. William M. Dietel, "Adsum Absentibus," *Bulletin of Emma Willard School*, February 1966, 6.

32. "Adsum Absentibus," *Bulletin of Emma Willard School*, February 1966, 6.

33. Richard Allen Zajchowski, "The William Moore Dietel Library," *Bulletin of Emma Willard School*, June 1968, 13.

34. William M. Dietel to Helen Snell Cheel, May 27, 1968, EWSA.

35. *Minutes of the Emma Willard Board of Trustees*, May 14, 1962, EWSA.

36. As of June 30, 2012, it has been twenty years since a faculty member has died while employed at the school.

37. William M. Dietel to Helen Snell Cheel, August 20, 1968, EWSA.

38. William M. Dietel, *State of the School*, August 27, 1965, 6, EWSA.

39. Dietel was not alone in choosing this comparison. As late as 1986, when she was over ninety and confined to a wheelchair, Anne Wellington asked the author if we had "caught up with Exeter."

40. William M. Dietel to David Knowlton, January 22, 1968, EWSA.

41. Darcy M. Curwen, "Comparison Enforced," *Bulletin of Emma Willard School*, June 1964, 4–5.

42. William M. Dietel, "Report of the Principal," *Bulletin of Emma Willard School*, June 1967, 15.

43. *Minutes of the Board of Trustees, Emma Willard School*, March 11, 1968, EWSA.

44. Dietel conversation, May 4, 2009.

45. William M. Dietel, "Endowment: A Matter of Survival," *Bulletin of Emma Willard School*, Winter 1969.

46. *Report of the Principal to the Board of Trustees*, August 1965, EWSA.

47. Peter Schrag to William M. Dietel, April 22, 1968, EWSA.

48. Jane Steinberg, "The Boarding School Mystique," *Mademoiselle*, May 1966, 215.

49. Jane Wales '66, "Editorial," *CLOCK*, December 10, 1965, 2.

50. *Report of the Principal to the Board of Trustees*, February 9, 1968, EWSA.

51. Ibid.

52. *Minutes of the Emma Willard Board of Trustees*, May 13, 1968, EWSA.

53. Her name was Ann Hart, and she taught French from 1963 to 1965 before moving on to Germantown Friends School in Philadelphia where she presumably had more colleagues of color and most certainly a larger, more diverse community outside the school.

54. Margaret Miller to William M. Dietel, January 18, 1968, EWSA.

55. William M. Dietel to Alexander Aldrich, August 9, 1968, EWSA.

56. "Troy's Inhospitality to Negro Told Factually for Rotarians," *The Times Record*, May 5, 1968.

57. Franciena King, "My White Brother," *Triangle*, Spring, 1967, 24.

58. Richard M. Nixon, *www.presidency.ucsb.edu/ws*, retrieved July 7, 2012.

59. Martha Weinman Lear, "The Second Feminist Wave," *New York Times Magazine*, March 10, 1968, 62.

60. Loretta Adams '65, "Happiness," *CLOCK*, November 27, 1963, 2–3.

61. "Letter to the Editor," *CLOCK*, January 20, 1969, 2.

62. *Emma Willard School Handbook, 1966–67*, EWSA.

63. William M. Dietel to School Affairs Committee, December 5, 1966, EWSA.

64. *Emma Willard School Handbook, 1967–68*, 18, EWSA.

65. Cartoon, *CLOCK*, November 29, 1965, 2.

66. "Editorial," *CLUCK*, April 19, 1965, 2.

67. *Handbook of Emma Willard School, 1963–64*, 3, EWSA.

68. "The Boarding School Mystique," 177.

69. *Handbook of Emma Willard School, 1968–69*, 7, EWSA.

70. Abby Merriam, "Poll Probes Smoking Rules," *CLOCK*, October 27, 1967, 6.

71. Jack Betterly to William M. Dietel, December 3, 1966 EWSA.

72. "Editorial," *CLOCK*, May 26, 1969, 2.

73. "Poll Results on Drugs," *CLOCK*, December 19, 1969, 1.

74. Judy Collins and Sandy Mardigian, "Drug Problem Acknowledged, Raid Possible," *CLOCK*, March 6, 1970, 1.

75. Ellen Manchester to William Dietel, January 5, 1969, EWSA.

76. "On Becoming a Senior," *CLOCK*, October 4, 1963, 2.

77. Jane Wales, "Should Juniors Have Rings?" *CLOCK*, November 25, 1964, 3.

78. "Flame Ceremony Held: Junior Receive New Roles," *CLOCK*, June 3, 1970, 1.

79. "Editorial," *CLOCK*, February 5, 1965, 2.

80. JMW (Jane Wales '66), "The New Morality," *CLOCK*, January 21, 1966, 2.

81. Sarah McBrian, "Lecture Clears Up Sex Problems," Ibid., 3.

82. Damien O'Leary, "Sex Lectures Improve," *CLOCK*, October 7, 1966, 2.

83. "Glance at Prank Reveals Results," *CLOCK*, June 5, 1968, 2.

84. William M. Dietel to Helen Cheel, August 20, 1968 EWSA.

85. Day's daughter is Lydia Day Hart '70; his granddaughter is Beckett Hart '01.

86. William M. Dietel, "When Is Emma Willard Going to Go Co-Ed?" *Bulletin*, Spring 1969, 1.

87. Ibid.

88. William W. Van Alstyne, "The Tentative Emergence of Student Power in the United States," *American Journal of Comparative Law* 17, no. 3 (Summer 1969): 403.

89. "Letter to the Editor," *CLOCK*, May 26, 1969, 2.

90. J. L. R., "Let Sleeping Co-Eds Lie," *CLOCK*, May 10, 1968, 2.

91. William M. Dietel to Helen Cheel, June 18, 1969 EWSA.

92. E-mail message, William M. Dietel to the author, May 11, 2009.

93. William M. Dietel to Kathryn and Willard Kiggins, October 9, 1969, EWSA.

94. Conversation between William M. Dietel and the author, September 26, 2008.

95. "Headmaster Resigns," *CLOCK*, October 27, 1969, 1.

96. William M. Dietel to Anne Wellington and Clemewell Lay, September 22, 1969, EWSA.

97. Barbara Colbron to William M. Dietel, October 13, 1969 EWSA. One of the women she nominated, Elizabeth Rouner, was the sister of Louise Rouner '50. Elizabeth Rouner became head of St. Agnes School. The other, Agathe Keliher, headed both Springside and Hewitt schools.

98. William M. Dietel to Barbara Colbron, October 17, 1969, EWSA.

99. Liz Armstrong, "Man in the News," *CLOCK*, December 19, 1969, 1.

100. *Ideal Applicant for the Position* EWSA. At least one member of the search committee was disturbed by the sexist approach to potential candidates. Janet Maly's copy of this document contains the notation next to the list of qualities sought in the head's wife, "good little woman!!!"

101. Dietel to Wellington, September 22, 1969, EWSA.

102. William M. Dietel to Richard Quaintance, October 16, 1969, EWSA.

103. Liz Santos, "Dorm Rules Changed; Trend Is to Unregimented Life," *CLOCK*, February 11, 1970, 3.

104. William Moore Dietel to Richard Davis, January 8, 1970, EWSA.

105. *Gargoyle*, 1970, 1.

106. Ibid., 93

These Will Not Be Easy Years

1. "Bicentennial," *Bulletin of Emma Willard School*, Winter 1975, 5.

2. Jack Betterly, "The Price of Pretension," *Bulletin of Emma Willard School*, Winter 1975, 2.

3. "The Inauguration," *Bulletin of Emma Willard School*, Winter 1970, 4.

4. Ibid.

5. Robert S. Ryf, "The Trouble with Education Is . . . ," *Papers of Dennis Collins*, Emma Willard School Archives (hereafter EWSA).

6. Ibid.

7. "Dennis Collins, 11th Principal, Inaugurated," *CLOCK*, October 2, 1970, 1.

8. Ibid.

9. *Report of the Director of Admissions to the Board of Trustees*, March 9, 1970, EWSA.

10. *Report of the Director of Admissions to the Board of Trustees*, May 18, 1970, EWSA.

11. Virginia Lee Warren, "After 25 Years, the Waiting Lists at Girls' Boarding Schools Begin to Thin Out," *New York Times*, May 31, 1970.

12. In contrast, Miss Porter's had 290 students in 1977; 12 were African American.

13. Peggy Parker, "January 17 Trustee Meeting with Afro-Am Students Spurs Comment," *CLOCK*, January 28, 1971, 3.

14. Vicky Beck, "Black Commentary: A Dark Situation in the Classroom," *CLOCK*, September 30, 1971, 3.

15. Parker, "January 17 Trustee Meeting," 3.

16. Arthur Homan to Dennis Collins, June 8, 1971, EWSA.

17. Beverley Marvin to Dennis Collins, August 13, 1971, EWSA.

18. *Principal's Report to the Board of Trustees*, May 10, 1971, EWSA.

19. Beverley Marvin to Dennis Collins, September 28, 1971, EWSA.

20. "Editorial," *CLOCK*, October 2, 1970, 2.

21. *Security Report*, February 19, 1971, EWSA.

22. Dennis A. Collins to students, January 2, 1973, EWSA.

23. Dennis Collins to Administrative Staff, Guidance Counselors, January 19, 1971, EWSA.

24. Barbara Keyser to Madeira parents, September 1970, EWSA.

25. Bernard Carragher, "There Really Was a Super Suicide Society," *New York Times*, October 8, 1972, Arts and Leisure, 18.

26. Mrs. Edwin G. Reade to Dennis Collins, February 23, 1973, EWSA.

27. Emmy Benjamin, "Emma Willard Student Drug Poll," *CLOCK*, May 10, 1973, 1.

28. Dennis Collins to Harold Edwards, Jr., May 27, 1971, EWSA.

29. Dennis Collins to Richard Zajchowski, November 10, 1971, EWSA.

30. William M. Dietel to Dennis Collins, February 13, 1973, EWSA.

31. *Report of the Director of Admission to the Board of Trustees*, November 8, 1971, EWSA.

32. *Implications of the New Curriculum for Admissions*, EWSA. In the margins of the extant copy of this document, someone has penciled, "The implications for Admissions are almost beyond believing."

33. *Principal's Report to the Board of Trustees*, November 5, 1971, EWSA.

34. Warren, "After 25 Years," *New York Times*, May 31, 1970.

35. Jack Betterly, *The View from Down Here*, 1988, EWSA.

36. *Principal's Report to the Board of Trustees*, August 27, 1965, EWSA.

37. William Dietel, "A Pathway through the Seventies," *Bulletin of Emma Willard School*, Spring 1970, 2.

38. *CWW Committee Report, 1967–68*, EWSA.

39. Ibid.

40. Four-School Study Committee, *16-20: The Liberal Education of an Age Group* (New York: College Entrance Examination Board, 1970), viii.

41. Ibid., 80.

42. Ibid., 3.

43. Ibid.

44. Ibid., 4.

45. Ibid., 80.

46. Dietel, "A Pathway through the Seventies," 2.

47. *The Report of the Curriculum Committee June, 1969, as Amended by the Faculty, September, 1969*, EWSA.

48. Ibid.

49. Ibid.

50. Ibid.

51. Ibid.

52. Ibid.

53. Ibid.

54. Ibid.

55. Ibid.

56. Dennis Arthur Collins, "The Future: Shock or Challenge," *Bulletin of Emma Willard School*, Spring 1971, 3.

57. *The Report of the Curriculum Committee, 1969*.

58. Conversation between Jack Easterling and the author, June 15, 2012.

59. Elizabeth Moore, "Applying to Bates or Bowdoin," *CLOCK*, December 12, 1977, 1.

60. Beth Waddums, "The Spring of Seventy-Two," *CLOCK*, May 11,1972, 2.

61. *Minutes, Emma Willard Board of Trustees*, November 7, 1974, EWSA.

62. Dennis Collins to Richard Zajchowski, June 22, 1971, EWSA.

63. Dennis Collins to Richard Zajchowski, March 11, 1971, EWSA.

64. Dennis Collins to Richard Zajchowski, March 8, 1971, EWSA.

65. Ironically, the faculty seemed unaware of his attempts to impose rigor. Increasingly scornful of his leadership and the curriculum, a group of them created an elaborate board game, complete with "Irony" cards. A typical one of these read, "All your books are ordered for British Literature; all of your students are illiterate." EWSA.

66. Collins to Zachowski, March 11, 1971.

67. Dennis Collins to Jean Bolgatz, November 1971, EWSA.

68. Beverley Marvin to Mrs. Harry C. Morgan, May 25, 1971, EWSA.

69. *Minutes, Emma Willard Board of Trustees*, March 15, 1971, EWSA.

70. Alicia Wille, "Thoughts on Here and Why," *CLOCK*, March 15, 1972, 2.

71. Andrea Lotze, "Yale Comes to Emma," *CLOCK*, February 15, 1973, 4.

72. "Ms Wallace Joins English Faculty," *CLOCK*, April 21, 1972, 2.

73. Adeline Scovil to Dennis Collins, February 15, 1972, EWSA.

74. *Report of the Long Range Planning Committee, Emma Willard Board of Trustees*, September 16, 1977.

75. In terms of purchasing power, these amounts in today's dollars range from less than $100 to over $700 per month. At least one alumna personally subsidized the retirement fund for a favorite retired teacher.

76. *Minutes, Emma Willard Board of Trustees*, March 15, 1971, EWSA.

77. Dennis A. Collins, "The Principal's Page," *Bulletin of Emma Willard School*, Winter 1971, 7.

78. H. Mark Johnson and Franklin F. Moon, "The Emma Willard Dollar: How Goes It?" *Bulletin of Emma Willard School*, Winter 1971, 9.

79. Walter Maguire to Mr. and Mrs. James Neighbors Jr., May 25, 1870, EWSA.

80. *Minutes, Emma Willard Board of Trustees,* March 13, 1972, EWSA.

81. *Minutes, Emma Willard Board of Trustees,* November 13, 1972, EWSA.

82. *Report of the Committee of the Board of Trustees on Co-Education,* September 1971, EWSA.

83. Ibid.

84. Ibid.

85. Ibid.

86. Ibid.

87. At least three Emma Willard alumnae are married to men they met on the Thacher exchange.

88. *Report of the Curriculum Review Committee, 1974,* EWSA.

89. *Survey on Women's Rights in Girls' Secondary Schools,* 1972, EWSA.

90. Rita Rief, "In Many Schools, the Headmistress Is a Man," *New York Times,* February 27, 1972.

91. Dennis Collins to Richard Zajchowski, EWSA.

92. Gwen Krause '78, untitled essay, 1977.

93. Ibid.

94. "About Us," *www.sfuhs.org,* retrieved July 10, 2012.

95. "DAC Becomes Organization Man," *CLOCK,* March 7, 1974, 1.

96. Collins had hoped to call Headmaster's Holiday in conjunction with the birth of his second daughter in 1972, but the baby did not arrive until too late in the spring to make it feasible to call the holiday at that time. Thus there was no holiday in 1971–72, much to student dismay.

97. Edward B. Fiske, "Tough Duties Replace Ceremony for School Trustees," *New York Times,* April 21, 1976, 25.

98. Sue Pringle, "Search Committee Makes Progress," *CLOCK,* January 25,1974, 3.

99. Audrey Peele, "Hail to the Chief," *CLOCK,* October 1974, 1.

100. Russell Locke, "Faculty Welcome to Dr. Frances R. O'Connor," EWSA.

101. Frances R. O'Connor, *Inaugural Address,* EWSA.

102. *Minutes, Emma Willard Board of Trustees,* November 11, 1974, EWSA.

103. Budget numbers vary slightly, according to who was doing the reporting: the business office, the budget committee of the board of trustees, or the audit. I have chosen to use the numbers compiled by Marcia P. Easterling from trustee minutes and reported in *Company Analysis: Emma Willard School,* April 1984.

104. *Minutes,* November 11, 1974.

105. In 1973–74, with 29 percent of the student body on financial aid, financial aid had accounted for 10 percent of the operating budget. By 1976–77, financial aid accounted for only 5 percent of the operating budget, and the number of students on aid had dropped below 14 percent of the student body.

106. *Minutes, Emma Willard Board of Trustees,* February 7, 1977, EWSA.

107. The dance studio was a gift from the Hattie M. Strong Foundation. Strong family members who attended the school included Alice Trowbridge Strong '17, Sigrid Strong Reynolds '70, Barbara Strong Kirk '71, and Dana Strong Van Loon '73.

108. Educational Amendments of 1972, Public Law No. 92-318, 86 Stat. 235, 20 U.S.C. Sections 1681-88, June 23, 1972.

109. Melissa Ludtke, "In the Wake of Title IX," *Wellesley,* Summer 2012, 25.

110. In 1972 fewer than 300,000 of the nation's several million high school athletes were girls. By 2005 about 3 million girls played high school sports compared with 4.2 million boys.

111. "Taft Girls in Sports: A Life Style Improved," *New York Times,* November 10, 1974.

112. "Bridges to Strengthen Competition," *CLOCK,* September 15, 1978, 3.

113. Peter Scales, "Sex Education in the '70s and '80s: Accomplishments, Obstacles, and Emerging Issues," *Family Relations,* October 1981, 563.

114. Ibid.

115. J.F., "Too Many Male Mentors," *CLOCK,* December 12, 1977, 2.

116. Ibid., 6.

117. Frances R. O'Connor, *Address to the Faculty,* May 2, 1978, EWSA.

118. *Minutes, Emma Willard Board of Trustees,* May 31, 1978, EWSA.

119. Frances R. O'Connor to Jack Betterly, June 21, 1976, EWSA.

120. Ibid.

121. Conversation between Donald Myers and the author, May 18, 2012.

122. *Minutes*, May 31, 1978.

Listening to Voices We Have Not Heard

1. Adrienne Rich, "In Those Years," *www.phys.unm.edu~tw/fas/yits/archive/rich_inthoseyears.html*, retrieved June 20, 2012.

2. One of the notable things about the show was its frequent use of the Cosby grandparents to teach their grandchildren—and the weekly viewers—about the importance that the civil rights movement had made in their lives.

3. "Looking Onward Today," *CLOCK*, September 28, 1979, 1.

4. Robert C. Parker to Kendra Stearns O'Donnell, March 26, 1982, Emma Willard School Archives (hereafter EWSA).

5. Welles's wife was Ann Thom Welles '41, his daughters, Nancy Welles Leahy '65, and Amy Welles '82.

6. *Minutes, Emma Willard Board of Trustees*, September 11, 1978.

7. "Facts," *CLOCK*, October 10, 1978, 3.

8. Jack Betterly to Philip S. Deely, *The View from Down Here*, 1988, EWSA.

9. Donald Myers to the author, e-mail, June 9, 2012.

10. Kathleen Howell, "The Stately Groves of Academe," program, Robert C. Parker installation, October 14, 1978, EWSA.

11. Peter Camp, *Installation Speech for Robert C. Parker*, EWSA.

12. Petra Perkins, *Welcome for Mr. Parker*, EWSA.

13. Susan Hunter, *Remarks for the Installation of Robert C. Parker*, EWSA.

14. Marcia P. Easterling, *Installation Speech,* October 14, 1978, EWSA.

15. Linda R. Dietel, *Charge to Robert C. Parker*, EWSA.

16. Robert C. Parker, *Installation Speech*, EWSA.

17. Carol Gilligan, "Woman's Place in Man's Life Cycle," *Harvard Educational Review* (Winter 1979): 431–46.

18. Bob Parker hired me in the spring of 1980 to replace the outgoing college counselor, Susan Edwards, who was also his associate head of school, a position she had assumed under Frances O'Connor. She and Parker had not been a good match, and he hired me as college counselor, but promised that if we worked together as well as he thought we would, I would be named associate principal. This in fact happened within the year, in large measure because of our close working relationship on this project.

19. *Proposal to the Geraldine Rockefeller Dodge Foundation*, March 1981, EWSA.

20. *Report to the Geraldine Rockefeller Dodge Foundation*, June 1983, EWSA.

21. Ibid.

22. Nina Mechta, "Taping of FSJ Hearings Proposed," *CLOCK*, November 5, 1981, 1.

23. Carol Gilligan, Nona P. Lyons, and Trudy J. Hanmer, eds., *Making Connections: The Relational Worlds of Adolescent Girls at Emma Willard School* (Troy: Emma Willard School, 1989). A second edition was published by Harvard University Press in 1990.

24. *Minutes, Emma Willard School Faculty Meeting*, June 1981, EWSA.

25. Ibid.

26. He actually hired co-chaplains, David and Kate Kotfila. Kate was the first female chaplain the school had ever had.

27. Jeanne Walker, "Issue of the Issue," *CLOCK*, November 5, 1981. Quotations from Lisa Goldthwaite '82, Tina Rahr '84, and Katrina Butcher '85.

28. "Issue of the Issue," *CLOCK*, September 16, 1983, 2.

29. Dana Pillsbury, "Chapel Controversy Explored," *CLOCK*, April 29, 1983, 2.

30. *Minutes, Faculty Meeting*, June, 1981.

31. *Report of Findings by Kane, Parsons & Associates,* March 1981, EWSA.

32. Sheila Raman, "The Steering Committee Hangs a Right," *CLOCK*, January 18, 1980, 2. Selina Peyser, "Student Rebuttal to Recent Changes Made in Curriculum and Schedule," *CLOCK*, February 22, 1980, 2.

33. *Minutes, Emma Willard Board of Trustees*, May 17, 1982, EWSA.

34. K. A. Major, "New Rules 'Smother,'" *CLOCK*, October 8, 1981, 2.

35. Regan Andrews, "Diehards Reflect on Four Years at Emma," *CLOCK*, June 4, 1981, 3.

36. Quoted in John A. Parker, John C. Parker, and Margaret Parker, eds., *The Book of Bob* (Pittsboro, NC: Kachergis Book Design, 1993), 13.

37. Christine Smith and Joo Mee Song, "MTV," *CLOCK*, October 26, 1984, 2.

38. Jenny Plane, "MTV Aggravates Television Addiction," *CLOCK*, February 25, 1982, 2.

39. Jane Maggard, "A Matter of Particular Concern," *CLOCK*, March 11, 1982, 2.

40. K. A. Major, "A Yearning for Quality," *CLOCK*, April 13, 1984, 2.

41. Robert C. Parker, *Charge to the Curriculum Committee*, May 10, 1983, EWSA.

42. Ibid.

43. Ibid.

44. Curriculum Review Committee 1984, *Summary Statement*, March 1984, EWSA.

45. Robert C. Parker to Emma Willard Board of Trustees, February 23, 1984, EWSA.

46. *Minutes, Emma Willard Board of Trustees*, February 6, 1984, EWSA.

47. Kathy Delaney, "Letter to the Editor," *CLOCK*, June 4, 1981, 2.

48. "Class Cut Policy," *CLOCK*, September 17, 1982, 2.

49. "More Gym a Burden," *CLOCK*, February 25, 1983, 2.

50. Sandy Denison, "Letter to the Editor," *CLOCK*, May 27, 1983, 2.

51. Liz Bogner, Vivian Brady, Jenny Dryfoos, Kim Jones, Tammy Kafin, Margarete Krueger, Bronwyn Poole, Jill Wendell, and Anne Wright, "Letter to the Editor," *CLOCK*, February 24, 1984, 2.

52. Kristin A. Major, "Senior Column: A Yearning for Quality," *CLOCK*, February 24, 1984, 3.

53. Curriculum Committee, *Summary Statement*, EWSA.

54. Ibid. The faculty vote on the semester system was the closest of any taken during the deliberations, but it passed 2:1.

55. Ibid.

56. *Points of Classroom Practice*, 1984, EWSA.

57. Curriculum Committee, *Summary Statement*, EWSA.

58. *Findings, Kane, Parsons*, EWSA.

59. *Minutes, Emma Willard Board of Trustees*, September 28, 1981, EWSA.

60. Ibid.

61. Robert C. Parker to the Executive Committee, Emma Willard Board of Trustees, June 18, 1981, EWSA.

62. *Minutes, Emma Willard Board of Trustees*, September 27, 1982, EWSA.

63. John Klingenstein to Kendra Stearns O'Donnell, November 12, 1985, EWSA.

64. *Minutes, Emma Willard Board of Trustees*, September 28, 1981.

65. Robert C. Parker to job applicant, February, 1985, EWSA.

66. Josephine Schmidt, "Teachers to Be Houseparents," *CLOCK*, April 29, 1980, 1.

67. Robert C. Parker to John Estey Jr., February 7, 1984, EWSA.

68. "Winning Isn't Everything," *Bulletin*, Spring 1983, 10.

69. Emma Hart Willard, "Address on the Time and Teaching of Little Children," December 30, 1853, EWSA.

70. *Report of the Strategic Planning and Policy Council*, May 1985, EWSA.

71. Robert C. Parker to Emma Willard Board of Trustees, November 1985, EWSA.

72. Robert C. Parker to Clementine Tangeman, February 27, 1986, EWSA.

73. Robert C. Parker to Judy Moon, April 4, 1986, EWSA.

74. "Bob Parker: A Pillar in the Cause of Woman," *Bulletin, Emma Willard School*, Winter 1986–87, 17.

75. Ibid., 16.

76. Ibid., 21.

77. Barbara Jones, *Eulogy for Robert C. Parker*, EWSA.

If You've Been to Emma Willard, You've Been to the Mountain

1. *Ten-Year Report of the N.Y.S.A.I.S. Evaluation Team*, March 1987, Emma Willard School Archives (hereafter EWSA).

2. Robert C. Parker to Jameson A. Baxter, July 10, 1985, EWSA.

3. Ibid.

4. A crew shell at Groton named the "Robert C. Parker" entered the water in the spring of 1986, just as he began new treatment. He telephoned his thanks, but with characteristic humor and optimism, he assured the donors, "I'm not gone yet."

5. Kendra S. O'Donnell '60 to the Emma Willard Community, April 1987, EWSA.

6. Alexandra Powell, "Introducing Mr. Deely," *CLOCK*, May 11, 1987, 1.

7. Among these were roof and masonry repairs, outdated plumbing in the dormitories, lighting and heating infrastructure. Money raised in memory of Bob Parker was earmarked for dormitory renovation, particularly the improvement of adult spaces, and it was included in the proposed major maintenance projects.

8. The percentage of students scoring over 500 on the verbal half of the PSAT declined from 55 percent for the class of 1987 to 37 percent in 1991; for the mathematics section of the test, the scores were less dramatic, moving from 63 to 52 percent. The downward trend in verbal scores was partially attributable to the increasing numbers of international students for whom English was a second language.

9. Mike Esposito, "Preparing for the Holidays Fifty Years Ago," *Troy United Newsletter, www.uncle-sams-home.com/tui/199712/a19971201120504.html*, retrieved August 7, 2012.

10. "Reason for Optimism," *The Troy Record*, January 31, 1970.

11. Amy Halloran, "Development in Troy Still a Guessing Game," *Albany Times-Union*, February 28, 2008.

12. Grimm's wife was Jeannette Smart Grimm '26, and his daughter is Carolyn Grimm '57.

13. Alison Easterling, "I Hate Troy," *CLOCK*, January 24, 1986, 2.

14. *Report of the Business Manager to the Board of Trustees*, September 23, 1988, EWSA.

15. "Three Seniors Feel Jilted," *CLOCK*, March 11, 1988, 2.

16. "Soon-to-Be-Senior Column," *CLOCK*, June 10, 1988, 2.

17. Keven Ryan Bellows '55, "Alumnae Respond to the 20th Century Survey," *Emma Willard School Bulletin*, Spring 1989, 13.

18. Amy H. Shouse, "Senior Column: Is '89 Blessed?" *CLOCK*, September 30, 1988, 2.

19. Peter Buttenheim, *Speech at Phil Deely's Installation*, EWSA.

20. Philip S. Deely to members of the Board of Trustees, February 26, 1988, EWSA.

21. "Trustees Appoint Robertson Principal," *CLOCK*, April 27, 1990, 1.

22. Letter to "The Alumnae and Friends of Emma Willard School" from Jameson A. Baxter, May 4, 1990, EWSA.

23. Bari Nan Cohen, "Robertson Inspired by First Visit," *CLOCK*, June 1, 1990, 1.

24. "Robertson Installed as Fifteenth Principal," *CLOCK*, October 26, 1990, 1.

25. The elected members of the committee were Kurt Boluch, science instructor; Judy Bridges, dean of students and athletic director; Françoise Chadabe, French instructor and chair of the language division; Marilyn Hunter, Spanish instructor; Kathleen McNamara, English instructor; Judy Price, mathematics instructor; and Ken Turner, history instructor and chair of the humanities division. In 2012, all but Turner and Boluch were still at the school.

26. Amy Chiaro, "Robertson Makes Weekend Life, Curriculum Priorities," *CLOCK*, April 15, 1991, 1.

27. *Emma Willard School Curriculum Review Report*, December 1991, 1, EWSA.

28. Ibid., 2.

29. *Minutes, Emma Willard Faculty Meeting*, September 9, 1991, EWSA.

30. *Curriculum Review Report*, 2.

31. Ibid., 3.

32. Ibid., 5.

33. Ibid., 6.

34. Ibid., 12.

35. "English III: To Be or Not to Be," *CLOCK*, March 5, 1992, 6.

36. "Issue of the Issue," *CLOCK*, March 5, 1992, 6.

37. "Qualifications Win Out in Battle over Gender," *CLOCK*, January 31, 1992, 6.

38. *Minutes of the Board of Trustees*, February 8, 1993, EWSA.

39. Ibid.

40. *Minutes of the Board of Trustees*, February 11, 1991, EWSA.

41. Ibid.

42. *Emma Willard Bulletin*, Winter/Spring 1992, cover.

43. *Minutes of the Board of Trustees*, February 10, 1992, EWSA.

44. "What We've Heard from You," *Emma Willard Bulletin*, Winter/Spring 1992, 9.

45. American Association of University Women, *Shortchanging Girls, Shortchanging America*, Executive Summary (Washington, DC: AAUW, 1991), title page.

46. Christy Kissileff, "*Alarm Clock* Rings with Spirit of Revolution," *CLOCK*, March 5, 1992, 4.

47. Anjali Dayal, "Do Financial Realities Define School's Identity?" *CLOCK*, February 18, 1999, 3.

48. Ibid.

49. *Minutes of the Board of Trustees*, November 3, 1990, EWSA.

50. *Faculty Meeting Minutes*, April 15, 1993, EWSA.

51. Margery G. Whiteman, "Dormitory Mastermind," *Bulletin*, Fall/Winter 1990, 8.

52. "Calling All Alumnae," *Emma Willard Bulletin*, Spring 1995, 19.

53. Grimmer succeeded Margery G. Whiteman, who had resigned in the fall of 1991. Adrienne Larys, who had a very successful career in alumnae relations and annual giving, served as acting director until Grimmer came on board. A native of England, Grimmer was a development professional whose organizational skills, understated British humor, no-nonsense affect, and unflappability complemented Robertson's style and ensured the success of the campaign.

54. "Campaign Kick-off," *Emma Willard Bulletin*, Winter 1993/1994, 11.

55. The Hunter children included Elizabeth '63, Barbara '66, and Susan '68.

56. *The Hunter Science Center, Emma Willard School, a New Paradigm for Science Education*, EWSA.

57. Helen O'Neill, "Long Weekend Schedule Upsets Student Plans," *CLOCK*, October 13, 1995, 6.

58. Branwen Buckley, "Symposium Promotes 'Curiosity and Confidence,'" *CLOCK*, April 18, 1997.

59. *Minutes, Emma Willard Board of Trustees*, February 9, 1998, EWSA.

60. *Minutes, Emma Willard Board of Trustees*, December 8, 1991, EWSA.

61. *Minutes, Emma Willard Board of Trustees*, February 8, 1993, EWSA.

62. *Mission Statement, Emma Willard School*, adopted by the board of trustees, May 1997, EWSA.

63. Rachel Wade Westmoreland, "Sex and Literature: Let's Not Bury Our Heads in the Sand," *CLOCK*, October 21, 1994, 4.

64. Email from Parker Hamilton to the author, November 11, 1997.

65. "Guiding Emma Willard School into the Next Millenium [sic]," *Emma Willard Bulletin*, Winter 1997–98, 9.

66. *Minutes, Emma Willard Board of Trustees*, February 9, 1998, EWSA.

67. Sonya Smelyansky, "Head of School to Leave Effective June 30," *CLOCK*, February 18, 1999, 1.

68 Robin Prout, "Celebrating the Robertson Years," *Emma Willard Bulletin*, Spring, 1999, 2.

69 Ibid., 3

Charting the Way for Others to Follow

1. In 1993 an audit of the condition of the windows by Mesick, Cohen and Waite had found that only 710 of the 3,000 leaded-pane windows on the campus were in "good condition." They estimated that restoring all of the windows in an historically accurate and energy-efficient way would cost approximately $1,000 per window. Furthermore, the work would have to be done by skilled artisans in good weather. Because a limited number of either of these two things was available, the project could take fifteen years to complete.

2. *Minutes, Emma Willard Board of Trustees*, May 16, 1999, Emma Willard School Archives (hereafter EWSA).

3. *Minutes, Emma Willard Board of Trustees*, May 22, 2000, EWSA.

4. *Minutes, Administrative Council*, November 10, 1999, EWSA.

5. Trudy E. Hall, "Faculty Column: A School-Wide Conversation," *CLOCK*, October 8, 1999, 3.

6. Three of the internships were endowed: the Isabel Davis Wise Teaching Fellow in History, the Sara Lee and Tillie K. Lubin Teaching Fellow in Science, and the Gordon B. and Mary J. Tweedy Fellow for the Humanities.

7. Lauren Dorgan, "Hall Appointed 16th Head," *CLOCK*, December 17, 1999, 1.

8. *http://www.parkerschool.org/about/history/*, retrieved September 25, 2012.

9. Lucia Bartholomew, "The Real Die-Hards," *CLOCK*, November 5, 1999, 3. In addition to Bartholomew, the others were Kate Wiley, Nicole Lemanski, and Tory Peterson.

10. *Minutes, Emma Willard Board of Trustees*, October 23, 1997, EWSA.

11. *Minutes, Emma Willard Board of Trustees*, February 9, 1998, EWSA.

12. *Minutes, Emma Willard Board of Trustees*, October 19, 1998, EWSA.

13. James E. Morley Jr., "Entrusting the Mace," October 5, 2000, EWSA.

14. Trudy E. Hall, "Accepting the Trust," October 5, 2000, EWSA.

15. Ibid.

16. *Minutes, Emma Willard Board of Trustees*, February 15, 2003, EWSA.

17. Her daughters are Alyssa Bernstein '05 and Natalie Alexander '09.

18. In keeping with the tradition of the nineteenth century, the school in the twenty-first century continued to send educators out to head other schools. In addition to Conard, Eric Niles left to head the Athenian School and Lisa Schmitt the Austin School for Girls. Two interns from the late twentieth century also became school heads: Elizabeth English at the Archer School and Danielle Boyd Heard at Nashoba Brooks.

19. *Minutes, Executive Committee, Emma Willard Board of Trustees*, December 9, 2004, EWSA.

20. "Helen Snell Cheel," *Emma*, Fall 2005, 5.

21. *Minutes, Emma Willard Board of Trustees*, October 28, 2006, EWSA.

22. Steven Ricci, "Wrought with Steadfast Will," *Emma*, Spring/Summer 2006, 3.

23. IMOW, retrieved September 29, 2012.

24. *Minutes, Emma Willard Board of Trustees*, May 16, 2009, EWSA.

25. *Minutes, Emma Willard Board of Trustees*, October 14, 2008, EWSA.

26. *The Plan for Emma Willard's Third Century: A Bicentennial Call to Action—2010–2014*, EWSA.

27. *Minutes, Emma Willard Board of Trustees*, October 23, 2010, EWSA.

28. Many of the details in this section are adapted from the Beloit College "Mindset" lists, which can be found at *http://www.beloit.edu/mindset/*.

29. Trudy E. Hall, "Accepting the Trust," *Values & Vision: The Leadership Venture*, 31.

30. Gillian Osborne, "Spunk, Pluck, and Other Winning Attributes of Emma Willard Women," *Emma*, Fall 2001, 26.. Select Bibliography

Bibliography

Author's Note: This bibliography does not include all of Emma Willard's writings. It also omits the many newspaper articles cited in the text of *Wrought with Steadfast Will*. All of those, plus the many letters written to Emma Willard and about her school, are fully cited in the endnotes of the chapters where they appear. A complete list of Emma Willard's writings is available on the Emma Willard School Web site: www.emmawillard.org/archive. Finally, the bibliography does not include individual citations for articles found in Emma Willard publications (for example, *CLOCK, Triangle,* or the school's alumnae bulletin). Those articles, like Emma Willard's letters, are fully cited in the endnotes of the chapters in which they appear.

Abir-Am, G. Pnina, and Dorinda Outram, eds. *Uneasy Careers and Intimate Lives: Women in Science, 1789-1979* (New Brunswick, NJ: Rutgers University Press, 1989).

Adams, Oscar Fay. *Some Famous American Schools* (Boston: Dana Estes and Co., 1903).

Adler, Jeanne Winston. *The Affair of the Veiled Murderess: An Antebellum Scandal and Mystery* (Albany: State University of New York Press, 2011).

Anderson, George Baker. *Landmarks of Rensselaer County, New York.* (Syracuse, NY: D. Mason, 1897).

Annual Report of the Commission of Colleges in New England (Boston: Commission of Colleges in New England, 1897).

Baldwin, Lydia Wood. *A Yankee Schoolteacher in Virginia* (New York: Funk & Wagnalls, 1884).

Baxter, James Phinney. "Inflation Hits the Colleges." *The Atlantic,* March 1948, 59–62.

Beecher, Catharine E. *Treatise on Domestic Economy, For the Use of Young Ladies at Home and at School* (New York: Harper and Brothers, 1856).

———. *The True Remedy for the Wrongs of Woman; With a History of an Enterprise Having That for Its Object* (Boston: Phillips, Sampson, and Co., 1851).

Beecher, Charles, ed. *The Autobiography, Correspondence, Etc. of Lyman Beecher* (New York: Harper and Bros., 1866).

Bernstein, Peter L. *Wedding of the Waters: The Erie Canal and the Making of a Great Nation* (New York: W.W. Norton, 2005).

Boisseau, T. J., and Abigail M. Markwyn, eds. *Gendering the Fair: Histories of Women and Gender at World's Fairs* (Urbana: University of Illinois Press, 2010).

Bolzau, Lydia. "Almira Hart Lincoln Phelps: Her Life and Work." PhD diss., University of Pennsylvania, 1936.

Brainerd, Ezra. *Mrs. Emma Willard's Life and Work in Middlebury.* Prepared originally for the Emma Willard Society of New York; reprinted by Middlebury College, 1918.

Brickley, Lynne Templeton, "Sarah Pierce's Litchfield Female Academy." PhD diss., Harvard Graduate School of Education, 1985.

Brockett, L. P., and Mary C. Vaughan. *Woman's Work in the Civil War: A Record of Heroism, Patriotism and Patience* (Philadelphia: Zeigler, McCurdy and Co., 1867).

Brown, Ralph S., Jr. "Upholding Professional Standards in the 70's." *AAUP Bulletin* 56, no. 2 (1970): 118–22.

Camp, David N. *History of New Britain, with Sketches of Farmington and Berlin, Connecticut, 1640–1889* (New Britain, CT: William B. Thomson, 1889).

Clarkson, Anna Howell. *A Beautiful Life and Its Associations* (New York: The Historical Department of Iowa, 1903).

Cohen, Sol. *Education in the United States: A Documentary History*, Vol. 3, 1571–91. [need place of publication and publisher and date; does Vol. 3 have a specific title?]

Cohen, Stanley. "The Assault on Victorianism in the Twentieth Century." *American Quarterly* 27, no. 5 (1975): 604–25.

Cornog, Evan. *The Birth of Empire: DeWitt Clinton and the American Experience, 1769–1828* (New York: Oxford University Press, 1898).

Cott, Nancy. *No Small Courage* (New York: Oxford, 2000).

Crocker, Ruth. *Mrs. Russell Sage: Women's Activism and Philanthropy in Gilded Age and Progressive Era America* (Bloomington: Indiana University Press, 2006).

Davis, Nancy, and Barbara Donahue. *Miss Porter's School: A History* (Farmington, CT: Miss Porter's School, 1992).

Degree, Kenneth A. "Malfeasance or Theft? What Really Happened at the Middlebury Branch of the Vermont State Bank." *Vermont History* 68 (Winter/Spring 2000): 5–34.

Eagle, Mary Kavanaugh Oldham, ed. *The Congress of Women Held in the Woman's Building, World's Columbian Exhibition, Chicago, U.S.A., 1893* (Philadelphia: International Publishing Co., 1895).

Evaluation of Secondary Schools: General Report on the Methods, Activities and Results of the Cooperative Study of Secondary School Standards (Washington, DC: Cooperative Study of Secondary School Standards, 1939).

Fairbanks, Mrs. A. W. *Emma Willard and Her Pupils* (New York: Mrs. Russell Sage, 1898).

Faust, Drew Gilpin. *This Republic of Suffering: Death and the American Civil War* (New York: Alfred A. Knopf, 2008).

Fitzpatrick, Edward A. *The Educational Views and Influence of DeWitt Clinton* (New York: Teachers' College, Columbia University, 1911).

Four-School Study Committee. *16-20: The Liberal Education of an Age Group* (New York: College Entrance Examination Board, 1970).

Fowler, Henry. "Educational Services of Mrs. Emma Willard." *American Journal of Education* (March 1859): 125-168.

Gardner, Mary Russell. *English History in Rhyme* (New York: Mary Russell Gardner, 1887).

Gilchrist, Beth Bradford. *The Life of Mary Lyon* (Boston: Houghton Mifflin, 1910).

Gilligan, Carol. "Woman's Place in Man's Life Cycle." *Harvard Educational Review* (Winter 1979): 431–46.

Gilligan, Carol, Nona P. Lyons, and Trudy J. Hanmer, eds. *Making Connections: The Relational Worlds of Adolescent Girls at Emma Willard School* (Troy: Emma Willard School, 1989).

Goddard, Abba A., ed. *The Trojan Sketchbook* (Troy: Young and Hart, 1846).

Gouverneur, Marion Campbell. *As I Remember: Recollections of American Society During the Nineteenth Century* (New York: D. Appleton and Co., 1911).

Hagy, James William. *This Happy Land: The Jews of Colonial and Antebellum Charleston* (Tuscaloosa: University of Alabama Press, 1993).

Hammersley, Sydney Earnest. *History of Waterford, New York* (Waterford: Privately published, 1957).

Harper and Brothers. *The Tourist, or Pocket Manuel for Travellers on the Hudson River, the Western Canal and Stage Road to Niagara Falls Down Lake Ontario and the St. Lawrence to Lebanon, Ballston, and Saratoga Springs* (New York: Harper and Brothers, 1834).

Harvard University. *General Education in a Free Society* (Cambridge: Harvard University Press, 1945).

Holcomb, James F., and Helen H. Holcomb. *In the Heart of India* (Philadelphia: Westminster Press, 1905).

Holcomb, Mrs. Helen Harriet Howe. *Bits about India* (Philadelphia: Presbyterian Board of Publication, 1888).

Holland, Mary A. Gardner. *Our Army Nurses* (Boston: B. Wilkins and Co., 1895).

Holman, Alfred L., ed. *Hinsdale Genealogy: Descendants of Robert Hinsdale of Dedham, Medfield, Hadley and Deerfield* (Privately printed by Alfred Hinsdale Andrews, 1906).

Homberger, Eric. *Mrs. Astor's New York: Money and Social Power in the Gilded Age* (New Haven: Yale University Press, 2002).

Hough, Franklin B. *Historical and Statistical Record of the University of the State of New York during the Century 1784 to 1884* (Albany: Weed, Parsons, and Co., 1885).

House, Harriet. "Sight-Seeing in Bangkok," in *Siam and Laos as Seen by Our Missionaries,* ed. Mary Backus (Philadelphia: Presbyterian Board of Publication, 1884).

Howard, George L. "Russell Sage as a Philanthropist." *Broadway Magazine,* September 1904, 22–26.

Hunter, Jane. *How Young Ladies Became Girls* (New Haven: Yale University Press, 2002).

Johnston, Ethel Stanwood, and Eva Johnston Coe. *American Samplers* (Boston: Colonial Dames, 1921).

Kelley, Mary. *Learning to Stand and Speak: Women, Education, and Public Life in America's Republic* (Chapel Hill: University of North Carolina Press, 2006).

Kerber, Linda. *Women of the Republic: Intellect and Ideology in Revolutionary America* (Chapel Hill: University of North Carolina Press, 1997).

Kimmel, Michael, and Thomas E. Mosmiller. *Against the Tide: Pro-Feminist Men in the US* (Boston: Beacon Press, 1992).

Korabel, Jerome. *The Chosen: The Hidden History of Admission and Exclusion at Harvard, Yale and Princeton* (Boston: Houghton Mifflin, 2005).

Lafarge, Phyllis. "A Warm-Hearted Guide to Certain Girls' Schools." *Harper's Magazine,* April 1963, 73–79.

Lane, Ann J. "'Consensual' Relations in the Academy: Gender, Power, and Sexuality." *Academe* 84, no. 5 (1998): 24–31.

Lay, Clemewell, and Anne Wellington. *Emma Willard Plan of Education* (Troy: Emma Willard School, 1961).

Lee, W. Storrs. *Stagecoach North: Being an Account of the First Generation in the State of Vermont* (New York: Macmillan, 1941).

Lerner, Gerda. *The Creation of Feminist Consciousness* (Oxford: Oxford University Press, 1993).

Lockwood, John H. *Westfield and Its Historical Influences, 1669–1919,* Vol. 2 (Privately printed, 1922).

Lord, John. *The Life of Emma Willard* (New York: D. Appleton, 1873).

Lutz, Alma. *Emma Willard: Daughter of Democracy* (Boston and New York: Houghton Mifflin, 1929).

Lynes, Russell. "Can The Private School Survive?" *Harper's Magazine,* January 1948, 39–60.

Mattingly, Paul H. *The Classless Profession: American Schoolmen in the Nineteenth Century* (New York: NYU Press, 1975).

McDougall, Walter A. *Throes of Democracy: The American Civil War Era 1829–1877* (New York: HarperCollins, 2008).

Mitchell, Helen Buss. "The North and South Meet: Almira Hart Lincoln Phelps and the Patapsco Female Institute, 1841–56." PhD diss., University of Maryland, 1990.

Morse, Jedediah. *The American Universal Geography* (Boston: Isaiah Thomas and Ebenezer Andrews, 1801).

Nash, Margaret. *Women's Education in the United States: 1780–1840* (New York: Palgrave Macmillan, 2005).

North, Catharine. *History of Berlin, Connecticut* (New Haven, CT: The Tuttle, Morehouse and Taylor Company, 1916).

Oates, Mary J., and Susan Williamson. "Women's Colleges and Women Achievers." *Signs* 3, no. 4 (1978): 795–806.

Olsen, Deborah M. "Remaking the Image: Promotional Literature of Mount Holyoke, Smith and Wellesley Colleges in the Mid-to-Late 1940s." *History of Education Quarterly* 40, no. 4 (2000): 418–59.

"On the Slopes of Mount Ida." *Time,* June 26, 1964, 60.

Paley, William. *Natural Theology or Evidence of the Existence and Attributes of the Deity Collected from the Appearances of Nature* (London: Hallowell, 1826).

Palmieri, Patricia Ann. *In Adamless Eden: The Community of Women Faculty at Wellesley* (New Haven: Yale University Press, 1995).

Parley, Peter. *Peter Parley's Universal History, On the Basis of Geography* (London: John W. Parker, 1837).

Patton, Julia. *Russell Sage College: The First Twenty-Five Years, 1916–1941* (Troy: Walter Snyder, printer, 1941).

Perry, Belle McArthur. *Lucinda Hinsdale Stone: Her Life Story and Reminiscence* (Detroit, MI: Blinn, 1902).

Phelps, Mrs. Almira Lincoln. *Botany for Beginners: An Introduction to Mrs. Lincoln's Lectures on Botany* (New York: Huntington and Savage, 1849).

———. *Lectures to Young Ladies* (Boston: Carter, Hendee and Co., 1833).

———. *Natural Philosophy for Beginners: Designed for Common Schools and Families* (New York: F. J. Huntington, 1840).

———. *Reviews, Essays on Art, Literature and Science* (Philadelphia: Claxton, Remsen and Haffelfinger, 1873).

Potwine, Elizabeth B. *Faithfully Yours, Eliza Kellas* (Troy: Emma Willard School, 2000).

———. "Hartford in an Old Account Book." *Bulletin of the Society for the Preservation of New England Antiquities* 53, no. 1 (1962): 17–22.

Pratt, Daniel J., compiler. *The Regents' Questions from the First Examination in 1866* (Syracuse, NY: C. W. Bardeen, 1880).

Proceedings of the Second Anniversary Convocation of the University of the State of New York (Albany: Charles Van Benthuysen and Sons, 1866).

Proceedings of the Sixth Anniversary Convocation of the University of the State of New York (Albany: Weed, Parsons and Co., 1870).

Reddy, William, and W. S. Smyth. *First Fifty Years of Cazenovia Seminary, 1825–1875* (New York: Nelson and Phillips, 1877).

Reichel, William C., and William H. Bigler. *A History of the Moravian Seminary for Young Ladies at Bethlehem, Pa., with a Catalogue of its Pupils, 1785 to 1870* (Bethlehem, PA: Moravian Seminary, 1901).

Report of the Commissioner of Education for the Year 1894–95, Vol. 2 (Washington, DC: U.S. Government Printing Office, 1896).

Report of the Committee of Ten on Secondary School Studies with the Reports of the Conferences Arranged by the Committee, 2nd ed. (New York: American Book Co., 1894).

Repousis, Angelo. "The Trojan Women: Emma Hart Willard and the Troy Society for the Advancement of Female Education in Greece." *Journal of the Early Republic* 24, no. 3 (2004): 445–76.

Riley, Glenda. *Inventing the American Woman*, 3rd ed. (Wheeling, IL: Harlan Davidson, 2001).

Roberts, Karen, ed. *New Year in Cuba: Mary Gardner Lowell's Travel Diary, 1831–32* (Boston: Massachusetts Historical Society and Northeastern University Press, 2003).

Robinson, Charles Edward. *Herrick Johnson: An Appreciative Memoir* (New York: Fleming H. Revell Co., 1914).

Rockwell, M. Emilia. *A Home in the West, or, Immigration and Its Consequences* (Dubuque, IA: Dubuque Express and Herald, 1858).

Rothbard, Murray. *The Panic of 1819: Reactions and Policies* (New York: Columbia University Press, 1962).

Rush, Benjamin. *Essays, Literary, Moral and Philosophical* (Philadelphia: Thomas and William Bradford, 1806).

Scales, Peter. "Sex Education in the '70s and '80s: Accomplishments, Obstacles, and Emerging Issues." *Family Relations* (October 1981): 557–66.

Schulter, Susan. "Emma Willard and the Graphic Foundations of American History." *Journal of Historical Geography* (July 2007): 542–64.

Scott, Anne Firor. "The Ever Widening Circle: The Diffusion of Feminist Values from the Troy Female Seminary, 1822–1872." *History of Education Quarterly* 19 (Spring 1979): 3–25.

Seccombe, Mike. "Historian Looks at Americans in Paris." *Vineyard Gazette,* July 14, 2009. **[page ref?]**

Seelye, L. Clark. *Early History of Smith College, 1871–1910* (Boston and New York: Houghton Mifflin, 1923).

Seller, Maxine Schwartz, ed. *Women Educators in the United States, 1820–1993: A Bio-Bibliographical Sourcebook* (Westport, CT: Greenwood Press, 1994).

Sherman, Michael, Gene Sessions, and P. Jeffrey Potash. *Freedom and Unity: A History of Vermont* (Barre: Vermont Historical Society, 2004).

Silliman, Benjamin. *A Tour to Quebec in the Autumn of 1819* (London: Sir Richard Phillips, 1822).

Slade, Mary B. *Thetford Academy's First Century: 1819–1919* (Montpelier, VT: Capital City Press, 1956).

Steinberg, Jane. "The Boarding School Mystique." *Mademoiselle,* May, 1966, 176, 212-216.

Stevenson, Louise L. *Miss Porter's School: A History in Documents, 1847–1948* (New York: Garland Press, 1987).

Swift, Samuel. *History of the Town of Middlebury in the County of Addison, Vermont* (Middlebury: A. H. Copeland, 1859).

Synnott, Marcia G. "The Admission and Assimilation of Minority Students at Harvard, Yale and Princeton, 1900–70." *History of Education Quarterly* 19 (Autumn 1979): 285–304.

Townsend, Lucy F., and Barbara Wiley. "The Divorce of a Domestic Educator: The Case of Emma Willard Yates." *Review Journal of Philosophy and Social Science* 27, nos. 1 and 2 (2002): 163–205.

Troy Chamber of Commerce. *New Troy* (Troy: Troy Times Art Press, printer, 1913).

Tuckerman, Bayard, ed. *The Diary of Philip Hone, 1828–1851* (New York: Dodd, Mead, 1889).

Valentine, John A. *The College Board and the School Curriculum: A History of the College Board's Influence on the Substance and Standards of American Education, 1900–1980* (New York: College Entrance Examination Board, 1987).

Van Alstyne, William W. "The Tentative Emergence of Student Power in the United States." *American Journal of Comparative Law* 17, no. 3 (1969): 403–17.

Vanderpoel, Emily Noyes, ed. *Chronicles of a Pioneer School from 1792 to 1833* (Cambridge, MA: University Press, 1903).

———. *More Chronicles of a Pioneer School, from 1792 to 1833, Being Added History of the Litchfield Academy Kept by Miss Sarah Pierce and Her Nephew, John Pierce Brace* (New York: The Cadmus Bookshop, 1927).

Weise, Arthur James. *Troy's One Hundred Years* (Troy: William H. Young, 1891).

White, Lynn T. *Educating Our Daughters: A Challenge to the Colleges* (New York: Harper Brothers, 1950).

Whitney, Caspar, and Albert Britt, eds. "Field Hockey as a Woman's Sport." *Outing* (October 1904–March 1905): 475–79.

Wilkeson, Frank. *Recollections of a Private Soldier in the Army of the Potomac* (New York: G.P. Putnam's Sons, 1887).

Willard, Emma. *Abridged History of the United States or Republic of America* (New York: A.S. Barnes, 1850).

———. *An Address to the Public; Particularly to the Members of the Legislature of New-York, Proposing a Plan for Improving Female Education* (Middlebury, VT: J.W. Copeland, 1819).

———. *Advancement of Female Education: Or, A Series of Addresses, in Favor of Establishing at Athens, in Greece, A Female Seminary Especially Designed to Instruct Female Teachers* (Troy: Norman Tuttle, Printer, 1833).

———. *History of the United States or The Republic of America* (New York: A.S. Barnes, 1845).

———. *History of the United States, or Republic of America: With a Chronological Table and a Series of Progressive Maps* (New York: A.S. Barnes, 1852).

———. *Journal and Letters, From France and Great-Britain* (Troy: Norman Tuttle, Printer, 1833).

———. *Last Leaves of American History Comprising A Separate History of California* (New York: A.S. Barnes, 1853).

———. *Late American History, Containing a Full Account of the Courage, Conduct, and Success of John C. Fremont; By Which, Through Many Hardships and Sufferings He Became the Explorer and the Hero of California* (New York: A. S. Barnes, 1856).

———. *Via Media: A Peaceful and Permanent Settlement of the Slavery Question* (Washington, DC: Charles H. Anderson, Bookseller, 1862).

Woloch, Nancy. *Women and the American Experience*, 3rd ed. (New York: McGraw-Hill, 2000).

Woody, Thomas. *A History of Women's Education in the United States,* 3rd ed. 2 vols. (New York: Octagon Books, 1980).

Yates, Christopher C. *Observations on the Epidemic Now Prevailing in the City of New-York Called the Asiatic or Spasmodic Cholera with Advice to the Planters of the South, for the Medical Treatment of Their Slaves* (New York: George C. Scott and Co., 1832).

Index

A

B

Barnard College, 215, 304
Barnes, A. S., 169
Barnes, Edward Larrabee, 438, 442
Barnum, P. T., 212
Bartholomew, Gracie, 422, 611n77
Barton, George Washington and
   Elizabeth, 74
baseball, 319
basketball, 292, 319, 354, 457
Bates, Elizabeth, 183
Bates College, 215
Battey, Katharine, 34, 47–48, 59
Battey, Robert, 240
Baxter, Jameson, 531, 532, 533, 550–51,
   557–58
Baxter, Mary Lillie, 245
Baxter, William W., 245
Beach, Ann, 570
Beatles, 453
Beaucheau, Charles, 389, 390
Beaucheau, Roy, 389
Bedell, Anna, 168
Bedell, Martha, 168
Bedell, Prudence, 168
Beebe, Bill, 444
Beecher, Catharine
   departure from Hartford, 145
   "Essay on the Education of Female
    Teachers, An," 133
   Hartford Female Seminary and, 43, 103
   Litchfield School and, 38, 41
   republican motherhood and, 35
   teacher training and, 131, 132–33
   Treatise on Domestic Economy, A, 54
   True Remedy, 133
Beecher, Harriet. See Stowe, Harriet
   Beecher
Beecher, Henry Ward, 189, 216
Beecher, Lyman, 41
Belgium, 336–37
Bell, Alexander Graham, 212
Bell, John, 199–200
Belloc, Louise, 115
Bellows, Keven R., 526, 540, 547
Belmont Hill School, 194
Beman, Nathan, 162, 192, 193, 292
Benet, Laura, 362, 408, 428
Berith Sholom synagogue, 8
Berkshire Reporter, 37
"Bernice Bobs Her Hair" (Fitzgerald), 361
Bernstein, Alyssa, 621n17
Betterly, Jack, 433–34, 456, 460, 465
Betts, Edgar H., 373, 385, 392
Betts, Robert G., 435
Bicentennial Call to Action, A, 574
bicentennial celebration, 574
Bickham, Edith, 282
Bigelow, Jane Ruth. See Storrs, Jane
   Bigelow
Bigelow, Mary, 138, 139–40
Big Parade, The (silent film), 340
Billy the Kid, 213
biographical record committee, 255–56
biology, 114–15

Birmingham church bombing, 448
Bisbee, Lucius, 127
Bisharat, Josephine, 413, 428
Bishop, Isadora, 204
Bissell, Melville, 212
Bissell, Taylor, 296
Black Bear (Arapaho chief), 8
blacklisting, 538
Blackmun, Nancy, 459
black political leadership conference
   (1967), 451
blacks
   college admission of, 216
   colonization movement and, 202
   NY voting requirements for, 86, 88
   progress in acceptance by whites, 503–4
   segregation and, 452, 465
black students at Emma Willard School,
   448, 449–53, 470–71
black students at Groton School, 505
black teachers, 452, 613n53
black trustees, 449, 451
Blatch, Harriot Stanton, 285–86
Blatchford, Samuel, 59, 62, 92
Blenheim Palace, 222, 237
Blessner, Gustave, 167–68
blind date dances, 421–22
Bliss, William, 67
Bloomingdale, Joseph and Lyman, 212
Bloustein, Edward J., 466–67
Blum, Arlene, 514
"Boarding School Mystique" (Steinberg),
   449
Bodel, Phyllis, 404, 610n35
Boluch, Kurt, 619n25
Bonney, Charles C., 256, 257
Bonney, Mary L. See Rambault, Mary L.
   Bonney
Bonz, Margaret, 549
Boone, Pat, 402
Borst, Elizabeth, 270
Boston Globe, 549
Boston stagecoach, 21
Bostwick, Lucy Watson, 254
Bosworth, Jane Foster, 242
Botany for Beginners (A. Phelps), 40
Bowers, Maria, 127, 128
boys and men on campus, 359–61, 421–23
Brace, John, 39, 41
Brackett, Mary, 259
Bradley, Agnes, 306–7
Bradley, Jonathan Dorr, 78, 79
Bradley, Laura, 306–7
Bradley, Merab, 78, 79, 84, 97
Bradley, William, 70
Brainerd, Mary C., 174
Brandow, Grace, 392
Brann, Ada, 277
Breakfast at Tiffany's, 431
Brearley school, 411
breast cancer, 443
Breasted, James, 363
Brewster, Lucretia Root, 204
Brewster, William, 204

Briarcliff School for Girls, 283
Bridge at San Luis Rey, The (Wilder), 362
Bridges, 571–72
Bridges, Judy
   on curricular review committee,
    619n25
   as dean of students, 523, 558, 561, 571
   as director of athletics, 498, 523, 546,
    561
Britain, Eliza, 205
British, 18, 24, 25, 27–28, 32. See also
   England
Brome, Quebec, 128
Brooke, Avery, 487
Brooke, Joel, 487, 491–92
Brooke, Sarah, 487
Brooklyn Eagle, The, 152
Brooks, Phillips, 189
Brooks School, 505
Brown, Charles and William, 5
Brown, Ellen Hathaway, 206–7
Brown, John, 198–99
Brunaud, Lydia, 484
Bryant, William Cullen, 106
Bryn Mawr College, 215, 249, 253, 272,
   304
Buchanan, James, 74
Buckingham, Belinda, 74
Bucktails, 86, 89
Buel, David, 67
Buel, David, Jr., 70
Buel, Jesse, 148
Buell, Martha, 5
Bull, Hannah, 26
Bull, Helen, 435
Bulletin
   on appointment of Dietels, 426
   capital campaign announcement in, 418
   comparison of Exeter and Emma
    Willard in, 445
   Dietel's case for larger endowment in,
    446, 447
   "Emma Willard Plan for Education"
    described in, 401
   on hard ten years, 465
   on social life on campus, 421
Bullitt, Virginia Anderson, 205, 259
Bullitt, William
Bulova, Joseph, 212
Burbank, Luther, 212
Burden, Henry, 4
Burlington Seminary, 174
Burnham School, 272
Burns, Cornelius, 326
Burns, James MacGregor, 514
Burr, Aaron, 38
Burritt, Jane, 131, 139, 142–43, 155
Burroughs, Catherine, 75
Burton, LeRoy, 327–28
Bush, Julia Howard, 368, 435
Bushnell, Ericsson F., 286
Butler, Aimee Mott, 498
Butler, Amy Pfau, 382–83
Butler, Elizabeth, 378

D

E

I

IBM, 504

I Know Why the Caged Bird Sings (Angelou), 449

"Implications of the New Curriculum for Admissions," 475, 614n32

In a Different Voice (Gilligan), 508

"In Behalf of Female Education in Greece" (E. Willard), 119

Independent School Management (ISM), 565

independent schools, 396

India, 188, 190

Indian Wars, 213, 595n3

indoor smoking areas, 472, 473

industrialization in United States, 85–86

Industry (ship), 71

infantile paralysis epidemic, 324

infant mortality, 158–59

infirmary, 319, 323–24, 368

inflation, 465, 495

influenza outbreak of 1918, 324–25, 335

information overload, 402

information vs. knowledge, 575

Ingalls, Sarah, 72

Ingram, Mary Warren, 205

In Our Own Voices (Martin), 542

Inslee, Louise, 388

intellectual perfection, 575

International Museum of Women, 573

Internet access on campus, 554, 561

internship program for teachers, 388

internships for students, 476–77, 478

In the Heart of India (Holcomb), 190

In the Heat of the Night, 449

Irish, Joy, 563–64

Irish Catholics, 197. See also Catholicism, distrust of; Roman Catholics

irony cards, 615n65

Irvine, Julia, 271

Irving, Ethel M., 284

Irving, Washington, 106

Irwin, Agnes, 297, 307, 309–10, 312–13

Isabel Davis Wise Teaching Fellow in History, 6260n6

"I Speak for Democracy" contest, 412

Italian language instruction, 113, 290

Ives, Elsa Mott, 439, 498

Ivy Day exercises, 353, 358

J

Jackson, Andrew, 94

Jackson, Jesse, 503

Jackson Five, 449

Jacksonian democracy, 86

Jacobs, Frederic, 138

Jacotot, Joseph, 109–10

James, Henry, 74

James, Jesse, 213

Jameson A. Baxter Award, 557–58

Jamieson, Caroline Woodward, 205

Jamieson, Martha, 204

Japanese, 363, 392

Jefferson, Thomas, 25, 29–30, 35, 49, 89, 94

Jeffersonian Democrats, 86

Jeffersonian Republicans, 15, 25, 127. See also Republican Party

Jeffersons, The, 503–4

Jeffries, Fleta Puckette, 205

Jersey ships, 24

Jesdale, Todd, 529

Jewish students, 195, 196, 197, 332–33, 343, 410, 448

Jews, persecution of, 340

Johnson, Anna, 115, 147

Johnson, Herrick, 189

Johnson, H. Mark, 477, 485

Johnson, Lyndon, 448

Johnson, Mary T., 189

Johnson Trust, 414

Johnston, William B., 205

John Willard Award, 557

joint inquiry, 467

Jones, Barbara, 529

Jones, Ella, 282, 293, 294, 313

Jones, Lucy, 171

Jones, Mary Field, 72, 74

Jordan, Mary Augusta, 297

Jordan, Wilbur K., 398, 400–401, 434–35

Judd, Alice, 362

Judson, Sarah, 222

June Day, 353, 358–59

K

Kafin, Robert, 524

Kalamazoo College, 244

Kappler, Lara, 541

Kappler, Serge, 541, 554, 561

Kapps, John, 381

Kay, Katty, 572

Keep, Robert Porter, 283

Keliher, Agathe, 613n97

Kellas, Alexander (Eliza's father), 310

Kellas, Alexander "Sandy" (Eliza's brother), 310, 311

Kellas, Eliza
academics under, 329–32
accomplishments of, 365
board of trustees and, 434
care for campus grounds, 367–68
centennial celebration and, 325–28
character building by, 348–53
Cheel donation in honor of, 438–39, 442
college prep emphasis of, 329
commencement traditions and, 358–59
competition emphasis of, 354–55
construction during tenure of, 368–75
early life of, 311
European travel of, 371–72
evening study halls and, 442
as gifted student and teacher, 310, 603n5

during Great Depression. See Great Depression
hiring of and arrival at EWS, 307, 309, 310–11, 312–13, 312–15
Hutchins and, 443
increase in boarding by, 317–18, 321
influence on Ruth Cheney, 604n10
leadership development by, 353–54
nursing of flu-stricken students by, 324
Olivia Sage and, 315, 325–26, 331
post-retirement presence of, 393–94, 609n78
religious discrimination by, 332–33
retirement of, 391, 392
Revels and, 355–58
as Russell Sage College president, 341–43, 344, 369
school culture and, 346–48

Kellas, Eliza (Eliza's mother), 310

Kellas, John, 310, 311

Kellas, Katherine, 310, 345–46, 369, 372, 392, 603n5

Kellas Hall, 368–71, 444, 571, 572

Kellas Hall, Potsdam, 345

Kelley, Florence, 296

Kellogg, Anna Shankland, 166, 167, 174, 177, 179, 182, 197

Kellogg, Day O., 184

Kellogg, Frances, 1

Kellogg, Giles, 3, 4

Kelsey, Keenan, 272

Kemp, William, 3, 4, 5, 224, 596n28

Kennedy, John Fitzgerald, 412, 429, 431

Kennedy, William S., 243

Kenney, Maria. See Gurley, Maria Kenney

Kent, Chancellor, 96–97

Kent, Elizabeth, 328

Kent State shootings, 453

Kern, Rebecca, 460

Kerner Commission report, 451

Ketchum, Mary, 134

Keyes, Emma Willard Scudder, 327

Keyser, Barbara, 474

Kiggins, Evelyn, 444

Kiggins, Kathryn Schafer, 444

Kiggins Hall, 444, 458

Kilby, Mr., 59, 60

Kimball, Sarah Hinsdale, 74, 600n45

Kimball Union, 174

Kimberly, Christopher, 570, 572

Kimberly, Hazard, 66

King, Caroline, 169, 227, 248

King, Franciena, 452–53

King, Harriet C., 243

King, H. M., 253

King, Martin Luther, Jr., 448, 505

King Philip's War, 13

Kinney, Priscilla O'Connell, 351

L

M

Y

Z

Photo Credits

Cover Photo courtesy of Fantasia Hanmer '05.

Photo of gargoyle courtesy of Steven Ricci.

Photos of Amos Eaton, Troy waterfront in the 1840s, Troy citizens greeting Union soldiers, and the interior of a collar factory all courtesy of Collection, Rensselaer County Historical Society.

All other photos are courtesy of the Emma Willard School archives or the author's personal photography collection.

Toya Dubin, vice-president of Hudson Micro-Imaging, Inc., digitized all of the photographs for publication.

Acknowledgements

As is inevitably true with any work of this magnitude, I have had the help of many people. Every head of school from Bob Parker to Trudy Hall has supported the project, and by making the book a centerpiece of the upcoming Bicentennial, the latest administration set a deadline that insured that the research would eventually have to stop and the writing begin. Although the research will probably not completely end until I draw my final breath, it has been satisfying to organize what I have and set it down on paper.

For the record, the opinions expressed in this work are mine and mine alone, and I also take full responsibility for any factual errors, although I have had the able editorial assistance of Anne Lesser, whose patience with my inconsistencies and quirks has been remarkable.

A small group of friends has read the manuscript almost as fast as I have written it, and their comments have been invaluable. I thank each of the following for their keen insights and valuable observations: Alice Dodge Wallace '38, P '70, Kath Howell '58, Jamie Baxter '61, Barbara Wiley, Christine Carroll, Kathleen McNamara, Bob Nielsen, and Lynn Parry. Alice Wallace and Barb Wiley had eagle eyes that caught the slightest typographical errors, Kath Howell had an unerring eye for historical inaccuracy, and Chris Carroll offered her particularly keen perspective on school traditions. Jamie Baxter added a much needed corrective on all things financial, and Bob Nielsen and Lynn Parry are representative of men who respect Emma Willard's history as much as any alumna. As for Kathleen McNamara, she has been the ultimate sounding board for questions literary and political: a perfect combination of Molly Maguire, Jane Austen, and Mother Teresa. In spite of her demanding schedule, Trudy Hall has made time to read each chapter of the manuscript as it has been written and has offered immediate feedback that is interesting, helpful, and illuminating—and provides important context gleaned from her wide experience at other girls' schools.

Other colleagues and friends have offered assistance at various points along the way. Fred Colson, Ace Ellis, and Brian Grandjean have provided me with helpful comparative data and ledger analysis. Several members of the history department have shared sources and wisdom: Bob Naeher, Ruth Burday, Carol Bendall, and Emily Snyder. Armand Herald, Ken McGivern, Dan Miller, and Ian Smith willingly sought out answers to my questions about the original buildings and grounds. Kevin Moore filled me in on the connections between the Watervliet Arsenal and the school's early years. Cheryl MacNeil gave me an inside tour of the original Emma Willard buildings on the Russell Sage campus. Frances O'Connor unstintingly shared her wisdom about and resources in publishing. Robyn Naeher did the legwork necessary to procure the copyright for the book. Lindsay Slaughter and Mark Van Wormer offered artistic guidance and photographs. The school's computer experts, Judith Curry, Pete Mc-Corkle, Ken Westfall, and Danny Whelchel saved my manuscript from numerous technical disasters. Jim Hanley was my go-to guy for any detail about the town of Watervliet. Cheryl Ackner, my steadfast associate, uncomplainingly formatted, copied and collated for me—and always did her best to keep me from taking myself too seriously. Countless members of the faculty and staff have cheered me along; their simple inquiries about the book's progress gave me daily boosts. Among them are Suzanne Baker, Alan and Sarah Berry, Brenda Brunelle, Laura Burgess '02, Stacey Dodd, John Evans, Gerri Biggins, Nina Fleishman '72, Maureen Harrison, Chris Hill, Kent Jones, Sue Lauther, Meredith Legg, Nicole Lynch, Diana Maleki, Meg McClellan, Linda McClusky, Anne Mossop, Janice Nimetz, Mary Moore, Angela Richard, Melissa Salmon, Sabra Sanwal, Jill Smith, Debra Spiro-Allen, Barbara Todd, and Jenn Ulicnik.

Other longtime colleagues and friends have read excerpts of the book from time to time, have assumed my duties when deadlines loomed, have traded memories and have generally been a source of deep encouragement. They are Judy Bridges, Françoise Chadabe, Marilyn Hunter, Pat Jones, Elizabeth Parry, Robin Prout, and Katie Wilson '84. I would be remiss if I did not acknowledge as well the help and support I have received from my former colleagues Jack and Marcia Easterling, Don and Susan Myers, Russell Locke, and Larry Lichtenstein.

Special thanks go to the crowd that has most often filled my lunch table for the past two years; they have good-naturedly listened to tales of Emma Willard history day after day when I emerged from a morning in the archives with yet another "fascinating" anecdote. They are Jeremy Bollam, Julie Clancy, Heather Cordes, Kelly Finnegan, Joe Hefta, and Hilary Kellogg.

The late Peter Shaver and my good friend and neighbor, Dan Keating, were invaluable sources on the history of Troy.

I have visited many archives during the course of my research, and the exact citations for material found elsewhere can be located in the appropriate endnotes. However, in my off-campus forays, I found the staff at the following institutions to be unfailingly helpful: the Troy Public Library, the Russell Sage College Library, the Smith College Archives, the Wellesley College Archives, the New York Public Library, the New-York Historical Society, the Rensselaer County Historical Society, the Wisconsin Historical Society, and the Radcliffe Institute.

As important as these resources have been, nothing has been more invaluable to my work than the Emma Willard School Archives and their extraordinary custodian, Nancy Iannucci. Nancy has been with me every step of the way for the past four years, cheerfully looking up the most obscure details, helping to find and organize photos, tracking down lost sources, filling my numerous interlibrary loan requests, and helping me decipher nineteenth century handwriting. I can honestly say this book might not have seen the light of day without her help.

As important as Nancy has been to my archival research, Marti Ohmart has been to my search for connections among our living alumnae. Time and again Marti has gone above and beyond to search out some random fact that seemed all-important to me at the time. She has also proved to be a fascinating sounding board to test my thinking about cultural changes in late twentieth century America and their impact on women's roles in general and Emma Willard in particular.

One of the most remarkable things that I discovered about the Troy Female Seminary was the myriad connections between its students and the students at West Point. Col. Charles Johnson has been a steady source of wisdom and information about all things West Point, lending me books, directing me to articles, and even driving me to the West Point archives. For all his support, he deserves my special thanks.

The wonderful world of FaceBook means that I have heard from more alumnae during this process than I could possibly acknowledge. However, certain women have sent me memorabilia, books and other material from their time—or their mothers' times—at the school. Others have willingly answered my specific questions about their days on campus. The following deserve my special thanks: Lauren King Buscone '95, Sandra Collins '95, Mags Caney Conant '67, Patricia Connally '41, Rachel Crow Dose '61, Jane Gale '44, Barbara Jones Higbee '64, Wendy Pestel Lehmann '64, Jaci Canning Murphy '64, Biddy Harte Owen '68, Nina Pattison '46, Karen Lundquist Peterson '68, Elissa Robison Prout '52, Jane LeFever Ruehle '51, Sigrid Strong Reynolds '70, Bonnie Sontag '69, Heidi Porter Webster '68, and Victoria Thompson Winterer '61.

In addition, I owe my thanks to Val and Stuart Schultz P '02, '05, '08 who generously contributed to my research budget. Special thanks also go to Katherine Deane Shubart '60 for her munificent support of this project; her gift underwrote the reproduction of the book's photographs. Last in this category, but by no means least, is Alice Wallace. Alice not only believed in this project from the first, she committed to underwriting the publication of the first edition of the book. Her support financed the editing, the formatting, the indexing, and the printing: in short, practically everything needed to produce this volume. I will be forever grateful for her generosity.

Among those people who have been most supportive are my students, both those who have studied history with me and the young women whom I have coached on Emma Willard quiz teams over the years. These students have been particularly inspiring, and their interest in the history of their *alma mater* has helped shape my thinking. To them I owe a particularly personal vote of thanks.

And, finally, as is probably true for every author, my deepest thanks go to the two people who lived through this project with me. Each in her own way sees me as somewhat crazily obsessed by the history of Emma Willard School. While I doubt either will ever fully understand my fascination with this subject, they both love me anyway, and nearly always tolerated yet another dinnertime rendition of Emma stories that I found exciting and they found mind-numbing; they never left the table, and they always came back for the next meal. Tasia and Linda, I thank you.